Ovid
Amores
Book 3

Ovid

Amores Book 3

Edited with an Introduction, Translation, and Commentary
by
P. J. DAVIS

Great Clarendon Street, Oxford, OX2 6DP,
United Kingdom

Oxford University Press is a department of the University of Oxford.
It furthers the University's objective of excellence in research, scholarship,
and education by publishing worldwide. Oxford is a registered trade mark of
Oxford University Press in the UK and in certain other countries

© P. J. Davis 2023

The moral rights of the author have been asserted

All rights reserved. No part of this publication may be reproduced, stored in
a retrieval system, or transmitted, in any form or by any means, without the
prior permission in writing of Oxford University Press, or as expressly permitted
by law, by licence or under terms agreed with the appropriate reprographics
rights organization. Enquiries concerning reproduction outside the scope of the
above should be sent to the Rights Department, Oxford University Press, at the
address above

You must not circulate this work in any other form
and you must impose this same condition on any acquirer

Published in the United States of America by Oxford University Press
198 Madison Avenue, New York, NY 10016, United States of America

British Library Cataloguing in Publication Data

Data available

Library of Congress Control Number: 2023932874

ISBN 978–0–19–887130–9

Printed and bound in the UK by
Clays Ltd, Elcograf S.p.A.

Links to third party websites are provided by Oxford in good faith and
for information only. Oxford disclaims any responsibility for the materials
contained in any third party website referenced in this work.

For Joshua and Posey

Preface

This book aims to meet the long-felt need for a detailed commentary on the third book of Ovid's *Amores*. Its primary goal is to present readers with the information required for understanding Book 3, its place in the *Amores*, in Ovid's work more generally, and in the tradition of erotic elegy. It has a particular focus on such matters as Ovid's allusion to and engagement with the works of earlier Roman love poets; the connections between elegies in Book 3 and poems in Books 1 and 2; the reworking of ideas and themes from *Amores* in Ovid's other erotic works; the verbal texture of Ovid's poetry, particularly his use of rhetoric and wit, and his employment of metrical and verbal patterns; the relationship between *Amores* and the political and cultural context of Augustan Rome; the elucidation of linguistic difficulties; and the discussion of textual problems, particularly the explanation of my choice of readings in disputed passages.

Close engagement with *Amores* inevitably leads to grappling with textual difficulties. Although I have consulted digital images of the principal manuscripts for *Amores* 3 (P, S, and Y), the text that I offer is based primarily on printed editions, especially those of Munari, Kenney, Showerman and Goold, McKeown, and Ramirez de Verger. A list of differences from these editions follows the text and translation.

I have taken a relatively conservative approach to textual matters. Even though I particularly admire Kenney's edition of *Amores*, I have not followed him in claiming that 3.5 is inauthentic because (a) it holds its place in the three best and oldest manuscripts and (b) its style is not significantly different from that of Ovid's other elegies.[1] Nor have I divided 3.11. If 3.5 is retained, there is no need to split 3.11 into two poems in order to bring the number of elegies in Book 3 up to the magical number of 15.[2]

My translation makes no claim to grace or elegance. It is intended primarily to clarify the surface meaning of the Latin.

I have tried to make this edition as inclusive as possible. The overall Introduction and the introductions to individual poems are intended to be comprehensible to anyone with an interest in Latin love poetry and the place of *Amores* within that tradition. While the Commentary is obviously aimed at readers with a knowledge of Latin, it does not require familiarity with Greek or other languages. On the other hand, I have not thought it necessary to keep reminding readers that Virgil

---

[1] For discussion of these issues see the introduction to 3.5.
[2] I also treat *Her.* 15 as authentically Ovidian. See Thorsen (2014: Chapter 4).

wrote *Eclogues* (*Ecl.*), *Georgics* (*G.*), and *Aeneid* (*A.*) and that Ovid wrote *Amores* (*Am.*), *Heroides* (*Her.*), *Metamorphoses* (*Met.*), and so on.

As I argue in the Introduction, I view *Amores* as a set of performances by different speakers, not all of whom can be identified with the poet or even with the lover of Corinna. For that reason I have labelled the speakers of the various poems in different ways and reserved the word 'Ovid' for the author of the fifteen poems of Book 3 and the poet's other works.

I have made extensive use of the Packard Humanities Institute's database of Classical Latin Texts. My claims concerning the occurrence or non-occurrence of words and phrases in Latin literature are based upon searches of this important resource.

Thanks to the internet, I have also been able to use not only some of the oldest printed texts of *Amores* (including Naugerius' Aldine edition [1515]), but also some of the earliest commentaries (including those of the Venetian scholar Marius Niger [Domenico Mario Negri; 1518]) and the German humanist Micyllus [Jacob Moltzer; 1549]), as well as the more famous works of seventeenth- and eighteenth-century editors Nicolaus Heinsius and Petrus Burmannus (Pieter Burman). When discussing textual matters, I have made a point of giving precise references to their works and those of other textual critics.

I am grateful to the following friends and colleagues for their critical reading of large portions of this book: A. J. Boyle (University of Southern California), Jacqueline Clarke (University of Adelaide), Robert Cowan (University of Sydney), and Carole Newlands (University of Colorado). I have also profited from the advice and assistance of Ben Nagy (University of Adelaide/Polish Academy of Sciences), Franziska Schnoor (Stiftsbibliothek St Gallen), and Ioannis Ziogas (Durham University). Finally, I would like to express my gratitude to my colleagues in Classics at the University of Adelaide (Han Baltussen, Jacqueline Clarke, and Margaret O'Hea) for their friendship and for providing such a supportive research environment.

I would also like to thank OUP's anonymous reader for helpful suggestions and corrections. Remaining errors are of course my own.

University of Adelaide

Contents

List of Abbreviations	xi
INTRODUCTION	1
1. Ovid's Life and Works	1
2. Dating *Amores*	2
3. The Design of the Three-Book Collection	4
4. The Place of Book 3 in the Collection	6
5. *Amores* as Performance	6
6. A Multiplicity of Masks	7
7. Corinna	8
8. Extending the Range	8
9. *Amores* and Politics	10
10. Verbal Patterning	12
11. *Amores* and Love Elegy	14
TEXT AND TRANSLATION	21
Differences from the texts of Munari, Showerman and Goold, McKeown, Kenney, and Ramirez de Verger	70
COMMENTARY	73
Bibliography	343
1. Latin Texts: Editions, Commentaries, Translations	343
2. Other Works	346
Indexes	359
1. Latin Words	359
2. Passages Quoted from Latin and Greek Texts	361
3. General Index	381

List of Abbreviations

1. Manuscripts of Ovid's *Amores* consulted

F	Francofurtanus Barth. 110. 12th/13th C
P	Parisinus Latinus 8242 (Puteaneus). 9th C
Ph	Parisinus Latinus 8245. 13th C
R	Parisinus Latinus 7311 (Regius). 9th C
S	Sangallensis 864. 11th C
Y	Berolinensis Hamiltonensis 471. 11th C
Vb	Vaticanus Palat. Lat. 1655. 13th C

2. Other Works

AR	Apollonius of Rhodes
Bornecque	Bornecque, H. (1930), Ovide: Les Amours. Paris.
Brandt	Brandt, P. (1911), P. Ouidi Nasonis Amorum Libri Tres. Leipzig.
Burman	Burman, P. (1727), Publii Ovidii Nasonis Opera Omnia IV. Voluminibus Comprehensa; cum Integris Jacobi Micylli, Herculis Ciofani, et Danielis Heinsii Notis, et Nicolai Heinsii Curis Secundis...Cura et Studio Petri Burmanni, 4 vols. Amsterdam.
Ceccarelli	Ceccarelli, L. (2018), Contributions to the History of the Latin Elegiac Distich. Turnhout.
CIL IV	Zangemeister, C. (1871), Corpus Inscriptionum Latinarum Consilio et Auctoritate Academiae Litterarum Regiae Borussicae Editum. Volumen Quartum. Inscriptiones Parietariae Pompeianae Herculanenses Stabianae. Berlin.
Goldberg and Manuwald (1)	Goldberg, S. M. and Manuwald, G. (2018), Fragmentary Republican Latin. Ennius. Testimonia, Epic Fragments. Cambridge Mass.
Goldberg and Manuwald (2)	Goldberg, S. M. and Manuwald, G. (2018), Fragmentary Republican Latin. Ennius. Dramatic Fragments, Minor Works. Cambridge Mass.
Harder	Harder, A. (2012), Callimachus: Aetia, 2 vols. Oxford.
Heinsius	Heinsius, N. (1658), Publii Ouidii Nasonis Operum Tomus I. Scripta Amatoria Complexus. Amsterdam.
Hollis	Hollis, A. S. (2007), Fragments of Roman Poetry C.60 BC–AD 20. Oxford.

Ingleheart and Radice	Ingleheart, J. and Radice, K. (2012), Ovid Amores III. A Selection: 2, 4, 5, 14. London.
Kenney	Kenney, E. J. (1961 and 1994), P. Ouidi Nasonis: Amores; Medicamina Faciei Femineae; Ars Amatoria; Remedia Amoris. 1 and 2 edns. Oxford.
Kenney (1)	Kenney, E. J. (1961), P. Ouidi Nasonis: Amores; Medicamina Faciei Femineae; Ars Amatoria; Remedia Amoris. 1 edn. Oxford.
Kenney (2)	Kenney, E. J. (1994), P. Ouidi Nasonis: Amores; Medicamina Faciei Femineae; Ars Amatoria; Remedia Amoris. 2 edn. Oxford.
LIMC	(1981–2009), Lexicon Iconographicum Mythologiae Classicae. Zurich.
Marius	Niger, Marius (1518), P. Ouidii Nasonis Amorum Libri Tres, De Medicamine Faciei Libellus: et Nux. Venice.
Marx	Marx, F. (1904), C. Lucilii Carminum Reliquiae. Leipzig.
McKeown	McKeown, J. C. (1987), Ovid: Amores. Text, Prolegomena, and Commentary. I. Text and Prolegomena. Liverpool.
Micyllus	Micyllus, I. (1549), P. Ouidii Nasonis Poetae Sulmonensis Opera Quae Vocantur Amatoria. Basel.
Müller	Müller, L. (1861), P. Ouidii Nasonis Carmina Amatoria. Berlin.
Munari	Munari, F. (1970), P. Ouidii Nasonis Amores: Testo, Introduzione, Traduzione e Note di Franco Munari. 5 edn. Florence.
Naugerius	Naugerius, A. (1515), P. Ouidii Nasonis...Heroidum Epistolae, Amorum Libri III, de Arte Amandi Libri III, de Remedio Amoris Libri II, de Medicamine Faciei. Venice.
Némethy	Némethy, G. (1907), P. Ovidii Nasonis Amores. Budapest.
OLD	Glare, P. G. W. (2012), Oxford Latin Dictionary. 2nd edn. Oxford.
PA	Tueller, M. A. and Paton, W. R. (2014–), The Greek Anthology, 5 vols. Cambridge, Mass.
Pinkster	Pinkster, H. (2015–21), Oxford Latin Syntax: 1: The Simple Clause. Oxford.
	Oxford Latin Syntax: 2: The Complex Sentence and Discourse. Oxford.
Ramirez de Verger	Ramirez de Verger and Socas, F. (1991), Ovidio. Obra Amatoria I: Amores. Madrid and
	Ramirez de Verger, A. (2006), Publius Ouidius Naso. Carmina Amatoria 2 edn. Munich.
Ramirez de Verger (1)	Ramirez de Verger and Socas, F. (1991), Ovidio. Obra Amatoria I: Amores. Madrid.
Ramirez de Verger (2)	Ramirez de Verger, A. (2006), Publius Ouidius Naso. Carmina Amatoria 2 edn. Munich.
Ribbeck	Ribbeck, O. (1897), Tragicorum Romanorum Fragmenta 3 edn. Lipsiae.

Showerman and Goold	Showerman, G. and Goold, G. P. (1977), Ovid: Heroides and Amores 2 edn. Cambridge, Mass.
TLG	(1972–) Thesaurus Linguae Graecae (http://stephanus.tlg.uci.edu)
TLL	(1900–) Thesaurus Linguae Latinae. Berlin. http://thesaurus.badw.de/en/tll-digital/tll-open-access.html
VF	Valerius Flaccus
Warmington	Warmington, E. H. (1936), Remains of Old Latin 2: Livius Andronicus, Naevius, Pacuvius and Accius. Cambridge, Mass.
Woodcock	Woodcock, E. C. (1959), A New Latin Syntax. London.

Introduction

1. Ovid's Life and Works

Ovid tells us more about his life than other Augustan poets. Following Propertian precedent,[1] he refers in *Amores* to his homeland, Sulmo, in the territory of the Paeligni (2.1.1, 2.16.1–10, 3.15.2–14). In addition, he provides evidence in *Amores* of his social status, with the lover of 1.3 and the speaker of the collection's final poem claiming to have inherited equestrian status (1.3.7–8, 3.15.5–6). These details are confirmed in *Tr.* 4.10, the autobiographical sketch that the poet wrote in exile.[2] There too he tells us that he came from Sulmo,[3] adding that he was born on 20 March, 43 BCE,[4] and that, although he was an *eques*,[5] he chose literature over politics.[6] Politics intervened, however, when the emperor relegated the poet to the shores of the Black Sea in 8 CE.[7] There he died in roughly 17 CE.[8]

Ovid's works, however, are our main concern. Broadly speaking, we can say that they fall into three distinct phases.[9] He began by writing love elegy in various forms (*Amores, Heroides, Ars Amatoria, Remedia Amoris, Medicamina*); around the turn of the millennium he shifted his focus to narrative poetry (*Metamorphoses, Fasti*); and after 8 CE he was engaged in writing works whose central theme is exile: *Tristia, Epistulae ex Ponto*, and *Ibis*. This schema, however, fails to account for *Medea* (a relatively early work mentioned in *Amores*) or the double *Heroides*.[10] Nor does it include the revising and polishing of *Amores, Metamorphoses*,[11] and *Fasti*.[12]

---

[1] Prop. 1.22, 4.1a.63–4,121–6.
[2] I assume that Ovid was actually exiled to the shores of the Black Sea. For ancient testimony see Plin. *Nat.* 32.152.1. One major deficiency in sceptical arguments is that they focus on details in *Tristia* and *ex Ponto* and ignore other exilic works. Some passages in *Fasti* (e.g. 1.481–2, 4.81–2, 6.665–6) depend for their effect on the reader's awareness of the poet's exile, while *Ibis*' climax (637–8) lacks all point if the reader thinks that its author is safely ensconced in Rome.
[3] *Tr.* 4.10.3.
[4] *Tr.* 4.10.6 (43 BCE: 'the year in which two consuls fell'), 13–14 (20 March: 'the first day of Minerva's festival which was stained with blood'; cf. *Fast.* 3.809–14).
[5] *Tr.* 4.10.7–8. See also *Tr.* 2.89–90, 113–14.
[6] *Tr.* 4.10.35–8. For his legal career, such as it was, see *Tr.* 2.93–6.
[7] For the date see Syme (1978: 37), Ingleheart (2010: 5).
[8] For the date see e.g. Syme (1978: 47).
[9] Thorsen (2014: 1) puts it slightly differently: 'His poetic career displays a tripartite structure in the sense that three themes mark his output: love, myth and exile'.
[10] Kenney (1996: 21) views *Her.* 16–21 as contemporaneous with *Metamorphoses* and *Fasti*. There are, however, good reasons for dating the double *Heroides* to the exile period. See e.g. Barchiesi (1995 and 1999), Heyworth (2016), and Thorsen (2018).
[11] At *Tr.* 1.7.29–30, 2.555–6, and 3.14.19–24 Ovid claims that *Metamorphoses* lacked their final polish.
[12] For *Fasti* as a revised text see e.g. Syme (1978: 21–36), Newlands (1995: 1–5), Boyle (1997a), Martelli (2013: 104–44).

2. Dating *Amores*

That *Amores* are an early work is clear. In *Tristia* 2 (9 CE),[13] the newly exiled Ovid described *Amores* as youthful poems (339–40):

> ad leue rursus opus, iuuenalia carmina ueni
> et falso moui pectus amore meum.

I came again to my lightweight task, youthful poems, and I stirred my heart with a fictional love.

At *Pont.* 3.3.29–30 he uses similar language to remind Cupid of his role in shaping his erotic verse. In particular he recalls the god's intervention in *Am.* 1.1:

> tu mihi dictasti iuuenalia carmina primus,
> apposui senis te duce quinque pedes.

You were the first to dictate to me my youthful poems, under your guidance I juxtaposed five feet with six.

But how early are *Amores*? At *Tristia* 4.10.57–8 Ovid seems to tell us that he began writing them when he was in his teens:

> carmina cum primum populo iuuenalia legi,
> barba resecta mihi bisue semelue fuit.

When I first began to read my youthful poems in public, my beard had been trimmed once or twice.

Given that Ovid was born in 43 BCE, scholars infer that he began writing *Amores* around 25.[14]

If so, Ovid must have been engaged in writing *Amores* for well over a decade after 25 BCE because some poems were written substantially later. 3.9, the 'Lament for Tibullus', obviously post-dates that elegist's death in 19, while 3.1's allusion to Horace's fourth book of *Odes* suggests a date later than 13,[15] and reference to 'a people over whom a triumph has been won' (1.14.46: *triumphatae...gentis*) points, as Syme suggests,[16] to a date later than 7 BCE.

This situation is complicated by the fact that in the epigram to *Amores* 1 the poet tells us that this is a revised work, that five (probably separate) books have been reduced to a single three-book collection (1–2):

---

[13] For the date see Syme (1978: 37–8), Ingleheart (2010: 5).
[14] E.g. McKeown (84), Knox (2009a: 5).
[15] *Am.* 3.1.19: *saepe aliquis digito uatem designat euntem* alludes to *Carm.* 4.3.22–3: *monstror digito praetereuntium | Romanae fidicen lyrae.* For the publication date of *Odes* 4 see Thomas (2011: 5–7).
[16] Syme (1978: 5) notes that '"triumphatus" in Ovid carries a proper and precise meaning'. Tiberius' triumph over the Sugambri took place in January, 7 BCE.

> qui modo Nasonis fueramus quinque libelli,
> tres sumus; hoc illi praetulit auctor opus.

We who were recently Naso's five books are three; the author preferred this work to that.

The exiled poet confirms the claim (*Tr.* 4.10.61–2):[17]

> multa quidem scripsi, sed, quae uitiosa putaui,
> emendaturis ignibus ipse dedi.

In fact I wrote a lot [about Corinna], but what I thought was faulty I handed over to the flames to improve.[18]

But the chronology of Ovid's early works is notoriously difficult to untangle. When, for example, did he write his tragedy, *Medea*? From *Am.* 3.1 and 3.15 we understand that the elegist is about to write a tragedy. But if we turn to 2.18, we discover that the tragedy has already been written (13–14):

> sceptra tamen sumpsi, curaque tragoedia nostra
> creuit et huic operi quamlibet aptus eram.

However, I took up the sceptre and with care my tragedy grew and I was suited to this genre.

Medea seems to have been written both before and after *Amores*.

But what of other works? It is generally accepted that *Ars Amatoria* was written later than *Amores*. After all, the Teacher gives this advice to his female students at *Ars* 3.343–4:[19]

> deue tribus libris, titulus quos signat Amorum,
> elige, quod docili molliter ore legas.

Or choose from the three books marked with the label *Amores* to read with softness and skill.

The inference is obvious: a three-volume edition of *Amores* exists.

But if we return to *Am.* 2.18, we learn that after composing his tragedy Ovid returned to writing erotic poetry (2.18.15–18):

> risit Amor pallamque meam pictosque cothurnos
> sceptraque priuata tam cito sumpta manu.

---

[17] Barchiesi (2001b: 159–61) questions whether there were two editions of *Amores*. He ignores *Tr.* 4.10.61–2.

[18] These lines constitute evidence that Ovid excised some of his earlier poems. I agree, however, with Martelli (2013: 37) that the precise nature of the transformation of the original *Amores* is 'destined to remain unknowable'.

[19] Gibson (2003: 39) dates *Ars* 3 to before 2 CE.

> hinc quoque me dominae numen deduxit iniquae,
> cothurnato uate triumphat Amor.

Love laughed at my cloak and painted buskins and the sceptre that I had taken up so quickly in my unroyal hand.

And from this too the power of my unjust mistress dragged me away and Love triumphs over the buskined seer.

What poems are these? They could be *Amores*. But the poet's language suggests that he has already written or is currently writing *Ars Amatoria* (2.18.19–20):[20]

> quod licet, aut artes teneri profitemur Amoris
> (ei mihi praeceptis urgeor ipse meis)...

As far as I can, I either expound the arts of tender Love (ah me! I am pressed hard by my own doctrines)...

Thus *Ars Amatoria* turns out to be either contemporary with or earlier or later than *Amores*.

The best explanation of these contradictions is that proposed by Syme (1978: 20) and developed by Thorsen (2013: 114–17; 2014: 25–6).[21] Syme argued that in 1 BCE (or before 2 CE at the latest),[22] Ovid revised his erotic poetry and produced a collected edition including *Amores*, *Heroides*, *Ars Amatoria*, and *Remedia*. If that is so, he made no attempt to harmonize the chronology of the various books; he was willing to let the contradictions stand. One advantage of this solution is that, as Thorsen (2014: 26) puts it, 'it forces the reader to look at the artistic design, rather than the actual making in time of the individual works'.[23] For Ovid the aesthetic arrangement of his poems was more important than informing readers of the order in which they were composed.

3. The Design of the Three-Book Collection

How did Ovid organize *Amores*? As transmitted to us in the oldest and best manuscripts, the collection consists of three books with 15 poems in the first and third books and 19 in the second.

---

[20] For this view see e.g. Hollis (1977: 150–1), Syme (1978: 7). McKeown (1998: 385) disagrees. However, as he notes, '*artes*, *profitemur* and *praeceptis* readily suit the *Ars*'. This is true. *praecipio* and cognates occur 23 times in *Ars* and *Remedia*, but only here in *Amores*. The comparable figures for *ars* are 66 in *Ars* and *Remedia* and 18 in *Amores*. The claim that 'love elegy in general could be represented as fundamentally didactic' is unpersuasive because it could be made of any and every literary genre.

[21] See also Harrison (2002: 84) who emphasizes the interconnectedness of Ovid's erotic works.

[22] References in *Ars Amatoria* to the mock sea-battle (1.171–4) and to Gaius Caesar's imminent eastern campaign (1.177–228), establish firm dates for that poem. The sea-battle formed part of the celebrations for the dedication of the Augustan forum in 2 BCE, while the dispute with Parthia was resolved peacefully in the spring of 2 CE.

[23] See also Barchiesi and Hardie (2010: 61 n.5): 'Ovid is more interested in the gesture politics of career construction than in presenting a consistent and coherent account of the chronology of his works'.

3. THE DESIGN OF THE THREE-BOOK COLLECTION

For some this lack of an obvious numerical pattern is troubling. A Book 2 with 20 poems would be much neater. We would then have three books each based on a multiple of five.[24] It is not clear, however, that Ovid was attracted to designs of this kind. Consider *Metamorphoses*, a work on which the poet was engaged around the time of the revised edition of *Amores*. Anderson (1968: 103) highlighted the importance of the artistic contest between Arachne and Minerva (*Met.* 6.70–128) for our understanding of Ovid's aesthetic principles. He concluded correctly that 'symmetry is no prerequisite to Ovidian art'. The same can be said for *Amores*. In each book the first poem reflects on the nature of elegy. And each book contains a signature poem. In Books 1 and 3 that poem closes the book (1.15, 3.15). In Book 2, however, it is 2.18, not 2.19, which constitutes a signature and identifies the *Amores*-poet as author of *Ars Amatoria* and *Heroides*. Just as in *Metamorphoses*, Ovid took pains in *Amores* to avoid accusations of an interest in numerical patterns.[25] In both *Amores* and *Metamorphoses* he avoided the four-square symmetry that characterizes *Aeneid*.

What principles of organization are discernible? Around a century ago, Port (1926: 452) established that Ovid employed a principle of variation, that he 'avoided the danger of uniformity within each book by the distribution of similar poems to different books'. The following table illustrates the point:[26]

1.5: I had sex with Corinna	2.12: I had sex with Corinna
1.6: To a nameless doorman	2.2: To a named doorman (Bagoas)
1.13: To a natural obstacle (the dawn)	3.6: To a natural obstacle (a river)
2.5: Your infidelity is obvious	3.14: Conceal your infidelity
2.6: Funerary poem (a parrot)	3.9: Funerary poem (Tibullus)
2.19: To a foolish husband	3.4: To a foolish husband

By assigning poems on similar themes to different books Ovid not only ensured variety within individual books but also created surprise when a subject reappeared. Part of the pleasure of reading 3.4 (Be less strict) is that it contradicts the advice given in 2.19 (Be more strict).

A countervailing principle can also be discerned. Some poems on similar themes are not only in the same book but are juxtaposed with each other. In these cases, however, there is dramatic continuity.

---

[24] See e.g. Port (1926: 452): 'It is certainly no coincidence that Ovid united 15 poems in the first and third books and 20 in the second'; Kenney (1962: 13): 'The three-book edition of *Amores* originally contained in its three books 15, 20, and 15 poems respectively'.

[25] It is notable that the various patterns proposed for *Amores* in PhD theses in the 1970s have had no impact, e.g. Hofstaedter (1973), Lawrence (1973), McCaffrey (1974), and Lörcher (1975). The same is true of Rambaux (1985), whose schema for Book 3, for example, pairs 3.2 (at the races) with 3.14 (conceal your infidelity); and 3.7 (the lover's impotence) with 3.9 (lament for Tibullus).

[26] This is my table not Port's. Some of his examples of similar poems are not convincing. For example, he links 1.5, 2.12, and 3.2 as illustrations of 'undisturbed togetherness with the beloved' (1926: 453). 1.5 and 2.12 recall sex with Corinna. 3.2, however, is set in the Circus Maximus. Nor do I accept Port's (1926: 453) and Cameron's (1968: 328) pairing of 1.4 with 2.5. Cameron claims: 'In 1.4 Ovid is at a party where his mistress is sitting next to her husband: in 2.5 he is the husband at the same party'. 1.4 is set at a party; 2.5 is not.

1.11: Nape, take a letter to Corinna
2.2: Bagoas, let me in
2.7: I did not sleep with Cypassis
2.13: Corinna has had an abortion

1.12: My letter failed
2.3: Curse you, Bagoas
2.8: Cypassis, how did she find out?
2.14: Abortion is wicked

These poems are so closely connected that, as J. T. Davis (1977: 19) put it, 'the second poem serves not just as the thematic companion piece to the preceding but as its dramatic sequel'.[27] There is no such pair in Book 3.

4. The Place of Book 3 in the Collection

All three books of *Amores* present remarkably varied material. Nevertheless, all begin with reflections on love elegy and all include signature-poems. And all three incorporate material of the kind familiar to readers of Catullus, Tibullus, and Propertius, particularly concerning the joys and difficulties involved in an erotic relationship. Book 3, however, moves away from the focus on the poet-lover's relationship with Corinna that so characterized Book 2. It is significant that Corinna is named only three times in this book (compared with nine times in Book 2) and then only in the past tense (3.1.49: *didicit…Corinna* ['Corinna learned'], 3.7.25–6: *Corinnam…memini* ['I remember that Corinna'], 3.12.16: *mouit… Corinna* ['Corinna inspired']). Book 3 also takes us into new territory with the attempt of a pickup artist to seduce a girl at the races (3.2), with an enormously influential dream vision poem (3.5), and with a married couple's pilgrimage to a festival of Juno (3.13). Explicit reflection on Ovid's elegiac predecessors, Tibullus (3.9), Catullus (3.11), and Propertius (3.12) makes Book 3 an appropriate conclusion to a collection of love elegies.

5. *Amores* as Performance

> hoc quoque iussit Amor. procul hinc, procul este, seueri.
> non estis teneris apta theatra modis. (2.1.3–4)

> Love also gave this order. Away from here, be far away from here, you moralists.
> You are not the right theatre for tender verse.

Ovid's *Amores*, as Boyd points out, resemble Horace's first set of *Odes* in being a three-book collection designed 'to be read and comprehended together and in their present sequence'.[28] They also resemble *Odes* 1–3 in not presenting a unified

---

[27] I do not include 2.9 and 3.11 in this category because (a) I do not think that they should be divided and (b), even if they were divided, they would not meet J. T. Davis's criteria.
[28] Boyd (1997: 136).

narrative. Ovid's *Amores* are neither 'a novel' nor a 'narrative of a love affair':[29] they do not present a movement from initial infatuation through love affair to final disillusionment.[30] Indeed it might be said that the collection is structured so as to obviate readings of this kind.

Central to love elegy, as we find it in Tibullus and Propertius, is a pose, to use Wallis's phrase, of 'fictitious realism'.[31] The first poem of *Amores* 1, with its depiction of Cupid's intervention in the poet's life, immediately establishes that Ovid has rejected that stance. In *Amores* Ovid gives us not the appearance of narrative continuity but a series of discontinuous performances, occasionally put on by a character who shares properties with the collection's author, sometimes by a man in a relationship with a woman called Corinna, but most often by a person who can be identified only by the mask that he chooses to adopt.

6. A Multiplicity of Masks

The authorship of *Amores* is not in doubt. It is not always clear, however, who speaks any particular poem. Sometimes the speaker provides enough information to suggest that he can be identified in some way with the poet. Perhaps he calls himself Naso (1.Epigr, 1.11, 2.1, 2.13) or claims authorship of other Ovidian works (2.18) or mentions his social status or origins in the Abruzzi (1.3, 2.1, 2.16, 3.15). At other times he behaves like a Tibullan or Propertian lover, celebrating his sexual successes or lamenting his failures with his mistress Corinna (1.5, 1.11 and 12, 2.7 and 8, 2.11, 2.12, 2.13 and 14, 2.17). But he also presents his relationship with Corinna as finished, as firmly in the past (2.19, 3.7, 3.12). More often, however, he presents himself as the lover of an unnamed girl (1.3, 1.4, 1.6, 1.7, 1.10, 1.13, 1.14, 2.2, 2.3, 2.5, 2.9, 2.15, 2.16, 2.17, 3.3, 3.5, 3.6, 3.7 [not Corinna], 3.8, 3.10, 3.11, 3.12, 3.14). Or he may be the lover of many girls (2.4) or just two (2.10). Then again he may be an aggressive pursuer of another man's wife (2.19 [not Corinna], 3.4), or a pickup artist (3.2), or a devoted husband (3.13). Elsewhere he eavesdrops on a procuress (1.8), offers paradoxical reflections (1.9), or mourns the death of a parrot (2.6) or a poet (3.9). There is no consistent 'I' in *Amores*.[32]

---

[29] For *Amores* as a novel see Holzberg (2002: 46–70); for 'narrative of a love affair' see Boyd (2002: 95). Closer to the mark is Oliver (1945: 201): 'I frankly see no way of avoiding agreement with the majority of modern scholars, who deny that *Amores* contain a continuous narrative'.

[30] I agree with McKeown's assessment (94): 'chronological ordering is not a significant principle in the arrangement of the collection'; (95): 'there is no clear narrative framework'.

[31] For Propertius' abandonment of this strategy in Book 3 see Wallis (2018: 201–16; for the phrase see 202).

[32] Unlike Oliensis (2019: 18), if I understand her correctly, I believe in 'dismantling the intratextual ego'. Nor do I agree with Volk (2005: 94): 'I see no point in further splitting up the persona of the *Amores*, a work that gives no indication that the speaker of the individual poems does not remain the same throughout the three books'.

7. Corinna

Ovid claims in both *Amores* (3.12.16) and *Tristia* (4.10.59–60) that a woman whom he called Corinna had inspired his verse. While Corinna may have been central to *Amores* in their original form, she is not a major player in the extant three-book edition: her name occurs 14 times in 49 poems. Comparison with Catullus, Tibullus, and Propertius only underlines that fact. Catullus' Lesbia is named nine times in his elegiac verse (poems 65–116; 15 times in all), while Tibullus' Delia appears in his first elegy (1.1.57, 61, 68) and subsequently in 1.2, 1.3, and 1.6. The case of Propertius' Cynthia is even more striking. Her primacy is obvious: Propertius begins his first poem with the words *Cynthia prima* ('Cynthia first' 1.1.1) and names his mistress 29 times in Book 1 alone.

Also important is the way in which Corinna is introduced into *Amores*. Her entry makes clear that readers should not expect an (auto)biographical text. In 1.1 it is Cupid who turns our poet towards love elegy; in 1.2 the poet experiences love's pangs in the abstract; in 1.3 he offers to make a girl famous in his poetry, while in 1.4 he is about to go to the same dinner as an unnamed girl and her partner. Corinna does not even appear until 1.5. And there is nothing in that poem to suggest that this was their first sexual encounter. When does Corinna's name appear next? At 1.11.5, when the lover is speaking to her hairdresser. If the opening poems of Book 1 are not enough to convince readers this is not a biographical text, they should attend to the closing lines of 3.12 (43–4):

> et mea debuerat falso laudata uideri
> femina; credulitas nunc mihi uestra nocet.

> It should have been obvious that the praises of my girlfriend were fictitious; your gullibility (i.e. of readers) is now harming me.

While it is possible that Ovid had employed Propertian-style 'fictitious realism'[33] in his representation of Corinna in the earlier version of *Amores*, what remains is a set of largely discontinuous scenarios confined mainly to Book 2:[34] I had sex with Corinna (1.5, 2.12), I wrote a letter to Corinna (1.11 and 1.12), Corinna's parrot died (2.6), I had sex with Corinna's slave (2.7 and 2.8), Corinna's voyage (2.11), Corinna's abortion (2.13 and 2.14), enslavement to Corinna (2.17).

8. Extending the Range

But Ovid did more than reduce the obsessive focus on a mistress that characterized earlier love elegy. He extended the genre's range to take in the social, economic,

---

[33] The phrase comes from Wallis (2018: 202).
[34] There is, however, continuity between 2.12 (note especially 27: *sine caede* ['without slaughter']) and the abortion poems which follow. See Gamel (1989).

and political context in which sexual relationships between freeborn men and 'disreputable' women took place.[35]

Consider, for example, that characteristic Propertian trope, the *seruitium amoris*,[36] the idea that being involved with a *domina* enslaves a freeborn male, that a woman becomes his mistress and his owner. Ovid also employs this metaphor (1.2.18, 1.3.5, 2.17.1, 3.8.14, 3.11.3, 10). More prominent in *Amores*, however, is literal slavery.[37] When the lover addresses an unnamed doorkeeper in 1.6 he begins with the words (1): *ianitor, indignum!, dura religate catena* ('Doorman, shocking!, bound with a harsh chain'). Also striking is that he praises his girlfriend's hair because it resembles a compliant slave (1.14.25): *quam se praebuerunt ferro patienter et igni* ('How patiently it submitted to iron and fire') and because it does not cause pain to an actual slave (1.14.15–16): *non acus abrupit, non uallum pectinis illos. | ornatrix tuto corpore semper erat* ('No needle tore it, no comb's palisade. The hairdresser's body was always safe').

It is noteworthy that three of the four sets of paired poems involve slaves. In each case Ovid highlights the psychological cruelty involved in the lover's treatment of his social inferiors. In 1.11 he acknowledges that Corinna's hairdresser, Nape, has human and possibly even sexual feelings (9–11). He also blames her for his lack of success with Corinna (1.12.3–6). In 2.2 and 2.3 he emphasizes Bagoas' status as a slave and a eunuch (2.2.15–16, 39–40, 61–2, 2.3.1–4), while in 2.7 and 2.8, after insisting that he would never have stooped to having sex with a slave (2.7.19–22), he tries to blackmail Cypassis into having sex with him again (2.8.21–8).[38]

It is also characteristic of Ovid that he refers to bodily aspects of sex that are avoided or passed over briefly by other elegists. In *Amores* he refers to violence against a girlfriend (1.7). He also confronts pregnancy and abortion as consequences of sexual intercourse (2.12: I had sex with Corinna; 2.13: Corinna's abortion; 2.14: Abortion is wicked), while in *Ars Amatoria*, he refers perhaps to menstruation (3.237–8) and certainly to the effects of childbirth on women's bodies (3.785; cf. *Am.* 2.14.7). And then there is a man's inability to have sex. At 1.5.39–44 the Tibullan lover refers to impotence caused by thinking of his regular girlfriend. In *Am.* 3.7 this becomes the subject of an 84-line poem in which the Ovidian lover (he refers to Corinna at line 25) reports his embarrassment and reflects on the reasons for his failure.

Ovid is also more explicit than his predecessors about the economic aspects of the relationship between the poet-lover and his mistress. From Tibullus we learn

---

[35] Cf. McKeown (17): 'Ovid restricts the genre's range of subject-matter'.
[36] On this trope see e.g. Lyne (1979), Murgatroyd (1981), McCarthy (1998), Fitzgerald (2000: 72–5). The Propertian lover addresses one poem (3.6) to a literal slave, Lygdamus.
[37] For discussion of Ovid's treatment of slavery in *Amores* see Henderson (1991, 1992), James (1997), Fitzgerald (2000: 59–67), De Boer (2010; 2021).
[38] For discussion of Ovid's representation of subaltern women in *Amores* see e.g. James (1997), De Boer (2010), and Wise (2019).

that Delia has a preference for rich lovers (1.5.47–8) and is fond of gifts (1.5.59–60). The Propertian lover expresses anxiety about Cynthia's greed (e.g. 2.16.11–12) and promiscuity (2.16.21–2).[39] But it is not until his final book, when Propertius gives voice to Acanthis, a procuress (4.5), that we find a clear hint that the relationship between mistress and lover actually resembles that between prostitute and client. Ovid also has a procuress, Dipsas (1.8), whose speech is over twice as long as Acanthis' and occupies the central position in Book 1. When a lover (perhaps the man who reported Dipsas' speech) is given a chance to reply he invokes the image of the lowly prostitute (1.10.21–2): *stat meretrix certo cuiuis mercabilis aere, | et miseras iusso corpore quaerit opes* ('The prostitute stands for purchase by anyone at a fixed price and acquires wretched money with her body on demand'). The issue is raised again in 3.12, a poem which names Corinna and alludes to her quasi-divine entry in 1.5,[40] but suggests that she has capitalized on her Ovid-given reputation to increase her market value.

9. *Amores* and Politics

The elegiac stance is implicitly countercultural because it places the highest value on a sexual relationship outside of marriage.[41] Fundamental to the genre is a man's love for a woman whom he cannot marry. Not surprisingly elegists like Tibullus and Propertius also reject other values prized by moralizing Romans. Both, for example, favour love over war. Tibullus closes his first elegy by stating a preference for erotic over actual warfare (1.1.75–6): *hic ego dux milesque bonus: uos, signa tubaeque, | ite procul* ('here [i.e. in love] I am a general and a good soldier. Away with standards and trumpets!'). And Propertius says much the same (1.6.29–30): *non ego sum laudi, non natus idoneus armis: | hanc me militiam fata subire uolunt* ('I was not born suitable for glory, for warfare: fate wants me to undergo this kind of military service'). He goes further and refuses to sing of Caesar (2.1.41–2) *nec mea conueniunt duro praecordia uersu | Caesaris in Phrygios condere nomen auos* ('My heart is not compatible with harsh verse and establishing Caesar's name back to his Trojan ancestors').

But between the composition of Tibullus' and Propertius' love elegies in the 20s BCE and the publication of the three-book edition of *Amores* much had changed. Moral codes which had once been enforced by the family and the power of social disapproval were now enshrined in law. The *lex Iulia de adulteriis coercendis* ('The Julian law on the suppression of adultery') had been passed in 18 BCE,

---

[39] For more detailed discussion of Propertius' anxieties see the Introduction to *Am.* 3.11.
[40] For this see Hinds (1987: 7–8; 2006: 19–21). Gale (2021: 220) notes that 'Like Catullus, the elegiac lover typically oscillates between idolisation and denigration of the beloved'.
[41] For fuller discussion Ovid's treatment of politics in *Amores* see Davis (2006: 71–84).

establishing a criminal court to deal with cases of adultery, and proposing punishments for guilty couples and compliant husbands.[42] While risqué poets might freely flaunt their indifference to traditional morality in the 20s, there was no guarantee that such freedom would be possible two decades later.

How did Ovid confront this new situation? When the Ovidian lover talks of sexual success with Corinna he is evasive (2.12.2–4): *in nostro est, ecce, Corinna sinu, | quam uir, quam custos, quam ianua firma, tot hostes, | seruabant* ('Look, Corinna is in my embrace, she who was protected by her man, her guard, a stout door, so many enemies'). That word *uir* ('man', but also 'husband') both suggests and resists an accusation of adultery.[43] Elsewhere, however, he ventriloquizes an aggressive adulterer: in 2.19, where he tries to increase his fun by asking a husband to defend his wife more carefully, and in 3.4, where he urges a husband to allow his wife more freedom. In case readers miss the point, he uses the word *adulter* repeatedly in 3.4: *adultera mens* (5 'her purpose is adultery'), *adulter* (8 'adulterer'), *adultera cara* (29 'a highly prized adulteress'), *adultera coniunx* (37 'a wife's adultery'). Ovid responds to Augustus' marriage legislation by having speakers in *Amores* parade their indifference to traditional morality and the law.

Also important to the Augustan regime was the attempt to justify its existence by manipulating history, or, as Propertius put it (2.1.42): 'by establishing Caesar's name back to his Trojan ancestors'. Virgil had laid out the connection between Augustus and his 'Trojan ancestors' in *Aeneid*,[44] while Augustus himself had formalized his lineage in stone in his forum in 2 BCE—that is, around the time when Ovid reduced five books of *Amores* to three.

How then does Ovid treat the myth of Trojan ancestry? Characters in *Amores* refer frequently to the two most prominent gods in the Augustan version of history: Venus, mother of Aeneas, and Mars, father of Romulus. Given the familiarity of the story (1.9.40: *notior in caelo fabula nulla fuit*, cf. *Ars* 2.561, *Met.* 4.189), it is not surprising that readers are reminded of their adultery (1.8.41–2, 1.9.40–1, 2.5.28, 2.9.47–8). As for Venus' love for Anchises, the Ovidian lover recalls their story when denouncing abortion (2.14.17–18): *si Venus Aenean grauida temerasset in aluo, | Caesaribus tellus orba futura fuit* ('If Venus when pregnant had defiled Aeneas in her womb, the world would have been bereft of Caesars'). Even more important, because treated at greater length, is the story of the origins of Romulus and Remus. At 3.4.39–40 the adulterer points out that the twins were born 'not without crime', while at 3.6.45–82 the frustrated lover tells the story of Ilia's double rape by Mars and the river Anio. He highlights her lack of consent and allows Ilia to express the pain and anguish that she feels. In both phases of the myth, the

---

[42] For details see the Introduction to 3.4.   [43] For the word's ambiguity see *OLD uir* 2.
[44] I do not claim that Virgil presents the connection as unproblematic. See e.g. Rogerson (2017: 37–56).

Trojan and the proto-Roman, Ovid highlights all that is most difficult, all that is most awkward in the Augustan version of Rome's origins.

10. Verbal Patterning

The elder Seneca tells the well-known story that when asked to nominate the lines of which he was most proud of Ovid chose (*Con.* 2.2.12.12):

>*Ars* 2.24: semibouemque uirum semiuirumque bouem

>Half-bull man and half-man bull

and

>*Am.* 2.11.10: et gelidum Borean egelidumque Notum

>And the chilly North wind and unchilly South wind.

Why would Ovid select these lines? One answer is that both lines display lexical ingenuity. *semibos*, for example, is an Ovidian coinage. While *semiuir* is not new, it is used here in a novel sense to mean not 'effeminate' (as at *A.* 4.215, 12.99, Liv. 33.28.8) but 'half-human being'. And while *gelidus* ('chilly') is relatively common, *egelidus* (*OLD*: 'having the chill taken off') is not. The adjective had been invented by Catullus (46.1: *iam uer egelidos refert tepores* ['now spring brings back unchilly warmth']) and then used in precisely the opposite sense by Manilius (5.131) and Virgil (*A.* 8.610; with Servius: '*egelido*', *id est nimium gelido* ['*egelido*, i.e. excessively chilly']). Ovid restores its Catullan sense. A second reason is that both lines embody antithesis and balance. Each consists of two phrases, each of which combines an adjective and a noun. And within each line each adjective and noun is antithetical to the other: *semibouemque / semiuirumque, uirum / bouem; et gelidum / egelidumque, Borean / Notum*. A third is metrical. In each case opposing phrases confront each other across the compulsory caesura. A fourth is sonic. Note the chiastic arrangement of sounds in *Ars* 2.24: *bouem uirum / uirum bouem*, and echoic sounds in *Am.* 2.11.10: *et gelidum / egelidum*. These two pentameters embody in compressed form much of what makes Ovid's verse so attractive: lexical creativity, the use of verbal patterns, ingenuity within a strict metrical schema, and a concern with the interplay of sounds.

Ovid is a also visual poet concerned with the architecture of lines and couplets. Consequently concern with verbal patterning, with the appearance of words on the page, is a marked characteristic of his poetry at every stage.[45] To illustrate this aspect of Ovid's style, I propose to examine 3.7.1–14, a passage which embodies within a narrow compass the features that I would like to discuss:

---

[45] For excellent surveys of the principle features of Ovid's style see McKeown (1987) and Kenney (2002).

> At non formosa est, at non bene culta puella,
>   at, puto, non uotis saepe petita meis.
> hanc tamen in nullos tenui male languidus usus,
>   sed iacui pigro crimen onusque toro
> nec potui cupiens, pariter cupiente puella, 5
>   inguinis effeti parte iuuante frui.
> illa quidem nostro subiecit eburnea collo
>   bracchia Sithonia candidiora niue
> osculaque inseruit cupida luctantia lingua
>   lasciuum femori supposuitque femur 10
> et mihi blanditias dixit dominumque uocauit
>   et quae praeterea publica uerba iuuant.
> tacta tamen ueluti gelida mea membra cicuta
>   segnia propositum destituere meum.

No, she wasn't lovely. No, she wasn't a sophisticated girl. No, I suppose, she wasn't the frequent object of my desire.

Nevertheless, I was distressingly limp when I held her to no purpose, but lay there a guilty burden on an idle bed.

I was eager (and the girl was equally eager) but couldn't enjoy the pleasant part of my feeble groin.

She placed her ivory arms, more radiant than Sithonian snow, beneath my neck,

With eager tongue she thrust in vigorous kisses and placed sexy thigh beneath my thigh,

and flattered me and called me master and used common words to help me as well.

But my sluggish penis, as if touched by icy hemlock, abandoned my goal.

The first line of this passage illustrates Ovid's use of repetition to achieve balance, with *at non* placed at the start of each phrase and with each phrase framing the main caesura.[46] Indeed *at non* articulates the whole couplet with the phrase being repeated, though broken up, in the pentameter (*at...non*). Line 5 works in a similar way, with sense units framing the main caesura. This time, however, balance is underlined by the use of repetition and polyptoton (*cupiens...cupiente*) and alliteration of *c* and *p*: *nec potui cupiens, pariter cupiente puella*. Similar are the placing of different forms of the same word at the caesura and the end of the line in line 10: *femur...femori*,[47] and the placing of an adjective at the caesura which agrees with the final word in lines 3, 4, and 7 (*nullos...usus*; *pigro...toro*; *nostro...collo*). In this latter case, the effect is, as Wilkinson observed, 'something very like rhyme'.[48]

---

[46] For Ovid's tendency to have a syntactic break at the main caesura see Commentary on 3.7.37.
[47] See also 1.4.32: *biberis...bibam*, 2.2.34: *fieri...facit*, 2.4.20: *placeo...placet*.
[48] Wilkinson (1955: 40).

A different kind of verbal patterning can be seen in lines 9 and 13, lines which contain four (or more) words ending in *a* in different cases (9): *osculăque inseruit cupidā luctantiā linguā*; (13): *tactă tamen ueluti gelidā meă membră cicuta*.[49] The fact that Ovid employs two such lines in succession at the collection's most critical juncture, the entry of Corinna (*Am.* 1.5.9–10):

> ecce, Corinnă uenit, tunicā uelată recinctā,
> candidă diuiduă collă tegente comā

suggests that he particularly prizes this verbal pattern.[50]

Also important are lines consisting of two nouns, two adjectives, and a verb (sometimes including a minor word). The best known of these is the line that Dryden called 'golden': abVAB.[51] Line 7 gives us an apparent golden line, with a centrally placed verb, *subiecit*, and with *illa* appearing to agree with *eburnea*, and *nostro* actually agreeing with *collo*. There are two patterned lines in this passage (6): *inguinis effeti parte iuuante frui* (AaBbV); and (9): *osculaque inseruit cupida luctantia lingua* (AVbaB). The first of these patterns also occurs at 1.6.28 and the second at 2.4.2 and 3.6.16. The most frequently-used patterns in *Amores* are VabBA (30 times), abVAB (24 times), and abAVB (20 times).

How does this concern with repetition and variation, with antithesis and balance, affect our understanding of Ovid's poetry? First, it opens up varied perspectives by suggesting different possibilities. Even when words and phrases are repeated precisely, a change of context gives them different meanings. Second, the use of verbal patterns (an elaborate form of hyperbaton) forces even practised readers to attend more closely to the relationships between the nouns and adjectives that they see or hear.

11. *Amores* and Love Elegy

One distinctive mark of *Amores* is their awareness of elegy as a genre. Both Tibullus and Propertius use the word 'elegy' only once. Tibullus complains that 'elegiacs are useless' (*nec prosunt elegi* 2.4.13), while Propertius' Horus labels elegy as *fallax* (4.1b.135): *at tu finge elegos, fallax opus* ('Compose your elegies, deceptive work'). Ovid, also employs *elegi* when reflecting on the genre's nature (2.1.21, 3.15.2, 19). But he takes this one step further when he personifies the genre, addressing Elegy in his lament for Tibullus (3.9.3), and making her a character in the drama of 3.1.

---

[49] Lines 7 and 8 give us a similar run of words ending in *a*: *eburnea collo | bracchia Sithonia candidiora niue*.

[50] For further discussion and a list of such lines in *Amores* see Commentary on 3.4.16. More striking still is *Met.* 7.204: *uiuăque saxă suă conuulsăque roboră terrā*.

[51] For this see Commentary on 3.3.21.

As Wallis observes (2018: 209): 'Ovid presents himself explicitly as one who has inherited an amatory tradition'.

That Ovid is aware of his place in this tradition is made explicit in *Tr.* 4.10.51–4:

> Vergilium uidi tantum, nec auara Tibullo
> tempus amicitiae fata dedere meae.
> successor fuit hic tibi, Galle, Propertius illi;
> quartus ab his serie temporis ipse fui.

> I only saw Virgil, and greedy fate did not give Tibullus enough time for friendship with me. He was your successor, Gallus, Propertius his. I was the fourth in temporal sequence after these.

It is also clear in *Amores*, where poems in Book 3 engage with Tibullus by name (3.9), and with Catullus (3.11) and Propertius (3.12) by means of clear and frequent allusion. It is not impossible that a poem in Book 3 alludes to poems written by Gallus, the genre's founder.

What is the nature of this engagement? It was once fashionable to use terms like 'burlesque' and 'parody'.[52] This, however, as McKeown pointed out,[53] underestimates the complexity of the relationship between *Amores* and earlier love elegy.

Ovid's approach to his predecessors is sometimes flippant. Consider, for example, the Propertian lover's attitude to his mistress's hair.[54] When in moralizing mood, he takes a firm stand against the use of hair dye (2.18.27–8):[55]

> illi sub terris fiant mala multa puellae,
> quae mentita suas uertit inepta comas.

> I hope that numerous misfortunes befall that girl in the underworld who dishonestly and foolishly alters her hair.

When Ovid takes up the theme in 1.14, misfortune befalls a girl in this world: she loses all her hair. Zetzel (1996: 76) pointed to the connection between 1.14.1 (*dicebam 'medicare tuos desiste capillos'* ['I kept on saying "stop medicating your hair"']) and Prop. 1.2, particularly the use of *capillo* (1.2.1 ['hair']) and *medicina* (1.2.7). There is also a link with Prop. 2.18, because in both poems the lover labels the girl as *inepta* ('foolish': Prop. 2.18.28, *Am.* 1.14.36). But the differences between *Am.* 1.14 and either Propertian treatment of the theme are remarkable. First, 1.14 is substantially longer than both of the Propertian lover's denunciations (Prop. 1.2: 32 lines, 2.18.23–38: 16 lines; *Am.* 1.14: 56 lines). Second, Ovid's poem lacks

---

[52] E.g. J. T. Davis (1981): 'burlesque'; Luck (1961: 173, 183, 185, 187, 188, 191, 193, 196): 'parody'.
[53] McKeown (1987: 17–18).
[54] The Tibullan lover also expresses anxiety about his girlfriend's hair (1.8.9–10).
[55] It is not clear whether all of Prop. 2.18.23–38 concerns hair dye (Lee: 1994; Fedeli: 2005) or cosmetics more generally (Goold: 1990). I quote only the lines that clearly concern hair. Different editors divide 2.18 differently and so I give only line numbers. For anxiety over Cynthia's hair see also 1.15.5.

Propertius' moralizing. The only reason for avoiding the use of hair dye seems to be practical: it causes hair loss. Third, the situation gives Ovid the opportunity for a virtuoso display of wit, praising the hair's beauty, its teachability, and its innocence. Fourth, there is an immediate solution: German wigs are available. And finally, the problem will eventually solve itself: hair grows back. While Ovid's treatment is lighter than Propertius', more entertaining in fact, words like 'burlesque' and 'parody' are inappropriate because they suggest dependence on a Propertian or other original.[56]

There are also poems which take up themes not handled by earlier elegists. Consider, for example, 2.13. If there is a model for this poem, it is Prop. 2.28,[57] a poem in which the lover's prayers rescue his girlfriend from a self-inflicted illness (2.28.5–6): *sed non tam ardoris culpa est neque crimina caeli, | quam totiens sanctos non habuisse deos* ('But it's not so much the heat's fault or heaven's crimes, as that she failed repeatedly to treat the gods as holy'). In *Am.* 2.13 the girlfriend's sickness is also self-inflicted: Corinna has had an abortion.

How does Ovid handle this subject? With complete seriousness.[58] 2.13 begins with a surprise: Corinna was pregnant (1–2): *dum labefactat onus grauidi temeraria uentris, | in dubio uitae lassa Corinna iacet* ('Because she recklessly undermines the burden of her pregnant belly, Corinna lies ill in danger of losing her life'). The situation surprises because, despite the fact that pregnancy must have been a frequent consequence of erotic liaisons, Tibullus and Propertius never mention it.[59] While *grauidus/grauida* ('pregnant') occurs in female-voiced *Heroides* (6.61, 120, 7.133, 16.44),[60] in *Amores* it occurs only here and in the next poem (2.14.17). It does not appear in the works of Ovid's elegiac predecessors.

And how does the lover respond? With fear and anger (4). Although he expresses disapproval of Corinna's action (she was 'reckless', *temeraria* 1), he also takes responsibility for the pregnancy (5): *sed tamen aut ex me conceperat, aut ego credo* ('But, however, she had conceived by me, or I think so'). He also prays to

---

[56] The term 'burlesque' is appropriately applied to a play like Aristophanes' *Thesmophoriazusae* because it parodies scenes from Euripides' *Helen* and *Andromeda*. For parody of Greek tragedy in both comedy and tragedy see Taplin (1986: 170–2). For discussion of Wright's (1674) burlesque of Seneca's *Thyestes* see Davis (2003: 121–2).

[57] Prop. 2.28 is sometimes treated as one poem (e.g. Fedeli [1994], Goold [1990], Heyworth [2007b]) or two (e.g. Lee [1994]) or three (e.g. Barber [1960]).

[58] Connor (1974: 34–5) observes that 'the reader is impressed with the delicate seriousness of it all'. J. T. Davis's (1977: 113) claim that lines 3 (*clam me* 'without my knowledge') and 5–6 are 'doubly humorous' is mistaken. The Romans viewed both abortion and miscarriage as primarily affecting the father's rights. See Watts (1973: 92): 'The sole legal grounds for punishing a woman who sought abortion in Rome was the violation of the father's patriarchal rights over all his family, born or potential, whether legal *personae* or not. In Roman law it was the father's rights, not the child's, that were essentially at stake'. From the lover's perspective 'without my knowledge' points to a significant wrong against himself.

[59] Due (1980: 136) makes this point.

[60] Although *grauida* is not used, pregnancy is also important in *Her.* 11.37–44 where Canace fails in her attempt to procure an abortion.

Isis, a goddess to whom elegiac mistresses, including Corinna, seem particularly devoted (Tib. 1.3.23, Prop. 2.33a, 4.5.34, *Am.* 1.8.74, 2.2.25). While Romans sometimes revile Isis (e.g. Prop. 2.33a.19–20),[61] here the prayer to the Egyptian goddess (7–14) takes the standard form, naming the places with which she is connected and listing her attributes and associates. It also makes clear that the lover's prime concern is the preservation of Corinna's life (15–16):

> huc adhibe uultus, et in una parce duobus:
> nam uitam dominae tu dabis, illa mihi.

Turn your gaze this way, and in one spare two: for you will give life to my mistress, she to me.

The lover is distressed by Corinna's possible death and the prospect of his own bereavement.[62] He closes with a prayer to Ilithyia, promising votive gifts and an inscription, and advice to Corinna that she should not try again.

Like 1.14, 2.13 shows a distinct lack of moralizing. (That will come in 2.14.) 2.13 differs from 1.14 in being deeply serious. While use of hair dye can lead to hair loss, a harm that is easy to fix, the use of drugs and implements (2.14.27–8) to procure abortion puts Corinna's life in danger. Note too that while Ovid's rhetorical skill is fully on display in this poem (especially in the prayer to Isis), flippancy and humour are absent. A girlfriend's death is no laughing matter. Consideration of 1.14 and 2.13 reveals that Ovid approaches his predecessors in widely divergent ways. Sometimes he responds to their work in ways that we think of as typically Ovidian—that is, with wit and humour. But sometimes he is deadly serious. There is no simple formula which encapsulates Ovid's reworking of Tibullus and Propertius.

Indeed there is no simple way of characterizing *Amores*.[63] This should not surprise us because Ovid's work is nothing if not varied. Consider, for example, how violence against women is presented in *Heroides* and *Amores*. We find, for example, that Paris, one of Ovid's sleaziest characters, makes light of Helen's abduction/rape by Theseus (*Her.* 16.149–53):

> ergo arsit merito qui nouerat omnia Theseus,
>   et uisa es tanto digna rapina uiro,
> more tuae gentis nitida dum nuda palaestra
>   ludis et es nudis femina mixta uiris.
> quod rapuit laudo, miror quod reddidit umquam.

---

[61] Due (1980: 142) notes the absence of the usual contempt for Isis' cult.

[62] Gamel (1989: 188) expresses concern that there is no 'vivid reference to the life inside Corinna'. We need to remember that (1) under Roman law the unborn child was not a legal person, (2) abortion was not prohibited, and (3) there was no agreement among the ancients as to when an unborn child could be considered a human being. For discussion of these issues see Watts (1973). Nor should we forget that under certain circumstances the ancients endorsed the practice of infanticide.

[63] Failure to recognize the diversity of *Amores* is one reason why some question the authenticity of 3.5.

18   INTRODUCTION

Therefore Theseus, who knew all this [how beautiful Helen was], was right to burn and you seemed rape-worthy to this great hero, when you played naked in ancestral manner in the gleaming palaestra and when you mingled as a woman with naked men. I praise the fact he raped you, I am amazed that he ever gave you back.

More complex is the case of the lover in *Am.* 1.7. Here we have a different kind of sexual violence: the speaker has struck his girlfriend and torn her hair and clothes. How is this presented? He begins powerfully, with a command that he be put in chains. He then resorts to mythological analogies (7–10), comparing himself to famously mad tragic heroes, Ajax and Orestes. He invokes mythology again, this time to characterize his girlfriend (13–18). But how does she resemble the heroines of old? This is how the lover introduces a set of three similes (11–13):

> ergo ego digestos potui laniare capillos?
>   nec dominam motae dedecuere comae.
> sic formosa fuit.

So was I able to tear her carefully arranged locks? Messed up hair was not unbecoming to my mistress. She was lovely like that.

And which heroines are these? They are huntress Atalanta, abandoned Ariadne, and Trojan Cassandra. What do they have in common? Presumably all were beautiful; and all had untidy hair.[64] Well, all of them except Cassandra, who wore a priestess's ribbons (*uittatis...capillis* 17). Cavalier comments like these make it difficult to take seriously all the lover's subsequent protestations, all his expressions of regret. And the final couplet makes clear that the reader's scepticism was well-founded (67–8):[65]

> neue mei sceleris tam tristia signa supersint,
>   pone recompositas in statione comas.

And so that there are no grim signs of my crime, rearrange your hair, put it back in place.

As with Corinna's hair loss in 1.14, the lover treats a problem as trivial. Here, however, the cause is not her overuse of hair dye but his violence.

But Ovid presents other perspectives, most notably those of women. Thus Oenone (writing to Paris, of course) describes her rape by Apollo as follows (*Her.* 5.140–4):[66]

---

[64] Greene (1999: 413) draws attention to the similar treatment of Daphne and Leucothoe (*Met.* 1.530: *auctaque forma fuga est* ['her beauty was increased by flight']; 4.230: *ipse timor decuit* ['fear itself became her']).

[65] For the effect of the final couplet see Parker (1969: 86–7) and Connor (1974: 24).

[66] These lines, queried by Merkel (1862), with no reason given, are wrongly consigned to a note by Showerman and Goold's Loeb edition and not translated. Consequently they are missing from most

> ille meae spolium uirginitatis habet
> id quoque luctando. rupi tamen ungue capillos,
> oraque sunt digitis aspera facta meis.
> nec pretium stupri gemmas aurumque poposci:
> turpiter ingenuum munera corpus emunt.

He has the spoils of my virginity, that too by struggle. However, I tore his hair with my nails and my fingers roughened his face. Nor did I demand gems and gold as a reward for my violation: it is shameful to buy a freeborn body with gifts.

One striking feature of *Her.* 16 is that the speaker, Paris, does not raise the issue of consent. Oenone does. And not only does she describe her struggle, she rejects the 'compensation' that sometimes follows rape by a divinity.[67] Her choice of *emunt* ('buy') in the last line implies that accepting a 'reward' would be tantamount to prostitution (144).

Close to Oenone's account of her resistance is the story of Ilia in *Am.* 3.6.45–82. The lover starts by describing Ilia's physical state, her torn clothing, her nail-torn hair and cheeks, her groaning, and her isolation. And what is the cause? The wickedness of her uncle and the crime of Mars (49). It is Ilia's misfortune, however, to face a second rapist. Her distress is made clear by her reaction to Anio's proposed marriage, by her efforts to escape, and most importantly by her speech: Ilia is a Vestal committed to virginity, a woman who should not be confronted with the possibility of marriage. Her final act, an attempt at suicide by drowning (80), leads to the 'marriage' that she refused.

Amores is a brilliantly written collection of poems that are sometimes frivolous, sometimes confronting, and sometimes both. Ovid clearly did not prize consistency of tone or approach either within these three books or across his earliest works. These elegies present not one man's perspective on a love affair with a single beloved but reflections on the related experiences of being in love and writing love poetry.

---

texts available on the internet and from English-language translations. They are included in Rosati (1989) and Knox (1995). Omission of these lines actually destroys the point that Oenone wishes to make, viz. that, unlike Helen, she resisted the advances of sexual predators.

[67] Cf. Daphne's 'reward' for being raped by Apollo (*Met.* 1.557–65).

Text and Translation

P. Ouidi Nasonis Amorum
Liber Tertius

3.1

Stat uetus et multos incaedua silua per annos;
  credibile est illi numen inesse loco.
fons sacer in medio speluncaque pumice pendens
  et latere ex omni dulce queruntur aues.
hic ego dum spatior tectus nemoralibus umbris, 5
  quod mea quaerebam Musa moueret opus.
uenit odoratos Elegeia nexa capillos
  et, puto, pes illi longior alter erat.
forma decens, uestis tenuissima, uultus amantis,
  et pedibus uitium causa decoris erat. 10
uenit et ingenti uiolenta Tragoedia passu:
  fronte comae torua, palla iacebat humi.
laeua manus sceptrum late regale mouebat,
  Lydius alta pedum uincla cothurnus erat.

et prior 'ecquis erit' dixit 'tibi finis amandi, 15
  o argumenti lente poeta tui?
nequitiam uinosa tuam conuiuia narrant,
  narrant in multas compita secta uias.
saepe aliquis digito uatem designat euntem
  atque ait: "hic, hic est, quem ferus urit Amor". 20
fabula (nec sentis) tota iactaris in Vrbe,
  dum tua praeterito facta pudore refers.
tempus erat thyrso pulsum grauiore moueri.
  cessatum satis est: incipe maius opus.
materia premis ingenium. cane facta uirorum: 25
  "haec animo" dices "area facta meo est".
quod tenerae cantent lusit tua Musa puellae,
  primaque per numeros acta iuuenta suos.
nunc habeam per te Romana Tragoedia nomen:
  implebit leges spiritus iste meas'. 30
hactenus, et mouit pictis innixa cothurnis
  densum caesarie terque quaterque caput.

Ovid Amores
Book 3

3.1: ELEGY OR TRAGEDY?

[1–14] There stands a forest ancient and uncut through many years; you could believe that a divinity is present in that place.
In the middle is a sacred spring and there's a cave vaulted with pumice and on every side birds moan sweetly.
While I was strolling here, protected by forest shadows, asking what genre my Muse should inspire,
Elegy came, her hair perfumed and braided, and, I think, one foot was longer than the other.
Her appearance was lovely, her clothing very fine, her face a lover's, the fault in her feet a source of loveliness.
Tragedy came too, aggressively, with giant stride: hair covered her pitiless brow, her robe the ground.
Her left hand brandished a royal sceptre, a tall Lydian buskin confined her feet.

[15–32] And she spoke first: 'Oh poet persistent in your choice of subject matter, will there be an end to your loving?
Boozy party-goers tell tales, crossroads divided into many streets tell tales of your depravity.
Often some stranger points out the poet as he passes by and says "That's him, that's him, he's the one that's burned by brutal Love".
You don't realise it, but you're the subject of gossip throughout the City, while you ignore decency and write about what you've been doing.
It's time you were excited, struck by a weightier thyrsus. Enough of hesitation: get started on more important work.
You are cramping your talent with your choice of subject matter. Sing the deeds of heroes: "This field", you will say, "suits my spirit".
Your Muse has had fun with songs for delicate girls to sing. Your earliest youth was spent in an appropriate metre.
Now I, Roman Tragedy, would like to win glory through you: that inspiration of yours will carry out my terms'.
This much and, standing tall on her embroidered buskins, three or four times she shook her head and luxuriant locks.

altera, si memini, limis surrisit ocellis.
　　　fallor, an in dextra myrtea uirga fuit?
　　'quid grauibus uerbis, animosa Tragoedia', dixit, 35
　　　'me premis? an numquam non grauis esse potes?
　　imparibus tamen es numeris dignata moueri.
　　　in me pugnasti uersibus usa meis.
　　non ego contulerim sublimia carmina nostris:
　　　obruit exiguas regia uestra fores. 40
　　sum leuis, et mecum leuis est, mea cura, Cupido:
　　　non sum materia fortior ipsa mea.
　　rustica sit sine me lasciui mater Amoris:
　　　huic ego proueni lena comesque deae.
　　quam tu non poteris duro reserare cothurno, 45
　　　haec est blanditiis ianua laxa meis. 46
　　per me decepto didicit custode Corinna 49
　　　liminis astricti sollicitare fidem 50
　　delabique toro tunica uelata soluta 51
　　　atque impercussos nocte mouere pedes. 52
　　et tamen emerui plus quam tu posse ferendo 47
　　　multa supercilio non patienda tuo. 48
　　uel quotiens foribus duris infixa pependi 53
　　　non uerita a populo praetereunte legi!
　　quin ego me memini, dum custos saeuus abiret, 55
　　　ancillae miseram delituisse sinu.
　　quid, cum me munus natali mittis, at illa
　　　rumpit et apposita barbara mersat aqua?
　　prima tuae moui felicia semina mentis.
　　　munus habes, quod te iam petit ista, meum'. 60

　　desierat. coepi: 'per uos utramque rogamus,
　　　in uacuas aures uerba timentis eant.
　　altera me sceptro decoras altoque cothurno:
　　　iam nunc contracto magnus in ore sonus.
　　altera das nostro uicturum nomen amori: 65
　　　ergo ades et longis uersibus adde breues.
　　exiguum uati concede, Tragoedia, tempus:
　　　tu labor aeternus, quod petit illa, breue est'.
　　mota dedit ueniam. teneri properentur Amores,
　　　dum uacat: a tergo grandius urget opus. 70

[33–60] The other one, if I remember rightly, smiled with sidelong glance: am I wrong, or was there a myrtle branch in her right hand?
'Why, proud Tragedy', she said 'do you cramp me with your serious words? Or are you never unable to be serious?
But you did see fit to advance in uneven rhythm. You attacked me using my own metre.
I would not compare exalted poetry to mine: your royal palace overwhelms my humble doors.
I'm a lightweight and Cupid, my concern, is a fellow lightweight: I'm not more heroic than my subject matter.
Without me the mother of mischievous Love would be a rustic: I've come forward to be procuress and companion for this goddess.
The door that you can't open with your harsh buskin is loosened by my flattery.
It was through me that Corinna learned to deceive a guard and undermine confidence in a locked doorway
And, covered in a loose dress, to slip out of bed and move around at night without stumbling.
But I have earned greater power than you because I've suffered many things your stern looks would not tolerate.
For instance, how many times have I hung fixed to stubborn doors, unafraid of being read by the passing population!
No, I recall hiding miserably in a maid's bosom until the brutal guard went away.
What about the time you sent me as a birthday present, but she ripped me up and barbarically drowned me in some nearby water?
I was the first to inspire your mind's fertile seeds. You have my reward: that woman's now pursuing you'.

[61–70] She had stopped. I began: 'In the names of both of you I ask, pay attention to the words of a fearful man.
You honour me with the sceptre and high buskin: even now there is grand eloquence in my narrow mouth.
You give our love fame that will live on: so come and help me and add short lines to long.
Tragedy, allow your poet a little time: your work lasts forever, what she wants is short'.
She was moved and gave permission. Hurry on, tender Loves, while there's a chance: grander work presses close behind me.

3.2

Non ego nobilium sedeo studiosus equorum.
  cui tamen ipsa faues, uincat ut ille, precor.
ut loquerer tecum ueni, tecumque sederem,
  ne tibi non notus quem facis esset amor.
tu cursus spectas, ego te. spectemus uterque 5
  quod iuuat atque oculos pascat uterque suos.

o, cuicumque faues, felix agitator equorum!
  ergo illi curae contigit esse tuae.
hoc mihi contingat, sacro de carcere missis
  insistam forti mente uehendus equis 10
et modo lora dabo, modo uerbere terga notabo,
  nunc stringam metas interiore rota.
si mihi currenti fueris conspecta, morabor,
  deque meis manibus lora remissa fluent.
at quam paene Pelops Pisaea concidit hasta, 15
  dum spectat uultus, Hippodamia, tuos!
nempe fauore suae uicit tamen ille puellae:
  uincamus dominae quisque fauore suae.

quid frustra refugis? cogit nos linea iungi.
  haec in lege loci commoda Circus habet. 20
tu tamen a dextra, quicumque es, parce puellae:
  contactu lateris laeditur ista tui.
tu quoque, qui spectas post nos, tua contrahe crura,
  si pudor est, rigido nec preme terga genu.
sed nimium demissa iacent tibi pallia terra: 25
  collige, uel digitis en ego tollo meis.
inuida uestis eras, quae tam bona crura tegebas.
  quoque magis spectes—inuida uestis eras.
talia Milanion Atalantes crura fugacis
  optauit manibus sustinuisse suis. 30
talia pinguntur succinctae crura Dianae,
  cum sequitur fortes fortior ipsa feras.
his ego non uisis arsi. quid fiet ab ipsis?
  in flammam flammas, in mare fundis aquas.
suspicor ex istis et cetera posse placere, 35
  quae bene sub tenui condita ueste latent.
uis tamen interea faciles arcessere uentos,
  quos faciet nostra mota tabella manu?

3.2: AT THE RACES

[1–6]   I'm not sitting here because I'm keen on thoroughbred horses. I pray your favourite wins.
I've come to talk to you, to sit with you, so that the love you cause does not go unnoticed.
You watch the races, I you. Let's both watch what we like, and let's both feast our eyes.

[7–18] O, your favourite, what a fortunate charioteer! So it seems that he was lucky enough to interest you.
If I'm lucky enough, once my horses leave the sacred barrier, I'll press on riding bravely
and now I'll slacken the reins, now I'll mark their backs with the lash, now with wheel too close I'll scrape the turning-post.
If I catch sight of you when I'm racing, I'll pause, the reins will fall slack from my hands.
But how close Pelops came to falling to Pisa's spear, while looking at your face, Hippodamia!
But of course he won because of his girlfriend's favour. May each of us win because of his mistress's favour.

[19–42] Why pull back? It's pointless. The rope forces us together. The Circus's seating rules have this advantage.
But you, on the right, whoever you are, don't hurt the girl: the touch of your body annoys her.
You too, watching behind us, pull back your legs, if you have any decency, and don't push her back with your rough knee.
But your robe lies too low on the ground: gather it up, or, look, I'm even lifting it up with my own fingers.
You were a selfish dress to cover up such gorgeous legs. And the more you look—you were a selfish dress.
That's what swift Atalanta's legs were like, the ones Milanion longed to hold in his hands.
That's how they paint Diana's legs with her dress hitched up, when she hunts bold beasts, but she's bolder.
I was on fire before I saw those legs. What will happen now that I actually have? You pour flame on flames, waters on the sea.
From these I guess that the rest is attractive too, all that's neatly hidden under your fine dress.
In the meantime, would you like me to summon favourable breezes and wave my program with my hand?

an magis hic meus est animi, non aeris aestus,
   captaque femineus pectora torret amor?   40
dum loquor, alba leui sparsa est tibi puluere uestis:
   sordide de niueo corpore puluis abi.

sed iam pompa uenit: linguis animisque fauete.
   tempus adest plausus: aurea pompa uenit.
prima loco fertur passis Victoria pinnis: 45
   huc ades et meus hic fac, dea, uincat amor.
plaudite Neptuno, nimium qui creditis undis:
   nil mihi cum pelago. me mea terra capit.
plaude tuo Marti, miles: nos odimus arma.
   pax iuuat et media pace repertus amor.   50
auguribus Phoebus, Phoebe uenantibus adsit.
   artifices in te uerte, Minerua, manus.
ruricolae, Cereri teneroque assurgite Baccho.
   Pollucem pugiles, Castora placet eques.
nos tibi, blanda Venus, puerisque potentibus arcu   55
   plaudimus; inceptis adnue, diua, meis
daque nouae mentem dominae, patiatur amari.
   adnuit et motu signa secunda dedit.
quod dea promisit, promittas ipsa rogamus:
   pace loquar Veneris, tu dea maior eris.   60
per tibi tot iuro testes pompamque deorum
   te dominam nobis tempus in omne peti.

sed pendent tibi crura: potes, si forte iuuabit,
   cancellis primos inseruisse pedes.
maxima iam uacuo praetor spectacula Circo   65
   quadriiugos aequo carcere misit equos.
cui studeas, uideo. uincet, cuicumque fauebis.
   quid cupias ipsi scire uidentur equi.
me miserum! metam spatioso circuit orbe.
   quid facis? admoto proximus axe subit.   70
quid facis, infelix? perdis bona uota puellae.
   tende, precor, ualida lora sinistra manu.
fauimus ignauo. sed enim reuocate, Quirites,
   et date iactatis undique signa togis.
en reuocant. ac ne turbet toga mota capillos,   75
   in nostros abdas te licet usque sinus.
iamque patent iterum reserato carcere postes,
   euolat admissis discolor agmen equis.

Or maybe it's my mind's that's hot, not the air, and it's a woman's love that takes my heart prisoner and scorches it?
While I've been talking, a speck of dust has spoiled your white dress: filthy dust, get off her snow-white body!

[43–62] But the procession is already on its way: show your favour with voice and heart. It's time for applause: the golden procession is on its way.
In first place comes Victory with outspread wings: come this way, goddess, and make my love a winner.
Applaud Neptune, if you have too much confidence in the waves: I'll have nothing to do with the sea. My land is my delight.
Applaud your Mars, soldier: I hate war. Peace is my pleasure and love is found in the midst of peace.
Let Phoebus give help to augurs, Phoebe help to hunters. Minerva, turn craftsman hands in your direction.
Country-dwellers, stand up for Ceres and tender Bacchus. Boxers, win over Pollux, riders, Castor.
We applaud you, charming Venus, and bow-powerful boys; agree to my plans, goddess,
give my new mistress the inclination, I hope she lets herself be loved. She has agreed, she nodded, a positive sign.
I ask you to promise what the goddess promised: I'll say it with Venus' permission, you will be the greater goddess.
I swear to you by all these witnesses and the gods' procession: I want you to be my mistress forever.

[63–84] But your legs are dangling: perhaps if you like, you can slip your toes into the railings.
Now that the Circus is clear, the praetor has let loose from the impartial starting-gate the greatest of spectacles, the four horses yoked abreast.
I see the one you're keen on. Your favourite will win. Even the horses seem to know what you desire.
Oh no! He's too wide in taking the turning-post. What are you doing? The next driver scraped his axle. He's catching up.
You loser, what are you doing? You're destroying a girl's fine hopes. Come on, pull on the left rein with all your strength.
We've supported a coward. Call them back, Quirites, flap your togas and give the signal, everyone.
Look, they're calling them back. Don't let those waving togas mess your hair, you can hide yourself in my arms.
The starting-gate's unbarred now, the doors are open again, the horses are racing, a multi-coloured mass is flying out.

nunc saltem supera spatioque insurge patenti:
  sint mea, sint dominae fac rata uota meae.   80
sunt dominae rata uota meae, mea uota supersunt.
  ille tenet palmam, palma petenda mea est.
risit et argutis quiddam promisit ocellis.
  hoc satis est, alio cetera redde loco.

3.3

Esse deos, i, crede. fidem iurata fefellit,
  et facies illi, quae fuit ante, manet.
quam longos habuit nondum periura capillos,
  tam longos, postquam numina laesit, habet.
candida candorem roseo suffusa rubore   5
  ante fuit: niueo lucet in ore rubor.
pes erat exiguus: pedis est artissima forma.
  longa decensque fuit: longa decensque manet.
argutos habuit: radiant ut sidus ocelli,
  per quos mentita est perfida saepe mihi.   10
scilicet aeterni falsum iurare puellis
  di quoque concedunt, formaque numen habet.

perque suos illam nuper iurasse recordor
  perque meos oculos: en doluere mei.
dicite, di, si uos impune fefellerat illa,   15
  alterius meriti cur ego damna tuli?
at non inuidiae uobis Cepheia uirgo est,
  pro male formosa iussa parente mori?
non satis est, quod uos habui sine pondere testes
  et mecum lusos ridet inulta deos?   20
ut sua per nostram redimat periuria poenam,
  uictima deceptus decipientis ero?

aut sine re nomen deus est frustraque timetur
  et stulta populos credulitate mouet
aut, siquis deus est, teneras amat ille puellas: 25
  nimirum solas omnia posse iubet.
nobis fatifero Mauors accingitur ense.
  nos petit inuicta Palladis hasta manu.
nobis flexibiles curuantur Apollinis arcus.
  in nos alta Iouis dextera fulmen habet.   30

Anyhow, get to the front now, charge into open space: make my, make my mistress's prayers successful.
My mistress's prayers are successful, my prayers await fulfilment. He holds his victory palm, I have to ask for mine.
She laughed and with expressive eyes she made a promise. That's enough, pay me the rest somewhere else.

3.3: MY GIRLFRIEND LIED

[1–12] Go on, believe the gods exist: she made an oath and broke her promise, and yet her appearance, the one she had before, remains unchanged.
The long hair she had before her perjury, is just as long after she gave divinities offence.
She was radiant before, her radiance suffused with a rosy blush: the blush still glows on her snow-white face.
Her foot was small: her foot still looks very slender. She was tall and lovely: she remains tall and lovely.
They were expressive: her eyes shone like a star. By those eyes the traitor often lied to me.
Obviously even the eternal gods let girls lie under oath, and beauty has supernatural power.

[13–22] I recall that she swore just now by her own, by my eyes too: look, mine are the ones in pain.
Tell me, gods, if she cheated you and got away with it, why do I suffer the punishment that someone else deserves?
But didn't Cepheus' virgin daughter make everyone hate you, when you ordered her death because of her mother's stupid beauty?
Isn't it enough, that I had you as weightless witnesses and that she mocks both the gods and me with impunity?
Will I be a deceiver's deceived victim so that she can atone for her perjury through my punishment?

[23–40] Either a god is a name without reality, is wrongly feared, and worries people because they are gullible and stupid
or, if a god exists, he loves delicate girls: of course he insists that they alone are all-powerful.
Mavors puts on his death-dealing sword for *us*. Pallas' spear attacks *us* with invincible force.
Apollo bends his pliant bow at *us*. High above Jupiter's hand holds his thunderbolt aimed at *us*.

formosas superi metuunt offendere laesi
    atque ultro, quae se non timuere, timent.
et quisquam pia tura focis imponere curat?
    certe plus animi debet inesse uiris.
Iuppiter igne suo lucos iaculatur et arces   35
    missaque periuras tela ferire uetat.
tot meruere peti: Semele miserabilis arsit.
    officio est illi poena reperta suo.
at si uenturo se subduxisset amanti,
    non pater in Baccho matris haberet opus.   40

quid queror et toto facio conuicia caelo?
    di quoque habent oculos, di quoque pectus habent.
si deus ipse forem, numen sine fraude liceret
    femina mendaci falleret ore meum.
ipse ego iurarem uerum iurare puellas   45
    et non de tetricis dicerer esse deus.
tu tamen illorum moderatius utere dono,
    aut oculis certe parce, puella, meis.

3.4

Dure uir, imposito tenerae custode puellae
    nil agis: ingenio est quaeque tuenda suo.
siqua metu dempto casta est, ea denique casta est.
    quae, quia non liceat, non facit, illa facit.
ut iam seruaris bene corpus, adultera mens est   5
    nec custodiri ne uelit ulla potest.
nec corpus seruare potes, licet omnia claudas:
    omnibus exclusis intus adulter erit.
cui peccare licet, peccat minus: ipsa potestas
    semina nequitiae languidiora facit.   10
desine, crede mihi, uitia irritare uetando:
    obsequio uinces aptius illa tuo.

uidi ego nuper equum contra sua uincla tenacem
    ore reluctanti fulminis ire modo;
constitit ut primum concessas sensit habenas   15
    frenaque in effusa laxa iacere iuba.
nitimur in uetitum semper cupimusque negata:
    sic interdictis imminet aeger aquis.

Offended gods are afraid of upsetting lovely girls and actually fear the
ones who don't fear them.
Does anyone bother to put pious incense on their fires? Men should
certainly have more spirit.
With his usual fire Jupiter strikes at groves and citadels, but he tells the
missiles that he throws not to strike perjured girls.
So many have deserved attack: poor Semele was the one who burned.
Because of her service a punishment was devised for her.
If she had stayed away when her lover was approaching, his father would
not have played the mother's role in the case of Bacchus.

[41–8] Why do I complain and hurl abuse at all of heaven? The gods have eyes
too, the gods have feelings too.
If I were a god, I would let a woman's lying mouth cheat my divinity
unharmed.
I would swear myself that girls swear the truth and I would not be called
a glum god.
But use their gift with more restraint, or, darling, at least don't hurt my eyes.

3.4: SOME MARITAL ADVICE

[1–12] You're strict, but when you set a guard for a delicate girl, you lose:
a woman should be protected by her innate character.
If a woman is chaste without the need for fear, she is truly chaste; the
woman who doesn't do it, only because she's not allowed, actually does it.
Even though you watch over her body closely, her purpose is adultery
and no woman can be guarded from desire.
And you cannot watch over her body, even though you shut all: when all
are shut out, there will be an adulterer within.
Whoever is allowed to do wrong, does wrong less: the very power to
choose weakens the seeds of depravity.
Trust me, don't provoke her vices through prohibition: you will
overcome them more easily with kindness.

[13–18] Recently I saw a stallion, mouth struggling, stubborn against his
restraints, move like a thunderbolt;
he stopped as soon as he felt the cords loosen and the reins lie slack on
his flowing mane.
We always strive for what is banned and crave what is refused: just like a
patient determined to get the water that's been forbidden.

centum fronte oculos, centum ceruice gerebat
   Argus, et hos unus saepe fefellit Amor. 20
in thalamum Danae ferro saxoque perennem
   quae fuerat uirgo tradita, mater erat.
Penelope mansit, quamuis custode carebat,
   inter tot iuuenes intemerata procos.
quidquid seruatur cupimus magis, ipsaque furem 25
   cura uocat; pauci, quod sinit alter, amant.

nec facie placet illa sua, sed amore mariti:
   nescio quid quod te ceperit esse putant.
non proba fit, quam uir seruat, sed adultera cara:
   ipse timor pretium corpore maius habet. 30
indignere licet, iuuat inconcessa uoluptas:
   sola placet 'timeo' dicere siqua potest.
nec tamen ingenuam ius est seruare puellam:
   hic metus externae corpora gentis agat.
scilicet ut possit custos 'ego' dicere 'feci', 35
   in laudem serui casta sit illa tui?

rusticus est nimium, quem laedit adultera coniunx,
   et notos mores non satis Vrbis habet
in qua Martigenae non sunt sine crimine nati
   Romulus Iliades Iliadesque Remus. 40
quo tibi formosam, si non nisi casta placebat?
   non possunt ullis ista coire modis.
si sapis, indulge dominae uultusque seueros
   exue nec rigidi iura tuere uiri
et cole quos dederit (multos dabit) uxor amicos: 45
   gratia sic minimo magna labore uenit.
sic poteris iuuenum conuiuia semper inire
   et, quae non dederis, multa uidere domi.

3.5

Nox erat et somnus lassos summisit ocellos;
   terruerunt animum talia uisa meum.

colle sub aprico creberrimus ilice lucus
   stabat et in ramis multa latebat auis.
area gramineo suberat uiridissima prato 5
   umida de guttis lene sonantis aquae.

[19–26] Argus had a hundred eyes in front, a hundred behind: and Love, all by himself, cheated them many times.
Danae, a virgin when consigned to a bedroom enduring with iron and stone, became a mother.
Even though she lacked a guardian, Penelope remained unsullied when surrounded by numerous youthful suitors.
What is watched we crave more and anxiety itself invites the thief; few men love because they have permission.

[27–36] It's not her appearance that makes her attractive, but her husband's love; they suppose that there is something that has taken hold of you.
A husband's protection does not make a woman virtuous, but a highly-prized adulteress; fear itself is actually more highly-valued than her body.
You can protest, but forbidden pleasure pleases: a woman is only attractive if she can say 'I'm afraid'.
It's not legal to maintain possession of a freeborn girl; this terror should afflict non-Roman bodies.
Really, is she going to be virtuous to boost a slave's pride, so the guard can say 'I'm responsible for that'?

[37–48] A man's a rustic if his wife's adultery offends him; he doesn't know enough of the City's ways,
the place where the Mars-begotten sons were born not without crime, Romulus, son of Ilia, and Ilia's son, Remus.
Why choose a beauty, if only virtue pleases? There is no way those things can be combined.
If you're smart, let a lady have her way, cast off those stern looks, and don't uphold a strict husband's legal rights,
And cultivate the friends your wife will bring (there'll be lots). In this way there'll be great reward for minimal effort;
in this way you'll get to go to young people's parties and see at home lots of gifts you haven't given.

3.5: A LOVER'S DREAM

[1–2] It was night and sleep lowered my weary eyes; this vision terrified my mind.

[3–32] At the foot of a sunny hill there stood a grove packed with ilex trees and many a bird was hidden in its branches.
At the edge of a grassy meadow lay a very green space, damp with drops of gently sounding water.

ipse sub arboreis uitabam frondibus aestum,
  fronde sub arborea sed tamen aestus erat.
ecce petens uariis immixtas floribus herbas,
  constitit ante oculos candida uacca meos,   10
candidior niuibus, tunc cum cecidere recentes,
  in liquidas nondum quas mora uertit aquas,
candidior, quod adhuc spumis stridentibus albet
  et modo siccatam, lacte, reliquit ouem.
taurus erat comes huic, feliciter ille maritus,   15
  cumque sua teneram coniuge pressit humum.
dum iacet et lente reuocatas ruminat herbas
  atque iterum pasto pascitur ante cibo,
uisus erat, somno uires adimente ferendi,
  cornigerum terra deposuisse caput.   20
huc leuibus cornix pinnis delapsa per auras
  uenit et in uiridi garrula sedit humo,
terque bouis niueae petulanti pectora rostro
  fodit et albentis abstulit ore iubas.
illa locum taurumque diu cunctata reliquit,   25
  sed niger in uaccae pectore liuor erat;
utque procul uidit carpentes pabula tauros
  (carpebant tauri pabula laeta procul),
illuc se rapuit gregibusque immiscuit illis
  et petiit herbae fertilioris humum.   30
dic age, nocturnae, quicumque es, imaginis augur,
  si quid habent ueri, uisa quid ista ferant.

sic ego; nocturnae sic dixit imaginis augur,
  expendens animo singula dicta suo:

quem tu mobilibus foliis uitare uolebas,   35
  sed male uitabas, aestus amoris erat.
uacca puella tua est: aptus color ille puellae;
  tu uir et in uacca compare taurus eras.
pectora quod rostro cornix fodiebat acuto,
  ingenium dominae lena mouebit anus.   40
quod cunctata diu taurum sua uacca reliquit,
  frigidus in uiduo destituere toro.
liuor et aduerso maculae sub pectore nigrae
  pectus adulterii labe carere negant.

dixerat interpres. gelido mihi sanguis ab ore   45
  fugit et ante oculos nox stetit alta meos.

I was avoiding the heat by sheltering under the trees' leaves, beneath the trees' leafage but it was hot nevertheless.
Look, making for the grass mixed with different kinds of flowers, there stood before my eyes a radiant white cow,
more radiant white than snow when freshly fallen, which time has not yet transformed to flowing water;
more radiant white than milk, still white with hissing froth, which has just left the sheep drained dry.
A bull accompanied her, who had the luck to be her husband, and together with his wife, he pressed upon the delicate earth.
While he lies there and slowly chews the cud and eats again already eaten food,
He seemed, since sleep had taken away his power to support it, to lower his horned head to the ground.
Gliding down on light wings through the breezes to this spot a talkative crow came and sat upon the green earth,
and three times it pecked aggressively at the cow's snow-white breast and stole some white hairs in its mouth.
After lingering for a long time, the cow left behind the place and the bull, but there was a black bruise on her breast;
and as she saw the bulls far off cropping fodder (the bulls were cropping lush fodder far off)
she raced over there and mingled with those herds and made for earth with more abundant grass.
Come, whoever you are, tell me, interpreter of night's imaginings, what this vision means, if it is in any sense truthful.

[33–4] So I; the interpreter of night's imaginings spoke like this, weighing individual words in his mind:

[35–44] What you wanted to avoid by means of shifting leaves, but hardly could avoid, was passion's heat.
The cow is your girlfriend: that colour suits a girl; you, a man, were the bull with the cow, his partner.
The fact that a crow was pecking her breast with its sharp beak: an aged procuress will interfere with your mistress's nature.
The fact that a cow, after lingering for a long time, left the bull: you will be abandoned cold in an empty bed.
The bruise and black spots on the front of her breast tell us that her breast does not lack adultery's stain.

[45–6] The expounder had spoken. Blood fled from my cold face and deep night stood before my eyes.

3.6

Amnis, harundinibus limosas obsite ripas,
  ad dominam propero: siste parumper aquas.
nec tibi sunt pontes nec quae sine remigis ictu
  concaua traiecto cumba rudente uehat.
paruus eras, memini, nec te transire refugi   5
  summaque uix talos contigit unda meos.
nunc ruis apposito niuibus de monte solutis
  et turpi crassas gurgite uoluis aquas.
quid properasse iuuat, quid parca dedisse quieti
  tempora, quid nocti conseruisse diem,   10
si tamen hic standum est, si non datur artibus ullis
  ulterior nostro ripa premenda pede?
nunc ego, quas habuit pinnas Danaeius heros,
  terribili densum cum tulit angue caput,
nunc opto currum, de quo Cerealia primum   15
  semina uenerunt in rude missa solum.
prodigiosa loquor ueterum mendacia uatum:
  nec tulit haec umquam nec feret ulla dies.

tu potius ripis effuse capacibus amnis,
  sic aeternus eas: labere fine tuo.   20
non eris inuidiae, torrens, mihi crede, ferendae,
  si dicar per te forte retentus amans.

flumina deberent iuuenes in amore iuuare,
  flumina senserunt ipsa quid esset amor.
Inachus in Melie Bithynide pallidus isse   25
  dicitur et gelidis incaluisse uadis.
nondum Troia fuit lustris obsessa duobus,
  cum rapuit uultus, Xanthe, Neaera tuos.
quid? non Alpheon diuersis currere terris
  uirginis Arcadiae certus adegit amor?   30
te quoque promissam Xantho, Penee, Creusam
  Pthiotum terris occuluisse ferunt.
quid referam Asopon, quem cepit Martia Thebe,
  natarum Thebe quinque futura parens?
cornua si tua nunc ubi sint, Acheloe, requiram,   35
  Herculis irata fracta querere manu;
nec tanti Calydon nec tota Aetolia tanti,
  una tamen tanti Deianira fuit.
ille fluens diues septena per ostia Nilus,
  qui patriam tantae tam bene celat aquae,   40

3.6: TO A RIVER

[1–18] River, you with your slimy banks all overgrown with reeds, I'm hurrying to see my mistress: halt your waters for a little while.
You have no bridges, no hollow skiff with threaded rope to carry me across without an oarsman's efforts.
You used to be tiny, I recall, nor did I shun crossing you, and your wave tops barely touched my ankles.
Now when the snows dissolve on the nearby mountain you rush down and roll your muddy waters in a foul eddy.
What good is hurrying, what good is giving too little time to rest, joining day to night,
if I have to stand here, if I have no means of treading the further bank?
Now I crave the wings of Danae's heroic son, when he carried that head thickly covered with terrifying snakes,
now the chariot from which Ceres' seeds were first thrown and reached uncultivated soil.
I am uttering the marvellous lies of ancient poets: no day has ever brought such things or ever will.

[19–22] River overflowing your capacious banks, may you run forever, but on this condition: flow within your limits.
Trust me, torrent, you won't be able to endure my hatred, if by chance I, a lover, should be said to be held up by you.

[23–44] Streams should help young lovers; streams have felt what love is.
Inachus is said to have run pale in the case of Bithynian Melie and to have grown hot in icy waters.
Troy had not yet been besieged for twice five years, when Neaera seized your gaze, Xanthus.
What? Did not true love for an Arcadian maid compel Alpheus to run to distant lands?
They say that you too, Peneus, concealed Creusa, promised to Xanthus, in the territory of the people of Phthia.
Why mention Asopus, captivated by Thebe, descendant of Mars, Thebe destined to be mother of five daughters?
If I should ask where your horns are now, Achelous, you will complain that they were broken by Hercules' angry hand;
nor was Calydon worth that much, nor all of Aetolia worth that much, but Deianira alone was worth that much.
They say that the wealthy Nile, flowing through seven mouths, which conceals so well the homeland of so much water,

fertur in †Euadne† collectam Asopide flammam
   uincere gurgitibus non potuisse suis.
siccus ut amplecti Salmonida posset Enipeus,
   cedere iussit aquam; iussa recessit aqua.

nec te praetereo, qui per caua saxa uolutans 45
   Tiburis Argei pomifera arua rigas,
Ilia cui placuit, quamuis erat horrida cultu,
   ungue notata comas, ungue notata genas.
illa gemens patruique nefas delictaque Martis
   errabat nudo per loca sola pede. 50
hanc Anien rapidis animosus uidit ab undis
   raucaque de mediis sustulit ora uadis
atque ita 'quid nostras' dixit 'teris anxia ripas,
   Ilia, ab Idaeo Laomedonte genus?
quo cultus abiere tui? quid sola uagaris, 55
   uitta nec euinctas impedit alba comas?
quid fles et madidos lacrimis corrumpis ocellos
   pectoraque insana plangis aperta manu?
ille habet et silices et uiuum in pectore ferrum,
   qui tenero lacrimas lentus in ore uidet. 60
Ilia, pone metus: tibi regia nostra patebit.
   teque colent amnes: Ilia, pone metus.
tu centum aut plures inter dominabere nymphas,
   nam centum aut plures flumina nostra tenent.
ne me sperne, precor, tantum, Troiana propago: 65
   munera promissis uberiora feres'.
dixerat. illa oculos in humum deiecta modestos
   spargebat teneros flebilis imbre sinus.
ter molita fugam ter ad altas restitit undas,
   currendi uires eripiente metu. 70
sera tamen scindens inimico pollice crinem
   edidit indignos ore tremente sonos:
'o utinam mea lecta forent patrioque sepulcro
   condita, cum poterant uirginis ossa legi!
cur, modo Vestalis, taedas inuitor ad ullas 75
   turpis et Iliacis infitianda focis?
quid moror et digitis designor adultera uulgi?
   desint famosus quae notet ora pudor'.
hactenus, et uestem tumidis praetendit ocellis
   atque ita se in rapidas perdita misit aquas. 80
supposuisse manus ad pectora lubricus amnis
   dicitur et socii iura dedisse tori.

could not overcome with his rolling waves his concentrated flame in the case of Evadne (?), Asopus' daughter.

So that Enipeus could be dry when he embraced Salmoneus' daughter, he ordered his water to retreat; the water retreated when ordered.

[45–84] And I won't leave you out, you who roll over hollowed rocks and irrigate Argive Tibur's fruitful fields,

To whom Ilia proved attractive, even though her clothes were ragged, her hair nail-torn, her cheeks nail-torn.

Lamenting her uncle's impious actions and the crime of Mars, she roamed barefoot through solitary places.

From his raging waters spirited Anio caught sight of her and raised his hoarse voice from the waves' midst

and spoke thus: 'Why do you tread my banks in such distress, Ilia, descended from Ida's Laomedon?

Why has your costume gone? Why do you wander all alone, why is there no white ribbon to tie and bind your hair?

Why weep and spoil your moist eyes with tears and furiously pound your bare breast?

He has flint and living iron in his breast, who looks unmoved at tears on a delicate face.

Ilia, set aside your fears: my kingdom will be open to you. Rivers will honour you: Ilia, set aside your fears.

You will lord it over a hundred or more nymphs; for our river holds a hundred or more.

Only do not reject me, I beg you, offspring of Troy: you will gain rewards more abundant than I promise'.

He had spoken. Casting modest eyes to the ground, she tearfully sprinkled her delicate bosom with rain.

Three times she attempted flight, three times she halted at the deep water, fear snatching away her ability to run.

After some time, tearing her hair with hostile hands, with trembling lips she spoke unworthy words:

'If only my bones had been gathered and hidden in my ancestral tomb, when they could have been gathered belonging to a virgin!

Why am I (a Vestal not long ago) summoned to any marriage, disgraced and excluded from the Ilian hearth?

Why wait and be pointed out by the people as an adulterer? Away with a face marked by infamous shame'.

So much, and she stretched a robe over her swollen eyes and, distraught, hurled herself into the swift-flowing waters.

They say that the slippery river placed his hands on her breast and granted her the rights of the marriage bed.

te quoque credibile est aliqua caluisse puella,
 sed nemora et siluae crimina uestra tegunt.

dum loquor, increuit latis spatiosus in undis, 85
 nec capit admissas alueus altus aquas.
quid mecum, furiose, tibi? quid mutua differs
 gaudia? quid coeptum, rustice, rumpis iter?
quid si legitimum flueres, si nobile flumen,
 si tibi per terras maxima fama foret? 90
nomen habes nullum, riuis collecte caducis,
 nec tibi sunt fontes nec tibi certa domus.
fontis habes instar pluuiamque niuesque solutas,
 quas tibi diuitias pigra ministrat hiems.
aut lutulentus agis brumali tempore cursus, 95
 aut premis arentem puluerulentus humum.
quis te tum potuit sitiens haurire uiator?
 quis dixit grata uoce 'perennis eas'?
damnosus pecori curris, damnosior agris.
 forsitan haec alios, me mea damna mouent. 100
huic ego uae demens narrabam fluminum amores?
 iactasse indigne nomina tanta pudet.
nescioquem hunc spectans Acheloon et Inachon amnem
 et potui nomen, Nile, referre tuum?
at tibi pro meritis, opto, non candide torrens, 105
 sint rapidi soles siccaque semper hiems.

3.7

At non formosa est, at non bene culta puella,
 at, puto, non uotis saepe petita meis.
hanc tamen in nullos tenui male languidus usus,
 sed iacui pigro crimen onusque toro.
nec potui cupiens, pariter cupiente puella, 5
 inguinis effeti parte iuuante frui.
illa quidem nostro subiecit eburnea collo
 bracchia Sithonia candidiora niue
osculaque inseruit cupida luctantia lingua
 lasciuum femori supposuitque femur 10
et mihi blanditias dixit dominumque uocauit
 et quae praeterea publica uerba iuuant.
tacta tamen ueluti gelida mea membra cicuta
 segnia propositum destituere meum.

I can believe that you have been hot for a girl, but groves and forests conceal your crimes.

[85–106] While I spoke, the river grew expansive in its broad waves, and the deep channel could not contain its free-flowing waters.
You're crazy. What do you have against me? Why postpone shared delights? You rustic, why interrupt my journey?
What if you were a legitimate river, if you were a noble river, if you had a reputation as the greatest throughout the world?
You have no renown, you're just a gathering of overflowing streams, you have no source and you have no undisputed home.
You have as a source rain and melted snow, wealth provided by winter's sloth.
In winter's season you run your course all muddy, or you're a dusty burden on dry ground.
Then what thirsty traveller could drink from you? Who has said with gratitude: 'May you run all year'?
You run ruinous to flocks, more ruinous to fields. Perhaps this ruin worries others, mine worries me.
Ah! Am I crazy? Was I telling this stream stories of rivers' loves? It's embarrassing that I mentioned such great names unworthily.
While gazing on this nobody, could I speak of Achelous, the river Inachus, and of your name, Nile?
Untransparent torrent, I hope you get what you deserve: devouring suns and winter always dry.

3.7: AN EMBARRASSING PROBLEM

[1–16] No, she wasn't lovely. No, she wasn't a sophisticated girl. No, I suppose, she wasn't the frequent object of my desire.
Nevertheless, I was distressingly limp when I held her to no purpose, but lay there a guilty burden on an idle bed.
I was eager (and the girl was equally eager) but couldn't enjoy the pleasant part of my feeble groin.
She placed her ivory arms, more radiant than Sithonian snow, beneath my neck,
with eager tongue she thrust in vigorous kisses and placed sexy thigh beneath my thigh,
and flattered me and called me master and used common words to help me as well.
But my sluggish penis, as if touched by icy hemlock, abandoned my goal.

truncus iners iacui, species et inutile pondus, 15
  et non exactum, corpus an umbra forem.

quae mihi uentura est, siquidem uentura, senectus,
  cum desit numeris ipsa iuuenta suis?
a, pudet annorum! quo me iuuenemque uirumque?
  nec iuuenem nec me sensit amica uirum. 20
sic flammas aditura pias aeterna sacerdos
  surgit et a caro fratre uerenda soror.
at nuper bis flaua Chlide, ter candida Pitho,
  ter Libas officio continuata meo est.
exigere a nobis angusta nocte Corinnam 25
  me memini numeros sustinuisse nouem.

num mea Thessalico languent deuota ueneno
  corpora? num misero carmen et herba nocent,
sagaue poenicea defixit nomina cera
  et medium tenuis in iecur egit acus? 30
carmine laesa Ceres sterilem uanescit in herbam,
  deficiunt laesi carmine fontis aquae,
ilicibus glandes cantataque uitibus uua
  decidit et nullo poma mouente fluunt.
quid uetat et neruos magicas torpere per artes? 35
  forsitan impatiens fit latus inde meum.
huc pudor accessit: facti pudor ipse nocebat.
  ille fuit uitii causa secunda mei.

at qualem uidi tantum tetigique puellam!
  sic etiam tunica tangitur illa sua. 40
illius ad tactum Pylius iuuenescere possit
  Tithonosque annis fortior esse suis.
haec mihi contigerat, sed uir non contigit illi.
  quas nunc concipiam per noua uota preces?
credo etiam magnos, quo sum tam turpiter usus, 45
  muneris oblati paenituisse deos.
optabam certe recipi: sum nempe receptus;
  oscula ferre: tuli; proximus esse: fui.
quo mihi fortunae tantum? quo regna sine usu?
  quid, nisi possedi diues auarus opes? 50
sic aret mediis taciti uulgator in undis
  pomaque, quae nullo tempore tangat, habet.
a tenera quisquam sic surgit mane puella,
  protinus ut sanctos possit adire deos?

A lifeless log I lay there, a semblance, a useless weight, and it wasn't clear whether I was a body or a shadow.

[17–26] What sort of old age will I have, if I live that long, when my youth is already deficient?
Ah, I'm ashamed of my age! What's the point in being young and manly? My girlfriend found me neither young nor manly.
That's how a priestess, forever destined to approach the flame, gets out of bed and a sister respected by her dear brother.
But not long ago blonde Chlide received my attentions twice, radiant Pitho three times, Libas three times.
I recall that Corinna insisted on undergoing nine workouts from me in one short night.

[27–38] Is my body limp, cursed by Thessalian poison? Are incantations and herbs doing me harm,
or has some sorceress bewitched my name with crimson wax and driven sharp needles into my liver?
When harmed by incantations Ceres disappears into sterile grass, spring water when harmed by incantations fails,
acorns fall from oak trees, grapes from vines when enchanted, and fruit slips off without being touched.
What's to stop my muscle from being paralysed by magic arts? Perhaps that's why my body lacks all sensation.
In addition there was embarrassment: embarrassment at what I'd done made things worse; that was the next reason for my failure.

[39–62] What a girl! But I only saw and touched. I touched her as closely as her dress.
At her touch the man from Pylos could grow young and Tithonus be stronger than his age.
She met me, but a man did not meet her. What new favours can I pray for? Actually I think that the great gods regret the gift they offered me. I used it so shamefully.
Certainly I prayed that I would be welcome: indeed I was welcomed; that I could kiss her: I did; that I would be next to her: I was.
But what's the point of me having so much good luck? Of power if you don't use it? What was I? Just a wealthy skinflint owning millions.
That's how that whistle-blower thirsts, though surrounded by water, and possesses fruit he can never touch.
Does anyone get up in the morning and leave a tender girl so pure that they can immediately approach the blessed gods?

      sed, puto, non blanda est: non optima perdidit in me   55
          oscula; non omni sollicitauit ope.
      illa graues potuit quercus adamantaque durum
          surdaque blanditiis saxa mouere suis.
      digna mouere fuit certe uiuosque uirosque,
          sed neque tum uixi nec uir, ut ante, fui.   60
      quid iuuet, ad surdas si cantet Phemius aures?
          quid miserum Thamyran picta tabella iuuet?

      at quae non tacita formaui gaudia mente
          quos ego non finxi disposuique modos?
      nostra tamen iacuere uelut praemortua membra   65
          turpiter hesterna languidiora rosa,
      quae nunc, ecce, uigent intempestiua ualentque,
          nunc opus exposcunt militiamque suam.
      quin istic pudibunda iaces, pars pessima nostri?
          sic sum pollicitis captus et ante tuis.   70
      tu dominum fallis, per te deprensus inermis
          tristia cum magno damna pudore tuli.
      hanc etiam non est mea dedignata puella
          molliter admota sollicitare manu.

      sed postquam nullas consurgere posse per artes   75
          immemoremque sui procubuisse uidet,
      'quid me ludis?' ait, 'quis te, male sane, iubebat
          inuitum nostro ponere membra toro?
      aut te traiectis Aeaea uenefica lanis
          deuouet, aut alio lassus amore uenis'.   80
      nec mora, desiluit tunica uelata soluta
          (et decuit nudos proripuisse pedes)
      neue suae possent intactam scire ministrae,
          dedecus hoc sumpta dissimulauit aqua.

                                  3.8

      Et quisquam ingenuas etiam nunc suspicit artes
          aut tenerum dotes carmen habere putat?
      ingenium quondam fuerat pretiosius auro,
          at nunc barbaria est grandis habere nihil.
      cum pulchre dominae nostri placuere libelli,   5
          quo licuit libris, non licet ire mihi;

But, I suppose, she was not enticing: she didn't waste glorious kisses on me; didn't use every possible means of exciting me.
She was capable of exciting ponderous oaks and hard adamant and deaf rocks with her enticements.
Certainly she deserved to excite anyone who was alive and male; but I was neither alive nor male as in the past.
What pleasure would it give, if Phemius sang to deaf ears? What pleasure would a painted panel give to wretched Thamyras?

[63–74] But what joys had I not secretly imagined, what positions had I not pictured and organized?
But my penis lay there as if prematurely dead, shamefully more limp than yesterday's rose.
But look, now it's vigorous, it's robust at the wrong time, now it demands work and active service.
Why don't you just lie there? You're a disgrace, my very worst part. I've been cheated by your promises before.
You deceive your master, because of you I was caught unarmed and suffered grim loss as well as deep embarrassment.
Even so my girlfriend did not disdain exciting it with gentle application of her hand.

[75–84] But after she saw that none of her skills would make it rise and that it lay there prostrate, forgetful of its true self,
'Why do you cheat me?', she said, 'You're sick. Who told you to put your body in my bed when you're not really willing?
Either Aeaea's witch has cursed you by piercing wool, or you're here worn out by some other love'.
Without delay, covered in a loose tunic she leaped up (she looked lovely rushing off barefoot)
and so that her servants could not know that she had not been touched, she concealed her disgrace with a bit of water.

3.8: MONEY RULES NOWADAYS

[1–8] And does anyone still admire the free-born arts, or think that delicate poetry receives its proper endowment?
Once upon a time talent was more precious than gold, but now owning nothing is utter barbarism.
When my books have pleased my mistress perfectly, where my books can go I cannot.

48 OVIDI AMORUM LIBER TERTIUS

cum bene laudauit, laudato ianua clausa est.
   turpiter huc illuc ingeniosus eo.

ecce, recens diues parto per uulnera censu
   praefertur nobis sanguine pastus eques.   10
hunc potes amplecti formosis, uita, lacertis?
   huius in amplexu, uita, iacere potes?
si nescis, caput hoc galeam portare solebat;
   ense latus cinctum, quod tibi seruit, erat.
laeua manus, cui nunc serum male conuenit aurum,   15
   scuta tulit; dextram tange, cruenta fuit.
qua periit aliquis, potes hanc contingere dextram?
   heu, ubi mollities pectoris illa tui?
cerne cicatrices, ueteris uestigia pugnae:
   quaesitum est illi corpore, quidquid habet.   20
forsitan et, quotiens hominem iugulauerit, ille
   indicet: hoc fassas tangis, auara, manus?

ille ego Musarum purus Phoebique sacerdos
   ad rigidas canto carmen inane fores.
discite, qui sapitis, non quae nos scimus inertes,   25
   sed trepidas acies et fera castra sequi
proque bono uersu primum deducite pilum:
   nox tibi, si belles, possit, Homere, dari.

Iuppiter, admonitus nihil esse potentius auro,
   corruptae pretium uirginis ipse fuit.   30
dum merces aberat, durus pater, ipsa seuera,
   aerati postes, ferrea turris erat.
sed postquam sapiens in munere uenit adulter,
   praebuit ipsa sinus et dare iussa dedit.

at cum regna senex caeli Saturnus haberet,   35
   omne lucrum tenebris alta premebat humus.
aeraque et argentum cumque auro pondera ferri
   Manibus admorat, nullaque massa fuit.
at meliora dabat, curuo sine uomere fruges
   pomaque et in quercu mella reperta caua.   40
nec ualido quisquam terram scindebat aratro,
   signabat nullo limite mensor humum.
non freta demisso uerrebant eruta remo:
   ultima mortali tum uia litus erat.

OVID, AMORES BOOK 3 [8.7–44] 49

After she commends them favourably, her door is closed to the author she commends. I may be talented but I wander here and there in disgrace.

[9–22] Look, newly rich, his property acquired by wounds, a knight fattened on blood is preferred to me.
My darling, can you embrace this man with your lovely arms? My darling, can you lie in this man's embrace?
If you are unaware, that head used to carry a helmet; his flank, the one that's enslaved to you, was equipped with a sword.
His left hand, so ill-suited to the golden ring he's just acquired, once carried shields; touch his right hand, once it was bloody.
Can you touch that right hand? It killed someone. Ah, where is your softness of heart?
Examine those scars, traces of a battle long ago: everything he owns he acquired with his body.
Perhaps he discloses how often he's slaughtered human beings: greedy woman, do you touch hands that make this confession?

[23–28] Do I, blameless priest of the Muses and Phoebus, sing a futile song before unyielding doors?
If you are smart, learn not what we slackers know, but how to follow fearful soldiers and the brutal camp.
And instead of fine verse, draw down the first javelin: Homer, if you went to war, you could get laid.

[29–34] Advised that nothing has more power than gold, Jupiter himself was the bribe for seducing a virgin.
As long as there was no payment, the father was stern, she severe, the doors bronze, the tower iron.
But after a wise adulterer came in the form of a gift, she offered her embrace and, when ordered to give, she gave.

[35–44] But when elderly Saturn held kingship over heaven, the earth's depths concealed all profit in darkness.
He had moved bronze and silver and, along with gold, the weight of iron down to the shades and metal-ore did not exist.
But he provided better things, crops without the curved plough and fruit and honey discovered in a hollow oak.
And no one split the earth with a strong plough, and no surveyor marked the ground with boundaries.
They did not thrust oars in, churn up, and sweep the waters: at that time the seashore was the furthest journey known to mortals.

contra te sollers, hominum natura, fuisti 45
  et nimium damnis ingeniosa tuis.
quo tibi turritis incingere moenibus urbes?
  quo tibi discordes addere in arma manus?
quid tibi cum pelago? terra contenta fuisses.
  cur non et caelum tertia regna facis? 50
qua licet, affectas caelum quoque: templa Quirinus
  Liber et Alcides et modo Caesar habent.

eruimus terra solidum pro frugibus aurum.
  possidet inuentas sanguine miles opes.
curia pauperibus clausa est, dat census honores; 55
  inde grauis iudex, inde seuerus eques.
omnia possideant. illis Campusque forumque
  seruiat, hi pacem crudaque bella gerant.
tantum ne nostros auidi liceantur amores,
  et (satis est) aliquid pauperis esse sinant. 60
at nunc, exaequet tetricas licet illa Sabinas,
  imperat ut captae qui dare multa potest.
me prohibet custos, in me timet illa maritum.
  si dederim, tota cedet uterque domo.
o si neglecti quisquam deus ultor amantis 65
  tam male quaesitas puluere mutet opes!

3.9

Memnona si mater, mater plorauit Achillem
  et tangunt magnas tristia fata deas,
flebilis indignos, Elegeia, solue capillos:
  a, nimis ex uero nunc tibi nomen erit.
ille tui uates operis, tua fama, Tibullus 5
  ardet in exstructo corpus inane rogo.

ecce, puer Veneris fert euersamque pharetram
  et fractos arcus et sine luce facem.
aspice, demissis ut eat miserabilis alis
  pectoraque infesta tundat aperta manu. 10
excipiunt lacrimas sparsi per colla capilli
  oraque singultu concutiente sonant.
fratris in Aeneae sic illum funere dicunt
  egressum tectis, pulcher Iule, tuis.

[45–56] Human nature, you were shrewd against your own interests and too talented in self-destruction.
Why must you enclose cities with towered walls? Why must you fit discordant hands to weapons?
What's the sea to you? You should have been content with land. Why not make heaven your third realm?
Where you can, you strive to conquer heaven too: Quirinus has a temple, Liber and Alcides, and now Caesar too.

[53–66] We dig up solid gold from the earth instead of crops. A soldier owns riches acquired by blood.
The senate-house is closed to the poor, wealth bestows rank; it creates the stern judge, it creates the austere knight.
Let the rich own everything. Let the Campus and the forum be enslaved to them, let them wage peace and savage wars.
Only the greedy should not bid for the ones we love and let the poor have something (it's enough).
But now, a man with lots of gifts, even though she's the equal of those dreary Sabine women, orders her around like a prisoner.
A guard shuts *me* out; if it's *me*, she's afraid of her husband. If I handed over gifts, both will vacate the whole house.
Oh, if there is any god at all who avenges disregarded lovers, may he transform wrongly acquired wealth into dust!

3.9: LAMENT FOR TIBULLUS

[1–6] If his mother mourned for Memnon, if his mother mourned for Achilles, and grim fates affect great goddesses,
Plaintive Elegy, untie your undeserving hair: ah, now your name will be all too accurate.
Tibullus, your genre's poet, your glory, blazes on a built-up pyre, a lifeless body.

[7–16] Look, Venus' boy brings his quiver upside-down, his bow broken and his torch lightless.
Behold how he advances, mourning, his wings downcast, how furiously he pounds his bare breast.
His hair spread out over his neck absorbs tears and his lips sound with a shaking sob.
They say that he was like that at the funeral of his brother, Aeneas, when he came out from your house, handsome Iulus.

nec minus est confusa Venus moriente Tibullo 15
    quam iuueni rupit cum ferus inguen aper.

at sacri uates et diuum cura uocamur;
    sunt etiam qui nos numen habere putent.
scilicet omne sacrum mors importuna profanat,
    omnibus obscuras inicit illa manus. 20
quid pater Ismario, quid mater profuit Orpheo?
    carmine quid uictas obstipuisse feras?
et Linon in siluis idem pater 'aelinon' altis
    dicitur inuita concinuisse lyra.
adice Maeoniden, a quo ceu fonte perenni 25
    uatum Pieriis ora rigantur aquis.
hunc quoque summa dies nigro submersit Auerno.
    defugiunt auidos carmina sola rogos.
durat opus uatum: Troiani fama laboris
    tardaque nocturno tela retexta dolo; 30
sic Nemesis longum, sic Delia nomen habebunt,
    altera cura recens, altera primus amor.

quid uos sacra iuuant? quid nunc Aegyptia prosunt
    sistra? quid in uacuo secubuisse toro?
cum rapiunt mala fata bonos (ignoscite fasso) 35
    sollicitor nullos esse putare deos.
uiue pius: moriere pius; cole sacra: colentem
    mors grauis a templis in caua busta trahet.
carminibus confide bonis: iacet ecce Tibullus:
    uix manet e toto parua quod urna capit. 40

tene, sacer uates, flammae rapuere rogales
    pectoribus pasci nec timuere tuis?
aurea sanctorum potuissent templa deorum
    urere, quae tantum sustinuere nefas.
auertit uultus, Erycis quae possidet arces; 45
    sunt quoque qui lacrimas continuisse negant.

sed tamen hoc melius, quam si Phaeacia tellus
    ignotum uili supposuisset humo.
hic certe madidos fugientis pressit ocellos
    mater et in cineres ultima dona tulit. 50
hic soror in partem misera cum matre doloris
    uenit inornatas dilaniata comas.

Venus was no less troubled when Tibullus died than when a savage boar ruptured her young lover's groin.

[17–32] But we are known as sacred poets and the gods' concern; some even suppose that we have divine power.
Obviously relentless death violates all that is sacred, she lays dark hands on everything.
What good was his father, what good his mother to Ismarian Orpheus? What good wild beasts overwhelmed and stunned by song?
They say that the same father sang 'aelinos' for Linus in the forest's depths even against his lyre's will.
Add in Homer, from whom, as from an unfailing spring, the mouths of poets are nourished by Pierian waters.
The final day drowned him too in black Avernus. Only poems escape the greedy funeral-pyre.
Poets' work endures: the story of Troy's suffering and the loom slowly unwoven by night's deceit;
in the same way Nemesis, in the same way Delia, will have an enduring name, one your latest care, the other your first love.

[33–40] What good are sacred rites to you? What good are Egyptian rattles now? What good is lying alone in an empty bed?
When an evil fate seizes hold of good people (forgive my confession) I am tempted to believe that the gods do not exist.
Live a pious life: you will die a pious death; worship the gods: stern Death will drag the worshipper from temples to hollow tombs.
Have confidence in fine poetry: look, Tibullus lies dead; from all of him there barely survives what a tiny urn can hold.

[41–6] Sacred poet, did funeral flames lay hold of you, not afraid to feed upon your breast?
Those flames, which dared to commit this dreadful sacrilege, could have burned the golden temples of the holy gods.
The goddess who occupies the citadels of Eryx turned aside her face; and some say that she could not restrain her tears.

[47–58] But this is better than if Phaeacia's land had buried him, a stranger, in worthless earth.
Here at least his mother closed his moist eyes as he escaped and brought final gifts to his ashes.
Here his sister came to share grief with her poor mother, her hair torn and dishevelled.

cumque tuis sua iunxerunt Nemesisque priorque
   oscula nec solos destituere rogos.
Delia discedens 'felicius' inquit 'amata 55
   sum tibi: uixisti dum tuus ignis eram'.
cui Nemesis 'quid' ait 'tibi sunt mea damna dolori?
   me tenuit moriens deficiente manu'.

si tamen e nobis aliquid nisi nomen et umbra
   restat, in Elysia ualle Tibullus erit. 60
obuius huic uenias hedera iuuenalia cinctus
   tempora cum Caluo, docte Catulle, tuo;
tu quoque, si falsum est temerati crimen amici,
   sanguinis atque animae prodige Galle tuae.
his comes umbra tua est, siqua est modo corporis umbra; 65
   auxisti numeros, culte Tibulle, pios.
ossa quieta, precor, tuta requiescite in urna,
   et sit humus cineri non onerosa tuo.

3.10

Annua uenerunt Cerealis tempora sacri:
   secubat in uacuo sola puella toro.
flaua Ceres, tenues spicis redimita capillos,
   cur inhibes sacris commoda nostra tuis?
te, dea, munificam gentes, ubi quaeque, loquuntur, 5
   nec minus humanis inuidet ulla bonis.
ante nec hirsuti torrebant farra coloni,
   nec notum terris area nomen erat,
sed glandem quercus, oracula prima, ferebant;
   haec erat et teneri caespitis herba cibus. 10
prima Ceres docuit turgescere semen in agris,
   falce coloratas subsecuitque comas.
prima iugis tauros supponere colla coegit
   et ueterem curuo dente reuellit humum.
hanc quisquam lacrimis laetari credit amantum 15
   et bene tormentis secubituque coli?
nec tamen est, quamuis agros amet illa feraces,
   rustica nec uiduum pectus amoris habet.

Cretes erunt testes; nec fingunt omnia Cretes.
   Crete nutrito terra superba Ioue. 20

And Nemesis and the earlier one added their kisses to your family's and did not abandon your pyre to isolation.
As she left Delia said 'Loving me brought you better luck: as long I was your flame, you stayed alive'.
To her Nemesis replied: 'Why are you sorry for my loss? As he died, I was the one he gripped with failing hand'.

[59–68] But if any part of us survives, other than name and shadow, Tibullus will be in Elysium's valley.
Garland your youthful brows with ivy and come to meet him, learned Catullus, with your dear friend Calvus;
You too, Gallus, wasteful of your life and blood, if the accusation of violating friendship is false.
Your shadow accompanies them, if the body's shadow actually exists; elegant Tibullus, you have increased the numbers of the pious.
Bones, rest quietly in a sheltering urn, and may the earth not lie heavy on your ashes.

3.10: PRAYER TO CERES

[1–18] The annual season of Ceres' festival has come: my girlfriend sleeps apart, alone in an empty bed.
Golden Ceres, your fine hair crowned with ears of grain, why do you restrain our benefits with your festival?
Goddess, all peoples, wherever they are, speak of you as bountiful; no goddess is less resentful of human wellbeing.
Previously hairy farmers used not to parch their emmer, and the threshing-floor was a name unknown to the earth,
but oak trees, the earliest oracles, bore acorns; these and the blades of tender turf were food.
Ceres was the first to teach seeds to swell in fields and to sever sun-darkened ears of grain with a scythe.
She was the first to compel bulls to place their necks beneath the yoke and to tear up ancient soil with the curved ploughshare.
Does anyone believe that she rejoices in lovers' tears and is properly worshipped by the torture of sleeping apart?
Even though she loves fruitful fields, she is certainly no rustic and her heart is not devoid of love.

[19–42] The Cretans will bear witness: not everything the Cretans say is false.
The land of Crete takes pride in having nurtured Jupiter.

illic sideream mundi qui temperat arcem
  exiguus tenero lac bibit ore puer.
magna fides testi: testis laudatur alumno.
  fassuram Cererem crimina nostra puto.
uiderat Iasium Cretaea diua sub Ida 25
  figentem certa terga ferina manu.
uidit, et ut tenerae flammam rapuere medullae,
  hinc pudor, ex illa parte trahebat amor.
uictus amore pudor: sulcos arere uideres
  et sata cum minima parte redire sui. 30
cum bene iactati pulsarant arua ligones,
  ruperat et duram uomer aduncus humum,
seminaque in latos ierant aequaliter agros,
  irrita decepti uota colentis erant.
diua potens frugum siluis cessabat in altis; 35
  deciderant longae spicea serta comae.
sola fuit Crete fecundo fertilis anno:
  omnia, qua tulerat se dea, messis erat.
ipse locus nemorum canebat frugibus Ide
  et ferus in silua farra metebat aper. 40
optauit Minos similes sibi legifer annos;
  optasset Cereris longus ut esset amor.

qui tibi secubitus tristes, dea flaua, fuissent,
  hos cogor sacris nunc ego ferre tuis.
cur ego sim tristis, cum sit tibi nata reperta 45
  regnaque quam Iuno sorte minora regat?
festa dies ueneremque uocat cantusque merumque;
  haec decet ad dominos munera ferre deos.

3.11

Multa diuque tuli; uitiis patientia uicta est:
  cede fatigato pectore, turpis amor.
scilicet asserui iam me fugique catenas
  et quae non puduit ferre, tulisse pudet.
uicimus et domitum pedibus calcamus Amorem. 5
  uenerunt capiti cornua sera meo.
perfer et obdura. dolor hic tibi proderit olim:
  saepe tulit lassis sucus amarus opem.

It was there that the ruler of the world's starry citadel gently drank milk when he was a tiny child.
I have great confidence in the witness: the witness is approved by the child it fostered. I think that Ceres will accept the truth of my accusations.
The goddess had seen Iasius at the foot of Cretan Ida accurately piercing the backs of wild beasts.
She watched, and just as tender marrow seizes flame, modesty dragged her this way, love in that direction.
Love defeated modesty: you could see furrows drying up and the crops returning with only a tiny fraction of themselves.
When the mattocks were vigorously applied and struck the ploughlands and the hooked ploughshare had burst through the hard soil,
seeds went evenly spaced into the broad fields, but the farmer was cheated and his prayers were vain.
The powerful goddess of crops was lingering in the forest's depths; the grain garlands had fallen from her long hair.
Crete alone was fertile in the fruitful year: where the goddess had passed everything was harvest.
Ida, the very home of forests, was white with crops and the wild boar were reaping emmer in the woods.
Lawgiver Minos prayed for years like this; he should have prayed for Ceres' love affair to be long-lasting.

[43–8] Golden goddess, the sleeping apart that would have been distressing for you, I am forced by your festival to endure.
Why should I feel distressed, when your daughter has been found and rules by lot a kingdom lesser than only Juno?
A holiday calls for sex, song, and wine; these are the gifts it's right to bring to the gods who rule us.

3.11: REFLECTIONS ON CATULLUS

[1–8] I've endured a lot and for a long time; my patience has been overcome by your faults: shameful love, withdraw from my exhausted heart.
Clearly I have now freed myself and run away from chains, and I'm ashamed at having endured what I was not ashamed to endure.
I have overcome. Love has been subdued and I trample him underfoot. Horns are finally growing on my head.
Endure and be strong. One day this pain will profit you: bitter juice has often helped the sick.

ergo ego sustinui, foribus tam saepe repulsus,
   ingenuum dura ponere corpus humo? 10
ergo ego nescio cui, quem tu complexa tenebas,
   excubui clausam seruus ut ante domum?
uidi, cum foribus lassus prodiret amator,
   inualidum referens emeritumque latus.
hoc tamen est leuius, quam quod sum uisus ab illo: 15
   eueniat nostris hostibus ille pudor.
quando ego non fixus lateri patienter adhaesi,
   ipse tuus custos, ipse uir, ipse comes?
scilicet et populo per me comitata placebas:
   causa fuit multis noster amoris amor. 20
turpia quid referam uanae mendacia linguae
   et periuratos in mea damna deos?
quid iuuenum tacitos inter conuiuia nutus
   uerbaque compositis dissimulata notis?
dicta erat aegra mihi: praeceps amensque cucurri. 25
   ueni et riuali non erat aegra meo.

his et quae taceo duraui saepe ferendis:
   quaere alium pro me, qui queat ista pati.
iam mea uotiua puppis redimita corona
   lenta tumescentes aequoris audit aquas. 30
desine blanditias et uerba potentia quondam
   perdere: non ego nunc stultus, ut ante fui.

luctantur pectusque leue in contraria tendunt
   hac amor hac odium. sed, puto, uincit amor.
odero, si potero; si non, inuitus amabo. 35
   nec iuga taurus amat; quae tamen odit, habet.
nequitiam fugio, fugientem forma reducit;
   auersor morum crimina, corpus amo.
sic ego nec sine te nec tecum uiuere possum,
   et uideor uoti nescius esse mei. 40
aut formosa fores minus aut minus improba uellem:
   non facit ad mores tam bona forma malos.
facta merent odium, facies exorat amorem:
   me miserum! uitiis plus ualet illa suis.

parce, per o lecti socialia iura, per omnes 45
   qui dant fallendos se tibi saepe deos,
perque tuam faciem magni mihi numinis instar,
   perque tuos oculos qui rapuere meos.

OVID, AMORES BOOK 3 [11.9–48] 59

[9–26] So have I, after being driven away so often from your doors, put up with placing my freeborn and delicate body on the hard earth?
So have I, for the benefit of some stranger, whom you held in your embrace, kept watch outside your locked house like a slave?
I saw when your lover left your house exhausted, taking home his feeble body, service done.
But this is easier to bear than the fact that he saw me: I hope this embarrassment happens to my enemies.
When have I not pressed close and clung patiently to your body, not been your guard, your lover, your companion?
Of course my company made you attractive to the people: my love made many love you.
Why mention your vacuous tongue's shameful lies and the gods you lied by to ruin me?
Why the young lovers' silent nods at parties, the agreed signals and secret words?
I was told she was sick: I ran to her, impetuous and frantic. I arrived and she was not sick for my rival.

[27–32] By enduring all of this, and more I will not mention, I have grown strong: look for my replacement, someone willing to tolerate these humiliations.
And now my ship, crowned with votive garlands, hears unmoved the sea's swelling waters.
Stop wasting flattery and words once powerful: I am no longer as foolish as I was.

[33–44] They struggle and drag my lightweight heart in opposite directions, love on this side, hate on that. But love wins, I suppose.
If I can, I'll hate; if not, I'll love against my will. No bull loves the yoke; he tolerates what he hates.
Her depravity I flee, but when I flee her beauty draws me back; I shun her criminal ways, I love her body.
So I cannot live with you or without you and I don't seem to know what I want.
I would like you to be less beautiful or less wicked; such good looks do not suit bad character.
Your actions deserve hatred, your appearance wins love: poor me! her faults are her strength.

[45–52] Be merciful, Oh by our bed's marriage laws, by all the gods who often let you cheat them,
By your beauty, a great god in my sight, by your eyes which snatched mine away.

quidquid eris, mea semper eris; tu selige tantum,
   me quoque uelle uelis, anne coactus amem.   50
lintea dem potius uentisque ferentibus utar
   et, quam, si nolim, cogar amare, uelim.

3.12

Quis fuit ille dies, quo tristia semper amanti
   omina non albae concinuistis aues?
quodue putem sidus nostris occurrere fatis,
   quosue deos in me bella mouere querar?
quae modo dicta mea est, quam coepi solus amare,   5
   cum multis uereor ne sit habenda mihi.
fallimur, an nostris innotuit illa libellis?
   sic erit: ingenio prostitit illa meo.
et merito: quid enim formae praeconia feci?
   uendibilis culpa facta puella mea est.   10
me lenone placet, duce me perductus amator,
   ianua per nostras est adaperta manus.

an prosint dubium, nocuerunt carmina semper;
   inuidiae nostris illa fuere bonis.
cum Thebae, cum Troia foret, cum Caesaris acta,   15
   ingenium mouit sola Corinna meum.
auersis utinam tetigissem carmina Musis,
   Phoebus et inceptum destituisset opus!

nec tamen ut testes mos est audire poetas:
   malueram uerbis pondus abesse meis.   20
per nos Scylla patri caros furata capillos
   pube premit rabidos inguinibusque canes;
nos pedibus pinnas dedimus, nos crinibus angues:
   uictor Abantiades alite fertur equo.
idem per spatium Tityon porreximus ingens,   25
   et tria uipereo fecimus ora cani;
fecimus Enceladon iaculantem mille lacertis,
   ambiguae captos uirginis ore uiros.
Aeolios Ithacis inclusimus utribus Euros;
   proditor in medio Tantalus amne sitit.   30
de Niobe silicem, de uirgine fecimus ursam.
   concinit Odrysium Cecropis ales Ityn;

Whatever you will be, you will always be mine; only choose whether you will me to love willingly or under compulsion.

May I rather spread my sails and experience favourable winds and may I love willingly a woman whom I would be forced to love if I were unwilling.

3.12: REFLECTIONS ON PROPERTIUS

[1–12] What a day was that, unwhite birds, when you sang grim omens to the perpetual lover?
What star should I suppose runs counter to my destiny, what gods should I complain of for stirring war against me?
The girl who has just been called mine, the one that I alone have begun to love, I'm afraid that I might have to share her with lots of men.
Am I wrong, or did she become famous through my books? That's right: my talent put her up for sale.
It serves me right. Well, why did I auction off her beauty? It's my fault that my girlfriend's marketable.
I'm the pimp who rendered her attractive, I'm the guide who brought her lovers, mine are the hands that opened the door.

[13–18] I doubt its usefulness: poetry is always harmful; it's caused resentment at my success.
Though Thebes was there to write about, and Troy, and Caesar's deeds, Corinna alone stirred my talent.
If only the Muses had turned away when I put my hand to poetry, if only Phoebus had abandoned the work I started!

[19–40] But it's not customary to listen to poets like witnesses in court; I had preferred my words to lack that kind of weight.
It's down to us that Scylla, after stealing her father's precious hair, confines rabid dogs with her private parts and groin;
we gave wings to feet, snakes to hair: Perseus is borne aloft on a winged horse.
We're the ones who stretched Tityos over a vast area and invented a snaky dog with three mouths.
We invented Enceladus hurling javelins with a thousand arms and men enthralled by a hybrid maiden's voice.
We imprisoned Aeolus' east winds in the Ithacan's leather bag; traitor Tantalus is thirsty in the middle of a river;
we invented flint from Niobe, a bear from a virgin; the Cecropian bird sings of Odrysian Itys;

Iuppiter aut in aues aut se transformat in aurum
   aut secat imposita uirgine taurus aquas.
Protea quid referam Thebanaque semina, dentes,   35
   qui uomerent flammas ore, fuisse boues,
flere genis electra tuas, auriga, sorores,
   quaeque rates fuerint, nunc maris esse deas,
auersumque diem mensis furialibus Atrei,
   duraque percussam saxa secuta lyram?   40

exit in immensum fecunda licentia uatum,
   obligat historica nec sua uerba fide.
et mea debuerat falso laudata uideri
   femina; credulitas nunc mihi uestra nocet.

3.13

Cum mihi pomiferis coniunx foret orta Faliscis,
   moenia contigimus uicta, Camille, tibi.
casta sacerdotes Iunoni festa parabant
   et celebres ludos indigenamque bouem.
grande morae pretium ritus cognoscere, quamuis   5
   difficilis cliuis huc uia praebet iter.
stat uetus et densa praenubilus arbore lucus;
   aspice, concedes numinis esse locum.

accipit ara preces uotiuaque tura piorum,
   ara per antiquas facta sine arte manus.   10
huc, ubi praesonuit sollemni tibia cantu,
   it per uelatas annua pompa uias.
ducuntur niueae populo plaudente iuuencae,
   quas aluit campis herba Falisca suis,
et uituli nondum metuenda fronte minaces   15
   et minor ex humili uictima porcus hara
duxque gregis cornu per tempora dura recuruo.
   inuisa est dominae sola capella deae:
illius indicio siluis inuenta sub altis
   dicitur inceptam destituisse fugam.   20
nunc quoque per pueros iaculis incessitur index
   et pretium auctori uulneris ipsa datur.

qua uentura dea est, iuuenes timidaeque puellae
   praeuerrunt latas ueste iacente uias.

Jupiter transforms himself into either birds or gold, or a bull slices through waves with a virgin on his back.
Why should I mention Proteus or that there were Theban seeds, teeth, bulls which spewed forth flames,
that your sisters, charioteer, wept amber down their cheeks, that sea goddesses now exist who once were ships,
or that the day was turned back by Atreus' frenzied feast, or that hard rocks followed after a strummed lyre?

[41–4] Poets' fertile freedom extends limitlessly and does not bind its words with historical truth.
It should have been obvious that the praises of my girlfriend were fictitious; your gullibility is now harming me.

3.13: JUNO'S FALISCAN FESTIVAL

[1–8] Since my wife was born in fruitful Faliscan territory, we arrived at the city that you conquered, Camillus.
The priests were preparing the holy festival for Juno, crowded shows and a local cow.
Lingering to become familiar with these rites is worthwhile, even though the road there with its slopes presents a difficult journey.
There stands a grove ancient and deeply shaded by massed trees; inspect it, you will concede that the place belongs to a divinity.

[9–22] An altar receives the prayers and votive incense of pious worshippers, an altar created artlessly by ancient hands.
To here, when the pipe has made its opening call with solemn music, the annual procession makes its way through covered streets.
To the people's applause snow-white heifers are led, nurtured in local fields by Faliscan grass,
And calves that menace with brows not yet fearsome, and a lesser victim, a pig from a lowly sty,
and the flock's leader with horns curving back over his hard temples. The lady goddess hates only the she-goat:
On her information, they say, she was discovered deep in the forest and had to abandon her exile.
Even now boys assail the informer with missiles and she is given as a prize to the one responsible for wounding her.

[23–36] Along the route the goddess is to take, young men and shy girls sweep the broad streets in advance with trailing clothes.

uirginei crines auro gemmaque premuntur, 25
   et tegit auratos palla superba pedes;
more patrum Graio uelatae uestibus albis
   tradita supposito uertice sacra ferunt.
ore fauent populi tum cum uenit aurea pompa,
   ipsa sacerdotes subsequiturque suas. 30
Argiua est pompae facies; Agamemnone caeso
   et scelus et patrias fugit Halaesus opes
iamque pererratis profugus terraque fretoque
   moenia felici condidit alta manu.
ille suos docuit Iunonia sacra Faliscos. 35
   sint mihi, sint populo semper amica suo.

3.14

Non ego, ne pecces, cum sis formosa, recuso,
   sed ne sit misero scire necesse mihi;
nec te nostra iubet fieri censura pudicam
   sed tamen ut temptes dissimulare rogat.
non peccat, quaecumque potest peccasse negare, 5
   solaque famosam culpa professa facit.
quis furor est, quae nocte latent, in luce fateri,
   et quae clam facias facta referre palam?
ignoto meretrix corpus iunctura Quiriti
   opposita populum summouet ante sera; 10
tu tua prostitues famae peccata sinistrae,
   commissi perages indiciumque tui?
sit tibi mens melior, saltemue imitare pudicas,
   teque probam, quamuis non eris, esse putem.
quae facis, haec facito: tantum fecisse negato 15
   nec pudeat coram uerba modesta loqui.

est qui nequitiam locus exigat; omnibus illum
   deliciis imple, stet procul inde pudor.
hinc simul exieris, lasciuia protinus omnis
   absit, et in lecto crimina pone tuo. 20
illic nec tunicam tibi sit posuisse pudori
   nec femori impositum sustinuisse femur;
illic purpureis condatur lingua labellis,
   inque modos uenerem mille figuret amor;
illic nec uoces nec uerba iuuantia cessent, 25
   spondaque lasciua mobilitate tremat.

Virginal locks are weighed down with gold and gems, and a proud robe covers golden feet.
In the Greek manner of their ancestors, veiled in white robes, they bear inherited sacred objects on their heads.
The people maintain a respectful silence when the golden procession comes, the goddess herself follows behind her priestesses.
The procession is Argive in appearance; after Agamemnon's death Halaesus fled crime and ancestral wealth
and now, after wandering land and sea as a refugee, happily founded these high walls.
He taught his Faliscans Juno's rites. May they always be dear to me and to her people.

3.14: CONCEAL YOUR INFIDELITIES

[1–16] I don't object, because you're lovely, to your misdeeds, but to the misery of being forced to know about them;
My censor's duty does not insist that you turn to chastity, but it does request that you try to fake it.
A girl who can deny that she offends, commits no offence; it's admitting guilt that wrecks her reputation.
What madness is this, to confess the night's mysteries in daylight and openly reveal the deeds that you do in secret?
When a prostitute is about to have sex with an unknown Roman, she first bolts the door and excludes the people;
will you publicly expose your offences to vicious rumour and inform against your own misdeeds?
Have better sense, at least simulate chastity, then I could imagine you were virtuous even though you won't be.
Do what you do: only say you didn't do it, and don't be ashamed to speak decorously in public.

[17–30] There is a place for depravity; fill it with every kind of delight, keep modesty well away.
As soon as you go outside, immediately forget all fun, leave your crimes behind in your bed.
When you're *there*, don't be ashamed of leaving your tunic behind or of placing thigh beneath thigh;
When you're *there*, bury your tongue in purple lips and let love shape sex in a thousand ways;
When you're *there*, whispers and encouraging words should not stop, and the couch should shake with unrestrained agility.

indue cum tunicis metuentem crimina uultum,
  et pudor obscenum diffiteatur opus.
da populo, da uerba mihi: sine nescius errem,
  et liceat stulta credulitate frui.   30

cur totiens uideo mitti recipique tabellas?
  cur pressus prior est interiorque torus?
cur plus quam somno turbatos esse capillos
  collaque conspicio dentis habere notam?
tantum non oculos crimen deducis ad ipsos;   35
  si dubitas famae parcere, parce mihi.
mens abit et morior, quotiens peccasse fateris,
  perque meos artus frigida gutta fluit.
tunc amo, tunc odi frustra, quod amare necesse est;
  tunc ego, sed tecum, mortuus esse uelim.   40

nil equidem inquiram, nec quae celare parabis
  insequar, et falli muneris instar erit.
si tamen in media deprensa tenebere culpa,
  et fuerint oculis probra uidenda meis,
quae bene uisa mihi fuerint, bene uisa negato: 45
  concedent uerbis lumina nostra tuis.
prona tibi uinci cupientem uincere palma est,
  sit modo 'non feci' dicere lingua memor.
cum tibi contingat uerbis superare duobus,
  etsi non causa, iudice uince tuo.   50

3.15

Quaere nouum uatem, tenerorum mater Amorum:
  raditur hic elegis ultima meta meis;
quos ego composui, Paeligni ruris alumnus,
  (nec me deliciae dedecuere meae)
si quid id est, usque a proauis uetus ordinis heres,   5
  non modo militiae turbine factus eques.

Mantua Vergilio gaudet Verona Catullo;
  Paelignae dicar gloria gentis ego,
quam sua libertas ad honesta coegerat arma,
  cum timuit socias anxia Roma manus.   10
atque aliquis spectans hospes Sulmonis aquosi
  moenia, quae campi iugera pauca tenent,

When you dress, clothe your face with a horror of wrongdoing and let your modesty deny your immoral work.
Deceive the people, deceive me: let me be wrong through ignorance and allow me to enjoy my stupid gullibility.

[31–40] Why do I have to see letters going back and forth so often? Why is the outer as well as the inner part of the couch crushed?
Why do I see your hair messed up by more than sleep and your neck with toothmarks?
You almost draw my eyes to your guilt; if you want to spare your reputation, spare me.
I'm losing my mind and I die when you admit to your offences, and icy drops of sweat flow over my body.
At one time I love, at another time I hate without success, because I have to love; at another, I'd rather be dead, but with you.

[41–50] For my part, I won't make inquiries, nor will I pursue what you're trying to conceal, and being deceived will be like a gift.
But if you are caught, surprised in mid offence, and my eyes have to see your disgrace,
Deny that I have actually seen what I have actually seen: I will believe your words and not my eyes.
It will be an easy victory for you to conquer a man eager to be conquered, as long as your tongue remembers to say 'Not guilty'.
Since you can win with just two words, conquer, if not with your argument, then with your judge.

3.15: GOODBYE, LOVE ELEGY

[1–6] Look for a new poet, mother of delicate Loves: here I am grazing the final turning-post with my elegies;
I composed them, a child of the Paelignian countryside, (nor did erotic verse fail to suit me),
long-standing heir to rank, if that's worth anything, from my great-grandfathers' time, not some knight recently created by the dizziness of a military campaign.

[7–14] Mantua rejoices in Virgil, Verona in Catullus; I shall be called the glory of the Paeliginian nation,
a people whom their own freedom drove to honourable warfare, when troubled Rome feared her allies' troops.
And a stranger gazing at well-watered Sulmo's walls, which protect the plain's few acres,

'quae tantum' dicet 'potuistis ferre poetam,
    quantulacumque estis, uos ego magna uoco'.

culte puer puerique parens Amathusia culti, 15
    aurea de campo uellite signa meo.
corniger increpuit thyrso grauiore Lyaeus:
    pulsanda est magnis area maior equis.
imbelles elegi, genialis Musa, ualete,
    post mea mansurum fata superstes opus. 20

will say 'You were able to produce a great poet. However small you are, I call you mighty'.

[15–20] Elegant boy and elegant boy's Amathusian mother, pluck your golden standards from my plain.
Horned Lyaeus has strummed with a weightier thyrsus: I have to pound a larger area with great horses.
Unwarlike elegies, cheerful Muse, goodbye, work destined to live on after my death.

Differences from the texts of Munari, Showerman and Goold, McKeown, Kenney, and Ramirez de Verger

	Davis	Munari (1970)	Showerman and Goold (1977)	McKeown (1987)	Kenney (2) (1994)	Ramirez de Verger (2) (2006)
3.1.45	poteris	poteris	poteris	poteris	poteris	poteras
3.1.47–8	after 52	after 46	after 46	after 52	after 52	after 46
3.1.51	soluta	soluta	soluta	soluta	soluta	recincta
3.1.53	infixa	incisa	infixa	infixa	infixa	incisa
3.1.64	contracto	contracto	contracto	contracto	contracto	contracto
3.2.15	at	at	at	a	a	a
3.2.22	ista	illa	ista	ista	ista	ista
3.2.75	ac	at	ac	ac	ac	ac
3.2.83	speaker	narrator	narrator	speaker	narrator	narrator
3.2.84	speaker	narrator	speaker	speaker	speaker	speaker
3.3.11	aeterni	aeterno	aeterni	aeterno	aeterni	aeterni
3.3.17	at	at	an	at	an	an
3.3.26	nimirum	et nimium	et nimium	nimirum	nimirum	nimirum
3.3.45	iurare	iurasse	iurare	iurasse	iurare	iurasse
3.4.8	exclusis	occlusis	exclusis	exclusis	occlusis	exclusis
3.4.29	fit	sit	fit	fit	fit	fit
3.5	genuine	doubtful	not genuine	not genuine	not genuine	genuine
3.5.6	umida	umida	umida	umida	umida	uuida
3.5.25	reliquit	reliquit	relinquit	reliquit	reliquit	reliquit
3.5.40	mouebit	movebit	movebat	mouebit	mouebit	mouebit
3.6.12	pede	pedi	pedi	pedi	pede	pedi

3.6.25	Inachus	Inachus	Inachus	Inachos	Inachus
3.6.31	Xantho	Xutho	Xutho	Xutho	Xutho
3.6.41	†Euadne†	Evanthe	Euanthe	Euanthe	Euanthe
3.6.46	pomifera	pomifer	pomifera	pomifer	pomifer
3.6.74	cum	dum	cum	cum	cum
3.6.85	spatiosus in	spatiosus in	spatiosior	spatiosus in	spatiosior
3.7.4	sed	sed	sed	sed	et
3.7.9	cupida…lingua	cupide…linguis	cupida…lingua	cupida…lingua	cupidae…linguae
3.7.37	accessit: facti	accessit: facti	accessit: facti	accessit facti:	accessit facti,
3.7.55	sed, puto, non blanda est	sed, puto, non †blanda†	sed, puto, non blanda	†sed puto non blanda†	sed, puto, non blanda est
3.7.62	iuuet	iuvat	iuvat	iuuet	iuuet
3.7.81	soluta	soluta	soluta	soluta	recincta
3.8.5	pulchre	pulchre	pulchrae	pulchre	pulchrae
3.8.28	nox tibi, si belles, possit	hoc tibi, si velles, posset	nox tibi, si belles, possit	nox tibi, si belles, possit	hoc tibi, si uelles, posset
3.8.50	facis	facis	petis	facis	facis
3.8.51–2	accept	accept	accept	accept	accept
3.9.23	et Linon	et Linon	et Linon	et Linon	aelinon
3.9.29	durat opus uatum	durat opus vatum	durant vatis opus	durat opus uatum	durat opus uatum
3.9.37	uiue pius: moriere pius; cole	vive pius: moriere. pius cole	vive pius – moriere; pius cole	uiue pius: moriere; pius cole	uiue pius: moriere pius; cole
3.9.40	toto	toto	toto	tanto	toto
3.9.49	hic	hic	hinc	hic	hic
3.9.51	hic	hic	hinc	hic	hic

Continued

Continued

	Davis	Munari (1970)	Showerman and Goold (1977)	McKeown (1987)	Kenney (2) (1994)	Ramírez de Verger (2) (2006)
3.9.61	uenias	venies	venias	uenies	uenies	uenies
3.10.24	nostra	nostra	nostra	nota	nota	nostra
3.10.39	ipse	ipse	ipsa	ipse	ipse	ipsa
3.10.42	optasset	optavit	optasset	optasset	optasset	optasset
3.10.43	qui	qui	quod	qui	qui	qui
3.10.44	hos	hos	hoc	hos	hos	hos
3.10.46	minora	minore	minore	minora	minora	minora
3.10.47	ueneremque	veneremque	Veneremque	ueneremque	Veneremque	Veneremque
3.11	One poem	Two poems	Two poems	One poem	Two poems	One poem
3.11.35–6	retain	retain	retain	retain	exclude	exclude
3.11.52	et, quam, si…uelim	ut, quam, si…uelim	ut, quam, si…velim	ut, quam, si…uelim	et quam, si…uelim	quam quamuis…tamen
3.12.15	Thebae	Thebe	Thebae	Thebae	Thebae	Thebae
3.13.8	concedes numinis esse locum	concedes numinis esse locum	concedas numen inesse loco	concedes numinis esse locum	concedes numinis esse locum	concedes numen inesse loco
3.13.11	huc	huc	hinc	huc	huc	huc
3.13.29	ore	ore	ora	ore	ore	ore
3.13.36	sint…sint	sit…sit	sint…sint	sint…sint	sint…sint	sint…sint
3.15.13	dicet	dicet	dicat	dicet	dicet	dicet

Commentary

3.1: ELEGY OR TRAGEDY?

Am. 3.1 is a drama with three speaking characters. It poses a key question: what should the poet write? All three books of *Amores* begin with meditations on the decision to write love elegy. Both 1.1 and 2.1 represent the poet as already engaged in composing an epic (1.1.1–2, 2.1.11–22) and as distracted by Love (1.1) or love (2.1). 3.1 similarly offers the poet a choice between frivolous and serious verse, this time between elegy and tragedy. 3.1 resembles 1.1 in employing personification to dramatize the poet's situation: Love determines the poet's subject matter in 1.1 by forcing him to write elegiac couplets, while in 3.1 Tragedy and Elegy compete for his allegiance. *Pont.* 3.3 looks back to all of these programmatic poems by staging an interview with Love in which the poet blames the god for *Amores* (*Pont.* 3.3.29): *tu mihi dictasti iuuenalia carmina primus* ('You were the first to dictate to me my youthful verse').

Claiming that the poet's work has been shaped by an encounter with one or more divinities has a long history. At the beginning of *Theogony* (22–34) Hesiod asserts that the Muses inspired his verse when he pastured sheep on Mt Helicon, while in *Aetia* Callimachus combines a dream of meeting Hesiod on Helicon (fr. 2.1–2 Harder) with the claim that Lycian Apollo advised him to employ a 'slender' style (fr. 1.21–4 Harder). Virgil adopts this same trope when reporting that Cynthian Apollo appeared and instructed him to 'utter fine-spun song' (*Ecl.* 6.5: *deductum dicere carmen*). Closest to Ovid, however, in both time and content, is Propertius. In elegy 3.3 Propertius places himself squarely in this tradition by invoking both Hesiod (he dreams of resting on Mt Helicon [3.3.1]) and Callimachus (it is Apollo who gives advice [3.3.14], presumably Lycian Apollo [cf. 3.1.38: *Lycio...deo*]).

The similarities between *Am.* 3.1 and Prop. 3.3 make it clear that Ovid engages most closely with Propertius. For example, the poems share similar settings, places which feature a sacred spring (Prop. 3.3.2, 5–6, 15, 51–2; cf. *Am.* 3.1.3) and a cave with overhanging pumice (*pendebantque cauis tympana pumicibus* Prop. 3.3.28; cf. *speluncaque pumice pendens Am.* 3.1.3). Each poem also has a cast of three characters, the poet, Apollo, and Calliope in Propertius; the poet, Tragedy, and Elegy in Ovid. And both poems reflect on the choice to write love elegy. Nevertheless, they differ in significant ways. Propertius presents himself as dreaming (*uisus eram* 3.3.1), as already writing epic (3–12), and as being rebuked in silence by two divinities in turn. Ovid, by contrast, presents a drama. He is not sleeping, but actively contemplating his next literary move. Elegy and Tragedy are present simultaneously and overtly critical, Tragedy of the poet and Elegy of Tragedy. Moreover, the poet responds by addressing them both. And of course the results differ. Propertius abandons epic for erotic elegy (3.3.51–2). Elegy is successful in persuading the poet, perhaps because her speech is longer (26 lines as opposed to Tragedy's 16) or perhaps because she speaks second. Nevertheless, Ovid's decision for love poetry is temporary: he will write tragedy.

Ovid differs not only from Propertius but from all his poetic predecessors in having the poet confront not a god or gods offering straightforward advice, but quarrelling personifications, each seeking a devotee, with, as Wyke (2002: 120; 2006: 174) points out, physical features functioning 'as a catalogue of stylistic practices'. While we might see this situation as prefiguring that which confronts the poet at the beginning of *Fasti* 5 and 6,[1] it is perhaps more important to observe that it resembles the dilemma facing Xenophon's Heracles when he has to choose between Virtue and Vice (*Mem.* 2.1.21.4–22.9):[2]

> For Prodicus says that when Heracles was hastening from boyhood to youth, a time when young men, who are already becoming independent, make clear whether they will choose the path of virtue (*aretē*) in life or that of vice (*kakia*), he came to a quiet spot and sat down wondering which path he should take; and that two tall women seemed to approach him, one fair to see and frank in nature, her body adorned with purity, her eyes with modesty, her appearance with restraint, her clothes with white; the other nourished to plumpness and softness, wearing cosmetics so that she looked whiter and redder in colour than she really was, so that she seemed more upright in her appearance than was natural, her eyes wide open and her clothing such that her beauty shone through.

Heracles, of course, chooses Virtue. Our poet picks both.[3] Also important, as Acosta-Hughes (2002: 192) notes, is Callimachus' *Iambus* 4, a poem which reports a squabble between a lowly olive and a noble laurel on Mt Tmolus.

---

[1] At the beginning of *Fasti* 5 the Muses dispute the origins of 'May', while in Book 6 goddesses argue over 'June'. For discussion see Newlands (1995: Chapter 2).

[2] Brandt (ad loc.) seems to have been the first to make this connection.

Cicero discusses this passage at *Off.* 1.118.2. His Hercules, however, faces a choice between two paths; he does not confront personifications of *Voluptas* and *Virtus*.

Zgoll's argument that the judgement of Paris is a more important model than Prodicus' 'Hercules at the Crossroads' is not persuasive because (a) the judgement of Paris involves three goddesses not two and (b) Zgoll's primary intertext (*Her.* 16) is almost certainly later than *Am.* 3.1.

[3] Silius Italicus' depiction of Scipio's choice between Pleasure (*Voluptas*) and Virtue (*Virtus*) (15.18–137) clearly engages with both Xenophon's Heracles and *Amores* 3.1, with Pleasure being modelled on Ovid's Elegy and Virtue on Tragedy. Like Elegy, Pleasure has styled and scented hair (15.23, 26; cf. 3.1.7: *odoratos... nexa capillos*) and a lover's gaze (*lasciuaque... lumina* 26–7; cf. 3.1.9: *uultus amantis*), while Virtue's indifference to coiffure and masculine gait make her resemble Tragedy (Sil. 15.28–9: *frons hirta nec umquam | composita mutata coma*, cf. 3.1.12: *fronte comae torua*; Sil. 15.30: *incessuque uiro propior*; cf. 3.1.11: *ingenti... passu*).

Fragmentary though the poem is, it seems to treat these trees as emblems of different kinds of verse.[4]

Because of its position in the collection, 3.1 arouses contradictory expectations. On the one hand, since the poem introduces the third volume of a collection labelled *Amores*, the reader expects the poet to choose erotic verse. On the other, a reader who has just finished Book 2 might suppose that the poet will choose tragedy because in 2.18, Book 2's penultimate poem, the poet claims that he is now a tragedian (2.18.13–14): *sceptra tamen sumpsi, curaque tragoedia nostra | creuit, et huic operi quamlibet aptus eram* ('Nevertheless, I took up the sceptre, and as a result of my devoted care a tragedy has grown, and I was quite suited to this task'). Although the poet chooses elegy in this opening poem, the collection's very last poem suggests that his commitment to erotic poetry is only temporary, because he finally accepts Tragedy's insistence that now is the time for 'a weightier thyrsus' (*thyrso grauiore* 3.15.17; cf. *thyrso...grauiore* 3.1.23).[5]

This wavering between Elegy and Tragedy prompts questions not only about Ovid's aesthetic choices but about chronology. While 3.1's dramatic situation implies that the poet has yet to write a tragedy, it does not follow that the poem was written before he composed *Medea*. In fact, it suggests the opposite: this poem reflects on the fact that Ovid's achievements include such disparate elements as books of erotic verse and a highly-regarded tragedy.[6] (For the date of the three-book collection see Introduction §2.)

Secondary literature: Wimmel (1960: 295–7); Schrijvers (1976); Morgan (1977: 17–21); Cahoon (1985); Kershaw (1986); Buchan (1995); Boyd (1997: 195–202); Keith (1994); D'Anna (1999); Deremetz (1999); Mazzoli (1999); Bretzigheimer (2001: 61–76); Wyke (2002: Chapter 4) = Wyke (2006); Hutchinson (2008); Karakasis (2010); Zgoll (2010); Perkins (2011); Davies (2013); Gardner (2013: Chapter 5); Westerhold (2016); Oliensis (2019: 151–2, 162–4, 169–70, 186–8); Fulkerson (2022).

1–2. Stat uetus et multos incaedua silua per annos;
credibile est illi numen inesse loco.
Primeval woods are often associated with the presence of divinities and uncanny forces. For other Ovidian examples see 3.13.7–8: *stat uetus et densa praenubilus arbore lucus; | aspice, concedes numinis esse locum*, *Met.* 2.418 (where Jupiter rapes

---

[4] It is possible that Ennius' dispute between Death and Life is also relevant (Quint. 9.2.36.4).
[5] For discussion of *Am.* 3.1 and 3.15 as 'frame poems' see Hutchinson (2008: 177–99).
Wimmel (1960: 295–6) speaks of *Am.* 3.1 as a 'fundamental transformation of the type' of *recusatio* (rejection of writing on serious/patriotic subjects) that we find in Horace and Propertius and lists themes that this poem has in common with rejections in the other poets. The idea that this poem is a *recusatio* is still current (e.g. Gardner [2013]: Chapter 5; Fulkerson [2022: 51]: 'not a typical *recusatio*'). Given that the poet does not reject the possibility of writing on serious subjects, the term is not applicable here. For a sceptical treatment of *recusatio* in *Amores* generally see D'Anna (1999).
[6] For the high regard in which *Medea* was held see Quintilian's comment (10.1.98.2): 'Ovid's *Medea* seems to me to show how much that man could have achieved if he had preferred to control his talent rather than indulge it'.

Callisto: *nemus quod nulla ceciderat aetas*), 3.28 (home of the Theban serpent: *silua uetus stabat nulla uiolata securi*), 3.155–62 (Gargaphie, Diana's sacred valley), 8.329 (hiding-place of the Calydonian boar: *silua frequens trabibus, quam nulla ceciderat aetas*), 8.741–50 (the tree/forest violated by Erysichthon); *Fast.* 2.435–6 (*monte sub Esquilio multis incaeduus annis | Iunonis magnae nomine lucus erat*), 3.261–76 (Diana's sanctuary at Aricia), 3.295–6, 4.649–50: *silua uetus nullaque diu uiolata securi | stabat, Maenalio sacra relicta deo*, 6.9–10 with line 13 (*ecce deas uidi*). See also Catul. 63.2–3 and Evander's words at *A.* 8.351–2: *hoc nemus, hunc inquit frondoso uertice collem | (quis deus incertum est) habitat deus*, together with Seneca's exegesis (*Ep.* 41.3): 'the tallness of the forest, the mystery of the place and the wonder of such thick, continuous shade will convince you of the divine presence'. Pliny (*Nat.* 12.3) observes that trees were the earliest sites of worship. Perhaps the best-known sacred forest in Latin literature is the one destroyed by Lucan's Caesar (3.399–405). See also Stat. *Theb.* 6.84–113, where the gods' forest home is cut down for Opheltes' funeral. For the importance of forests in Roman religion see Hunt (2016); for Virgil on the sacredness of forests see Armstrong (2019: 53–92).

1. Stat: As opposed to *est*, *stat* emphasizes endurance through time (*OLD sto* 15, 17).

incaedua: An Ovidian coinage, the adjective is used only at *Fast.* 1.243, 2.435, and Stat. *Theb.* 6.90.

silua: While the primary meaning of *silua* here is obviously 'forest', the word's association with the idea of 'subject matter' can hardly be ignored in a metaliterary poem. Hinds explains (1998: 12): '*Silua* is used metaphorically in various contexts in Latin to represent ὕλη [hulē], in the sense "matter", "mass of material", "raw material"'. (For detailed discussion of *silua* as a metapoetic term see Wray [2007] on the title of Statius' *Siluae*.) Westerhold (2016) detects a possible reference to the title of Ennius' *Annales* and allusion via sound and substance to Enn. *Ann.* 6.175 Goldberg and Manuwald (1): *incedunt arbusta per alta, securibus caedunt* and *A.* 6.179: *itur in antiquam siluam, stabula alta ferarum*.

2. credibile est illi numen inesse loco: For the association between forests and *numina* see also 3.13.7–8 (quoted above) and *Fast.* 3.295–6: *lucus Auentino suberat niger ilicis umbra, | quo posses uiso dicere numen inest*. Here an assertion of faith is cast in sceptical terms: *credibile est*. (Cf. the mix of scepticism and condescension the lover uses when addressing enslaved Nape [1.11.11]: *credibile est et te sensisse Cupidinis arcus*.) In 3.13 and *Fasti* the speaker is less doubtful: *concedes; posses…dicere*. Note too that the lover, not entirely seriously, makes the same claim for poets at 3.9.17–18: *at sacri uates et diuum cura uocamur; | sunt etiam qui nos numen habere putent* and *Ars* 3.547–8: *uatibus Aoniis faciles estote, puellae: | numen inest illis*. Cf. Tib. 1.5.57: *sunt numina amanti*.

illi...inesse loco: As is usual in Ovid, *insum* here takes the dative (rather than *in* plus the ablative).

3–4. fons sacer in medio speluncaque pumice pendens
et latere ex omni dulce queruntur aues.

Description of the drama's setting continues with emphasis not only on its sanctity but also its beauty.

3. fons sacer: That springs are sacred is an ancient commentator's commonplace. See e.g. Servius' observation on *Ecl.* 1.52: *FONTES SACROS quia omnibus aquis nymphae sunt praesidentes* and Porphyrio's explanation of Hor. *Carm.* 1.1.22: *id est: apud fontem; omnes autem fontes sacri habentur.* Ovid follows suit. See e.g. *Her.* 15.158 (with Thorsen [2014: 166]): *fons sacer: hunc multi numen habere putant*, *Ars* 3.688, *Met.* 2.464, 5.573, *Fast.* 3.303, 4.759–60, 5.674. Particularly important for this passage is the beginning of Prop. 3.1, where the poet combines the ideas of grove, spring, and poetic choice (1–4):

> Callimachi Manes et Coi sacra Philitae,
>   in uestrum, quaeso, me sinite ire nemus
> primus ego ingredior puro de fonte sacerdos
>   Itala per Graios orgia ferre choros

important because in the first three poems of Book 3 Propertius sets out a rationale for choosing to write erotic elegy rather than poetry on so-called serious themes. (For discussion of Prop. 3.1–3 see e.g. Wallis [2018: Chapter 1]).

speluncaque pumice pendens: Here too Ovid alludes to the set of metaliterary poems which open Propertius' third book (3.3.27–8): *spelunca...| pendebantque cauis tympana pumicibus*. See also Prop. 3.1.5: *quo pariter carmen tenuastis in antro*; and 3.3.13–14: *Phoebus | sic ait aurata nixus ad antra lyra*. For the association between poetry and caves more generally see e.g. Catul. 61.28, *Ecl.* 5.6, 19 (where a cave is chosen as a site for song), Hor. *Carm.* 2.1.39, 3.4.40, 3.25.4, Stat. *Silu.* 4.5.59–60.

For alliteration of *p* in similar contexts see Cic. *Tusc.* 1.37.5, quoting an unidentified tragedy (Ribbeck [1897] p. 283; Warmington [1936] p. 602): *per speluncas saxis structas asperis pendentibus*; *G.* 4.374: *postquam est in thalami pendentia pumice tecta*. For this use of *pendeo* see *OLD* 6b.

4. queruntur aues: For Latin poets the plaintive sounds of birds are a key feature of an ideal rural landscape. See e.g. Horace's list of rural pleasures (*Epod.* 2.26): *queruntur in siluis aues*; and Hippolytus' description of the prelapsarian world (Sen. *Phaed.* 508): *hinc aues querulae fremunt*. For Ovid's Sappho, by contrast, their absence underlines her distress (*Her.* 15.152): *et nullae dulce queruntur aues*.

That birds moan is perhaps a reminder that complaint is intrinsic to the elegiac stance (e.g. Tib. 1.2.9; Prop. 1.7.8: *cogor et aetatis tempora dura queri*, 1.18.1, 2.4.1; cf. Hor. *Carm.* 2.13.24–5, *Rem.* 644–5).

dulce: Like other poets, Ovid prefers the adverbial accusative over the prose form *dulciter*.

5–6. hic ego dum spatior tectus nemoralibus umbris,
   quod mea quaerebam Musa moueret opus.
Into this ideal location the poet enters casually pondering his next poetic move.

5. spatior: The verb suggests relaxed walking, typically (in erotic poetry at least) taking a stroll in a colonnade. Cf. Prop. 4.8.75 (Cynthia's ghost): *tu neque Pompeia spatiabere cultus in umbra, Am.* 2.2.3–4: *hesterna uidi spatiantem luce puellam,* | *illa, quae Danai porticus agmen habet, Her.* 21.97, *Ars* 1.67.

nemoralibus umbris: For shade as protective of poetry see, for example, Meliboeus' description of Tityrus (*Ecl.* 1.4–5: *tu, Tityre, lentus in umbra* | *formosam resonare doces Amaryllida siluas*) and Propertius' account of his meeting with Apollo (3.3.1: *molli recubans Heliconis in umbra*). Ovid also associates shade with poetry, especially love poetry e.g. 2.18.3: *nos, Macer, ignaua Veneris cessamus in umbra; Ars* 3.542: *contempto colitur lectus et umbra foro*; while in *Metamorphoses* woodland shade provides a congenial place for Minerva to listen to song (5.336): *Pallas ait nemorisque leui consedit in umbra*.

6. quod mea quaerebam Musa moueret opus: Bretzigheimer (2001: 62) notes that, as in 1.1, this inner dilemma is projected outwards by means of personification. Alliteration of *m* perhaps places emphasis on the poet's search for his own source of inspiration: *mea...Musa*.

For the suggestion that the juxtaposition of *Musa* and *quaerebam* hints at the Platonic (*Crat.* 406a4) derivation of *Musa* (Greek: *Mousa*) from μῶσθαι (*mōsthai*, 'seek after') see McKeown (57–8); also Maltby (1991: 399).

moueret: Imperfect subjunctive used in an indirect question after a main verb in a historic tense (Woodcock [§180]).

opus: For opus as 'genre' see e.g. Prop. 3.3.15–16: *quis te* | *carminis heroi tangere iussit opus?*; *Am.* 1.1.24: *'quodque canas, uates, accipe' dixit 'opus!'*; 2.18.14: *huic operi* (i.e. tragedy) *quamlibet aptus eram*; 3.9.5: *ille tui uates operis* (i.e. elegy), *tua fama, Tibullus; Ars* 3.346: *ignotum hoc aliis ille nouauit opus* (i.e. *Heroides*).

7–10. uenit odoratos Elegeia nexa capillos
   et, puto, pes illi longior alter erat.
forma decens, uestis tenuissima, uultus amantis,
   et pedibus uitium causa decoris erat.

As Wyke (2002: 140; 2006: 192) points out, the description of Elegy recalls not only Prodicus' picture of Vice (see introduction above) but representations of the elegiac mistress, particularly of Tibullus' Nemesis (2.3.53-4): *illa gerat uestes tenues, quas femina Coa | texuit*; and Propertius' Cynthia (1.2.1-3): *quid iuuat ornato procedere, uita, capillo | et tenuis Coa ueste mouere sinus, | aut quid Orontea crines perfundere murra*. It also alludes to Callimachus' address to the Graces (*Aet*. fr. 7.11-14 Harder):

> κάλλη τε καὶ αἰόλα βεύδε' ἔχουσαι
> ...ἀπ' ὀστλίγγων δ' αἰὲν ἄλειφα ῥέει,
> ἔλλατε νῦν, ἐλέγοισι δ' ἐνιψήσασθε λιπώσας
> χεῖρας ἐμοῖς, ἵνα μοι πουλὺ μένωσιν ἔτος.

With lovely and shining dresses...and always oil flows from your tresses, be kind now, and wipe your radiant hands upon my elegies, so that they may endure for many a year.

For discussion of Ovid's use of double allusion (to Callimachus and to this poem) in the treatment of Flora in *Fasti* 4 and 5 see McKeown (44-5).

7. The careful placing of words in the line, often involving the combination of two adjectives, two nouns, and a verb is a frequent feature in all of Ovid's works. That Ovid prizes such effects is clear from the remarkable runs of patterned lines at *Her*. 2.113-20 and *Her*. 16.107-14 (with Kenney [1996: ad loc.]). Similar is 2.6.4-6. For other examples of this verbal pattern (VaBbA), in which a line begins with a verb followed by a chiastic arrangement of adjectives and nouns, see *Am*. 1.5.2, 1.8.52, 1.13.18, 1.15.34, 2.1.24, 2.5.52, 3.1.18, 40, 3.6.86, 3.9.6, 28, 3.10.26, 32, 3.13.26, 3.15.18. For Ovid's use of patterned lines see Introduction §10.

odoratos...capillos: For the association between perfumed hair and luxury see *Med*. 18-19 (to the contemporary generation of women): *uultis inaurata corpora ueste tegi, | uultis odoratos positu uariare capillos*; and *Fast*. 2.309-10 (Omphale): *ibat odoratis umeros perfusa capillis | Maeonis, aurato conspicienda sinu*. For the erotic associations of perfumed hair outside elegy see Virgil's description of Venus at *A*. 1.403-4: *ambrosiaeque comae diuinum uertice odorem | spirauere*; and Silius' depiction of Pleasure at 15.23-4: *altera Achaemenium spirabat uertice odorem | ambrosias diffusa comas*.

Elegeia: Recent editors print *Elegia*, the usual Roman transliteration of the Greek ἐλεγεία (*elegeia*). I use the spelling found in the principal manuscripts, P, S, and Y. The Greek diphthong ει (*ei*) is to be scanned as one long syllable.

Ovid treats *a* in this word as long. See Am. 3.9.3: *flebilis indignos, Elegeia, solue capillos*, Rem. 379: *blanda pharetratos Elegeia cantet Amores*, Her. 15.7 (with Knox [1995: ad loc.]): *flendus amor meus est: elegeia flebile carmen*.

8. puto: While the *o* in *puto* is usually scanned as long, Ovid treats it as short in both his elegies and in *Metamorphoses*. For a list of such verbs (usually disyllabic) see Platnauer (1951: 51–2). For *putŏ* in *Am.* 3 see 7.2, 7.55, and 11.34. Note also *tollŏ* (3.2.26), *oderŏ* (3.11.35), and *amŏ* (3.14.39).

pes illi longior alter erat: Reference to elegy's employment of lines of differing length is common in Ovid's elegiac works e.g. 1.1.4, 1.1.30; *Rem.* 390; *Fast.* 2.567–8; *Tr.* 3.1.11–12, 3.1.56, 3.7.9–10; *Pont.* 3.3.29–30, 4.3.85–8, 4.5.1–4. For personification combined with punning on 'foot' see *Tr.* 1.1.15–16: *uade, liber, uerbisque meis loca grata saluta:* | *contingam certe quo licet illa pede*; *Pont.* 4.5.3 (to *leues elegi*): *longa uia est nec uos pedibus proceditis aequis*. Hinds (1998: 56–7) notes that punning on the two senses of *pes* goes back to the first line of Ennius' *Annales*.

illi: Possessive dative.

9. uestis tenuissima: Elegy's diaphanous clothing links her both to Xenophon's Vice (*Mem.* 2.1.22; quoted above) and to representations of the elegiac mistress e.g. Tib. 1.10.61: *sit satis e membris tenuem rescindere uestem*, 2.3.53–4 (quoted above on 7–10), 2.4.29–30, Prop. 1.2.2 (quoted above on 7–10); *Am.* 3.2.36. The elder Seneca associates filmy female garments with adultery (*Con.* 2.7).

As the Latin equivalent of Callimachus' *leptaleēn* (*Aet.* fr. 1.24: Μοῦσαν… λεπταλέην, with Harder's note), *tenuis* is also a key metaliterary term. Ovid deploys it, for example, when explaining to Augustus why he shunned grander themes (*Tr.* 2.327): *tenuis mihi campus aratur*. Cf. *Ecl.* 6.8: *agrestem tenui meditabor harundine Musam*, Hor. *Ep.* 2.1.225: *tenui deducta poemata filo*.

10. pedibus uitium causa decoris erat: Ovid is fond of the paradox that a blemish can be a source of beauty: *Ars* 3.295 (lisps can be attractive), *Fast.* 3.495 (with Heyworth [2019: ad loc.]: *uitio tibi gratior ipso est*). See also Cic. *N. D.* 1.79: *etiam uitia saepe iucunda sunt*. The elder Seneca quotes Ovid as saying that a mole or birthmark made a face more beautiful (*Con. ex.* 2.2.1.36): *aiebat interim decentiorem faciem esse, in qua aliquis naeuus esset*.

11–14. uenit et ingenti uiolenta Tragoedia passu:
   fronte comae torua, palla iacebat humi.
laeua manus sceptrum late regale mouebat,
   Lydius alta pedum uincla cothurnus erat.
The four-line description of Elegy is now balanced by four lines describing Tragedy. Key details here recall the poet's claim that he is now a tragic poet (2.18.13–16):

> sceptra tamen sumpsi, curaque tragoedia nostra
>   creuit, et huic operi quamlibet aptus eram.
> risit Amor pallamque meam pictosque cothurnos
>   sceptraque priuata tam cito sumpta manu

and foreshadow his description of his own *Medea* (*Tr.* 2.553–4):

> et dedimus tragicis sceptrum regale tyrannis,
>   quaeque grauis debet uerba cothurnus habet.

11. This verbal pattern (VabBA), the most frequent in *Amores*, varies the golden line (see below on 3.3.21), placing the verb at the beginning and not in the centre. See also 1.1.8, 29; 1.2.20, 1.6.14, 1.7.8, 1.8.52, 60, 98, 1.14.26, 30, 42; 2.1.22, 2.5.26, 30, 2.16.6; 3.2.32, 38, 78; 3.5.9; 3.9.2; 3.10.2, 36; 3.12.32, 42, 3.13.12; 3.15.10. (For discussion see Introduction §10.)

uiolenta Tragoedia: Frequently used of destructive natural forces (*OLD* 2) or wild animals (*OLD* 1), *uiolentus* is typically used of characters in serious genres like epic (e.g. *A*. 10.151: *uiolentaque pectora Turni*; Stat. *Theb.* 2.466: *uiolente* [addressed to Eteocles]) and tragedy (e.g. Sen. *Her. F.* 43 [of Hercules], *Ag.* 825 [of Hercules again], *Oed.* 960 [of Oedipus about to blind himself], *Thy.* 33 [of the whole house of Atreus]). And note Ovid's description of his own attempt at a serious poem: 1.1.1–2: *uiolentaque bella parabam | edere*. Here it is applied to Tragedy herself, violence being one of the genre's defining features (Arist. *Poet.* 1453b10–14).

ingenti...passu: Tragedy's giant stride suggests that she does not follow the standards of female decorum laid down by the Teacher at *Ars* 3.298–9: *discite femineo corpora ferre gradu: | est et in incessu pars non temnenda decoris*. Cf. his description of a peasant's wife (*Ars* 3.303–4): *illa uelut coniunx Vmbri rubicunda mariti | ambulat, ingentes uarica fertque gradus*. In *Metamorphoses* Ovid describes the Cyclops in the same way (13.776): *gradiens ingenti litora passu*. Cf. Silius' description of Virtue's gait (15.30): *incessuque uiro propior*.

12. fronte...torua: Similarly, Tragedy's pitiless brow implies that she does not conform to the norms of feminine beauty: Virgil uses the phrase of the Cyclops (*A*. 3.635–6), while Seneca uses it of Hector (*Tro.* 467) and of Jupiter disguised as a bull (*Phaed.* 303). Like Tragedy, Silius' Virtue shows no concern for her appearance (15.28–9).

palla: Worn by women as an outdoor garment (*OLD* 1), the *palla* is also associated with tragic performances e.g. Hor. *Ars* 278–9: *post hunc personae pallaeque repertor honestae | Aeschylus*; 2.18.15 (quoted above on 11–14). For Silius' Virtue the *palla* is linked to modesty (15.30–1).

iacebat: The verb is to be construed with both *comae* and *palla*. For similar ellipse of a verb form see e.g. 1.2.48: where *fuisti* is supplied from *fuit*, 2.13.16: *dabit* from *dabis*, and 3.2.5: *specto* from *spectas*.

13. sceptrum...regale: For the *sceptrum* as emblematic of tragedy see 2.18.13, 16, line 63 below, and *Tr.* 2.553. Tragedy's sceptre reminds us of the genre's concentration on the doings of royalty and its focus on power. *sceptrum* occurs 49 times in Seneca's tragedies.

late...mouebat: As *TLL* 1023.68 suggests, *late* here implies arrogance. Cf. *Her.* 9.127 (Iole as imagined by Deianira): *ingreditur late lato spectabilis auro*; Sen.

Ep. 76.31 (of tragic actors): *non magis quam ex illis quibus sceptrum et chlamydem in scaena fabulae adsignant: cum praesente populo lati incesserunt et cothurnati.*

14: Lydius…cothurnus: For the thick-soled boot or buskin as an emblem of tragedy see e.g. Ar. *Frogs* 47, 557; *Ecl.* 8.10; Hor. *S.* 1.5.64, *Ars* 280; Prop. 2.34.41; *Am.* 1.15.15: *nulla Sophocleo ueniet iactura cothurno*. For the association of the *cothurnus* (Greek: *kothornos*) with Lydia see Hdt. 1.155.17–21. The epithet is also appropriate here because Bacchus, tragedy's god, is associated with Lydia (e.g. Eur. *Bacch.* 13, 464). Micyllus (p. 332), citing *Ars* 1.111–12, suggests that since *Lydius* can mean 'Etruscan' (*Lydius* OLD 2), Ovid may have in mind the Etruscan origins of some Roman theatrical practices. (For this see Boyle [2006: 7–10].)

alta pedum uincla: For *uincla* of footwear see e.g. *A.* 8.458: *et Tyrrhena pedum circumdat uincula plantis*, Tib. 1.5.66, *Fast.* 1.410, 2.324, 5.32. For the *cothurnus* as a high-fitting boot see *A.* 1.337: *purpureoque alte suras uincire cothurno*; and line 63 below. In this context *alta* might also point to Tragedy's literary aspirations. Given Ovid's penchant for punning on the biological and metrical senses of 'foot' (see above on line 8), there are metaliterary possibilities here. Cf. [Tib.] 3.7.36: *undique quique canent uincto pede quique soluto*.

15–16. et prior 'ecquis erit' dixit 'tibi finis amandi,
 o argumenti lente poeta tui?
After the grand four-line description of Tragedy's attributes, her abrupt intervention comes as a surprise. Her language is well calculated to convey her annoyance at the poet's behaviour.

15. Use of informal language (*ecquis* is particularly common in comedy, 94 times in Plautus) suggests exasperation. See e.g. Pan's remark to Gallus dying of love (*Ecl.* 10.28): *ecquis erit modus?* and Turnus' impatient question (*A.* 9.51, with Hardie [1994: ad loc.]: 'vigorously colloquial'): *ecquis erit mecum, iuuenes, qui primus in hostem—?* Bretzigheimer (2001: 72) notes that the line's disjointedness helps convey Tragedy's vehemence.

erit…finis: For the complaint that there is no end to love's pain see *Ecl.* 10.28 (quoted above) and Prop. 1.16.21: *nullane finis erit nostro concessa dolori?*

16. o argumenti lente poeta tui: For *lentus* as 'persistent' see OLD 6. *TLL* 1165.37–8 notes that the genitive after *lentus* resembles that after *tenax* (e.g. Hor. *Carm.* 3.3.1: *tenacem propositi uirum*). McKeown (108) points out that 'the slowness of the rhythm, accentuated by the hiatus, well conveys Tragedy's disgust at Ovid's persistence with love-elegy'. Repeated *t* sounds may be intended to reinforce that effect.

17–18. nequitiam uinosa tuam conuiuia narrant,
 narrant in multas compita secta uias.

This couplet consists of two patterned lines (AbaBV and VaBbA), each with interwoven nouns and adjectives, but with the second line mirroring the first, with the hexameter ending with a verb and the pentameter beginning with that same verb (anadiplosis). For other examples of this form of repetition see Wills (1996: 394–7).

The repetition of *narrant* underlines the universality of such gossip. Tragedy's claim that the poet's *nequitia* has made him a subject of conversation varies an accusation made by the Propertian lover against Cynthia (2.5.1–2): *hoc uerum est, tota te ferri, Cynthia, Roma, | et non ignota uiuere nequitia?* For crossroads as sites of gossip see Prop. 2.20.21–2: *septima iam plenae deducitur orbita lunae, | cum de me et de te compita nulla tacent.*

17. nequitiam: Moral worthlessness is an important characteristic of both lover and beloved in Ovid's elegiac predecessors (e.g. Gallus [145.1 Hollis]): *tristia nequit[ia fact]ạ, Lycori, tua*; Prop. [1.6.25–6]: *me sine, quem semper uoluit fortuna iacere, | huic animam extremam reddere nequitiae*). For the *Amores*-poet it is definitive (2.1.1–2): *hoc quoque composui Paelignis natus aquosis, | ille ego nequitiae Naso poeta meae.* Cf. *Tr.* 2.279–80, where the poet defends his *Ars* by arguing that elegy is not the only genre that promotes immorality: *ludi quoque semina praebent | nequitiae.* See also 2.4.1–2, where the poet refuses to defend his *mendosos… mores* and to take up arms *pro uitiis… meis.* For discussion of elegiac *nequitia* see e.g. Sharrock (2013).

uinosa…conuiuia: *uinosus* seems to be an informal word; while common in prose, it is rare in verse (twice in Horace's *Epistles*, once each in *Ars* and *Fasti*; high poetry prefers *ebrius* or a periphrasis [e.g. *uino sepultus/solutus, A.* 2.265, 9.189; cf. 1.4.53: *compositus somno uinoque, Fast.* 2.333: *somno uinoque solutos*]). *TLL* 885.54–80 records *conuiuium* here as the earliest metonymic use ('partygoer', not 'party').

18. in multas compita secta uias: At *Fast.* 1.142 (*in ternas compita secta uias*), the Teacher associates crossroads with the number three because of their connection with Hecate-Trivia. Here Tragedy follows the usual definition (cf. Porph. on Hor. *S.* 2.3.25–6: 'places where many roads meet'), because it makes her point more effectively.

19–20. saepe aliquis digito uatem designat euntem
    atque ait: 'hic, hic est, quem ferus urit Amor'.
Tragedy attempts to embarrass the poet by drawing attention to his status as a notorious lover. Vestal Ilia uses similar language when propositioned by the river Anio (*Am.* 3.6.77–8): *quid moror et digitis designor adultera uulgi?| desint famosus quae notet ora pudor!*

19. saepe aliquis digito uatem designat euntem: Tragedy implicitly rebukes the *Amores*-poet by alluding to Horace's claim to serious achievement in a major

84   *Commentary*

genre (*Carm.* 4.3.22–3): *monstror digito praetereuntium | Romanae fidicen lyrae*. (For the dating implications of allusion to *Odes* 4 see Introduction §2.) Cf. Ilia's expression of shame at 3.6.77: *digitis designor adultera uulgi*.

uatem: Originally used of prophets speaking in verse, *uates* is used sparingly and solemnly by earlier Augustan poets to designate their sacred role. See e.g. *A.* 7.41 (with Horsfall [2000: ad loc.]): *tu uatem, tu, diua, mone*, Hor. *Carm.* 1.1.35 (with Nisbet and Hubbard [1970: ad loc.]): *quodsi me lyricis uatibus inseres, Ars* 400–1, Tib. 2.5.114–15, Prop. 2.10.19–20, 4.6.1; cf. Ov. *Ars* 3.407–8: *sanctaque maiestas et erat uenerabile nomen | uatibus*. In *Amores* it is Ovid's standard term for a poet: 1.1.6, 24; 1.8.57, 59; 2.1.34; 2.4.21; 2.18.18, 35, 3.1.67, 3.6.17, 3.9.5, 17, 26, 29, 41; 3.12.41, 3.15.1.

20. For repeated *hic* combined with *est* used to single out a person of particular note see *A.* 6.791 (of Augustus Caesar): *hic uir, hic est*. Wills observes (1996: 76): 'Both poets use the expected phrase of public recognition'. Tragedy's description of *Amor* as *ferus* recalls the poet's own description of the god at 1.2.8: *et possessa ferus pectora uersat Amor*. See also *Ars* 1.17–18: *Aeacidae Chiron, ego sum praeceptor Amoris: | saeuus uterque puer*.

21–2. fabula (nec sentis) tota iactaris in Vrbe,
    dum tua praeterito facta pudore refers.
Tragedy continues speaking in a conversational manner (note the use of parenthesis) in her attempt to embarrass the poet-lover into changing his ways. This claim that his writing and behaviour had become a source of scandal is one that the exiled poet would explicitly deny (*Tr.* 2.349–50): *sic ego delicias et mollia carmina feci, | strinxerit ut nomen fabula nulla meum*; (*Tr.* 4.10: 67–8): *cum tamen hic essem minimoque accenderer igni, | nomine sub nostro fabula nulla fuit*.

21. fabula: For *fabula* as 'subject of gossip' see *OLD* 1d and *TLL* 26.8–20. For *fabula* used of a lover's notoriety see e.g. Hor. *Epod.* 11.8 (*fabula quanta fui*; with Watson [2003: ad loc.]), Tib. 1.4.83, 2.3.31–2, Prop. 2.24.1–2. Cf. Propertius' warning that mistreating Cynthia leads to instant scandal (1.5.26): *quam cito de tanto nomine rumor eris*.

22. praeterito...pudore: Tragedy complains not only that the poet has let himself be burned by sexual passion, but that he has ignored the claims of decency by writing about it. Propertius' critic seems to make a similar point at 2.24a.1–4 (the text, however, is disputed; see Heyworth [2007a: 211–12]).
    This verbal pattern (abABV) varies the golden line (see below on 3.3.21), placing the verb at the end and not in the centre. See also: 1.2.28, 30, 46, 2.9.28, 2.19.22, 3.6.4, 3.7.72, 3.10.34, 3.12.30, *Her.* 2.132, 4.78, 6.84, 7.56, 154, 15.64, 148, 18.116, 19.192.

23–4. tempus erat thyrso pulsum grauiore moueri;
    cessatum satis est: incipe maius opus.

Tragedy's exasperation becomes even more obvious as she switches from grand statement in the hexameter to abrupt and forceful censure and command in the pentameter.

23. Tragedy looks back to 1.1.1–2 and 2.1.11–16, where the poet professed to be working on an epic, and to 2.18.13–14, where he claimed to have written a tragedy. (For discussion of the dating problem see Introduction §2.)

For the association between the Bacchic thyrsus and poetic inspiration see Lucr. 1.922–3: *sed acri | percussit thyrso laudis spes magna meum cor*; *Am.* 3.15.17: *corniger increpuit thyrso grauiore Lyaeus*, *Tr.* 4.1.43: *sic ubi mota calent uiridi mea pectora thyrso*. *grauis* is a key term in this poem. See below on 35–6.

tempus erat: The imperfect is used here without past temporal significance to express impatience. Cf. Liv. 8.5.3.1, Hor. *Carm.* 1.37.4 (with Nisbet and Hubbard [1970: ad loc.]), 2.9.24, *Tr.* 4.8.25, Sen. *Med.* 111.

24. ces_sa_tum _sat_is: Repeated *sat* underlines Tragedy's exasperation with the poet.

maius opus: Tragedy adopts a phrase that Virgil uses (*A.* 7.45: *maius opus moueo*) of the more serious, i.e. Iliadic, portion of the *Aeneid*. Elsewhere, Ovid uses it when alluding to *A.* 7.45 (*Met.* 8.328; noted by Bömer [1977: ad loc.] and Kenney [2011: ad loc.]) and when referring to *Metamorphoses* (*Tr.* 2.63: *inspice maius opus*). See also *Ars* 3.370, *Rem.* 109, *Met.* 15.751, *Fast.* 5.568, 6.592.

25–6. materia premis ingenium. cane facta uirorum:
  'haec animo' dices 'area facta meo est'.
Tragedy continues with forceful censure and abrupt command in the hexameter and follows with a prediction that the poet will find this new subject matter congenial.

25. This line's dactylic character (DDDD) and the absence of a third-foot caesura make it remarkable. Having *ingenium* occupy the whole of the third foot throws the word into particular prominence.

If we pass over cases where the caesura is blurred by elision, there are only four other examples in Ovid's elegiac works of hexameters lacking a third-foot caesura: 3.9.53 (see below), *Her.* 2.37 (Knox [1995: ad loc.]: 'the unusual rhythm lends emphasis to *iurasti*'), 15.113 (where Sappho's *dolor* is highlighted), *Fast.* 2.43 (a three-word hexameter). Ceccarelli (74) infers that 'Ovid does not like lines of this type'. It seems more likely that Ovid reserves such lines for special effects.

materia: Tragedy's criticism of Ovid's choice of *materia* recalls the poet's initial resistance to erotic poetry and the elegiac couplet in 1.1 (1–2: *arma graui numero uiolentaque bella parabam | edere, materia conueniente modis*, 19: *nec mihi materia est numeris leuioribus apta*). We might also see reference to the advice given to a foolish husband in Book 2's last poem (2.19.44): *daque locum nostris materiamque dolis*.

The idea that certain metres suit certain kinds of subject matter is pervasive in Ovid (e.g. *Her.* 15.5–6, *Rem.* 371–4, *Tr.* 2.219–24, 331–2, *Fast.* 2.3–6, 121–6, 6.21–2, *Pont.* 3.4.85–6, *Ib.* 45–6, 643–4). Ovid may have been the first to use *materia* of poetic subject matter (cf. Hor. *Ars* 38–9 [around 10 BCE]: *sumite materiam uestris, qui scribitis, aequam | uiribus*).

ingenium: This is a key term in Ovid's critical lexicon, denoting natural ability or talent (*OLD* 4, 5). Ovid famously uses it to characterize the differing poetic achievements of Callimachus and Ennius (Callimachus: *Am.* 1.15.13–14: *Battiades semper toto cantabitur orbe; | quamuis ingenio non ualet, arte ualet*; Ennius: *Am.* 1.15.19: *Ennius arte carens, Tr.* 2.424: *Ennius ingenio maximus, arte rudis*). Above all, however, *ingenium* is the definitive property of Ovid's own work, particularly when viewed from the exiled poet's perspective e.g. *Am.* 3.8.3: *ingenium quondam fuerat pretiosius auro*, 3.8.8: *turpiter huc illuc ingeniosus eo*, 3.12.16: *ingenium mouit sola Corinna meum; Ars* 3.58: *dum facit ingenium* (with Gibson's [2003] note: 'while my poetic talent functions successfully'); *Fast.* 1.18, 2.123; *Tr.* 1.1.36, 2.2 (with Ingleheart's [2010] note on the importance of Prop. 3.2.25–6), 3.3.74, 4.10.59–60; *Pont.* 1.5.2–3. Though hardly justified, Quintilian's comment (10.1.89) that Ovid is 'excessively in love with his own talent' underlines the importance of *ingenium* in the poet's conception of his own achievement.

Discussion of the opposition between innate talent and acquired skill in Latin goes back at least as far as Cicero (e.g. *de Or.* 1.113–15). For roughly contemporary discussion of the roles of *ingenium* and *ars* in literary composition see Hor. *Ars* 408–18.

premis: For this sense of *premo* see *TLL* 1180.34–48.

cane facta uirorum: Allusion to *Aeneid*'s opening words, suggests that Tragedy requires epic seriousness from Ovid's work.

26. area: Ovid employs this distinctly concrete term (*OLD* 1: 'space clear of buildings'; *OLD* 2: 'threshing-floor') as a metaphor for the scope of his literary activity. Elsewhere he highlights its connection with horse racing (3.15.18).

27–8. quod tenerae cantent lusit tua Musa puellae,
    primaque per numeros acta iuuenta suos.
After censure comes forgiveness: love elegy was appropriate when the poet was young. Tragedy implies, however, that now is the time to grow up.

27. tenerae...puellae: Connoting both youth (*OLD* 2) and sensuality (*OLD* 6), *tener* defines beloveds whether female or male (e.g. Tib. 1.3.63, 1.4.58, Prop. 2.25.41, *Am.* 2.1.33, 2.14.37, 3.3.25, 3.4.1, 3.7.53, *Ars* 3.31), as well as *amor*/Amor (Tib. 1.3.57, *Am.* 2.18.4, *Ars* 1.7), and elegiac poetry itself (*Am.* 2.1.4, 3.8.2).

lusit: The idea of poetry as a form of play is not unusual in earlier Latin poetry (e.g. Catul. 50, *Ecl.* 1.10, 6.1, 7.17, *G.* 4.565). The notion that love and love poetry are a form of play, however, is unusual in early Ovid (cf. 2.3.13, *Her.* 15.21: *sunt apti lusibus anni*, *Ars* 2.599–600: *nisi lege remissum | luditur*). It is in the exile poetry that Ovid stresses that his erotic works were merely a game (e.g. *Fast.* 2.6 [quoted below on 28], *Tr.* 1.9.61, 2.223, 3.1.7–8, 5.1.7, *Pont.* 1.4.4). Indeed, he comes to define his earlier self as a player of games (*Tr.* 3.3.73, 4.10.1): *tenerorum lusor amorum*.

cantent: The present subjunctive is used here in a purpose/final clause introduced by the relative pronoun *quod* (Woodcock [§148]).

28. Tragedy's characterization of Ovid's youthful poems foreshadows the poet's own description in later works. In addition to the passages just cited, see *Fast.* 2.6: *cum lusit numeris prima iuuenta suis* (which clearly rewrites this line) and 4.9: *quae decuit primis sine crimine lusimus annis*. Time, however, has passed and it is time for the poet to move on.

numeros: A double entendre is possible here. Cf. 3.7.18: *cum desit numeris ipsa iuuenta suis*, 26: *numeros sustinuisse nouem*.

29–30. nunc habeam per te Romana Tragoedia nomen:
 implebit leges spiritus iste meas'.
Although very little pre-Senecan tragedy survives, it is clear that Roman tragedy had already had a distinguished history under the Republic. Ovid speaks highly of Accius in particular (*Am.* 1.15.19: *animosique Accius oris*; *Tr.* 2.359: *Accius esset atrox*; for Accius' spirited ferocity see Boyle [2006: 113–19]).

29. Tragedy's wish is probably accomplished fact.

30. For other examples of this verbal pattern (VABba), which combines an initial verb with the chiastic arrangement of adjectives and nouns, see *Am.* 1.1.22, 1.8.80, 1.13.28, 2.1.18, 2.19.58, 3.7.38, 3.10.4, 3.11.6, 3.14.44, 46.

implebit: For *impleo* in this sense see *OLD* 9b. Hall (1999: 98) claims: 'As was perceived by Heinsius, what would be true to the facts is *impleat et*'. Heinsius printed *implebit*. No change is necessary.

31–2. hactenus, et mouit pictis innixa cothurnis
 densum caesarie terque quaterque caput.
Tragedy's standing tall and tossing her hair presumably reflect the behaviour typical of tragic actors. The language seems to foreshadow the narrator's description of Jupiter at the council of gods at *Met.* 1.178–80: *celsior ipse loco sceptroque innixus eburno | terrificam capitis concussit terque quaterque | caesariem*. Perhaps both Tragedy and Jupiter are over-acting.

31. pictis…cothurnis: For Tragedy's characteristic *cothurni* see above on 14. For the buskins as embroidered see 2.18.15: *pictosque cothurnos*. Virgil represents (non-tragic) *cothurni* as red or purple in colour (*Ecl.* 7.32, *A.* 1.337).

innixa cothurnis: For standing tall on tragic buskins see Hor. *Ars* 279–80: *Aeschylus... | et docuit magnumque loqui nitique cothurno*, *Pont.* 4.16.29: *Musaque Turrani tragicis innixa cothurnis.* Tragedy's height hints at the genre's aspiration to sublimity.

32. caesarie: Occurring only three times in prose (in Livy, the younger Pliny, and Apuleius), *caesaries* is a high-style poetic word for hair (e.g. Catul. 66.8: *e Bereniceo uertice caesariem*, Hor. *Carm.* 1.15.14, *G.* and *A.* (five times), and *Met.* (seven times). Here it suggests Tragedy's importance or self-importance.

terque quaterque: The phrase is found mainly in epic (*A.* 1.94, 4,589, 12.155; *Met.* 1.179, 2.49, 9.217, 12.288; Luc. 5.497) and at more solemn moments in elegy (Prop. 3.7.6). Use of double *que* (the first *que* being redundant) is characteristic of the high style (Davis [2020: 120]). Lateiner (1990: 234) notes that in this line 'the third and fourth words mean "thrice and four times"'.

33–4. altera, si memini, limis surrisit ocellis.
 fallor, an in dextra myrtea uirga fuit?
If Tragedy is all bluster, Elegy embodies sexual allure: all smiles and glances, and Venus' myrtle.

33. limis...ocellis: The phrase suggests Elegy's seductiveness. Cf. Apuleius' account of Lucius' encounter with Photis (*Met.* 2.10): 'Then she twisted her neck and, turning towards me with sidelong looks and fluttering eyes (*limis et morsicantibus oculis*), she spoke'. Marius suggests that *limis ocellis* implies either annoyance (*subirata*) or sexiness (*lasciuiae*). The context (*surrisit*, the erotically-charged diminutive *ocellis* [cf. Catul. 3.17–18: *tua nunc opera meae puellae | flendo turgiduli rubent ocelli*, Prop. 1.1.1: *Cynthia prima suis miserum me cepit ocellis*], and the reference to Venus' myrtle) suggests that sexiness is closer to the mark. Marlowe (1603) translated: 'The other smiled (I wot) with wanton eyes'.

34. fallor, an: These words give the line the character of a stage direction. Cf. 1.6.49: *fallimur, an uerso sonuerunt cardine postes.*

myrtea uirga: The myrtle's association with Venus, lovers, and love poets (e.g. *Ecl.* 7.61–2: *populus Alcidae gratissima, uitis Iaccho, | formosae myrtus Veneri*, Tib. 1.3.65–6, *Am.* 1.15.37) makes it an appropriate emblem for Elegy to carry.

35–6. 'quid grauibus uerbis, animosa Tragoedia', dixit,
 'me premis? an numquam non grauis esse potes?
Elegy begins not by criticizing the poet, but by attacking Tragedy. Repetition of *grauis* underlines tragedy's claim to be the pre-eminently serious genre. Cf. *Tr.* 2.381: *omne genus scripti grauitate tragoedia uincit.* Gravity also characterizes its practitioners. See Cicero's description of Accius as *grauis et ingeniosus poeta* (*Planc.* 59.13) and Quintilian's claim that Aeschylus was *sublimis et grauis* (*Inst.* 10.1.66.3).

Given Elegy's preference for being *leuis* (41 below), *grauis* will have negative connotations here (cf. *OLD* 10: 'obnoxious').

35. animosa Tragoedia: Elegy describes Tragedy in terms that Ovid had used to define the style of Accius (1.15.19): *animosique Accius oris*.

36. me premis: Cf. the language that Tragedy had used when criticizing the poet (25): *materia premis ingenium*.

numquam non: Understatement, suggested by the double negative, is sometimes more powerful than plain statement. Here it implies impatience with Tragedy's endless seriousness. Cf. Prop. 2.20.23–4: *interea nobis non numquam ianua mollis, | non numquam lecti copia facta tui*, where repeated *non numquam* implies frequent sexual success.

37–8. imparibus tamen es numeris dignata moueri.
    in me pugnasti uersibus usa meis.
Elegy capitalizes on the fact that in order to speak in this poem Tragedy has had to employ the elegiac couplet. Ovid's Sappho makes a similar point when she suggests that Phaon will wonder why she now writes elegiacs (*Her.* 15.5–6): *forsitan et quare mea sint alterna requiras | carmina, cum lyricis sim magis apta modis*.

37. imparibus…numeris: The combination of a line of six feet with a line of five makes the elegiac form inherently 'uneven'. Ovid employs the image at all stages of his elegiac career e.g. 2.17.21: *carminis hoc ipsum genus impar*; *Ars* 1.264, *Tr.* 2.219–20, *Pont.* 4.16.11–12, *Pont.* 4.16.36. Frampton (2019: 111) observes that the practice of indenting pentameter lines that we see in the Gallus papyrus (Hollis [2007: 224]) is almost certainly the origin of this trope.

39–40. non ego contulerim sublimia carmina nostris:
    obruit exiguas regia uestra fores.
For conservative critics like Quintilian sublimity belongs exclusively to the higher genres, like epic (*Inst.* 1.8.5: *sublimitate heroi carminis animus adsurgat*) and (at a pinch) tragedy (*Inst.* 1.8.6: *utiles tragoediae*). At 1.15.23–4 the poet declares the poetry of *sublimis…Lucreti* to be immortal.

39. contulerim: As at 1.14.33 (*illis contulerim* [with McKeown ad loc.]), Ovid employs the perfect potential subjunctive. (For other examples see Woodcock [§120]).

40. The front of a palace is a regular setting for tragedies (e.g. Acc. fr. 244 Warmington [1936]: *sed ualuae resonunt regiae*; Sen. *Phaed.* 384: *patescunt regiae fastigia*). Elegy's lovers, by contrast, often find themselves outside the doors of less exalted dwellings (e.g. Tib. 1.1.56, Prop. 3.7.72, *Am.* 1.9.8).

exiguas: Suggests the modesty to which elegiac poets aspire. For *exiguus* as an appropriate description of *Amores* see *Fast.* 2.3–6 (with line 6 reworking line 28 of this poem):

> nunc primum uelis, elegi, maioribus itis:
> exiguum, memini, nuper eratis opus.
> ipse ego uos habui faciles in amore ministros,
> cum lusit numeris prima iuuenta suis.

See also Prop. 2.1.72, 2.13.33, 4.1.59.

41–2. sum leuis, et mecum leuis est, mea cura, Cupido:
    non sum materia fortior ipsa mea.
Elegy switches from a negative to a positive account of the literary values for which she stands.

41. leuis...leuis: For lightness as elegy's defining property see e.g. Tib. 1.1.73: *nunc leuis est tractanda Venus*, Prop. 2.12.22: *haec mea Musa leuis*, Am. 1.1.19: *nec mihi materia est numeris leuioribus apta*, 2.1.2, *Rem.* 379–80, *Pont.* 4.5.1. For Cupid as *leuis* see 2.9.49: *tu leuis es multoque tuis uentosior alis*, *Ars* 2.19; for love poetry in general as *leuis* see the proem to Orpheus' song at *Met.* 10.152: *nunc opus est leuiore lyra* (cf. Hor. *Carm.* 2.1.40: *leuiore plectro*).

42. non sum materia fortior ipsa mea: For *materia* as literary subject matter see above on 25. Elegy's claim that she lacks strength recalls the excuses given by earlier Augustan poets for refusing to take on epic themes (e.g. Hor. *Carm.* 1.6, Prop. 2.1.17–26). Cf. *Tr.* 1.5.55–6 (where his own sufferings really are beyond the poet's strength): *non tamen idcirco complecterer omnia uerbis, | materia uires exsuperante meas*. For discussion see Morgan (2010: 355–8).

43–4. rustica sit sine me lasciui mater Amoris:
    huic ego proueni lena comesque deae.
But literary values imply moral values, and the values for which Elegy stands are urban sophistication and sexual freedom.

43. rustica: In Ovid *rusticus/rustica* is almost always a pejorative term, with particular emphasis on *OLD* 7: 'lacking the townsman's sophisticated outlook, provincial, old-fashioned'. In *Ars* it is opposed to the *cultus* that the Teacher prizes (3.127–8: *sed quia cultus adest, nec nostros mansit in annos | rusticitas, priscis illa superstes auis*). In erotic contexts (*OLD* 7b) it connotes either indifference to sexual passion or an old-fashioned attitude to sexual morality. For *rusticitas* as lack of interest in sex see e.g. 2.4.13–14: *siue procax aliqua est, capior quia rustica non est, | spemque dat in molli mobilis esse toro*, *Ars* 1.672 (rebuking a lover who stops at kisses): *ei mihi, rusticitas, non pudor ille fuit*, cf. *Met.* 11.767–8: *non agreste tamen nec inexpugnabile amori | pectus habens*; for *rusticitas* as adherence to old-fashioned morality see e.g. 3.4.37 (a man troubled by his wife's adultery): *rusticus est nimium, quem laedit adultera coniunx*, *Her.* 1.77–8 (Penelope imagining what Ulysses tells his girlfriends): *quam sit tibi rustica* *coniunx* | *quae tantum lanas non sinat esse rudes*, Her. 4.131–2: *ista uetus pietas, aeuo moritura futuro,* | *rustica Saturno regna tenente fuit*, Rem. 330: *et poterit dici rustica, siqua proba est.*

Ovid's attitude to *rusticitas* (a word he seems to have invented) contrasts sharply with that of Tibullus, who regularly pictures himself in the countryside and even imagines himself as a farmer (1.1.7–8): *ipse seram teneras maturo tempore uites* | *rusticus*, 2.3.3–10, esp. 4: *uerbaque aratoris rustica discit Amor.*

lasciui…Amoris: Meaning both 'mischievous' (*OLD* 3) and 'free from restraint in sexual matters' (*OLD* 4), *lasciuus/lasciua* is applied by the elegists to poets like Catullus (Prop. 2.34.87, *Tr.* 2.427) and Sappho (*Ars* 3.331), to sexual relationships outside the scope of the law (*Ars* 3.27: *nil nisi lasciui per me discuntur amores*), and to the god of Love himself (Tib. 1.10.57, *Ars* 2.497, *Met.* 1.456). For Quintilian (*Inst.* 10.1.93.3) *lasciuia* is the defining quality of Ovid's love poetry: *Ouidius utroque lasciuior.*

huic ego: The juxtaposition of third and first person pronouns emphasizes the value of the services that Elegy performs for Venus.

lena: That Elegy should speak of herself as Venus' 'procuress' may seem shocking, not only because brothel-keepers were legally defined as *infames* (*Dig.* 3.2.1), but because all three male elegists treat the *lena* with unreserved hostility (Tib. 1.5.48, 2.6.44; Prop. 4.5; *Am.* 1.8). On the other hand, Ovid speaks of his poetry as turning his girlfriend into a prostitute (*ingenio prostitit illa meo* 3.12.8) and of himself as a procurer (*me lenone* 3.12.11).

45–6. quam tu non poteris duro reserare cothurno,
    haec est blanditiis ianua laxa meis.
Elegy, moreover, has advantages: it opens doors that Tragedy cannot.

45. poteris: Most editors print the reading of the major manuscripts P, S, and Y. Ramirez de Verger (2) prefers *poteras* found in P4. The difference in meaning is not great.

duro: For *durus* as an epithet for serious poetry see e.g. Prop. 2.1.41, 2.34.44.

46. blanditiis ianua laxa meis: Elegy repeats the poet's claim that doors give way to poetry (2.1.27–8): *carminibus cessere fores, insertaque posti,* | *quamuis robur erat, carmine uicta sera est.* For flattery as an essential weapon in the lover's armoury see e.g. Tib. 1.2.93, 1.9.77, *Am.* 1.2.35 (where *Blanditiae*, along with *Error* and *Furor*, accompany the lover in Cupid's triumphal procession), 2.1.21: *blanditias elegosque leuis, mea tela, resumpsi.* It is particularly important when the lover faces his girlfriend's bolted door (Prop. 1.16.16, *Am.* 1.6.15).

ianua laxa: The phase also occurs at 1.8.77.

**47–8. et tamen emerui plus quam tu posse ferendo
multa supercilio non patienda tuo.**
I accept the transposition of these lines, proposed in Kenney (1) and printed in Kenney (2), which has been accepted by McKeown, but not Ramirez de Verger. The reordering markedly improves the logical sequence, with Elegy's claims (a) that she has power to open doors (45–6) and (b) that she has suffered (47–8) being followed by appropriate evidence.

47. et tamen emerui: While these three words begin Prop. 4.11.61, it is not clear that we should speak of allusion here.

**49–52. per me decepto didicit custode Corinna
liminis astricti sollicitare fidem
delabique toro tunica uelata soluta
atque impercussos nocte mouere pedes.**
Elegy now claims to be a teacher. While the Ovidian lover gives his girlfriend much advice on deceiving a partner in 1.4, it is the Tibullan lover who claims to have taught his mistress the skills she needs for deceiving guards (1.6.9–10): *ipse miser docui, quo posset ludere pacto | custodes* and opening doors in silence (1.6.12): *cardine nunc tacito uertere posse fores.* Ovid claims as much at *Tr.* 2.449: *fallere custodes idem* (i.e. Tibullus) *docuisse fatetur.* In *Ars,* however, the Teacher gives far more detailed advice on deceiving guards than Tibullus ever offered (3.617–58). For the *custos* see below on 3.4.1–2.

49. Corinna: The central female figure of *Amores* has remarkably little presence in the collection. Whereas Tibullus' Delia is named 15 times in Book 1 (and she has to compete with the poet's boyfriend, Marathus) and Propertius' Cynthia is named 59 times in four books (in the first poem's first line in fact [1.1.1]: *Cynthia prima suis miserum me cepit ocellis*), Corinna does not enter until 1.5, is mentioned only 14 times across three books, and sometimes in ways that make clear that she is not the poem's subject or addressee (2.19, 3.7). Her problematic status is highlighted by the poet himself at *Ars* 3.538 (*et multi, quae sit nostra Corinna, rogant*) and is explored in *Am.* 3.12 (see below; see also Introduction §7).

50. sollicitare fidem: Elsewhere Ovid uses this expression (which is used by no other author) of attempts to undermine a woman's chastity (*Her.* 17.3–4: [Helen rejecting Paris]: *ausus es…| legitimam nuptae sollicitare fidem, Met.* 6.463–4 [Tereus and Philomela], 7.720–1: [Cephalus and Procris]: *statuo donisque pudicam | sollicitare fidem*). Here it is transferred from the woman herself to the locked doorway which protects her chastity.

51. tunica uelata soluta: The significance of this phrase (and its variation *tunica uelata recincta*) changes according to context. At 1.5.9 it signifies Corinna's readiness for sex: *ecce, Corinna uenit, tunica uelata recincta*; at 3.7.81 it highlights the speedy departure of a disappointed girlfriend: *desiluit tunica uelata soluta*; while at *Ars* 1.529 and *Fast.* 3.645 it marks the unpreparedness of Ariadne and Anna

Perenna when just aroused from sleep: *tunica uelata recincta*. Here it underlines Corinna's interest in sexual adventure.

52. impercussos: An Ovidian coinage, this word appears nowhere else in Latin. Its meaning, however, 'not struck (against anything)' (*OLD*) is clear. *inoffensus* is the usual word in such contexts e.g. Tib. 1.7.62, *Am*. 1.6.7–8: *ille* (i.e. *amor*) *per excubias custodum leniter ire | monstrat: inoffensos derigit ille pedes*, *Tr*. 3.4.33.

53–4. uel quotiens foribus duris infixa pependi
   non uerita a populo praetereunte legi!
Speaking of her own suffering, Elegy emphasizes her status as a written text. Reference to the material nature of writing is frequent in *Heroides* (e.g. 3.3: *lacrimae fecere lituras*; 11.1–2, 15.1–4). The exiled Ovid often refers to the book as a material object (e.g. *Tr*. 1.1, 3.1, *Pont*. 2.10.1–4). For this see Frampton (2019: Chapter 6).

53. uel: This is the reading of the major manuscripts and is printed by Munari, Kenney, and McKeown. For *uel* meaning 'for instance' see *OLD* 4b and Kershaw (1986: 407). Cf. Tib. 1.8.53–4 (with Maltby's [2002] note): *uel miser absenti maestas quam saepe querelas | conicit*. Showerman and Goold and Ramirez de Verger (2) follow Goold (1965: 45) in printing Vb's *a*.

foribus duris: The doors are hard because (a) that is the nature of wood and (b) they guard the homes of unresponsive girlfriends (*dura* being the elegiac lover's standard epithet for a woman whom he regards as difficult [*TLL* 2308.75–2309.17]). Cf. Tib. 1.8.75–6: *nunc displicet illi* (i.e. Marathus) | *quaecumque opposita est ianua dura sera*; *Am*. 1.6.62 (addressed to a doorkeeper): *o foribus durior ipse tuis*.

infixa: P and Y offer *incisa*, a reading accepted by most editors, including Heinsius, Munari, and Ramirez de Verger. (S has the clearly unsatisfactory *illisa*). McKeown and Kenney (2) print *infixa* (Vb). Goold (1965: 46) asks the key question: 'Surely nothing *incised* upon a door can be said to *have hung* (as though temporarily) upon it?'. The parallels cited by Ramirez de Verger (2) do not persuade. Cf. *A*. 8.196–7: *foribusque adfixa superbis | ora uirum tristi pendebant pallida tabo*, *Fast*. 1.557: *ora super postes adfixaque bracchia pendent*. For lovers' poems on doors see Plaut. *Merc*. 409, Prop. 1.16.9–10.

54. Elegy confirms Tragedy's claim that the Ovidian lover is notorious throughout the City (21).

55–6. quin ego me memini, dum custos saeuus abiret,
   ancillae miseram delituisse sinu.
Elegy speaks as if she were a letter passed between lovers rather than a poetry collection.

55. For the cruel *custos* (cruel because he frustrates lovers' desires) see *Am*. 2.2 and 3.4. See also Tib. 1.2.5: *nostrae custodia saeua puellae*, Prop. 2.23.9: *uultum custodis amari*, Ars 2.635: *custos odiose puellae*.

56. For maids as bearers of letters between lover and beloved see 1.11, 2.19.41, *Ars* 1.383. For the bosom as a hiding-place for letters see Tib. 2.6.45-6, *Ars* 3.621-2.

delituisse: *delitesco* frequently connotes concealment for nefarious purposes e.g. *G.* 3.417 (a viper), *A.* 2.136 (Sinon), *Her.* 8.68 (Jupiter's rape of Leda), *Met.* 4.340 (Salmacis' rape of Hermaphroditus).

**57-8. quid, cum me munus natali mittis, at illa
   rumpit et apposita barbara mersat aqua?**
Elegy now addresses the poet himself and complains of brutal treatment at the hands of a girlfriend unhappy with receiving poetry as a birthday present. Cf. the contradictory advice offered by Dipsas the procuress and the Ovidian teacher: at *Am.* 1.8.57-62 girls are told to seek wealthy lovers, not poets, while at *Ars* 3.533-52 they are urged to accept gifts of verse from poet-lovers.

57. quid, cum me munus natali mittis, at illa: Use of spondees in the first four feet makes this line unusual. (In *Amores* there are only 19 other examples: 1.2.49, 1.5.21, 1.8.27, 1.8.43, 1.8.85, 1.10.61, 1.13.21, 1.13.35, 1.14.39, 1.15.5; 2.5.43, 2.11.11, 2.11.27, 2.14.23, 2.19.29; 3.3.39, 3.6.29, 3.9.17, 3.14.33). Here it expresses Elegy's disgust at her treatment by the poet's girlfriend.

For the lover's obligation to give his girlfriend a birthday gift see *Am.* 1.8.93-4, *Ars* 1.405, 417-18, 429-30, Prop. 4.5.35-6.

barbara: The term is used here with its full emotional force. Cf. 1.7.19: *quis non mihi 'barbare!' dixit?* Discarding poetry is tantamount to violence against a girlfriend.

**59-60. prima tuae moui felicia semina mentis.
   munus habes, quod te iam petit ista, meum'.**
Elegy closes by reminding the poet of his obligation to her as his talent's first inspiration.

59. prima...semina mentis: At line 28 Tragedy used the concept of primacy (*primaque...iuuenta* 28) to encourage the poet to grow up and move on. Elegy employs the same concept to persuade the poet to stay put.

Ovid reworks this line at *Fast.* 6.6: *impetus hic sacrae semina mentis habet*, where he claims divine inspiration for his work. When Silius (see introduction n. 3 above) reuses *semina mentis* in the context of Scipio's choice, he clearly has *Fasti* in mind rather than *Amores* (15.71-2): *cui ratio et magnae caelestia semina mentis | munere sunt concessa deum?*

felicia: When juxtaposed with *semina*, *felicia* will suggest fertility (*OLD* 1), in this case, fertility of invention. But the adjective also suggests success (*OLD* 5), as at 2.17.27-8: *sunt mihi pro magno felicia carmina censu, | et multae per me nomen habere uolunt.* For a love elegist success consists in attracting women.

60. munus habes, quod te iam petit ista, meum: It is ironic, however, that the poet's success as a love elegist has also attracted the attention of 'that woman', i.e. Tragedy.

Commentary, 1.56–65

61–2. desierat. coepi: 'per uos utramque rogamus,
   in uacuas aures uerba timentis eant.
The poet responds to these speeches with a request and an expression of fear. Like the Teacher of *Fasti* 6, who is all too conscious of his Paris-like position (97–100), the *Amores*-poet is aware of the risks inherent in choosing.

61. desierat. coepi: The use of asyndeton to mark an abrupt transition seems paralleled only in the poet's brisk interview with Erato at *Fast.* 4.215, 217: *desierat. coepi...|...desieram. coepit.*

per uos utramque rogamus: As Némethy observes, Ovid here combines two expressions, with *uos utramque* functioning as object of both *rogamus* ('I ask both of you, pay attention') and *per* ('in the name of you both').

62. uacuas aures: *uacuus* is regularly used of ears 'as ready to listen' (*OLD* 11c) e.g. Lucr. 1.50, Hor. *Ep.* 1.16.26, *Met.* 12.56.

63–4. altera me sceptro decoras altoque cothurno:
   iam nunc contracto magnus in ore sonus.
The poet flatters Tragedy in terms that suggest that he has or is about to yield to her advice.

63. For Tragedy's *cothurnus* see above on 14 and 31; for her *sceptra* see on 13.

64. contracto: I follow Heinsius, McKeown, Kenney (2), and Ramirez de Verger (2) in printing *contracto* found written in a later hand in Y (y$_S$). The major manuscripts (P, S, and Y) offer *contacto*. The juxtaposition *contracto magnus* is particularly attractive. More importantly, *contracto* has greater point than the majority reading, because, when used of poetic style (*TLL* 761.64–762–14), it suggests less grandiloquent language. Statius, for example, uses *contraho* when marking a shift from epic to lyric poetry (*Silu.* 4.7.1–4):

> iam diu lato sociata campo
> fortis heroos, Erato, labores
> differ atque ingens opus in minores
>   contrahe gyros.

magnus in ore sonus: The claim that the poet feels grandiloquence coming on adapts Virgil's commitment to more elevated song (*G.* 3.294): *magno nunc ore sonandum*. Cf. Prop. 2.10.12 (praising Augustus): *magni nunc erit oris opus*; *Am.* 2.1.12 (as the poet begins his gigantomachy): *et satis oris erat*; *Ars* 1.206 (promising an epic for Gaius Caesar): *et magno nobis ore sonandus eris*.

65–6. altera das nostro uicturum nomen amori:
   ergo ades et longis uersibus adde breues.
The poet flatters Elegy and asks for help in terms that imply that he will continue writing erotic poetry.

Commentary

65. nostro uicturum nomen amori: Ovid's concern with literary survival is evident at every stage of his career e.g. 1.15.7–8: *mihi fama perennis | quaeritur, in toto semper ut orbe canar*, 42: *uiuam, parsque mei multa superstes erit*, *Met.* 15.878–9, *Tr.* 3.7.50–2. In *Amores* he also claims to be able to confer immortality upon the women whom he loves (1.3.25–6; 1.10.57–8, 62; 2.17.27–8).

66. ades: This imperative is regularly used in invocations to gods e.g. Catul. 62.5 (and eight more times): *Hymen ades o Hymenaee*, *Am.* 2.13.21: *lenis ades precibusque meis faue, Ilithyia*, *Ars* 1.30, *Rem.* 704, *Fast.* 2.17–18 (to Caesar).

longis uersibus adde breues: In *Amores* and elsewhere Ovid's treatment of the elegiac couplet is playful (see on 8 and 37 above). For a similarly literal description of the elegiac couplet (a long line followed by a shorter one) see 2.17.22: *iungitur herous cum breuiore modo*.

67–8. exiguum uati concede, Tragoedia, tempus:
   tu labor aeternus, quod petit illa, breue est.
The poet does not reject Tragedy's demands outright, but merely requests a postponement. For the chronological implications see Introduction §2.

67. exiguum...tempus: For *exiguum* see above on 40.

uati: For the connotations of *uates* see above on 19.

68. labor aeternus: The long/short contrast is now applied to the time involved in composing tragedy as opposed to love elegy. The poet contradicts the claim for love elegy's importance that he made in Book 1's signature poem (1.15.7–8): *mortale est, quod quaeris, opus. mihi fama perennis | quaeritur, in toto semper ut orbe canar*. It is tragedy that lasts, not elegy.

69–70. mota dedit ueniam. teneri properentur Amores,
   dum uacat: a tergo grandius urget opus.
The poem closes with a compromise: the poet will continue writing love elegy but will soon switch to something grander.

69. mota dedit ueniam. teneri properentur Amores: The wholly dactylic line underlines the speaker's impatience and the need for speed.

The description of Amor/*amor* as *tener* derives from Tibullus (1.3.57, 2.6.1) and is frequent in Ovid (2.18.4, 19, 3.15.1; *Ars* 1.7, *Fast.* 4.196) until it comes to define the poet's sense of his own achievement: *Tr.* 2.361: *denique composui teneros non solus amores*, 3.3.73: *hic ego qui iaceo tenerorum lusor amorum*, 4.10.1: *ille ego qui fuerim, tenerorum lusor amorum*. It is not just Amor who needs to be hurried along, but this collection of elegies, *Amores*.

70. grandius urget opus: The poet yields in terms which recall Amor's command at 1.1.24: *quodque canas, uates, accipe dixit opus* and Tragedy's order (24): *incipe* *maius opus.* Cf. *Fast.* 4.948 (concluding the description of Flora; see above on 7–10): *nunc me grandius urget opus.*

3.2: AT THE RACES

Am. 3.2 takes the form of a dramatic monologue delivered by a single speaker, an anonymous pickup artist, who addresses an unnamed young woman and others in an identifiable location. The symbolic landscape of 3.1 now gives way to an actual place, the Circus Maximus in Rome,[1] and allegorical figures yield to apparently real human beings watching the chariot races.

Located between the Aventine and Palatine hills, the Circus Maximus, Rome's largest venue for public spectacle,[2] figures prominently in Ovid's poetry. In *Ars Amatoria* it is singled out as a place for meeting women (1.135–62; cf. *Tr.* 2.283–4), while in *Fasti* it is the site for a procession and horseracing on the 10th and 19th of April (4.389–92, 679–80) and for games on the 12th of May (5.189–90, 597–8). *Fasti*'s Teacher also underlines its association with Rome's remote past (1.391–2) and with temples of Mercury (5.669–70) and Mater Matuta (6.477–8). In *Tristia* it is referred to as an arena for bullfights (4.9.29–30; cf. *Met.* 12.102–4), while in *Metamorphoses* the poet mentions the resemblance between pinecones and the racetrack's turning-points (10.106).

Who are these people? While we might be tempted to identify the speaker with the poet-lover, the Naso who is named in four poems in Books 1 and 2 (the initial epigram, 1.11, 2.1, and 2.13), but not at all in Book 3, there is no indication that this is so. When alluding to this poem in *Tristia* 2, the exiled Ovid refers to the speaker as 'unknown' (*Tr.* 2.283–4): *non tuta licentia Circi est:* | *hic sedet ignoto iuncta puella uiro* ('the freedom of the Circus is unsafe: here a girl sits right next to an unknown man'); unknown to the girl certainly, but unknown to readers too. And who is the girl? There is no indication that she is Corinna. Perkins (2015: 142) tells us that she is 'freeborn and unmarried'. According to Cairns (2012: 75), she is a 'prostitute there to be picked up'.[3] In fact, there is no evidence to support either of these claims.[4] All we can assert with confidence is that, if it is true that

---

[1] There was one other circus in Augustan Rome where horse races could be held: the Circus Flaminius. Claridge (1998: 221) describes it as follows: 'It was not a proper circus for chariot-racing in the sense of Circus Maximus; it had no seating, nor starting gates, nor was it necessarily even circus-shaped, though it could be used for horse-racing'. Given *Am.* 3.2's references to sitting (1, 3, 23–6, 63–4) and starting gates (9, 66, 77), the poem is clearly not set in the Circus Flaminius. For more positive identification of the Circus Maximus see the note on line 65 below.
[2] A contemporary writer, Dionysius of Halicarnassus (*Ant. Rom.* 3.68.3), estimated that the Circus Maximus held 150,000 people.
[3] It is strange therefore that Cairns (2012) classifies *Am.* 3.2 as belonging to his genre of 'wooing' poems.
[4] Perkins (2015: 141) acknowledges this lack of evidence when she comments: 'The status of the woman is unspecified'. One of Cairns's (2012: 69) key pieces of evidence is his claim that the *pallium* is

seating at the Circus Maximus was organized by rank (Humphrey [1986: 76–7]), the would-be seducer and his target belong to the same social class.

What kind of poem is this? Some scholars focus on the fact that the speaker is present at a ritual and a spectacle. Schwarz (1952: 32–3) and J. T. Davis (1979: 54), for example, treat Theocritus *Idylls* 2 and 15, Callimachus *Hymns* 2, 5, and 6, and Tibullus 2.1 as 'foundations' or 'models' for 3.1, because each of these poems involves description of or participation in a religious ritual. However, these works are very different both from each other and from 3.2. *Idyll* 2 dramatizes the prayer of a woman abandoned by her lover, while *Idyll* 15 presents the conversation of two women making their way to a festival of Adonis. Callimachus' *Hymns* are prayers, but prayers with dramatic elements, particularly instructions to fellow worshippers. Tibullus 2.1, by contrast, presents the poet as a priest in charge of a rustic festival. Moreover, all of these 'models' differ from *Am.* 3.2, because here the speaker has no interest in the ritual or spectacle, only in the opportunity they provide for picking up a sexual partner. These Greek poems are not Ovid's models. And there is nothing similar in earlier Roman elegy. This is a radically new kind of poem.

3.2 is primarily an attempt at persuasion: it is the speech of a man trying to seduce a young woman. Its affinities lie, as Tarrant (1995: 66) points out, with other poems in *Amores*, particularly 1.6 (addressed to an uncooperative doorman), 1.13 (to the goddess of dawn), 2.2 (to Bagoas, another unhelpful doorman), and 3.6 (to a river in flood). This is, in the words of *Fasti*'s Teacher, an example of the earliest form of eloquence (4.111): *eloquiumque fuit duram exorare puellam* ('eloquence was persuading an obstinate girl'). It is not surprising, therefore, that in *Ars Amatoria* the Teacher recycles *Am.* 3.2's techniques of seduction when advising his students how to pick up women at the races (1.135–64).

These techniques include the insistent repetition of words and ideas. Note, for example, the way in which the poem's end mirrors its beginning: *studeas* (67) echoes *studiosus* (1), while *cetera* (84) recalls *cetera* (35); *uincet cuicumque fauebis* (67) picks up *cui tamen ipsa faues, uincat ut ille* (2); the driver is said to be *felix* at line 7, but *infelix* at 71; the seducer imagines the horses leaving the *carcer* at line 9, describes how they actually leave at 66, and again at 77; and, similarly, he imagines himself plying the reins at 11 and 14, and then urges the driver to pull them tight at 72. Also notable is the use of repetition or near-repetition of individual words and phrases in close proximity: 5: *spectas......spectemus*; 27–8: *inuida uestis eras...*|*...inuida uestis eras*; 32: *fortes, fortior*; 34: *in flammam flammas, in mare... aquas*; 51: *Phoebus, Phoebe*; 59: *promisit, promittas*; 81: *uota meae, mea uota*; 82: *palmam; palma*). There are also recurrent ideas. There is, for example, repeated emphasis on the concepts of sight (especially on the male gaze: 5 [x2], 16, 23, 28,

---

associated with prostitutes. This is not the case. See below on 25. Cairns also notes that the woman seems to be unveiled (line 75). This observation only supports Cairns's case if he establishes that the only unveiled women in Rome were prostitutes. He does not.

Commentary, 2.1–3 99

65, 67, 68) and victory (both equestrian and sexual: 2, 17, 18, 45, 46, 67). While all of these devices are typical of Ovid, when used in close combination they underline this speaker's persuasive skills.

Secondary literature: Fränkel (1945: 23–4); Schwarz (1952: 32–47); Thomas (1969); Frécaut (1972: 137–9, 185–6), Connor (1974); J. T. Davis (1979); Lyne (1980: 280–2); Miller (1989); Tarrant (1995); Boyd (1997: 204–10); Ramirez de Verger (1999); Henderson (2002); Boyle (2003: 199–202); Morwood et al. (2011); Shea (2011: Chapter 4); Ingleheart and Radice; Cairns (2012); Welch (2012); Perkins (2015); Oliensis (2019: 166–7).

On the Circus Maximus and the Circus procession: Dionysius of Halicarnassus (*Ant. Rom.* 3.68, 7.72–3); Humphrey (1986); Richardson (1992); Claridge (1998); Feeney (1998: 96); Dodge (1999); Coarelli (2007); Latham (2016: Chapter 2).

1–2. Non ego nobilium sedeo studiosus equorum.
 cui tamen ipsa faues, uincat ut ille, precor.
As in 1.1, Ovid makes an impressive opening with a wholly dactylic couplet. Here it may suggest the speed that we associate with the racetrack or perhaps the smooth talk of the pickup artist. The fact that there are only 17 such couplets in *Amores* (i.e. around 1.5 per cent in total; for a list see McKeown [117]) underlines its exceptional character. Ceccarelli (260, table 3a) calculates that only 6.55 per cent of hexameters in Ovid's erotic works have the pattern DDDD.

1. Ovid establishes the speaker's character and location with brilliant economy. The Teacher alludes to this line when shifting focus from the theatre to the Circus in *Ars Amatoria* (1.135): *nec te nobilium fugiat certamen equorum*. Though repeated, *nobilium…equorum* works differently in the different contexts. Here the phrase helps to individualize the seducer (he has no interest in horse racing), whereas in *Ars* the conventional epithet *nobilis* (used of horses by Cicero, Livy, and Tacitus among others) serves primarily to signal allusion to this poem.

studiosus: Cf. *studeas* (67).

2. At *Ars* 1.146 the Teacher advises students to follow this aspiring seducer's practice: *cui fauet illa, faue*.

faues: *faueo* and *fauor* occur six times in this poem (2, 7, 17, 18, 43, 67; there are only 10 examples in *Amores*). They are used to vary a religious formula (43), to denote a 'real' or mythical girl's support for her preferred charioteer (2, 7, 17, 18, 67, 73), and a girl's goodwill towards a lover (17, 18, 67).

faues, uincat ut ille, precor: The speaker's prayer is transformed into a prediction at line 67: *uincet, cuicumque fauebis*.

3–4. ut loquerer tecum ueni, tecumque sederem,
 ne tibi non notus quem facis esset amor.

This couplet consists of two purpose clauses dependent on *ueni*, with the first line offering a blunt statement of the reason for the seducer's presence, and the second softening his approach through the use of the double negative: *ne... non*.

3. This is a superbly structured line, with the main verb *ueni* in the centre, framed by *tecum* on either side and then by two verbs in the imperfect subjunctive.

5–6. tu cursus spectas, ego te. spectemus uterque
  quod iuuat atque oculos pascat uterque suos.
Emphasis on gazing in this couplet could hardly be stronger, with *spectas, spectemus* and implied *specto* in the hexameter and a near synonym in the pentameter. The repetition of *uterque*, with its suggestion of mutual gazing, misleads, for while the speaker watches the woman, she watches the races.

5. spectas...spectemus: Ovid uses repetition of forms of *specto* to create remarkable lines e.g. *Am.* 2.5.43: *spectabat terram: terram spectare decebat*, *Her.* 21.103: *forsitan haec spectans a te spectabar, Aconti*, *Ars* 1.99: *spectatum ueniunt, ueniunt spectentur ut ipsae*, *Met.* 3.98: *serpentem spectas? et tu spectabere serpens*.

ego te: The juxtaposition of the first and second person pronouns is often associated with love of various kinds (e.g. Catul. 64.149, Hor. *Carm.* 1.23.9, Prop. 2.20.27, *A.* 4.333, *Her.* 17.180: *tua me, te mea*, *Met.* 4.142: *quis te mihi casus ademit*, Stat. *Achil.* 1.253). Here it also reflects the physical location of the seducer and the woman.

cursus: Showerman and Goold print Bentley's *currus*. For Bentley's justification see Hedicke (1905: 21; he cites *Ars* 3.634 and *Tr.* 4.2.63); for Goold's see Goold (1965: 46, citing Bentley and the same passages). Ovid, however, and this is hardly surprising, regularly uses *cursus* in connection with horses (e.g. *Ars* 1.629, *Met.* 6.226, 14.354, *Pont.* 1.2.84, 1.4.16, 3.9.26). For other authors see *TLL cursus* 1533.19–49 (*imprimis de equis*). Bentley's parallels are unconvincing and there is no need for change.

6. oculos pascat: For *pascere* used of gazing upon the beloved see Ter. *Phorm.* 85, Lucr. 1.36. It is used more frequently, however, for feasting the eyes on acts of cruelty (*TLL* 595.66–78).

7–8. o, cuicumque faues, felix agitator equorum!
  ergo illi curae contigit esse tuae.
There is a marked difference in tone between hexameter and pentameter, with the first line expressing enthusiasm for the woman's preferred charioteer, and the second, perhaps spoken as an aside, registering the speaker's disappointment in not being favoured.

7. o: The interjection is used here to introduce an evaluative exclamation with an implied main verb (*est*). See Pinkster (1.361) for discussion of exclamatory sentences.

felix: Though *felix* now, the charioteer will soon be *infelix* (71).

agitator equorum: Plautus (*Men.* 160) and Lucilius (*sustineas currum, ut bonus saepe agitator, equosque* 1305 Marx) use *agitator* as a synonym for the more commonplace *auriga*. The seducer prefers still grander language and quotes Virgil (*A.* 2.476–7): *equorum agitator Achillis,* | *armiger Automedon*.

8. Older editors printed this pentameter as a statement (e.g. Naugerius, Micyllus, Burman). Heinsius and more recent editors (Munari, Kenney, McKeown, Ramirez de Verger) present it as a question. The reasons for this are not clear. Even though the authors of the best English-language versions, Lee (1968) and Green (1982), use Kenney's text, they ignore his question mark. Either way, the line expresses disappointment or resentment.

ergo: For this use see *OLD* 4: 'elliptically with suppression of the preceding statement, introducing an exclamation or rhetorical question, often with a note of emotion. So it seems that...!'

curae...tuae: This is probably predicative dative with *esse*, with *tuae* being used in place of the expected *tibi*. Kenney (1958: 63), though noting that 'the two come to very much the same thing', preferred the genitive.

contigit: In this line and the next, the verb is used intransitively with the dative (*OLD* 8): 'to fall to one's lot, happen, be granted to one'. Cf. 1.3.18: *uiuere contingat teque dolente mori*, 2.10.35: *at mihi contingat Veneris languescere motu*, 3.7.43: *haec mihi contigerat; sed uir non contigit illi*.

9–10. hoc mihi contingat, sacro de carcere missis
   insistam forti mente uehendus equis
Unlike most couplets in *Amores*, this one, though making sense by itself, is not fully self-contained, because the sentence is not completed until the end of line 12. (Platnauer [1951: 27] reckons the number of enjambed couplets in Ovid at 5 per cent.) Continuity between couplets adds excitement to the speaker's vision of himself as a charioteer. The rhyme produced by vertical agreement (*missis... equis*) helps bind these two lines together.

9. contingat: As Burman (ad loc.) recognized, *contingat* here expresses a condition: 'understand, *si*'. *contingat* is sometimes treated by translators and commentators as expressing a wish. This leads to syntactic awkwardness, because the logical connection between the first clause and the following indicatives is not clear.

sacro de carcere: Dionysius of Halicarnassus provides contemporary evidence for the starting mechanism (*Ant. Rom.* 3.68.3.6): 'the other of the remaining sides [of the Circus Maximus], left unroofed, has vaulted starting lines all opened at the same time by a single cord'. It is not clear why the starting-gate is described as *sacer*. For discussion of the literary and archaeological evidence for the *carcer* at Rome and elsewhere see Humphrey (1986: 132–74).

10. The spondaic opening perhaps underlines the seducer's determination to demonstrate courage.

insistam: The form is ambiguous between the present subjunctive and the future indicative. While the present subjunctive in 9 encourages readers to take the verb as subjunctive, the futures in line 11 suggest that it may be future indicative.

forti mente: For the combination of an adjective and *mente* used adverbially see e.g. 1.4.23 (*tacita*), 2.15.3 (*laeta*), 3.7.63 (*tacita*), Her. 18.38 (*certa*), Ars 1.602 (*tacita*), Met. 5.275 (*tota*), 8.634 (*iniqua*), 9.473 (*dubia*), 13.214 (*placida*), 15.26 (*tacita*), Fast. 3.634 (*tacita*).

11–12. **et modo lora dabo, modo uerbere terga notabo,**
   nunc stringam metas interiore rota.
In imagining the race, the speaker first emphasizes his speed by employing as many dactyls as possible in line 11 and then highlights his resolution to take risks by using only spondees in the first half of the pentameter.

11. This is a brilliantly structured line, with parallel clauses separated by the main caesura, with four words on either side, with each half introduced by *modo* as the first main word, and with balance reinforced by internal rhyme (*dabo...notabo*). To cap it off, it is a wholly dactylic line perhaps reflecting the charioteer's imagined speed. For Ovid's preference for a syntactic break at the main caesura see on 3.7.37.

modo...modo: For repeated *modo* used to articulate different racing strategies see Ars 2.433–4: *aspice, ut in curru modo det fluitantia rector | lora, modo admissos arte retentet equos.*

lora dabo...uerbere terga notabo: For loosening the reins and plying the lash as techniques for achieving speed in a chariot race see G. 3.106–7: *illi instant uerbere torto | et proni dant lora, uolat ui feruidus axis.*

12. For the importance of cleaving to the turning-post as tightly as possible see Homeric Nestor's advice to Antilochus (*Il.* 23.338–40): 'Let the horse on the left almost touch the post, so that the hub of the well-made wheel seems to graze the surface'. Cf. Hor. Carm. 1.1.4–5: *metaque feruidis | euitata rotis*, Virgil's description of a boat race (esp. A. 5.159–64), Prop. 2.25.25–6, Am. 3.15.2, Ars 2.426: *interior curru meta terenda meo est*, 3.396: *metaque feruenti circueunda rota*, Luc. 8.199–201 (likening a ship's movement to a chariot's), and Statius' account of Amphiaraus' hopes (*Theb.* 6.440–2).

13–14. **si mihi currenti fueris conspecta, morabor,**
   deque meis manibus lora remissa fluent.

The sense pause after the first short syllable in the hexameter's fifth foot makes for an unusual rhythm and perhaps highlights the importance of both *conspecta* and *morabor* and, by implication, the elaboration of *morabor* in the pentameter. We see a similar effect in other examples in *Amores*: 1.13.47: *iurgia finieram. scires audisse: rubebat*; and 2.3.17: *aptius ut fuerit precibus temptasse: rogamus*. For a complete list see McKeown (1989) on *Am*. 1.4.11.

13. fueris conspecta: Equivalent to *eris conspecta*, this combination of future perfect and perfect participle passive stresses the brevity of the moment. Cf. Canace's claim that she will kill her baby and then herself (*Her*. 11.120): *nec mater fuero dicta nec orba diu*; and the poet's advice to his book (*Tr*. 1.1.105–6): *cum tamen in nostrum fueris penetrale receptus, | contigerisque tuam, scrinia curua, domum*.

conspecta: For explicit statement of the role of the eyes and sight in sexual attraction see Prop. 2.15.12: *oculi sunt in amore duces*. For Ovidian examples see e.g. *Her*. 20.55–6: *tu facis hoc oculique tui, quibus ignea cedunt | sidera, qui flammae causa fuere meae*, *Met*. 4.316 (Salmacis and Hermaphroditus), 6.478 (Tereus and Philomela), *Fast*. 3.21 (Mars and Silvia). Cf. Hom. *Il*. 14.293–4: ἴδε δὲ νεφεληγερέτα Ζεύς. | ὡς δ' ἴδεν, ὥς μιν ἔρως πυκινὰς φρένας ἀμφεκάλυψεν ('Zeus who gathers the clouds saw her. When he saw her, desire enfolded his shrewd mind').

14. lora remissa: Letting the reins go signifies loss of control. Cf. Phaethon's response to the sight of the Scorpion (*Met*. 2.200): *mentis inops gelida formidine lora remisit* and the description of Niobe's son Ismenus when struck by an arrow (*Met*. 6.228): *frenisque manu moriente remissis*.

15–16. at quam paene Pelops Pisaea concidit hasta,
   dum spectat uultus, Hippodamia, tuos!
Mythological allusion is unexpected at this point and is made all the more striking by the marked alliteration of *p* in the hexameter, perhaps intended to highlight the name Pelops, and by the apostrophe to Hippodamia in the pentameter.

Roman poets assume their readers' knowledge of the story of Pelops' 'winning' of Hippodamia. Hence Virgil asks 'Who has not told this story?' (*G*. 3.6–8). Consequently we find only brief references to this myth in Latin poetry e.g. *Her*. 8.70, 16.266, *Ars* 2.7–8, Prop. 1.2.19–20, 1.8b.35–6, Germ. *Arat*. 161–2, Sen. *Thy*. 409–10, 660–2, VF 7.276–8.

For fuller narratives we have to turn to the Greeks. AR provides a somewhat elliptical account in his description of Jason's cloak (1.752–8). Diodorus Siculus, however, provides more detail (4.73.4–5):

> Oenomaus used to sacrifice a ram to Zeus and the suitor would set out driving a four-horse chariot; after the sacred rites had been performed, Oenomaus would begin the race and chase the suitor, holding a spear and with his charioteer Myrtilus; if he caught up with the chariot he was chasing, he would strike the suitor with his spear

and kill him. In this way he always caught the suitors because of the speed of his horses and he wiped out many. Pelops, son of Tantalus, arriving in Pisa, and seeing Hippodamia, desired marriage; having bribed Myrtilus, Oenomaus' charioteer, and taking him as partner in his victory, he reached the altar of Poseidon at the Isthmus first. Oenomaus, thinking that the oracle was being fulfilled, and disheartened with grief, committed suicide. In this way Pelops married Hippodamia.

The myth is relevant here because it involves a chariot race and men competing for possession of a woman. Presumably the seducer expects the girl to ignore Pelops' use of bribery.

15. at: This is the reading of major manuscripts P and Y (S reads *ad*). Kenney, McKeown, and Ramirez de Verger (2) prefer *a*, based on *ah*, proposed by a later hand in Y and conjectured by Heinsius (p. 266). *a* is attractive because Ovid often uses this interjection to introduce an exclamation. He does, however, use *at* for the same purpose at 2.8.18 and 3.7.39.

Whether a sentence should be punctuated as an exclamation or a plain statement is often a matter of judgement. Despite their different editorial practices, Kenney, Showerman and Goold, McKeown, and Ramirez de Verger are agreed in treating 2.8.17 and 3.7.39 as exclamations. Kenney has three examples of *at* followed by an exclamation mark; Showerman and Goold have thirteen.

paene Pelops Pisaea concidit hasta: As is clear from Diodorus Siculus (quoted above), Oenomaus carries a spear in order to kill unsuccessful suitors. See also Pindar (*Ol.* 1.76) and Apollonius of Rhodes (1.756). The spear is *Pisaea* because Oenomaus is king of Pisa. Accius (*Atreus* fr. 196 Ribbeck, fr. 162 Warmington [1936]) makes one of his characters refer to Hippodamia as *Pisaea praemia*.

16. spectat: McKeown (58) detects a possible reference to the suggestion in Plato's *Cratylus* (395c2–d3) that Pelops' name means 'the man who sees only what is immediately at hand, i.e. "close" (*pelas*)'.

Hippodamia: Here Hippodamia embodies beauty; for the Propertian lover she represents beauty unadorned (1.2.19–20): *nec Phrygium falso traxit candore maritum | auecta externis Hippodamia rotis.*

17–18. nempe fauore suae uicit tamen ille puellae:
  uincamus dominae quisque fauore suae.
  Rhyme, both internal and external, is marked in this couplet, with *suae* at the main caesura and *puellae* at line's end in 17; and *dominae* at the main caesura in 18 and *suae* at line's end. *suae* in 18 of course also rhymes with *puellae* in 17. The repetition *fauore suae uicit...| uincamus...fauore suae* underlines the connection between the myth and present circumstances.

17. fauore suae...puellae: Unfortunately for the seducer's argument it is not clear that Pelops' victory owed anything to Hippodamia's *fauor*. *puella* is ambiguous between 'young woman married or otherwise' (*OLD* 2) and 'girlfriend' (*OLD* 3), a word used by love poets of their sexual partners (e.g. Catul. 2.1, Tib. 1.1.55, Prop. 1.5.19, *Am*. 1.4.3). Hippodamia is a *puella* in the sense of *OLD* 2.

18. uincamus: The meaning of *uinco* shifts in these lines. In 17 it refers solely to victory in a chariot race. Now it refers to the charioteer's hope for victory and the seducer's desire for sexual conquest.

domina: The ambiguity of *puella* makes this shift in the argument plausible. *domina*, used by elegists of the woman with whom they have a sexual relationship (e.g. Catul. 68b.68, Gallus 145.7 Hollis, Tibullus 2.4.1, Propertius 1.1.21, *Am*. 1.4.47), is the equivalent of *puella* in the sense of *OLD* 3.

19–20. quid frustra refugis? cogit nos linea iungi.
   haec in lege loci commoda Circus habet.
These lines are notable for their use of alliteration and assonance, with the repetition of *f, r, g, n*, and *u* sounds in the hexameter emphasizing the futility of trying to escape the speaker's attentions and the *c* sounds in the pentameter underlining the place in which they find themselves. In *Ars* Ovid converts these lines into detailed advice (1.139–42):

> proximus a domina, nullo prohibente, sedeto,
>   iunge tuum lateri qua potes usque latus;
> et bene, quod cogit, si nolis, linea iungi,
>   quod tibi tangenda est lege puella loci.

19. quid frustra refugis?: The lover finally turns from self-centred fantasy to observing the woman's reaction to his advances: she finds him repulsive. *frustra* underlines the fact that she is trapped.

cogit nos linea iungi: There is a paradox here: the line which is intended to separate actually joins couples together. (For the logical connection between *linea* and separation see *TLL* 1437.27–79, citing this passage as the first example). The precise meaning of *linea* is disputed. It may refer to a line marking off a section of seating (*OLD* 6b: 'a line or rope marking off a block of seats in the theatre') or individual seats (Hollis on *Ars* 1.141–2: 'A line marks the space for each individual on the bench'). Humphreys (1986: 76–7), using the evidence of this passage and *Ars* 1.139–42, offers both possibilities. The paradox, however, is more effective if the *linea* is understood as separating groups but bringing individuals together, i.e. if *OLD* 6b is correct.

iungi: For the sexual overtones of *iungo* see Adams (1982: 179–80).

20. in lege loci: While the *lex Iulia theatralis* enforced the separation of the sexes in the theatre (Suet. *Aug*. 44, cf. *Am*. 2.7.3–4; for discussion see Rawson [1987]), this poem and *Ars* 1.139–42 imply that no such law applied in the Circus. This is confirmed by Juvenal's reference to young men sitting in the Circus beside their girlfriends during the Megalesia (11.201–2): *spectent iuuenes, quos clamor et audax | sponsio, quos cultae decet adsedisse puellae.*

commoda: Cf. *Ars* 1.136: *multa capax populi commoda Circus habet.*

21–2. tu tamen a dextra, quicumque es, parce puellae:
   contactu lateris laeditur ista tui.
In an apparent show of solicitous concern, the speaker turns to another person in the crowd, reminding us that he is actually making his advances in public. Here too alliteration and assonance are pronounced, with marked repetition of consonants in adjacent words: *tu tamen, parce puellae, lateris laeditur.*

21. parce puellae: Cf. Hero's very different request to Leander, one that arises out of genuine love (*Her.* 19.205): *dilectae parce puellae.*

22. contactu lateris: For use of the genitive with *contactus* compare the introduction to the story of Pyramus and Thisbe (*Met.* 4.51–2): *quae poma alba ferebat | ut nunc nigra ferat contactu sanguinis arbor.*

ista: Principal manuscripts divide between *ista* (PY) and *illa* (S). Munari and Kenney (1) print *illa*, while Showerman and Goold, McKeown, Kenney (2), and Ramirez de Verger print *ista*. Goold (1965: 51) argues for *ista* on the grounds that it is 'more colloquial and peremptory than the formal *illa*'.

23–4. tu quoque, qui spectas post nos, tua contrahe crura,
   si pudor est, rigido nec preme terga genu.
In this couplet too the seducer conjures up the sense of a pressing crowd by addressing one of its members. He also conveys concern for the woman's welfare by solving a possibly imaginary problem. Alliteration of *c, r,* and *g* adds vigour to the request. Reinforcing *tu* with *tua* and using three verbs in the second person help to suggest the reality of the person whom our speaker is addressing. At *Ars* 1.157–8 the Teacher converts the would-be lover's behaviour into advice: *respice praeterea, post uos quicumque sedebit, | ne premat opposito mollia terga genu.*

25–6. sed nimium demissa iacent tibi pallia terra:
   collige, uel digitis en ego tollo meis.
The speaker turns his attention back to the woman and, in a seeming show of concern, lifts her dress from the ground. At *Ars* 1.153–4 the Teacher offers advice based on our seducer's practice: *pallia si terra nimium demissa iacebunt, | collige, et immunda sedulus effer humo.*

25. pallia: As Varro (*Ling.* 8.28) observes, the *pallium* is a garment worn by Roman women as a practical alternative to the *stola*, the male equivalents being the *tunica* and the toga. Cairns's claim (2012: 69) that the *pallium* is evidence that the woman is a prostitute will not stand. Among poets Ovid and Martial provide evidence to the contrary. Ovid's Cydippe wears the *pallium* (*Her.* 21.170), while Martial complains that his moralistic wife wears this form of dress (11.104.7): *fascia te tunicaeque obscuraque pallia celant*. If we turn to the law, we find that Ulpian treats the *pallium* as a garment typical of respectable women (*Dig.* 34.2.23.2): 'All clothes are either manly or boyish or womanly or common or for slaves.... Those are womanly which are purchased for the sake of the *mater familias*, which cannot easily be worn by men without censure, for example, *stolae, pallia…*'.

tibi: The dative denotes both possession and disadvantage.

26. uel…meis: The combination of *uel* in the sense of 'even' (*OLD* 5) and *meis* placed in the emphatic final position underlines the seducer's extraordinary willingness to help (and his interest in seeing a woman's legs).

en: Ovid uses *en*, not only to call attention to what is happening, but to underline how momentous the event is. Cf. 1.2.19: *en ego confiteor*, 1.8.31–2: *en aspice: diues amator | te cupiit*, line 75 below, 3.3.14.

tollo: Ovid here treats final *o* as short. For other examples see above on 3.1.8.

27–8. inuida uestis eras, quae tam bona crura tegebas.
 quoque magis spectes—inuida uestis eras.
After addressing fellow spectators and the girl herself, the seducer now apostrophizes her dress. Use of the first two and a half feet of the hexameter for the second half of the pentameter gives a formal strictness to the couplet and an appearance of logical tightness to the argument. See also 1.9.1–2 (*militat omnis amans*), 3.6.61–2 (*Ilia, pone metus*, with discussion below), *Her.* 5.117–18 (*Graia iuuenca uenit*), *Rem.* 71–2 (*Naso legendus erat/erit*), 385–6 (*Thais in arte mea est*), *Fast.* 4.365–6 (*qui bibit inde furit*). For a similar effect in a non-elegiac text see *Met.* 8.38–9: *impetus est illi, liceat modo, ferre per agmen | uirgineos hostile gradus, est impetus illi*.

Ovid employs apostrophe frequently in *Amores*. Addresses to a god (often Venus or Cupid), to a personification (Aurora in 1.13, an unnamed river in 3.6, Elegy in 3.9), to a mistress or other fictional character, to a (probably) real human being (Atticus in 1.9, Graecinus in 2.10, Macer in 2.18, Tibullus in 3.9) are not uncommon. More surprising are addresses to his own hands (1.7.27–8) or inanimate objects like garlands (1.6.67–70), doors (1.6.73–4), writing tablets (1.12.7–14), triumphal laurels (2.12.1), a ring (2.15.1–8), or mountains and valleys (2.16.51–2). Apostrophe of this latter kind sometimes suggests that the lover is overcome by emotion. Here, and at 56 below, it underlines the speaker's wit and is intended to amuse both listener and reader.

The Teacher rewrites this couplet in more overtly self-interested terms (*Ars* 1.155–6): *protinus, officii pretium, patiente puella | contingent oculis crura uidenda tuis*.

28. inuida uestis eras: As well as creating formal balance, the repetition of this phrase enables the speaker to avoid completing his sentence (aposiopesis): 'The more you look, …'. It is up to the reader to supply the rest.

**29-30. talia Milanion Atalantes crura fugacis
   optauit manibus sustinuisse suis.**
In this couplet and the next the seducer invokes the glamour of mythological precedent. The hexameters have similar structures: both identify the model and emphasize the key point of comparison by placing *talia* and *crura* in the same metrical positions. Here the pentameter introduces a surprise by referring not just to Milanion's admiration of Atalanta's legs but to his preferred position for having sex with her. For successive hexameters with similar verbal structures see Prop. 1.17.21: *illa meo caros donasset funere crinis* and 23: *illa meum extremo clamasset puluere nomen*.

Ovid uses mythology in a variety of ways in his erotic poetry. In *Amores* mythological examples are used to advance a quasi-serious argument (e.g. Tarpeia and Eriphyle were examples of female greed [1.10.47–52]) or an entirely paradoxical argument (e.g. the capture by Ulysses and Diomedes of Rhesus' horses at night [1.9.21–4]) or for the sake of humour (e.g. the resemblance of Atalanta, Ariadne, and Cassandra to Corinna in having lovely hair [1.7.13–18]). Here, humour is combined with sexual innuendo. (Cf. Dipsas' version of Penelope's activities with the suitors [1.8.47–8].) The didactic character of *Ars Amatoria* allows for extended use of mythological stories for humorous purposes e.g. the rape of the Sabine women as proof that theatres are good places for meeting women (1.100–134), Pasiphae's love for a bull as evidence that women are more sexual than men (1.295–310), Menelaus' responsibility for the adultery of Paris and Helen (2.359–72), and the excellent fashion choices of Briseis and Andromeda (3.189–92). For a catalogue of examples see Frécaut (1972: 104–34).

29. Atalantes…fugacis: Earlier in the collection Atalanta is presented as a hunter (1.7.13–14): *talem Schoeneida dicam | Maenalias arcu sollicitasse feras*. Here the choice of *fugax* makes it plain that the speaker thinks of her primarily as a runner.

Perhaps an amalgam of more than one myth, Atalanta's story is varied. (For discussion see Janka [1997: on *Ars* 2.185–6].) She is the daughter of either Iasius (e.g. Prop. 1.1.9, Hyg. 70.1.8) or Schoeneus (e.g. *Am*. 1.7.13, *Her*. 16.265) and she is a hunter (e.g. *Am*. 1.7.13–14, *Met*. 8.317–23) or a runner (e.g. *Her*. 16.265-6, *Met*. 10.560-680), or perhaps both (Prop. 1.1.9–16, where reference to Milanion gazing upon *hirsutas…feras* [12] might suggest the hunter, while reference to *uelocem…puellam* [15] implies the runner). The names of her lover/s differ: she is involved with Milanion (Prop. 1.1.9, *Ars* 2.188, 3.775) or Hippomenes (*Met*. 10.681–704) or Meleager (*Met*. 8.317–28, where she is referred to as *Tegeaea*).

30. The Teacher revisits this line when advising women how to show off their legs when having sex (*Ars* 3.775–6): *Milanion umeris Atalantes crura ferebat: | si* *bona sunt, hoc sunt accipienda modo.* (For references to this sexual position in Greek comic writing see Gibson [2003: ad loc.])

sustinuisse: For similar use of *sustineo* of the male role in sexual intercourse see 2.4.21–2: *est etiam, quae me uatem et mea carmina culpet | culpantis cupiam sustinuisse femur.* (At 3.14.22 *sustinuisse* is used of the female role.)

Ovid uses the perfect infinitive of this verb because the present cannot be accommodated in dactylic verse (*sūstĭnērĕ*). Elegiac poets (including Martial) always place *sustinuisse* in this metrical position.

31–2. talia pinguntur succinctae crura Dianae,
 cum sequitur fortes fortior ipsa feras.
As noted on 28–9, the structure of the hexameter underlines the fact that these are paired similes, both naming females who excel in conventionally male activities. Both lines are superbly designed, with the hexameter employing a pattern which varies the golden line (aVbAB) and the pentameter employing Ovid's most frequently used pattern (VabBA). (See Introduction §4.) For other examples in *Amores* see note on 3.1.11.

31. pinguntur: For similes comparing humans to representations of gods in works of art see e.g. 1.14.33–4: *illis contulerim, quas quondam nuda Dione | pingitur umenti sustinuisse manu*, *Met.* 10.515–17: *qualia namque | corpora nudorum tabula pinguntur Amorum, | talis erat.* (For images of Diana as hunter see *LIMC* II.2 Artemis / Diana 590–6.)

succinctae: Female hunters are regularly described in this way (e.g. *A.* 1.323, *Ars* 3.143–4, *Met.* 3.156, 10.536). Tucking the skirts under a belt allowed women a freedom of movement they would not normally have. Cf. Phaedra's attempt to seduce Hippolytus (*Her.* 4.87): *quid iuuat incinctae studia exercere Dianae* and the narrator's description of Arachne and Minerva at work (*Met.* 6.59–60): *utraque festinant cinctaeque ad pectora uestes | bracchia docta mouent.*

32. Marked alliteration of *f* and the juxtaposition of *fortes* and *fortior* stress Diana's status as hunter. For alliteration of *f* in a similar context see Actaeon's words (*Met.* 3.148–9): *ferrumque cruore ferarum | fortunaeque dies habuit satis.* For this variation on the golden line (aVbAB) see 1.5.5, 2.11.29, 3.6.17, 3.11.21. (For the golden line see below on 3.3.21.)

fortes fortior: Ovid is fond of symmetry emphasized by repetition (often with polyptoton) which frames the main caesura. Examples in Book 3 are: 51 (*Phoebus // Phoebe*), 59 (*promisit // promittas*), and 82 below (*palmam // palma*); 3.3.22 (*deceptus // decipientis*); 3.4.40 (*Iliades // Iliades*); 3.5.18 (*pasto // pascitur*); 3.8.7 (*laudauit // laudato*); 3.9.1 (*mater // mater*); 3.10.23 (*testi // testis*); 3.11.37 (*fugio // fugientem*), 50 (*uelle // uelis*); 3.14.8 (*facias // facta*). See also 1.2.41, 42; 2.4.39, 2.5.31, 43, 58; 2.6.59; 2.16.41; 2.19.5; *Her.* 1.41, 65; 2.95, 110; 6.29 (*timidus // timidum*); 7.6, 41; 8.75; 9.108, 13.19, 135, 150; 15.43; 16.291, 349, 356.

33-4. his ego non uisis arsi. quid fiet ab ipsis?
   in flammam flammas, in mare fundis aquas.

Although flawed, this couplet's logic is psychologically plausible: I am excited when I see your legs; therefore you are responsible for making me more and more excited. The hexameter's rhetorical question is answered with a brilliant conceit, made striking by balance at the main caesura and by use of repetition and variation.

33. This line is notable for its repetition of *s* and *i*, highlighting perhaps the importance of *arsi* immediately after the main caesura.

34. The repetition *flammam flammas* in the first half of the line picks up *arsi* in the hexameter, while *in mare...aquas* offers variation (a) by shifting from fire to its opposite and (b) by employing synonyms rather than identical language. For similar repetition see *Met.* 2.313: *saeuis compescuit ignibus ignes*, *Met.* 15.181: *unda impellitur unda*. For similar use of variation see 2.10.14: *in freta collectas alta quid addis aquas?* For similar combination of repetition and variation see *Met.* 11.488: *egerit hic fluctus aequorque refundit in aequor*.

35-6. suspicor ex istis et cetera posse placere,
   quae bene sub tenui condita ueste latent.

This phase of the argument concludes with the seducer's suggestion that the loveliness of the woman's legs hints at beauties not yet seen. Cf. the equally sleazy Acontius (*Her.* 20.61-2): *cetera si possem laudare, beatior essem, | nec dubito, totum quin sibi par sit opus*; and the far more sinister Tereus (*Met.* 6.492): *qualia uult fingit quae nondum uidit*.

35. Alliteration of *s*, *p*, and *c* throw the last three words into prominence.

cetera: Ovid sometimes uses *cetera* to avoid sexual explicitness e.g. 1.5.25: *cetera quis nescit*; *Her.* 18.105: *cetera nox et nos et turris conscia nouit*; *Ars* 1.669: *oscula qui sumpsit, si non et cetera sumet*; *Met.* 2.863: *uix cetera differt*; *Fast.* 2.349-50: *cetera temptantem subito Tyrinthius heros reppulit*.

placere: For *placeo* in the sense of 'be sexually attractive to' see *OLD* 1d. Cf. *Her.* 4.63 (Phaedra to Hippolytus): *placuit domus una duabus* and Sen. *Phaed.* 683-4 (Hippolytus to Phaedra): *sum nocens, merui mori; | placui nouercae*.

36. quae bene...latent: Recalls the language used by the aspiring lover to refer to his girlfriend's beauty at *Am.* 1.4.41: *sed quae bene pallia celant*. Linguistic similarity, however, underlines situational difference. In 1.4 the lover fears (*timoris* 42) a partner's forced access to a woman's body (*iure coacta* 64), while here he flatters his mark by implying that still greater beauties remain to be discovered. Perhaps closer to our passage is Prop. 1.4.14: *gaudia sub tacita ducere ueste libet* ('the joys it is a pleasure to practise under the covers'). (The text of this line is disputed: some read *dicere* or *discere*. For this interpretation see Fedeli [1980: 146].)

37-8. uis tamen interea faciles arcessere uentos,
   quos faciet nostra mota tabella manu?
The speaker now turns from innuendo to apparent concern for the woman's comfort, with a pompous line followed by impressive verbal patterning.

37. faciles arcessere uentos: The seducer uses inflated language to impress the girl. Elsewhere Ovid, and he is the only author to use *facilis* in this way (*TLL* 60.75-8), describes winds (*uenti/aurae*) as *facilis* in the context of sailing (*Her.* 16.23, 18.45, *Tr.* 1.2.81). Similarly, *arcesso*, with its military and legal associations (*OLD* 1, 2), seems a grandiose substitute for the straightforward *uoco* favoured even by epic poets (e.g. *A.* 8.707-8 [Cleopatra]: *ipsa uidebatur uentis regina uocatis | uela dare*, *Met.* 7.202 [Medea]: *uentos abigoque uocoque*).

38. For other examples of this verbal pattern (VabBA) in *Amores* see on 3.1.11.

tabella: The *praeceptor Amoris* gives similar advice at *Ars* 1.161: *profuit et tenui uentos mouisse tabella*. Elsewhere in elegy *tabella* signifies either writing tablets (e.g. Tib. 2.6.45, Prop. 3.23.1, *Am.* 1.11.15) or a painted panel (e.g. Tib. 1.3.28, Prop. 2.6.27, *Am.* 3.7.62). Here, as Hollis (1977: on *Ars* 1.161) suggests, it seems to refer to an improvised fan.

39-40. an magis hic meus est animi, non aeris aestus,
   captaque femineus pectora torret amor?
The speaker turns attention back to himself by asking whether the heat that he feels is caused by the air or by his own passion. The couplet combines two conceptions of love common in Roman erotic poetry viz. that love is a form of heat and that the lover is a captive. For love as heat or fire see e.g. Catul. 45.15-16, 100.5-7; *Ecl.* 2.1, *A.* 1.660, 4.2; Prop. 1.6.7, 1.9.17, *Am.* 2.19.15-16, 3.5.36; for the lover as prisoner see e.g. Tib. 1.1.55, 1.9.79; Prop. 3.11.1-4; *Am.* 1.2.

39. an magis: While it would be possible to read this couplet as a statement, it is more likely that the scribe of S and editors are right in treating it as a question because (a) *an* is regularly used to introduce direct questions (*OLD* 1) and (b) the phrase *an magis* is usually (though not always) used to introduce questions in both verse and prose.

40. For a similar combination of the ideas of heat and captivity see Prop. 3.24.13-14: *correptus saeuo Veneris torrebar aeno; | uinctus eram uersas in mea terga manus*. For this verbal pattern (abAVB), which varies the golden line (see below on 3.3.21) by placing the verb in the penultimate position, see the following examples in *Amores*: 1.1.28, 1.2.8, 1.5.7, 1.7.28, 1.9.14, 2.3.14, 2.4.9, 2.5.40, 2.6.4, 2.8.12, 20, 2.9.19, 2.9.34, 2.16.10, 3.5.16, 3.6.8, 3.7.30, 3.9.30, 3.12.40. This is the third most frequent verbal pattern in *Amores*.

41-2. dum loquor, alba leui sparsa est tibi puluere uestis:
   sordide de niueo corpore puluis abi.

This phase of the argument is rounded off with a humorous address to the (possibly non-existent) speck of dust which mars the appearance of the girl's dress. *Ars* 1.149–50 reworks these lines, converting the seducer's practice into the Teacher's advice: *utque fit, in gremium puluis si forte puellae | deciderit, digitis excutiendus erit*. The following couplet, however, hints at the way in which the seducer's concern should be interpreted (1.151–2): *etsi nullus erit puluis, tamen excute nullum | quaelibet officio causa sit apta tuo*. It is the appearance of concern that counts, not actual concern.

41. While the line itself embodies no particular verbal pattern, the main clause is golden (abVAB; see below on 3.3.21).

dum loquor: For the present indicative in a *dum*-clause, followed by a main verb in the past tense see Woodcock (§221).

42. The witty address, as Thomas (1969: 719) points out, gives the seducer an opportunity for flattery by contrast, for he juxtaposes *sordide* with *niueo* and *corpore* with *puluis*.

For other examples of this verbal pattern (abBAV), which combines the chiastic arrangement of adjectives and nouns with a verb placed at the end, see 1.2.4, 1.6.6, 1.8.104, 1.9.26, 1.14.12, 2.1.14, 2.6.50, 2.9.52, 3.13.28. For Ovid's use of apostrophe in *Amores* see above on 27–8.

43–4. sed iam pompa uenit: linguis animisque fauete.
 tempus adest plausus: aurea pompa uenit.
Repetition of *pompa uenit*, placed just before hexameter's caesura and at the end of the pentameter, marks a major shift in the argument, because the arrival of the procession provides our speaker with fresh material. 20 lines of seducer's chatter (43–62) are reduced to just two lines of advice in *Ars* (1.147–8): *at cum pompa frequens caelestibus ibit eburnis, | tu Veneri dominae plaude fauente manu*.

Dionysius of Halicarnassus (7.72–3) gives us the fullest account of the Circus procession. Having described the entry of young Romans on horseback and on foot, of charioteers and other contestants, of dancers and musicians, he turns to the climax (7.72.13):

> Finally images of all the gods entered in procession carried on men's shoulders... not only of Zeus, Hera, Athena, Poseidon, and of the others whom the Greeks count among the twelve...and of the demigods whose souls, leaving behind their mortal bodies, are said to have ascended to heaven and been assigned god-like honours, of Heracles, Asclepius, the Dioscuri...

While there is overlap between Dionysius and Ovid, with both explicitly referring to Neptune, Minerva, Castor, and Pollux, there are important differences. Dionysius is primarily concerned to stress the Greek origins of the procession and so summarizes by referring to the twelve Olympians. Ovid's seducer, by contrast, says nothing of human involvement and names a few of the twelve Olympian gods, but puts most emphasis on Victory (not mentioned by Dionysius) and Venus (one of the twelve, but not named). The selection of details is clearly shaped by the speaker's erotic agenda.

43. pompa: For Roman references to the Circus procession see *Fast.* 4.391: *Circus erit pompa celebre numeroque deorum* and 6.405: *qua Velabra solent in Circum ducere pompas*, Liv. 30.38.11, Suet. *Aug.* 16.3 (with Wardle [2014: 142]).

linguis animisque fauete: This command and its variations, calling for respectful silence, occur regularly in poetry in sacrificial or quasi-sacrificial contexts e.g. Tib. 2.2.2; Hor. *C.* 3.1.2–4; *Met.* 15.677: *animis linguisque fauete; Fast.* 1.71: *linguis animisque fauete*. Servius on *A.* 5.71, however, reminds us that when Aeneas says *ore fauete omnes*, 'he uses language that is suitable for both sacrifice and the games', suitable because the games were an important part of religious ritual (Beard, North, and Price [1998a: 262–3]).

44. aurea pompa: The procession is golden because the gods' statues are made of or dressed in gold. Cf. 3.13.29: *ore fauent populi tum cum uenit aurea pompa*.

45–6. prima loco fertur passis Victoria pinnis:
  huc ades et meus hic fac, dea, uincat amor.

45. prima loco: It is possible that Victory normally took first place in Circus processions. Here, however, the reason for her primacy is clear: the seducer prays for sexual conquest (*uincat amor*).

passis…pinnis: Victory is commonly represented as a winged goddess in both literature (e.g. *Met.* 8.13: *uolat dubiis Victoria pennis*; Tib. 2.5.45, Sil. 14.675) and the visual arts (*LIMC* VIII.1 Victoria 237–69, VIII.2.167–94). Livy records (29.14.14) that there was a shrine to Victory on the Palatine and that the temple of Jupiter Optimus Maximus housed a golden statue of the goddess (22.37). *passus* is regularly used of parts of the body (*TLL pando* 194.35–57).

46. huc ades: This formula is normal when addressing a god e.g. 1.6.54 (Boreas), 2.12.16 (Triumphus), *Tr.* 5.3.43 (Bacchus) or humans conceived of as godlike e.g. *Ecl.* 2.45 (Corydon to Alexis) with Clausen's note (1994: ad loc.), *Her.* 15.95 (Sappho to Phaon) with Knox's note (1995).

47–8. plaudite Neptuno, nimium qui creditis undis:
  nil mihi cum pelago. me mea terra capit.
The speaker marks Neptune's entry into the Circus with a couplet in which both lines consist of two clauses and have a syntactic break at the main caesura. The couplet surprises because of its sudden shift in tone. While the first two words,

with their alliteration of *p* suggesting the crowd's applause, imply a positive attitude to the god of the sea, the rest of the couplet is entirely negative.

47. plaudite: The verb is common in the context of processions (*TLL* 2362.60-9). In Ovid it takes the dative of the person applauded e.g. *Am.* 1.2.39-40: *triumphanti…* | *plaudet*, *Ars* 1.148: *Veneri dominae plaude*.

Neptuno: Suetonius' claim (*Aug.* 16.3) that in response to a maritime disaster, Octavian/Augustus ordered Neptune's removal from the Circus procession confirms Dionysius' view that the god's statue was a normal part of the ceremony.

nimium qui creditis undis: The characterization of seafarers as rash is consistent with the representation of the hazards of sailing in Augustan poetry (e.g. Tib. 1.3, Hor. *Carm.* 1.3, Prop. 1.17.13-14, *Am.* 2.11).

48. nil mihi cum: The expression is apparently colloquial. See e.g. Plaut. *Cist.* 646-7, *Cur.* 465, *Men.* 648. Cf. *Rem.* 386, *Fast.* 1.253, 2.308.

me mea terra capit: The alliteration of *m* and the interplay of *e* and *a* is striking in this half line. For the verbal play (polyptoton) *me mea* cf. Tib. 1.1.5, Prop. 2.10.10, 4.9.65. Ovid employs it six times in his erotic poetry (*Am.* 1.8.109, 2.10.21, 3.6.100, *Her.* 6.136, 10.45, 12.35), 16 times in all. For other examples see Wills (1996: 242).

49-50. plaude tuo Marti, miles: nos odimus arma.
    pax iuuat et media pace repertus amor.
This couplet employs the same strategy as its predecessor: after calling for applause for the god, the speaker rejects all that the god stands for.

49. plaude tuo Marti, miles: The placing of the possessive adjective before the god's name immediately distances the speaker from the god of war: he is your god, not mine. Alliteration of *m* perhaps underlines the connection between Mars and his followers.

nos odimus arma: The seducer adopts the standard elegiac stance. The speaker of Tibullus' elegies, for example, rejects conventional soldiering (1.1.75-6): *uos, signa tubaeque,* | *ite procul* and devotes a whole poem (1.10) to denouncing war and praising peace. Similarly, the Propertian lover declares himself unsuited to war (1.6.29): *non ego sum laudi, non natus idoneus armis* and devotes an entire elegy to the subject of peace (3.5). For the apparent contradiction between the elegists' rejection of warfare and the concept of the *militia amoris* (found in all three elegists, but especially in *Am.* 1.9) see Davis (2006: 74-7).

50. pax iuuat et media pace repertus amor: Perhaps alludes to Prop. 3.5.1: *pacis Amor deus est, pacem ueneramur amantes*. Both lines have a form of *pax* as the first word and as the first word after the caesura. In each case the commitment to peace is emphatic.

51-2. auguribus Phoebus, Phoebe uenantibus adsit.
   artifices in te uerte, Minerua, manus.

After two critical couplets devoted to a single divinity comes a neutral couplet naming three: Apollo, Diana, and Minerva.

51. This is a superbly structured line with brother and sister, Phoebus and Phoebe, on either side of the main caesura, each flanked by four-syllable words designating his/her devotees. While Ovid prefers to refer to Apollo's sister as Diana (52 times in all), using the goddess's other name enables him to create a visual pattern (chiasmus). For similar verbal play and a not dissimilar pattern see *Fast.* 5.699 (Phoebe and Hilaira): *abstulerant raptas Phoeben Phoebesque sororem*, Sen. *Phaed.* 654 (Phaedra speaking): *tuaeque Phoebes uultus aut Phoebi mei*. For repetition used to frame the main caesura see above on 32.

auguribus: For Apollo's association with various forms of prophecy, including augury, see Tib. 2.5.11-16.

adsit: On the use of forms of *adsum* in prayers see above on 1.66 and line 46.

52. artifices...manus: For *artifex* used adjectivally of hands see Prop. 4.2.62: *tellus artificis ne terat Osca manus* and *Met.* 15.218: *artifices natura manus admouit*.

In his hymn to the goddess, *Fasti*'s Teacher (3.815-34) emphasizes Minerva's association with artisans as varied as woolworkers, shoemakers, doctors, schoolteachers, engravers, painters, and poets.

53-4. ruricolae, Cereri teneroque assurgite Baccho.
   Pollucem pugiles, Castora placet eques.

The pace of the catalogue speeds up with four gods crammed into a single couplet.

53. ruricolae: Ovid perhaps coined this word (this is its first occurrence) as a neutral equivalent to the pejorative *rusticus*. See also *Met.* 5.479, 6.392, 11.91, 15.124, *Fast.* 1.384, 1.580, 2.628, *Tr.* 1.10.26, 4.6.1, *Pont.* 1.8.54. It was picked up by Columella, Lucan, Valerius Flaccus, Silius, Statius, and Apuleius.

teneroque: This is a standard epithet for Bacchus (e.g. *Ib.* 497, Tib. 2.3.63, Sen. *Her. F.* 472), perhaps because of his youth (*OLD* 1), perhaps because of his association with sexual passion (*OLD* 6; see above on 3.1.69).

54. For Ovid's preference for parallel clauses separated by the main caesura see above on line 11 and below at 3.7.37. The connection between Castor and horse riding and Pollux (Polydeuces) and boxing goes back to Homer ('Castor tamer of horses and Polydeuces skilled with the fist' [*Il.* 3.237, *Od.* 11.300]). Latin poets compete in contriving brilliant ways of naming the twins e.g. Catul. 4.27, Prop. 2.26a.9, Hor. *Carm.* 3.29.64, *Ars* 1.746, VF 2.427.

placet: Jussive subjunctive from *placare*. While we might expect *placent* after the plural subject *pugiles*, the verb's form has been has been attracted into the singular by the proximity of *eques*.

55–8. nos tibi, blanda Venus, puerisque potentibus arcu
   plaudimus; inceptis adnue, diua, meis
daque nouae mentem dominae, patiatur amari.
   adnuit et motu signa secunda dedit.

After one couplet devoted to four gods, we now have three couplets (55–60) devoted to the seducer's patron goddess, Venus. We also have an address which overruns the couplet and occupies three full lines. Alliteration of *p* in 55–6 both suggests the sound of clapping and underlines the power of Cupid. For similar alliteration of *p* with *plaudo* see e.g. A. 6.644, Am. 3.13.13, Ib. 165, Met. 8.237–8: *perdix | et plausit pennis*.

55. Venus is introduced with a wholly dactylic line, balanced at the main caesura.

blanda Venus: For the erotic associations of *blandus* see e.g. Tib. 1.4.71, Prop. 4.1b.137, Am. 1.2.35 (*Blanditiae* are Cupid's companions along with *Error* and *Furor*), 2.1.21 (the poet resumes *blanditiae* and *elegosque leuis*), Ars 1.362: *blanda tum subit arte Venus*; Rem. 379: *blanda pharetratos Elegeia cantet Amores*.

puerisque potentibus arcu: The bow as a symbol of Love's power is apparently Hellenistic in origin (e.g. AR 3.281–4). More importantly, however, the connection of Amor/Cupid with archery symbolizes his power over lovers and the love poet in *Amores* (1.1.21–5, 1.11.11, 1.15.27, 2.1.7, 2.7.27, 2.9.5). It is not unusual for Amor/Cupid to be represented as plural in poetry (especially Ovid) and in the visual arts: Catul. 3.1: *lugete, o Veneres Cupidinesque*, 13.12; Prop. 3.1.11; Am. 3.1.69: *tenerorum mater Amorum*, 3.15.1, Her. 16.203: *uolucrum cui mater Amorum*, Rem. 379 (quoted above), Met. 10.516: *corpora nudorum tabula pinguntur Amorum*, Fast. 4.1: *geminorum mater Amorum*; VF 7.171; Stat. Silu. 3.3.131; LIMC III.1 Eros / Amor, Cupid 1049–850, III.2.609–727).

56. plaudimus: The seducer's practice becomes precept at Ars 1.148: *tu Veneri dominae plaude fauente manu*.

inceptis adnue: Varies a formula used in Virgilian prayers: G. 1.40: *da facilem cursum atque audacibus adnue coeptis*, A. 9.625: *Iuppiter omnipotens, audacibus adnue coeptis*.

57–8. The framing of this couplet by forms of *dare* (*da | dedit*) suggests the power of the seducer's prayer.

57. daque nouae mentem dominae: If the text is sound (some less authoritative manuscripts read *nouam mentem*), the seducer is supremely confident of success: this woman will be his new mistress.

mens has a wide range of meanings. Here it seems to mean something like 'inclination' (*OLD* 9), i.e. eagerness to have sex. Perhaps the closest parallel is G. 3.267 (speaking of mares in heat): *et mentem Venus ipsa dedit*. For *mens* in a similar context see *Ars* 1.358: *quo facilis dominae mens sit et apta capi*.

patiatur amari: Recalls the hopes and prayer of the lover in *Am.* 1.3, who having hoped for lasting love, prays to Venus that his mistress might at least tolerate his passion (1.3.3–4): *tantum patiatur amari, | audierit nostras tot Cytherea preces*. For the idea of putting up with passion see Ovidian Sappho's hope that Phaon might allow her love (*Her.* 15.96): *non ut ames oro, uerum ut amere sinas*.

58. adnuit: Venus' agreement to the seducer's wish resembles the consent given by other female characters in Ovid, i.e. it depends on the interpretation of a self-interested male observer. Cf. Acontius' account of Diana's approval of his deception of Cydippe (*Her.* 20.19–20): *adfuit et, praesens ut erat, tua uerba notauit | et uisa est mota dicta tulisse coma*. For further discussion of consent in 3.2 see below on 83–4.

59–60. quod dea promisit, promittas ipsa rogamus:
   pace loquar Veneris, tu dea maior eris.
After the four-line prayer to Venus, the seducer turns now his attention to the girl. Both hexameter and pentameter exhibit balance at the main caesura, with repetition (*promisit, promittas*) underlining symmetry in the hexameter and rhyme being used to similar effect in the pentameter (*Veneris... eris*).

59. For similar play with *promitto* in an erotic context see *Her.* 20.195; *Ars* 1.443, 631, 3.461. *rogamus* is followed by an indirect command from which *ut* has been omitted.

60. pace...Veneris: *pace* (*OLD* pax 3: 'by your leave or favour, with all due respect to you') is used to preface a remark that will not please the hearer. Thus Cephalus, realizing that Aurora will be offended by the truth, declares (*Met.* 7.704–5): *liceat mihi uera referre | pace deae*. Cf. *Pont.* 3.1.7, 9: *pace tua*, where the Exile hopes to avoid offending the land of Pontus. Clearly there is risk in claiming that your girl-friend is superior to Venus.

61–2. per tibi tot iuro testes pompamque deorum
   te dominam nobis tempus in omne peti.
The seducer's commentary on the procession closes with a promise of undying love. Alliteration of *t*, particularly marked in the hexameter, is presumably intended to throw the first word of the pentameter into particular prominence.

The seducer's practice is offered as advice at *Ars* 1.631–2: *nec timide promitte: trahunt promissa puellas. | pollicito testes quoslibet adde deos*.

61. per tibi: Placing an unstressed pronoun after *per* is normal in oaths and other forms of appeal e.g. *A.* 4.314–19: *per ego has lacrimas...oro, Her.* 10.73: *per ego*

118   *Commentary*

ipsa pericula iuro, 15.107–8: *per tibi... iuro*, *Fast.* 2.841: *per tibi ego hunc iuro*, Sen. *Med.* 285–8: *per ego auspicatos regii thalami toros... precor.*

62. tempus in omne: Cf. Medea's report of Jason's equally sincere plea (*Her.* 12.82): *effice me meritis tempus in omne tuum.*

63–4. sed pendent tibi crura: potes, si forte iuuabit,
    cancellis primos inseruisse pedes.
With this couplet the speaker shifts attention from the procession to the race.

63. Given that the third-foot weak caesura (*crŭră // pŏ*) is rare in Ovid's erotic works (8.68 per cent; Ceccarelli [277, table 11]; – // uu accounts for 91.25 per cent of cases), it is possible that its use here is intended to suggest the girl's discomfort. See below on 81 and on 3.9.15.

64. cancellis: Humphrey (1986: 74) explains: 'The first section [of the seating] was divided from the second (and likewise the second from the third) by metal gratings (*cancelli*) into which adjacent spectators might slip their toes'.

65–6. maxima iam uacuo praetor spectacula Circo
    quadriiugos aequo carcere misit equos.
Alliteration of *c* in this couplet highlights key words (*Circo, carcere, equos*) and is perhaps intended to underline the event's significance: the race has finally begun.

65. The verbal pattern varies the 'Golden Line' (abVAB), replacing the verb with a noun designating the presiding magistrate. Note too that the line is framed by *maxima... Circo*, a combination of adjective and noun, which, even though they are not in agreement, suggests the poem's setting. For the role of the praetor urbanus in presiding over Circus races see e.g. Liv. 8.40 (*ludi Romani*), 25.12 (*ludi Apollinares*), Juv. 11.193–204 (Megalesia).

66. For other examples of this verbal pattern (abBVA), which combines the chiastic arrangement of adjectives and nouns with a verb in the penultimate position see 1.4.22, 36, 44; 1.6.2; 1.8.18, 1.10.22, 3.10.14.

quadriiugos: This adjective is most commonly used of prestigious forms of transport e.g. *A.* 12.163 (Latinus' ceremonial entry); *Met.* 9.272 (Jupiter taking Hercules to Olympus); *Tr.* 4.2.54 (Caesar in triumph). For images of four-horse chariots in the Circus Maximus see Humphrey (1986: 142–3, 178–254).

aequo carcere: The *carcer* is described as *aequus* because it was designed, as Humphrey (1986: 134) notes, so that 'the arrangement and mechanism of the gates gave every competitor an equal chance'.

misit: This is the standard term for the starting of the chariot race. See e.g. Enn. *Ann.* 1.79–81 Goldberg and Manuwald (1): *expectant ueluti consul quom mittere signum | uolt, omnes auidi spectant ad carceris oras | quam mox emittat pictos e faucibus currus*, Varr. *Ling.* 5.153.4: *carceres dicti, quod coercuntur equi, ne inde* *exeant antequam magistratus signum misit*, Her. 18.166: *ut celer Eleo carcere missus equus*, Tr. 5.12.26. For more details see Humphrey (1986: 153).

67–8. cui studeas, uideo. uincet, cuicumque fauebis.
quid cupias ipsi scire uidentur equi.

As the event begins, the seducer begins to use shorter sentences that suggest his excitement at the race and its hoped-for sequel.

67. The language here recalls the seducer's opening gambit, with *studeas* looking back to *studiosus* (1), *uideo* to the language of the gaze (*spectas, spectemus* 5, *spectat* 16, *spectas* 23, *spectes* 28), *uincet* to ideas of conquest and victory (*uincat* 2, *uicit* 17, *uincamus* 18, *Victoria* 45, *uincat* 46), and *fauebis* evoking the hope that the girl's favour will turn in his direction (*faues* 2, *faues* 7, *fauore* 17, *fauore* 18). For repetition as one of the seducer's persuasive techniques see the introduction above.

cui studeas: Indirect question depending on *uideo*.

68. quid cupias: Indirect question depending on *scire uidentur*.

69–70. me miserum! metam spatioso circuit orbe.
quid facis? admoto proximus axe subit.

This description of the charioteer's failure to cling closely to the turning-point, recalls the seducer's earlier image of himself as heroic driver. For the importance of a tight turn see above on 12.

69. me miserum: Although common in comedy and prose, this phrase (an exclamatory accusative) is rare in Augustan poetry (Propertius uses it twice; Tibullus, Horace, and Virgil not at all). Ovid, by contrast, uses it eight times in *Amores* alone. Knox (1986: 56) notes that the exclamatory accusative lends a 'colloquial coloring', while Hinds (1998: 30) observes that it is 'common in lively speech'. Here, as often in Ovid's erotic poetry, *me miserum* seems to be used flippantly. See e.g. 1.1.25 (of Cupid's darts): *me miserum! certas habuit puer ille sagittas*; 1.14.51 (of a girlfriend's baldness): *me miserum! lacrimas male continet*; 2.5.8 (the evidence of a girlfriend's infidelity is so good): *me miserum! quare tam bona causa mea est?*; Ars 3.552 (of girls expecting gifts from poets): *me miserum! scelus hoc nulla puella timet*.

spatioso...orbe: Cf. Statius' description of a horse recovering from a wide turn (*Theb.* 6.446): *laxo...ab orbe reductus*.

70. quid facis?: Ovidian characters or narrators use this phrase to express frustration and/or incredulity: e.g. Her. 5.115 (Cassandra to Oenone, warning of Helen's arrival): *quid facis, Oenone? quid harenae semina mandas?*; Ars 1.691 (Teacher to transvestite Achilles): *quid facis Aeacide? non sunt tua munera lanae*; Fast. 2.386 (Teacher to Amulius plotting to kill the twins): *quid facis? ex istis Romulus alter erit*. Of the 28 examples in classical Latin, 17 are in Ovid.

120   Commentary

71–2. quid facis, infelix? perdis bona uota puellae.
   tende, precor, ualida lora sinistra manu.

71. Cf. the Teacher's melodramatic apostrophe to Cephalus as he kills his wife (*Ars* 3.735–6): *quid facis, infelix? non est fera, supprime tela! | me miserum! iaculo fixa puella tuo est.*

quid facis?: Repetition underlines the seducer's incredulity and frustration.

infelix: While in *Aeneid* Virgil uses this adjective in deeply tragic contexts (e.g. Priam: 3.50; Dido: 1.749, 4.68, 450, 529, 596, 6.456), in *Amores* Ovid uses it humorously (e.g. 2.5.53 [of a lover fearing that his rival is receiving equally sweet kisses], 2.6.20 [of a dead parrot], 2.9.39 [of a man who can sleep all night], 2.19.53 [of a lover who is not deprived of his girlfriend's company]).

72. tende…lora sinistra: The driver is urged to pull on the left-hand reins because, as is clear from Manilius' (5.76–84) and Silius' descriptions of chariot races (16.302–456), the turning-point lay to the left. Here is Silius' praise of a horse named Pelorus (16.360–1): *non umquam effusum sinuabat deuius axem, | sed laeuo interior stringebat tramite metam.* Cf. Gyas' advice to Menoetes in Virgil's boat race (*A.* 5.163): *litus ama et laeua stringat sine palmula cautes.* Humphrey (1986: 5) notes that turning in an anticlockwise direction was universal in Greco-Roman chariot racing.

73–4. fauimus ignauo. sed enim reuocate, Quirites,
   et date iactatis undique signa togis.

73. fauimus: For *faueo* in this poem see above on 2.

ignauo: While love poets sometimes revel in the charge of being *ignauus* (Prop. 3.11.3, *Am.* 1.15.1, 2.18.3), here it is used as a term of disapproval.

reuocate: Humphrey (1986: 156) notes that it was customary 'to recall the teams after a false start'. Here, however, the seducer seems to want the race restarted because of the incompetence of his girlfriend's preferred charioteer.

Quirites: This formal term for addressing Roman citizens occurs most frequently in speeches made before the assembly (e.g. Cic. *Man., Agr., Rab. Perd., Catil.* 2 and 3, *Phil.* 4 and 6; *Met.* 15.600). Ovid uses it in connection with Circus games at *Fast.* 5.597: *sollemnes ludos Circo celebrate, Quirites.* Here this form of address is, as Fantham (1998: 129) notes, 'a poetic fantasy'. For *Quirites* in the singular see below on 3.14.9.

74. iactatis…togis: For audience members at the games waving togas see Mart. 13.99: *delicium paruo donabis dorcada nato: | iactatis solet hanc mittere turba togis.*

75–6. en reuocant. ac ne turbet toga mota capillos,
   in nostros abdas te licet usque sinus.

The couplet begins abruptly, opening with a vivid *en* and then offering an unexpected sense pause in the second foot. The speaker, however, recovers quickly and turns the situation to his advantage.

75. en: See above on line 26.

ac ne: Munari and Kenney (1) print *at, ne*, while McKeown, Kenney (2) and Ramirez de Verger read *ac ne*. The principal manuscripts offer different readings: P has *agne*, but with the correction *c* written above the *g*; S has *et ne*; while Y has *agne* with the correction *et ne* superscript. Goold (1965: 47) argued persuasively for *ac ne*: 'A sense-pause after the second foot followed by a monosyllable occurs only twice in Ovid, at *Fast.* 6.443 and *Her.* 12.89, in each of which instances the monosyllable is the proclitic *et*.... Instead of the adversative *at*, read the continuative *ac*, which coalesces with *ne* to form a metrical word-group'.

76. sinus: While this could refer to garment folds (*OLD* 1, 4; as at 3.1.56), it seems more likely that *sinus* here means 'embrace' (*OLD* 2b), i.e. the seducer offers to put his arms around the girl with the 'unselfish' aim of protecting her from the breeze. Cf. *Am.* 2.12.2: *in nostro est ecce Corinna sinu*, *Her.* 15.95: *huc ades inque sinus, formose, relabere nostros*. For the discussion of the ambiguity of *sinus* see below on 3.8.34.

77–8. iamque patent iterum reserato carcere postes,
   euolat admissis discolor agmen equis.
The crowd's protest is quickly successful and the race begins again.

77. carcere: On the starting-gate see above on 9.

78. For this verbal pattern (VabBA) see above on 3.1.11.

discolor: Refers to the different colours worn by teams of charioteers. Tertullian (*De spect.* 9) claims that the original teams were 'white and red' (*albus et russeus*) and that 'green' (*prasinum*) and 'blue' (*uenetum*) were added later. Earlier writers confirm some of these details. Suetonius tells us that Caligula was devoted to the 'green faction' (*prasinae factioni* 55.2) and Vitellius to the 'blue' (*uenetae* 7.1). For the 'reds' and the 'whites' see Plin. *Nat.* 7.186, 8.160.

79–80. nunc saltem supera spatioque insurge patenti:
   sint mea, sint dominae fac rata uota meae.
The speaker now shifts from description of the restarted race, to encouragement of the driver and his twin hopes for success.

79. Alliteration of *s* is marked in this line, perhaps to convey the excitement of racing in the hexameter, perhaps to reinforce the sound of repeated *sint* in the pentameter.

80. For similarly structured lines see 3.13.36: *sint mihi, sint populo semper amica suo* and *Ars* 1.518: *sit coma, sit trita barba resecta manu*.

dominae...meae: For the connotations of *domina* see above on 18. Here it implies that the seducer will be successful.

81–2. sunt dominae rata uota meae, mea uota supersunt.
 ille tenet palmam, palma petenda mea est.
This is a superbly constructed couplet involving repetition, chiasmus, and parallelism: repetition of key words from the preceding pentameter (*dominae...rata uota meae*), chiasmus (*uota meae, mea uota*) in the hexameter, and parallelism built around the main caesura in the pentameter. The hexameter even begins and ends with *sunt*, while the whole couplet is framed by forms of *esse*.

81. Like lines 1, 11, and 55, this hexameter is wholly dactylic. Here perhaps it reflects the seducer's smooth confidence in his own success. For the rarity of the third-foot weak caesura (*uōtă // mĕ*) in Ovid's erotic works see above on 63 and below on 3.9.15.

82. palmam, palma: Often awarded to competition winners, the 'palm' is sometimes equivalent to 'victory'. *TLL* 146.73–147.10 lists some notable examples, including Catul. 62.11, Prop. 4.1.139–40, *Am.* 2.5.12, 3.14.47. Triple alliteration of *p* underlines the speaker's focus on both equestrian and, more importantly, sexual victory. For repetition which frames the main caesura see above on 32.

mea est: The principal manuscripts divide between reading *mea* (PY) and *mihi* (S). Both are syntactically acceptable. The line's assonance (*palmam, palma petenda*), however, makes *mea (e)st* more attractive than *mihi (e)st*.

83–4. risit et argutis quiddam promisit ocellis.
 hoc satis est, alio cetera redde loco.
Who speaks these lines? The would-be seducer or an external Ovidian narrator? Munari places lines 1–82 in quotation marks, treating the final two lines as narratorial comment. Kenney, Showerman and Goold, and Ramirez de Verger place lines 1–82 and line 84 in quotation marks, treating only line 83 as external comment, while McKeown and the two best English translators, Lee and Green, use no quotation marks and leave it to the reader to decide.

At this point it is important to remember, as Feeney (2011: 50–1, 62–3) points out, that (a) classical Latin texts lacked modern punctuation, including quotation marks, and (b) Roman writers used words like *inquit* (e.g. 3.9.55) and *dixerat* (3.5.45, 3.6.67) to mark the beginnings and ends of speeches. There are no such markers here. Ovid uses words like *hactenus* (3.1.31) and *desierat* (3.1.61), and phrases like *uox erat in cursu* (1.8.109), *sic ego* (3.5.33), and *haec ego* (2.5.33) to indicate a shift from speech to narrative.

Why is this important? If quotation marks are inserted around lines 1–82 and line 84 (or lines 1–82 à la Munari) line 83 becomes a stage direction guiding the reader to a particular interpretation: the seducer has succeeded and the girl has consented. The text, however, is open to another possibility: the girl's agreement may be the product of the seducer's imagination. Ovid regularly highlights the ability of men to interpret women's seeming consent in their own interests e.g. *Am.* 1.13.47 (a lover and Aurora): *iurgia finieram. scires audisse: rubebat*; *Met.* 1.566–7 (Apollo and Daphne): *factis modo laurea ramis | adnuit utque caput uisa est agitasse cacumen, Fast.* 2.846 (Lucretia and Brutus): *uisaque concussa dicta probare coma*. This is an issue that readers should be left to decide for themselves. For further discussion see Henderson (2002: 51–2) and Morwood et al. (2011: 14–21).

83. argutis…ocellis: Boyd (1997: 204 n. 1) notes a connection with the next poem (3.3.9): *argutos habuit: radiant ut sidus ocelli*.

84. cetera: For the use of *cetera* to avoid sexual explicitness see above on 35.

3.3: MY GIRLFRIEND LIED

This poem's premise, that the gods are indifferent to lovers' perjuries, was to find its most famous expression at *Ars* 1.633: *Iuppiter ex alto periuria ridet amantum* ('From on high Jupiter laughs at lovers' lies').[1] In fact, however, it had long been commonplace. In *Catalogue of Women*, for example, Hesiod had claimed (fr. 73 Most [2018]): ἐκ τοῦ δ' ὅρκον ἔθηκεν ἀποίνιμον ἀνθρώποισι | νοσφιδίων ἔργων πέρι Κύπριδος ('From that time on he [Zeus] made an oath free of punishment for human beings if it concerned Aphrodite's clandestine deeds'). Characters in Plato make similar statements (*Symp.* 183b, *Phlb.* 65c) and Callimachus had written an epigram on the subject (*AP* 5.6):

> Callignotus swore to Ionis that he would never have a boyfriend or girlfriend above her.
> He swore. But they speak the truth who say that lovers' oaths do not reach the ears of the immortals.
> Now he's hot with fire for a male and, as of the Megarians, there is no account or reckoning for his poor bride.

The Tibullan lover asserts its truth (1.4.23–4): *uetuit pater ipse ualere, | iurasset cupide quidquid ineptus amor* ('the father himself denied validity to whatever foolish love has rashly sworn'), while the Propertian lover has reservations

---

[1] Cf. Juliet's words in Shakespeare's *Romeo and Juliet* 2.2.92–3: 'At lovers' perjuries | They say Jove laughs'. For the same thought less memorably expressed see *Rem.* 687–8: *at tu nec uoces (quid enim fallacius illis?) | crede, nec aeternos pondus habere deos* ('But do not suppose that words [for what is more deceptive than them?] or the eternal gods have weight'). See also 2.8.19–20 (to Venus): *tu, dea, tu iubeas animi periuria puri | Carpathium tepidos per mare ferre Notos* ('Goddess, order the warm south winds to carry a pure heart's perjuries over the Carpathian sea'), [Tib.] 3.6.49–50: *nulla fides inerit: periuria ridet amantum | Iuppiter et uentos irrita ferre iubet* ('There will be no good faith in her: Jupiter laughs at lovers' perjuries and tells the winds to carry them off as useless').

(2.16.47–8): *non semper placidus periuros ridet amantes | Iuppiter* ('Jupiter does not always smile indulgently at perjured lovers').[2] It was Horace, however, who wrote the most important poem on the subject before Ovid. His treatment is far from commonplace (*Carm.* 2.8):[3]

> If any punishment for perjury had ever harmed you, Barine, if you became black-toothed or uglier by one fingernail,
> I would believe: but just when you pledge your treacherous head by vows, you shine out far more beautiful and emerge as a public concern to young men.
> It profits you to swear falsely by your mother's concealed ashes and night's silent constellations along with all of heaven and the gods free from chill death.
> Venus herself laughs at this, I say, the guileless Nymphs laugh and brutal Cupid who always sharpens his burning arrows with a blood-stained whetstone.
> Throw in the fact that all the young are growing up for your benefit, a fresh band of slaves grows up, nor do their predecessors, despite their many threats, abandon their impious mistress's home.
> Mothers are afraid of you for their calves' sake, stingy old men are afraid of you, and wretched brides, virgins not long ago, lest your scent detain their husbands.

As third-century commentator Porphyrio noted, this ode's opening is strikingly dramatic (*scaenicum principium*). Horace gives us part of a continuing conversation, a dramatic monologue responding to a woman's promise which the speaker thinks is false. Even though a variation of the Hesiodic cliché (here it is Venus who is indifferent to perjury, not Zeus or Jupiter [cf. *Am.* 1.8.86: *commodat in lusus numina surda Venus*]) constitutes the poem's central idea, the idea takes life by being embedded in a rant addressed to a particular woman, by being combined with other striking ideas (perjury does not harm Barine's beauty, it actually makes her more attractive) and insults (she invokes her mother's ashes when she lies), and by emphasizing the dangers that Barine poses not only to young men but to society in general.

When we turn to 3.3, we find another histrionic opening, a like emphasis on the lying girlfriend's continuing beauty, and a similar assertion of divine indifference to lovers' perjuries (11–12). In other respects, however, 3.3 could hardly be more different. First, this is not a dramatic monologue but a soliloquy: it is not until the final couplet that the speaker turns from absorption in his own thoughts to addressing his delinquent, unnamed girlfriend. Second, it raises philosophical or quasi-philosophical problems. When the Horatian speaker raises the question of belief (*crederem* 5), he means faith in what Barine says. Here, by contrast, his

---

[2] Cf. Prop. 1.15.25–6: *desine iam reuocare tuis periuria uerbis, | Cynthia, et oblitos parce mouere deos* ('Stop reminding me of your perjuries with your words, Cynthia, and refrain from provoking the forgetful gods').

[3] For the connection between *Carm.* 2.8 and love elegy see Harrison (2017: 112).

girlfriend's perjury prompts Ovid's speaker ('the boyfriend') to question belief in the gods' existence (*esse deos*......*crede* 1) and to reflect upon the different ways in which the gods treat men and women (25–40). Third, Ovid's poem develops its case at twice the length, with its primary pleasure coming not from the vehemence of the speaker's attack, but from the ingenuity of his arguments and the brilliance of their presentation. Fourth, where Horace's speaker ends with a seemingly serious warning of the fear provoked by Barine's behaviour (21–4), Ovid's actually retracts his own argument and claims that he shares the gods' indifference to a girlfriend's falsehoods. While both *Carm.* 2.8 and *Am.* 3.3 treat the same well-worn proposition with glittering wit and humour, they employ different means to different ends.

Secondary literature: Frécaut (1972: 187–8); Du Quesnay (1973: 13–15); Boyd (1997: 41–6); Keith (1994); Bretzigheimer (2001: 201–3, 215–20); Zimmermann Damer (2019).

1–2. Esse deos, i, crede. fidem iurata fefellit,
  et facies illi, quae fuit ante, manet.
The opening of 3.3 is exceptionally dramatic: a brief command is followed by a powerful assertion which completes the hexameter, and is then combined with a quieter expression of surprise in the pentameter. For a similarly abrupt start to an elegy see Prop. 1.17.1–2: *et merito, quoniam potui fugisse puellam,* | *nunc ego desertas alloquar alcyonas* (with Fedeli [1980: 401], who notes that beginning '*ex abrupto*' underlines the speaker's excitement).

1. Esse: This is a surprising choice for a poem's first word. The only earlier example is *Am.* 1.2 where it expresses puzzlement (1.2.1): *esse quid hoc dicam*. For similar emphasis on initial *esse* see *Pont.* 4.13.27, 29, 31.

Esse deos...crede: Belief that gods sustain the world's moral ordering is conventional in Greco-Roman thinking. For Ovidian examples of the denial of the gods' existence as a response to injustice, see the reaction to Tibullus' death (3.9.35–6): *cum rapiunt mala fata bonos (ignoscite fasso)* | *sollicitor nullos esse putare deos* and Hercules' response to his persecutor's health (*Met.* 9.203–4): *at ualet Eurystheus!* *et sunt qui credere possint* | *esse deos*. Also notable in poetry are Prop. 1.6.8: *et queritur nullos esse relicta deos*, Luc. 3.447–8, Sen. *Med.* 1027: *testare nullos esse, qua ueheris, deos, Thy.* 789–884.

The principal gods of both Greeks and Romans had responsibility for ensuring that oaths were observed, with Zeus having the title Horkios ('protector of oaths' e.g. Soph. *Phil.* 1324, Eur. *Hipp.* 1025; for the statue of Zeus Horkios at Olympia see Paus. 5.24.9), and with Fides having a temple next to that of Jupiter on the Capitol (Cic. *Off.* 3.104; Enn. fr. 165 Goldberg and Manuwald [2]): *nam praeclare Ennius: 'O Fides alma apta pinnis et ius iurandum Iouis'. qui ius igitur iurandum uiolat, is fidem uiolat, quam in Capitolio uicinam Iouis optimi maximi...maiores nostri uoluerunt.*

126   Commentary

i: Ovid uses this form of *ire* more than any other Latin poet. While he sometimes uses it to state a simple command (e.g. *Rem.* 214 [to an unhappy lover]: *i procul et longas carpere perge uias*, *Met.* 2.464 [Diana to Callisto]: *i procul hinc…nec sacros pollue fontis*, *Tr.* 1.1.57 [to his book]: *tu tamen i pro me*), he typically uses it to express sarcasm e.g. *Am.* 1.7.35 (to himself after striking his girlfriend): *i nunc, magnificos uictor molire triumphos* (with McKeown [1989: ad loc.]), *Her.* 3.26 (Briseis to Achilles): *i nunc et cupidi nomen amantis habe*, 4.127, 9.105, 12.204, 17.57, *Ars* 2.222, 2.635, *Met.* 12.475, *Pont.* 1.3.61, 4.3.53. Cf. *A.* 4.381 (Dido to Aeneas): *i, sequere Italiam uentis*, 9.634 (Ascanius to slain Remulus): *i, uerbis uirtutem illude superbis*. See also the Pompeian graffito (*CIL* 4.5296.3): *i nunc, uentis tua gaudia, pupula, crede.* For text, translation, and discussion of this poem see Graverini (2012–13; 2019), and Milnor (2014: 191–232).

fidem…fefellit: The phrase *fidem fallere* has both moral and legal overtones. See, for example, Cicero's praise of Regulus for refusing to break his oath to the Carthaginians (*Off.* 1.39): *ad supplicium redire maluit quam fidem hosti datam fallere*, Polynices' objection to being exiled (Sen. *Phoen.* 588–9): *quid paterer aliud, si fefellissem fidem? | si peierassem?*, and the observation in Justinian's *Digest* (13.5.1): *graue est fidem fallere.*

iurata fefellit: Ovid's Teacher recycles these words, when advising how to fall out of love: (*Rem.* 303): *sic mihi iurauit, sic me iurata fefellit.*

2. et: The conjunction here has adversative force, i.e. it is equivalent to 'and yet'. See *TLL et* 893.4–39. Other Ovidian examples are *Her.* 5.133–4: *at manet Oenone fallenti casta marito | et poteras falli legibus ipse tuis* and *Pont.* 1.5.37–8: *saucius eiurat pugnam gladiator, et idem | immemor antiqui uulneris arma capit.*

facies…fuit: Alliteration of *f* echoes the alliteration in the previous line and draws attention to the connection between appearance (*facies*) and falsehood (*fidem fefellit*).

quae fuit…manet: Surprise at continuity, based on the juxtaposition of *fuit* and *manet*, is exploited here (and at line 8 below) for comic effect. In *Tristia* continuity underlines the Exile's tragic circumstances (*Tr.* 4.6.6, 4.10.30, 5.2.8).

3–4. quam longos habuit nondum periura capillos,
    tam longos, postquam numina laesit, habet.
The couplet's use of verbal repetition (*quam longos habuit | tam longos…habet*) and structural parallelism (with corresponding phrases *nondum periura* and *postquam numina laesit* centrally placed) makes for straightforward statement and perhaps underlines the boyfriend's naïve surprise.

4. numina laesit: This expression is used of the different ways in which it is possible to give serious offence to the gods: by neglect (e.g. *Met.* 4.8), by accident

(*Tr.* 2.108), or by crimes of various kinds (e.g. *A.* 1.8: *quo numine laeso*, 2.183), but especially perjury (e.g. *Her.* 2.43, 20.100; Tib. 1.9.6; Hor. *Epod.* 15.3–4).

5–6. candida candorem roseo suffusa rubore
 ante fuit: niueo lucet in ore rubor.
  These lines make essentially the same point as the previous couplet but by different means, using enjambment rather than end-stopped lines and elaborate verbal play. The origin of poetic interest in the red–white contrast probably lies in the Homeric simile (*Il.* 4.141–6) comparing Menelaus' bloodstained thigh to ivory stained with purple. Among Roman poets it is used to suggest an embarrassed blush e.g. *A.* 12.64–9 (with Tarrant [2012: ad loc.]) or, as here, beauty e.g. Prop. 2.3.11–12 (on his girlfriend's loveliness; with Fedeli [2005: 128–32]): *ut Maeotica nix minio si certet Hibero* | *utque rosae puro lacte natant folia*; *Her.* 21.217 (illness robs Cydippe of her looks): *candida nec mixto sublucent ora rubore*; *Met.* 3.423 (Narcissus admires himself): *et in niueo mixtum candore ruborem*; 10.594–5 (Atalanta running): *inque puellari corpus candore ruborem* | *traxerat*.

  For other examples of what we may call vertical polyptoton (*rubore* / *rubor*) see *Her.* 20.31–2 (*dolosus* / *dolus*), *Met.* 15.186–7 (*noctes* / *nocti*), 15.343–4 (*spiramenta* / *spirandi*), *Fast.* 2.778–9 (*amor* / *amoris*), 2.805–6 (*minisque* / *minis*), *Tr.* 5.7.11–12 (*Getasque* / *Getis*), *Pont.* 1.7.5–6 (*tuorum* / *tuus*), 3.6.59–60 (*amare* / *ama*).

5. This line is notable for its alliteration and polyptoton: *candida candorem*; *roseo…rubore*.

candida candorem: For similar verbal play on forms of *candidus* (as well as words for 'black') see *Met.* 11.314: *candida de nigris et de candentibus atra*.

candida…rubore: For the opposition between *candor* and *rubor* (and cognates) in erotic contexts see e.g. *Her.* 21.217, *Met.* 3.423, 10.594–5 (all quoted above); *Ars* 3.199–200, *Met.* 3.491, 4.332, [Tib.] 3.4.29–34.

candorem: This is perhaps best described as a 'retained' accusative dependent on *suffusa*, a passive participle with middle force. For discussion see Tarrant (2012: 106, on *A.* 12.64–5) and Pinkster (1.242).

roseo suffusa: Combines elements from Virgil's description of Lavinia's blush (*A.* 12.65: *flagrantis per*fusa *genas*; 68–9: *lilia multa* | *alba* rosa).

roseo…rubore: Cf. the description of Narcissus' breast (*Met.* 3.482): *pectora traxerunt roseum percussa ruborem*.

6. For *niueus* and *rubor* (and cognates) used to suggest erotic beauty see *Her.* 20.119–20: *seruentur uultus ad nostra incendia nati*, | *quique subest niueo lenis in ore rubor*, *Met.* 3.423 (quoted above), Sen. *Med.* 99–100 (of Jason's bride): *ostro sic niueus puniceo color* | *perfusus rubuit*, Stat. *Silu.* 1.2.244–5 (of Lavinia and Turnus).

7–8. pes erat exiguus: pedis est artissima forma.
   longa decensque fuit: longa decensque manet.
For this third example of continuity between past and present, Ovid employs the simplest of syntax, repetition (*pes erat…pedis est* | *longa decensque…longa decensque*), and formal balance, with each line consisting of two self-contained clauses separated by the main caesura. Wills (1996: 415) classifies line 8 as consisting of 'parallel half lines'. The same is effectively true of line 7, with *artissima forma* being equivalent to *exiguus*.

7. pes…exiguus: For the praiseworthiness of the tiny foot see Ars 1.621–2: *nec faciem, nec te pigeat laudare capillos | et teretes digitos exiguumque pedem.*

8. longa: For the attractiveness of tall women see e.g. Hom. Od. 18.248–9 (Eurymachus addressing Penelope): 'You surpass women in form and stature (*megethos*) and well balanced mind within'; Catul. 86.1–2: *Quintia formosa est multis. mihi candida, longa, | recta est*; Prop. 2.2.5–6 (describing his girlfriend, presumably Cynthia): *fulua coma est longaeque manus, et maxima toto | corpore, et incedit uel Ioue digna soror*; Am. 2.4.33–4: *tu, quia tam longa es, ueteres heroidas aequas | et potes in toto multa iacere toro.* (Note, however, that the lover of 2.4 likes short girls too [35]: *haec habilis breuitate sua est.*)

9–10. argutos habuit: radiant ut sidus ocelli,
   per quos mentita est perfida saepe mihi.
This fourth example is the most important, for it is by her eyes that the speaker's girlfriend swore. Here the syntax is slightly more complex than in the previous couplet, with the reader needing to supply *ocellos* as object of *habuit* from *ocelli* in the following clause.

9. argutos [ocellos]: Boyd (1997: 204 n. 1) notes that Ovid used similar language at 3.2.83: *argutis quiddam promisit ocellis.*

radiant ut sidus ocelli: As Boyd (1997: 44) observes, the comparison links 3.3 with 2.16, another poem in which the lover accuses his girlfriend of perjury (43–4): *at mihi te comitem iuraras usque futuram: | per me perque oculos, sidera nostra, tuos.* For the image see e.g. Prop. 2.3.14: *non oculi, geminae, sidera nostra, faces*; Her. 20.55–6: *tu facis hoc oculique tui, quibus ignea cedunt | sidera,* Met. 1.498–9 (Apollo and Daphne): *uidet igne micantes | sideribus similes oculos,* 3.420 (of Narcissus): *geminum, sua lumina, sidus*; Sen. Phaed. 1174 (Theseus to Hippolytus): *oculique nostrum sidus.*

10. per quos mentita est: For the girlfriend swearing by her eyes (in addition to 2.16.44, quoted above) see Prop. 1.15.33–6, [Tib.] 3.6.47–8.

perfida: Links the girlfriend with Horace's Barine (Carm. 2.8.6): *perfidum… caput* and Propertius' Cynthia 1.15.33–4: *ocelli, | per quos saepe mihi credita perfidia est.*

Commentary, 3.7-15

11-12. scilicet aeterni falsum iurare puellis
   di quoque concedunt, formaque numen habet.
The boyfriend rounds off this phase of the argument by concluding that if the gods fail to punish this case of perjury, they must be tolerant of women telling lies.

11. scilicet: As often (*OLD* 4), *scilicet* underlines a speaker's disapproval of a state of affairs.

aeterni: The principal manuscripts (P, S, and Y) offer *aeterno* (corrected to *aeterni* in Y). Kenney (1958: 64) notes, however, that Ovid does not employ this form of the adverb (he uses *aeternum* at *Met.* 6.369 and *Tr.* 5.3.41) and that, as Némethy (1907: 228) had pointed out, *aeterni* alludes to Horace's description of the gods at *Carm.* 2.8.11-12: *gelidaque diuos | morte carentis*.

falsum iurare: For the expression see Cic. *Off.* 3.108.2: *falsum iurare periurare est*; *Ars* 1.635: *per Styga Iunoni falsum iurare solebat | Iuppiter*, *Met.* 13.558-9: *spectat... | falsaque iurantem*.

12. formaque numen habet: Perhaps recalls the Tibullan lover's reaction to his boyfriend's lies (1.9.5-6): *aequum est impune licere | numina formosis laedere uestra semel*, a sentiment that foreshadows this poem's conclusion. For beauty's power see *Met.* 10.573 (of Atalanta): *tanta potentia formae est*. Here, however, beauty's power is specifically divine.

13-14. perque suos illam nuper iurasse recordor
   perque meos oculos: en doluere mei.
Use of anaphora (*perque suos / perque meos*) combined with the postponement of *oculos* makes for a powerful couplet and underlines the strength of the boyfriend's feelings. Ovid's Briseis is even more emphatic in her use of anaphora when swearing that she has not had sex with Agamemnon (*Her.* 3.105-10: *perque trium fortes animas...perque tuum nostrumque caput...perque tuos enses...iuro*). Cf. 3.11.47-8; *Pont.* 2.8.29, 31, 33; Sen. *Phaed.* 869-70.

13. nuper: The adverb drags us back from generalization to the current situation.

14. en doluere mei: *en* introduces a moment of self-dramatization. Cf. 1.2.19: *en ego confiteor*; 1.8.31: *en aspice*; 3.2.26: *uel digitis en ego tollo meis*; 3.2.75: *en reuocant*. These three words underline the injustice of the situation, for while the girlfriend swore by her eyes and his, only his are in pain.

15-16. dicite, di, si uos impune fefellerat illa,
   alterius meriti cur ego damna tuli?
The boyfriend now turns attention from himself to the gods and poses pertinent questions in this and the next three couplets. Alliteration (especially of *d, f*, and *l*) and assonance (note the frequency of *i*) perhaps reinforce the speaker's anger at divine injustice.

15. dicite, di: Alliteration and assonance, especially the repetition of initial *di*, make the speaker's demand particularly emphatic.

16: alterius meriti…damna: For the genitive used of the cause of the loss, rather than what is lost see e.g. *Am*. 1.13.20: *unius ut uerbi grandia damna ferant*; *Ars* 1.186, 2.174, *Rem*. 102.

17-18. at non inuidiae uobis Cepheia uirgo est,
   pro male formosa iussa parente mori?
The mythological example of 'Cepheus' virgin daughter' illustrates the point exactly: Neptune punishes innocent Andromeda because her mother, Cassiope, had boasted that she was more beautiful than the Nereids (Apollod. 2.43; at *Met*. 4.670-1 it is 'unjust Ammon' [i.e. Jupiter in Egyptian guise] who exposes the girl to the sea monster). The gods need to understand that punishing the wrong person exposes them to hostility and resentment.

   Although Goold (1965: 48) reckons that the mythology is 'irrelevant' and that 'the couplet was fabricated by a pasticheur', he prints it without comment in Showerman and Goold.

17. at non: Goold, Kenney, and Ramirez de Verger (2) print *an non*, found in some minor manuscripts. S and Y read *at non*, while P offers *ad non*. *at non* yields excellent sense and should not be altered. Ovid never uses *an non*. In late Republican and Augustan poetry *an non* is used only twice and only in alternative indirect questions (Catul. 17.22, Hor. S. 2.3.260).

inuidiae: Use of this noun in the predicative dative is rare. See, however, *Am*. 3.12.14 and *Met*. 10.731, as well as Cic. *Ver*. 2.3.144, Sal. *Jug*. 73.4, Prop. 1.12.9. For the predicative dative more generally see Woodcock (§68) and Pinkster (1.778).

18. male formosa: While *male* sometimes negates the adjective it modifies (e.g. Tib. 1.10.51: *male sobrius*, i.e. 'drunk', A. 4.8: *male sana*, i.e. 'distraught' [*OLD* 5]), here it creates a paradox: 'beautiful to ill effect' (*OLD* 7).

19-20. non satis est, quod uos habui sine pondere testes
   et mecum lusos ridet inulta deos?
Failure to punish perjury not only exposes the gods to hatred, but renders them useless. What is the point of invoking them as witnesses?

19. sine pondere testes: For *pondus* in a quasi-legal sense (*OLD* 6) see 3.12.19-20, *Tr*. 1.6.17-18, *Pont*. 3.9.49-50. Cf. Cic. *Top*. 73.4: *persona autem non qualiscumque est testimoni pondus habet*.

mecum: *cum* is used here as equivalent to *et* (*TLL cum* 1377.42-1378.6), *et* having already been used to link the two clauses.

20. inulta: It is conventional for despisers of the gods to suffer e.g. Virgil's Mezentius (*A*. 7.648), Ovid's Pentheus and Polyphemus (*Met*. 3.514, 13.761),

Seneca's Ajax (*Ag.* 528–38), and Statius' Capaneus (*Theb.* 3.602). The lying girlfriend, however, remains unpunished.

21–2. ut sua per nostram redimat periuria poenam,
   uictima deceptus decipientis ero?
The boyfriend rounds off this phase of the argument with an impressive couplet, remarkable for verbal patterning and alliteration.

21. For this line the speaker adopts the verbal pattern which John Dryden labelled 'golden' (1685: Preface [unnumbered page]: 'that Verse commonly which they call golden, or two Substantives and two Adjectives with a Verb betwixt them to keep the peace'), or, to put it less colourfully, a line consisting of two adjectives, a verb in the centre (or some other significant word), followed by two nouns in the same order as the adjectives (abVAB). For discussion see Wilkinson (1963: 215–17), Conrad (1965: 234–41), and Ross (1969: 132–7). For other examples in *Amores* see 1.3.9, 1.7.25, 1.8.50, 1.9.16, 1.13.10, 2.3.8, 2.6.5 (the centrepiece of three patterned lines in succession: abAVB | abVAB | aVBbA), 2.9.21, 2.14.41, 2.15.17, 2.18.2, 3.6.14, 3.6.52, 3.7.27, 3.7.63, 3.9.43, 3.11.10, 3.12.26. It is the second most frequent verbal pattern in *Amores*.

periuria poenam: Alliteration underlines the expected connection between perjury and punishment. Cf. Hor. *Carm.* 2.8.1–2 *peierati* | *poena* and Tib. 1.9.3–4: *primo periuria celat* | *sera tamen tacitis Poena uenit pedibus*.

22. uictima deceptus decipientis: The use of alliteration and polyptoton underlines the boyfriend's status as victim. Ovid uses similar verbal play to describe Dido's death (*Met.* 14.81): *incubuit ferro deceptaque decipit omnes*. In *Metamorphoses* the narrator works by contrast: she who was deceived now deceives. Here the speaker reinforces: she deceives; he is deceived. For this form of symmetry in which repetition frames the main caesura see on 3.2.32.

23–6. aut sine re nomen deus est frustraque timetur
   et stulta populos credulitate mouet
aut, siquis deus est, teneras amat ille puellas
   nimirum solas omnia posse iubet.
In these two couplets the boyfriend recapitulates the poem's opening: the gods do not exist; and raises a new possibility: the gods are prejudiced in favour of women. He clearly rejects the first proposition and favours the second, with the following 14 lines advancing mythological examples to support this new argument.

23. sine re nomen: The distinction between *res* ('fact', 'reality' OLD 6) and *nomen* ('a mere name' OLD 16) is pervasive in Roman thinking. See e.g. Cic. *Ver.* 2.1.11: *monumenta, quae nomine illorum, re uera populi Romani et erant et habebantur*; *Off.* 1.105.11: *sunt enim quidam homines non re sed nomine*; *Am.* 1.8.3 (the etymology of 'Dipsas'): *ex re nomen habet*. For the emptiness of names see e.g. *A.* 4.324 (Dido): *hoc solum nomen quoniam de coniuge restat?*; *Met.* 14.396: *nec quidquam antiquum Pico nisi nomina restat.*

deus...timetur: McKeown (1987: 48) argues that Ovid here alludes to 'the derivation of *deus* from δέος (*deos*)', citing Servius on *A.* 12.139: 'that which is called *deos* in Greek is called *timor* in Latin, hence the word *deus*, because all religion is characterized by fear'. See also Maltby (1991: 185).

frustraque: The adverb's effect is to undermine the link between Greek *deos* and Latin *deus*: the girlfriend's perjury proves that the gods should not be feared.

24. stulta...credulitate: Unlike the speaker of this poem, the speaker of 3.14 actually prizes a lying girlfriend and prefers to be gullible (29–30): *sine nescius errem, | et liceat stulta credulitate frui.* For the phrase see also *Pont.* 2.4.32.

25. teneras...puellas: For *tener* in elegiac poetry see on 3.1.27.

26. nimirum: This is Némethy's (1907: 229) correction of the manuscripts' *et nimium*. The transmitted text yields awkward sense: 'and he insists that girls alone are excessively all-powerful'. It is noteworthy that editor-translators who retain *et nimium* do not offer literal versions: Bornecque (1930: *trop exclusivement* ['too exclusively']); Showerman and Goold (1977: 'too quick'). Often used ironically, *nimirum* is appropriate because the boyfriend is about to argue a paradoxical case: the gods treat women more favourably than men. Némethy points to Paris' praise of Venus as an appropriate parallel (*Her.* 16.23–4): *illa dedit faciles auras uentosque secundos: | in mare nimirum ius habet orta mari.*

27–8. nobis fatifero Mauors accingitur ense.
    nos petit inuicta Palladis hasta manu.
Use of anaphora in this and the following couplet (*nobis...nos...nobis...in nos*) underlines the boyfriend's identification with the male sex. Although each line makes the same argument, begins with a form of *nos*, and uses a god's name to separate an adjective from the noun it qualifies, Ovid achieves variation by placing the verbs in different positions, second last in 27 and second in 28.

27. The argument that Mars attacks only men gains plausibility from the fact that he is a god of the battlefield, a place usually reserved for males.

fatifero...ense: The language is drawn from epic, the most masculine of genres, with *fatifer*, a Virgilian coinage, being used only in epic poetry (*A.* 8.621: *fatiferumque ensem*, 9.631: *fatifer arcus*; *Met.* 6.251: *fatifero...ferro*, 12.492: *ensem fatiferum*; Sil. 1.641, 2.116).

accingitur ense: Again the language is characteristic of epic poetry: *A.* 7.640: *fidoque accingitur ense*, 11.849: *laterique accinxerat ensem*; *Met.* 6.551: *quo fuit accinctus, uagina liberat ensem*; Stat. *Theb.* 1.428–9: *et accinctos lateri (sic ira ferebat) | nudassent enses*; VF 5.513: *accinctum gemmis fulgentibus ensem*.

Mauors: This form of Mars' name is archaic and occurs mostly in epic e.g. Enn. *Ann.* 1.99 Goldberg and Manuwald (1), *A.* 6.872 (and six more times); Luc. 7.569 (and one more time); Sil. 2.365 (and 34 more times); Stat. *Theb.* 2.718 (and 25 more times); VF 5.667 (and seven more times).

28. While Minerva resembles Mars in being a warrior god, it is not true that she attacks only men. For her assault on Arachne see *Met.* 6.129–45.

hasta: In the visual arts Minerva is regularly represented as holding a spear, as she herself acknowledges (*Met.* 6.78): *at sibi dat clipeum, dat acutae cuspidis hastam.* Her best-known attack on a man, however, on Ajax son of Oileus, involves Jupiter's thunderbolts (Sen. *Ag.* 528–43).

29–30. nobis flexibiles curuantur Apollinis arcus.
 in nos alta Iouis dextera fulmen habet.
These lines present the same argument and embody the same verbal pattern as those in the previous couplet: with anaphora of forms of *nos* combined with a god's name separating an adjective from the noun it qualifies. As before, Ovid effects variation by the artful placing of the verb, in the centre in line 29, at the end in 30.

29. While the bow is Apollo's characteristic weapon (his standard epithets in the *Iliad* include *hekēbolos* ['far-shooting'] and *argurotoxos* ['with the silver bow']), it is not true that men are his only victims. See, for example, his killing of pregnant Coronis (*Met.* 2.603–5).

flexibiles: While common in prose (Cicero, Seneca, Quintilian), this adjective is rare in poetry. See Laber. 160, Maec. 188 (Hollis), *Laus Pis.* 53.

30. The association between Zeus/Jupiter and the thunderbolt is pervasive in Greco-Roman thinking. The author of the *Priapea* is explicit on the point (20.1–2): *fulmina sub Ioue sunt; Neptuni fuscina telum; | ense potens Mars est; hasta, Minerua, tua est.*

While it may be true that Jupiter does not use the thunderbolt against women, he does kill women and men indiscriminately when he visits a deluge upon the earth (*Met.* 1.253–312) and destroys the neighbours of Baucis and Philemon (*Met.* 8.696–8).

31–2. formosas superi metuunt offendere laesi
 atque ultro, quae se non timuere, timent.
From these four examples the boyfriend concludes that the gods are afraid of lovely girls.

31. This line is superbly structured, with the main verb placed in the centre and flanked by two substantives on the one side and two other verb forms on the other.

formosas superi: The poet uses word order to represent the relationship between gods and lovely girls: they confront each other on the page.

offendere laesi: While the meanings of these verbs overlap, there is an important difference: *laedo* is used of giving serious offence (see above on 4), while *offendo* can be used of triggering a minor upset e.g. *Ars* 3.211 (a girl's cosmetics): *quem non offendat toto faex illita uultu*; Hor. *Ars* 351–2 (a poem's blemishes): *uerum ubi plura nitent in carmine, non ego paucis | offendar maculis*; Mart. 1.53.10 (a magpie among nightingales): *improba Cecropias offendit pica querelas*. The difference underlines a power imbalance: though seriously offended, the gods refuse to upset a pretty girl.

32. timuere, timent: Juxtaposition of two forms of *timere* highlights an important distinction between gods and girls: the former are afraid, the latter not.

se: As usual, the reflexive pronoun in the subordinate clause refers to the subject of the main verb. For discussion see Woodcock (§36) and Pinkster (1.1124).

33–4. et quisquam pia tura focis imponere curat?
  certe plus animi debet inesse uiris.
Having asserted that the gods are prejudiced against men, the speaker questions whether they deserve to be worshipped.

33. Incense-burning is of course a standard part of Roman religious ritual. In Tibullus it is essential to birthday celebrations (2.2.3) *urantur pia tura focis*. Ovid's beautician recognizes its value (*Med.* 83): *quamuis tura deos irataque numina placent* and even his sceptical Teacher recommends the practice (*Ars* 1.637–8): *expedit esse deos, et, ut expedit, esse putemus. | dentur in antiquos tura merumque focos.* See also 2.13.23: *ipse ego tura dabo fumosis candidus aris*, 3.13.9: *uotiuaque tura piorum.*

While the speaker's questioning of the value of burning incense seems to echo a Tibullan sentiment (1.8.70: *nec prodest sanctis tura dedisse focis*), there is an important difference: in Tibullus it is a woman's arrogance that is criticized, not the gods. Juno poses the same question from a divine perspective (*A.* 1.48–9): *et quisquam numen Iunonis adorat | praeterea aut supplex aris imponet honorem?*

quisquam: The pentameter suggests that *quisquam* here really means not 'anyone' but 'any man'.

pia tura: The adjective is regularly used of objects associated with religious worship, including blood, grain, knives, and garlands (*TLL pius* 2239.46–64). For *pia tura* see e.g. Tib. 2.2.3 (quoted above); *Her.* 21.7, *Met.* 11.577, *Tr.* 2.59; Luc. 9.996.

34. If, as we expect, the pentameter develops the thought expressed in the hexameter, the implication is that men should be more manly and stop worshipping the gods.

35–6. Iuppiter igne suo lucos iaculatur et arces
  missaque periuras tela ferire uetat.

Commentary, 3.32–8

The argument now switches from criticism of lesser gods (27–30) and sceptical speculation (31–4) to an attack on Jupiter himself (35–40).

35. Recalls Horace's description of Jupiter at *Carm.* 1.2.2–4: *et rubente | dextera sacras iaculatus arces | terruit urbem.*

lucos…et arces: Jupiter actually takes aim at hallowed spaces. In this context *luci* are sacred groves (*OLD* 1; cf. *Am.* 3.13.7–8), while, as in Horace, *arces* refers to the summit of the Capitol, the site of Jupiter's chief temple (Nisbet and Hubbard [1970: 22]).

igne suo: Jupiter's *ignis* is of course the thunderbolt (see line 30 above). *suo* underlines the fact that this is his characteristic weapon. See also *Tr.* 5.3.29–30 (of Capaneus): *quem magna locutum | reppulit a Thebis Iuppiter igne suo.*

36. Whereas Horace's Jupiter terrifies the whole city, Ovid's is concerned to hit only men (30) and to miss female perjurers.

37–8. tot meruere peti: Semele miserabilis arsit.
 officio est illi poena reperta suo.
In this and the following couplet, the boyfriend highlights the absurd injustice of Jupiter's behaviour, pointing out that the only woman whom he destroyed by thunderbolt was Semele. And she was innocent.

37. peti: For *peti* used in this context see *Tr.* 1.1.82: *me reor infesto cum tonat igne peti.*

Semele…arsit: Semele's story is hinted at in Euripides' *Bacchae*. See, for example, the chorus's response to the palace miracle (596–9): 'Do you not see, discern the fire around Semele's sacred tomb here, the fire which once Zeus' thunder-hurling lightning left behind?' For a detailed narrative see *Met.* 3.259–315, especially 308–9: *corpus mortale tumultus | non tulit aetherios donisque iugalibus arsit.*

miserabilis: Underlines the tragedy of Semele's fate. Elsewhere Ovid uses the adjective of Dido (2.18.25, *Fast.* 3.545: *Dido miserabilis*) and her unborn child (*Her.* 7.135: *miserabilis infans*).

38. officio…suo: In this context *officium* is a euphemism for sexual services. See e.g. Prop. 2.22a.23–4: *saepe est experta puella | officium tota nocte ualere meum*; *Am.* 1.10.46: *non manet officio debitor ille tuo*; 3.7.24: *ter Libas officio continuata mea est*. For discussion see Adams (1982: 163–4).

Use of the reflexive adjective without reference to the subject of the sentence (*poena*) emphasizes the injustice of Jupiter's actions. Pinkster explains (1.1132): '*suus* is especially used in this way when it is emphatic, for example in an unexpected situation'. That punishment should be devised for Semele (*illi*) because of her 'services' (*officio* is causal ablative) is certainly unexpected.

Apparently unaware of *officium*'s sexual meaning, Hall (1999: 98) proposed altering *officio* to *obsequio*. This is unnecessary.

poena reperta: The phrase suggests that a particularly cruel punishment was devised to punish Semele. Cf. *Tr.* 2.12: *ingenio est poena reperta meo* (with Ingleheart [2010: ad loc.]), 3.10.78: *haec est in poenam terra reperta meam*, 3.11.51 (the tyrant Phalaris addressing a deviser of torture): *poenae mirande repertor*.

39-40. at si uenturo se subduxisset amanti,
    non pater in Baccho matris haberet opus.
To close this phase of the argument the boyfriend refers to the story, familiar from Euripides' *Bacchae* (88–98), of the birth of Bacchus from the thigh of Zeus. Ovid retells the story in *Metamorphoses* (3.310–12) and *Fasti* (3.715–18). While this version is consistent with Euripides and with Ovid's subsequent accounts, it differs in one important respect: it insists on Semele's agency. Had she chosen to reject Jupiter, Bacchus would not exist.

39. In *Metamorphoses* Semele is presented as a victim of Juno's malevolence and Jupiter's rashness. In *Amores*, her willingness to have a relationship with Jupiter highlights his culpability, while the spondees (SSSS) perhaps underline her responsibility. (For similarly spondaic lines see above on 3.1.57.)

40. pater…matris…opus: Ovid reworks this phrase at *Fast.* 3.718: *expletum patrio corpore matris opus*. Euripides also underlines Zeus' paradoxical role as mother-father to Dionysus (*Bacch.* 526–7): Ἴθι, Διθύραμβ᾽, ἐμὰν ἄρ- | σενα τάνδε βᾶθι νηδύν ('Come, Dithyrambus, enter this male womb of mine').

in: For this use of *in* (*OLD* 42: 'in the matter of') see e.g. 3.6.25, 40; Prop. 1.1.17 (with Fedeli [1980]), 2.18.2, 2.20.11.

41–2. quid queror et toto facio conuicia caelo?
    di quoque habent oculos, di quoque pectus habent.
Having criticized Jupiter for failing to punish female perjurers and for mistreating Semele, the speaker changes tack and decides that if he were a god, he would do the same. Both lines are notable for their alliteration of *c/q*.

41. For alliteration of c/q used to reinforce the sounds of key words see e.g. *Am.* 1.7.21: *sed taciti fecere tamen conuicia uultus*; *Her.* 6.17: *quid queror officium lenti cessasse mariti?*; 9.2: *uictorem uictae succubuisse queror*; *Met.* 14.522: *addidit obscenis conuicia rustica dictis*.

toto…caelo: Alludes to Hor. *Carm.* 2.8.10–11: *toto taciturna noctis | signa cum caelo*.

42. Repetition makes this a formally balanced line with almost identical clauses separated by the main caesura. It falls into Wills's (1996: 415) class of 'parallel half lines' (see above on 7–8).

As we expect, the pentameter develops the thought of the preceding line. We should not abuse the gods, because they are just like us (males): they have eyes for pretty girls and they have feelings.

**43-4. si deus ipse forem, numen sine fraude liceret
femina mendaci falleret ore meum.**
Having suggested that the gods are just like humans, the speaker imagines how he would behave if he were a god. As in lines 1 and 2, alliteration of *f* draws attention to the connection between key terms: *femina*, *fraus* (which often means 'deceit' [*OLD* 4]), and *fallere* (which means 'deceive' [*OLD* 1]).

43. sine fraude: While in this context *sine fraude* must mean 'without harm to oneself, in safety, unscathed' (*OLD* 1), the proximity of words like *mendaci* and *falleret* can only activate the other meaning of *fraus*.

44. mendaci...ore: Cf. *Met.* 9.322-3: *quae quia mendaci parientem iuuerat ore | ore parit*, where a figure of speech in *Amores* becomes literal: a midwife's deception explains why weasels give birth through their mouths. For another literal reading see [Tib.] 3.6.44: *nec bene mendaci risus componitur ore* (with Fulkerson [2017: ad loc.]).

falleret: While *licet* regularly takes an infinitive, it can, as here, be followed by a subjunctive usually without *ut* (Woodcock [§124.iii]).

**45-6. ipse ego iurarem uerum iurare puellas
et non de tetricis dicerer esse deus.**
Not only does the speaker claim that he would not punish girls for lying, but that he would swear that their oaths are always true.

45. iurare: The main manuscripts divide between *iurare* (P and Y) and *iurasse* (S); as do editors, with Showerman and Goold, and Kenney, favouring *iurare*; and Munari, McKeown, and Ramirez de Verger preferring *iurasse*. I print *iurare* for two reasons. First, this line looks back to lines 11 and 13. When the speaker generalizes about women he uses a plural noun with the present infinitive (11): *falsum iurare puellis*; when he speaks of a particular event in the past he uses a singular noun with the perfect infinitive (13): *illam nuper iurasse recordor*. This is clearly a generalization (note *puellas*) and therefore the present infinitive is more appropriate. Second, *iurare*, with its repetition of all but one letter of *iurarem* and its improved alliteration of *r*, produces a more playful line. For similar play with forms of *iurare* see Cydippe's self-defence at *Her.* 21.133, 135, 143.

46. tetricis: A term of approval in moralizing authors (see Livy on Numa and the Sabines [1.18]), *tetricus* suggests disapproval in Ovid. See 3.8.61 (the Sabine women) and *Fasti*'s praise of Flora (5.351-2): *non est de tetricis, non est de magna professis: | uolt sua plebeio sacra patere choro.*

47-8. tu tamen illorum moderatius utere dono,
  aut oculis certe parce, puella, meis.
The poem closes with an address to the speaker's girlfriend, requesting merely that she refrain from swearing by his eyes.

47. Alliteration of *t* underlines the fact that the speaker has ceased his rant and is now addressing his girlfriend: *tu tamen*.

48. The speaker's final request is made more emphatic through alliteration of *c* and *p*. Unlike the girlfriends' oaths in Propertius and [Tibullus] (see above on line 10), this girlfriend has sworn by her lover's eyes and they hurt (14).

3.4: SOME MARITAL ADVICE

Am. 3.4 purports to offer advice to an unwise husband. That advice, however, is couched in terms that can only remind readers of Augustus' attempts to regulate sexual morality.

In 18 BCE the *princeps* had introduced two marriage laws, the *lex Iulia de maritandis ordinibus* ('The Julian law on upper class marriage') and the *lex Iulia de adulteriis coercendis* ('The Julian law on the suppression of adultery'). The first restricted the classes of persons whom Roman citizens, especially members of the senatorial order and their families, could marry.[1] The second established a permanent criminal court to deal with irregular sexual relationships, the *quaestio perpetua de adulteriis*; and punishments not only for the guilty pair (including loss of property and relegation to an island) but also for a lenient husband who could be charged as a pimp (*leno*).[2] Under this law it was the status of the female partner in a sexual act that counted: extramarital sex with a *mater familias* or *matrona* was now subject to the criminal law, with a *mater familias* being defined negatively as 'any woman not a slave, prostitute, procuress, peregrine, or convicted adulteress'.[3] In *Ars Amatoria* and elsewhere Ovid offers a positive definition based on the *matrona*'s clothing: she wears a long dress, the *stola*, with its characteristic hem, the *instita*, and woollen ribbons, *uittae*:[4] *Ars* 1.31-2 (cf. *Tr.* 2.247-8), 2.600, 3.483-4 with Gibson (2003: ad loc.), *Rem.* 386, *Pont.* 3.3.51-2; cf. Tib. 1.6.67-8.

For our understanding of erotic elegy the date is important. In Tibullus, who died in 19 BCE, *adulter* and its cognates do not occur, while in Propertius they appear only twice in four books (2.9.38, 2.34.7; Book 2 was published around

---

[1] For details of these restrictions see McGinn (1998: 93).
[2] For the punishments see Treggiari (1991: 290); for the charge of *lenocinium* see Treggiari (1991: 288-9), McGinn (1998: 171-94).
[3] McGinn (1998: 155).
[4] For these woollen ribbons see below on 3.6.56.

26 BCE). In the three-book edition of *Amores*, by contrast, published nearly two decades after the passing of the marriage legislation (Introduction §2), *adulter* and *adultera* occur nine times, four times in this poem alone. While we might expect poets writing before the legislation to have spoken freely of adulterous relationships and the poet writing after to be more circumspect, the opposite is the case. In *Amores* and *Ars Amatoria* Ovid actually draws attention to the fact that his poetry deals with matters covered by the new marriage laws.[5] Indeed, the speaker ('the adulterer') of *Am.* 3.4 speaks freely of his desire to have sex with a free-born, married woman.

Early in 3.4 the speaker uses ambiguous language, words like *uir* and *puella* (1), words which leave marital status undefined. As the poem progresses, however, troubling words like *adulter* occur (5, 8), and the language becomes more explicit: the man is a husband (*maritus* 27) and the woman is both free-born (*ingenuam......puellam* 33) and a wife (*coniunx* 37, *uxor* 45).

It has been argued that terms like *maritus* and *uxor* are ambiguous. Booth (1991: 91), for example, claims that in 2.19 'there is just enough ambiguity in the terms *maritus* and *uxor*, used of the man and the girl, to cover Ovid, should he so wish, against the charge of posing as an adulterer'. Stroh (1979: 333–4) makes the same case in greater detail, arguing that the terms *uxor*, *maritus*, and *coniunx* are ambiguous because they are sometimes used of unmarried people. But this argument is not persuasive. Consider the words 'husband' and 'wife' in English. They can be used as courtesy titles of unmarried people, but there is no doubt that 'husband' means 'a married man' and that 'wife' means 'a married woman'. Even if there were any ambiguity about Ovid's terms, their juxtaposition in 2.19 and 3.4 would remove it. Moreover, if *coniunx*, *uxor*, and *maritus* are ambiguous, what terms were available to Ovid should he wish to speak unambiguously? I might add that calling yourself and your partner *adulter* and *adultera* is a strange way of resisting the charge of 'posing as an adulterer'.

2.19 and 3.4 are companion poems: both invoke the examples of Io (2.19.29, 3.4.19–20) and Danae (2.19.27–8, 3.4.21), both involve persuasion of a husband, both refer to the woman and her partner as *uxor* and *maritus*. And both poems make explicit reference to the marriage legislation, with 2.19 suggesting that his girlfriend's husband is a pimp (*lenone marito* 57), and 3.4 making clear that the girlfriend does not belong to a category exempt from the law, that she is in fact free-born and not a slave or ex-slave. Nevertheless, the two poems differ in offering contradictory advice, with 2.19 urging the husband to be more strict and 3.4 demanding that he be less harsh. Note too that while the speaker of 3.4 remains unnamed, the speaker of 2.19 refers to his relationship with Corinna and so identifies himself as the Ovidian lover.

---

[5] For adultery in *Ars* see e.g. Davis (2006: 85–95).

140   *Commentary*

In the context of Rome in the late first century, 3.4 is a highly provocative poem, because it presents a speaker who flaunts his indifference not only to traditional morality but also to the values enshrined in the marriage legislation of 18 BCE. And we should not forget that appearing to promote adultery was one of the reasons given for Ovid's banishment to the shores of the Black Sea (*Tr.* 2.212): *arguor obsceni doctor adulterii* ('I am accused of being a teacher of foul adultery').

Secondary literature: Lee (1962: 159–60); Stroh (1979); Frécaut (1972: 129–30); Du Quesnay (1973); Greene (1994); Davis (2006: Chapter 5); Hutchinson (2008); Ross in Morwood et al. (2011), Ziogas (2021:123–39).

1–2. Dure uir, imposito tenerae custode puellae
   nil agis: ingenio est quaeque tuenda suo.
The opening couplet makes a striking beginning, with both hexameter and pentameter beginning with two assertive words followed by a justification for their use. The couplet's message is summed up in those four forceful words: *dure uir, nil agis.*

For the pointlessness of guards and the importance of a woman's character see Euripides (fr. 1061 Collard and Cropp: 2008): 'In keeping watch over the female sex we labour in vain. For if a woman is naturally upright, why is it necessary to guard her and fail even more?'; (fr. 1063 Collard and Cropp: 2008): 'A wise man must never guard his wife too much in the inner recesses of the house; for sight craves outdoor pleasure; but if she wanders about in the midst of plenty, gazing at everything and being present everywhere, having sated her sight, she is released from evil'; and Propertius 2.6.39–40: *nam nihil inuitae tristis custodia prodest: | quam peccare pudet, Cynthia, tuta sat est*, 4.1b.145–6: *nec mille excubiae nec te signata iuuabunt | limina: persuasae fallere rima sat est.*

1. Dure uir: Starting a poem with a word or words in the vocative is unusual. Of the other examples in *Amores* the opening of 1.6 provides the closest parallel (*Ianitor, indignum, dura religate catena*) because it is addressed to precisely the kind of guard envisaged in 3.4. (In 2.15 and 3.6 the use of the vocative is remarkable because the addressees are not human.)

Ovid employs the phrase *durus uir* in various ways e.g. of a cruel husband or boyfriend (*Her.* 7.84 [Aeneas], *Rem.* 554) or a sturdy farmer (*Fast.* 4.692). Closest to this one is the Teacher's claim that lovers are excited by the (pretended) presence of a stern man (*Ars* 3.601–2).

Dure: In the elegiac lexicon *durus/dura* often connotes someone or something that frustrates the lover's desires e.g. an 'uncooperative' girlfriend (e.g. Tib. 2.6.28, Prop. 1.7.6, *Am.* 1.9.19) or a locked door (e.g. Tib. 1.1.56, Prop. 1.16.18, *Am.* 1.6.28). It is also used of people whose values are antithetical to those of the elegiac lover e.g. Prop. 2.1.41 (the epic poet who sings *duro...uersu*; also 2.34.44: *dure poeta*); 2.32.47 (*durosque Sabinos*), 3.20.3 (*durus, qui lucro potuit mutare* *puellam*); Tib. 1.10.49–50 (*duri* | *militis*); *Am.* 1.6.62 (the *ianitor* who is *durior* than his own door; cf. *Ars* 3.587). While some of these meanings are pertinent here, 'strict, austere, unbending' (*OLD* 6) is uppermost. Cf. Prop. 2.30b.13: *ista senes licet accusent conuiuia duri* (with Fedeli [2005: ad loc.]).

uir: At this stage the word is ambiguous between *OLD* 2a 'husband' and *OLD* 2b 'lover'.

imposito…custode: For the guard whose job it is to protect women from men like the speaker of this poem see Tib. 1.2 (esp. line 5: *nam posita est nostrae custodia saeua puellae*), *Am.* 1.6, 2.2, and 2.3. See also *Am.* 1.6.7, 1.9.27–8, 2.12.3, 3.1.49, 3.8.63, 3.11.18. For *custodem imponere* see e.g. Nep. *Cim.* 4.1.3., Sen. *Ep.* 25.5.3.

tenerae…puellae: See above on *tenerae…puellae* at 3.1.27.

2. nil agis: The expression is colloquial and blunt. *nil/nihil agis* is frequent in Plautus (*Cas.* 78 and 11 more times). Horace uses it in *Epodes* and *Satires*, but not in *Odes*; Virgil never uses it. See also *Met.* 8.140 (Scylla to departing Minos), *Fast.* 2.807: (Tarquinius about to rape Lucretia): *nil agis: eripiam, dixit, per crimina uitam*, 6.123–5 (Teacher to Carna about to be raped by Janus): *stulta…* | *nil agis, et latebras respicit ille tuas.* | *nil agis, en!*

ingenio est quaeque tuenda suo: This apparently moralizing advice summarizes the argument to follow, that the enforcement of chastity is useless. The Nurse in Seneca's *Phaedra* makes a similar argument when promoting adultery (459–60): *ingenia melius recta se in laudes ferunt,* | *si nobilem animum uegeta libertas alit.*

3–4. siqua metu dempto casta est, ea denique casta est.
   quae, quia non liceat, non facit, illa facit.
For the first full statement of his argument, the adulterer uses repetition in the hexameter to create the appearance of a necessary truth (*casta est…casta est*) as well as alliteration of *c/q* and repetition in the pentameter to create a sense of paradox (*non facit, illa facit*).

3. metu dempto: Ziogas (2021: 131) notes that *metus* recalls the legal concept of 'duress' (a *delictum* or private crime) and that Ovid shares Cicero's view (*Leg.* 1.50–1) that 'following the law out of fear does not make a man or woman chaste'. Cf. Tibullus' advice to Delia (1.6.75): *nec saeuo sis casta metu, sed mente fideli.*

casta: The adjective denotes sexual purity whether of virgins, human or divine, or married women e.g. Tib. 1.6.67–8: *sit modo casta, doce, quamuis non uitta ligatos* | *impediat crines nec stola longa pedes*; *Ars* 2.400 (of Helen before she meets Paris): *casta fuit: uitio est improba facta uiri*; *Fast.* 2.139 (comparing Romulus with Augustus): *tu rapis, hic castas duce se iubet esse maritas*, 4.313 (of Claudia Quinta): *castarum processit ab agmine matrum*.

While sexual purity is prized in other Ovidian contexts (e.g. *Her.* 5.133: *at manet Oenone fallenti casta marito*, *Met.* 7.724–5 [Cephalus' narrative]: *culpa domus ipsa carebat | castaque signa dabat*, *Fast.* 2.139 [quoted above], 4.305–25 [Claudia Quinta]), some characters in *Amores*, characters like the aged procuress Dipsas (1.8.43: *casta est, quam nemo rogauit*) and the speaker of this poem offer a more cynical view.

4. The argument highlights the importance of intent. The speaker claims that there is no difference between willingness to perform an action and its performance.

quia non liceat: The subjunctive presumably reflects the woman's subjective point of view (Woodcock [§240]). Cf. *Ars* 2.685: *odi quae praebet, quia sit praebere necesse*.

facit: For *facere* 'substituted for indelicate verbs' see Adams (1982: 204). He notes that it is used in various sexual senses.

5–6. ut iam seruaris bene corpus, adultera mens est
 nec custodiri ne uelit ulla potest.
The speaker now develops the argument by appealing to the mind–body distinction: even if you can keep a woman's body safe, her mind will be that of an adulteress.

5. ut iam: As noted by McKeown (1989: 5), the expression is prosaic. It is found in poetry, however, more often than he claims: in Catullus, Lucretius, Virgil, Horace, and Silius, as well as Juvenal and Ovid.

seruaris: In this poem *seruare* (also at lines 7, 25, 29, and 33) shifts between 'keep under observation' (*OLD* 2) and 'maintain possession of' (*OLD* 7c), these being the twin goals of the *durus uir*.

The shortened form of the perfect subjunctive *seruaueris* is used here in a concessive clause (*ut* = 'though').

corpus…mens: For the mind–body distinction in elegy see e.g. Prop. 3.5.9–10 (of Prometheus creating humans): *corpora disponens mentem non uidit in arto | recta animi primum debuit esse uia*, *Her.* 18.30: *quo non possum corpore, mente feror*, *Tr.* 4.6.43: *corpore sed mens est aegro magis aegra*.

mens: A word with a wide semantic range, here it denotes both 'the mind' (*OLD* 1) and 'frame of mind, attitude' (*OLD* 8). But given the emphasis on intent in line 4, *OLD* 7 is particularly pertinent: 'purpose, design, intention'.

adultera: Use of this term invokes the reader's awareness of Augustan legislation on the subject. See also 8 (*adulter*), 29 (*adultera*), and 37 (*adultera*).

6. For the claim that women are willing to commit adultery see *Ars* 1.274–5: *haec quoque, quam poteris credere nolle, uolet | utque uiro furtiua uenus, sic grata puellae*.

nec…ulla: The combination *non ullus / haud ullus* is used as 'an emphatic variation of *nullus*' (*OLD ullus*). *ulla* underlines the fact that adulterer makes claims about all women, not just the partner of the *durus uir*.

custodiri: Recalls *custode* in line 1 and functions as a verb of prevention (hence *ne* followed by the subjunctive).

7–8. nec corpus seruare potes, licet omnia claudas:
    omnibus exclusis intus adulter erit.
This couplet takes the argument of the previous two lines and develops it in more vivid terms: even if you could shield a woman's body by barring every entrance and excluding every lover, you cannot control her mind.

7. nec corpus seruare potes: For the sake of argument the speaker assumed in the previous couplet that guarding women's bodies was possible. Now, replacing the subjunctive with the indicative, he asserts that it is not.

omnia claudas: Ovid uses this expression with the same meaning but to opposite effect at *Ars* 2.53: *aera non potuit Minos, alia omnia clausit*. Minos 'closes all' to prevent Daedalus from leaving, while the *durus uir* 'closes all' to stop lovers from coming in.

8. omnibus exclusis: With slight variation (the simple verb becomes a compound, the concessive clause an ablative absolute), this phrase repeats the closing words of the hexameter. (For discussion of this form of repetition in Ovid see Wills [1996: 316–21].) There is, however, an important semantic shift: while *omnia* referred to barriers of every kind, *omnibus* refers to men.

exclusis is the reading of P, Y, and most other manuscripts. S offers *occlusis*. Goold (1965: 51) rightly rejects *occlusis*, accepted by Munari and Kenney, on the grounds of sense, because it implies that even though every entrance has been blocked, there will be a lover 'hiding under your wife's bed'. As Goold notes, *exclusis* also produces a superior line, with *ex*clusis juxtaposed with *in*tus, and *omnibus* contrasted with (just one) *adulter. excludo* is regularly used of shutting out lovers (e.g. Tib. 2.4.39, *Am.* 1.6.31, 1.8.78, *Ars* 3.69, *Rem.* 36).

intus, as Goold observes, means 'in her mind' (*OLD* 4; *TLL* 105.32–61). Marlowe's translation suggests that he understood the argument in this way (1603): 'Nor canst by watching keep her mind from sin; | all being shut out, the adulterer is within'.

9–10. cui peccare licet, peccat minus: ipsa potestas
    semina nequitiae languidiora facit.
The speaker now develops the other side of the argument: if people have the power to choose they are less likely to do wrong.

9. cui peccare licet: The adulterer offers an apparently universal maxim (*cui* is gender neutral) as an argument. The language recalls that of moralists like Cicero e.g. (*Parad.* 3.20.13): *peccare certe licet nemini*; (*Tusc.* 5.55.16): *etsi peccare nemini licet*.

peccare...peccat: For *peccare* as a euphemism for committing adultery see e.g. Hor. *Carm.* 3.24.22–4, *Ars* 2.365 (excusing Paris and Helen): *nil Helene peccat, nihil hic committit adulter*. For *peccare* used of illicit sex generally see Adams (1982: 202).

potestas: The word is rarely used in poetry in this sense. The only other examples in *TLL* (314.3–29) come from Lucan and Statius.

10. semina nequitiae: Ovid uses the same language at *Tr.* 2.279–80: *ludi quoque semina praebent | nequitiae*. The image seems to be drawn from moral philosophy e.g. Plutarch (*Mor.* fr. 141.10): 'the seeds of virtue' (σπέρματ' ἀρετῆς), Arrian (*Epict.* 2.20.34.5): 'seeds of nobility' (τὰ τῆς εὐγενείας σπέρματα).

nequitiae: For the elegiac resonance of this word see above on 3.1.17.

languidiora: While *languidus* and its cognate verbs, *langueo* and *languesco*, are regularly used of plants (e.g. *A.* 9.435–6, Germ. *Arat.* 338, Sen. *Phaed.* 768), they also have sexual connotations (e.g. Tib. 1.9.56, Prop. 1.13.15, *Am.* 2.10.35). *semina* activates the first sense, the context the second. For further discussion of *languidus* see below on 3.7.3, 66.

11–12. desine, crede mihi, uitia irritare uetando:
  obsequio uinces aptius illa tuo.
This phase of the argument closes with a command and a prediction.

11. crede mihi: Only the untrustworthy ask for trust in *Amores*: 1.8.62 (Dipsas the procuress), 1.9.2 (a proponent of a paradoxical case: *militat omnis amans*), 2.2.51 (an aspiring adulterer).

uitia irritare: Morally-minded writers regularly use *irritare* and cognates with *uitia* e.g. Liv. 22.3.5, Sen. *Ep.* 51.5, Plin. *Nat.* 33.4.9. Ovid adapts this claim at *Rem.* 133, using *uitia* in the sense of 'disease': *quin etiam accendas uitia irritesque uetando*.

12. obsequio: Recalls Priapus' advice to a man in love (Tib. 1.4.40): *cedas: obsequio plurima uincet amor*.

13–16. uidi ego nuper equum contra sua uincla tenacem
  ore reluctanti fulminis ire modo;
constitit ut primum concessas sensit habenas
  frenaque in effusa laxa iacere iuba.
The next stage in the argument opens with an appeal to evidence from the natural world. References to the behaviour of animals, particularly horses and cattle, are common in Ovid's erotic poetry e.g. 1.2.13–16, 1.10.25–8, 2.9.29–30, 2.12.25–6, 3.5, *Her.* 4.21–2, *Ars* 1.19–20, 1.279–80, 1.471–2, 2.483–8, 3.555–6, *Rem.* 235–6,

Commentary, 4.10–16 145

633–4. Cf. Prop. 2.3.47–8, 2.34.47–8. Developed over four lines, this example of a stallion is longer than most and gains vividness and authority by claiming to be based on recent personal experience. While the first couplet pictures the horse's violent reaction to being reined in, the second images his docility when restraints are relaxed.

13. uidi ego nuper: The claim to be a recent eyewitness has persuasive force. Not surprisingly we find Cicero employing it in forensic speeches e.g. *Ver.* 2.5.44, *Flac.* 53.1, *Sest.* 13.4.

uincla: The use of *uinclum/uinculum* of the restraints applied to animals (reins, leashes, yokes etc.) is almost exclusively poetic e.g. Enn. *Ann. sedinc.* 535–6 Goldberg and Manuwald (1): *sicut equos qui de praesepibus fartus | uincla suis magnis animis abrumpit*, A. 11.492–3 (of a horse), *Met.* 8.332 (of dogs), VF 7.602 (of bulls). But see Tac. *Ann.* 1.66.1: *forte equus abruptis uinculis uagus*.

tenacem: The description of the horse as *tenax* seems paradoxical because the adjective is typically applied to *uincla* e.g. *G.* 4.412: *tenacia uincla*, *Met.* 11.252: *uincloque innecte tenaci*, Plin. *Ep.* 4.15.2.3: *tenacissimum uinculum*.

14. ore reluctanti: Perhaps recalls Virgil's depiction of the struggles of a dying calf (*G.* 4.300–1): *huic geminae nares et spiritus oris | multa reluctanti obstruitur*.

fulminis...modo: Comparison of an animal to a thunderbolt suggests both violence and speed. It is commonly used of boars (e.g. *Ars* 2.373–4, Stat. *Theb.* 6.868, *Achil.* 2.124, Mart. 11.69.9), but also of lions (Sen. *Ag.* 830) and tigers (Sil. 12.461).

15. concessas...habenas: Varies the usual idioms for loosening reins (*habenas immittere*: OLD *immitto* 9, TLL *habena* 2394.49–52; and *habenas effundere* (OLD *effundo* 14, TLL *effundo* 218.78–219.3). (This is the only example of *concedo* used with *habenae*.) Using *concedo*, a word usually applied to human beings, reminds the reader that behind this image is a request that the *durus uir* make concessions to his wife and her lover. It also foreshadows the speaker's preference for *inconcessa uoluptas* (31).

16. The interweaving of four words ending in *a* makes for a particularly attractive line: *frenăque in effusā laxă iacere iubā*. Other examples in *Amores* are: 1.3.20, 1.5.9, 1.5.10, 1.7.4, 1.8.80, 1.11.14, 2.3.10, 2.5.12, 2.6.6, 2.10.26 (five), 2.11.42, 2.13.4, 3.7.13 (five), 29, 81, 3.8.40, 3.11.29, 3.12.10. The fact that Ovid employs two such lines in succession at the collection's most critical juncture, the entry of Corinna (*Am.* 1.5.9–10): *ecce, Corinnă uenit, tunică uelată recincta, | candidă diuiduă collă tegente comā*), and that he even has lines with five words ending in *a* (2.10.26, 3.7.13) suggests that he particularly prizes this verbal pattern.

Lines of this kind occur in every book of *Metamorphoses*. Especially impressive are those which combine interwoven final *a* with golden form (abVAB) e.g. 3.57

146 Commentary

(the Theban serpent): *tristia sanguinea lambentem uulnera lingua*, 12.606 (Paris killing Achilles): *certaque letifera derexit spicula dextra*. See also *Met*. 7.204 (with all six words ending in *a*): *uiuaque saxa sua conuulsaque robora terra*. Such lines are also common in the later works: *Her*. 16.148, 249, 18.20, 19.106, 20.198; *Fast*. 1.280, 2.326, 4.870, 5.511, 6.580; *Tr*. 1.1.128, 3.7.8, 5.9.31; *Pont*. 2.9.69, 4.14.55.

For the other elegists see e.g. Tib. 1.10.26: *hostiaque e plena rustica porcus hara*, 1.10.40: *occupat in parua pigra senecta casa*; Prop. 1.11.10: *paruula Lucrina cumba moretur aqua*, 2.6.32: *turpia sub tacita condita Laetitia*, 4.10.20: *et galea hirsuta compta lupina iuba*.

17–18. nitimur in uetitum semper cupimusque negata:
sic interdictis imminet aeger aquis.

The speaker now sums up this phase of the argument with a moral generalization and a medical analogy.

17. This line can be interpreted as quasi-proverbial: 'We humans strive…we humans crave'. However, given that the plural is often used for the singular and that *cupio* is a sexually loaded term (*OLD* 2), it might also be read as a statement of an adulterer's creed: 'I strive…I crave'.

nitimur in uetitum: Rewrites Horace's denunciation of human failings (*Carm*. 1.3.25–6): *audax omnia perpeti | gens humana ruit per uetitum nefas*. At this stage of the argument the speaker seems to sympathize with Horatian moralizing.

18. Recalls the advice offered by medical writers like Celsus (early first century CE; 3.6.1): 'For fever inflames thirst and demands water most when it is most dangerous. But the patient (*aeger*) must be taught that when the fever calms down, the thirst will immediately calm down too…the person who does not drink will stop being thirsty more quickly'. The adulterer, however, is incapable of following such instructions.

19–20. centum fronte oculos, centum ceruice gerebat
Argus, et hos unus saepe fefellit Amor.

This and the following mythological examples are intended to prove that restrictions are pointless because they never succeed.

Argus is a familiar character in Io's story, a story to which the poet refers at 1.3.21 *carmine nomen habent exterrita cornibus Io*; 2.2.45–6: *dum nimium seruat custos Iunonius Io, | ante suos annos occidit. illa dea est*; 2.19.29–30: *dum seruat Iuno mutatam cornibus Io, | facta est, quam fuerat, gratior illa Ioui*; and tells in detail at *Met*. 1.588–721. This version differs in making no mention of Io and in indicating that Argus performed this task more than once.

19. The repetition of *centum* and the placing of opposite terms *fronte* and *ceruice* highlight the line's symmetry, particularly its balance at the main caesura. Whereas Argus has a hundred eyes in total in *Metamorphoses* (quoted on line 20 below), here he has a hundred eyes on both sides of his head.

20. unus: Contrasts with repeated *centum* in the previous line: one Amor could defeat two hundred eyes.

unus saepe: Ovid achieves a similar kind verbal play when describing Argus' death at *Met.* 1.721: *centumque oculos nox occupat una*. For similar close collocation of words denoting unity and multiplicity see e.g. *Am.* 2.10.4: *duas uno*, *Her.* 3.38: *una...tribus*, *Her.* 16.368: *unus...innumeri*, *Met.* 13.241 *milibus unum*, *Met.* 15.529 *unum...omnia*.

21–2. in thalamum Danae ferro saxoque perennem
  quae fuerat uirgo tradita, mater erat.
Like other myths, Danae's story was adaptable. Whereas Horace had used it to demonstrate the power of money (*Carm.* 3.16.1–8) and Propertius to argue that women lack concern for sexual morality (2.32.59–60): *nec minus aerato Danae circumdata muro | non potuit magno casta negare Ioui*, Ovid invokes Danae's pregnancy both here and at 2.19.27–8: *si numquam Danaen habuisset aenea turris, | non esset Danae de Ioue facta parens* as evidence that confining women is futile. At 3.8.29–34 Danae exemplifies the female susceptibility to bribes.

21. thalamum...perennem: Enclosing word order images Danae's imprisonment.

perennem: Usually used of such things as *fama* (*A.* 9.79, *Am.* 1.10.62, 1.15.7, *Met.* 15.875) and water (Prop. 3.5.30, *Am.* 3.6.98, 3.9.25, *Rem.* 652, *Fast.* 2.820, 3.298), the adjective is here used of rock and iron, things more commonly thought of as 'enduring' (cf. Hor. *Carm.* 3.30.1: *aere perennius*, *Met.* 15.813: *adamante perenni*). In this case, however, rock and iron do not 'endure' in any meaningful sense.

22. fuerat uirgo...mater erat: The presence of *uirgo* and *mater* in the same line, as well as internal rhyme, underlines tactfully, if candidly, the failure of Acrisius' attempt to protect his daughter's virginity.

23–4. Penelope mansit, quamuis custode carebat,
  inter tot iuuenes intemerata procos.
After establishing the identity of its mythological subject in the first word, this couplet postpones its key terms until the very end: *intemerata procos*.

23. Penelope: Despite the claims advanced by elegiac brothel-keepers (Prop. 4.5.7–8, with Hutchinson [2006: ad loc.]; *Am.* 1.8.47–8, with McKeown [1989: ad loc.]) and the author of the *Priapea* (68.27–38), Ulysses' wife embodies marital fidelity. She was familiar to contemporary readers not only from Homer's *Odyssey* but also from *Heroides* 1. Her faithfulness is lauded in erotic elegy: Propertius contrasts her with Cynthia both implicitly (1.3.41 with Fedeli [1980: ad loc.]) and explicitly (2.9.3–8); and even the Teacher of *Ars* 3 claims to admire her *pietas* (15–16): *est pia Penelope lustris errante duobus | et totidem lustris bella gerente uiro*.

mansit: Waiting is one of Penelope's characteristic activities e.g. Prop. 2.9.7–8: *uisuram et quamuis numquam speraret Vlixem, | illum exspectando facta remansit anus*, Her. 1.49: *si maneo qualis Troia durante manebam*.

24. iuuenes: Like Dipsas the brothel-keeper (1.8.47): *Penelope iuuenum uires temptabat in arcu*, the adulterer emphasizes the suitors' youth in order to underline their sexual attractiveness. Cf. line 47 below: *iuuenum conuiuia*.

intemerata: When used of women, the adjective suggests sexual purity hallowed by religion e.g. A. 11.582–4 (of Camilla): *sola contenta Diana | aeternum telorum et uirginitatis amorem | intemerata colit*, Stat. *Theb.* 1.572–3 (of Crotopus' daughter): *mira decore pios seruabat nata penates | intemerata toris*). Relatively rare in both verse and prose, it is used nowhere else in Ovid.

25–6. **quidquid seruatur cupimus magis, ipsaque furem
   cura uocat; pauci, quod sinit alter, amant.**
This couplet recapitulates the conclusion of the previous phase of the argument (*quidquid seruatur cupimus magis* rewrites *cupimusque negata*) and draws out its implications: an owner's anxiety attracts thieves and a husband's refusal invites lovers.

25. quidquid seruatur cupimus magis: Némethy compares a poem of Philodemus in the *Greek Anthology* (*PA* 12.173) in which the speaker chooses to pursue a virgin rather than a professional (5–6): οὐ γὰρ ἕτοιμα | βούλομαι, ἀλλὰ ποθῶ πᾶν τὸ φυλασσόμενον ('For I do not want what is available, but I desire everything that is under guard').

seruatur: For the importance of this verb see above on line 5.

cupimus: As at line 17, *cupimus* is ambiguous between 'we humans crave' and 'I desire'. Here too the sexual sense is not far from the surface.

furem: The argument that an owner's concern to protect property may invite theft is persuasive. Note, however, that while *fur* means 'thief' or 'burglar', two of its cognates, *furtiuus* and *furtum*, are frequently used of adultery (*furtiuus*: TLL 1644.41–74; *furtum*: 1649.68–1650.28; Adams [1982: 167–8]). There are different kinds of thieves. Marius, the poem's earliest commentator, was more explicit: *furem: adulterum*.

26. cura: This too can be an amatory term, meaning either love itself (most famously at A. 4.1: *at regina graui iamdudum saucia cura*; TLL 1474.80–1475.41) or the beloved (e.g. *Ecl.* 10.22–3: '*Galle, quid insanis?*' inquit. '*tua cura Lycoris | perque niues alium perque horrida castra secuta est*'; TLL 1475.42–60).

pauci, quod sinit alter, amant: The speaker's true concern is now made explicit: if the *durus uir* were more permissive, his partner would be safe from adulterers.

Virtual repetition of 2.19.4: *ferreus est, si quis <u>quod sinit alter amat</u>*, underlines the connection between these two poems. (For this see introduction above.)

quod: For the impersonal neuter used of a woman see *Am.* 2.2.14, 2.5.9, 2.19.4 (quoted above), 8, 31, 36 (twice), 3.14.39; *Her.* 19.179 (Hero of herself), *Ars* 1.35, 91 (twice), 92 (twice), 175, 263, *Rem.* 13, 89, 297, 345.

27-8. nec facie placet illa sua, sed amore mariti:
    nescio quid quod te ceperit esse putant.
The speaker now turns back from examples drawn from the natural world and mythology to explicit denunciation of the practice of protecting women from adulterers.

27. placet: For *placeo* as 'be sexually attractive to' (*OLD* 1d) see above on 3.2.35.

facie...amore: Causal ablatives.

amore: The major manuscripts (P, S, and Y) offer *more*. Since the fifteenth century editors have printed the correction found in Y (ᴀᵃmore) and later manuscripts. While it is a priori more likely in a collection of erotic poems that *more* would be corrupted to *amore*, *amore* is the better reading because the pentameter effectively rewrites the hexameter. In this context *amor*, not *mos* = *quod te ceperit*.

mariti: If there were any doubt, even after the use of *adultera* in 5 and *adulter* in 7, about the nature of the relationship between the *durus uir* and his *puella*, it is now removed: they are husband and wife. For the alleged ambiguity of *maritus* see the introduction above.

28. I translate: 'they suppose that there is something (i.e. about her) that has taken hold of you'. Another possibility is 'they suppose that she's something special because she's taken hold of you'. The difference in meaning is not great and both versions fit the context well. However we construe, the perfect subjunctive is used for a subordinate clause in indirect speech.

ceperit: For *capio* in this erotic sense see e.g. Tib. 1.4.3, Prop. 1.1.1, 2.3.9, *Am.* 1.10.10, 2.4.39: *candida me capiet, capiet me flaua puella*, *Rem.* 554.

29-30. non proba fit, quam uir seruat, sed adultera cara:
    ipse timor pretium corpore maius habet.
Recalling the language of line 5 (*seruat/seruaris, adultera/adultera*), this couplet transforms the quasi-psychological claims of lines 5-6, arguing that it is precisely the husband's protection and the fear it causes that make his wife a desirable target.

29. proba: For being *proba* as a specifically female virtue involving chastity and faithfulness in marriage see *TLL* 1486.54–1487.10.

fit: The major manuscripts (P, S, and Y) offer *sit*. All or most other manuscripts (ω in Kenney and McKeown) read *fit*. Munari prints *sit*. Kenney, Showerman and

Goold, McKeown, and Ramirez de Verger prefer *fit*. The indicative *fit* is preferable because it is not clear what the point of subjunctive *sit* would be.

adultera cara: The expression shocks because when used of people *carus/cara* is a term of approval, meaning 'regarded with affection, beloved, dear' (*OLD* 2). Here, however, it means 'highly-prized' (cf. *OLD* 1: 'expensive, costly, dear'). Moreover, the epithet typically used of adulterers and adultery is the pejorative *turpis* e.g. *Her.* 4.34: *peius adulterio turpis adulter obest*, 13.133 (Laodamia speaking of Helen): *quid petitur tanto nisi turpis adultera bello*, Hor. *Carm.* 1.33.9: *quam turpi Pholoe peccet adultero*. The adjective even has legal standing in Justinian's code (*Dig.* 50.16.42): *adulterium natura turpe est*.

The rarity of this hexameter ending (Ovid avoids following a noun which ends in short *a* with a similar adjective; this is the only example in *Amores* and single *Heroides*) perhaps underlines the shock. For statistics see Holmes (1995).

30. ipse timor: Whose fear? Comparison with 2.19.55–6 (*nil metuam? per nulla traham suspiria somnos?* | *nil facies, cur te iure perisse uelim?*) suggests that it is the speaker's fear that is at stake. And that is how Bornecque (1930) understood the line: *La crainte même que l'on a d'être surpris lui donne plus de prix que ses charmes* ('The very fear one has of being surprised gives her more value than her charms'). In that poem the lover complains that the husband is too lax because he likes taking risks in order to commit adultery.

Here, however, the speaker makes the opposite case: the husband is too strict. Marius explains: *ipsa puella magis censetur timore mariti illam claudentis, quam corporis pulchritudine*, i.e. the girl's main value lies more in the fear that her husband causes in her than in her physical beauty. This interpretation fits the poem's overall argument and is confirmed by lines 32: *sola placet, 'timeo' dicere siqua potest* and 34: *hic metus externae corpora gentis agat*.

pretium corpore maius: Cf. *Rem.* 232 (of mental health): *at pretium pars haec corpore maius habet*.

31–2. indignere licet, iuuat inconcessa uoluptas:
    sola placet 'timeo' dicere siqua potest.
If the adulterer's argument in the previous couplet was somewhat compressed and in need of explication, here he states his position in terms that could not be more blunt.

31. iuuat inconcessa uoluptas: The lover of 2.19 reaches a similar conclusion, deciding that he has had enough of permitted love (51–2): *lentus es et pateris nulli patienda marito;* | *at mihi concessi finis amoris erit*. In both 3.4 and 2.19 Ovid's speaker unambiguously states an immoralist position. Cf. *Ars* 1.749: *nil nisi turpe iuuat*.

Moralizing Romans were more likely to single out 'permitted pleasures' for toleration, on the assumption that most pleasures are to be condemned. Tacitus, for

Commentary, 4.30–3 151

example, speaks of the attempts of Seneca and Burrus to restrain Nero *uoluptatibus concessis* (*Ann.* 13.2.7).

uoluptas: Sometimes serves in Ovid (but not the other elegists) as a euphemism for sexual intercourse e.g. 1.4.47, 1.10.35, 2.10.25, *Ars* 2.477, 2.623, 2.687, 2.717, 2.727, *Rem.* 413. That may well be the case here: 'I like illicit sex'.

32. placet: For *placeo* as 'be sexually attractive to' see above on 27.

timeo: The adulterer claims to prefer the challenge presented by a woman who fears her husband. In *Ars* the Teacher gives complementary advice, instructing his female students to pretend to fear a *durus uir* (3.601–4).

By contrast, the Propertian lover claims to despise men who like locked doors (2.23.12) and to prefer unguarded girls who have no fear (2.23.19: *nec dicet 'timeo'*). For a similar view see Hor. *S.* 1.2.127–31.

33–4. nec tamen ingenuam ius est seruare puellam:
   hic metus externae corpora gentis agat.
The adulterer now claims the moral and legal high ground by arguing that this over-zealous husband is depriving his wife of her rights as a free-born Roman.

33. ingenuam...puellam: While *ingenua* here primarily signals that the woman is free-born (*OLD* 2), the pentameter suggests that the other sense 'native to a place' (*OLD* 1) is also present. For other meanings of *ingenuus* see below on 3.8.1 and 3.11.10.

In *Ars* the Teacher argues, whether correctly or incorrectly, that freedwomen were not covered by the marriage legislation (*Ars* 3.615–16: *te quoque seruari, modo quam uindicta redemit, | quis ferat?*). Our speaker makes it plain that in this case there is no such defence: this woman is not an ex-slave.

For the idea that the presence of a guard robs a woman of the freedom to which she is entitled see 2.2.15–16 (to the guard Bagoas): *huic furtiua tuo libertas munere detur | quam dederis illi, reddat ut illa tibi.* The lover of 1.4 implies that a woman's partner will treat her as a slave (61): *nocte uir includet.*

ius: There is irony in the fact that while accusing the *durus uir* of illegality, the speaker's own activities are punishable by law. Cf. 33 below: *iura...uiri.*

seruare: While the meaning 'watch over, guard' (*OLD* 1) is obviously pertinent, the perceived etymological link between *seruare* and *seruus* suggests that the sense 'retain possession of' (*OLD* 7b) is also in play, implying that the autocratic husband treats his free-born wife as a slave. For the etymology see Maltby (1991: 563–4). Gibson (2003: 335) notes that Ovid engages in identical word-play to different ends at *Ars* 3.615–16 (quoted above) and cites Justinian's *Digest* for the connection (50.16.239.1): 'The appellation of "slaves" (*seruorum*) flowed from the fact that our generals are accustomed to sell prisoners and so save (*seruare*) and not kill them'.

Commentary

34. externae corpora gentis: The phrase denotes foreign-born slaves, with *externa* functioning as the opposite of *ingenua* in the senses of both 'native' and 'free-born'. Burman (ad loc.) puts it succinctly: *Corpora.] Id est ancillas.*

For *corpora* used of slaves see Briseis' description of the gifts offered to Achilles (*Her.* 3.35–6): *forma praestante puellae | Lesbides, euersa corpora capta domo.* Barchiesi (1992: ad loc.) labels this use of *corpora* 'legal-military' and cites as examples Liv. 5.22.1, 31.46.16.

For the contrast between *ingenua* and *externa* meaning 'native-born' as opposed to 'foreign' see Lucr. 1.230–1 (with Bailey [1947: ad loc.]): *unde mare <u>ingenuei</u> fontes <u>externaque</u> longe | flumina suppeditant*, contrasting native springs (i.e. those which rise from the sea's floor) with rivers from outside. For the association between being *externa* and being enslaved see Aulus Gellius' advice on wet-nurses (12.1.17.4–6): 'Especially if she whom you introduce to offer milk is either a slave (*serua*) or slavish (*seruilis*) and belongs, as is usually the case, to a foreign (*externae*) and barbarian nation'.

35–6. scilicet ut possit custos 'ego' dicere 'feci',
  in laudem serui casta sit illa tui?
This phase of the argument closes with a sarcastic question, implying that if a slave is to be responsible for his wife's virtue, then they should get the credit.

35. scilicet: For ironic use of *scilicet* in a question see e.g. 2.14.7–8 (denouncing abortion): *scilicet, ut careat rugarum crimine uenter, | sternetur pugnae tristis harena tuae?*, 2.19.53 (complaining of the husband's carelessness): *scilicet infelix numquam prohibebor adire?*

36. in laudem serui…tui: For the idea that a woman's behaviour benefits a slave see 2.2.17: *domina est obnoxia seruo.*

serui: Lovers in *Amores* typically emphasize the servile status of the guards they face. When addressing a doorkeeper at 1.6.1, for example, the lover speaks of his chain (*dura religate catena*), while the lover of 2.2 speaks of Bagoas' loss of *libertas* (15–16), of his *peculium* (19), and of the flogging that awaits him (61).

sit: Deliberative subjunctive.

37–40. rusticus est nimium, quem laedit adultera coniunx,
  et notos mores non satis Vrbis habet
in qua Martigenae non sunt sine crimine nati
  Romulus Iliades Iliadesque Remus.
The adulterer now adopts an overtly cynical position, arguing that concern for traditional sexual morality marks the husband as boorish, as lacking in that urban sophistication which has characterized Rome from its very foundation.

37. rusticus: When used in the masculine, *rusticus* denotes either an actual farmer (e.g. 2.16.35) or an obstacle to the lover's sexual fulfilment (e.g. 3.6.87–8 [to an annoying river]: *quid mutua differs | gaudia? quid coeptum, rustice, rumpis iter?*). Combined with a negative, it suggests an attractive sexual partner (*Ars* 2.369 [of Paris in Sparta]): *non rusticus hospes*. For the wider connotations of this term in Ovid see above on see 3.1.43. Here, as the following couplet makes clear, the contrast is drawn not just between city and country, but between the City, the only one that counts, and the countryside.

quem laedit adultera coniunx: Declaring that a husband should not be troubled by his wife's adultery runs counter not only to conventional morality but also to Augustan legislation, for the law required that husbands divorce delinquent wives. We find this in Justinian's *Digest* (4.4.37.7–11): 'But when we come to the rules set out in the Julian law on the suppression of adultery…if one of them [i.e. a minor] commits one of these offences which the same law punishes as adultery, for example, if he knowingly marries a woman condemned for adultery, or does not divorce a wife caught in adultery (*in adulterio deprehensam uxorem non dimiserit*)…'.

38. For the association between Rome and sexual freedom see e.g. Prop. 2.6.22, 3.12.17–18, *Am.* 1.8.42: *at Venus Aeneae regnat in urbe sui*, *Ars* 1.59–60, 173–4. Conversely the countryside is sometimes perceived as a place of sexual innocence e.g. Prop. 2.19.3–4 (to Cynthia leaving Rome): *nullus erit castis iuuenis corruptor in agris | qui te blanditiis non sinat esse probam*.

39. Martigenae: This seems to be an Ovidian coinage. Cf. *Fast.* 1.199 (with Green [2004: ad loc.]): *Martigenam…Quirinum*. It is also used by Statius and Silius.

non…sine crimine: Understatement makes for powerful indictment. Here and elsewhere Ovid presents Mars' treatment of Ilia unambiguously as rape. See 3.6.49: *illa gemens patruique nefas delictaque Martis* and *Fast.* 3.21–2 (with Heyworth [2019: ad loc.]): *Mars uidet hanc uisamque cupit potiturque cupita, | et sua diuina furta fefellit ope*.

40. This is a virtuoso line, which is arranged chiastically (abba), which is balanced at the main caesura, and which employs repetition of a newly-invented matronymic to frame that caesura. (For balance at the main caesura see note on 3.7.37 below; for repetition framing the main caesura see above on 3.2.32.) It is also entirely dactylic.

Iliades: Ovid is the only author to use this word as a matronymic, reserving the epithet for Romulus (*Met.* 14.781, 824; *Fast.* 4.23, 5.565) or Remus (*Tr.* 4.3.8) or both (*Fast.* 3.62: *Iliadae fratres*). Cf. *Met.* 10.160 (of Trojan Ganymede). Others use *Iliades* of the Trojan women (e.g. *A.* 1.480, Sen. *Tro.* 144).

41–2. quo tibi formosam, si non nisi casta placebat?
  non possunt ullis ista coire modis.
Breathtaking in his cynicism, the adulterer now employs colloquial candour (note the omission of a verb meaning 'you chose' from the first line) to query the

husband's assumption that beauty and virtue are compatible and to assert bluntly that they are not.

41. quo: The lack of a following verb conveys urgency. For ellipsis of the verb see *OLD quo*[1] 2. Though found in prose writers (e.g. Cic. *Fam.* 7.23.2.13, V. Max. 9.13(ext).2.7–8 [*quo* x3]) and other poets (e.g. *A.* 4.98, Hor. *Ep.* 1.5.12, Phaed. 3.18.9, Mart. 9.66.2, Stat. *Theb.* 9.55), the idiom seems particularly common in Ovid e.g. 2.19.7, 3.7.19, 49 (x2), 3.8.47, 48, *Her.* 2.53, *Ars* 1.303, *Met.* 13.103.

formosam…casta: For the impossibility of being both *formosa* and *casta* (and similar contempt for traditional morality, this time from the lips of a brothel-keeper) see 1.8.43–4: *ludunt formosae. casta est quam nemo rogauit | aut, si rusticitas non uetat, ipsa rogat.* Cf. Prop. 2.16.26: *formosis leuitas semper amica fuit.*

si non nisi: This jingling phrase provides attractive alliteration and throws *casta* into prominence.

placebat: For *placeo* as 'be sexually attractive to' see above on 3.2.35.

42. non…ullis: For the force of this combination see above on 6.

coire: For this use of *coeo* (*OLD* 9b: 'be found together') see *Met.* 8.785–6: *neque enim Cereremque Famemque | fata coire sinunt* (cf. *Met.* 8.814 where *Fames* is *contraria semper* to Ceres), Luc. 8.494–5: *uirtus et summa potestas | non coeunt.*

43–4. si sapis, indulge dominae uultusque seueros
    exue nec rigidi iura tuere uiri
The conversational tone continues with the speaker advising the husband to loosen up and not to insist on his legal rights.

43. si sapis: The phrase is colloquial, with 50 per cent of examples coming from Plautus (15) and Terence (3). See also *Am.* 2.2.9, *Rem.* 372.

seueros: In erotic poetry *seueritas* characterizes love's opponents and the loveless life. See e.g. Catul. 5.2–3, Prop. 2.34.23, *Am.* 2.10.15–16: *sed tamen hoc melius, quam si sine amore iacerem | hostibus eueniat uita seuera meis.*

44. rigidi: Suggests a stern morality of which lovers disapprove e.g. 2.4.15, *Her.* 4.73–4 (of Hippolytus), *Ars* 2.663–4: *nec quo sit nata, require, | consule, quae rigidus munera Censor habet.*

iura…uiri: Recalls not only *ius* at 33, but the language of the *lex Iulia de adulteriis coercendis* setting out a husband's rights (*iure mariti / iure uiri*) when dealing with an adulterous wife e.g. *Dig.* 4.4.37, 23.2.34, 48.5.2, 5, 12, 14, 15, 39, 41.

45–8. et cole quos dederit (multos dabit) uxor amicos:
    gratia sic minimo magna labore uenit.
sic poteris iuuenum conuiuia semper inire
    et, quae non dederis, multa uidere domi.

After merely invoking the law, the adulterer now outlines the advantages of breaking one of its specific provisions, viz. the rule against profiting from a wife's adultery. See *Dig.* 48.5.2.2: 'The crime of pandering (*lenocinii... crimen*) is laid down by the Julian law on adultery because a penalty is established for a husband who takes possession of anything as a result of his wife's adultery'; 48.5.30.3: 'Anyone who profits from his wife's adultery, is punished: for a man has committed no minor offence who has practised pandering (*lenocinium*) in the case of his wife'.

45. This is a remarkable line which, by placing the relative clause before its antecedent, surprises readers with its final word *amicos*. The parenthesis combined with polyptoton (*dederit... dabit*) underlines the conversational tone.

At 3.8.64 a lover takes an opposing stance and criticizes husbands who accept gifts from their wife's lovers.

46. The overall advantage of cultivating a wife's friends is expressed in a patterned line (AbaBV; cf. 1.14.6, 3.1.17) which juxtaposes its two key adjectives: *minimo magna*.

47-8. The speaker reserves his most outrageous suggestion for the final couplet: the husband can profit from his wife's infidelities. As the passages from the *Digest* quoted above make clear, accepting gifts from his wife's lovers exposed a husband to the charge of pandering, of *lenocinium*. Conviction for pandering incurred *infamia* (*Dig.* 3.2.1), i.e. it placed the guilty person in the same category as dishonourably discharged soldiers, paid actors, and those guilty of robbery, theft, and fraud. Note too that whereas the lover of 2.19 insults a lazy husband by implying that he is guilty of pandering (57): *quid mihi cum facili, quid cum lenone marito?*, this lover proposes that the *durus uir* should become a pander.

3.5: A LOVER'S DREAM

Is this poem by Ovid or not? This question has dominated discussion of *Am.* 3.5 for nearly two centuries.[1]

What evidence supports 3.5's place in the collection? First, it is transmitted in this position by the three principal manuscripts, P, S, and Y.[2] Second, its style is not significantly different from that of Ovid's other elegies.[3] Third, a line from 3.5

---

[1] In the first printed edition (Johannes Andreas [Rome: 1471]) 3.5 was placed between 2.5 and 2.6. Marius (1518), as he himself observes, was the first editor to place 3.5 in its present position. The poem was accepted as genuine by sixteenth-, seventeenth- and eighteenth-century editors. Weise (1845: ad loc.) seems to have been the first to reject that consensus: *absque dubio spuria* ('undoubtedly spurious').

[2] Kenney (1962: 12; writing before the revaluation of Y) notes that it occurs in its present position in PSObTXZ.

[3] I base this claim on Ben Nagy's stylometric work on *Her.* 15 (2023). He advises me that: (1) the style of *Amores* is very variable; (2) while 3.5 is not entirely typical, it is more so than 1.15; (3) there is no stylometric evidence to support non-authenticity; and (4) caution is needed because of the poem's size.

is attributed to Ovid in Servius Auctus' commentary (seventh to eighth century) on Virgil: *Ecl.* 6.54: *PALLENTES RVMINAT HERBAS reuomit et denuo consumit: 'atque iterum pasto pascitur ante cibo'* (= *Am.* 3.5.18), *sic Ouidius*.[4] Given the strength of the evidence, the burden of proof lies on those who doubt Ovid's authorship and 3.5's place in *Amores*. Important too is the judgement of Ovid's greatest editor, Nicolaus Heinsius (p. 273): *haec elegia...huc revocanda est ex fide optimorum ac veterrimorum codicum. uti pater meus jampridem monuit* ('This elegy...must be restored to this position on the evidence of the best and oldest codices. As my father [Daniel Heinsius in his edition of 1629] advised long ago').

Why has 3.5's authenticity been doubted? Important twentieth-century editors either expressed serious reservations or declared that 3.5 was not genuine because of oddities in the manuscript tradition. Munari (1948: 148–9), for example, notes that the poem that we call 3.5 is found after 2.5 in some manuscripts, as well as after 3.8, 3.9, 3.12, 3.13, and 1.15. He also observes (144) that a poem entitled *de Somnio* was condemned as non-Ovidian in the fourteenth century.[5] Kenney (1962: 12) went further, pointing out that 3.5 is sometimes transmitted with *Amores*, sometimes separately, and sometimes not at all; and inferring that 'it follows from this that the *Somnium* was not in the "archetype", but gained entry into the tradition at a subsequent date'. McKeown (2002) agreed.

But this explanation is not without problems. As Bertini (1976: 152) pointed out, if Kenney is right, something remarkable has happened: a spurious poem has found its way into 20 or so unrelated manuscripts of different date and provenance. It has, moreover, turned up in in exactly the same position in the best and oldest codices. In those circumstances it seems safest to accept Ramirez de Verger's (1) conclusion (LII): 'On the authenticity or not of the *Somnium* (*Amores* III 5) I do not dare to make a definitive pronouncement. Now, until more evident proofs are offered that it does not belong to Ovid, it must continue to be edited, as coming from Ovid's pen, in the place where it is transmitted in PYS'.

But there are other difficulties. Perhaps the most obvious objection to 3.5 is that this elegy is very different from the other poems that make up *Amores*. Müller (1863: 81), for example, complained that 'the whole poem has such a morose seriousness, such a solemn mood, that it is strangely out of harmony...with Ovid's familiar tone'.[6] Different it certainly is. But so is 3.13, a poem in which a serious husband accompanies his wife on a solemn pilgrimage. And then there are 2.13 and 2.14, poems which raise the issue of abortion. The problem with this objection is that it underestimates the collection's tonal variety.

---

[4] For allusions to 3.5 in the Carolingian poets Paul the Deacon and Theodulf of Orleans see below on 2.

[5] Munari (144, n. 1), however, is aware that this rejection may refer to a different poem. For the fourteenth-century condemnation see Ghisalberti (1946: 50–1). For the text (with translation) of the medieval *de Somnio* see Hexter, Pfuntner, and Haynes (2020: 308–13).

[6] See also Kenney (1962: 12): 'The content, tone, and style are un-Ovidian and accord ill with the collection as a whole. Gloom and mystery...pervade the poem'.

Another objection is that 3.5 is not very good. Again, this was the view of Müller (1856: 75): 'I agree with Merkel that all of this poem seems unworthy of Ovid'.[7] That is hardly a reason for rejecting Ovid's authorship. Even Ovid nods. Note too that Kenney (1962: 13) disagrees: 'The *Somnium* is, in its way, a fine poem, and the work of an accomplished poet'.

Kenney (1962: 12) raises different kinds of problems, arguing that 'the language and style present specifically un-Ovidian features'.[8] These include (a) un-Ovidian repetitions at 7–8, 27–8, and 31–3; (b) the use of hyperbaton at 14 and 18; and (c) miscellaneous other verbal details. Some years later Kenney (1969b: 2) added an additional argument: 'the narrator of the dream is a married man'. Since I propose to deal with these objections in the appropriate place below, I will content myself with noting that both repetition[9] and hyperbaton[10] are marked features of Ovid's style. Note too that Kenney (1969b: 4) acknowledges what he calls the poem's '*Ouidianus character*' and recognizes it as a 'successful essay in the Ovidian manner'.[11]

If 3.5's subject matter, a dream and its interpretation, is exceptional in *Amores*, it is not unusual in the poetic tradition or even in love elegy. In *Iliad* 2, for example, Zeus sends Destructive Dream to Agamemnon (2.5–75), whose message the king either misinterprets or misuses. And in *Odyssey* 19 Penelope reports a dream in which animals symbolize humans (535–43), a dream which is then interpreted correctly by both the eagle within the dream and the disguised Odysseus (544–58). Closer still is the dream that Tarquinius reports in Accius' *Brutus* (17–28 Warmington; 651–74 Dangel [1995]), a dream in which the king sacrifices one ram but is brought down by its brother; closer to 3.5 because a seer is used to explain the dream's obvious significance.[12]

If we turn to elegy we find that Propertius reports several dreams, one in which Cynthia comes close to drowning (2.26a), another in which he encounters Apollo on Mt Helicon (3.1), and a third in which he is abused by Cynthia's ghost (4.7). And Ovid's Hero (*Her.* 19.199–202) reports a vision of a stranded dolphin, while the exiled poet would return to dream vision in *Pont.* 3.3. Important too is

---

[7] Cf. Merkel (1862: X): *Vereor ut in Amor. de solo carmine III 5 integro sit ambigendum* ('I am afraid that in *Amores* there is doubt about only one poem in its entirety, 3.5').

[8] Stylometric analysis (n. 3 above) does not support Kenney's claims.

[9] For Ovid's use of hyperbaton see e.g. Kenney (2002: 43): 'Of hyperbaton (artificial dislocation of word-order)...his use in his hexameters is relatively restrained. In his elegies license in this area has to some seemed to shade into abuse'. For Ovidian examples of hyperbaton see Platnauer (1951: 105–8).

[10] For Ovid's use of repetition see Kenney (2002: 47–8). For Ovid's repetitions see the Index Locorum to Wills (1996), where the list of references occupies five whole pages.

[11] McKeown's argument that 3.5 is not by Ovid because it lacks the expected allusions to Propertius or other elegists is not persuasive. For his argument to be convincing McKeown needs to establish that 3.5 is the *only* poem in *Amores* which fails to allude to appropriate models. He does not attempt to do this.

I pass over Zwierlein's (1999: 372–5) claim that Julius Montanus, a minor poet from the reign of Tiberius, is author of 3.5 (along with 3.9, 3.11, 3.13, and 3.14).

[12] Della Corte (1972: 321–4) lists other literary dreams involving animals.

Lygdamus' ([Tib.] 3.4) vision in which Apollo accuses the dreamer's girlfriend of unfaithfulness.[13]

How then does 3.5 fit with the rest of the collection? First, like many of the poems in Book 3, it reflects a man's concern with a woman's infidelity (cf. 3.3, 3.4, 3.8, 3.11, 3.12, and 3.14). Second, it invokes the language of the law, using such terms as *maritus* (15; cf. 1.9.25, 1.13.1, 2.2.51, 2.19.51, 57, 3.4.27, 3.8.63), *coniunx* (16; cf. 2.12.25 [of cattle], 3.4.37), and *adulterium* (44; cf. 1.3.22, 1.10.4, 2.18.37, 3.4.5, 8, 29, 37, 3.6.77, 3.8.33). Third, the poem opens with a description of an ideal landscape (2–8) reminiscent of the setting described in 3.1. Fourth, it uses the animal world as an analogue for human behaviour (e.g. 1.2.13–16, 1.10.25: *sumite in exemplum pecudes* ['take cattle as an example'], 2.12.25–6: *uidi ego pro niuea pugnantes coniuge tauros:* | *spectatrix animos ipsa iuuenca dabat,* ['I have seen bulls fighting over a snow-white wife: the watching cow gave them courage'], 3.11.36).[14] Fifth, as in 1.8, the lover fears the power of the procuress, the *lena*.[15]

Nevertheless, it has to be acknowledged that 3.5 surprises. But so do many other poems in the collection. 3.5 harmonizes so well with the rest of *Amores* that its *Ouidianus character*, to use Kenney's phrase, suggests that it was written by a poet very much like Ovid or, to apply Ockham's razor, by Ovid himself.[16]

Secondary literature: Munari (1948: 143–52); Kenney (1962); Frécaut (1968); Kenney (1969b); Della Corte (1972); Bertini (1976); Rambaux (1985: 145–7); Semmlinger (1988); Navarro Antolín (1996); Weinlich (1999: 181–3, 206–13); Bretzigheimer (2001: 263–72); McKeown (2002); Heyworth (2009); Knox (2009b); Heyworth in Morwood et al. (2011: 21–6); Ingleheart and Radice (2012); Martín Puente (2012); Scioli (2015: 43–54).

1–2. Nox erat et somnus lassos summisit ocellos;
    terruerunt animum talia uisa meum.

The beginning of this poem misleads: it is not until lines 31–2 that we discover that this is not a dramatic monologue, that the speaker is actually addressing a dream-interpreter. Others had adopted a similar tactic. In *Epode* 2, Horace reveals

---

[13] See below on 31.
[14] The dream is of the kind that Artemidorus calls 'allegorical' (1.2.11): 'Allegorical dreams are those which signify something by means of something else, when the soul says something obscurely in them by reference to the physical world'.
[15] Kenney (1969b: 3) lists 'echoes and parallels presented by the *Somnium*' with Ovid's other works. These might establish that the author of 3.5 knew Ovid very well; or that Ovid, one of the most self-referential of poets, was intimately familiar with 3.5, i.e. that he was the poem's author.
[16] Scholars have used structural arguments to support the authenticity of 3.5. Della Corte (1972: 329) and Bertini (1976: 156) claim that there are important thematic links between 1.5, 2.5, and 3.5. Holzberg (2002: 61) goes further: 'In fact, when one compares all fifteen elegies in Book 3 with all fifteen in Book 1 (something I cannot do in detail here) one discovers, at every turn, thematic affinities between the poems designated by the same number'. See also Holzberg (2014: 226). Lörcher (1975: 81–2) reckons that it is important that 3.6 and 3.10 be flanked by the non-mythological elegies 3.5 and 3.11. None of these arguments is persuasive.

Commentary, 5.1–3 159

in the last four lines that a moralizing discourse is delivered by a money-lender, while in *Elegy* 1.5 Tibullus withholds key information (the speaker is outside his girlfriend's house) until lines 67–8. Modern editors, apart from Munari, insert quotation marks and ruin the effect. (For the use of quotation marks in Latin texts see on 3.2.83–4.)

1. Nox erat: The phrase introduces reliable dream visions at *A.* 3.147 (Penates appear to Aeneas), 8.26 (Tiber to Aeneas), *Fast.* 3.639 (Dido to Anna). Consequently Lenz's (1966: 220) claim that the dream's timing (i.e. at night, and not just before dawn) undermines its plausibility is not persuasive.

summisit ocellos: Kenney (1962: 12) objects: '*somnus lassos submisit ocellos*: the omission of *mihi* or *nobis*, the use of *submittere* of lowering the eyes of another person, and the diminutive are all odd'.

The omission of *mihi* or *nobis* is not difficult. Readers of Latin are used to supplying personal pronouns. For examples with *summitto* see e.g. Stat. *Theb.* 4.761–2 (thirst lowers our courage): *sitis...| summittitque animos*, *Ach.* 1.327 (Thetis lowers Achilles' shoulders): *summittitque graues umeros. deicio ocellos/oculos*, however, is the more frequent expression (e.g. 1.8.37, 2.4.11, 3.6.67). For similar use of *deicio ocellos* without *mihi* or *nobis* see *Her.* 11.35 (shame lowers Canace's eyes): *gremioque pudor deiecit ocellos*.

It is hard to say whether using *summittere ocellos/oculos* of lowering another person's eyes is odd because the expression occurs only three times (also *Fast.* 3.372, Sen. *Dial.* 4.12.5.5).

Use of the diminutive *ocelli* is not unusual in *Amores*: 1.8.37, 1.14.37, 2.8.15, 2.19.19, 3.1.33, 3.2.83, 3.3.9, 3.6.57, 79, 3.9.49.

2. For this verbal pattern (VAbBa), in which a line begins with a verb followed by a chiastic arrangement of nouns and adjectives, see 1.1.18, 2.1.8, 2.5.48, 2.6.8, 3.5.10, 34, *Her.* 7.188, 10.22, 134, 11.22, 12.38, 188, 15.72, 74.

We know that 3.5 circulated in the eighth century because two Carolingian poets rework this line: Paul the Deacon 14.4 (Duemmler [1881: 51]): *terruerunt animum fortia uerba meum*; and Theodulf of Orleans 3.6 (Duemmler [1881: 525]): *mouerunt animum talia uisa meum?* For discussion see Munari (1948: 146), Semmlinger (1988: 473), and Lenz (1966: 220).

terruerunt: The speaker clearly intuits the import of his nightmare and this fact motivates his narrative.

3–4. colle sub aprico creberrimus ilice lucus
    stabat et in ramis multa latebat auis.
The speaker begins to describe the dream's setting, picturing an ideal landscape.

3. colle sub aprico: For the sunny hill as part of a *locus amoenus* see *Ecl.* 9.49, Tib. 1.4.19.

creberrimus ilice lucus: For the association of the ilex or holm oak with a perfect setting see 2.6.49, *Fast.* 3.295–6: *lucus Auentino suberat niger ilicis umbra, | quo posses uiso dicere 'numen inest'*.

4. in ramis multa latebat auis: Recalls the forest described at 3.1.4: *et latere ex omni dulce queruntur aues*.

5–6. area gramineo suberat uiridissima prato
 umida de guttis lene sonantis aquae.
The speaker turns to describing the meadow and stream. Kenney (1969b: 5) compares *Fast.* 4.427–8 and objects to 3.5's 'singularly unconvincing waterfall'. This, however, is not a description of a waterfall but of a stream passing through a meadow. Proximity to water, particularly in Mediterranean climates, makes fields more green. See, for example, the description of the territory around Sulmo (2.16.5–6, 9–10): *arua pererrantur Paeligna liquentibus undis, | et uiret in tenero fertilis herba solo; perque resurgentes riuis labentibus herbas | gramineus madidam caespes obumbrat humum.* Note too that the speaker is recounting a dream not describing an actual landscape.

5. Reworks the description of Elysium at 2.6.50: *udaque perpetuo gramine terra uiret*.

For the verbal pattern (AbVaB), a variation on the golden line, see 1.8.29, 2.14.24, 3.6.56, 58, 3.8.43, 3.9.10, 3.13.34, *Her.* 1.7, 2.94, 7.138, 151, 10.26, 47, 11.90, 12.52, 156, 14.24.

6. umida: Ramirez de Verger (2) follows Heinsius in printing *uuida*. Heinsius claimed the authority of his Puteaneus (=P) for this reading. P, however, clearly reads *umida*. Y has *umida*, S *humida*.

guttis...aquae: Not spray from a waterfall (*aspergine Fast.* 4.427), but fine drops of water vapour visible above a stream.

7–8. ipse sub arboreis uitabam frondibus aestum,
 fronde sub arborea sed tamen aestus erat.
This elegantly phrased couplet uses repetition and variation (*sub arboreis... frondibus | fronde sub arborea; aestum |...aestus erat*) to underline the speaker's failure to achieve his stated goal. Kenney (1962: 12) observes that this repetition 'might pass as Ovidian'. Repetition with variation within lines and couplets is standard Ovidian practice. Here are three comparable examples from different erotic works: (3.8.11–12): *hunc potes amplecti formosis, uita, lacertis? | huius in amplexu, uita, iacere potes?*; *Her.* 3.5–6: *si mihi pauca queri de te dominoque uiroque | fas est, de domino pauca uiroque querar*, *Ars* 1.191–2: *auspiciis annisque patris, puer, arma mouebis, | et uinces annis auspiciisque patris*.

aestum |...aestus erat: As becomes clear at line 36, the day's heat symbolizes sexual passion: *aestus amoris erat*. Allusion to the opening words of 1.5 underlines a change in tone: what was positive is now entirely negative.

7. arboreis...frondibus: Ovid uses similar language when describing Io's plight (*Met.* 1.632) and Atlas' realm (*Met.* 4.637).

9–10. ecce petens uariis immixtas floribus herbas,
   constitit ante oculos candida uacca meos,
With *ecce* comes a shift in focus from the environment to the first of its occupants.

9. uariis...floribus: As in lines 3 and 5, the details imply an ideal landscape, in this case a Virgilian one (*Ecl.* 9.40–1): *hic uer purpureum, uarios hic flumina circum | fundit humus flores*; (*A.* 6.707–8): *ac ueluti in pratis ubi apes aestate serena | floribus insidunt uariis*.

10. For this verbal pattern (VAbBa) see above on 2.

candida uacca: The emphasis on the cow's radiant whiteness (also at 11 and 13) points to the cow symbolizing the dreamer's partner, the ideal woman often being represented as *candida* in erotic poetry (e.g. Catul. 68b.70, 86.1; Prop. 2.3.9, 2.22a.5, 8, 3.11.16; *Am.* 1.5.10, 1.7.40, 2.7.5, 2.18.29).

11–14. candidior niuibus, tunc cum cecidere recentes,
   in liquidas nondum quas mora uertit aquas,
candidior, quod adhuc spumis stridentibus albet
   et modo siccatam, lacte, reliquit ouem.
To highlight the cow's whiteness the dreamer turns to two similes. While each image might be considered conventional (whiter than snow, whiter than milk), each is enlivened by remarkable precision. For multiple similes in *Amores* see 1.5.11–12, 1.7.13–18, 1.10.1–6, 2.5.35–40 (five similes for the colour red).

11. For a similarly precise comparison to snow see *Met.* 2.852–3 (of Jupiter as bull): *quippe color niuis est, quam nec uestigia duri | calcauere pedis nec soluit aquaticus auster*, *Pont.* 2.5.37–8: *non ego laudandus, sed sunt tua pectora lacte | et non calcata candidiora niue*.

candidior: For the shift from positive to comparative form of an adjective see 2.16.7: *ferax...feracior*, 3.2.32: *fortes...fortior*, Her. 16.85–6: *pulchrae...pulchrior*, 18.73: *formosis formosior*.

12. Implicit here is a contrast with the stream described at 3.6.7–8: *nunc ruis apposito niuibus de monte solutis | et turpi crassas gurgite uoluis aquas*.

13–14. Kenney (1962: 12), while acknowledging that 'Ovid's predilection for this figure is notorious', found the use of hyperbaton in this couplet (the displacement of *lacte*) so 'violent' that he used it as evidence for non-Ovidian authorship. This example, however, is no more difficult than *Her.* 7.147–8: *utque latet uitatque tuas abstrusa carinas, | uix tibi continget terra petita seni*; and certainly less 'violent' than 2.2.4 (*illā, quae Danai porticus agmen habet = illā porticu quae habet Danai agmen*), where the antecedent of a relative clause (*porticu*) has been transferred to the relative clause and attracted into a different case (*porticus*). And see Housman's (1889: 7) list of his top ten Ovidian hyperbata. More extraordinary still is Met. 7.593–5:

> <u>admoti</u> quotiens templis, dum uota sacerdos
> concipit et fundit durum inter cornua uinum,
> haud exspectato ceciderunt uulnere <u>tauri</u>.

The displacement of *lacte* to the next line may be daring, but it is more likely to be the daring of an original poet than an imitator.

13. candidior: For the use of anaphora to highlight multiplicity of similes see 1.10.1–6: *qualis... qualis... qualis*; 2.5.35–8: *quale... quale*.

14. lacte...ouem: McKeown (2002: 119) criticizes the comparison of a cow's colour to sheep's milk. The simile might be odd if the Romans associated cows with milk. But they did not. The Romans used cattle for sacrifice, labour, and meat; they used sheep for cheese-making and wool (Chandezon [2015]).

15–16. taurus erat comes huic, feliciter ille maritus,
 cumque sua teneram coniuge pressit humum.
Having described an exquisitely beautiful cow, the dreamer turns now to the cow and her bull as a married couple. Use of matrimonial language of animals (and trees) is normal not only in poetry but in agricultural handbooks. See e.g. *Ecl.* 7.7: *uir gregis ipse caper*, *G.* 3.125 (of a horse): *quem legere ducem et pecori dixere maritum*, Hor. *Carm.* 1.17.7 (of goats): *olentis uxores mariti*, Col. 7.6.4.5 (of goats): *maritos gregum*, 8.2.11.5 (of birds): *coniugalem gregem*.

Not surprisingly, the language of elegiac poetry is not used of the farmyard: Columella uses *puella* only once and then of a human being (12.1.1: an estate manager's wife should not be *nimium puella*). He does not use *domina* at all. Bretzigheimer points out (2001: 264) that the worlds of the dream and the dreamer are distinct, that the language of marriage (*maritus, coniunx*) is confined to the vision, and that it is the *augur* who links bovine spouses with elegiac lovers. It follows that we cannot infer that 'the narrator of the dream is a married man' (Kenney [1969b: 2]).

16. For this verbal pattern (abAVB), the third most frequent in *Amores*, see above on 3.2.40.

17–18. dum iacet et lente reuocatas ruminat herbas
 atque iterum pasto pascitur ante cibo,
Focus now shifts to the 'husband'. While the description of the bull's digestive processes may be physiologically accurate, the language suggests complacency.

17. iacet: Perhaps recalls the description of the girlfriend's *uir* (1.4.53): *si bene compositus somno uinoque iacebit*.

ruminat: The verb first occurs in its literal sense at *Ecl.* 6.54: *ilice sub nigra pallentis ruminat herbas*. Clausen (1994: ad loc.) notes that earlier writers treat the verb as deponent and employ it metaphorically. Its only other occurrence in verse is at *Hal.* 119, in a passage which may imitate this one: *ut scarus* (a sea fish) *epastas solus qui ruminat escas*.

18. pasto pascitur: As often in Ovid (see on 3.2.32), repetition frames the main caesura. Kenney (1962: 12) claims that '*pasto* used passively of the food eaten seems not to be paralleled except by *Hal.* 119 *epastas*' (quoted above). But see Prop. 2.33a.12 (with Camps [1967: ad loc.] and Fedeli [2005: ad loc.]): *stabulis arbuta pasta tuis*. Virgil uses *depasco* in the same way *A.* 5.93 (of a serpent): *successit tumulo et depasta altaria liquit*.

As it happens, Ovid's authorship of this line is better attested than most (see Servius on *Ecl.* 6.54 [quoted in the introduction above]). For Ovid's presence in Servius see Haynes (2015) and Delvigo (2019).

19-20. uisus erat, somno uires adimente ferendi,
  cornigerum terra deposuisse caput.
The bull's complacency of the previous couplet now becomes complete inattention to his 'wife's' behaviour.

19. uires: The bull's lack of *uires* perhaps suggests the dreamer's lack of sexual attentiveness or vigour. Cf. 1.8.47: *Penelope iuuenum uires temptabat in arcu*, 2.10.25: *et lateri dabit in uires alimenta uoluptas*.

20. cornigerum...deposuisse caput: Bretzigheimer (2001: 271) notes that if a bull's horns are its weapons, this phrase implies unwillingness to fight. For *deponere arma* see e.g. *A.* 12.707, Sen. *Ag.* 229, Sil. 16.218.

21-2. huc leuibus cornix pinnis delapsa per auras
  uenit et in uiridi garrula sedit humo,
Into this apparently idyllic scene, however, comes a talkative crow.

21. cornix: In Artemidorus' dream-handbook crows symbolize, among other things, old women (2.20.50): 'Because of its longevity the crow signifies a long time, delay in business, and an old woman'. And that is how the *augur* interprets the crow at 39-40. For the association between crows and old age see e.g. Hes. fr. 254.1 (Most), *Am.* 2.6.35-6, *Met.* 7.274.

delapsa per auras: The phrase is used of unexpected apparitions e.g. *A.* 11.595 (Opis comes for Camilla's corpse), *Ars* 1.43 (a girl will not appear *delapsa per auras*), *Met.* 3.101 (Minerva).

22. garrula: For the crow as talkative see *Met.* 2.547-8 (*garrula...cornix*), *Fast.* 2.89 (*loquax...cornix*). Given that this crow will be interpreted as a *lena* (40), the conventional garrulity of the procuress is also relevant (McKeown [1989: 212], citing Plaut. *Cist.* 120-2,149).

Commentary

**23–4. terque bouis niueae petulanti pectora rostro
fodit et albentis abstulit ore iubas.**
In a couplet notable for its alliteration (*petulanti pectora, albentis abstulit ... iubas*), the dreamer reports the crow's assault on the bull's 'wife'.

23. bouis niueae: Recalls the simile likening the cow to fresh snow (11–12).

petulanti ... rostro: While *petulanti* primarily underlines the crow's aggressive behaviour (*OLD* 1), the adjective's other meaning (*OLD* 2c: 'wanton, immodest') is also present.

pectora ... | fodit: The phrase is used in both physical and psychological contexts. Within the dream it denotes the action of piercing the cow's breast. When applied to the dreamer's world, however, it suggests the arousal of unhealthy emotions (see 39–40). Cf. Sil. 5.158-9: *is uero ingentia sumat | e medio, fodiant quae magnas pectus in iras.*

24. albentis: Ovid is the first poet to use the participle of *albeo* as a metrically convenient synonym for *albus*. See also *Her.* 11.67, *Ars* 2.666, 3.182, *Met.* 3.516, 5.110, 7.415, 11.176, 13.534, 15.519, 15.676, *Pont.* 4.12.30. Manilius, Seneca, and the three Flavian epicists follow suit.

abstulit ... iubas: This motif drawn from sacrifice, as at *A.* 4.698-9 (with Pease [1935: ad loc.]), perhaps signifies the cow's (i.e. the girl's) destruction.

iubas: Usually used of lions and horses, *iuba* is sometimes used of cattle e.g. *Fast.* 5.607, Sen. *Phaed.* 1037, Calp. *Ecl.* 7.62.

**25–6. illa locum taurumque diu cunctata reliquit,
sed niger in uaccae pectore liuor erat;**
The crow's pecking prompts the cow to abandon her 'husband'.

25. The line is reworked and its meaning expounded at 40–1 below.

diu cunctata: The phrase occurs twice in 3.5, here and (with slight variation: *cunctata diu* 41) in the augur's exposition. See also *Epic. Drusi* (*Consolation to Livia*) 253: *flamma diu cunctata caput contingere sanctum.* Richmond (1981: 2780) and Knox (2009b: 214) date the *Consolation* to before 37 CE.

reliquit: Showerman and Goold follow some older editors in printing *relinquit*. Most modern editors accept *reliquit* transmitted in P, S, and Y.

26. niger ... liuor: As at *Met.* 10.258 ([of Pygmalion]: *pressos ueniat ne liuor in artus*) and *Tr.* 2.455 (*quibus e sucis abeat de corpore liuor*), *liuor* is used here in its primary physical sense. Elsewhere (1.15.1, 39; *Rem.* 365, 369, 389; *Met.* 6.129, 515; *Fast.* 4.85; *Tr.* 4.10.123, *Pont.* 3.1.65, 3.3.101, 3.4.74), it is a term of moral condemnation: 'envy, spite, malice' (*OLD* 2). The secondary sense is pertinent here too, as the dream-interpreter makes clear (43–4).

27-8. utque procul uidit carpentes pabula tauros
   (carpebant tauri pabula laeta procul),
Kenney (1962: 12) objects to this repetition as 'un-Ovidian'. But repetition in parenthetic 'stage directions' is characteristic of Ovid e.g. *Her.* 11.95: *'Aeolus hunc ensem mittit tibi' (tradidit ensem), Ars* 3.53-4: *dixit, et e myrto (myrto nam uincta capillos | constiterat), Met.* 6.358-9: *qui nostro bracchia tendunt | parua sinu, (et casu tendebant bracchia nati),* 10.556-7: *libet hac requiescere tecum" | (et requieuit), Fast.* 3.171-2: *sic posita dixit mihi casside Mavors | (sed tamen in dextra missilis hasta fuit),* 4.691: *'hoc' ait 'in campo' (campumque ostendit).* For three 'stage directions' in six lines (two with repetitions) see *Ars* 2.131-5:

> ille leui uirga (uirgam nam forte tenebat)
>   quod rogat, in spisso litore pingit opus.
> 'haec' inquit 'Troia est' (muros in litore fecit):
>   'hic tibi sit Simois; haec mea castra puta.
> campus erat' (campumque facit).

For parenthetic repetitions in Ovid and others see Wills (1996: 337-41).

29-30. illuc se rapuit gregibusque immiscuit illis
   et petiit herbae fertilioris humum.
The account of the dream closes with the bull's 'wife' leaving him for other herds and greener pastures.

29. se rapuit: Alcyone uses similar language when addressing the dream-figure of Ceyx (*Met.* 11.676): *mane! quo te rapis? ibimus una.* The expression is rare. *TLL* (104.59-71) also lists Hor. *S.* 2.7.117-18, VF 6.581.

se...immiscuit illis: This phrase is perhaps adapted by Phaedrus (15 BCE - 50 CE: 1.3.7 [of a jackdaw consorting with peacocks]): *se immiscuit pauonum formoso gregi.*

30. Recalls the proverbial idea that 'the grass is always greener'. The Teacher uses a similar image when explaining female desire *Ars* 1.349-50: *fertilior seges est alienis semper in agris, | uicinumque pecus grandius uber habet.* For other examples of the proverb see Otto (1890: 13).

herbae fertilioris: For the genitive of description see Woodcock (§84-5) and Pinkster (1.1002-3).

31-2. dic age, nocturnae, quicumque es, imaginis augur,
   si quid habent ueri, uisa quid ista ferant.
The dreamer closes his speech with a surprise: we have not been reading a monologue, but an address to a dream-interpreter.

31. dic age: For the phrase used when addressing an authoritative source of information see e.g. *A.* 6.343 (Aeneas to Palinurus), *Met.* 12.177 (Achilles to Nestor), *Fast.* 1.149 (Teacher to Janus).

nocturnae...imaginis: Lygdamus reworks this phrase when reporting a dream in which Apollo accuses his girlfriend, Neaera, of infidelity [Tib.] 3.4.55-6: *et cum te fusco Somnus uelauit amictu,* | *uanum nocturnis fallit imaginibus.*

quicumque es: Adds to the poem's strangeness: the dream-interpreter's identity is unknown.

augur: Technically denoting an interpreter of bird behaviour, especially a member of the college of augurs, the term is commonly transferred to prophets of any kind (*OLD* 2).

32. si quid habent ueri: Adapts *A.* 7.273: *si quid ueri mens augurat.* Ovid reuses the phrase at *Met.* 15.879: *si quid habent ueri uatum praesagia, uiuam* and *Tr.* 4.10.129: *si quid habent igitur uatum praesagia ueri.* For hesitation about the reliability of prophets in Augustan poets and Lucan see O'Hara (1990: 55-6).

33-4. sic ego; nocturnae sic dixit imaginis augur,
  expendens animo singula dicta suo:
With this couplet the speaker marks a transition between his own speech and that of the dream-interpreter. *Fasti*'s Teacher employs the same technique at 3.171-2, 4.195-6, 5.193-4, and 6.655-6.

33. sic ego: Marks the end of a speech to a divinity in each of the *Fasti* passages cited above (Mars, Erato, Flora, Minerva) and at *Fast.* 6.801 (Clio), Mart. 6.10.11 (Minerva).

nocturnae...imaginis auctor: The phrase is repeated from 31. For repetition with variation see above on 7-8.

sic dixit: The phrase introduces Cupid's speech at *Rem.* 555-6: *is mihi sic dixit (dubito, uerusne Cupido,* | *an somnus fuerit: sed puto, somnus erat).*

34. For this verbal pattern (VAbBa) see above on 2.

expendens...singula dicta: For this metaphorical use of *expendere* (*OLD* 5) see e.g. *Met.* 13.150: *meritis expendite causam.* Closer still is Tac. *Ann.* 13.3.15: *Tiberius artem quoque callebat qua uerba expenderet.*

35-6. quem tu mobilibus foliis uitare uolebas,
  sed male uitabas, aestus amoris erat.
The dream-interpreter begins by considering the symbolism of the landscape described in 2-8.

35. mobilibus foliis: The image, as Kenney (1969b: 6-7) notes, derives from Hor. *Carm.* 1.23.5-6: *nam seu mobilibus ueris inhorruit* | *aduentus foliis.* Kenney rightly observes that shifting leaves would imply 'a breeze' that would bring 'some sort of relief'. He is wrong, however, to criticize the image for that reason. The dreamer hopes to find relief by means of a breeze (instrumental ablative) but cannot, because there is no breeze and the leaves are not 'shifting'. *Her.* 5.109–10 adapts Horace differently and is not relevant.

36. male uitabas: As Kenney notes, *male* here effectively means *non*.

aestus amoris: The use of *aestus* in erotic contexts (e.g. 1.5.1, 3.2.39–40 [with note above]) eases the shift from literal to metaphorical heat.

37–8. uacca puella tua est: aptus color ille puellae;
   tu uir et in uacca compare taurus eras.
From the landscape the interpreter turns to the symbolism of the cow and bull.

37. puella: When the interpreter shifts from the symbolic to the 'real' world he employs the language of love elegy, not that of marriage. While the cow was a *coniunx* (16), the woman is a *puella*. (For *puella* as an elegiac term see on 3.2.17.)

color ille: Recalls the emphasis on the cow being *candida* (10, 11, 13) and avoids repetition of an adjective that has already been used three times. For the colour's appropriateness for a *puella* see above on 10. Kenney's [1969b: 5] claim that the phrase is evidence of 'careless plagiarism' from *Ars* 1.729 is not persuasive.

38. uir: Frequently designates the elegiac lover. For its ambiguity (lover / husband) see the introduction to 3.4.

39–40. pectora quod rostro cornix fodiebat acuto,
   ingenium dominae lena mouebit anus.
And the pecking crow symbolizes a procuress's incitement to wrongdoing.

39. Recalls the description of the crow's behaviour at 21–4.

40. ingenium…mouebit: Ovid uses this expression in different ways. Here it suggests that the *lena* perverts the beloved's character. At *Ars* 2.43 (with Janka [1997: ad loc.]) it is used to restate the proverb 'Necessity is the mother of invention': *ingenium mala saepe mouent*. At 3.12.16 and *Tr.* 4.10.59–60 it asserts that Corinna inspired his talent as an erotic poet: *ingenium mouit sola Corinna meum; mouerat ingenium…|…Corinna mihi.*

Kenney (1996: 13) suggests that *mouere* means 'inspire' at 3.12.16, *Ars* 2.43, and *Tr.* 4.10.59–60. If so, 'inspire' at *Ars* 2.43 (does Corinna count as a *malum*?) is very different from 'inspire' in the other two cases. Semmlinger (1988: 466–7) also notes the shift in meaning between the examples of Corinna (3.12.16 and *Tr.* 4.10.59–60) and Daedalus (*Ars* 2.43).

dominae: As in 37–8, the interpreter translates the dream vision into elegiac language. (For *domina* as an elegiac term see on 3.2.18.)

lena…anus: The *lena*'s age links her with the crow (see on 21) and the procuress of Book 1 (1.8.1–2): *est quaedam (quicumque uolet cognoscere lenam, | audiat), est*

168   *Commentary*

quaedam nomine Dipsas anus. Fear that greed may transform a mistress into a prostitute is a persistent concern in Book 3 (3.1, 3.8, 3.11, 3.14).

mouebit: This is the reading of S and possibly P. (P is very hard to read at this point.) Y offers *mouebat*. The future is preferable because, as *destituere* (42) makes clear, the point of the dream is its predictive force.

41–2. quod cunctata diu taurum sua uacca reliquit,
     frigidus in uiduo destituere toro.
While the hexameter restates a key element in the dream (*taurumque diu cunctata reliquit* 25), the pentameter underlines its significance for the dreamer.

42. frigidus: For 'cold' as the equivalent of 'sexless' or 'loveless' see 2.1.5: *frigida uirgo*, 2.7.9: *in te quoque frigidus esse*.

uiduo…toro: For an empty bed as a misfortune see 2.10.17–18: *hostibus eueniat uiduo dormire cubili | et medio laxe ponere membra toro, Her.* 5.106, 10.14, 16.317–18.

43–4. liuor et aduerso maculae sub pectore nigrae
      pectus adulterii labe carere negant.
As in the previous couplet, the hexameter looks back (*sed niger in uaccae pectore liuor erat* 26), while the pentameter expounds its significance.

43. liuor: For *liuor* see above on 26.

aduerso…pectore: The adjective indicates that the mark is on the cow's front (*OLD aduersus* 4b). Despite Kenney's (1969b: 5) claim, *aduerso pectore* does not always imply 'an encounter of some kind'. See e.g. *Met.* 4.803 (of Minerva wearing the Gorgon): *pectore in aduerso, quos fecit, sustinet angues.* Hill (1985) translates: 'She keeps the snakes she made on the front of her breast'. Rosati (in Barchiesi and Rosati [2007: ad loc.]) agrees: '*in aduerso* because her gaze is at the front and therefore effective'.

44. adulterii: Kenney (1969b: 2), arguing that the speaker must be a married man, comments: '*adulterium*…must mean "adultery" not merely "infidelity"'. But see Propertius' account of an early morning visit to Cynthia (2.29b.37–8): *aspice ut in toto nullus mihi corpore surgat | spiritus admisso motus adulterio.*

45–6. dixerat interpres. gelido mihi sanguis ab ore
      fugit et ante oculos nox stetit alta meos.
The poem's final lines recall its opening. The fear that the dreamer felt in the first couplet (*terruerunt* 2) has proved justified. For ring composition in this poem see Bertini (1976).

45. gelido mihi sanguis ab ore: For the association of blood and cold with fear see e.g. *A.* 3.30, 259, 12.905. For fear and cold see e.g. *Her.* 5.37, 11.82, 15.112, 16.67.

46. nox…alta: The literal night of the poem's first words has become a metaphor for despair.

3.6: TO A RIVER

Persuasion is central to many poems in *Amores*. Sometimes speakers attempt to defend themselves (e.g. 2.7: I did not sleep with your slave; 2.10: I can love two girls), sometimes to make a paradoxical case (1.9: a lover's life is like a soldier's). More often they try to change someone else's behaviour (e.g. 1.10: Don't ask for gifts; 1.14: Stop dyeing your hair; 2.11: Don't leave me; 3.2: Have sex with me). 3.6 falls into this latter category. It differs from the other examples, however, in having no possible chance of success. In fact, the elegy that 3.6 most closely resembles is 1.13, a poem which attempts to persuade the sun from rising. In 3.6 the speaker's goal is to induce a flooding river to lower its waters and let him cross.[1] What can be the point of such a poem?

The question becomes more pressing when we consider the poem's length: at 106 lines this is the second longest poem in the three-book collection.[2] One answer must be that it gives the poet an opportunity for a display of wit and rhetorical skill. Readers can only marvel at the speaker's ingenuity, at the ability to produce more and more evidence and arguments to support an impossible case.

Some claim that the poem has a metaliterary dimension. Barchiesi (1989: 63; 2001a: 54),[3] for example, notes that 'the river is described in essentially "anti-Callimachean" terms'. In support of this case we can point to seeming allusions to Callimachus' defence of his aesthetic principles at the end of the *Hymn to Apollo* (105–12):

> Envy spoke secretly into the ears of Apollo: 'I do not like a poet who does not sing as much as the sea'. Apollo kicked Envy with his foot and spoke as follows: 'The Assyrian river's flow is great, but it drags a lot of the earth's filth and much rubbish on its water. The bees do not carry water from every source to Deo, but the tiny trickle which springs up pure and undefiled from the sacred fountain, the very best'.

Callimachus had also employed water imagery when speaking of both his literary and his amatory choices (*Epigr.* 28.1–4):

> I loathe the cyclic poem, nor do I take pleasure in a path which takes many people this way and that; I hate the wandering boyfriend and I do not drink from a fountain; I detest everything that's popular.

---

[1] Cf. Luc. 2.485–90 where Domitius urges a river to flood and halt Caesar's advance.
[2] *Am.* 1.8 is the longest (114 lines). [3] See also Suter (1989) and Boyd (1997: 212).

170   *Commentary*

It is possible that Ovid alludes to these passages when the lover expresses his erotic preferences at 2.19.31–2:[4] *quod licet et facile est quisquis cupit, arbore frondis | carpat et e magno flumine potet aquam* ('Whoever desires what's allowed and easy, should pluck leaves from a tree and drink water from a mighty river') and when he describes the recalcitrant stream at 3.6.7–8: *nunc ruis apposito niuibus de monte solutis | et turpi crassas gurgite uoluis aquas* ('Now when the snows dissolve on the nearby mountain you rush down and roll your muddy waters in a foul eddy').[5]

What would be the point of allusion to Callimachus' aesthetic principles in a poem that purports to express a lover's frustrations? One answer might be that 3.6 incorporates material that as yet has no parallel in *Amores*,[6] including a lengthy catalogue (25–44), catalogues being a fixture in epic poetry, and a central episode (45–82) which reworks an episode from Ennius' *Annales*. The inclusion of material familiar from heroic poetry, particularly from Rome's oldest hexameter epic, might well prompt reflection on the capacity of elegiac poetry to accommodate this alien subject matter.

It must be said, however, that 3.6 displays no signs of such reflection.[7] While this material may seem unfamiliar to readers of *Amores*, it does have parallels in works less grand than those of Homer, Ennius, and Virgil. After all, the catalogue in 3.6 is not a list of land or naval forces, but of sexually-active rivers. And lists had been a feature of non-heroic poetry from the beginning. Hesiod, for example, had written a poem that we call the *Catalogue of Women*, a genealogical account in several books of women prominent in Greek mythology, while his *Theogony* (337–45) had included a list of rivers. Moreover, catalogues were a regular feature of Hellenistic poetry, including Phanocles' *Erotes or Beautiful Boys*, Nicaenetus' *Catalogue of Women*,[8] and Callimachus' *Aetia*, described by Cameron as a 'catalogue poem in several books'.[9] Callimachus had included a list of not-yet-existing rivers in his *Hymn to Zeus* (18–27) and composed a prose treatise *On the Rivers of the Inhabited World*.[10] Even more importantly, as Courtney (1988: 20–1) points out, he had included in his *Hymn to Delos* a catalogue of rivers approached by the pregnant Leto, some of which also occur in Ovid's list (Inachus [*Hymn* 4.74], and Asopus [4.78]). Particularly telling is the fact that both Callimachus and Ovid refer to the nymph Melie (4.80; 3.6.25) and both address the river Peneus and refer to its location in Phthia: Πηνειὲ Φθιῶτα ('Phthiotian Peneius' 4.112);

---

[4] For discussion of the Callimachean implications of the language used in 2.19 see Lateiner (1978).
[5] For the metaliterary function of allusion to Callimachus' *Hymn to Apollo* in *Metamorphoses* 8, particularly the characterization of Achelous, see Hinds (1987: 19) and Barchiesi (2011: 523).
[6] There is an equally long catalogue at 3.12.19–40.
[7] In *Fasti*, by contrast, the inclusion of material more typical of epic does generate what Robinson (2011: 137–8) calls 'generic anxiety'.
[8] For Phanocles, Nicaenetus, and other Hellenistic catalogue poets see Asquith (2005), Cameron (1995: 380–6), and Hunter (2005).
[9] Cameron (1995: 382).   [10] For this see Krevans (2011: 128–9).

Commentary, 6.1   171

Penee...| Pthiotum terris ('Peneus in the territory of the Phthiotians' 31-2). The catalogue of rivers in 3.6 is very much in keeping with Hesiodic and subsequent traditions.[11]

The same argument applies to the inclusion of quasi-historical Roman subject matter. Aspiring to be the 'Roman Callimachus' (4.1a.64), Propertius had widened Latin love elegy's range in his fourth book with poems on Tarpeia (4.3), the foundation of the Ara Maxima (4.9), and the origins of the *spolia opima* (4.10). Given the *princeps*' concern with shaping perceptions of the Roman past,[12] it is clear that Propertius had extended elegy's engagement with politics from concern with purely sexual matters[13] into a new and potentially risky field. Thus the *spolia opima* ('the spoils of honour'), an award given to a commander who killed the enemy leader, were a matter of current concern to Augustus and not merely of antiquarian interest (Liv. 4.20). While no poem in *Amores* is exclusively concerned with early Roman history, Ovid can be seen as following Propertian precedent by recounting the aftermath of Ilia's rape, Ilia being the mother of Romulus, a figure central to the Augustan vision of history.[14]

Secondary literature: Morgan (1977: 88-90); J. T. Davis (1980), Courtney (1988), Suter (1989), Connors (1994); Keith (1994); Boyd (1997: 214-19); Davis (2006: 78-80); Barchiesi (2001a); Bretzigheimer (2001: 177-9), Brecke (2021).

1-2. Amnis, harundinibus limosas obsite ripas,
   ad dominam propero: siste parumper aquas.
As in 2.15 and 3.4, the speaker begins abruptly with a noun in the vocative. Here the vocative is followed by an offensive description of the addressee, a blunt statement, and a peremptory command.

1. Amnis: The only parallels for addressing a non-anthropomorphic being in love elegy are 1.12.7-30, where the poet curses writing tablets, and 2.15, where he apostrophizes a ring. Cf. Theoc. 28 (addressed to a distaff), *Tr.* 1.1.1 (*parue...liber*), and Mart. 3.2.1 (*libelle*).

harundinibus limosas...ripas: The description is not flattering. See Porphyrio's comment on Hor. *S.* 1.10.36-7: 'For in describing the Rhine, which is rightly called muddy, because of its eternally murky waters (*turbida semper aqua*) and

---

[11] For the Hellenistic fascination with Hesiod see e.g. Asquith (2005) and Hunter (2005). For Callimachus' prose treatise *On the Rivers of the Inhabited World* see Krevans (2011: 128-9). Also of interest is a six-line epigram of Antiphilus (*PA* 9.277) in which the poet confronts a raging stream that he wishes to cross. Given that Antiphilus seems to have dedicated a poem to the emperor Nero, the epigram is almost certainly later in date than 3.6. See Gow and Page (1969: Vol. 2, 119-20).

[12] This concern was most obviously embodied in the Augustan forum where the key figures of Roman history were represented together with descriptions of their achievements. For discussion see e.g. Zanker (1988: Chapter 5), Luce (1990), Boyle (2003: 205-11).

[13] However we interpret the poem, Prop. 2.7 is evidence of the poet's awareness that the law might affect his relationship with 'Cynthia'.

[14] For the importance of Romulus in Augustus' representation of the past see, for example, discussions of his role in the Augustan Forum in Zanker (1988: 201-10) and Barchiesi (2002).

172   *Commentary*

slimy banks (*limosis ripis*)…'. Cf. Virgil's sketch of the river that flows past his native Mantua (*Ecl.* 7.12–13): *hic uiridis tenera praetexit harundine ripas | Mincius*, where the choice of adjectives and word order (abVBA) suggest the speaker's affection for a beautiful site.

2. dominam: For the connotations of *domina* in love elegy see above on 3.2.18.

siste…aquas: Halting waters is usually associated (at least in poetry) with witchcraft. See e.g. AR 3.532 (Medea): 'She immediately halts the flow of noisy rivers', *A.* 4.489 (a priestess): *sistere aquam fluuiis et uertere sidera retro*, *Her.* 6.87 (Medea again): *illa refrenat aquas obliquaque flumina sistit*, *Met.* 7.153–4 (Medea yet again). The lover, however, is no sorcerer and his words fail.

3–4. nec tibi sunt pontes nec quae sine remigis ictu
    concaua traiecto cumba rudente uehat.
The lover continues by listing even more of the river's failings: it has no bridge or cable ferry.

The elaborate periphrasis, which occupies more than half the hexameter and all the pentameter, seems designed to avoid the use of a prosaic word like *ponto*, which occurs in utilitarian texts like Caesar (*BC* 3.29.3), Aulus Gellius (10.25.5.6: in a list of different kinds of boats), and the *Digest* (8.3.38): 'A *uia* can be established even if a river intervenes, if it can be crossed by ford or has a bridge: the situation is different if it has to be traversed by boats (*pontonibus*)'.

4. For this verbal pattern (abABV) see above on 3.1.22.

5–8. paruus eras, memini, nec te transire refugi
    summaque uix talos contigit unda meos.
nunc ruis apposito niuibus de monte solutis
    et turpi crassas gurgite uoluis aquas.
Contrasting the stream's former condition with its present state suggests that it has departed from its true nature. Its current violence, volume, and filth are not characteristic.

5. transire refugi: The use of *refugio* with a prolative infinitive is confined to poetry. See Hor. *Carm.* 1.1.34 (with Mayer [2012: ad loc.]), Sen. *Ag.* 419–20. For the prolative infinitive see Woodcock (§§22–3), Pinkster (2.204).

6. For this verbal pattern (aBVAb), a variation on the 'golden line' (see above on 3.3.21), see also 2.11.34, 3.15.16, *Her.* 2.68, 11.110, 13.116, 165, 15.150.

summaque…unda: The phrase has an epic ring e.g. *A.* 1.147 (of Neptune): *atque rotis summas leuibus perlabitur undas*, 6.357 (Palinurus), *Met.* 2.457 (of Diana), Luc. 3.702. Here, however, it underlines the stream's previous lack of epic qualities.

7–8. The description of the river's present state, by contrast, evokes Homeric similes e.g. *Il.* 11.492–5: 'As when a swollen river descends to the plain, winter-flowing, down from the mountains, forced on by the rain of Zeus, and it brings many dry oaks and many pines and throws much filth into the sea'. See also *Il.* 4.452–4, 5.87–92, 16.389–92, 17.263–5.

Both lines impress with their interweaving of nouns and adjectives. For the form of the hexameter (VaBAb) see *Her.* 18.211; for the pentameter (abAVB) see above on 3.2.40.

9–12. **quid properasse iuuat, quid parca dedisse quieti**
tempora, quid nocti conseruisse diem,
si tamen hic standum est, si non datur artibus ullis
ulterior nostro ripa premenda pede?
Given Ovid's strong preference for self-contained couplets (Platnauer [1951: 27–33]), a sentence that occupies four lines will have particular force. The speaker begins with three emphatic interrogative words (*quid... quid... quid*) in the hexameter, follows that with two conditions in the next hexameter (*si... si*), and closes the pentameter with marked alliteration and assonance: *ripa premenda pede*.

9. Repetition of *quid* underlines the fact that, as often, the line is balanced at the main caesura. For this see note on 3.7.37.

parca: This is the reading of P. A corrector's intervention has left Y ambiguous between *parca* and *pauca*. Munari (1965: 52) comments: '*pauca:...fuisse uid. parca*'. S and early editions (including Marius) offer *pauca*.

For *parcus* used of times of rest see Sil. 7.339–40: *cui parca quies minimumque soporis, | nec notum somno noctes aequare*, Plin. *Pan.* 49.8.3: *inde tibi parcus et breuis somnus*. In Silius and Pliny absence of rest implies a commitment to duty. Here it signifies eagerness to see a girlfriend.

10. **nocti conseruisse diem:** As the second half of the previous line makes clear, this is an elaborate way of saying that the lover set out before dawn. Moralizing Romans (and their mythological characters) see the separation of night and day as evidence of virtue, e.g. Sen. *Ep.* 122.9, *Thy.* 467–8 (Thyestes): *nec somno dies | Bacchoque nox iungenda peruigili datur*.

11. As in the previous hexameter, repetition (this time of *si*) highlights balance at the main caesura.

12. **ulterior...ripa:** As befits a highly rhetorical sentence, the phrase has overtones of epic and history (e.g. *A.* 6.314: *tendebantque manus ripae ulterioris amore*, Stat. *Theb.* 1.296–7, Liv. 21.26.6, 22.44.3, 39.31.5, 42.60.5, 44.33.4, 44.40.8).

pede: This is the reading of P and Y. (S has *die*.) Heinsius (1658: 275) emended to *pedi* as 'more correct'. Munari, Showerman and Goold, McKeown, and Ramirez de Verger follow suit. Kenney (1958: 64), however, compares *Ars* 1.40: *haec erit admissā meta terenda rotā*, where the gerundive is followed by an ablative, and notes that '*pede* at the end of the pentameter... is far commoner than *pedi* in Ovid in this position (sixteen times/twice). Equally important is the fact that *pede* produces superior assonance.

13–16. **nunc ego, quas habuit pinnas Danaeius heros,**
    terribili densum cum tulit angue caput,
nunc opto currum, de quo Cerealia primum
    semina uenerunt in rude missa solum.
Ovid follows one two-couplet sentence with another that is equally impressive. This time anaphora (repetition of *nunc*) articulates the two halves of the sentence, while each couplet alludes obliquely to a well-known mythological episode, the story of Perseus in 13–14, that of Triptolemus in 15–16.

Ovid reworks these lines in *Tr.* 3.8, when longing for escape from Tomis. He employs similar anaphora of *nunc* but more straightforward language (1–2, 5–6):

> Nunc ego Triptolemi cuperem consistere curru,
>   misit in ignotam quo rude semen humum...
> nunc ego iactandas optarem sumere pennas,
>   siue tuas, Perseu, Daedale, siue tuas.

13. Danaeius heros: For the story of Perseus see *Met.* 4.604–5.241. The use of *heros* with an adjective denoting ancestry suggests epic diction e.g. ἥρως Ἀτρεΐδης ('hero son of Atreus'; Hom. *Il.* 1.102, 7.322, 13.112, *Od.* 15.52, 15.121), *Laomedontius heros* (*A.* 8.18), *Daunius heros* (*A.* 12.723), *Cadmeius heros* (Stat. *Theb.* 1.376, 3.366, 7.492). Ovid is particularly creative with this quasi-formula in *Metamorphoses* (where *Danaeius heros* is recycled [5.1]; but note especially the shocking *Cinyreius heros* [10.730], where Cinyras is both father and grandfather of Adonis). The adjective *Danaeius* surprises not only because this is its first outing but also because matronymic adjectives are rare. But see *Autonoeius heros* (*Met.* 3.198: for Actaeon son of Autonoe) and *Cythereius heros* (*Met.* 13.625, 14.584, *Fast.* 3.611: for Aeneas son of Venus).

14. Ovid tells the story of Medusa's rape and transformation at *Met.* 4.790–803. Here the head of Gorgon Medusa is given a golden line (abVAB).

15–16. For the story of Triptolemus see *Met.* 5.642–661 and *Fast.* 4.503–60.

15. Cerealia...semina: Ovid uses the phrase again in a more naturalistic account of agriculture's origins: *semina tum primum longis Cerealia sulcis | obruta sunt* (*Met.* 1.123–4).

16. For this verbal pattern (AVbaB) see 2.4.42, 3.7.9, *Met.* 13.24.

17–18. prodigiosa loquor ueterum mendacia uatum:
    nec tulit haec umquam nec feret ulla dies.
After using grand language to invoke the authority of heroic myth, the lover dismisses the stories of Perseus and Triptolemus as falsehoods. There is irony in the

Commentary, 6.13-18   175

fact that, as Bretzigheimer points out (2001: 178), the lover acknowledges the fictional character of myth precisely when he is about to tell a series of even less credible stories.

Rosati (1983: 86-92) notes that drawing attention to the fictionality of myth is characteristic of Ovid, especially in the exile poetry. Thus the passage from *Tr.* 3.8 quoted above (on 13-16) concludes with words that rewrite this couplet (11-12): *stulte, quid haec frustra uotis puerilibus optas,* | *quae non ulla tibi fertque feretque dies?* See also *Tr.* 1.5.79-80, 4.7.11-18, *Pont.* 1.4.25-6. In *Metamorphoses* Pirithous denies the poem's premise in the epic's central book (8.614-15): *'ficta refers nimiumque putas, Acheloe, potentes* | *esse deos', dixit 'si dant adimuntque figuras'.* While the narrator implicitly condemns Pirithous as *deorum* | *spretor* (8.612-13), the exiled poet actually endorses the sceptic's view when he writes to the *princeps* (*Tr.* 2.63-4): *inspice maius opus, quod adhuc sine fine tenetur,* | *in non credendos corpora uersa modos.* (For discussion of myth's fictionality in *Metamorphoses* see Feeney [1991: 224-32].)

17. For the verbal pattern (aVbAB) see above on 3.2.31.

prodigiosa: Implies that these lies are obviously unbelievable. See Pliny on the customs of remote peoples (*Nat.* 7.6.6): *in quibus prodigiosa aliqua et incredibilia multis uisum iri haud dubito.*

mendacia: Propertius introduced *mendacium*, a word common in comedy and prose, into Augustan verse, placing it in the mouth of a brothel-keeper (4.5.27-8): *sperne fidem, prouolue deos, mendacia uincant,* | *frange et damnosae iura pudicitiae.* Ovid uses it more frequently (eight more times), usually in vigorously moralizing contexts e.g. 3.11.21: *turpia quid referam uanae mendacia linguae,* Her. 15.55: *nec uos decipiant blandae mendacia linguae.*

mendacia uatum: Drawing attention to the unreality of myth foreshadows the poet's assertion of the fictionality of his own work in 3.12. Ovid recalls this passage at *Fast.* 6.253-4, when declaring that he is about to speak the truth about Vesta (with Littlewood [2006: ad loc.]): *non equidem uidi (ualeant mendacia uatum)* | *te, dea, nec fueras aspicienda uiro.*

The idea that poets sometimes lie is at least as old as Hesiod (*Theog.* 27-8: the Muses speaking): ἴδμεν ψεύδεα πολλὰ λέγειν ἐτύμοισιν ὁμοῖα, | ἴδμεν δ' εὖτ' ἐθέλωμεν ἀληθέα γηρύσασθαι ('We know how to speak many falsehoods that resemble reality, but we know how to utter the truth when we want to'). For discussion of this passage and other examples in early Greek poetry see Bowie (1993: esp. 20-3).

18. **nec tulit haec umquam nec feret ulla dies:** The allusion to this line at *Tr.* 3.8.12 (*quae non ulla tibi fertque feretque dies*) underlines the hopelessness of the poet's situation in both cases. Here, however, his difficulties are trivial.

feret: For this sense of *fero* see *OLD* 30d.

176   Commentary

19–20. tu potius ripis effuse capacibus amnis,
    sic aeternus eas: labere fine tuo.
The lover turns now from mythological to a different kind of fantasy and gives orders to the river.

Wide separation of subject and adverb (*tu potius*) from the main verb (*labere*) helps bind together the couplet's disparate elements (apostrophe, prayer, and command).

19. tu…ripis effuse capacibus amnis: As at 2.15.1 (*Anule, formosae digitum uincture puellae*), elaborate apostrophe to a non-anthropomorphic being is intended to be flattering but has comic effect. Even more impressive are the addresses to enslaved women Nape (1.11.1–2) and Cypassis (2.8.1–2).

20. sic aeternus eas: Imposing a condition on a wish or prayer is frequent in Augustan poetry. See Fordyce (1961) on Catul. 17.5, who cites *Ecl.* 9.30 (with Clausen [1994]: 'first attested in Catullus'), Hor. *Carm.* 1.3.1–8, *Met.* 8.857, and Tib. 2.5.121. For other examples in *Amores* see 1.6.25–6 (with McKeown [1989]), 1.13.3, 2.13.12.

21–2. non eris inuidiae, torrens, mihi crede, ferendae,
    si dicar per te forte retentus amans.
After an effusive address and a command in the previous couplet, the lover now turns to a one-word vocative and a threat. If, as seems likely, *dicar* is subjunctive, we have a tentative protasis (present subjunctive) followed (logically at least) by an aggressive apodosis (future indicative).

21. inuidiae…ferendae: Burman (ad loc.) offers a paraphrase: 'That is, you will not be enough or sufficient for bearing and enduring all the hatred', and compares *Met.* 10.628: *non erit inuidiae uictoria nostra ferendae* (as well as Liv. 2.9.6.6 and 28.25.7.4). As Reed (2013: on *Met.* 10.628) observes, the dative is predicative. Woodcock (§205c) explains: 'There are a few idiomatic phrases in which the dative of the gerund or gerundive is used predicatively, e.g.…*esse oneri ferendo*, "to be capable of bearing a burden"'.

22. forte: Both increases the likelihood that *dicar* is subjunctive and reinforces by sonic repetition the river's responsibility ('held up b̲y̲ y̲o̲u̲': *per t̲e̲ f̲o̲r̲t̲e̲ r̲e̲t̲e̲n̲tus*). For similar repetition of *te* with similar accusatory effect see *Her.* 3.114 (with Barchiesi [1992: ad loc.]): *t̲e̲ t̲e̲net in t̲e̲pido mollis amica sinu*.

amans: The couplet's key term is held to the end: it is the speaker's status as a lover which makes his situation so pressing and his need so great.

23–4. flumina deberent iuuenes in amore iuuare,
    flumina senserunt ipsa quid esset amor.
The primary function of this couplet is to introduce the following catalogue of rivers. Anaphora of *flumina* and explicit statement emphasize the stream's duty to help young lovers.

23. iuuenes...iuuare: Sonic repetition not only underlines the lover's need for assistance, but also reflects ancient views on the etymology of *iuuenis*. See Maltby (1991: 320), who cites Censorinus and Isidore for the claim that *iuuenes* were so called because now they could help the state (Cens. 14.2): *quod rem publicam in re militari possent iuuare.* Here, however, it is the youth who needs help. For similar verbal play see *Pont.* 1.4.4 (with Helzle [2003] and Tissol [2014]): *nec iuueni lusus qui placuere iuuant.*

24. senserunt: Where characters in Theocritus (3.15: νῦν ἔγνων τὸν Ἔρωτα 'Now I know Eros'), Virgil (*Ecl.* 8.43: *nunc scio quid sit Amor*), and Lygdamus ([Tib.] 3.4.73: *nescis quid sit amor, iuuenis*) speak of knowing what love is, this lover talks of experiencing or feeling it. See also *Met.* 13.762 (of the Cyclops): *quid sit amor sentit.*

25-6. Inachus in Melie Bithynide pallidus isse dicitur et gelidis incaluisse uadis.
The lover begins his catalogue of lustful rivers and the women whom they love or rape with the obscure case of Inachus and Melie.

25. Inachus: Citing Goold (1965: 96), Kenney (2) rejects *Inachus*, found in all manuscripts, and prints Greek *Inachos*, the Greek accusative *Inachon* being used at 103. Ovid, however, is not consistent in his choice of Greek or Latin forms of names even in the same poem e.g. (Kenney [1996]): *Her.* 17.110: *Menelaus*, 154: *Menelaus*, 249: *Menelaon*. Showerman and Goold print *Inachus*.

Melie Bithynide: There are several nymphs named Melie/Melia who were impregnated by gods: (1) the mother of Ceos by Apollo (Callim. *Aet.* fr. 74.63); (2) the mother of Tenerus by Apollo (Pind. *Paean* 9.41-3); (3) the mother of Dolion by Silenus (Strab. 12.4.8.12); (4) the mother of Amycus by Poseidon (AR 2.4); and (5) the mother of Phoroneus and Aegialeus by Inachus.

Our only evidence for the last of these comes from the mythographer Apollodorus (2.1.3-5): 'Inachus was born a child of Oceanus and Tethys, from whom the river Inachus in Argos is named. Two sons were born from him and Melia, Phoroneus and Aegialeus'. Although this is clearly the Melie to whom Ovid's lover refers, the issue is complicated by the adjective *Bithynide*, because it recalls AR's account of the origins of Amycus (2.2-4): ὅν ποτε νύμφη | τίκτε Ποσειδάωνι Γενεθλίῳ εὐνηθεῖσα | Βιθυνὶς Μελίη ('Whom once the nymph Bithynian Melie bore, having been to bed with Poseidon Genethlios'). (See also Servius on *A.* 5.373 and VF 4.118-19, where Neptune claims that he raped Melie.) Ovid seems to be playing with the identity of these two nymphs, just as he does with the two Scyllas (3.12.21-2 [with note below], *Ars* 1.331-2, *Rem.* 737, *Fast.* 4.500; cf. *Ecl.* 6.74-7 [quoted below on 33]). On the two Scyllas see e.g. Hinds (1993: 11-21), Fantham (1998: 187), Kenney (2011: 222), and Cowan (2017).

in: For this use see above on 3.3.40.

Commentary

Melie: Many or most manuscripts (ω in Kenney and McKeown) offer *media*, a reading found in the earliest editions (e.g. Johannes Andreas [1471], Celsanus [1484]). Marius (1518) printed *Melia* on the authority of a manuscript *horrendae uetustatis*. Y offers *meliae* (and the correction *media*), while S has *melie*. On the authority of Heinsius, editors report P as reading *melie*. The text, however, is unreadable at this point.

pallidus: For the lover's typical pallor see e.g. Prop. 1.5.21: *nec iam pallorem totiens mirabere nostrum*, Ars 1.729: *palleat omnis amans: hic est color aptus amanti*.

26. dicitur: May suggest that the lover is sceptical concerning the truth of this story (see above on 17–18) or may allude to a particular earlier poem under the guise of a reference to tradition. Or it may do both of these things. See also notes on 32, 41, and 82 below.

For this kind of allusion (commonly called an 'Alexandrian footnote') see Ross (1975: 78); for discussion see Miller (1993) (= Miller [2006]) and Hinds (1998: 1–5).

gelidis incaluisse: Oxymoron, along with broader forms of paradox, is a marked feature of Ovid's writing at every stage, but especially in *Metamorphoses*. See e.g. 1.9.22: *armata... inermis*, Ars 3.578: *infida... fides*, Met. 2.627: *iniustaque iusta*, 3.5 (and 9.408): *facto pius et sceleratus eodem*, 6.635: *scelus est pietas*, 8.477: *impietate pia est*, 9.711: *pia... fraude*, Fast. 2.717: *stulti sapiens*, 2.805: *amans hostis*, 4.555: *stulte pia*, Tr. 3.8.41: *odio ciuiliter*, Pont. 2.10.49: *ades... absens*. For discussion of Ovid's use of paradox see Tissol (1997: Chapter 1), Hardie (2002: 42–4), and Kenney (2002: 74–8).

27–8. nondum Troia fuit lustris obsessa duobus,
    cum rapuit uultus, Xanthe, Neaera tuos.

Unfortunately, we have no other evidence for this myth. There seem to be seven mythological women called Neaera: (1) the mother of nymphs Lampetia and Phaethusa by Hyperion (Hom. *Od.* 12.133); (2) a daughter of Niobe and Amphion (Apollod. 3.45.5, Hygin. 11.1.2); (3) a daughter of Pereus (Paus. 8.4.6.6, Apollod. 3.102.7); (4) a daughter of Autolycus (Hygin. 243.4.1); (5) the wife of Hyspicreon, who fell in love with Promedon (Plut. *de mul. uir.* 254B4); (6) the wife of Strymon and mother of Euadne (Apollod. 2.3.4); (7) and the mother of Dresaeus by Theodamas (Quint. Smyrn. 1.292). We cannot be certain, however, that these are seven separate women. Nor can we identify the one who caught Xanthus' attention.

Xanthus is the Trojan river also known as Scamander (Hom. *Il.* 20.73–4): 'The great deep-whirling river, which the gods call Xanthus, but men Scamander'. Scamander is father of the Trojan king Teucer with the nymph Idaea (Diod. Sic. 5.75.1.2, Herodian 3.1.203.28) and of Glaucia, a woman who fell in love with a companion of Heracles during his expedition against Troy (Plut. *Quaest. Graec.* 301A9).

Commentary, 6.26–31

27. nondum: Dates the event to a time before Agamemnon's expedition to Troy or at least before the war's conclusion.

lustris…duobus: Ten years is the traditional length of the Trojan war (e.g. *A*. 2.198: *non anni domuere decem, non mille carinae*). While Livy (39.52.1.5: *cum superioribus duobus lustris Africanus fuisset*) uses this expression in the strict sense (i.e. of the censors' five-year term of office), Ovid uses it for the length of the Trojan war and Ulysses' wanderings: 2.12.9: *Pergama cum caderent bello superata bilustri*, *Ars* 3.15–16: *est pia Penelope lustris errante duobus | et totidem lustris bella gerente uiro*, *Pont*. 4.10.10, 4.16.14.

28. rapuit: We expect that a male will be the subject of this verb. The lover, however, surprises by suggesting that Neaera, whose name is withheld until the last possible moment, 'rapes' Xanthus' gaze. The adulterer of 2.19 uses similar language to address his girlfriend (19): *tu quoque, quae nostros rapuisti nuper ocellos*.

29–30. quid? non Alpheon diuersis currere terris
   uirginis Arcadiae certus adegit amor?
The story of the attempt by Alpheus (a river which flows through Arcadia and Elis) to rape the nymph Arethusa, of her flight under the sea to Sicily, and of her transformation into a Syracusan spring is familiar from both Greek (e.g. Pind. *Nem*. 1.1–2, Callim. fr. 407.45–7, Strab. 6.2.4.52–4, Paus. 5.7.2) and Roman sources. Virgil alludes to the myth at *Ecl*. 10.1–5, and Aeneas reports Achaemenides' version of the tale (minus the rape) at *A*. 3.694–6. Arethusa tells her own story as part of Calliope's narrative at *Met*. 5.577–641.

29. quid? For this way of introducing a mythological example see 1.7.7, 2.9.7, *Tr*. 2.385; Prop. 2.8.21, 2.22a.29, 31. The fact that it is particularly common in the comedies of Plautus (53 times) and Terence (43 times), and in Cicero's speeches (74 times in the speeches against Verres alone) suggests that it is a lively way of introducing a point.

diuersis…terris: For the extension of the dative to express direction, especially in verse, see Pinkster (1.813–14).

30. certus amor: The phrase connotes genuine passion and affection e.g. Prop. 1.8b.45 (of Cynthia): *nec mihi riualis certos subducet amores*; *Met*. 4.156 (of Pyramus and Thisbe): *quos certus amor…iunxit*. Even though this story is one of attempted rape, the lover's argument only works if *certus amor* has that same connotation here.

31–2. te quoque promissam Xantho, Penee, Creusam
   Pthiotum terris occuluisse ferunt.
After a familiar myth, the lover invokes a less well-known story, one that seems to combine two different Creusas, the wife of an Athenian king and mother of Ion, and the mother of Hypseus.

180 Commentary

31. The hexameter seems designed to be enigmatic, beginning with an unidentified *te* and closing with a run of three proper names, with the last word finally identifying the unknown woman.

Xantho: While all manuscripts offer *Xantho*, all current editions print *Xutho* and cite the authority of Heinsius. Heinsius printed *Xantho* and explains in his notes (276): 'At one time I used to suspect that we should write *promissam Xutho* and I thought the reference was to Creusa daughter of Erechtheus, king of Athens, who married Thessalian Xuthus, son of Hellen. Pausanias tells the story... But since Pindar in his ninth Pythian ode implies that Creusa, the Naiad daughter of Earth, was loved by Peneus, I have now changed my opinion'.

Emending to *Xutho* is attractive for two reasons: (1) the lover refers to a Xanthus (the river) in line 28; (2) the story the Creusa's marriage to Xuthus is well known not only from Pausanias, but from Euripides' *Ion*. Note, however, that the Athenian Creusa's husband is also known as Xanthus. An ancient commentator on Hom. *Il*. 13.685 ('the Ionians with long tunics') explains: Λέγει δὲ τοὺς Ἀθηναίους. ἀπὸ Ἴωνος τῆς Κρεούσης τῆς Ἐρεχθέως καὶ Ξάνθου τοῦ Ἕλληνος 'He means the Athenians. From Ion, son of Creusa, the daughter of Erechtheus, and Xanthus son of Hellen'. If Xanthus is an alternative name for Xuthus, retaining *Xantho* is consistent with a reference to the myth familiar from Euripides, Pausanias, and others. The river Peneus, however, has no role to play in this story.

Penee: As Heinsius points out, Pindar refers to a myth involving a Creusa and the river Peneus as ancestors of Hypseus (*Pyth*. 9.15–17): 'Creusa, Naiad daughter of Earth, having rejoiced in the bed of Peneus, once gave birth to him in Pindus' famous glens'.

Clearly lacking from Pindar's tale, however, is a man called Xanthus or Xuthus.

Creusam: Meaning 'female ruler', the name is used of various mythological princesses e.g. Jason's Corinthian bride (Prop. 2.16.30, 2.21.12, *Her*. 12.53, *Ars* 1.335), Aeneas' Trojan wife (*A*. 2.562), the daughter of Erechtheus (see above), and the wife of Cassandrus (Quint. Smyrn. 8.82). Here Ovid's lover seems to combine the myths of two Creusas, just as he does with the two Melies (see above on 25–6).

32. Pthiotum: For allusion to the *Hymn to Delos* see Courtney (1988: 21). Ovid follows Callimachus in addressing the river and defining it by its location (112): Πηνειὲ Φθιῶτα ('Phthian Peneus'). The Pthiotae/Phthiotae are the inhabitants of Phthia in Thessaly.

For the form see Cic. *Tusc*. 1.21.5, Liv. 33.32.6, 36.15.7, Plin. *Nat*. 4.28.9. Manuscripts divide over the spelling of this name. P is particularly hard to read at this point (Munari: *P**hiotum*; Kenney: *pithiotum [ut uid.]*), while S has *Pithiadum*. I print Y's version of the name.

ferunt: May imply the narrator's scepticism or work as an 'Alexandrian footnote' or perform both functions. See notes on 26, 41, and 82.

33–4. quid referam Asopon, quem cepit Martia Thebe,
     natarum Thebe quinque futura parens?

A less familiar myth is now followed by one that is even more obscure, its obscurity underlined by the fact that the couplet takes the form of a question. It seems likely that Ovid alludes to a text which is lost to us.

33. quid referam? The question implies that that the myth or the relevant text is so well known that elaboration is unnecessary. The myth and text, however, are far from familiar.

Asopon: There are two Greek rivers with the name Asopus: in Boeotia near Thebes and in the Peloponnese near Sicyon. It is possible that Ovid is conflating the two rivers. Certainly Virgil uses similar language when combining the Odyssean Scylla with Scylla daughter of Nisus (*Ecl.* 6.74–6): *quid loquar aut Scyllam Nisi, quam fama secuta est | candida succinctam latrantibus inguina monstris | Dulichias uexasse rates?*

cepit: For *capio* in this erotic sense see above on 3.4.28.

Martia: The inhabitants of both Thebes and Sicyon claimed Thebe as daughter of their Asopus (Paus. 2.5.2.2–3.1). The connection between Thebes and Mars suggests that Boeotian Asopus is uppermost in the lover's mind.

Mars is associated with Thebes because (a) Cadmus, the city's founder, married Harmonia, daughter of Mars and Venus, and (b) the first Thebans sprang to life from the teeth of the war-god's dragon (*Met.* 3.32: *Martius anguis*). Ovid's Pentheus cries out to the Thebans (*Met.* 3.531–2): *quis furor, anguigenae, proles Mauortia, uestras | attonuit mentes?* Cf. Polynices' self-identification (Stat. *Theb.* 1.680): *Cadmus origo patrum, tellus Mauortia Thebe* and the narrator's description of the Thebans (4.345 [with Parkes 2012: ad loc.]): *Cadmi Mauortia plebes*.

Thebe: The name is regularly applied to one of Asopus' daughters (e.g. Pind. *Isthm.* 8.16a–20, Hdt. 5.80.3, Diod. Sic. 4.72.1, Paus. 5.22.6, Callim. *Hymn* 4.87). It does not seem to be used of any of his sexual partners.

34. natarum...quinque: Asopus was famous for his many daughters. Nonnus even calls him (*Dion.* 7.212): Ἀσωποῖο, θυγατρογόνου ποταμοῖο ('Asopus, the daughter-fathering river'). The lover's numerical precision suggests that he alludes to a particular version of the myth.

Pausanias (2.5.2) claims that Peloponnesian Asopus had three daughters (Corcyra, Aegina, and Thebe), while Diodorus Siculus (4.72.1) lists twelve along with two sons. Others name other daughters (e.g. Hom. *Od.* 11.260: Antiope; Hdt. 9.51.10: Ōeroē; AR 2.946–7: Sinope).

35–8. cornua si tua nunc ubi sint, Acheloe, requiram,
     Herculis irata fracta querere manu;
nec tanti Calydon nec tota Aetolia tanti,
     una tamen tanti Deianira fuit.

182   *Commentary*

After obscure myths involving the rivers Peneus and Asopus, the lover now invokes a story familiar not only from Sophocles' *Women of Trachis* (9–27, 507–16), but also from the roughly contemporaneous *Heroides* 9 (Deianira's letter to Hercules) and *Metamorphoses* 8.879–9.88. The lover begins with complex syntax (an unreal condition combined with an indirect question) and an apostrophe in the first couplet, and follows in the second with a simple and emphatic assertion of Deianira's value (*tanti…tanti…tanti*, reinforced by marked alliteration of *t*), withholding her name until the last possible moment.

35. cornua…tua: Delz (1983) and Casali (1995: 187) claim that this is plural for singular, because otherwise this account is incompatible with *Met.* 9.85–8, where Hercules rips off only one of Achelous' horns. They also cite *Her.* 9.139: *cornua flens legit ripis Achelous in udis* and 16.267: *ut ferus Alcides Acheloia cornua fregit.* Here, however, there is emphasis on plurality: *cornua…tua…sint…fracta.* It is clear, moreover, that for Ovid narrative consistency within or across his works was not a primary consideration. For *Metamorphoses* see e.g. O'Hara (2007: Chapter 5); for *Fasti* see e.g. Barchiesi (1997: Chapter 2). For inconsistency across works see e.g. the accounts of Caesar's apotheosis at *Met.* 15.843–51 and *Fast.* 3.697–704.

Acheloe: The vocative introduces variety and makes for a vivid catalogue entry. For similar use of apostrophe see *Met.* 4.44–5 (in a list of possible narratives); 6.112–18 (in a catalogue of divine rapes); *Fast.* 4.499–500 (the places that Ceres avoids).

The river Achelous is in Aetolia in western Greece.

36. irata…manu: Anger is typical of Hercules, most obviously in the Heracles/ Hercules plays of Euripides and Seneca, but also in the *Aeneid*, where Virgil stresses his *ira* (8.230–1: *ter totum feruidus ira | lustrat Auentini montem*) and *furor* (8.219, 228).

37. While the couplet does not explicitly state who prizes Deianira so highly (Achelous, Hercules, or both), the force of the argument requires that it be Achelous. The threefold repetition of *tanti* (genitive of value) underlines Deianira's importance: for the river the whole region of Aetolia and its most famous city, Calydon, are less valuable than a woman.

38. The framing of the line (beginning with *una*, and with *Deianira* placed in the last possible position) and the alliteration of *t* and *n*, make the pentameter a particularly effective conclusion to this story.

39–42. ille fluens diues septena per ostia Nilus,
    qui patriam tantae tam bene celat aquae,
fertur in †Euadne† collectam Asopide flammam
    uincere gurgitibus non potuisse suis.

Commentary, 6.35-41

A well-known myth is followed by the most obscure of all, with a textual difficulty compounding the problem. The overall point, however, is clear: for all its waters, the Nile's 'fire' for Evadne (?) could not be extinguished. If we had the text to which Ovid alludes, these lines would present fewer difficulties.

39. ille...Nilus: For *ille* and an accompanying noun used as a framing device see below on 3.9.6.

diues...Nilus: The Nile is 'rich' because of the wealth that it confers upon Egypt. AR (fr. 5.1 Powell) writes of 'the gifts of the wealthy Nile' (δῶρα πλουσίου Νείλου), while Virgil (A. 9.31) compares Turnus' forces to *pingui flumine Nili*, where *pinguis* means both 'rich' and 'muddy'. See also Juv. 13.27: *diuitis ostia Nili*.

The only evidence for the Nile's sexual activities comes from Apollodorus, who lists two daughters: Memphis (2.10.1) and Anchinoe (2.11.2).

septena per ostia: Poets compete in creating new ways of describing the Nile's delta, with Catullus coining *septemgeminus* (11.7) and Ovid creating *septemfluus* (*Met.* 1.422) and recycling Virgil's *septemplex* (A. 12.925: of Turnus' shield; *Met.* 5.187). Ovid is the first to use *septeni* in this context. Cf. Sen. *Nat.* 4a.2.12: *Nilus, per septena ostia in mare emittitur*.

40. The source of the Nile was famously unknown in antiquity (e.g. Hdt. 2.28, Tib. 7.23-4, Luc. 1.20, 10.268-71). Callimachus reports the words of Nile himself (fr. 384.31-2 Pfeiffer): ὃν οὐδ' ὅθεν οἶδεν ὁδεύω | θνητὸς ἀνήρ ('No mortal man knows from where I journey'). In *Metamorphoses* the fault is Phaethon's (2.254-5).

41. fertur: May imply the narrator's scepticism or work as an 'Alexandrian footnote' or perform both functions. Cf. the use of *dicitur* at 26 and 82, and *ferunt* at 32.

in: For this use see above on 3.3.40.

†Euadne†...Asopide: The principal manuscripts offer differing versions of this name: Y: eb^Λeu^anthe; P: ebanthe; S: ebantẹ. Fifteenth- and sixteenth-century editors (including Johannes Andreas [Euannem], Marius, Naugerius, and Micyllus) printed Euanne, understanding, as Marius makes clear, that she shared a name with the wife of Capaneus, i.e. Evadne. Heinsius and Burman corrected the spelling to reflect that fact. Riese (1871) printed Euanthe and modern editors follow suit. Neither of these is listed by Diodorus Siculus (4.72.1) as one of the twelve daughters of Asopus.

Given the manuscript readings, the attraction of Evanthe is obvious. There is, however, only one mythological woman of that name, a possible mother of the Graces. A commentator on Callimachus' *Aetia* (fr. 7a.14-15 Harder) offers her as candidate number four: παρ' οἷς δ(ὲ) Ε[ὐάν-]θης τ(ῆς) Οὐρανοῦ κ(αὶ) Διός ('according to others Evanthe, the daughter of Ouranos and Zeus'). See also Cornut. *ND* 20.11. If Euanthe is the correct reading here, this is the only occurrence of her name in Latin. It seems unwise to insert into Ovid's text the poorly-attested name of a person about whom we know virtually nothing.

There are, by contrast, four women called Evadne: (1) the daughter of Iphis and wife of Capaneus (e.g. Apollod. 3.79.6, Stat. *Theb.* 12.801), (2) the daughter of Pitana and Poseidon, and mother of a child to Apollo (Pind. *Ol.* 6.27–30, 47–9), (3) a daughter of Pelias, whom Jason married off to Canes son of Cephalus (Diod. Sicul. 4.53.2), and (4) a daughter of Strymon and Neaera, who married Argos (Apollod. 2.3.4). Leaving aside the mythographer Hyginus, who mentions the wife of Argos (145.2.1) and the daughter of Neptune and Pitana (157.2.3), all references in Latin literature are to the wife of Capaneus, who famously incinerated herself on her husband's funeral pyre. Since we have no evidence linking any of these to the Nile, I prefer to obelize.

collectam...flammam: Varies the quasi-scientific *colligere flammas/ignes* (e.g. Lucr. 1.723, G. 1.427, Luc. 1.606–7, Sen. *Nat.* 2.12.4.1).

42. gurgitibus...suis: For the paradoxical combination of metaphorical heat and water see above on 25. Here water fails to quench flames.

43–4. siccus ut amplecti Salmonida posset Enipeus,
    cedere iussit aquam; iussa recessit aqua.

To close this sequence of lustful rivers drawn from Greek mythology the lover now reworks a tale familiar from Homer's *Odyssey*. In Book 11 Odysseus encounters Tyro, daughter of Salmoneus (*Od.* 11.235–54 [with omissions]):

> There the first whom I saw was noble Tyro, who said she was the offspring of blameless Salmoneus...who fell in love with the divine river Enipeus...and she used to visit Enipeus' fair streams. Making himself like him, the earth-supporter, the earth-shaker lay with her at the mouth of the whirling river; and a dark wave stood around them like a hill, piled high, and concealed the god and the mortal woman. And he undid her virgin belt and poured sleep upon her....'Rejoice, woman, in this love....But I am Poseidon, the earth-shaker.'...She conceived and bore Pelias and Neleus.

While the lover's version of the relationship between Tyro and Enipeus clearly alludes to the Homeric account (note especially the reference to the parting of the waters), it is not identical. In particular, there is no reference to Poseidon/Neptune because the lover's argument requires that a river, not the god of the sea, be in love with Salmoneus' daughter. On the other hand, allusion to Homer makes this example an effective bridge to the major Roman tale that is to follow, because the stories of Tyro and Ilia have major elements in common: divine rape and the birth of twins.

Ovid's Hero offers an account closer to Homer's at *Her.* 19.129–32 (Tyro and Neptune), while Arachne accuses Neptune of disguising himself as Enipeus and of fathering Otos and Ephialtes (*Met.* 6.116–17): *tu uisus Enipeus | gignis Aloidas*. Propertius also gives differing accounts, offering one that focuses on Neptune's rape (1.13.21–2): *non sic Haemonio Salmonida mixtus Enipeo | Taenarius facili pressit amore deus*; and another that stresses Tyro's lust for the river-god (3.19.13–14): *testis Thessalico flagrans Salmonis Enipeo, | quae uoluit liquido tota subire deo*.

43. siccus…Enipeus: Enclosing word order is used here to brilliant effect: we do not expect *siccus* to qualify the name of a river. The Enipeus is a river in Thessaly.

amplecti: While *amplector* is sometimes used as a euphemism for 'rape' (e.g. *Met.* 4.351, 6.707, 11.264), the emphasis on Tyro's passion for Enipeus in Homer and Propertius 3.19 suggests that it is used here of a consensual relationship.

Salmonis: This patronymic seems to have been invented by Propertius. It does not occur in Greek. (AR [4.1693] and others use 'Salmonis' as the name of a headland.)

44. The line is remarkable for its balance and simplicity. For other examples of parallel half lines see Wills (1996: 414–18).

Virgil's adaptation of *Od.* 11.243–4 ('and a dark wave stood around them like a hill, piled high') is closer to the Homeric original: *G.* 4.361: *curuata in montis faciem circumstetit unda*.

cedere iussit: The fact that the subject is still Enipeus (why can't a river-god withdraw his own waters?), underlines the key difference from the Homeric version.

45–8. nec te praetereo, qui per caua saxa uolutans
   Tiburis Argei pomifera arua rigas,
Ilia cui placuit, quamuis erat horrida cultu,
   ungue notata comas, ungue notata genas.
With a seemingly flippant remark ('I won't leave you out'), the lover introduces a local story of a lustful river, a story that focuses upon a key portion of Rome's foundation legend and occupies almost 40 per cent of the poem.

45. nec te praetereo: For the casual suggestion that a vital topic might have been omitted see e.g. *Ars* 3.612: *quaque uigil custos, praeteriturus eram*, *Fast.* 3.697: *praeteriturus eram gladios in principe fixos*.

te: While the river Anio is not named here, it is readily identified by allusion to Propertius in the next line and its role in myth in the next couplet.

46. Recalls Propertian lover's description of Cynthia's preferred burial place (4.7.81): *ramosis Anio qua pomifer incubat aruis*.

Tiburis Argei: According to Horace (*Carm.* 1.18.2, 2.6.5: *Tibur Argeo positum colono*) Tibur (now Tivoli) was founded by an Argive named Catilus.

pomifera arua: Tibur was famous for its fruit e.g. Hor. *S.* 2.4.70: *Picenis cedunt pomis Tiburtia suco*, *Carm.* 1.7.13–14: *et praeceps Anio ac Tiburni lucus et uda |*

mobilibus pomaria riuis. The agricultural writer Columella speaks of (10.1.1.138): *pomosi Tiburis arua.*

P and S offer *pomifer*, a reading accepted by recent editors apart from Showerman and Goold. Y's scribe seems to have been tempted by *pomifera*: *pomifer/a___ rua*, as was Bentley (Hedicke [1905: 22]). Goold (1965: 51) argues for *pomifera*: 'Here are four nouns and four attributes, exactly one for each. But *qui* (= Anio) has two, and *arua* has none'. This is persuasive: readers expect one adjective per noun (see Servius on *A.* 2.392: *non enim sunt duo epitheta, quod apud Latinos uitiosum est*). (Goold's other arguments are less convincing.) Also important is the fact that *pomifera* produces a more elegant line, with an attractive arrangement of nouns and adjectives (AabBV). Elision of the final *a* in speech easily accounts for the letter's loss in written texts.

rigas: Ovid notes Tibur's abundance of water at *Fast.* 4.71: *iam moenia Tiburis udi | stabant.* See also Hor. *Carm.* 1.7.13–14 (quoted above), 3.29.6: *semper udum Tibur.* This has not changed: Tivoli's Villa d'Este (sixteenth-century) is famous for its spectacular fountains.

47. Ilia: This is the name by which the mother of Romulus and Remus is most commonly known e.g. Enn. *Ann.* 1.56, 60 (Goldberg and Manuwald [1]), Hor. *Carm.* 1.2.17, *A.* 1.274, 6.778, *Am.* 2.14.15, 3.4.40, Tib. 2.5.52. Livy (1.3) calls her Rea Silvia, while in *Fasti* Ovid uses both names (e.g. Ilia: 2.598, 3.233, 4.54, 55; Silvia: 2.383, 3.11, 45). 'Ilia' has the advantage of underlining Rome's Trojan origins. Cf. 65 below: *Troiana propago.*

placuit: For *placeo* as 'be sexually attractive to' (*OLD* 1d) see above on 3.2.35.

quamuis erat horrida cultu: The state of Ilia's clothing suggests the distressing nature of her experience.

48. The use of parallel half lines emphasizes the pitiable nature of Ilia's condition. Her nail-torn cheeks and hair may result from the god's violence (cf. the Propertian lover's invitation to Cynthia [3.8.6]: *et mea formosis unguibus ora nota*; and the Ovidian lover's admission of guilt [*Am.* 1.7.49–50]: *sustinui... | ferreus ingenuas ungue notare genas*); or from Ilia's distress (cf. 2.6.4: *et rigido teneras ungue notate genas*, *Her.* 5.71–2: *tunc uero rupique sinus et pectora planxi, | et secui madidas ungue rigente genas*, 11.91–2: *tunc demum pectora plangi | contigit inque meas unguibus ire genas*).

49–50. illa gemens patruique nefas delictaque Martis
    errabat nudo per loca sola pede.
The focus now shifts from the river to Ilia herself: her anguish at her uncle's impious actions and the crime of Mars.

49. patruique nefas: Servius (on *A.* 1.273) tells the story: 'Amulius and Numitor were brothers. Amulius drove his brother from power and killed his son, but made his daughter Ilia a priestess of Vesta, to remove hope of offspring, by whom he knew he could be punished. Mars, as many say, raped her, and so were born Remus and Romus, whom Amulius ordered to be thrown into the Tiber with their mother. Then, as some say, Anien made Ilia his wife'.

delictaque Martis: Ovid regularly uses *delicta* of sexual wrongdoing e.g. 2.4.3, *Her.* 17.219, *Met.* 7.834, *Tr.* 2.541.

The lover is emphatic on the subject of Mars' guilt, as is *Fasti*'s Teacher (3.21–2): *Mars uidet hanc uisamque cupit potiturque cupita,* | *et sua diuina furta fefellit ope.* Others present matters differently. While acknowledging that Silvia was raped (*ui compressa Vestalis* 1.4.2.2), Livy suggests that Mars may not have been the perpetrator. Tibullus' Sibyl blames Ilia (2.5.51–4).

50. errabat...per loca sola: Alludes to Ilia's dream of the aftermath of her rape in Ennius' *Annales* (1.39–40 Goldberg and Manuwald [1]): *ita sola* | *postilla, germana soror, errare uidebar.*

nudo...pede: Perhaps suggests Ilia's innocence and vulnerability. Cf. the description of Proserpina before her rape (*Fast.* 4.426): *errabat nudo per sua prata pede.* It is also possible that going barefoot was as an aspect of Vesta's cult (*Fast.* 6.395–7). If so, this passage is the only evidence for the practice (Bömer [1958: 366]).

51–2. hanc Anien rapidis animosus uidit ab undis
      raucaque de mediis sustulit ora uadis
After a couplet devoted to Ilia, attention switches back to the river, now named as the Anien.

51. Anien: This form of the river's name is favoured in poetry. The Anio rises in the Apennines, flows past Tibur (hence Prop. 3.22.23: *Anio Tiburne*), and joins the Tiber just north of Rome.

rapidis undis: For the phrase see Lucr. 4.421: *in rapidas amnis despeximus undas,* in a context where words like *uis* and *raptim* underline the water's violence.

animosus: When used of natural forces (*OLD* 4), this adjective also suggests violence e.g. *Met.* 11.552–3 (of Ceyx' storm): *spoliisque animosa superstes* | *unda, uelut uictrix, sinuataque despicit undas.* McKeown ([1989] on 1.6.51) suggests a possible play on *anemos* ('wind' in Greek).

52. For the golden line see above on 3.3.21.

raucaque...sustulit ora: Combines two ideas, with Anio both raising his face (*ora*; cf. *Met.* 15.38: *ad superos tollens reus ora manusque*) from the water and using his lips (*ora*; cf. *Met.* 5.600 [Alpheus]: *iterum rauco mihi dixerat ore*; *Fast.* 5.638 [Tiber]): *raucaque dimouit talibus ora sonis*) to speak. *raucus* is commonly used of running water (*OLD* 2b), whether personified or not.

53–4. atque ita 'quid nostras' dixit 'teris anxia ripas,
   Ilia, ab Idaeo Laomedonte genus?

Anio begins his speech with a series of questions, with the first combining concern for Ilia's plight (he recognizes her distress) and flattery (a whole line is given to her name and pedigree).

53: anxia: Cf. Enn. *Ann.* 1.50 (Goldberg and Manuwald [1]): *aegro cum corde*.

ripas: Ilia's distress near a riverbank is not surprising, given the location of her rape by Mars. See Enn. *Ann.* 1.38–9 (Goldberg and Manuwald [1]): *nam me uisus homo pulcer per amoena salicta | et ripas raptare locosque nouos*. (On *raptare* see Skutsch [1985: 198]: 'there is the merest hint at her rape in the verb'.) Cf. *Fast.* 3.13: *uentum erat ad molli decliuem tramite ripam*.

54. It is not only Ilia's name that underlines her Trojan connections, but the reference to Laomedon, the city's founder, and use of the adjective *Idaeus*, which sometimes functions as a synonym for 'Trojan', e.g. *Her.* 19.177 (of Paris): *ut semel Idaeus Lacedaemona uenit adulter*, *Fast.* 2.145 (of Ganymede): *iam puer Idaeus*.

55–6. quo cultus abiere tui? quid sola uagaris,
   uitta nec euinctas impedit alba comas?

Anio follows with questions expressing puzzlement: Why is a Vestal Virgin roaming the countryside by herself? Why is she without the Vestals' insignia?

55. cultus: Refers to the costume worn normally by the Vestal Virgins. DiLuzio (2016: 155) defines it as follows: 'The full Vestal regalia included the *seni crines* (six-tressed) hairstyle, a headdress composed of the *infula* and *vittae* (woolen bands), a veil known as the *suffibulum*, a *palla* (mantle), the soft shoes of a priestess and...a long *tunica* (tunic), rather than a *stola*'. As a Vestal who is no longer a virgin, Ilia lacks the traditional costume because she is not entitled to wear it.

sola uagaris: The detail derives from Ilia's self-description in Ennius (*Ann.* 1.39–40 Goldberg and Manuwald [1]): *ita sola |...errare uidebar*.

56. For the verbal pattern (AbVaB) see on 3.5.5.

uitta: Anio refers to the woollen bands worn by the Vestals and other priests. Lindner (2015: 101), who uses both literary and material evidence, describes them as: 'four or six long loops of cloth that lay on the Vestal's breasts and/or on her upper back...The *vittae* were attached at the back of the Vestal's head, underneath the *infula* rows'.

For the loss of Ilia's/Silvia's *uittae* see *Fast.* 3.29–30: *lapsa capillis | decidit ante sacros lanea uitta focos*. For the forced removal of an unchaste Vestal's *uittae* see Dion. Hal. *Ant. Rom.* 8.89.5.3: 'Having removed the *uittae* (τὰ στέμματα) from the top of her head, and having escorted her through the forum, they buried her alive within the walls'.

For other priests see e.g. Virgil's Haemonides (*A.* 10.537–8): *Phoebi Triuiaeque sacerdos,* | *infula cui sacra redimibat tempora uitta*; together with Servius' explanation: '*infula*: a band in the shape of a diadem, from which *uittae* hang from either side: it is usually broad and usually twisted from white and scarlet thread'.

The Ovidian lover pictures virgin priestess Cassandra as a quasi-Vestal (1.7.17; with McKeown [1989: ad loc.]): *nisi uittatis quod erat Cassandra capillis*, while Lucan similarly Romanizes the Delphic priestess (5.142–4).

euinctas…comas: Refers to the braided *seni crines* (DiLuzio: 2016: 162–5; with illustrations).

57–8. quid fles et madidos lacrimis corrumpis ocellos
pectoraque insana plangis aperta manu?

Anio's next questions seem poised between sympathy for Ilia's plight and impatience.

57. quid fles: The question may express compassion or annoyance. For compassion see *Her.* 3.24 (Briseis reporting Patroclus' words): '*quid fles? hic paruo tempore*', dixit, '*eris*'; for annoyance Prop. 2.20.1–2: (to Cynthia): *quid fles abducta grauius Briseide? quid fles* | *anxia captiua tristius Andromacha?*) and Hor. *Carm.* 3.7.1: *quid fles, Asterie?* Here, however, the tone seems ambiguous.

madidos…ocellos: For the phrase see 3.9.49, where it is used of dying Tibullus.

corrumpis ocellos: May suggest genuine concern or merely worry that Ilia is spoiling her good looks. At Plaut. *Merc.* 501: *nimis stulte facis, oculos corrumpis tales* and *Ars* 1.129 (rapist to rape victim): *quid teneros lacrimis corrumpis ocellos?*, the speaker seems wholly devoid of sympathy.

58. For the verbal pattern (AbVaB) see above on 56.

pectora…plangis aperta: Alliteration of *p* is often used for onomatopoeic effect in contexts of mourning e.g. Catul. 64.351 (of Trojan mothers), *Am.* 2.6.3 (for Corinna's parrot), 3.9.10 (for Tibullus), *Met.* 13.491 (for Polyxena): *consuetaque pectora plangit*, Sen. *Tro.* 64 (Hecuba to the Trojan women): *ferite palmis pectora et planctus date*).

59–60. ille habet et silices et uiuum in pectore ferrum,
qui tenero lacrimas lentus in ore uidet.

Anio seems now to come down on the side of sympathy for Ilia with a denunciation of those who would be unmoved by a woman in her predicament.

59. ill(e) habet et silices et uiu(um) in: Multiple elisions are sometimes used to suggest monstrosity e.g. *A.* 3.658 (of the Cyclops): *monstr(um) horrend(um), inform(e), ingens, cui lumen ademptum*, *Met.* 13.550 (of Hecuba about to attack Polymestor): *non oblit(a) animor(um), annor(um) oblita suorum.* That seems appropriate here too: only a monster could be so unfeeling.

Hexameters with two elisions are rare in *Amores*. Ceccarelli (104) observes that Propertius has elisions in 26.58 per cent of his hexameters, Tibullus 12.4 per cent, Ovid 11.06 per cent. Ovid has two or more elisions in the following hexameters in *Amores*: 1.7.51, 1.8.53, 1.9.41, 1.11.5, 1.13.19, 2.7.13, 2.9.15, 2.11.45, 2.15.15, 2.19.21, 3.8.37. On multiple elisions in the pentameter see below on 80.

silices: The proverbial hardness of flint makes it an apt image for unconcern e.g. *A.* 6.471 (Dido before Aeneas): *si dura silex aut stet Marpesia cautes, Am.* 1.11.9, *Her.* 10.109–10.

silices et uiuum in pectore ferrum: The toughness of both materials sees them paired in both literal (e.g. Lucr. 1.571, Stat. *Silu.* 4.3.1) and figurative contexts. Ovid uses similar metaphorical language of Corinna's Nape (1.11.9): *nec silicum uenae nec durum in pectore ferrum* and Byblis' brother Caunus: (*Met.* 9.614): *nec rigidas silices solidumue in pectore ferrum*. See also Tib. 1.1.63–4, *Tr.* 1.8.41–2, and *Pont.* 4.10.3.

uiuum...ferrum: Pliny explains that 'living iron' inflicts harsher wounds (*Nat.* 34.147.2–5): 'Only this material (iron) catches an emanation from that stone (the magnet) and retains it for a long time, taking hold of other iron so that sometimes a chain of rings can be seen. The ignorant multitude call this "living iron". Injuries of this kind are more severe'.

60. tenero...in ore: For the connotations of *tener* see above on 3.1.27. Elsewhere Ovid uses this phrase only of children: 3.10.22 (infant Jupiter), *Her.* 16.256 (Helen's Hermione). Martial uses it of Amor himself (8.50.14). Here it suggests both innocence and sexual attractiveness.

lacrimas: Perhaps recalls Ennius' references to Ilia's weeping: *lacrimans* (1.35), *lacrumans* (1.49).

61–2. Ilia, pone metus: tibi regia nostra patebit.
  teque colent amnes: Ilia, pone metus.
This couplet is striking for its use of the first two and a half feet of the hexameter as the second half of the pentameter. Framed by Anio's attempt to assuage the Vestal's fears (*Ilia, pone metus*) are Anio's promises of a glorious future, each beginning with a form of *tu: tibi...te*. While in other examples repetition of whole phrases aims to amuse (3.2.27–8, with discussion above) or create a sense of logical coherence (1.9.1–2, *Rem.* 71–2, 385–6) or danger (*Her.* 5.117–18, *Fast.* 4.365–6), here it is supposed to soothe Ilia's anxieties. For other forms of framing repetition in Ovid and other poets see Wills (1996: 430–5).

61. Use of framing repetition helps to make this a wholly dactylic line.

pone metus: Characters in Ovid sometimes urge fearlessness when fear is needed e.g. *Her.* 16.68, 20.1, *Ars* 1.556, *Met.* 5.226. For Ilia's fear see Enn. *Ann.* 1.35: *exterrita*.

tibi regia nostra patebit: In Ennius' account of Ilia's dream, her father (i.e. Aeneas) predicts only that an encounter with a river will end her misfortunes (1.44–5 [Goldberg and Manuwald [1]]): *o gnata tibi sunt ante gerendae | aerumnae, post ex fluuio fortuna resistet.*

**63–4. tu centum aut plures inter dominabere nymphas,
  nam centum aut plures flumina nostra tenent.**
Repetition is an important element in this couplet too, with the phrase *centum aut plures* placed immediately after the first syllable in each line. Here repetition seems intended to underline the magnitude of Anio's promise and to add to its persuasiveness.

63. centum aut plures: Imprecision gives the impression of abundance. Cf. Catul. 22.4–5: *puto esse ego illi milia aut decem aut plura | perscripta*, Ars 3.185–7: *quot noua terra parit flores,… | lana tot aut plures sucos bibit.*

dominabere: The verb seems chosen to recall the *Aeneid*'s predictions of imperial greatness (1.285, 3.97, 6.766; cf. 7.70), perhaps linking Ilia's rape with Rome's future.

**65–6. ne me sperne, precor, tantum, Troiana propago:
  munera promissis uberiora feres'.**
Anio closes his plea with a request that Ilia not reject his advances and a promise of still more gifts to come.

65. ne…sperne: McKeown (1989: 195) cites Servius (on A. 6.544) for the claim that *ne* followed by the imperative was an archaism in the Augustan period.

Troiana propago: The grandeur of the phrase suggests flattery. Horsfall (2013: on A. 6.870) notes that *propago* is 'a weightier synonym for *proles, gens*, and…*stirps*'. See e.g. A. 6.870–1: *nimium uobis Romana propago | uisa potens*, 12.827: *Romana potens Itala uirtute propago*, Fast. 3.157: *ille deus* (i.e. Julius Caesar) *tantaeque propaginis auctor*. Here it is used not of a family or nation but an individual (*OLD* 2b). Cf. Lucr. 1.42: *Memmi clara propago* and (with irony) Luc. 6.589: *Pompei ignaua propago*.

66. Cf. Helen's sceptical response to Paris' promised gifts (*Her.* 17.222): *donaque promissis uberiora feram.*

**67–8. dixerat. illa oculos in humum deiecta modestos
  spargebat teneros flebilis imbre sinus.**
With the end of Anio's speech attention shifts to Ilia's response.

67. dixerat: Is here used as a single-word sentence to mark the close of an important speech and to mark a significant transition. The device is frequent in epic poetry, much less common in love elegy. (Its only other use in *Amores* is at 3.5.45.)

oculos in humum deiecta modestos: Keeping one's eyes on the ground is a generally recognized sign of *pudor* in both women and men (Kaster [1997: 7]).

For Ovidian examples see e.g. 2.4.11–12, *Her.* 6.25–6, *Her.* 21.242: *lumina fixa tenens plena pudoris humo*.

68. imbre: For rain as a metaphor for tears see *Her.* 10.138 (Ariadne): *et tunicas lacrimis sicut ab imbre grauis*, *Ars* 1.532: (of Ariadne) *indigno teneras imbre rigante genas*, *Tr.* 1.3.18, 3.2.19, 4.1.95–8. See also Sen. *Tro.* 965–6, *Oed.* 952–3.

69–70. ter molita fugam ter ad altas restitit undas,
  currendi uires eripiente metu.

69. ter…ter: For repetition of *ter* see *A.* 2.792–3 (Aeneas and Creusa): *ter conatus ibi collo dare bracchia circum;* | *ter frustra comprensa manus effugit imago*, 4.690–1 (Dido): *ter sese attollens cubitoque adnixa leuauit,* | *ter reuoluta toro est*, 6.700–1 (Aeneas and Anchises), *Ars* 1.552, *Fast.* 2.823 (Lucretia), 5.247 (Flora to Juno). Pease (1935: 527 [on *A.* 4.690–1]) notes that 'several of these instances describe a repeated attempt followed…by a repeated collapse or failure'. Although Pease does not cite this passage, repeated *ter* clearly signifies failure here too.

molita fugam: The expression comes from Virgil (*A.* 2.108–9): *saepe fugam Danai Troia cupiere relicta* | *moliri*. Servius (ad loc.) notes that *moliri* (as opposed to *parare*) underlines the difficulty of the task of leaving Troy. Here it highlights the difficulty of escaping Anio's clutches.

70. metu: Ilia clearly has not obeyed Anio (61–2) and given up her fear. For the paralyzing effects of fear on rape victims see *Ars* 1.121–4, *Met.* 4.228–9, 6.527–30, 6.706, *Fast.* 2.810.

71–2. sera tamen scindens inimico pollice crinem
  edidit indignos ore tremente sonos:
Having described Ilia's attempt to escape, the speaker reinforces the fact of Ilia's unwillingness in this transition to her speech.

71. sera: The adjective is used here with adverbial force (*OLD* 4b). Ilia is too distraught for an immediate reply.

scindens…crinem: Tearing the hair is a mark of deep distress. Cf. Juturna's reaction to the Fury fluttering in front of Turnus' face (*A.* 12.870): *infelix crinis scindit Iuturna solutos* and the exiled Ovid's advice to his wife (*Tr.* 3.3.51): *parce tamen lacerare genas, nec scinde capillos*.

inimico pollice: For *pollex* as 'hand' or 'hands' see Booth (1991: 116; on 2.4.27–8) and Kenney (1996: 145; on *Her.* 17.266). See also *Her.* 19.26, 20.139, *Met.* 9.395, 13.746.

72. edidit…sonos: This is an Ovidian way of introducing a speech: *Her.* 11.94, *Fast.* 1.100, 434, 2.840, *Ib.* 224.

indignos…sonos: Ilia's words are 'unworthy' because she should not have had to utter them. Cf. the tears that Ariadne should not have had to shed

(*Ars* 1.531–2): *Thesea crudelem surdas clamabat ad undas,* | *indigno teneras imbre rigante genas.*

73–4. 'o utinam mea lecta forent patrioque sepulcro
condita, cum poterant uirginis ossa legi!

Ilia begins with a remarkable couplet, with the maximum number of dactyls in both lines, with hiatus in the first foot of the hexameter, and the key word *ossa* postponed until the last possible moment. (For the dactylic couplet see above on 3.2.1–2.)

In *Heroides* 2 Phyllis also wishes that she had died before losing her virginity (59–60): *quae fuit ante illam, mallem suprema fuisset* | *nox mihi, dum potui Phyllis honesta mori.* Ilia expresses her similar desire in more colourful terms, picturing not just her last night alive but the gathering and burial of her bones.

73. o utinam: The context and other examples (e.g. Tib. 1.3.2; Prop. 1.3.39, 4.4.33; *Her.* 1.5, 4.125, 19.115, *Tr.* 4.4.87) suggest that the phrase conveys deep emotion.

Of the 35 examples in classical Latin verse, 13 are found in Ovid. Tibullus uses it once, Propertius five times. Bömer (1969: 563; on *Met.* 3.467) suggests that the phrase is 'comparatively rare' in epic. Although it is not found in Virgil, it was picked up by Lucan and all three Flavian epic poets.

lecta forent: Ilia imagines the collection of her bones and their burial after cremation. Cf. the closing lines of Virgil's description of Misenus' funeral (*A.* 6.226–8): *postquam conlapsi cineres et flamma quieuit,* | *reliquias uino et bibulam lauere fauillam,* | *ossaque lecta cado texit Corynaeus aeno.*

patrioque sepulcro: The importance of burial in the family tomb is usually highlighted when, as here, it is not possible e.g. *A.* 10.557–8, Hor. *S.* 2.3.196, Luc. 2.732.

74. cum: This is the reading of P and Y. S offers *dum*. Goold (1965: 52) explains why *cum* is preferable: 'Tenses of the indicative other than the present endow *dum* with the meaning "all the time that"… The reading of the best manuscript, *cum* "at a time when"… should dissuade us from outraging Silvia's syntax as well as her honor'. Kenney (1966: 269) agrees.

75–6. cur, modo Vestalis, taedas inuitor ad ullas
turpis et Iliacis infitianda focis?

Ilia now poses a rhetorical question that explains the powerful wish expressed in her opening couplet.

75. modo Vestalis: Rarely is *modo* used so effectively. The phrase underlines both Ilia's previous commitment to her Vestal duties and the anguish resulting from her loss of virginal status.

taedas…ad ullas: From Ilia's perspective, she is not worthy of any kind of marriage at all.

76. turpis: Enjambment throws *turpis* into prominence and highlights Ilia's sense of guilt at her perceived betrayal of her Vestal status. When used without irony, it is one of the most powerful terms of condemnation in the moral lexicon, being used of perjurers, of corrupted courts and jurors (*Am.* 1.10.39–41), of a married man's mistress (*Her.* 5.70, 6.133, 9.134), of an adulteress (*Her.* 13.133).

Iliacis…focis: The fire is Trojan because it was thought to have been brought from Troy. See e.g. Aeneas' report of the ghostly Hector's action (*A.* 2.296-7): *sic ait et manibus uittas Vestamque potentem | aeternumque adytis effert penetralibus ignem.* For the phrase see *Fast.* 3.142, 418, 6.456.

The choice of *focus* (as opposed to, say, *flamma* or *ignis* [cf. *Fast.* 3.29]) recalls the claimed derivation of Vesta's name from that of the Greek goddess of the hearth (Cic. *N.D.* 2.67.11): *Vestae nomen a Graecis (ea est enim quae ab illis Ἑστία [Hestia] dicitur).*

infitianda: Use of legal language underlines Ilia's pain at being disqualified from performance of her Vestal duties. For the legal significance of *infitiari* see Berger (1953: 501) and Casali (1995: 38). For Ovid's use of legal language see Kenney (1969a) and Ziogas (2016), (2021). Ovid is the only Augustan poet to use this verb (2.17.26, *Her.* 9.4, *Ars* 2.414, *Met.* 2.34, 11.205, *Tr.* 4.3.66, *Pont.* 1.3.87, 1.7.27, 4.6.42).

77-8. quid moror et digitis designor adultera uulgi?
 desint famosus quae notet ora pudor'.
Overwhelmed by shame, Ilia closes her speech with a decision to commit suicide.

77. quid moror: Recalls Dido's words hinting at suicide in her final speech to Aeneas (*A.* 4.325–6; with Pease [1935]): *quid moror? an mea Pygmalion dum moenia frater | destruat aut captam ducat Gaetulus Iarbas?* Cf. Hecuba's response to Polyxena's death (*Met.* 13.517): *quidue moror? quo me seruas, annosa senectus?*

digitis designor adultera uulgi: Alliteration of *d* underlines Ilia's conception of herself as an adulteress. The language recalls Tragedy's emphasis on the disgrace inherent in being a love poet (3.1.19): *aliquis digito uatem designat euntem.*

adultera: Philomela responds to rape by Tereus in a similar way, seeing herself as her sister's *paelex* (*Met.* 6.537, 606).

78. famosus…pudor: Like Ilia, other Ovidian rape victims experience profound shame e.g. *Met.* 2.450 (Callisto), 6.544–5 (Philomela), 6.604, *Fast.* 2.170 (Callisto), 2.819–20 (Lucretia): *illa diu reticet pudibundaque celat amictu | ora.*

quae notet ora pudor: *pudor* and its physical manifestation, the blush, are regular companions in Ovid e.g. 1.14.52, 2.5.34, *Her.* 21.167–8, *Met.* 1.484, 4.329, *Tr.* 4.3.50. *noto*, with its sense of 'brand or tattoo (as a sign of disgrace)' (*OLD* 1b) reinforces Ilia's sense of shame.

Commentary, 6.76-81

79-80. hactenus, et uestem tumidis praetendit ocellis
  atque ita se in rapidas perdita misit aquas.
Having completed her speech, Ilia covers her face and attempts suicide by hurling herself into the Anio.

79. hactenus: The abrupt transition from speech to action underlines the speed of Ilia's response.

uestem...praetendit: The gesture suggests a mixture of shame and grief. Cf. the Senecan Theseus' description of Phaedra's response to his threats (*Phaed.* 886-7): *quidnam ora maesta auertis et lacrimas genis | subito coortas ueste praetenta optegis?*

tumidis...ocellis: For *tumidus* used of eyes swollen with tears see Sen. *Med.* 1020 (Medea to Jason; with Boyle [2014: ad loc.]): *lumina huc tumida alleua.*

80. atq(ue) ita s(e) in: Elisions in the first two feet of a pentameter are striking. Here they may suggest the horrific nature of Ilia's action.
  Elision in the Ovidian pentameter is rare. Ceccarelli (105) notes that Propertius allows elision in 19.34 per cent of his pentameters, Tibullus 9.68 per cent, and Ovid 6.08 per cent in the erotic works. The only other pentameter in *Amores* with two elisions is 2.10.2: *uno poss(e) aliquem tempor(e) amare duas.*

se...misit: Ovid seems to reserve this expression for attempts at self-drowning: *Her.* 15.167-8, *Met.* 4.529-30, *Ib.* 499.

perdita: Recalls other women in a state of despair, women like Ariadne (Catul. 64.70, 177) and Dido (*A.* 4.541, *Her.* 7.61).

81-2. supposuisse manus ad pectora lubricus amnis
  dicitur et socii iura dedisse tori.
Leaping into the Anio, however, results not in Ilia's death but in rape by and marriage to the river. While the language of the hexameter suggests both positive and negative interpretations of Anio's intentions, that of the pentameter seems more positive.

81. supposuisse manus: This expression can be used in a positive sense e.g. of helping a person or ship endangered by water (e.g. *Met.* 14.561 [nymphs helping ships], *Pont.* 2.6.14 [aiding a drowning person]). It can also suggest stealth (e.g. *Met.* 4.776-7 [of Perseus stealing Phorcys' daughters' single eye]: *id se sollerti furtim, dum traditur, astu | supposita cepisse manu*).

manus ad pectora: For the overtones of sexual violence cf. *Met.* 4.359 (Hermaphroditus and Salmacis): *subiectatque manus, inuitaque pectora tangit, Fast.* 2.803-4 (Lucretia and Tarquinius): *positis urgentur pectora palmis, | tum primum externa pectora tacta manu.*

lubricus: Commonly used of rivers (e.g. Hor. *Epod.* 13.14: Simois; *Fast.* 4.337: Almo; 6.238: Tiber) the adjective is also applied to snakes e.g. *A.* 5.84 and, more importantly, to treacherous people e.g. *A*. 11.716 (with McGill [2020: ad loc.]): *nequiquam patrias temptasti lubricus artis*, VF 2.555–6: *illum torua tuens atque acri lubricus astu | rex*. For the word's sexual meaning in later texts see *TLL* 1690.45–66.

82. dicitur: Almost certainly alludes to Ennius' version of the story. It implies narratorial scepticism and suggests that the inherited version of the relationship between Ilia and Anio is not correct. For this scepticism see above on 26, 32, and 41.

socii…iura tori: The phrase *socii…tori* combined with *iura* implies legitimate marriage. Cf. *Her*. 16.285–6 (of Helen and Menelaus), *Fast*. 2.729 (of the royal wives), *Pont*. 2.8.29 (of Livia): *perque tori sociam*.

From one perspective, that of Ilia's father in Ennius' *Annales*, this is a satisfactory outcome (*Ann*. 1.44–5 Goldberg and Manuwald [1]): *o gnata, tibi sunt ante gerendae | aerumnae, post ex fluuio fortuna resistet*. Ovid's Anio presumably agrees. After all, even if his action results from miscommunication, as Bretzigheimer (2001: 179) suggests, he has made Ilia his lawful wife. Ilia, however, might not. Having expressed a Vestal virgin's horror of any kind of marriage (*taedas…ullas* 75), she is now raped for a second time.

83–4. te quoque credibile est aliqua caluisse puella,
    sed nemora et siluae crimina uestra tegunt.
The lover's speech closes with the suggestion that even this stream might have experienced sexual passion and been guilty of the crimes of all the others.

83. The lover closes his speech with a line combining a run of dactyls (DDDD) with utter disdain.

credibile est: For similar condescension see 1.11.11 (address to enslaved Nape): *credibile est et te sensisse Cupidinis arcus*. Ovid favours this sentiment (15 of its 18 occurrences in classical verse are his) perhaps because it invites scepticism.

caluisse: For *caleo* used of erotic excitement (*OLD* 6) see e.g. *Her*. 18.90, *Ars* 1.525–6, 3.571: *ista decent pueros aetate et amore calentes*. For the association between heat and sexual passion see above on 3.2.39–40.

84. crimina: For similar evaluation of the behaviour of rapist gods see e.g. 3.4.39: *non sunt sine crimine nati*, *Ars* 2.110: *Naiadumque tener crimine raptus Hylas*, *Met*. 6.131: *caelestia crimina*.

uestra: Given that the couplet begins with *tu*, it seems more likely that *uestra crimina* refers to Anio's misdeeds rather than to those of all the previously named rivers. This is another example of *uestra* being equal to *tua*. For *uester* used for *tuus* see *OLD uester* 2c, Housman (1909), Fordyce (1961: 188–9) on Catul. 39.20, Booth (1991: 175–6) on 2.16.24, and Davis (2020: 117) on VF 7.91.

Commentary, 6.82-9

85–6. dum loquor, increuit latis spatiosus in undis,
  nec capit admissas alueus altus aquas.
With the words *dum loquor* the lover turns from trying to persuade the river to observing that all his rhetorical efforts have been in vain: the stream has continued to rise.

85. dum loquor: For *dum* followed by a present indicative in the *dum*-clause, followed by a main verb in the past tense see Woodcock (§221).

spatiosus in: This is the reading of the major manuscripts (P, S, and Y). Goold (1965: 52) argued for Bentley's (Hedicke [1905: 22]) *spatiosior*, subsequently printed in Showerman and Goold. Ramirez de Verger (2) agrees. But the combination of the comparative adjective *spatiosior* flanked by an adjective and noun in the ablative, will encourage the reader to treat *latis…undis* as ablative of comparison: 'more spacious than its wide waters'. This is nonsense.

86. For this verbal pattern (VaBbA) see above on 3.1.7. Here the line images what it describes, with *admissas…aquas* overflowing the *alueus altus*.

87–8. quid mecum, furiose, tibi? quid mutua differs
  gaudia? quid coeptum, rustice, rumpis iter?
Recognition of failure leads to anger, with the lover posing three heated questions in two lines, each beginning with *quid*.

87. quid mecum…tibi: The expression is apparently colloquial. See 1.7.27, 2.19.57: *quid mihi cum facili, quid cum lenone marito?*, *Her.* 6.47–8: *quid mihi cum Minyis, quid cum Dodonide pinu? | quid tibi cum patria, nauita Tiphy, mea?*, *Fast.* 3.3 (with Heyworth [2019: ad loc.]), 4.3. Cf. Plaut. Cur. 688, St. 333: *quid mecum est tibi?*, Men. 369–70: *quid mecum tibi | fuit umquam?*

mutua…| gaudia: As in Lucretius (4.1205, 5.854), the phrase emphasizes the importance of shared sexual pleasure in keeping couples together. Here, however, the stream frustrates lovers' shared desires. For *gaudium* as a sexual term see Adams (1982: 197–8). See also 2.3.2 where the locked-out lover pities a eunuch's ignorance of such joys: *mutua… Veneris gaudia*; and *Ars* 2.682 where the Teacher prizes shared pleasure: *quod iuuet ex aequo femina uirque ferant*.

88. coeptum, rustice, rumpis iter: Alliteration and assonance help convey the lover's anger and frustration.

rustice: For the force of this term see above on 3.1.43.

89–90. quid si legitimum flueres, si nobile flumen,
  si tibi per terras maxima fama foret?
While adopting a rhetorical approach similar to that of the previous couplet (a single question with three parts, this time articulated by repetition of *si*), the

lover now turns to abusing the stream in terms applicable to both a flow of water and a quasi-person.

89. legitimum: Means 'properly so called, genuine, real' (*OLD* 5), but not without a hint at 'born in lawful wedlock, legitimate' (*OLD* 2c).

legitimum flueres...nobile flumen: The quasi-repetition *flueres...flumen* enables balance (*si* plus adjective plus *flu-* x2), alliteration of *l*, and avoidance of the more usual, but less interesting, *esses*. For other examples see below on 3.8.65.

90. Alliteration is notable in the pentameter too, of *t* in the first half and of *m* and *f* in the second.

foret: A metrically convenient alternative to *esset* (*foret* is used six times in *Amores*, *esset* five), it also has the advantage of reinforcing the *f* in *fama*.

91–2. nomen habes nullum, riuis collecte caducis,
   nec tibi sunt fontes nec tibi certa domus.
The lover now picks up the secondary sense of *legitimum* and begins questioning the stream's ancestry.

91. nomen nullum habes: This may be the literal truth: the stream may be so insignificant as to be nameless. But *nomen* also means 'good repute' or 'glory' (e.g. 3.1.29: *nunc habeam per te Romana Tragoedia nomen*, *G.* 3.47: *Caesaris et nomen fama tot ferre per annos*) and connote noble ancestry (e.g. *Pont.* 1.9.39: *si modo non census nec clarum nomen auorum*, *A.* 12.225–6: *cui genus a proauis ingens clarumque paternae | nomen erat uirtutis*). Even if the stream has a name, it remains insignificant.

riuis collecte caducis: This might be said to most rivers. After all, the Nile and Danube have tributaries. The point is that the stream is such a temporary assemblage of creeks and rivulets, that it has no actual identity.

92. The line's symmetry is highlighted by the repetition of *nec tibi* at the beginning of each half.

As at *A.* 6.673 (*nulli certa domus*) and 8.39 (*hic tibi certa domus*), *certa domus* here means 'fixed abode', i.e. the stream's course is variable. The absence of identifiable *fontes* confirms the point. But the use of *nec certa domus* as an insult reminds the reader that *certus* can mean 'legitimate' (*OLD* 4c). See e.g. Sen. *Phaed.* (ironically of bastard Hippolytus) 1112: *certus heres*; *Thy.* 1101–2 (Thyestes): *natos parenti* (Atreus): *fateor, et, quod me iuuat, | certos*.

93–4. fontis habes instar pluuiamque niuesque solutas,
   quas tibi diuitias pigra ministrat hiems.
The lover, focusing on the stream's condition in winter, develops the thought from the previous couplet that it lacks a proper source.

Commentary, 6.89-97

93. fontis...instar: Instead of having a standard *fons* (*OLD* 1: 'a flow of water issuing from the ground, spring'), this stream is fed by irregular supplies of water.

94. diuitias: Metonymy (wealth = water) helps preserve the stream's ambiguous status as both water and quasi-person.

pigra...hiems: The association between winter and inactivity or sluggishness is conventional e.g. *Ars* 3.186: *pigraque fugit hiems*, Sen. *Thy*. 863-4: *pigram referens hiemem gelidus | cadet Aegoceros*. Cf. Lucr. 5.746-7. Here, however, *pigra* is offensive and adds to the insult.

95-6. aut lutulentus agis brumali tempore cursus,
     aut premis arentem puluerulentus humum.
Indeed the stream barely has a continuing existence. Its true character is underlined by similar-sounding, polysyllabic adjectives: in winter it is a muddy flow (*lutulentus*); in summer it is a heap of dust (*puluerulentus*).

95. lutulentus: The word's rarity in poetry underlines its offensiveness. Horace employs it when criticizing Lucilius' style (*S*. 1.4.11, 1.10.50), while Ovid uses it of the earth's condition after the flood (*Met*. 1.434). Servius notes that Virgil (*Ecl*. 1.65) prefers to describe the river Oaxes as *rapidum cretae* ('chalk-snatching') rather than call it *lutulentum*.

agis brumali tempore cursus: The language is overly grand. *agere cursum* is appropriate not for muddy creeks but for the passage of stars and comets through the cosmos e.g. Manil. 4.863: *qua mundus agit cursus*; Sen. *Her. F.* 928-9, Plin. *Nat*. 2.23.5. So too with *brumali tempore*. This periphrasis for 'winter' recalls Cicero's translation of Aratus' poem on the stars (*N.D*. 2.112.14): *brumali flectens contorquet tempore currum*. The juxtaposition of astronomical language with *lutulentus*, an adjective more typical of comedy and prose, magnifies the speaker's rudeness.

96. premis...puluerulentus: The line manages to convey two ideas (reinforced by alliteration), not merely that the stream is mere dust in the summer, but it that lies a useless burden on the earth.

97-8. quis te tum potuit sitiens haurire uiator?
     quis dixit grata uoce 'perennis eas'?
After insulting assertions, the lover now returns to blunt questions (note the insistent effect of repeated *quis*) expressed in the plainest of language, focusing this time on the stream's condition in summer.

97. Alliteration of *t* perhaps highlights the line's key word: *sitiens*. Cf. *Ars* 2.231: *nec graue te tempus sitiensque Canicula tardet*, *Fast*. 4.940 *tosta sitit tellus*; Tib. 1.4.42: *et Canis arenti torreat arua siti*.

tum: Marks the transition from a couplet concerned with two seasons to one dealing only with summer.

98. perennis: In dry places streams that flow all year are prized. For *perennis* as a suitable epithet for a stream see e.g. Enn. *Scip.* fr. 5 Goldberg and Manuwald (2: p. 292), Lucr. 5.262, *Am.* 3.9.25, *Her.* 8.64, *Rem.* 652, *Fast.* 3.654.

99–100. damnosus pecori curris, damnosior agris.
  forsitan haec alios, me mea damna mouent.
After questions implying the stream's uselessness to thirsty travellers, the lover declares that it is emphatically ruinous (*damnosus...damnosior |...damna*) not only to flocks and fields but to the lover himself.

99. As Wills (1996: 234) observes, this line recalls and reverses the epitaph of Virgil's Daphnis (*Ecl.* 5.44): *formosi pecoris custos, formosior ipse.*

100. me mea damna mouent: Alliteration of *m* plus the combination of pronoun and possessive adjective (*me mea*) underline the lover's concern for his own interests. Wills (1996: 242) points out that while this form of repetition occurs in all or most poets, it is particularly frequent in Ovid (*me mea*: 17 times; *te tua*: seven times).

101–2. huic ego uae demens narrabam fluminum amores?
  iactasse indigne nomina tanta pudet.
Having denounced the stream, the lover realizes not the folly of addressing a body of water, but the stupidity of telling stories of great rivers to such an unworthy listener.

101. huic ego: Here the juxtaposition of third and first person pronouns underlines the lover's incredulity that he has actually been telling these stories to this stream. For *huic ego* used to different effect see above on 3.1.44.

uae: This exclamation is usually employed in contexts of genuine distress e.g. Catul. 8.15: *scelesta, uae te quae tibi manet uita, Ecl.* 9.28: *Mantua uae miserae nimium uicina Cremonae, Her.* 3.82: *hic mihi uae miserae concutit ossa metus.* Here, however, its use smacks of comic exaggeration.

fluminum amores: For the phrase see *Met.* 5.576: *fluminis Elei ueteres narrauit amores.*

  Elision within the fifth foot (*flūmĭn(um) ă|mōres*) is rare in *Amores*. (See also: 1.10.13, 2.1.13, 2.19.45, 3.9.67.) Platnauer (1951: 73) notes the exceptional character of this line: 'Cretics [*flūmĭnūm*] in *-m* are not elided before an initial short vowel except for "huic ego, vae, demens narrabam flūmĭn(um) ămores" (Ov. *Am.* III.6.101)— a unique instance'. The effect is perhaps to underline the lover's shock at his own folly.

102. iactasse...nomina: For *iactare nomina* as 'mention' (*OLD* 10b) see 3.1.21, *Ib.* 14: *iactat et in toto nomina nostra foro.* Cf. *Her.* 17.51: *sed genus et proauos et regia nomina iactas.*

**103–4. nescioquem hunc spectans Acheloon et Inachon amnem
et potui nomen, Nile, referre tuum?**
The lover's shock is given substance when realizes that he has implicitly likened this nobody to rivers like Achelous (35), Inachus (25), and the Nile (39).

103. nescioq(uem) hunc: *nescioquem*, particularly when combined with harsh elision, implies contempt, as when Dido's suitors are outraged by her choice of Aeneas (*Her*. 7.123–4): *qui me coiere querentes | nescioquem thalamis praeposuisse suis* or when Polyphemus speaks of Jupiter (*Met.* 13.843–4): *nam uos narrare soletis | nescioquem regnare Iouem.*

104. As one of the world's great rivers, the Nile is addressed and awarded a line to itself.

**105–6. at tibi pro meritis, opto, non candide torrens,
sint rapidi soles siccaque semper hiems.**
The lover closes with an insult and a powerful curse. His language recalls an earlier lover's imprecation against that other barrier to love, Dipsas the brothel-keeper (1.8.113–14): *di tibi dent nullosque Lares inopemque senectam, | et longas hiemes perpetuamque sitim.*

105. non candide: Restates one of the lover's main objections to the river: its lack of clarity (1, 8, 95). For the power of understatement see above on 3.1.36 and 3.4.39. Cf. Martial's praise of the water flowing from Rome's aqueducts (6.42.19–20): *quae tam candida, tam serena lucet, | ut nullas ibi suspiceris undas.*

106. rapidi soles: Given that *rapidus* is a standard epithet for the sun (e.g. Catul. 66.3, *G.* 1.92: *rapidiue potentia solis*, 1.424, 2.321, Hor. *Carm.* 2.9.12, *Met.* 8.225), it is clear that the lover hopes for normal Italian summers.

sicca...hiems: Mediterranean winters are usually wet (Varro even links *hiems* and *imber* [*L.* 6.9.2]: *huius temporis pars prima hiems, quod tum multi imbres*) and so the lover hopes for a reversal of the natural order. This will both harm the stream and assist future lovers.

3.7: AN EMBARRASSING PROBLEM

Roman love poets sometimes brag about their sexual prowess. Catullus is the most explicit, promising Ipsitilla *nouem continuas fututiones* ('nine straight fucks' 32.8). The elegists prefer more oblique language, with lovers in both Propertius and Ovid employing euphemism to boast of their abilities:[1] (Prop. 2.22a.23–4):

---

[1] For 3.7 as 'euphemistic' see Adams (1982: 224), Sharrock (1995: 157–9). For the poem's avoidance of 'anatomical terms' see Kennedy (1993: 58).

saepe est experta puella | officium tota nocte ualere meum ('A girl has often found my service good all night'); (*Am.* 2.10.26): *decepta est opera nulla puella mea* ('No girl has been disappointed by my performance').[2]

Some, however, write about sexual failure. Impotence is the subject of poems in the *Greek Anthology*, including one by Philodemus (c. 110–40 BCE),[3] and in Horace's *Epodes*.[4] Among love elegists, however, only Tibullus had referred to the inability to have sex (1.5.39–44):

> saepe aliam tenui, sed iam cum gaudia adirem,
>   admonuit dominae deseruitque Venus.
> tunc me discedens deuotum femina dixit
>   (a pudet!) et narrat scire nefanda meam.
> non facit hoc uerbis; facie tenerisque lacertis
>   deuouet et flauis nostra puella comis.

Often I held another girl, but when I was approaching joy, Venus reminded me of my mistress and abandoned me. Then, as she left, the woman pronounced me cursed and (how embarrassing!) reports that my girlfriend knows evil arts. My girlfriend does not achieve this with words; she curses me with her looks and tender arms and blonde hair.

The Tibullan lover fails because he is in thrall to Delia. Ovid's poem differs in treating the subject at length (84 lines versus six) and in its presentation of the lover's psychology (this lover is enslaved to no one.) As Adams (1982: 224) observed, '*Am.* 3.7 is quite unlike anything in Tibullus or Propertius'.

3.7 is exceptional because of its subject matter. It is one of those poems with which Ovid extended the range of love elegy in surprising ways, as when he introduced such topics as domestic violence (1.7), abortion (2.13 and 14), and travelling with one's wife (3.13).[5] On the other hand, as Keith (1994: 38) and Sharrock (1995: 154–5) observed, explicit allusion links 3.7 with 1.5, one of the collection's most significant poems: impotence is the flipside of success with Corinna. If 1.5 describes the fulfilment of a straight man's erotic fantasies, 3.7 reflects upon the lover's failure to match masculine desire with reality.[6]

Ovid's treatment of impotence differs markedly from those of Horace and Tibullus. In *Epod.* 8 the Horatian lover blames the woman's ugliness for his inability to have an erection, while the Tibullan lover attributes his failure to his girlfriend's power. In 3.7, by contrast, the Ovidian lover tries to understand his experience

---

[2] See Adams (1982) for *officium* (163–4) and *opera* (157) as sexual terms.
[3] *PA* 11.30. This and other examples are discussed below.
[4] Especially in *Epodes* 8 and 12, where impotence is the poet's response to a repulsive sexual partner. For discussion see e.g. Fitzgerald (1988) and Watson (2003: 287–8).
[5] For the widening of elegy's scope see Introduction §8.
[6] For the importance of reflection (as opposed to narrative) in 3.7 see Gärtner (2011: 104).

and ultimately accepts that he, the man, is responsible for his failure and not the woman.[7]

3.7 is also unusual in that the speaker identifies himself as Corinna's lover. One of the most striking aspects of Book 3 is that it presents a wide variety of speakers who cannot obviously be identified with the Ovidian lover, with the man who celebrated sexual success with Corinna in 1.5 and 2.12.[8] Conversely, there is no reason to identify any of the women in Book 3 with Corinna.[9] At 3.1.49 and 3.12.16 she functions as an emblem of Ovid's poetry, while in this poem reference to her name at line 25 establishes that the lover's partner is not Corinna.

Secondary literature: Morgan (1977: 91–2); Cahoon (1988); Baeza Angulo (1989); Richlin (1992: 117–19); Keith (1994); Sharrock (1995); Obermayer (1998: 283–9); Mauger-Plichon (1999); Bretzigheimer (2001: 139–40, 236–7); James (2003: 183–4); Holzberg (2009); Gärtner (2011); Lavery (2016: 42–51); Oliensis (2019: 184–5); Grant (2019: 122–50); Starnone (2019).

1–2. At non formosa est, at non bene culta puella,
  at, puto, non uotis saepe petita meis.
Triple repetition of *at non* makes for an arresting and powerful opening couplet, with the hexameter balanced at the main caesura and with *puto* dividing the third *at non* and undercutting the force of the speaker's assertions. The irony is patent: the girl is lovely; she is sophisticated; and she was the object of desire.

1. at non: As McKeown observes (201; on 1.8.1–2), opening a poem with a spondee is rare in *Amores*. The other examples are: 1.8, 1.14, 2.7, 2.8, 2.9, 2.16, and 3.8. As in 1.14 (Stop dyeing your hair!), 2.7 (I'm innocent!), and 3.8 (You're greedy!), the effect is to suggest the speaker's distress, whether real or fake.

formosa: In Catullus (poem 68) being *formosa* implies not just physical beauty but intelligence and wit, while in Ovid it suggests the opposite of being chaste (1.8.43): *ludunt formosae. casta est quam nemo rogauit*; (3.4.41): *quo tibi formosam, si non nisi casta placebat?*

culta: In *Amores* beauty and *cultus* are natural partners e.g. 1.8.25–6: *et cur non placeas? nulli tua forma secunda est. | me miseram, dignus corpore cultus abest*; (2.10.5): *utraque formosa est, operosae cultibus ambae*. See also *Met.* 9.461–2 (of Byblis): *uisuraque fratrem | culta uenit, nimiumque cupit formosa uideri*. Being *culta/cultus*, however, has varying connotations. It may suggest stylish hair or dress (*OLD cultus* 3; e.g. *Ars* 1.511: *Hippolytum Phaedra, nec erat bene cultus, amauit*) or some other form of refinement (*OLD* 4; e.g. *Ars* 3.341–2: *nostri lege culta magistri | carmina*; Tib. 1.9.74: *et senis amplexus culta puella fugit*). Both are possible here.

---

[7] As Gärtner (2011: 106) points out, Ovid's lover accepts that he is to blame and not his partner.
[8] For Ovid's use of different personae in *Amores* see Introduction §6.
[9] For the role of Corinna see Introduction §7.

2. puto: This is an example of *puto* used parenthetically as 'a pointer to the falsity or absurdity of the stance adopted or the claim made' (Booth [1991: 171, on 2.5.25]). See also 1.2.5, 1.12.9, 2.15.25, 3.1.8, 3.7.55, 3.11.34, *Her.* 2.105.

For the scansion *putŏ* see above on 3.1.8.

uotis saepe petita meis: For the character of the lover's desires see lines 63–4 below.

3–4. hanc tamen in nullos tenui male languidus usus,
    sed iacui pigro crimen onusque toro.
After the rhetorically vigorous opening come explanation and self-reproach.

3. male: For the force of *male* see above on 3.3.18.

languidus: For the connotations of this adjective and cognate verbs see above on 3.4.10 and below on line 66. For their association with impotence see e.g. Catul. 25.3, 67.21, Hor. *Epod.* 12.14, Tib. 1.9.56, Prop. 1.3.38, 1.13.15; and Adams (1982: 46).

4. sed: Ramirez de Verger (2) accepts *et*, suggested, though not printed, by Heinsius (280). Given that *sed* is the reading of all manuscripts and given that the poem's argument advances via assertion and contradiction (Gärtner [2011: 105] speaks of 3.7's 'adversative way of arguing' [*adversative Argumentationsweise*]; both *sed* and *at* occur in this poem more than any other in *Amores*), the inherited reading should be retained.

pigro...toro: Normally applied to living creatures, *piger* is here transferred from the man to the place which lacks an expected activity. Cf. *Met.* 2.770–1: *at illa | surgit humo pigrā*, where the adjective is used of the ground from which Envy arises, rather than the goddess herself.

crimen onusque: The phrase is best treated as a hendiadys, i.e. as two nouns used for a single idea ('guilt and a burden' = 'a guilty burden'). It recalls Achilles' self-description as 'a useless burden on the land' (Hom. *Il.* 18.104: ἐτώσιον ἄχθος ἀρούρης).

5–6. nec potui cupiens, pariter cupiente puella,
    inguinis effeti parte iuuante frui.
Using less emotive and evaluative language, the lover explains his problem: despite the eagerness of both partners, he was unable to have an erection.

5. This is a remarkable line, in which balance at the main caesura is highlighted by alliteration of *p* and *c*, by repetition of forms of *cupio*, and by use of *pariter*.

pariter: For *pariter* as a marker of different kinds of balance see 2.19.5: *speremus pariter, pariter metuamus amantes; Her.* 3.47: *uidi consortes pariter generisque necisque*; 12.198: *cum quo sum pariter facta parente parens*; 13.29: *ut rediit animus, pariter rediere dolores*; and *Rem.* 77: *tu pariter uati, pariter succurre medenti.*

cupiens...cupiente: This type of repetition (polyptoton) underlines formal balance at 1.2.42: *ibis in auratis aureus ipse rotis*; 1.4.27: *tange manu mensam, tangunt quo more precantes*; 1.4.32: *et, qua tu biberis, hac ego parte bibam*; 2.5.58: *lingua tua est nostris, nostra recepta tuis*; 2.16.7: *terra ferax Cereris multoque feracior uuis*. This is an example of what Wills (1996: 202–5) calls 'amorous polyptoton'.

cupiens...cupiente puella: In both *Amores* and *Ars* characters claim that men and women can and should experience sexual pleasure equally: 1.10.33, 2.10.29, *Ars* 2.682, 3.794: *et ex aequo res iuuet illa duos*.

For similar verbal play (polyptoton combined with balance at the main caesura) involving *cupio* see *Her.* 16.93 (Paris): *utque ego te cupio, sic me cupiere puellae*.

6. inguinis: Denoting 'the part of the body around the sexual organs' (*OLD* 2), *inguen* here is a euphemism for *mentula*. For the euphemism's widespread use see Adams (1982: 47–8).

effeti: Meaning 'worn out with bearing offspring' (*OLD* 2) or 'exhausted' (*OLD* 3) this too is a euphemism. Cicero is instructive here. When he declares that sexual excess in youth leads to an enfeebled body in old age (*effetum corpus tradit senectuti* Sen. 29.10), he is referring to general weakness, not sexual impotence. The word is so unusual in sexual contexts that Adams (1982) does not discuss it.

7–12. illa quidem nostro subiecit eburnea collo
   bracchia Sithonia candidiora niue
osculaque inseruit cupida luctantia lingua
   lasciuum femori supposuitque femur
et mihi blanditias dixit dominumque uocauit
   et quae praeterea publica uerba iuuant.

Given that 95 per cent of Ovid's couplets are grammatically self-contained (Platnauer [1951: 27]), a three-couplet sentence is exceptional. Such sentences are designed to impress. One is addressed to a potential girlfriend (1.3.7–14), another to a goddess (2.13.7–16), while at 2.16.33–40 a lengthy period underlines the lover's longing for his girlfriend. Here it highlights not just the girl's beauty, but her numerous attempts to stimulate her partner.

7. quidem: Use of this particle underlines the argumentative character of 3.7. See McKeown (1989: 219; on 1.8.35–6) on the frequency of its use in Ovid and other poets.

eburnea: For 'ivory-coloured' as an index of beauty see *Her.* 20.57 (Acontius of Cydippe), *Met.* 3.422 (Narcissus), 4.335, 354 (Hermaphroditus), 10.592 (Atalanta). For discussion of the importance of 3.7 for Pygmalion's ivory girl (*eburnea uirgo Met.* 10.275) see Starnone (2019).

8. Sithonia: Equals 'Thracian'. For reference to 'Sithonian snow' (both in erotic contexts) see *Ecl.* 10.66: *Sithoniasque niues hiemis subeamus aquosae*, Hor. *Carm.* 3.26.10: *Memphin carentem Sithonia niue*.

candidiora: As 3.5.11 (*candidior niuibus, tunc cum cecidere recentes*) and *Pont.* 2.5.38 (*et non calcata candidiora niue*) make clear, *candidus* is exactly the right epithet for freshly-fallen snow.

9. osculaque inseruit cupida luctantia lingua: This is a particularly elegant line, combining interwoven nouns and adjectives and four words ending in *a*. For Ovid's fondness for this kind of line see above on 3.4.16. This poem contains more such lines than any other in *Amores*.

For deep kissing see 2.5.24, 57–8, 3.14.23, *Her.* 15.129–30, and Tib. 1.8.37–8 (quoted below).

The major manuscripts (P, S, and Y) offer: *oscula inseruit cupide luctantia/ luctancia linguis*. Munari retains this reading and translates *e mi diede dentro la bocca baci che lottavano bramosamente colle lingue* ('and she gave me kisses in my mouth that fought longingly with tongues'). This presents several problems. First, it is not clear what it means. Second, the plural *linguis* is difficult. Marius draws attention to Tib. 1.8.37–8: *et dare anhelanti pugnantibus umida linguis | oscula*. This, however, is a case of mutual lust in which each lover inserts a tongue into the other's mouth. In 3.7, by contrast, only one tongue is involved: the woman inserts her tongue into her partner's mouth to stimulate his erection.

More recent editors print *cupida...lingua* (Kenney, Showerman and Goold, McKeown; also Marius, Naugerius, and Micyllus) or *cupidae...linguae* (Ramirez de Verger [2]; also Heinsius and Burman). Both have merits. *cupidae...linguae* has the advantages of preserving the *cupide* found in P, S, and Y; and of producing both good sense ('she thrust an eager tongue's vigorous kisses'); and an elegant line with interlacing of nouns and adjectives (AbaB). *cupida...lingua* also has manuscript support (Kenney: ω [*codices praeter* Rr Pp Yy S *omnes uel plures*]); produces perhaps slightly superior sense; and a line of even greater refinement (AbaB; plus four words ending in *a*).

luctantia: For *luctor* used of erotic struggle see Prop. 2.1.13, 2.15.5.

Superficially similar, *luctantiaque oscula* at *Met.* 4.358 has a different meaning. Bömer (1976: ad loc.) notes that by 'bold enallage' *luctantia* is equivalent to *luctantis* and applies not to the kisses but to Hermaphroditus.

10. lasciuum femori supposuitque femur: Wills (1996: 203) treats this as an example of 'amorous polyptoton'. See also 1.4.43–4: *nec femori committe femur nec crure cohaere | nec tenerum duro cum pede iunge pedem*, 3.14.22: *nec femori impositum sustinuisse femur*. For the phrase see Catul. 69.2: *tenerum supposuisse femur*.

Commentary, 7.8-15

11. blanditias: For the erotic importance of flattery see e.g. 1.2.35, 1.4.66, 2.9.45, and 2.19.17–18: *quas mihi blanditias, quam dulcia uerba parabat | oscula, di magni, qualia quotque dabat.*

dominumque uocauit: For *dominus* used by a woman of her lover see *Her.* 8.8 (with Pestelli [2007: ad loc.]), 15.145, *Ars* 1.314. At *Met.* 9.466 (with Kenney [2011: ad loc.]) it is ambiguous between a familial and an erotic term.

12. publica: The term is used of a commonplace subject: *Ars* 1.144 (how to start a conversation): *et moueant primos publica uerba sonos*; or ordinary language: *Ars* 3.480 (on letter writing): *sermonis publica forma placet*. Here it presumably denotes the (perhaps obscene) language commonly used by lovers.

iuuant: For words as helpful in lovemaking see 3.14.25, *Ars* 2.159–60: *blanditias molles auremque iuuantia uerba | affer*, 3.524: *'lux mea' quaeque solent uerba iuuare uiros*, 3.795–6.

13–14. tacta tamen ueluti gelida mea membra cicuta
  segnia propositum destituere meum.
This is a virtuoso couplet. It is wholly dactylic (DDDD | DD), contains notable alliteration of *t*, *c*, and *m*, as well as five words ending in *a* in the hexameter, and a solid run of five words ending in *a* in the hexameter and pentameter. (For the dactylic couplet see above on 3.2.1–2.)

13. Lines with five words ending in *a* are unusual and clearly the product of design. For lines which interweave four or more words ending in *a* see above on 3.4.16. Here the device ironically recalls 2.10.26, where the lover makes the opposite claim: *decepta est opera nulla puella mea*.

gelida...cicuta: For hemlock's traditional association with cold see e.g. Arist. *Frogs* 124–5: 'Dionysus: Are you speaking of hemlock? Heracles: Yes. Dionysus: That's a cold and wintry way [to Hades]'; Plin. *Nat.* 24.24.8: 'It (styrax) counteracts poisons which kill by cold and for that reason hemlock'.

membra: The word often means simply 'body' (1.4.9, 1.5.2, 1.6.6, 36, 1.7.53, 2.10.18, 3.7.78). Here it is euphemistic shorthand for *genitalia membra* (2.3.3); see also 2.15.25 and line 65 below. Adams (1982: 224) notes that this is one of 3.7's 'colourless' terms for the penis. See also Catul. 63.6, Tib. 1.4.70, Prop. 2.16.14.

14. segnia: For *segnis* of unsatisfactory sex see *Rem.* 403–4: *quamlibet inuenias, in qua tua prima uoluptas | desinat: a prima proxima segnis erit*. McKeown (50) observes that 'the derivation of *segnis* from *sine igni* enhances the point in *gelida*', citing Servius on *A.* 2.374: *segnis autem est proprie frigidus, sine igni*.

15–16. truncus iners iacui, species et inutile pondus,
  et non exactum, corpus an umbra forem.

208   *Commentary*

Whereas the previous couplet was wholly dactylic, this one consists of a hexameter with the maximum number of dactyls (DDDD) and a pentameter with the maximum number of spondees (SS). The shift to spondees seems appropriate to the subject matter.

15. The language alludes, ironically perhaps, to words spoken by Priapus, a god whose iconography includes an erect penis (Hor. *S.* 1.8.1): *olim truncus eram ficulnus, inutile lignum*. For discussion see Gowers (2012: 266–7).

truncus: The image of a useless tree trunk (*OLD* 2) recalls Catullus' comparison of an impotent husband to an alder in a ditch (17.18–19): *nec se subleuat ex sua parte, sed uelut alnus | in fossa Liguri iacet suppernata securi.*
When used of humans, *truncus* suggest a lifeless body e.g. Catul. 64.370 (of Polyxena): *proiciet truncum summisso poplite corpus, A.* 2.557 (of Priam): *iacet ingens litore truncus* or possibly a castrated one (Obermayer [1998: 286]).

iners: Sometimes meaning 'lazy' or 'inactive' (*OLD* 2), *iners* is an appropriate description of the elegiac poet and his way of life (e.g. Tib. 1.1.5, Prop. 3.7.72, *Am.* 1.15.2). Here, however, it implies impotence as at Catul. 67.26, Hor. *Epod.* 12.17, and *Rem.* 780.

species et...pondus: The claim surprises because *species* ('a phantom appearance' OLD 9a) and *pondus* are contradictory terms: by definition a *species* lacks weight. The lover, however, feels himself to be both.

inutile: Perhaps recalls 2.3.7 (addressed to a eunuch): *non tu natus equo, non fortibus utilis armis* and 2.10.27–8: *saepe ego lasciue consumpsi tempora noctis, | utilis et forti corpore mane fui*. For *utilis/inutilis* in sexual contexts see also Sen. *Con.* 2.5.14.8: *inutilis in concubitu* and Mart. 11.81.3: *uiribus hic* [a eunuch], *operi non est hic* [an old man] *utilis annis*.

16. **corpus an umbra:** Recognizing the contradiction, the lover cannot decide whether he is a body or a ghost. For hesitation expressed in similar terms see (*Pont.* 3.3.3–4; of Amor's apparition): *dum tibi quae uidi refero, seu corporis umbra | seu ueri species seu fuit ille sopor*. For *umbra* and *species* as synonyms see Liv. 40.56.9: *cum identidem species et umbrae insontis interempti filii agitarent*.

17–18. **quae mihi uentura est, siquidem uentura, senectus,**
    cum desit numeris ipsa iuuenta suis?
The suggestion in the previous couplet that the lover may already be a ghost prompts him to wonder if he has a future, whether he will reach old age.

17. **senectus:** Although reflection on old age and the male lover occurs in the *Greek Anthology* (e.g. *PA* 5.129, 10.100, 11.30) and elsewhere in love elegy (e.g. Tib. 1.2.89–98, 1.4.27–39, 2.4.45–50; Prop. 2.18b, 2.25.9–10; *Am.* 1.9.3–4, 1.13.1–2), the lover's argument here is distinctive: he is so feeble that he may not reach old age at all.

18. numeris…suis: Most commonly used in *Amores* to denote the elegiac metre, *numerus* cannot have that sense here. 2.6.40, however, is helpful: *implentur numeris deteriora suis*. Kenney (1959: 241) explains: 'It seems more likely that *numerus* in the passage under discussion bears its not uncommon sense of "part" of a whole… If this explanation is correct, *inplentur numeris suis* means no more than "are complete"'. For other Ovidian examples of *numerus* in this sense (*OLD* 12) see e.g. *Met.* 1.427–8 *quaedam imperfecta suisque | trunca uident numeris*, *Tr.* 1.8.48 (with Luck [1977: ad loc.]): *ut careant numeris tempora prima suis*. As in these later examples, the phrase here underlines lack of wholeness.

Passages in which Ovid associates *iuuenta* with *numerus* in its metrical sense (3.1.28, *Fast.* 2.6) are only superficially similar.

19–20. a, pudet annorum! quo me iuuenemque uirumque?
    nec iuuenem nec me sensit amica uirum.
Thoughts of youth and old age prompt the lover to raise one of this poem's key concerns: the nature of masculinity.

19. pudet: Shame or embarrassment is this poem's dominant emotion (*pudor… pudor* 37, *pudibunda* 69, *pudore* 72). Only in 3.14 do *pudet* and cognates occur more often (five times in 3.7, six in 3.14). There, however, it is feminine modesty that is at stake.

quo: For *quo* used without a following verb to convey urgency see above on 3.4.41. A verb like *uoco* is to be understood.

iuuenemque uirumque: Use of two words denoting male persons (*TLL* 736.50–5 lists only five classical examples of *iuuenis* applied to a woman; there are more than 2000), their repetition in the next line, and the fact that *uir* occurs five times (19, 20, 43, 59, and 60) underline the poem's concern with masculinity.

The supposed etymological link between *uir* and *uires* (Maltby [1991: 647]) may be relevant here. See below on 59.

20. sensit: While *sentio* can have an intellectual element (*OLD* 2 'become aware of'; e.g. 2.8.6: *sensit concubitus unde Corinna tuos?*), its meaning here is bluntly physical (*OLD* 1b 'feel'). For this lover it is the ability to have penetrative sex that defines a man. At *Ars* 1.698 the Teacher takes a similar view: (Deidamia and Achilles): *haec illum stupro comperit esse uirum*.

21–2. sic flammas aditura pias aeterna sacerdos
    surgit et a caro fratre uerenda soror.
The humiliated lover now invokes images of a Vestal virgin and a chaste sister to describe his girlfriend's plight.

21. flammas…pias: The flames are those of Vesta's cult. Cf. *Fast.* 6.440 (Vesta's temple ablaze): *mixtaque erat flammae flamma profana piae*.

aditura: For sexual purity as a prerequisite for approaching the gods see lines 53–4 below and 3.10.

aeterna: Usually applied in religious contexts to the gods or the world or time (*TLL* 1142.72–1144.70), the adjective is applied to a human being only here. It is, however, used of Vesta's sacred fire (e.g. Cic. *Font.* 47.9, *A.* 2.297, Liv. 5.52.7.1, *Fast.* 3.421). Here it is transferred (enallage) from the flames to the priestess herself.

sacerdos: The point of the simile is the Vestals' abstention from sexual relationships. We should recall Ilia's horror at the prospect of any kind of marriage (3.6.75–6).

22. surgit: This is the standard verb for rising from bed: 1.13.13, 22, 25, 38; 3.7.53. Ironically, perhaps, it is also used of male sexual arousal (2.15.25).

a caro fratre: For the innocence of sister–brother relationships compare the lover's description of guilty kisses (2.5.25): *qualia non fratri tulerit germana seuero*.

uerenda soror: The epithet distinguishes this sister from one like Byblis who lusts after her brother (*Met.* 9.456: *non soror ut fratrem, nec qua debebat, amabat*).

23–4. at nuper bis flaua Chlide, ter candida Pitho,
   ter Libas officio continuata meo est.
After embarrassment comes boasting, with the lover listing sexual successes with other women.

23. bis: For the boast that the lover was once capable of sex several times a night see Philodemus (*PA* 11.30.1–2): ὁ πρὶν ἐγὼ καὶ πέντε καὶ ἐννέα, νῦν, Ἀφροδίτη | ἐν μόλις ('Aphrodite, I, who previously five or nine, now barely one' [the verb is omitted]).

flaua: It is conventional for Roman poets to describe attractive women (and indeed men) as having blonde hair e.g. Catul. 64.63 (Ariadne): *flauo…uertice*, *A.* 4.590 (Dido): *flauentisque…comas*, Tib. 1.5.44: *flauis nostra puella comis*, *Am.* 1.15.35: *flauus Apollo*, *Her.* 20.57 (Cydippe): *hoc faciunt flaui crines et eburnea ceruix*.

Chlide: Meaning 'delicacy' in Greek, the name occurs nowhere else in Greek or Latin literature.

candida: The ideal woman is often 'radiant white' e.g. Catul. 68b.70, 86.1; Prop. 2.3.9, 2.22a.5, 8, 3.11.16; *Am.* 1.5.10, 2.7.5, 2.18.29, 3.3.5.

Pitho: Meaning 'persuasion' in Greek, the name occurs nowhere else in Latin. In Greek it is the name of a personified abstraction e.g. Hes. *Theog.* 349, Aesch. *Cho.* 726, Hdt. 8.111.7.

24. Libas: The name occurs nowhere else in Latin or Greek. It may be connected with Greek λιβάς (*libas* 'a stream').

officio…meo: For *officium* as sexual service see above on 3.3.38.

Commentary, 7.22-7   211

continuata: Although it is a euphemism, the sexual meaning of *continuare* in this context is clear. (*TLL* 725.5-6 lists this as the only example of the verb used of sexual intercourse; it is not mentioned in Adams [1982].) Elsewhere in Ovid it hints at sex, especially the adultery of Venus and Mars e.g. *Ars* 1.406 (with Hollis [1977: ad loc.]), *Fast.* 4.130 (with Fantham [1998: ad loc.]).

25-6. exigere a nobis angusta nocte Corinnam
me memini numeros sustinuisse nouem.
Even more impressive than the lover's performance with unknown girls, was his workout with the collection's most prominent woman, Corinna.

25. angusta nocte: Not commonly used with expressions of time (e.g. G. 4.206 [*aeui*], *Trist.* 5.10.8 [*dies*], Luc. 1.98 [*temporis*]), *angusta* here has the paradoxical effect of magnifying the lover's achievement. Philodemus' definition of time, by contrast, underlines the Greek lover's failure: (*PA* 11.30.2): ἐν μόλις ἐκ πρώτης νυκτὸς ἐς ἠέλιον ('Barely one from night's beginning until sunrise').

Corinnam: For Corinna's problematic status in *Amores* see Introduction §7, the discussion of 3.1.49 above, and of 3.12 below. Mention of her name establishes that this is not a Corinna poem.

26. me memini: Expressions of memory often signal an 'Alexandrian footnote', i.e. an allusion to an earlier text. (See on 3.6.26.) As Sharrock (1995: 169-70) observes, *nouem* combined with *continuata* (24) suggests a reference to Catul. 32.8: *nouem continuas fututiones*.

numeros: Allusion to Catullus allows Ovid to have it both ways. He employs both euphemism (for *numerus* as 'exercises' see *OLD* 12b) and complete explicitness: *numeros = fututiones*. For discussion of this strategy see Sharrock (1995: 170).

nouem: For the number nine see also Catul. 32.8 (quoted above) and Philodemus (*PA* 11.30.1; quoted above on 23).

27-30. num mea Thessalico languent deuota ueneno
corpora? num misero carmen et herba nocent,
sagaue poenicea defixit nomina cera
et medium tenuis in iecur egit acus?
After recollection of past successes comes the search for an explanation. Perhaps witchcraft was the cause.

27. Thessalico: The association between Thessaly and witchcraft was of long standing (e.g. Ar. *Clouds* 749-50, Plat. *Gorg.* 513a5-6) and was common in Latin literature (e.g. Hor. *Epod.* 5.45-6, Tib. 2.4.55-6, Prop. 3.24.10, Luc. 6.434-506, VF 1.735-40, Apul. *Met.* 2.1). Indeed *Thessalis* (*OLD* b) often equals 'witch'.

languent: For the sexual connotations of *langueo* and cognates see above on 3.4.10, above on line 3 and below on 66. See also Adams (1982: 46).

deuota: Belongs to the language of witchcraft e.g. 80 below, *Her.* 6.91 (of Medea; quoted below on 29–30), Tib. 1.8.18: *deuouit tacito tempore noctis anus?*, Apul. *Met.* 2.29.13: *an non putas deuotionibus meis posse Diras inuocari*. The Tibullan lover uses the same language when linking his impotence with witchcraft (1.5.41): *tunc me discedens deuotum femina dixit*.

ueneno: While *uenenum* can signify any harmful substance (e.g. 1.14.44 [hair dye], *Rem.* 351 [cosmetics]), it is commonly used of magical drugs (e.g. Hor. *Carm.* 1.27.21–2, *Her.* 6.131, *Met.* 7.394: *sed postquam Colchis arsit noua nupta uenenis*). And *uenefica* means not only 'female poisoner' but also 'witch' (e.g. 79 below, *Her.* 6.19: *barbara narratur uenisse uenefica tecum*, *Met.* 7.316).

28. corpora: While this may be a euphemism for 'penis', as Adams (1982: 46) suggests, it may simply refer to the lover's enfeebled body.

carmen et herba: Because witches use both incantations and herbs, they are commonly found together in magical contexts e.g. Tib. 1.8.17, 1.8.23, Hor. *S.* 1.8.19–22, *Met.* 14.20–22, *Fast.* 2.425–6, Luc. 6.822: *carminibus magicis opus est herbisque*.

29–30: These lines rework (or are reworked by) Hypsipyle's description of Medea's activities (*Her.* 6.91–2): *deuouet absentis simulacraque cerea figit, | et miserum tenuis in iecur urget acus*.

Piercing a wax doll with needles is a practice prescribed in ancient magical texts. Here is Ogden's (2002: 248) translation of instructions for a spell intended for binding (Greek: *katadesmos*) a woman:

> Take thirteen bronze needles and insert one of them into the brain while saying, 'I pierce your brain (insert her name)'; insert two into her ears, two more into her eyes, one into her mouth, two below her rib cage, one into her hands, two into her vulva and anus, and two into the soles of her feet, while on each occasion saying once, 'I pierce the (insert name of part) of (insert her name), so that she may think of no one, except me alone, (insert your name)'.

For recent discussion of this and other erotic spells see Watson (2019: 23–56; including an illustration of the Louvre 'Voodoo Doll').

Here the lover imagines that a witch has employed this technique not to secure his love but to destroy his sexual potency. Although she does not employ the same method, Greek literature's earliest witch, Circe, has a similar power (*Od.* 10.301, 341).

29 cera: For wax dolls used for magical purposes elsewhere in Latin poetry see e.g. *Ecl.* 8.80–1: *limus ut hic durescit, et haec ut cera liquescit | uno eodemque igni, sic nostro Daphnis amore*; and Hor. *S.* 1.8.30 (with Gowers [2012: ad loc.]): *lanea et effigies erat altera cerea*.

Commentary, 7.28-31 213

defixit: For *defigo* used in magical contexts see e.g. [Sen.] *Her. O.* (523-4): '*hoc' inquit 'magae | dixere amorem posse defigi malo*'; Plin. *Nat.* 28.19.1 (discussing magic in the Twelve Tables): *defigi quidem diris precationibus nemo non metuit.* Cf. *Her.* 6.91: *figit.* For the piercing of curse tablets with nails (*defixio*, a modern term) see e.g. Watson (2019: 57-83).

30. iecur: The liver is pierced because of its association with lust; see e.g. Hor. *Epod.* 5.37-8, *Carm.* 1.25.15; Servius on *A.* 6.596: *dicit namque Tityon amorem esse, hoc est libidinem, quae secundum physicos et medicos in iecore est.*

acus: For the magical use of needles elsewhere in Latin poetry see *Her.* 6.92, *Fast.* 2.577.

31-4. carmine laesa Ceres sterilem uanescit in herbam,
 deficiunt laesi carmine fontis aquae,
ilicibus glandes cantataque uitibus uua
 decidit et nullo poma mouente fluunt.
As evidence of their power, the lover cites a claim frequently made for literary witches viz. that they can halt and even reverse the flow of rivers e.g. AR 3.532 (with Hunter [1989: on 531-3]), 1.8.6: *inque caput liquidas arte recuruat aquas*, 2.1.26: *inque suos fontes uersa recurrit aqua*, *Her.* 6.87, *Met.* 7.199-200, Tib. 1.2.46, Sen. *Med.* 762-4, VF 6.443; cf. Ov. *Med.* 40: *nec redit in fontes unda supina suos.* The claim that they exert power over crops is less common in literature (though see VF 6.443: *mutat agros*), but perhaps widely believed: Seneca (*Nat.* 4b.7.2.8 [with due scepticism]) and Pliny (*Nat.* 28.18) both cite the Twelve Tables' prohibition against the enchantment of other people's fields.

Notably missing from this list are some of the more spectacular claims for sorcery's power, that witches can draw down the moon (e.g. *Ecl.* 8.69, Tib. 1.2.45, Prop. 1.1.19, *Am.* 2.1.23, Luc. 6.499-500; cf. *Med.* 42: *numquam Luna suis excutietur equis*) or cause snakes to explode (*Ecl.* 8.71, *Am.* 2.1.25, Luc. 6.490; cf. *Med.* 39: *nec mediae Marsis finduntur cantibus angues*). These would perhaps invite scepticism and weaken the lover's case.

31-2. carmine…|…carmine: For repetition of *carmen* emphasizing the magical power of witches see 2.1.23-8: *carmina* (23), *carmine* (25), *carminibus* (27), *carmine* (28), *Met.* 14.20, *Fast.* 4.551-2.

31. Ceres…uanescit: *uanesco* and *euanesco* are used primarily of emotions (e.g. *luctus* Catul. 64.199, *amor* Ars 2.358), insubstantial things (e.g. *dicta* 2.14.41, *spiritus Her.* 12.85, *fumus* Luc. 9.76-7, Sen. *Tro.* 392-3), and supernatural beings (e.g. Mercury *A.* 4.278, Apollo *A.* 9.658, Romulus *Fast.* 2.509). Here it reminds us that Ceres is both grain and goddess.

sterilem…herbam: Implies either that the plants bear no fruit (*OLD* 2) or that the field is taken over by weeds (cf. Curt. 4.1.21: *hortum intrant, quem forte steriles herbas eligens Abdalonymus repurgabat*).

214 Commentary

33. cantata: For *canto* used of magical enchantment in *Amores* see 1.14.39: *non te cantatae laeserunt paelicis herbae*, 2.5.38: *aut ubi cantatis Luna laborat equis*.

34. fluunt: For this use of *fluo* see 2.14.23–5: *quid… | pomaque crudeli uellis acerba manu? | sponte fluant matura sua*.

35–6. quid uetat et neruos magicas torpere per artes?
 forsitan impatiens fit latus inde meum.
If witches have these powers over nature, what could stop them from exerting a malign influence over the lover's body?

35. neruos: This is another euphemism for 'penis' (Adams [1982: 38]). See e.g. *Priap.* 68.33, Hor. *Epod.* 12.19–20, Juv. 9.34: *nil faciet longi mensura incognita nerui*. For sexual innuendo involving *nerui* see 1.1.18 (Oliensis [2019: 132, 157]), 2.10.24 (with Booth [1991: 145]), *Rem*. 147.

torpere: Not common in sexual contexts, this verb and its cognates are not discussed in Adams (1982). See, however, *Ars* 3.799 (of female genitalia): *infelix, cui torpet hebes locus ille, puella*.

36. impatiens: The only other example of *impatiens* in the sense of 'lacking all sensation' seems to be Sen. *Ep*. 9.2: 'This objection to Stilbo is made by Epicurus and others who think that the unfeeling (*impatiens*) soul is the highest good. We must fall into ambiguity if we want to translate *apatheia* quickly with one word and say *impatientia*'.

latus: This is another euphemism for male genitalia. Adams (1982: 49) notes that, when used of men, *latus* is often associated with sexual exhaustion e.g. Catul. 6.13: *latera ecfututa, Am.* 2.10.25, 3.11.14, *Ars* 2.413.

37–8. huc pudor accessit: facti pudor ipse nocebat.
 ille fuit uitii causa secunda mei.
There is, however, an additional explanation, one that requires no reference to the supernatural: embarrassment at initial failure led to subsequent lack of success.

37. There is disagreement over the punctuation of this line: should a pause be placed after *accessit* or *facti*? Munari and Showerman and Goold pause after *accessit*, while McKeown, Kenney, and Ramirez de Verger pause after *facti*. Older editors were also divided: Naugerius, Daniel Heinsius (1629), Heinsius, and Burman punctuated after *accessit*, while Marius and Micyllus punctuated after *facti*.

I punctuate after *accessit* because in balanced lines like this one Ovid's usual practice is to have a syntactic break at the main caesura: 1.2.41, 48; 1.4.18, 27, 31, 32, 49; 1.5.3; 1.7.65; 1.8.89; 1.13.21; 1.14.9; 2.3.7, 13; 2.4.45, 46; 2.5.31, 43, 44, 58; 2.9.15; 2.10.3, 5, 7, 8, 13, 22; 2.11.10, 11, 18, 26, 36, 40; 2.16.7, 41; 2.18.24; 2.19.3, 5, 17, 36; 3.1.24; 3.2.11, 34, 51, 54, 59; 3.3.7, 8, 42; 3.4.19, 40; 3.6.9, 11, 44, 48, 61, 62, 100; 3.7.1, 5, 10, 17, 43, 47, 55; 3.8.6, 7, 56; 3.9.1, 21, 62; 3.10.19, 23; 3.11.34,

35, 36, 37, 39; 3.12.11, 13, 31, 33, 38; 3.14.8, 15. There are of course exceptions e.g. 2.12.13, 3.7.49, 3.12.23, 3.14.45.

The sense pause in the fifth foot is unusual and perhaps underlines the speaker's feelings of awkwardness.

pudor…pudor: Shame is here linked to the lover's belief that sexual performance is a key part of his masculine identity (see above on 19–20). Initial failure generates still more disappointment. For the importance of *pudor* for an elite male's sense of self see Kaster (1997: 10–11). For female *pudor* see above on 3.6.78.

38. secunda: The adjective has chronological (not logical) force here: shame resulting from failure becomes the second reason for lack of success.

39–40. at qualem uidi tantum tetigique puellam!
   sic etiam tunica tangitur illa sua.
After reflecting on the reasons for his failure, the lover turns to recollection and self-reproach. Polyptoton (*tetigi / tangitur*), reinforced by alliteration (*tantum tetigique / tunica tangitur*), underlines the limits to his sexual activity.

39. Alludes to the Ovidian lover's first successful encounter with Corinna (1.5.19): *quos umeros, quales uidi tetigique lacertos!* The addition of *tantum*, however, makes a striking difference. Here the lover can do no more than see and touch; there is no *cetera quis nescit?* (1.5.25).

40. tunica: In 1.5 Corinna's *tunica* was real; it was there to provoke (9) and be removed (13, 14). Here it is an image of futile proximity: the lover was as close to the girl as her dress, but he could do nothing.

41–2. illius ad tactum Pylius iuuenescere possit
   Tithonosque annis fortior esse suis.
Continuing with the focus on the sense of touch, the lover now returns to reflection on old age (cf. 17–18), arguing that even the most famous elderly men from mythology would find her exciting. Behind this argument may lie Homer's description of the oldest Trojans' reaction to Helen's beauty (*Il.* 3.156–8).

41. ad tactum: The phrase is rare, but see *G.* 3.501–2: *aret | pellis et ad tactum tractanti dura resistit.*

Pylius: Nestor is defined by the city he ruled. In both Greek and Latin he is 'Nestor the Pylian' (e.g. Soph. *Phil.* 422: Νέστωρ ὁ Πύλιος, Hor. *Carm.* 1.15.22: *Pylium Nestora*). Ovid sometimes omits the name: he is simply 'the Pylian' (e.g. *Met.* 8.365, 12.537, 542). Old age is his other essential property. Homer's claims that he has outlasted two generations and now rules over a third (*Il.* 1.250–2; cf. Prop. 2.13.46: *Nestoris est uisus post tria saecla cinis*), while Ovid's claims to be over 200 years old (*Met.* 12.187–8): *uixi | annos bis centum; nunc tertia uiuitur aetas.* Seneca's Pyrrhus (*Tro.* 212) sums him up: he is *Pylii senis.*

42. Tithonosque: Aurora's husband is famously old, his antiquity being one reason for Dawn's inconveniently early rising (1.13.37): *longo quia grandior aeuo*. See also Prop. 2.18.7: *at non Tithoni spernens Aurora senectam*.

For Nestor and Tithonus as paired examples of old age see Prop. 2.25.10, Sen. *Apoc.* 4.1.14, Stat. *Silu.* 4.3.150–1.

43–4. haec mihi contigerat, sed uir non contigit illi.
  quas nunc concipiam per noua uota preces?
Reflection on his inadequacy (Nestor and Tithonus would have done better) prompts a question: What's the point of making fresh promises to the gods?

43. contigerat...contigit: *contingo* here has the sense of 'fall to one's lot', 'be granted to one' (*OLD* 8, *TLL* 717.75–719.15). A personal subject, however, is unusual. Cf. *A.* 11.371: *scilicet ut Turno contingat regia coniunx*, *Met.* 3.132–3 (of Cadmus): *soceri tibi Marsque Venusque | contigerant*, 11.219–20 (of Peleus): *siquidem Iouis esse nepoti | contigit haut uni, coniunx dea contigit uni.* But given the emphasis on the sense of touch in lines 39–41 (*teitigi, tangitur, ad tactum*), there will also be overtones of *OLD* 1: 'to come into physical contact with'.

uir: For the poem's emphasis on masculinity see above on 19.

44. Looks back to line 2, where the lover reports that he had often prayed for the chance to sleep with this girl: *uotis saepe petita meis*. Given his failure to use his god-given opportunity, further prayer is pointless.

45–6. credo etiam magnos, quo sum tam turpiter usus,
  muneris oblati paenituisse deos.
Explaining why further prayer is pointless, this couplet generates initial uncertainty (Where is the noun to agree with *magnos*? Where is *quo*'s antecedent?) only to resolve it in the pentameter, withholding the key word until last.

45. magnos: This standard epithet for gods has epic ancestry e.g. Enn. *Ann.* 6.190 (Goldberg and Manuwald [1]): *uolentibus cum magnis dis*; *A.* 3.12, 8.679. Ovid uses it with equal solemnity at *Fast.* 6.187: *quam bene, di magni, pugna cecidisset in illa*, but with rather less at *Am.* 2.19.18 and *Her.* 18.102. Given that *magnos* follows closely upon *credo* (cf. 3.3.1: *esse deos, i, crede*), *deos* is perhaps the expected complement. Ovid, however, makes us wait.

For *magnus* used of gods see *TLL* 134.72–135.7.

turpiter: This powerful term of condemnation (e.g. 1.7.47 [of the lover's violence against his girlfriend], 2.12.20 [of the behaviour of Centaurs], *Her.* 6.133 [Hypsipyle on Medea's love for Jason]) underlines the lover's sense of shame. See also line 66 below.

46. paenituisse deos: Cf. Dido's view of the gods' escape from Troy (*Her.* 7.132): *paenitet elapsos ignibus esse deos.*

47–8. optabam certe recipi: sum nempe receptus;
   oscula ferre: tuli; proximus esse: fui.
With superb succinctness the lover sums up the situation, packing three antitheses into two lines and exploiting Latin's use of inflected forms to underline his seductive skills. McKeown (1998: 92; on 2.5.25–6) rightly speaks of 'brilliant *declinatio*'.

47: optabam: Governs all three infinitives.

recipi…receptus: For *recipio* in an erotic sense see Catul. 63.43, Prop. 2.14.28, 2.22b.48, *Am.* 1.8.78, *Her.* 2.29, 3.87, 6.20, 16.14, *Ars* 2.360, 2.407, *Rem.* 456.

48. ferre: tuli: For similar play with forms of *fero* see 2.5.25–8: *tulerit…tulerit… ferre…tulisse.*

49–50. quo mihi fortunae tantum? quo regna sine usu?
   quid, nisi possedi diues auarus opes?
But recollection of success prompts moralizing reflection: What good is winning if you can't use your achievement? As Marius pointed out, the couplet reworks Horace's words to Torquatus (*Ep.* 1.5.12–14): *quo mihi fortunam, si non conceditur uti? | parcus ob heredis curam nimiumque seuerus | adsidet insano.* The lover transforms an invitation to celebrate Caesar's birthday into criticism of his own sexual performance.

49. quo…quo: Repetition of *quo* within the line suggests that these are urgent questions. For omission of the verb after *quo* see above on 3.4.41.

quo mihi fortunae tantum: Recalls not only Horace, but (ironically) the adulterer's supreme self-confidence at 2.19.7–8: *quo mihi fortunam, quae numquam fallere curet?| nil ego, quod nullo tempore laedat, amo.*

sine usu: The expression is found nowhere else in classical poetry. Its use here ironically recalls its occurrence in moralizing texts emphasizing the importance of practice over theory e.g. Cic. *Off.* 1.60: 'But as neither doctors nor generals nor orators, even if they understand the rules of their art, can achieve anything worthy of great praise without practice (*sine usu*)'; Sen. *Ep.* 117.16: 'You surely say that wisdom, if it is given without practice (*sine usu*), is not to be welcomed'. Failure in sexual performance is implicitly equated to moral weakness.

50. diues auarus: The unsuccessful lover resembles a miser (Horace's *parcus*), a rich person who fails to use their wealth. Here too there is an equivalence between sexual and moral failure. For proper use of wealth as a moral ideal see e.g. Hor. *Carm.* 2.2 (with Harrison [2017: 59–66]); Sen. *Dial.* 6.23.3: *carentem uitio, diuitias sine auaritia, honores sine ambitione, uoluptates sine luxuria.*

51–2. sic aret mediis taciti uulgator in undis
   pomaque, quae nullo tempore tangat, habet.

Without using his name, the lover invokes the example of Tantalus, a familiar example of unfulfilled desire, the underworld criminal who is constantly cheated of food and drink.

51. aret mediis…in undis: The image of Tantalus parched with thirst in the middle of abundant water is strikingly appropriate to the lover's situation. For this version of Tantalus' punishment see e.g. Cic. *Tusc.* 1.10.3, Hor. *S.* 1.1.68–70, Tib. 1.3.77–8, Prop. 2.1.66, *Am.* 2.2.43–4: *quaerit aquas in aquis et poma fugacia captat | Tantalus*, 3.12.30: *in medio Tantalus amne sitit*. Most vivid of all is Sen. *Thy.* 152–75.

Tantalus is sometimes pictured as threatened by an overhanging rock e.g. Lucr. 3.980–1, Cic. *Fin.* 1.60.2, *Tusc.* 4.35.11.

taciti uulgator: For Ovid Tantalus is primarily a betrayer of the gods' secrets: 2.2.44: *hoc illi garrula lingua dedit*, 3.12.30: *proditor…Tantalus*. Cicero (*Tusc.* 4.35.12) refers to his *superbiloquentiam*. For a full list of his crimes see Murgatroyd (1980: 123; on Tib. 1.3.77–8).

52. tangat: For the poem's emphasis on touch see above on 39–40. The lover's situation is perhaps worse than that of Tantalus, because the lover can touch but not possess what he desires.

53–4. a tenera quisquam sic surgit mane puella,
    protinus ut sanctos possit adire deos?
After mythological analogy the lover shifts the focus from his failure (what man could leave a girl in this state?) to its effect (he was ritually pure).

53. tenera…puella: For the resonance of *tenera* see above on 3.1.27.

surgit mane puella: The verbal resemblance to 1.13.25 (*sed surgere mane puellas*) and *Rem.* 431 (*a Veneris rebus surgente puella*) perhaps underlines a contrast: in those cases a girl leaves after sex; here a man leaves after failure to have sex.

54. The speaker links abstinence from sex with the ritual purity necessary for participation in religious worship.

possit adire deos: The subject should be the same as the subject of *surgit* in 53, i.e. a male lover. For the insistence that a worshipper approach the gods pure in both mind and body see e.g. Cic. *Leg.* 2.24.12: *caste iubet lex adire ad deos, animo uidelicet in quo sunt omnia; nec tollit castimoniam corporis*; for general abstinence from sex before religious ritual see Tib. 2.1.11–12: *uos quoque abesse procul iubeo, discedat ab aris, | cui tulit hesterna gaudia nocte Venus*; for male avoidance of sex before worship see *SHA Alexander Severus* (29.2.1): 'This was his way of life: first, if he had the opportunity, i.e. if he had not had sex with his wife, in the morning hours he would worship in his lararium'. For discussion see Lennon (2014: 61–4).

Marlowe (1603) viewed the subject of *possit* as female: 'Hath any rose so from a fresh young maid | As she might straight have gone to church and prayed?' See also Melville, lightly adapting Marlowe, (1989): 'Does any man rise thus from a young maid | As she might have gone to church and prayed'. The frequency of the requirement that women in particular abstain from sexual activity before worship (e.g. Tib. 1.3.25–6 [Isis], Prop. 2.33.1–6 [Isis], *Am.* 3.10.1–2 [Ceres], *Met.* 10.431–5 [Ceres], *Fast.* 6.231–2 [among the rules governing the wife of the *flamen dialis*]) makes this attractive. But syntax dictates otherwise.

55–6. sed, puto, non blanda est: non optima perdidit in me oscula; non omni sollicitauit ope.
Recalls and varies the ironizing strategy of the opening couplet, with triple repetition of *non*, with *sed…non* replacing *at non*, and *puto* in the same metrical position: she was enticing, she wasted kisses, she did everything she could.

55. sed, puto, non blanda est: The principle manuscripts offer the following: Y: *sed puto non blanda* ᵉˢᵗ/; P: *sed puto non blanda*; S: *si puto non blanda*. The text is difficult because the metre needs *blandā*, while the sense requires *blandă*.

Heinsius solved the problem by transposition: *sed non blandā, pŭtō*. Ovid, however, (a) always treats the final *o* of *puto* as short and (b) either makes it the second word or places it in the second half of the line: 1.2.5: *nam, puto*; 1.12.9: *quam, puto*; 2.4.16: *uelle, sed ex alto dissimulare puto*, 2.15.25, 3.1.8: *sed, puto*; 3.7.2: *at, puto*; 3.10.24: *fassuram Cererem crimina nostra puto*, 3.11.34: *hac amor hac odium, sed, puto, uincit amor*.

Ehwald (1903: XII) wrote *blande* (also Brandt [1911], Harder and Marg [1956], Holzberg [2014: 228 'makeshift' *Notbehelf*]). Housman (1927: 11) labelled *blande* 'contemptible'. Although it improves the metre, it is meaningless.

Showerman and Goold print *sed, puto, non blanda*, accepting Housman's explanation: '*blanda* is abl. fem. in agreement with the *puella* of 53, and the sense is "*sed, puto, non blanda a puella sic surrexi*"'. While this is possible, *blanda* is too far from *puella* to be convincing.

Munari obelizes *blanda* (also Lenz [1966], Lee [1968], and Bertini [2017]), while Kenney and McKeown obelize the first four words.

I print *blanda est*, recorded as the reading of T by Ramirez de Verger and a correction found in Y. This was suggested by Riese (1871: XV) and subsequently printed by Némethy and Ramirez de Verger. It corrects the metre and completes the sense.

blanda: Recalls *blanditias* in line 11. For the adjective used of sexual stimulation see e.g. Juv. 6.196–7: *quod enim non excitet inguen | uox blanda et nequam?*; Mart. 6.23.3: *tu licet et manibus blandis et uocibus instes*, 10.68.10: *numquid, cum crisas, blandior esse potes?*

perdidit in me: For the idiom see 1.2.50: *parce tuas in me perdere, uictor, opes*.

56. omni...ope: The language is euphemistic. The lover is more explicit at 74.

sollicitauit: For *sollicitare* used in a sexual sense (*OLD* 5c) see e.g. 2.4.45: *me noua sollicitat*, line 74 below, *Met.* 7.720–1, *Tr.* 2.346.

**57–8. illa graues potuit quercus adamantaque durum
   surdaque blanditiis saxa mouere suis.**
The lover now invokes Propertius' advice to Ponticus (1.9.30–2): *quisquis es, assiduas tu fuge blanditias. | illis et silices et possint cedere quercus, | nedum tu possis, spiritus iste leui*s. The allusion is ironic, for, as Fedeli (1980: 248) notes, the situation in Prop. 1.9 is precisely the opposite of that in 3.7: this lover can and does resist a girlfriend's charms.

57. graues...quercus: Oaks are conventionally hard (e.g. *Ecl.* 4.30, 8.52–3, *Met.* 13.799), but not heavy. As McKeown (51) points out, however, *graues* echoes Propertius' *leuis*.

durum: This is the expected epithet for adamant e.g. *Her.* 2.137, Luc. 6.801. Servius (on *A.* 6.552) explains: 'it is the hardest stone and of such great solidity that it cannot be broken by iron'.

58. surdaque...saxa: That rocks are deaf is conventional e.g. Eur. *Med.* 28–9: 'She listens like a rock or wave of the sea', Hor. *Carm.* 3.7.21: *scopulis surdior Icari*. The lover perhaps reverses *Epod.* 17.54: *non saxa nudis surdiora nauitis*, where a woman is deaf to Horace's pleas.

blanditiis: The term's meaning shifts. At 11 the context implies that *blanditiae* are purely verbal (also 1.4.66, 2.9.45, 2.19.17, 3.11.31; *Ars* 2.159–60 [quoted on line 12]). At Prop. 1.9.30 (quoted above) it is equivalent to 'allurements' (Goold: 1990) or 'temptations' (Lee: 1994). Here it may suggest something more physical (cf. the use of *blandus* by Juvenal and Martial [quoted on line 55] and see 73–4 below).

saxa mouere: For *mouere* used of making rocks respond (as opposed to changing their physical location) see *Met.* 6.547 (Philomela): *implebo siluas et conscia saxa mouebo*, 13.48 (Philoctetes): *saxa moues gemitu*. Cf. *Ars* 3.321–2 (of Orpheus) where both senses are in play.

**59–60. digna mouere fuit certe uiuosque uirosque,
    sed neque tum uixi nec uir, ut ante, fui.**
In a couplet notable for its verbal play, the lover emphasizes both his partner's beauty and his own deficiencies.

59. dignus mouere: The use of the infinitive after *dignus* (and *indignus*) is primarily poetic. *TLL* 1152.32–70 lists examples in Catullus, Virgil, Horace, Tibullus, Ovid, and others; but no prose examples before Valerius Maximus. Bömer (1958: 176; on *Fast.* 3.490) notes the construction's Greek origins.

uiuosque uirosque: Alliteration of *u* and echoed vowel sounds help to make this phrase particularly effective.

The juxtaposition of *uiuus* and *uir* reminds the reader of their common (supposed) connection with *uires* (Maltby [1991: 649 *uis*; cf. *Fast.* 1.553: *dira uiro facies, uires pro corpore*]), *uires* being precisely the quality that this speaker lacks.

Use of double *que* (the first *que* actually being redundant) is a high-style mannerism. For its use in epic see Davis (2020: 120). In *Amores* Ovid uses it for grand events e.g. when describing a triumph 1.2.35: *blanditiae comites tibi erunt Errorque Furorque*, 37: *his tu militibus superas hominesque deosque*; or, as here, when indulging in verbal play e.g. 2.8.27-8 (with Wilkinson [1955: 68] on the use of *q*): *quoque loco tecum fuerim, quotiensque, Cypassi, | narrabo dominae, quotque quibusque modis*, 2.11.36: *Nereidesque deae Nereidumque pater*.

60. uixi nec uir: Reworks the verbal play of the previous line with alliteration of *u* and repetition of *i*.

ut ante: For unfavourable comparison of the present with the past see above on 23-6. The phrase is used to opposite effect at 3.11.32.

61-2. quid iuuet, ad surdas si cantet Phemius aures?
quid miserum Thamyran picta tabella iuuet?
In this elegant couplet the lover invokes two mythological examples to illustrate his circumstances. The use of the first two words of the hexameter to frame the pentameter seems exceptional. See, however, Sen. *Med.* 696-7:

> maior minorque, sentiunt nodos ferae
> (maior Pelasgis apta, Sidoniis minor).

61. ad surdas...aures: The futility of singing (or speaking) to the deaf is proverbial (Otto [1890: §1715]). See e.g. *Ecl.* 10.8, Prop. 4.8.47. The cliché, however, is enlivened by reference to a particular singer and by etymological play.

Phemius: Odysseus' Ithacan bard is mentioned only here in Latin poetry. Homer names him at *Od.* 1.154, 337, 17.263, and 22.330-1. The last of these is important:

> Τερπιάδης δ' ἔτ' ἀοιδὸς ἀλύσκανε κῆρα μέλαιναν,
> Φήμιος, ὅς ῥ' ἤειδε παρὰ μνηστῆρσιν ἀνάγκῃ.
> Terpiades, the bard, was still avoiding black doom,
> Phemius, who used to sing among the suitors under compulsion.

As McKeown (50) points out, the repetition of *iuuet* in the sense of 'give pleasure' recalls the derivation of Phemius' patronymic from *terpnos*, 'delightful'.

62. Thamyran: Alludes ironically to Prop. 2.22a.19-20, where, as Morgan (1977: 92) observes, reference to Thamyras and blindness is immediately followed by a claim to sexual prowess (21-4).

For Thamyras as blind bard see also Eur. *Rhes.* 924–5, Ov. *Ib.* 272. At Hom. *Il.* 2.595–600, by contrast, the Muses 'maim' Thamyris in an unspecified way (πηρὸν θέσαν 2.599) and rob him of memory.

iuuet: The principal manuscripts differ: S and Y offer *iuuat*, and P *iubet*. McKeown, Kenney, and Ramirez de Verger (2) rightly print *iuuet*. This makes sense of P's *iubet* and is the reading of Vb. It eases the couplet's syntax (*iuuet* followed by *iuuat* is clumsy) and refines its form.

Editors report P as reading *iuuat* in 62. Examination of the digitized manuscript, however, suggests that P offers *iubet* in both 61 and 62 (the third letter is clearly *b*, not *u*). Heinsius (281) records *jubet* as the reading of his Puteaneus (i.e. P) in line 61; and prints *juvet* in both 61 and 62.

63–4. at quae non tacita formaui gaudia mente
    quos ego non finxi disposuique modos?
The lover now shifts attention from the girl to himself, reflecting upon the stages of his experience. Here he thinks back to his plans for their meeting.

63. A golden line (abVAB) is used for the recollection of picturing future pleasures. (For the golden line see above on 3.3.21.)

tacita...mente: For the adverbial use of an adjective with *mente* see above on 3.2.10.

formaui: For the use of *formo* in this sense see (*OLD* 6): 'fashion a likeness of (in the mind)' e.g. Sen. *Ep.* 58.15.5: *Centauri, Gigantes et quidquid aliud falsa cogitatione formatum*, Plin. *Pan.* 4.4.2: *cum interea fingenti formantique mihi principem*.

gaudia: For *gaudia* as a sexual term see Adams (1982: 197–8) and note on 3.6.88.

64. finxi: For *fingo* as a near synonym of *formo* see Cic. *de Orat.* 3.177.7: *mollissimam ceram ad nostrum arbitrium formamus et fingimus*, Plin. *Pan.* 4.4.2 (quoted above).

Ovid presents imagination as a key element in the lust of Paris (*Her.* 16.101–2) and Tereus (*Met.* 6.478, 492).

disposuique: The lover had planned the order in which they would adopt particular positions. Cf. Tib. 1.9.63–4: *illa nulla queat melius consumere noctem | aut operum uarias disposuisse uices*.

modos: For *modi* as sexual positions see Lucr. 4.1263, Tib. 2.6.52, *Am.* 2.8.28, 3.14.24, *Ars* 2.680, Mart. 6.71.2, Juv. 6.406.

65–8. nostra tamen iacuere uelut praemortua membra
    turpiter hesterna languidiora rosa,
quae nunc, ecce, uigent intempestiua ualentque
    nunc opus exposcunt militiamque suam.

The lover now turns to consideration of the previous and present state of his penis, treating it as a person with an existence independent of himself, a being with its own desires and demands.

65. Rewrites in sexual terms Catullus' reaction to his meeting with Licinius (50.14–15): *at defessa labore membra postquam | semimortua lectulo iacebant.*

iacuere: This seems to be the standard verb for a flaccid penis. See e.g. 69 below, Mart. 10.55.5, Juv. 10.205, Apul. *Met.* 2.7.15.

praemortua: Relatively rare (five times in all), the word occurs only here in poetry. For the association between death and impotence in the *Greek Anthology* see e.g. *PA* 5.129.8: ἐξ ᾅδου τὴν κορύνην ἀνάγει 'she raises my staff from Hades'; 11.29.3–4: ἡ πρὶν ἀκαμπὴς | ζῶσα νεκρὰ μηρῶν πᾶσα δέδυκεν ἔσω 'What was once unbending, alive, now a corpse, has wholly sunk within my thighs'; 11.30.3–4: καὶ τοῦτο κατὰ βραχύ (πολλάκι δ' ἤδη | ἡμιθανές) θνῄσκει 'Slowly (it's often been half-dead already) this thing is dying'; 12.232.4 (quoted below on 67–8). See also Petr. 20.2.3, Mart. 13.34.

membra: See above on line 13.

66. hesterna…rosa: Alludes ironically to Propertius' commitment to the life of love (2.34.59): *mi libet hesternis posito languere corollis.* For the Propertian lover limpness is evidence of success (*ut regnem mixtas inter conuiuia puellas* 57), for this lover failure.

languidiora: The image is particularly effective because *languidus* and cognates are used in high poetry of flowers (e.g. *A.* 9.435–6: *purpureus ueluti cum flos succisus aratro | languescit moriens*, 11.69, Sen. *Phaed.* 768) and in obscene works of penises (e.g. Catul. 25.3: *uel pene languido senis situque araneoso*; Mart. 12.97.6–7). At *Her.* 21.156, 228 Cydippe uses *languida membra* of her own sickly body.

67–8. For the erection that comes too late see *PA* 12.216: 'Now you're upright, you bastard, and vigorous, when there's nothing; but yesterday, when there was something, you wouldn't take a breath at all'; 12.232.1–4: 'Now you stand upright, nameless thing, you're stiff as if you'll never stop; but when Nemesenus inclined his whole self to me, offered everything I wanted, you hung down dead'.

67. uigent…ualentque: Alliteration makes this a combination attractive to writers of both verse and prose e.g. Lucr. 5.1112: *nam facies multum ualuit uiresque uigebant*, Sal. *Cat.* 20.10.2, Cic. *Fin.* 5.35.5.

intempestiua: For *intempestiua/tempestiua* of untimeliness/timeliness in sexual contexts see Hor. *Carm.* 1.23.11–12: *desine matrem | tempestiua sequi uiro*, 3.19.27: *tempestiua petit Rhode*; *Met.* 10.689: *illic concubitus intempestiua cupido.*

68. opus: For *opus* used of sexual intercourse see 1.4.48, 2.10.36, 3.14.28, *Ars* 2.480, *Rem.* 399.

militiamque: Alludes to the idea that the lover is a kind of soldier. Though found elsewhere in elegy (e.g. Tib. 1.3.64, Prop. 1.6.30), the idea finds its fullest exposition in *Am.* 1.9. Elsewhere, most notably in the next poem, the Ovidian lover mocks military pretensions. For discussion see Davis (2006: 74–7) and on 3.8 below. For the Propertian lover's similarly complex stance see Gale (1997).

69–72. quin istic pudibunda iaces, pars pessima nostri?
  sic sum pollicitis captus et ante tuis.
tu dominum fallis, per te deprensus inermis
  tristia cum magno damna pudore tuli.
The lover takes personification one step further, addressing his penis in the manner of a Homeric hero speaking to his 'own great-hearted spirit' (e.g. *Il.* 11.403, 17.90). Richlin (1992: 118) labels the speech 'brief and dignified'. Dignified or not, the speech is certainly less explicit than the poems just quoted from the *Greek Anthology*, or the one that Horace's *mutto* ('prick') delivers at *S.* 1.2.68–71. Closer is Encolpius' criticism of his inert member (Petr. 132.9.3): *omnium hominum deorumque pudor.*

69. pudibunda...pars pessima: Alliteration of *p* is often associated with mourning (see above on 3.6.58).

pudibunda: A primarily poetic word (it occurs only once in prose), *pudibunda* is usually used in Ovid of women (or the faces of women) who feel themselves to have been shamed e.g. *Her.* 11.81 (Canace), *Met.* 3.393 (Echo), 6.604 (Philomela), 9.568 (Byblis), 10.421 (Myrrha), *Fast.* 2.819 (Lucretia). The incongruous adjective (reinforced by alliteration) underlines the speech's absurdity.

iaces: See above on 65.

pars pessima: *pars* is regularly combined with adjectives to form euphemisms for the penis (Adams [1982: 45]). Here, however, although it glances at those euphemisms, the phrase primarily denotes a major source of distress (cf. *Pont.* 3.1.9–10 [of the land of Pontus]): *tu pessima duro | pars es in exilio.*

70. pollicitis: For *pollicitum* used as a substantive see 2.16.48, *Her.* 6.110, 18.192, 20.180, *Ars* 1.268, 355, 444, 632.

71. dominum: Recalls the girl's attempts to arouse her lover by flattery (11): *dominumque uocauit*. This master is no master.

inermis: Recalls not only the idea that love is a form of *militia* (68), but that the penis is a kind of weapon e.g. Prop. 1.3.16 (*arma manu* [with Fedeli: 1980 ad loc.; and Heyworth: 2007a ad loc.]), *Am.* 1.9.26, 2.3.7, 2.9.48; Adams [1982: 19–22]).

72. This line reworks or is reworked by *Her.* 15.64: *mixtaque cum turpi damna pudore tulit*. Our speaker suffers deep embarrassment, while Sappho's brother suffers moral and financial loss. Thorsen (2006: 106) notes that these lines 'stage the same drama'.

For this variation on the golden line (abABV) see above on 3.6.4.

pudore: For masculine *pudor* see above on 19 and 37.

73-4. hanc etiam non est mea dedignata puella
molliter admota sollicitare manu.
One source of embarrassment for both the lover and his partner is the fact that she felt compelled to use her hand when trying to coax his penis into action.

73. hanc: Refers to *partem* in 69.

non est...dedignata: The claim that 'she/he did not disdain' only underlines the humiliation involved. See e.g. *Her.* 4.149 (Phaedra to Hippolytus): *non ego dedignor supplex humilisque precari*, 12.83 (Jason proposing to Medea), *Fast.* 4.35-6 (Venus and Anchises).

74. sollicitare: See line 56 above.

admota...manu: For this phrase in a different sexual context see Prop. 1.3.16: *osculaque admota sumere et arma manu*. For discussions of this line see above on 71.

75-6. sed postquam nullas consurgere posse per artes
immemoremque sui procubuisse uidet,
As elsewhere in Roman literature (e.g. Petr. 105.9, Mart. 11.29, Juv. 10.205-6), however, the partner's manipulations fail.

75. consurgere: Another euphemism, *consurgere* is most commonly used by Ovid and others of human beings (*OLD* 1-5). As noted at *TLL* 620.56, it continues the personification of the lover's penis.

Cf. 1.9.29: *uictique resurgunt*, where the speaker puns on the sexual and military meanings of both terms; and 2.15.25: *sed, puto, te nuda mea membra libidine surgent*, where *surgere* is a relatively polite term for an erection. Catullus is more blunt (32.11): *pertundo tunicamque palliumque*.

Dr Franziska Schnoor (Stiftsbibliothek St Gallen) advises me that verses 3.7.75–3.9.10 are misplaced in S (Cod. Sang. 864) and are to be found between 2.15.2 and 2.15.3.

76. immemoremque sui: Suggests that the penis has forgotten its true nature. Cf. *Met.* 10.171 (Apollo fails to act like a god): *immemor ipse sui non retia ferre recusat*, 13.453 (Polyxena behaves like a princess): *quae memor ipsa sui*. (Ter. *An.* 281 and *A.* 6.664 are only superficially similar.)

procubuisse: Frequently used of the dead or dying (*TLL* 1567.21–47; e.g. *Met.* 5.122 [of Pedasus slain by Perseus]: *procubuit terrae mactati more iuuenci*) or of worshippers or suppliants (*TLL* 1567.59–1568.21; e.g. 1.7.18 [of Cassandra]: *procubuit templo*), *procumbere* is a grandiose substitute for *iacere* (see above on 65).

77–8. 'quid me ludis?' ait, 'quis te, male sane, iubebat
    inuitum nostro ponere membra toro?

After the lover's elaborate euphemisms come the girl's straightforward questions: Why are you cheating me? Why are you in my bed?

77. ludis: While Ovid often uses *ludo* to mean 'deceive' in erotic contexts (e.g. 1.3.22, 1.10.4, *Ars* 1.643: *ludite, si sapitis, solas impune puellas; Her.* 17.45, 142, *Met.* 6.113, 124, *Fasti* 3.685), here there is a difference: this lover's deception is involuntary.

male sane: The adjective is used here in its most literal sense, i.e. 'physically sound' (*OLD* 1); not 'mentally sound' (*OLD* 3; cf. *A.* 4.8: *unanimam adloquitur male sana sororem*); or 'free from love' (*OLD* 3b; *Rem.* 504: *qui poterit sanum fingere, sanus erit*).

78. ponere membra toro: Alludes ironically to 2.10, a poem in which the lover boasts of his ability to satisfy two girlfriends (17–18): *hostibus eueniat uiduo dormire cubili | et medio laxe ponere membra toro.*

79–80. aut te traiectis Aeaea uenefica lanis
    deuouet, aut alio lassus amore uenis'.

Like the lover (27–38), the disappointed partner considers possible causes for failure, including witchcraft.

79. traiectis...lanis: For the use of woollen dolls by witches see Horace's account of the activities of Canidia and Sagana (*S.* 1.8.30–1): *lanea et effigies erat altera cerea: maior | lanea, quae poenis compesceret inferiorem.* For the piercing of dolls see above on 29. For the use of woollen threads in magic see Theoc. *Id.* 2.2, Ogden (2002: 241, 271).

Aeaea uenefica: Aeaea's witch is Circe (Hom. *Od.* 10.135–6, *A.* 3.386: *Aeaeaeque... Circae, Met.* 4.205: *Aeaeae... Circes*), famous for her ability to render men impotent (Hom. *Od.* 10.341 [Odysseus to Circe]: ὄφρα με γυμνωθέντα κακὸν καὶ ἀνήνορα θήῃς 'So that when I am naked you can make me cowardly and unmanned'). For *uenefica* see above on 27.

80. deuouet: See above on 27.

alio lassus amore uenis: For a woman's complaint that the lover is worn out from sex with another see Prop. 1.3.37–8: *namque ubi longa meae consumpsti tempora noctis, | languidus exactis, ei mihi, sideribus?* At *Rem.* 401–4 the Teacher urges his students to adopt this as a strategy. For *lassus* as 'sexually exhausted' see 3.11.13.

81–2. nec mora, desiluit tunica uelata soluta
    (et decuit nudos proripuisse pedes)

Speech is followed by immediate action when the girl leaps out of bed and abandons her lover.

81. desiluit tunica uelata soluta: Alludes ironically to Corinna's entry into *Amores* (1.5.9): *ecce, Corinna uenit, tunica uelata recincta*. Even though the language is similar, with *recincta* and *soluta* being very close in meaning (*TLL recingo* 325.40), the differences between the two passages are striking. 1.5 describes Corinna's entry into her lover's bedroom, her clothing (absence of a belt [*recincta*] implying readiness for sex), and a successful sexual encounter. 3.7 describes a girl's departure from her own bedroom, her clothing (absence of a belt [*soluta*] suggesting eagerness to leave quickly), and a failed attempt at intercourse. For discussion of this phrase and its variations in *Amores* and elsewhere see above on 3.1.51.

For the interweaving of four words ending in *a* see above on 3.4.16.

Ramirez de Verger's (2) acceptance of *recincta* is mistaken. Use of near synonyms underlines both similarity and difference.

82. decuit: The observation that embarrassment (e.g. 2.5.43) or fear (*Ars* 1.126, *Met.* 4.230, *Fast.* 5.608) or flight (*Met.* 1.530) or tears (*Fast.* 2.757) or (as here) bare feet made a woman more attractive is characteristic of some Ovidian narrators. For discussion see Richlin (2014: 139).

83–4. neue suae possent intactam scire ministrae,
    dedecus hoc sumpta dissimulauit aqua.
The poem closes with the girl's attempt to conceal her disgrace from her slaves.

83. intactam: Being *intacta* is usually presented as a positive thing in a woman e.g. *A.* 1.345 (of Dido): *cui pater intactam dederit*, Hor. *Carm.* 1.7.5: *intactae Palladis*, Prop. 2.6.21: *intactas… Sabinas*, Sen. *Phaed.* 668: *respersa nulla labe et intacta, innocens*. Here, however, it is a source of embarrassment.

84. dedecus: A powerfully pejorative term in sexual contexts (e.g. Plaut. *Amph.* 882-3 [Alcmena protesting her innocence]: *durare nequeo in aedibus. ita me probri, | stupri, dedecoris a uiro argutam meo*; *Fast.* 2.826 (of Lucretia's rape): *eloquar infelix dedecus ipsa meum*), *dedecus* is here used of the shame arising from a failure to have sex. For washing after (actual) sex see *Ars* 3.96: *quid, nisi quam sumes, dic mihi, perdis aquam?*

3.8: MONEY RULES NOWADAYS

Is the elegiac lover rich or poor? If by 'elegiac lover' we mean the authors of love elegies, the evidence suggests that most of these men had substantial wealth.[1]

---

[1] The only female elegist whose work survives, Sulpicia, was of higher social status than her male counterparts. Stevenson (2005: 37) describes her as 'an aristocratic young woman, whose family connections were of the highest respectability'.

Cornelius Gallus, usually regarded as the genre's founder,[2] was a member of the equestrian order,[3] and so, it seems, was Tibullus.[4] The same is true of Ovid, who, when writing to the *princeps* in 9 CE, draws attention to his equestrian status (*Tr.* 2.89–90, 541–2; see also *Fast.* 2.127). According to Horace the minimum qualification for membership of the order was 400,000 sesterces (*Ep.* 1.57–9).[5] That places Gallus, Tibullus, and Ovid among Rome's wealthier citizens.[6]

But if by 'elegiac lover' we mean the male speaker in the love poems of Tibullus, Propertius, and Ovid, the story is very different.[7] The Tibullan lover speaks of his poverty (*mea paupertas* 1.1.5; cf. 1.5.61–5, where he calls himself *pauper* four times in five lines), of his desire to 'live content with little' (*contentus uiuere paruo* 1.1.25), while the Propertian lover claims to come from a middling background (2.24c.37–8): *nec sanguine auito | nobilis et...non ita diues* (' not noble through ancestral blood and...not so rich') and to possess only modest wealth (2.34.55, 3.2.11–14). *Amores* present a similar picture. When describing his qualities to a potential girlfriend, the lover of 1.3 claims that although he comes from equestrian stock, his family is neither wealthy nor distinguished (7–9):

> si me non ueterum commendant magna parentum
> nomina, si nostri sanguinis auctor eques,
> nec meus innumeris renouatur campus aratris...

> If great names of ancient ancestors do not make me attractive, if the founder of my family was a knight, and if my lands are not renewed by countless ploughs...

And the collection's final speaker describes himself in complementary terms, as a 'long-standing heir to rank from my great-grandfathers' time' (*usque a proauis uetus ordinis heres* 3.15.5).[8]

Given the poet-lover's relative poverty, it is not surprising that elegists write poems concerning the possibility or reality of a wealthier rival. The Tibullan lover, for example, sees a brothel-keeper's influence behind Delia's favouring a wealthy partner (1.5.47–8), while the Propertian lover is delighted that Cynthia prefers a

---

[2] For the importance of Gallus see especially *Tr.* 4.10.53–4: *successor fuit hic tibi, Galle, Propertius illi; | quartus ab his serie temporis ipse fui* ('He [Tibullus] was your successor, Gallus, Propertius his. I was the fourth from them in time's sequence').

[3] For details of Gallus' career, including inscriptional evidence for his equestrian status, see Davenport (2019: 171–2).

[4] The remains of the 'Suetonian' life of Tibullus record that he was an *eques Romanus*. For Tibullus' *paupertas* see Maltby (2002: 40).

[5] For discussion of the property qualification for membership of the equestrian order see Davenport (2019: 34–8).

[6] We have no firm evidence for Propertius' social status.

[7] We do not know how the lover in Gallus' poetry represented his social and economic status.

[8] For the claim that the love poet is poor see also *PA* 5.50.1 ('Poverty and love are my two misfortunes...', 12.148.1 (Callimachus: 'I know that my hands are destitute of wealth...'). These and other examples are discussed in the commentary below.

poet to a man who can offer gold and Indian pearls (1.8b.37–40). Resentment of a moneyed rival is central to *Am.* 3.8.

Ovid explores the theme of wealth at several points in *Amores*. In 1.8 and 1.10, for example, he examines love's economic aspects from differing perspectives, from the woman's in 1.8 and from the man's in 1.10. For Dipsas, the despised brothel-keeper of 1.8, financial survival (her own, that of the young woman and her family) requires extracting presents from young men; while for the lover of 1.10 sex should entail pleasure freely given, not handing over gifts (1.10.35–6): *cur mihi sit damno, tibi sit lucrosa uoluptas, | quam socio motu femina uirque ferunt?* ('Why should pleasure bring me loss and you profit, pleasure which a woman and a man gain through cooperation?'). Although he has less to say about riches in Book 2, the lover does reject the pursuit of money (2.10.33–4) and claim that poetry is equivalent to great wealth (2.17.27–8).

But 3.8 is concerned not just with wealth, but with wealth derived from military service. Even though elegiac poets sometimes treat love as a form of soldiering (1.9 and 2.12 are the most obvious examples; for hints of the motif see e.g. Tib. 2.3.33–4: *Cupido | imperat, ut nostra sint tua castra domo* ['Cupid commands that your camp be at my house'], Prop. 2.7.15: *quod si uera meae comitarem castra puellae* ['But if I were following a real camp, the one that belongs to my girlfriend']),[9] they also represent the lover's life as antithetical to the soldier's. The Tibullan lover, for example, having refused to go on campaign, declares (1.1.57–8): *non ego laudari curo, mea Delia; tecum | dum modo sim, quaeso segnis inersque uocer* ('Delia, I don't care for glory; as long as I'm with you, I prefer to be called lazy and idle'); in similar fashion the Propertian lover regards himself as unsuitable for the army (1.6.29–30): *non ego sum laudi, non natus idoneus armis: | hanc me militiam fata subire uolunt* ('I was not born fit for glory, for warfare: the fates want me to undergo this kind of military service'). While the Ovidian lover rejects the army elsewhere (e.g. 1.15.3–4: *non me more patrum, dum strenua sustinet aetas, | praemia militiae puluerulenta sequi* '[Why complain that] I do not in the manner of my ancestors, while vigorous age supports me, pursue the dusty rewards of military service?'), it is in 3.8 that we find his most powerful assault on the values of the military.[10]

Secondary literature: Morgan (1977: 92–4); Barsby (1996); Greene (1994); James (2003: 101–4); Davis (2006: 74–7); Oliensis (2019: 94–9); Pietropaolo (2020: 175–7).

1–2. Et quisquam ingenuas etiam nunc suspicit artes
aut tenerum dotes carmen habere putat?

---

[9] For detailed discussion of the handling of this motif see Murgatroyd (1975) and Drinkwater (2013).
[10] For the complexities involved in Ovid's treatment of the military see Davis (2006: 74–7).

Commentary

The poem opens with an impassioned but misleading question, one which suggests that we are about to read an ethical discourse on a familiar theme viz. the greed of the current age and its undervaluing of the arts. For similar moralizing which is actually based on dissatisfaction with a sexual partner's greed see e.g. the ancient summary of Callim. *Ia.* 3 (fr. 193.col. 6.34–5 Pfeiffer): καταμέμφεται τὸν καιρὸν ὡς πλούτου μᾶλλον ἢ ἀρετῆς ὄντα... παρεπικόπτει δὲ καὶ Εὐθύδημόν τινα, ὡς κεχρημένον τῇ ὥρᾳ πορισμῷ ('He criticizes the time as one of wealth rather than virtue... he inserts a criticism of a certain Euthydemus as using his beauty for profit'); Tib. 1.4.57–8: *heu male nunc artes miseras haec saecula tractant:* | *iam tener adsueuit munera uelle puer*; Petr. 88.2.1 (Eumolpus): *tum ille, pecuniae, inquit, cupiditas haec tropica instituit. priscis enim temporibus, cum adhuc nuda uirtus placeret, uigebant artes ingenuae.*

1. Et: As first word, *et* makes a dramatic opening to the poem. Propertius adopts a similar strategy in 1.17 (1–2): *et merito, quoniam potui fugisse puellam* | *nunc ego desertas alloquor alcyonas.*

ingenuas...artes: While Cicero (*de Orat.* 1.11.2, 1.73.10, 3.21.4, *Fam.* 4.3.4.10, *Fin.* 3.4.7, 5.48.12, *Inu.* 1.35.20, *Tusc.* 5.63.10) and Ovid (*Ars* 2.121, *Fast.* 3.6, *Tr.* 1.9.45, *Pont.* 1.6.7, 2.5.66, 2.7.47, 2.9.47) are the authors who refer most to the *artes ingenuae/liberales*, it is perhaps Tacitus who gives us the clearest sense of what these studies included (*Dial.* 30.4): 'And so we can discover in Cicero's books that he was lacking in knowledge not of geometry, not of music, not of literature, not in short of any free-born art (*ingenuae artis*). He understood the subtlety of dialectic, the usefulness of ethics, the motions and causes of the universe'. Not surprisingly, Ovid puts most emphasis on poetry and eloquence (*Ars* 2.121, *Tr.* 1.9.45–6, *Pont.* 2.5.65–6, 2.7.47–8, 2.9.47–52).

These *artes* are *ingenuae/liberales* because, as Seneca makes clear, they are suitable for free (i.e. not enslaved) humans (*Ep.* 88.2.1): *quare liberalia studia dicta sint uides: quia homine libero digna sunt.* For other meanings of *ingenuus* see on 3.4.33 and 3.11.10.

2. tenerum...carmen: For *tener* used of elegiac poets/poetry see 2.1.4, *Ars* 2.273, 3.333, *Rem.* 757: *teneros... poetas, Tr.* 2.361, *Tr.* 3.3.73, 4.10.1: *tenerorum lusor amorum/Amorum*. For *tener* of beloveds and *amor/Amor* see above on 3.1.27.

dotes: For the connection between poetry and 'endowment' see 1.10.59–60: *est quoque carminibus meritas celebrare puellas* | *dos mea* and *Rem.* 758: *summoueo dotes impius ipse meas*, where the poet's *dos* is his service. Here, however, he is concerned not with the benefits which his poetry confers on others, but the rewards that it brings him.

3–4. ingenium quondam fuerat pretiosius auro,
 at nunc barbaria est grandis habere nihil.

Commentary, 8.1–5 231

The moralizing continues along lines familiar from Callimachus and Petronius, contrasting a virtuous past with an avaricious present.

3. ingenium: For the importance of *ingenium* in the Ovidian lexicon see above on 3.1.25.

pretiosius auro: For shock that profit is more highly prized than poetic talent see Hor. *Epod.* 11.11–12 (with Watson [2003: ad loc.]): *contrane lucrum nil ualere candidum | pauperis ingenium.*

4. barbaria: The word is rare in classical poetry (once in Horace; 11 times in Ovid, including eight in the exile poetry). It can be used descriptively e.g. Hor. *Ep.* 1.2.7 (of the Trojans): *Graecia barbariae lento collisa duello*, *Met.* 15.829–30 (of Caesar's conquests): *quid tibi barbariam gentesque ab utroque iacentes | oceano numerem?* Here, however, it has its full emotional and evaluative force. Cf. *Ars* 2.552 (of a jealous lover): *barbaria noster abundat amor*, *Tr.* 3.9.2 (of the Exile's surroundings): *inter inhumanae nomina barbariae.*

habere nihil: Conventional morality treats the simple life of the past as a model of perfection e.g. Lucr. 5.1117–19, Hor. *S.* 2.2.1, *Carm.* 2.16.13, Virg. *G.* 2.472, *A.* 9.607: *et patiens operum exiguoque/paruoque adsueta iuuentus.* Nowadays, however, according to our disillusioned speaker, that ideal is not just old-fashioned but uncivilized. In *Ars* the Teacher takes a cynical view of the present (2.277–8): *aurea sunt uere nunc saecula: plurimus auro | uenit honos: auro conciliatur amor.* *Fasti*'s Janus is appropriately ambivalent (1.223–4): *nos quoque templa iuuant, quamuis antiqua probemus, | aurea.*

5–8. cum pulchre dominae nostri placuere libelli,
   quo licuit libris, non licet ire mihi;
cum bene laudauit, laudato ianua clausa est.
   turpiter huc illuc ingeniosus eo.
In two neatly parallel couplets, the speaker sets out the erotic consequences of the contemporary obsession with wealth: while books can enter his mistress's house, he cannot; he is forced to hang around outside.

5. pulchre: Editors divide between *pulchre* (Munari, Kenney, McKeown, Ramirez de Verger [1]) and *pulchrae* (Showerman and Goold, Ramirez de Verger [2]). The principle manuscripts all offer *pulchrae* (P: *pulchrę* [ę = ae], S: *pulchrę*, Y: *pulchrae*). Many lesser manuscripts (Kenney's ω) read *pulchre*. Note, however, that the diphthong *ae* is often written as *e* and that *ae* and *ē* are easily confused.

In favour of *pulchrae* are: (1) it has the support of the main manuscripts; and (2) Ovid uses *pulchre* nowhere else.

In favour of *pulchre* are: (1) it has wide manuscript support; (2) it is used by Catullus, Lucretius, and Horace; (3) Ovid prefers to separate adjectives from nouns they qualify (e.g. only eight instances of *pulcher* [out of 52] are placed next to their accompanying noun); (4) the proximity of *dominae* is more likely to have corrupted *pulchre* into *pulchrae* than vice versa; and, most importantly, (5) parallelism between the two couplets requires an adverb in line 5 to balance *bene* in line 7: *cum pulchre / cum bene*.

pulchre also has the support of older editors including Naugerius, Marius, Micyllus, Daniel Heinsius (1629), Heinsius, and Burman.

dominae: For this term see above on 3.2.18.

libelli: For the books of *Amores* as *libelli* see 1.ep.1: *qui modo Nasonis fueramus quinque libelli*; 2.17.33, 3.12.7. See also Catul. 1.1: *cui dono lepidum nouum libellum*, 1.8: *quare habe tibi quidquid hoc libelli*; Prop. 2.25.3–4: *ista meis fiet notissima forma libellis, | Calue, tua uenia, pace, Catulle, tua*. It is perhaps the preferred term for a collection of love poetry.

6. quo licuit libris, non licet ire mihi: Ovid rewrites this line in tragic mode at *Tr.* 1.1.1–2: *parue (nec inuideo) sine me, liber, ibis in Vrbem, | ei mihi, quo domino non licet ire tuo.*

7. laudauit, laudato: For polyptoton used to frame the main caesura see above on 3.2.32.

ianua clausa: The girlfriend's locked door is a regular feature of Roman love poetry (and poetry about love) e.g. Lucr. 4.1177–9, Catul. 67, Prop. 1.16, Tib. 1.2, Hor. *Carm.* 3.10, *Am.* 1.6. Most pertinent here, however, is the Propertian lover's complaint when Cynthia sleeps with a wealthy praetor (2.16.6): *nunc sine me tota ianua nocte patet.*

8. huc illuc: The phrase is often used to suggest anxiety and helplessness e.g. *Her.* 13.34 (Laodamia): *huc illuc, qua furor egit, eo*, 20.129–30 (Acontius): *ad limina crebro | anxius huc illuc dissimulanter eo*, *Medea* 2 (Ribbeck [1897]): *feror huc illuc.*

ingeniosus: The term is used in *Amores* of the poet himself (here and at line 46) and of Corinna's highly skilled possessions, enslaved Nape (1.11.4) and her parrot (2.6.18). Here it also recalls Dipsas' cynical advice (1.8.62): *crede mihi, res est ingeniosa dare*. While the world treats wealth as talent, true ability goes unvalued.

turpiter: For the force of this adverb see above on 3.7.45.

**9–10. ecce, recens diues parto per uulnera censu
praefertur nobis sanguine pastus eques.**
This brings us to the real reason for the lover's moralizing: his girlfriend has found a newer and wealthier lover.

9. The poet-lover objects to both the newness of his rival's money and the means by which it was acquired. Cf. the poet's self-definition at 3.15.6: *non modo militiae turbine factus eques.*

Commentary, 8.6–13 233

ecce: Is often used to mark a significant transition in the argument (e.g. 1.5.9: *ecce, Corinna uenit*, 2.7.17: *ecce nouum crimen*). Here it also recalls a poem which raises similar questions (1.8.57–8: *ecce, quid iste tuus praeter noua carmina uates | donat?*).

parto...censu: Refers to both the man's wealth (*OLD* 3) and his socio-legal status as a member of the equestrian order (*OLD* 2b).

10. sanguine pastus: The lover's disgust is underlined by language that, as Pietropaolo (2020: 175–6) points out, suggests animality. We can go further and say that it implies monstrosity. See *Met.* 8.170 (of the Minotaur): *et Actaeo bis pastum sanguine monstrum*.

eques: For the acquisition of equestrian status through military service see also *Fast.* 4.383 (with Fantham [1998]): *hanc ego militia sedem* (i.e. a theatre seat next to Ovid's), *tu pace parasti*.

11–12. hunc potes amplecti formosis, uita, lacertis?
   huius in amplexu, uita, iacere potes?
Having expressed his disgust with this jumped-up knight, the lover expresses surprise that his girlfriend does not share his feelings. Use of similar language (*hunc potes amplecti/huius in amplexu...potes*) in the hexameter and pentameter underlines differences in perspective: How can she bear to embrace him? How can she bear to be embraced by him? Cf. the Propertian lover's description of Cynthia and his rival (2.16.23–4): *numquam septenas noctes seiuncta* (i.e. *a me*) *cubares, | candida tam foedo bracchia fusa uiro*.

11/12. uita: This term of endearment comes from ordinary speech (e.g. Plaut. *Cas.* 135: *mea uita, mea mellilla, mea festiuitas*, Cic. *Fam.* 14.2.3.7 [to his wife]: *obsecro te, mea uita*, 14.4.1.9: *ego uero te quam primum, mea uita, cupio uidere*). Among love poets it is found primarily in Catullus (45.13: *sic, inquit, mea uita, Septimille*, 109.1: *iucundum, mea uita, mihi proponis amorem*) and Propertius (1.2.1: *quid iuuat ornato procedere, uita, capillo*, 1.8a.22, 2.3.23, 2.5.18, 2.19.27, 2.20.11, 2.20.17, 2.24b.29, 2.26a.1, 2.30b.14). Ovid uses it only in this couplet and at 2.15.21.

13–14. si nescis, caput hoc galeam portare solebat;
   ense latus cinctum, quod tibi seruit, erat.
To increase the girl's revulsion the lover draws attention to his rival's body, to the head which used to carry a helmet and the flank that bore a sword.

13. galeam portare: The expression seems strange. While *portare* is used of bearing/wearing weapons (*TLL porto* 50.68–51.26), it is not usually used of helmets. At Sil. 4.214: *portans galeam* describes a victorious warrior who carries off a dead man's helmet, while at Sil. 12.236–8 *portare* seems to need the support of *gestare* to convey the appropriate sense: *tune, ignauissime, sacri | portabis capitis, quae non sine crimine uester | inuidiaque deum gestaret tegmina ductor? induo* is the expected verb for putting on and wearing a helmet in prose and verse (e.g. Caes. *Gal.* 2.21.5.4: *sed etiam ad galeas induendas scutisque tegimenta detrahenda tempus defuerit*, Hyg. *Astr.* 2.12.1.6: *praeterea galeam, qua indutus ex aduerso non poterat uideri*, A. 2.392-3, 5.673-4: *galeam ante pedes proiecit inanem, | qua ludo indutus*, 9.365-6). The oddness perhaps suggests the speaker's distaste for the soldier's way of life.

14. While *ense latus cinctum* is a standard poetic way of describing a man wearing a sword (*Fast.* 2.784: *ense latus cinxit*, Sen. *Phaed.* 547-8: *longo latus | mucrone cingens ensis*), *accingo* is actually more common (e.g. 3.3.27, A. 7.640, 11.489, VF 5.513). The descriptive clause *quod tibi seruit* activates the sexual sense of *latus* (see above on 3.7.36).

seruit: Recalls the elegiac concept of the *seruitium amoris*, an idea found in *Amores* (1.2.18, 1.3.5, 2.17.1), but central to Propertius' conception of love. For the elegists' use of this trope see Lyne (1979), Murgatroyd (1981), McCarthy (1998), Fitzgerald (2000: 72-5), and Fulkerson (2013).

15-16. laeua manus, cui nunc serum male conuenit aurum,
   scuta tulit; dextram tange, cruenta fuit.
Continuing the focus on his rival's body, the lover now concentrates on his hands as bearers of weapons.

15. laeua manus: While the left hand wears the gold ring worn by members of the equestrian order (Davenport [2019: 113-19]), it also carries a soldier's shield (e.g. A. 10.261-2: *clipeum cum deinde sinistra | extulit ardentem*; *Tr.* 4.1.73-4: *nunc senior gladioque latus scutoque sinistram, | canitiem galeae subicioque meam*). Seeing the ring should prompt thoughts of that hand's other use.

serum: Reminds the girlfriend that her lover's status is recently acquired. In Book 1 the Ovidian lover claimed that his rank was inherited (1.3.8): *nostri sanguinis auctor eques*; while in the collection's final signature, the poet defines his status as precisely the opposite of this soldier-lover (3.15.5-6): *usque a proauis uetus ordinis heres, | non modo militiae turbine factus eques*.

male conuenit: The ring does not suit the rival's hand precisely because of the way in which it was won.

16. scuta: The *scutum* is 'the oblong shield used by heavy infantry' (*OLD*).

dextram: Reflecting actual military practice, the speaker associates the sword with the soldier's right hand e.g. Liv. 6.12.8.4: *pilis ante pedes positis gladiis tantum dextras armemus*, Luc. 4.248: *ut dextrae iusti gladius dissuasor adhaesit*.

cruenta: Cognate with *cruor* (spilled or spattered blood), *cruentus* is an emotive term with connotations of cruelty and bloodthirstiness (*TLL* 1240.37: *sanguinis cupidus uel amans, crudelis*). Here it is intended to increase the girl's revulsion towards her partner. At *Ars* 2.713-14, by contrast, Briseis is praised for enjoying a bloodstained lover: *illis te manibus tangi, Brisei, sinebas, | imbutae Phrygia quae nece semper erant.*

17-18. qua periit aliquis, potes hanc contingere dextram?
heu, ubi mollities pectoris illa tui?
The speaker now draws out the implications of the previous pentameter and contrasts the brutality of the soldier's hand with the softness of the girl's breast.

17. qua periit aliquis: The couplet begins with an adjectival clause highlighting the reason why the soldier's hand is *cruenta*: he is a killer.

potes hanc contingere dextram: Rewrites the advice of the previous line. Whether a question (as usually printed) or a statement, it expresses incredulity.

18. heu: A marker of deep distress (e.g. Catul. 101.6: *heu miser indigne frater adempte mihi*, A. 6.882: *heu, miserande puer*), *heu* expresses the lover's dismay at his girlfriend's loss of her essential softness.

If we leave aside repeated *heu* in Tibullus, Ovid is the only elegist to allow hiatus after *heu* and then only with *ubi* (*Her.* 4.150, 6.41, *Fast.* 3.485, 5.465). The frequency of hiatus after interjections (Platnauer [1951: 57]) suggests that it is used to underline strength of feeling.

mollities: The Romans conceived of softness, both physical and emotional, as a quintessentially female quality to the point that the etymologist Isidore connects *mollis* with *mulier* (Maltby [1991: 389]). As Sharrock (in Elsner and Sharrock [1991: 173]) observes: 'For a woman to be *mollis* is to be sexually compliant and alluring; for a man it is to be effeminate. A man must be *rigidus* and a woman *mollis* and not the other way round'. Touching this man's hand endangers a woman's status as a female.

pectoris: The noun is used here in both its physical (*OLD* 1) and non-physical (*OLD* 3-4) senses, i.e. of the girlfriend's breast and of her moral and emotional life.

19-20. cerne cicatrices, ueteris uestigia pugnae:
quaesitum est illi corpore, quidquid habet.
But the girl does not need to imagine how this soldier's hands were used in the past. She should look at his body as it is now and think about the sources of his wealth.

19. The line is remarkable for its fourfold alliteration of *c*, underlining the ugliness of the word *cicatrix* and what it connotes; and alliteration of *u* after the caesura, hinting at the reality behind the euphemism, i.e. *uulnera*.

ueteris uestigia: The context makes allusion to Catullus' description of Prometheus (64.295: *extenuata gerens ueteris uestigia poenae*) more likely than reference to Virgil's Dido (*A.* 4.23: *agnosco ueteris uestigia flammae*).

Commentary

20. quaesitum...corpore: The phrase suggests that the soldier is akin to a prostitute. See e.g. Enn. *Euh.* 10 (Goldberg and Manuwald [2]): 'Venus was the first to establish the art of prostitution (*artem meretriciam*) and established for women in Cyprus how to make a profit by prostituting their bodies (*uti uulg<at>o corpore quaestum facerent*)', *Am.* 1.10.21-2: *stat meretrix certo cuiuis mercabilis aere, | et miseras iusso corpore quaerit opes*. In fact it reflects the language of the law e.g. *Dig.* 23.2.24, 23.2.43 (twice), 23.2.47, 38.1.38: 'For if a prostitute (*meretrix*) has been manumitted, she must not offer the same services to her patron, even though she is still making a profit with her body (*quamuis adhuc corpore quaestum faciat*)'. For law and the language of prostitution see McGinn (1998: 221-3), Flemming (1999: 50), and Strong (2016: 112). For a similar, if less insulting, view of the soldier's way of life see 2.10.31-2: *induat aduersis contraria pectora telis | miles et aeternum sanguine nomen emat*.

21-2. forsitan et, quotiens hominem iugulauerit, ille
  indicet: hoc fassas tangis, auara, manus?
This phase of the argument closes with a reminder in the most brutal terms that this man is a killer.

21. iugulauerit: A highly emotive word, it literally means 'kill by cutting the throat' (*OLD* 1). See e.g. *Met.* 12.80-1: *'quisquis es, o iuuenis', dixit 'solamen habeto | mortis, ab Haemonio quod sis iugulatus Achille!'*, 15.466-7 (vegetarian Pythagoras on animal sacrifice): *aut qui uagitus similes puerilibus haedum | edentem iugulare potest*.

22. indicet: Used of revealing secrets ('esp. of an incriminating nature' *OLD* 2), the verb implies a sense of shame or guilt.

fassas: Reinforces the implication of *indicet* (cf. 2.4.3: *siquid prodest delicta fateri*) and, when applied to *manus*, creates a striking phrase. For metaphorical use of *fateor* see *Ars* 1.573: *atque oculos oculis spectare fatentibus ignem*.

23-4. ille ego Musarum purus Phoebique sacerdos
  ad rigidas canto carmen inane fores.
Shifting attention from the soldier to himself, the lover now contrasts his exalted status as a poet with his current humiliation.

23. ille ego: Ovid uses this phrase in contexts of poetic self-definition e.g. 2.1.2: *ille ego nequitiae Naso poeta meae*, *Tr.* 4.10.1: *ille ego qui fuerim, tenerorum lusor amorum*, 5.7.55: *ille ego Romanus uates*, *Pont.* 4.3.11, 13, 15, 16, 17.

Musarum...Phoebique sacerdos: Combines claims made by Horace and Propertius at their most pompous: *Carm.* 3.1.2-4: *carmina non prius | audita Musarum sacerdos | uirginibus puerisque canto*; Prop. 3.1.3: *primus ego ingredior puro de fonte sacerdos*. While Horace claims to be a priest of the Muses, and Propertius (3.1.7) implies that he is a priest of Apollo, Ovid's poet-lover claims to be both.

Commentary, 8.20-6   237

purus: As in Prop. 3.1.3 (with Heyworth and Morwood [2011]), the adjective looks back to Callimachus (*Hymn to Apollo* 110-11): 'The bees do not bring water from every source to Deo, but whatever springs up pure and undefiled (καθαρή τε καὶ ἀχράαντος)'. (For the full passage see the introduction to 3.6.)

24. The hexameter's grandiose claim is undercut by a reminder that the poet is currently waiting outside his girlfriend's door.

rigidas...fores: Excluded lovers typically view doors as hard e.g. Tib. 1.1.56: *et sedeo duras ianitor ante fores, Am.* 2.1.22: *mollierunt duras lenia uerba fores.* rigidus, however, when used in connection with song, recalls claims made by Virgil's shepherd-poets at *Ecl.* 6.27-8: *tum uero in numerum Faunosque ferasque uideres | ludere, tum rigidas motare cacumina quercus* and 6.71: *cantando rigidas deducere montibus ornos.* In *Eclogues* song can move oaks and ash trees; in *Amores* it cannot even open a girlfriend's door.

canto...carmen: Recalls Hor. *Carm.* 3.1.2-4: *carmina...canto.* As Nisbet and Rudd (2004: ad loc.) observe, assonance 'suits the sacral style'. Cf. *Met.* 14.430: *carmina iam moriens canit exequialia cycnus, Fast.* 2.121: *dum canimus sacras alterno carmine Nonas.* Here the 'sacral style' underlines the poet's failure.

inane: Highlights love poetry's failure (*OLD* 13: 'serving no purpose, vain, futile') to achieve one its primary goals, success with women: 2.1.33-4: *at facie tenerae laudata saepe puellae, | ad uatem, pretium carminis, ipsa uenit.*

25-8. discite, qui sapitis, non quae nos scimus inertes,
    sed trepidas acies et fera castra sequi
proque bono uersu primum deducite pilum:
    nox tibi, si belles, possit, Homere, dari.
From his failure to win access to his girlfriend, the poet draws the only possible conclusion: poets should give up and join the army.

25. discite: With this dramatic imperative, the lover addresses the reader directly in the manner of a didactic poet. See e.g. *G.* 2.35: *quare agite o proprios generatim discite cultus; Med.* 1 (with Johnson [2016: ad loc.]): *discite quae faciem commendet cura, puellae; Ars* 1.459: *disce bonas artes, moneo, Romana iuuentus*; 3.298: *discite femineo corpora ferre gradu.*

qui sapitis: Varies the conversational *si sapis* (Plaut. *Am.* 311 and 14 more times) and *si sapitis* found at *Ars* 1.643 and 2.173 (with Janka [1997: ad loc.]).

inertes: For the elegiac poet as *iners* see Tib. 1.1.58: *dum modo sim, quaeso segnis inersque uocer,* Prop. 3.7.72: *ante fores dominae condar oportet iners,* Ov. *Am.* 1.15.2: *ingeniique uocas carmen inertis opus.*

26. castra sequi: The opposition between 'following the camp' and elegiac love is conventional. See *Ecl.* 10 where Gallus' mistress leaves him for a soldier (22-3):

tua cura Lycoris | perque niues alium perque horrida castra secuta est; Tib. 2.6.1: *castra Macer sequitur: tenero quid fiet Amori?*; and Prop. 2.10, where the poet promises to abandon elegy one day (19): *haec ego castra sequar.*

27. bono uersu: *bonus* belongs to the ordinary language of criticism. See e.g. 3.9.39: *carminibus confide bonis*; Sen. *Suas.* 6.27.1 (after quoting a lengthy passage from Cornelius Severus): *non fraudabo municipem nostrum bono uersu*; and Gellius citing Cicero on himself: (12.2.5.3): *Cicero summus orator agebat causam suam et uolebat suos uersus uideri bonos.*

primum...pilum: Recalls the standard term for legion's senior centurion: *primi pili centurio* (e.g. Caes. *Gall.* 3.5.2.1, *Civ.* 1.13.4.4, Cic. *Balb.* 34.9, Liv. 2.27.6.2).

deducite: Unlike *bonus*, *deduco* is a key literary term, often associated with adherence to Callimachus' poetic values. See e.g. *Ecl.* 6.4–5: *pastorem, Tityre, pinguis | pascere oportet ouis, deductum dicere carmen*, Hor. *Ep.* 2.1.225: *tenui deducta poemata filo*, Prop. 2.33b.38: *et mea deducta carmina uoce legis*, *Met.* 1.4 (with Kenney [1976: 51–2] and Barchiesi [2005: 144–5]): *ad mea perpetuum deducite tempora carmen.* Here, however, the literary term becomes a military one, used of taking down javelins.

28. nox tibi, si belles, possit, Homere, dari: I print Kenney's (1958: 64–5) brilliant reconstruction of this line because it gives exactly the sense required: even a poet of Homer's stature would have problems getting laid; but if he stopped being a poet and became a soldier he would succeed. For a similarly irreverent apostrophe to Homer see *Ars* 2.279–80: *ipse licet uenias Musis comitatus, Homere, | si nihil attuleris, ibis, Homere, foras.* The argument recalls Propertius' comment on the erotic uselessness of Homer (1.9.11): *plus in amore ualet Mimnermi uersus Homero* and the advice of Dipsas (*Am.* 1.8.61): *qui dabit, ille tibi magno sit maior Homero.*

The principal manuscripts offer the following: P: *hic tibi si uelles possit homere dari*; S: *hic tibi si uelles posseǫ homere dari*; Y: *hic tibi si uelles possit homere dari.* Munari and Ramirez de Verger print *hoc tibi, si uelles, posset, Homere, dari.* Munari translates: *Questo grado, se tu lo volessi, potrebbe essere dato a te, o Omero* ('This rank, should you wish it, could be given to you, Homer'). But this is pointless. Kenney comments (1958: 64): 'No admirer of Ovid's will acquiesce in such feebleness'.

Kenney accepts Madvig's (1873: 69) *belles* for *uelles* and Campbell's *nox* for *hoc*. As parallels for *noctem dare* ('make a night available for sex') Kenney cites *Rem.* 306, 520. See also Pl. *As.* 194, *Trin.* 250, *Truc.* 32, 279; Hor. *Epod.* 15.13; Prop. 2.15.39 (*si dabit et multas* [i.e. *noctes* 37]). For *nox* as 'night of sex' see e.g. 1.8.67, 1.10.30, 1.11.13, 2.19.54.

Kenney notes that 'P's *possit* [also in Y] may be a relic of the original reading', i.e. the present subjunctive in the apodosis implies a present subjunctive in the protasis.

29-30. Iuppiter, admonitus nihil esse potentius auro, corruptae pretium uirginis ipse fuit.

The argument now switches direction, with the lover employing mythology and turning from the sufferings of poets to female greed.

For the treatment of Danae's story in Horace, Propertius, and *Amores* see above on 3.4.21-2. The argument here is closer to Hor. *Carm.* 3.16.1-8 and Prop. 2.32.59-60 than to *Am.* 2.19 and 3.4, where the focus is on the futility of confining women.

29. Iuppiter...auro: The story is so well known that referring to Jupiter and gold is enough to conjure up Danae's story.

potentius auro: Recalls Hor. *Carm.* 3.16.9-11: *aurum...|...potentius | ictu fulmineo*.

30. corruptae...uirginis: Danae's story is capable of various interpretations. While her inclusion in Arachne's tapestry implies that she is raped (*Met.* 6.113), here the argument demands, and the choice of *corrumpo* (*OLD* 5b: 'to corrupt sexually, seduce') confirms, that this Danae is a willing participant. Propertius' overall argument (women are prone to infidelity) requires us to understand 2.32.59-60 in the same way: *nec minus aerato Danae circumdata muro | non potuit magno casta negare Ioui.*

pretium: Recalls Hor. *Carm.* 3.16.8: *conuerso in pretium deo* and confirms that in this account Danae succumbs to bribery.

31-2. dum merces aberat, durus pater, ipsa seuera, aerati postes, ferrea turris erat.

The argument continues: before money was involved, Acrisius and his daughter conformed to moral norms and the family's defences remained strong.

31. merces: Functions as a synonym for *pretium* and recalls Propertius' complaint about Cynthia (2.16.16): *indigna merce puella perit.*

durus pater: The stern father is a type familiar from comedy (Ter. *Hau.* 439, Ov. *Am.* 1.15.17 [on Menander]) and rhetorical exercises (Sen. *Con.* 1.7.2.4, 2.3.21.2, 9.3.11.10, 10.3.12.2). The phrase implies that Acrisius also took a bribe.

seuera: For the connotations of *seuerus* see above on 3.4.43. At 2.1.3 the poet explicitly excludes moralists from his readership: *procul hinc, procul este, seueri!*

32. aerati postes: Bronze (not iron) defences are a regular part of the myth e.g. Soph. *Ant.* 944-5, Hor. *Carm.* 3.16.1, Prop. 2.32.59, Paus. 10.5.11.3.

33-4. sed postquam sapiens in munere uenit adulter, praebuit ipsa sinus et dare iussa dedit.

Stripped of the glamour of myth (no more bronze posts and iron tower), the story of Jupiter and Danae becomes a tawdry tale of adultery and a bribe.

240   *Commentary*

33. sapiens...adulter: The phrase shocks. The expected epithet for an adulterer is *turpis* (see above on 3.4.29). The phrase recalls the description of Jupiter as *callidus...adulter* (1.10.4). *callidus*, however, is merely 'clever' or 'cunning', while *sapiens* has connotations of 'wisdom' and 'sound judgement' (*OLD* 2).

in munere: For Jupiter's appearance to Danae in the form of golden rain see Hyg. *Fab.* 63.1: *Iouis autem in imbrem aureum conuersus cum Danae concubuit, ex quo compressu natus est Perseus*; cf. *Met.* 4.611, 6.113.

Manuscripts and older editions offer *in munera*. *in* followed by the accusative, however, is used for purpose (*OLD in* 21) and gives the wrong meaning. Marlowe (1603) translated *in munera* incorrectly but supplied the correct sense: 'But when in gifts the wise adulterer came'. Kenney (1958: 65) argued for Francius's *in munere* (reported in Burman [ad loc.]), a correction accepted by subsequent editors.

34. praebuit: For *praebere* in a sexual sense see *Ars* 2.685: *odi quae praebet, quia sit praebere necesse*, 3.666.

sinus: What did Danae offer? *sinus* has a range of meanings (*OLD* suggests 12), several of which are pertinent here. It can be used of (*OLD* 4): 'the hanging fold of a toga or other garment used as a pocket, esp. for money' e.g. (1.10.17–18): *quid puerum Veneris pretio prostare iubetis?* | *quo pretium condat, non habet ille sinum*; or 'embrace' (*OLD* 2b) e.g. (2.12.2): *in nostro est, ecce, Corinna sinu*; or 'breast' (*OLD* 1b) e.g. (*Her.* 20.140–1): *candida per causam bracchia saepe tenet,* | *contrectatque sinus, et forsitan oscula iungit*. Although translators are obliged to choose, it would be wrong to insist on a single meaning here.

Pichon (1902: 264) suggests 'lap' (*gremium*) as a translation of *sinus*. While this is attractive, none of his female examples is persuasive.

dare...dedit: For *dare* used absolutely in a sexual sense see 1.4.64, 70; *Ars* 1.345, 670, 674, 2.576, 3.579.

iussa: If Danae is obeying her father's orders, as Marius suggests (*a patre, qui ante munera oblata durus erat*), then Acrisius is a father who prostitutes his daughter.

35–8. at cum regna senex caeli Saturnus haberet,
    omne lucrum tenebris alta premebat humus.
aeraque et argentum cumque auro pondera ferri
    Manibus admorat, nullaque massa fuit.

The poet-lover now follows various Roman predecessors (Catullus, Virgil, Horace, Tibullus) in adapting Hesiod's myth of the golden generation which lived at the time of Cronos (*Works* 109–20). Given the poem's focus on gold (3, 15, 29), it is not surprising that the lover begins with an item implied but not actually mentioned in Hesiod's picture of primal innocence, the absence of mining.

35. regna...caeli: For Cronos' rule of the sky see Hes. *Works* 111: 'They existed at the time of Cronos, when he ruled heaven'. Roman writers sometimes associate

Commentary, 8.33–40 241

Saturn's reign with early Italy e.g. Enn. *Ann.* 1.20–1 (Goldberg and Manuwald [1]), *A.* 6.793–4, *Fast.* 1.193.

senex…Saturnus: For Saturn as old see *A.* 7.180: *Saturnusque senex*. Horsfall (2000: ad loc.) notes that Livius Andronicus had identified Saturn with Cronos in the third century BCE.

36–8. For the idea that the creator decided to make metals inaccessible see *Met.* 1.139–40: *quasque recondiderat Stygiisque admouerat umbris,* | *effodiuntur opes*.

36. lucrum: A pejorative term in moralizing discourses e.g. Hor. *Carm.* 3.16.11–13 (first Danae, then Amphiaraus): *concidit auguris* | *Argiui domus ob lucrum* | *demersa exitio*; Ov. *Am.* 1.10.41–2: *turpe tori reditu census augere paternos,* | *et faciem lucro prostituisse suam*; Luc. 4.96: *pro lucri pallida tabes!*

37. The language is indebted to Lucretius' naturalistic account of the discovery of metals (5.1241–2): *quod superest, aes atque aurum ferrumque repertumst* | *et simul argenti pondus plumbique potestas*.

38. Manibus admorat: The phrase is adapted at *Met.* 1.139: *Stygiisque admouerat umbris*.

massa: Used of various metals, *massa* is frequently used in metal-working contexts e.g. *A.* 8.453: *uersantque tenaci forcipe massam*, Luc. 6.403, Stat. *Silu.* 3.3.104–5. Here it stands for 'metallurgy'.

39–40. at meliora dabat, curuo sine uomere fruges
   pomaque et in quercu mella reperta caua.
The argument now moves to a positive aspect of Saturn's reign: the abundance of easily-obtained food.

39. meliora: Here Saturn provides something 'better', i.e. food which is better than metal. At *Fast.* 4.401–2, by contrast, Ceres (i.e. agriculture) produces food which is 'better' than that of an earlier age: *prima Ceres homine ad meliora alimenta uocato* | *mutauit glandes utiliore cibo*.

curuo sine uomere: For crops without ploughing see e.g. Hes. *Works* 117–18: 'The wheat-giving ploughland used to bear grain of its own accord, in abundance, unstintingly', *Ecl.* 4.41 (of a future golden age): *robustus quoque iam tauris iuga soluet arator*, Tib. 1.3.41: *illo non ualidus subiit iuga tempore taurus*, *Met.* 1.101–2: *ipsa quoque immunis rastroque intacta nec ullis* | *saucia uomeribus per se dabat omnia tellus*.

40. in quercu mella reperta caua: For honey from oak trees see *Ecl.* 4.30: *et durae quercus sudabunt roscida mella*, Tib. 1.3.45: *ipsae mella dabant quercus*, *Met.* 1.112: *flauaque de uiridi stillabant ilice mella*. The idea perhaps derives from Hesiod's description of the rewards of justice (*Works* 232–3): 'In the mountains the surface of the oak bears acorns, the centre bees'.

41–2. nec ualido quisquam terram scindebat aratro,
signabat nullo limite mensor humum.

The speaker now returns to features that were not present in Saturn's time: ploughing and private property.

41. ualido…aratro: Given that Virgil and Ovid prefer to describe the plough as *curuus* or *incuruus* (*G.* 1.170, 494, 2.189, 513; *Her.* 1.55, 17.139, *Met.* 3.11, 15.123, *Fast.* 2.517, 3.781), the choice of *ualidus* is striking. Perhaps it underlines the difficulty of the task of splitting the soil. (See below on *scindebat*.)

VF alludes to this passage when describing Jason's attempt to plough Aeetes' field (7.602): *utque dedit uinclis ualidoque obstrinxit aratro*. Allusion to *Am.* 3.8 is not surprising in an epic centrally concerned with technological progress and the myth of ages.

scindebat: For *scindo* used of ploughing see *G.* 1.50, 2.399, 3.160. *scindo* is perhaps used here for *proscindo* i.e. of the first and hardest ploughing of the season (Var. *R.* 1.29.2.1: *terram cum primum arant, proscindere appellant*).

42. signabat nullo limite: Rewrites *G.* 1.126–7: *ne signare quidem aut partiri limite campum | fas erat*. Tibullus' golden age is similarly free of boundary-makers (1.3.43–4): *non fixus in agris, | qui regeret certis finibus arua, lapis.*

Both Virgil and Ovid, by contrast, draw attention to *limites* in the heroic era (*A.* 12.898): *limes agro positus litem ut discerneret aruis*; (*Met.* 1.136 [reversing the force of this line]): *cautus humum longo signauit limite mensor.*

43–4. non freta demisso uerrebant eruta remo:
ultima mortali tum uia litus erat.

To round off this phase of the argument the speaker invokes one of the most familiar golden age tropes, the absence of navigation. For Roman authors from Catullus onwards the invention of sailing and Argo's voyage constitute a pivotal moment marking the end of the golden age. See Tib. 1.3.37–40, Hor. *Carm.* 1.3.9–24, *Am.* 2.11.1–6, *Met.* 1.94–96. For later authors see Davis (2010).

43. For this verbal pattern (AbVaB) see above on 3.6.56.

uerrebant: Although *uerro* is regularly used of sailing (e.g. Enn. *Ann.* 14.377 Goldberg and Manuwald [1]): *uerrunt extemplo placidum mare, A.* 3.208: *et caerula uerrunt*), the context suggests allusion to Catul. 64.7 (of the Argonauts): *caerula uerrentes abiegnis aequora palmis.*

eruta: A verb with forceful overtones, used of uprooting trees (*TLL* 844.23–38) and destroying cities (*TLL* 845.70–846.6), *eruo* here suggests the violence involved in sailing. See also *Her.* 5.54: *et remis eruta canet aqua.*

44. The idea that golden age humans went no further than the seashore seems to be an Ovidian innovation. See also *Met.* 1.96: *nullaque mortales praeter sua litora* *norant.* Seneca develops the idea at *Med.* 331–2: *sua quisque piger litora tangens | patrioque senex factus in aruo.*

45–6. contra te sollers, hominum natura, fuisti
et nimium damnis ingeniosa tuis.

From reworking of golden age tropes, the lover turns to angry rebuke of human nature.

45. sollers: A contemptuous term to use of a grand philosophical abstraction. Elsewhere in *Amores* it is used only of enslaved women (1.8.87, 2.7.17, 2.19.41).

Fast. 3.839–40: *capitale uocamus | ingenium sollers* implies that *sollers* is not a particularly flattering compliment because, with very few exceptions, *capitalis* is a pejorative term.

hominum natura: For similar indignant apostrophes addressed to an abstraction see e.g. *A.* 3.56–7: *quid non mortalia pectora cogis, | auri sacra fames*, *Met.* 13.517: *quo me seruas, annosa senectus.* For discussion see Hampel (1908: 19–20). For other forms of apostrophe in *Amores* see above on 3.2.27–8.

The concept of 'human nature' (*hominum natura/natura humana*) is frequent in moralizing discourses, particularly in the philosophical works of Cicero and Seneca. In Seneca's *Phaedra*, a play in which nature is a central concept (Davis [1983], Boyle [1997b: 60–7]), both the chorus (959) and Theseus (1116) apostrophize *natura*.

46. Ovid reworks this line when writing of his own situation (*Tr.* 2.342): *inque meas poenas ingeniosus eram.* See also *Ib.* 188: *Aeacus in poenas ingeniosus erit.*

ingeniosa: For this adjective see above on line 8.

47–8. quo tibi turritis incingere moenibus urbes?
quo tibi discordes addere in arma manus?

Now follow passionate questions (repeated *quo tibi* suggests vehemence) addressed to 'human nature'.

47. quo tibi: For omission of the main verb to suggest urgency (something like *necesse est* is needed to complete the sense) see above on 3.4.41. For insistent repetition of *quo* see 3.7.49: *quo mihi fortunae tantum? quo regna sine usu?*

turritis: The use of defensive towers suggests instability and danger. For *turritus* of fortifications see e.g. *Pont.* 3.4.105 (for an imagined triumph): *oppida turritis cingantur eburnea muris*, Luc. 6.39–40 (Caesar at Dyrrachium): *pandit fossas turritaque summis | disponit castella iugis.*

incingere moenibus urbes: Recalls Virgil's description of the world's slow reversion to the golden age (*Ecl.* 4.32–3): *quae cingere muris | oppida.* Ovid varies the idea at *Met.* 1.97: *nondum praecipites cingebant oppida fossae.*

48. The Teacher takes an opposed stance in *Ars*, advising his students to be energetic when young (2.672–4): *aut fera belligeras addite in arma manus, | aut latus et uires operamque adferte puellis: | hoc quoque militia est.*

addere...manus: For the phrase, 'an Ovidian idiom' (Heyworth [2019: 144]), see 1.7.1: *adde manus in uincla meas*, *Ars* 2.672 (quoted above), *Fast.* 3.306: *uinclaque sopitas addit in arta manus*. Cf. *Met.* 7.788: *dum digitos amentis addere tempto*.

discordes...manus: The phrase is striking because we expect *discors* to be applied to *arma* e.g. *G.* 2.459: *quibus ipsa procul discordibus armis*, Tib. 2.3.37: *praeda feras acies cinxit discordibus armis*, Stat. *Theb.* 11.100–1: *ipsae discordibus armis | aptemur*. It suggests, as Putnam [1973: p. 171] observes, civil war.

49–50. quid tibi cum pelago? terra contenta fuisses.
   cur non et caelum tertia regna facis?
While the questions continue, the tone changes from passionate urgency to exasperation and sarcasm.

49. quid tibi cum pelago? For this idiom, an 'expression of impatience and disgust' (McKeown [1998: 431]), see 1.7.27: *quid mihi uobiscum, caedis scelerumque ministrae?*, 2.19.57: *quid mihi cum facili, quid cum lenone marito?* For the variation *nihil mihi cum* see above on 3.2.48.

terra contenta fuisses: Draws on a distinction made by Varro (*R.* 3.3.3, 3.10.1) between land-loving and amphibious birds. Humans should resemble peacocks and doves, not geese and ducks.

50. Having spoken of land and sea, the speaker now resorts to scorn and raises a third possibility: Why not try to rule the sky? For the folly of humans attempting flight see Hor. *Carm.* 1.3.34–8: *expertus uacuum Daedalus aera | pinnis non homini datis |... caelum ipsum petimus stultitia*.

tertia regna: Normally used of the underworld (*Fast.* 4.584, [Tib.] 3.5.22, Sil. 8.116), the phrase recalls the division of the world between Jupiter, Neptune, and Pluto. But if the gods were willing to share, human nature apparently aspires to rule all three available realms.

regna facis: This, the reading of S, is printed by most modern editors. P and Y offer *dona facis*. *dona* makes no sense in this context. Before Riese (1871) editors printed *regna petis*, *petis* being found as a suggestion in Y and lesser manuscripts. *facis* has the advantage of being found in P, S, and Y.

51–2. qua licet, affectas caelum quoque: templa Quirinus
   Liber et Alcides et modo Caesar habent.
But in fact some humans have aspired to heaven and have become divine. For the deifications of Quirinus, Liber, Hercules, and (Augustus) Caesar see Hor. *Carm.* 3.3.9–16.

Ehwald (1903: XII) declared these lines suspect. Here is his 'argument' in full: '51 sq. suspectae fidei mihi videntur'. Kenney agreed, citing as evidence Luc. 3.110, a line which links Julius Caesar's apotheosis with tyranny (3.109–11): *sedere patres censere parati, | si regnum, si templa sibi iugulumque senatus | exiliumque petat.* This couplet constitutes the climax of this section of the lover's argument. It is found in all manuscripts and should not be excised because editors dislike its political implications.

51. affectas caelum: Elsewhere Ovid uses this language of the giants' impious assault on the gods. See *Met.* 1.152: *affectasse ferunt regnum caeleste gigantas, Fast.* 3.439–40, *Pont.* 4.8.59. For the argument to work it must be equally pejorative here.

Quirinus: For the identification of Quirinus with the deified Romulus see e.g. Enn. *Ann.* 1.100 (Goldberg and Manuwald [1]; with Skutsch [1985: 245–6]), *A.* 1.292: *Remo cum fratre Quirinus, Fast.* 2.475–6: *at tertia dicta Quirino, | qui tenet hoc nomen (Romulus ante fuit).*

The temple of Quirinus, located on the Quirinal hill, held an image of Romulus and Remus taking the auspices in its pediment. It was restored by Augustus in 16 BCE. For details see Coarelli (2007: 233–4) and Cooley (2009: 190 [on *RG* 19.2]).

52. Liber et Alcides: Liber, an Italian god whom the Romans identified with Dionysus (*OLD* 1), and Hercules are commonly linked as divinities who had not always been gods. See e.g. Cic. *Leg.* 2.19.11, *Tusc.* 1.28.6, *N. D.* 2.62.8, Tac. *Ann.* 4.38.17–19: 'To be sure the best of mortals hold the loftiest ambitions: thus Hercules and Liber among the Greeks and Quirinus among us, have been added to the company of gods'.

Caesar: The temple of the deified Julius Caesar, at the eastern end of the Roman forum, was decreed in 42 and dedicated on 18 August 29 BCE. For details see Coarelli (2007: 79) and Cooley (2009: 185 [on *RG* 19.1]).

The inclusion of the *princeps*' adoptive father in a list of those who resembled the impious giants shocks. But it should not surprise because it is consistent with Ovid's treatment of the Julian family and its legend in this collection and elsewhere. For the politics of *Amores* see Davis (2006: 71–84) and Introduction §9.

53–4. eruimus terra solidum pro frugibus aurum.
   possidet inuentas sanguine miles opes.
In this final phase of the argument the lover turns from concern with the past (35–43) and criticism of human nature (44–56) to moralizing about the present and concern for his own situation.

53. For the absence of mining in the age of Saturn see above on 35–8. The choice of the present tense (*eruimus*) immediately marks a contrast between an idealized past and now.

eruimus: For the violent connotations of this verb see above on 43. This seems to be the first use of *eruo* for mining (*OLD* 1b, *TLL* 844.38–47). Cf. Luc. 4.223–4: *non chalybem gentes penitus fugiente metallo | eruerent*.

solidum...aurum: For the association between solid gold and wealth see e.g. Sen. *Ep.* 5.3.2 (of the philosophical mean): *non habeamus argentum in quod solidi auri caelatura descenderit*, Sil. 16.175 (of *ditissimus* Syphax): *nec foret aut ebore aut solido qui uinceret auro*.

54. inuentas sanguine miles opes: This may refer to the dangers involved in mining gold or to the means by which soldiers acquire their wealth (as in 10).

55–6. curia pauperibus clausa est, dat census honores;
   inde grauis iudex, inde seuerus eques.
Now follows moralizing based on the reality of Roman politics: there was a property qualification for membership of the senatorial and equestrian orders.

55. curia pauperibus clausa est: This is simple fact. Suetonius (*Aug.* 41.1) and Dio (54.17.3) report that Augustus raised the property qualification for membership of the senatorial order to a million or more sesterces. Whatever the precise figure, it was, in Talbert's (1984: 47) words, 'a colossal sum'.

dat census honores: For identical words and similar moralizing see Janus' discourse (*Fast.* 1.217–18): *dat census honores, | census amicitias; pauper ubique iacet*. See also *Ars* 2.277–8: *plurimus auro | uenit honos*, Sen. *Con.* 2.1.17.12: *census senatorium gradum ascendit*, Plin. *Nat.* 14.5.2: *postquam senator censu legi coeptus*.

honores: Not only esteem, but high political office e.g. *Fast.* 3.420: *accessit titulis pontificalis honor*, *Pont.* 4.4.25: *purpura Pompeium summi uelabit honoris*.

56. inde: Repetition of the adverb underlines the connection between wealth and legal status.

grauis iudex: For gravitas as an expected judicial attribute see e.g. Cic. *Flac.* 98.14: *semper graues et sapientes iudices in rebus iudicandis*, *Ars* 1.461: *quam populus iudexque grauis lectusque senatus*, Fro. *Aurel.* 2.1.2.4: *in omnibus causis iustum te et grauem et sanctum iudicem exhibuisti*. The speaker's point, however, is that wealth is no guarantee of judicial gravity.

seuerus eques: Nor does it guarantee legal strictness. For the prized *seueritas* of equestrian jurors see Davenport (2019: 77).

57–8. omnia possideant. illis Campusque forumque
   seruiat, hi pacem crudaque bella gerant.
But these things don't matter. The wealthy are welcome to their control of political office, the law, and matters of peace and war.

57. possideant: For a similarly dismissive use of the jussive subjunctive see e.g. Lucr. 3.135: *quidquid id est habeant*; Prop. 4.7.93: *nunc te possideant aliae*; Mart. 6.86.5: *possideat Lybicas messis*.

Campus: For the Campus Martius as the site for elections to senior magistracies (*honores* 55) see e.g. Hor. *Carm*. 3.1.11: *descendat in Campum petitor*, Luc. 1.180: *annua uenali referens certamina Campo*.

forumque: Important as (among other things) the site of the law courts (*grauis iudex, seuerus eques*).

58. seruiat: Draws out the implication of *possideant*: ownership of politics and the courts by the rich means that they are enslaved to their interests.

pacem…bella gerant: While *bellum gerere* is standard (*TLL gero* 1942.83–1943.54), and while *pax* and *bellum* are often paired as opposites, the combination *pacem gerere* is striking. See Sall. *Iug*. 46.8.3: *pacem an bellum gerens*, *A*. 7.444 (with Horsfall [2000: ad loc.], who notes the zeugma): *bella uiri pacemque gerent quis bella gerenda*, 9.279: *seu pacem seu bella geram*.

crudaque bella: This is a more powerful expression than the conventional *bellum crudele* (e.g. Cic. *Catil*. 3.25.10, *Pis*. 84.12, *Att*. 9.6.7.4; *A*. 8.146, 11.535), *crudus* connoting not just cruelty but primitive savagery (*TLL* 1236.16–76, *OLD* 2, 7).

59–60. tantum ne nostros auidi liceantur amores,
   et (satis est) aliquid pauperis esse sinant.
But the wealthy should restrict their control to public life and not interfere in the erotic lives of the poor.

59. auidi: While *census* (55), denoting wealth and/or socio-legal status, is a morally neutral term, *auidi* is not. Once the rich harm the speaker's interests they are described as 'greedy'.

liceantur: Perhaps because it is explicitly commercial, the verb is rare in verse. But see 1.10.30 (with Kenney [1966: 269]), Pers. 5.191.

First printed by Heinsius, *liceantur* is the universally accepted correction of unintelligible readings in the major manuscripts (P: *liciantur*; S: *uicientur*; Y: *liciantur* [corrected to *liceantur*]). Before Heinsius editors printed *lucrentur*.

60. pauperis: Parenthetic *satis est* suggests that the poor want only one thing: freedom from competition in their love lives. Clearly *pauper* is being used in that sense peculiar to elegiac poets (see introduction above).

amores: For *amores* used of the beloved see e.g. Catul. 45.1–2: *Acmen Septimius, suos amores, | tenens in gremio*; Prop. 4.4.37 (Hutchinson [2006: ad loc.]: 'perhaps rather colloquial'): *ille equus, ille meos in castra reponet amores*; *Met*. 4.137 (Thisbe sees Pyramus): *sed postquam remorata suos cognouit amores*.

61-2. at nunc, exaequet tetricas licet illa Sabinas,
  imperat ut captae qui dare multa potest.

From moral stricture the lover turns to jaundiced description of the present: rich men can control any woman they want.

61. tetricas: See above on 3.3.36.

Sabinas: As embodiments of traditional morality, the Sabine women are treated negatively in *Amores*. For Dipsas they are *immundae* (1.8.39), for the lover *rigidae* (2.4.15).

62. qui dare multa potest: Quotes Prop. 2.26b.28: *qui dare multa potest, multa et amare potest*. Quotation underlines difference. The Propertian lover argues that money has no power because (a) his girlfriend prefers poetry to wealth (25): *nam mea cum recitat, dicit se odisse beatos*; and (b) wealthy lovers are likely to prove unreliable (28): *multa et amare potest*. (For a similar claim see Prop. 1.8b.37-8.) In *Am*. 3.8, however, money captures and enslaves even women of Sabine virtue. (For discussion see Morgan [1977: 93-4]).

63-4. me prohibet custos, in me timet illa maritum.
  si dederim, tota cedet uterque domo.

A woman's protectors invoke morality only when dealing with people like me; if a lover offers gifts, they set aside morality and vacate the house.

63. For the complaint that money gives access see *PA* 5.30.3-4: ἢν μὲν γὰρ τὸ χάραγμα φέρῃς, φίλος· οὔτε θυρωρὸς | ἐν ποσὶν οὔτε κύων ἐν προθύροις δέδεται ('If you carry coin, she loves you; there is no doorkeeper before you, no dog chained in the doorway').

me…in me: The placing of *me* at the beginning of the line and immediately after the main caesura suggests a degree of self-pity.

custos: For the *custos* see above on 3.1.55 and 3.4.1.

in me: For this use of *in* plus the ablative see *OLD* 42 ('when dealing with', i.e. 'in the case of') and *TLL* 780-81.37 (in *occasionis*); e.g. Prop. 2.20.11: *in te ego et aeratas rumpam, mea uita, catenas*, *Met*. 6.116, *Fast*. 6.576 (of Fortune).

timet illa maritum: For a wife's fear of her husband see above on 3.4.32.

64. si dederim: Here the lover complains that a husband has taken the advice that he (or another lover) gave earlier (3.4.47-8): *sic poteris…| et, quae non dederis, multa uidere domi*.

65-6. o si neglecti quisquam deus ultor amantis
  tam male quaesitas puluere mutet opes!

The poem closes with the wish that some god might change his rival's wealth to dust.

65. si: For the omission of the verb in a condition (in each case a form of *esse* that is easily supplied) see 1.3.7, 3.6.89 (with note above), *Her.* 10.143, 13.166, *Ars* 1.595.

quisquam: The adjective, along with the implied *sit*, suggests that there is no such god.

66. male quaesitas: The phrase implies wrongful acquisition at the least (*Her.* 6.93), if not outright theft (e.g. Liv. 1.49.2.3, *Dig.* 16.3.31). Here it suggests merely the speaker's distaste at the source of his rival's wealth.

3.9: LAMENT FOR TIBULLUS

Greeks and Romans believed that the elegiac metre was originally associated with grief.[1] Horace, for example, underlines the connection (*Ars* 75): *uersibus impariter iunctis querimonia primum* ('lament first belonged to unequally joined verses'), as does Ovid's Sappho (*Her.* 15.7): *flendus amor meus est: elegeia flebile carmen* ('My love merits mourning: elegy is a song of mourning').[2] And the exiled Ovid presents the medium as particularly appropriate to his condition (*Tr.* 5.1.5–6): *flebilis ut noster status est, ita flebile carmen, | materiae scripto conueniente suae* ('As my state is mournful, so is my poetry mournful: my writing matches my subject matter'). As in 2.6, Ovid here takes the form back to its supposed origins.

It is not surprising that this lament for a dead person has elements in common with actual epitaphs and with more literary commemorations of the dead. Funerary inscriptions, for example, regularly include praise of the deceased's accomplishments and a prayer that the earth lie lightly upon them.[3] Not surprisingly, however, 3.9 has more in common with 2.6, Ovid's requiem for a parrot. In both poems the speaker summons mourners to attend, complains of fate's injustice, lists the subject's achievements, describes their death and burial, and imagines their afterlife.[4]

Closer in tone and subject matter, however, are two Hellenistic dirges: Bion's *Lament for Adonis* and [Moschus'] *Lament for Bion*.[5] The *Lament for Adonis* focuses not only on the mythical lad's death and Aphrodite's distress, but also, by means of shifting refrains, evokes the ritual associated with the Adonia festival.[6] More complex and more important is [Moschus'] *Lament for Bion*: more complex

---

[1] For discussion of the Greek belief that the elegiac couplet was originally used for lament see Harvey (1955: 170–2). Ennius introduced elegiacs to Rome (Isid. *Orig.* 1.39.15). All of his surviving couplets concern death (Goldberg and Manuwald [2: 228–36]).
[2] The precise wording of the text is disputed. I quote from Knox's (1995) edition.
[3] For these see Lattimore (1962: 65–73, 285–90).
[4] For detailed comparison of these two poems see Thomas (1965a).
[5] It is generally agreed that the *Lament for Bion* attributed to Moschus cannot have been written by him. Moschus is dated to the mid-second century BCE, while Bion belongs to the late second century. For convenience the author is usually referred to as [Moschus].
[6] For the connection between the *Lament* and the festival see Reed (1997a: 16–17).

because it widens the focus from the deceased and the bereaved; more important for readers of 3.9 because it emphasizes Bion's status as a poet and his place in a poetic tradition.[7]

Ovid and [Moschus] employ similar strategies. First, [Moschus] honours Bion as both a poet: καλὸς τέθνακε μελικτάς ('A fine/handsome singer has died' 7) and as a character from one of his own poems: Βίων τέθνακεν ὁ βουκόλος ('Bion the oxherd has died' 11); second, he pays tribute to a pastoral poet through the use of pastoral tropes: calling upon the natural world to mourn, for example, and employing a refrain characteristic of pastoral lament (line 8 and 13 more times):[8] 'Begin, Sicilian Muses, begin the dirge'; and, third, he engages with Bion's *Adonis*. Reed (1997b: 264) notes that [Moschus] uses ὦ τριπόθητε ('O triply desirable' 51) to allude to *Adonis* 58 and that he refers to the subject matter of Bion's poem (68–9): 'And Cypris kissed you much more than the kiss she kissed Adonis just now dead'. In the same way, *Am.* 3.9 focuses on Tibullus both as a poet, the *uates* whose body burns on a funeral pyre (5–6, 41–2), and as the lover of Delia in his first book of elegies and Nemesis in the second (31–2, 53–8); he also honours Tibullus the love poet by associating him with erotic predecessors like Calvus, Catullus, and Gallus (61–4); and he engages closely with Tibullus' poetry,[9] so closely that Bretzigheimer can fairly claim that the poem's 'reality is constructed from Tibullus' fantasies about his death'[10] and that Oliensis can call it 'a veritable pastiche of Tibullan phrases and scenes'.[11] But Ovid goes further than this, alluding not only to Tibullus, but to 3.9's Greek models, to Bion's *Adonis* and [Moschus'] *Lament for Bion*. He refers, for example, to the Adonis myth (16) and employs a Greek cry of anguish *aelinon* (23), which happens to be the first word of [Moschus'] *Lament*: αἴλινά μοι στοναχεῖτε νάπαι ('Cry *aelina*, you groves').[12]

In a book framed by poems reflecting on the elegiac genre, Ovid now offers the first of a series of reflections on his elegiac predecessors. Here he meditates on Tibullus, focusing on two of his major obsessions: love and death. Soon he will engage with Catullus (3.11) and Propertius (3.12).

Secondary literature: Thomas (1965a), (1965b); Taylor (1970); Frécaut (1972: 340–5); McLennan (1972); Morgan (1977: 94–6); Cahoon (1984); Cornacchia (1989); Kenney (in Melville [1989: xix, 208–9]); Perkins (1993); Boyd (1997: 181–9); Reed (1997b); Perkins (2000); Bretzigheimer (2001: 180–2); Williams (2003); Huskey (2005); Ramsby (2005); Maltby (2009); Thorsen (2014: 166–70); de Vasconcellos (2017); Oliensis (2019: 23–30, 90–8); Ingleheart (2021).

---

[7] For Ovid's debt to these two poems see Reed's valuable study (1997b).
[8] Cf. the use of refrains in Thyrsis' poem on the death of Daphnis (Theoc. 1.64 and 18 more times) and the repeated phrase ἀπώλετο καλὸς Ἄδωνις ('handsome Adonis has died') in Bion's *Lament for Adonis* (1 and five more times).
[9] For details see the Commentary below.
[10] Bretzigheimer (2001: 180–2).
[11] Oliensis (2019: 92).
[12] For further details see the Commentary below.

Commentary, 9.1

1-4. Memnona si mater, mater plorauit Achillem
   et tangunt magnas tristia fata deas,
flebilis indignos, Elegeia, solue capillos:
   a, nimis ex uero nunc tibi nomen erit.

Ovid's lament for Tibullus begins in a surprising way. First, he starts with a puzzle, withholding the name of the person to be mourned until line 5. Bion, by contrast, names Adonis twice in line 1 and [Moschus] names Bion in line 2, while 'parrot' is the first word of *Am*. 2.6. Even Virgil's poem on Gallus' quasi-death, with its enigmatic apostrophe to Arethusa (*Ecl*. 10.1), names the love elegist in line 2. Second, the speaker addresses not a divinity like Aphrodite (Bion 3) or the plants and animals that knew him ([Moschus] 1–18), but a personification of the genre to which Tibullus and Ovid were committed.

1. Memnona si mater, mater plorauit Achillem: Boyd (1997: 180) observes that this line is 'a gem of design: the heroes' names in first and last position (emphasized by the postponement of *si*) and the repetition of *mater* at the major caesura give the line an elegant balance'. (For repetition used to frame the main caesura see on 3.2.32; for balance at the main caesura more generally see on 3.7.37.) Note too the employment of chiasmus (ab/ba) and the predominance of spondees (DSSS). Particularly striking is what we could call either the twofold use of ellipse, with the verb being omitted from the first clause and the conjunction *si* from the second; or the *apo koinou* ('in common') construction, with each half of the line 'sharing' *si* and *plorauit*.

For similarly brilliant use of the double ellipse/*apo koinou* construction see *Her*. 2.26: *uela queror reditu, uerba carere fide*. Here too we have balance at the main caesura, with *carere* missing from the first clause (highlighted by the ablative *reditu*) and *queror* missing from the second. Here too there is chiasmus, though of a different kind, with *uela...uerba* reversing the word order of the previous line (*uerba et uela dedisti*). For discussion of the *apo koinou* construction see Mayer (1994: 25–8); for its use in Ovid see Kenney (2002: 73). For other examples in the erotic works see 1.2.48, 1.4.18, 1.6.60, 1.13.21, 1.14.53, 1.15.29, *Her*. 10.60, 11.70, 114, 13.104, 14.86, 19.74, *Ars* 2.36, 73, 3.300.

Memnona...mater: For Aurora's grief for Memnon, one of Achilles' victims, see *Met*. 13.576–622. The story is at least as old as the *Aethiopis* (7C BCE?). (For the date see West [2003a]; for text and translation see West [2003b] *Arg*. 2). For Aurora as Memnon's mother see 1.8.3–4, 1.13.3–4, *Fast*. 4.713–14, *Pont*. 1.4.57–8.

mater...Achillem: Thetis is a conspicuous mourner in the *Iliad*, most notably at 18.35–64, when she leads the dirge for Patroclus, and at 24.85–6, when she mourns Achilles' imminent death: κλαῖε μόρον οὗ παιδὸς ἀμύμονος, ὅς οἱ ἔμελλε | φθίσεσθ' ἐν Τροίῃ ἐριβώλακι τηλόθι πάτρης ('She was weeping for the fate of her blameless son who was destined to perish in fertile Troy far from his fatherland'). Her mourning for her dead son formed part of the *Aethiopis* (West [2003b] *Arg*. 4).

252   Commentary

2. For this verbal pattern (VabBA) in *Amores* see above on 3.1.11.

3. flebilis: The adjective is of course particularly associated with death and funerals. See e.g. *Her.* 12.140 (Medea speaking of the songs for Jason's wedding): *at mihi funerea flebiliora tuba, Met.* 11.52–3 (of Orpheus): *flebile nescio quid queritur lyra, flebile lingua | murmurat exanimis, respondent flebile ripae.*

Elegeia: For the spelling see above on 3.1.7.

indignos...capillos: The transferred epithet (enallage/hypallage; it is Elegy, not her hair, who does not deserve this suffering) suggests pathos. For enallage's association with pathos in *Aeneid* see Conte (2007: Chapter 3).

For *indignus* used of parts of the body in contexts of mourning see *Met.* 4.138 (Thisbe), *Met.* 10.723 (Venus sees Adonis dying), *Tr.* 1.3.18 (Ovid's wife on the poet's last night in Rome): *imbre per indignas usque cadente genas.* Cf. *Epic. Drusi* (*Consolation to Livia*) 40: *indignas, Liuia, solue comas.*

solue capillos: Alludes perhaps to Tibullus' request that Delia not behave in the conventional manner at his funeral (1.1.67–8): *tu manes ne laede meos, sed parce solutis | crinibus et teneris, Delia, parce genis.*

Plutarch (*Quaest. Rom.* 267A) treats the loosening of female hair as a Roman funerary practice. See e.g. *Ars* 3.431–2 (on picking up men at funerals): *ire solutis | crinibus et fletus non tenuisse decet.* Poets also attribute it to the Trojans e.g. Catul. 64.350, *A.* 3.65, 11.35, Sen. *Tro.* 85, 99.

4. Alludes to the belief that 'elegy' (ἐλεγεία *elegeia*) derives from the sounds of grief. Porphyrio (on Hor. *Carm.* 1.33.2) claims that 'elegiac verses are particularly suited to lament, and for that reason he calls them *miserabiles.* For they think that the very name of elegy comes from ἒ ἒ ('e e'), the sound made by mourners'. Other etymologies were available (see Maltby [1991: 201–2]): 'elegy' was said to be derived from εὖ λέγειν (*eu legein* 'speak well' i.e. of the dead) or τοῦ ἐλέου (*tou eleou* 'pity').

ex uero nunc tibi nomen: For the use of *nomen* when drawing attention to etymology see e.g. 1.8.3 (of Dipsas, 'thirsty') *ex re nomen habet, Met.* 13.569–70 (of Cynossema, 'the dog's tomb'): *locus exstat et ex re | nomen habet, Fast.* 2.859 (with Robinson [2011: ad loc.]): *ex uero positum permansit Equirria nomen.*

5–6. ille tui uates operis, tua fama, Tibullus
 ardet in exstructo corpus inane rogo.
After a highly rhetorical build-up, the speaker finally names Tibullus as the person who has died and pictures his funeral.

5. uates: For this term see on 3.1.19. While it is a standard word for a poet in *Amores*, elsewhere in Ovid it can have grander connotations. It is used, for example, of mythological figures like Orpheus (e.g. *Met.* 10.89), of Virgil as author of *Aeneid* (*Pont.* 3.4.84), and of himself as Hesiodic poet of the Roman calendar (e.g.

Fast. 1.101, 3.177). In this context grander connotations are appropriate. See also lines 17, 26, and 29 below. Tibullus uses it of a poet (himself) only once (2.5.113–14): *at tu, nam diuum seruat tutela poetas, praemoneo, | uati parce, puella, sacro.*

operis: For *opus* as 'genre' see on 3.1.6.

tua fama: For *fama* used of a person see e.g. Prop. 1.15.22 (of Evadne): *Argiuae fama pudicitiae*, Mart. 11.9.1 (of a poet): *Romani fama cothurni.*

6. For this verbal pattern (VaBbA) see above on 3.1.7.

This line reworks (or is reworked by) *Her.* 15.116: *portet ad exstructos corpus inane rogos.* For discussion of the connections between 3.9 and *Her.* 15 see Thorsen (2014: 166–70).

ille...Tibullus: Use of *ille* enables Ovid to frame the line with reference to his predecessor. (For similar framing see *A.* 5.609–10 [Iris]: *illa...|...uirgo*, Prop. 2.8.29: *ille etiam abrepta desertus coniuge Achilles*, *Am.* 3.6.39: *ille fluens diues septena per ostia Nilus.*) It also underlines the earlier poet's importance. For this use of *ille* (OLD 4b) see e.g. *Her.* 6.152: *Iuppiter ille*, *Met.* 1.79: *ille opifex rerum.*

corpus inane: This is shorthand for *animae corpus inane.* See e.g. Prop. 3.18.32, *Met.* 2.611, 13.488: *quae corpus complexa animae tam fortis inane.* Ovid uses the briefer expression at *Her.* 15.116, *Pont.* 1.10.22, *Ib.* 152.

7–8. **ecce, puer Veneris fert euersamque pharetram**
   et fractos arcus et sine luce facem.
If the previous line led readers to expect a realistic account of Tibullus' funeral, this couplet and those following establish that Ovid's prime concern is with imagining the kind of procession that might suit a love poet. This baroque confection is closer to Cupid's triumph in 1.2 than to real life.

7. **ecce:** For *ecce* used to mark transitions see above on 3.8.9.

euersamque pharetram: Amor's upside-down quiver reflects Roman funerary practice. See e.g. *A.* 11.93 (Pallas' funeral): *Tyrrhenique omnes et uersis Arcades armis.* Servius (ad loc.) notes that 'our ancestors used to do everything the wrong way round at a funeral'. For fasces reversed see e.g. *Epic. Drusi* (*Consolation to Livia*) (141–2): *quos primum uidi fasces, in funere uidi, | et uidi euersos indiciumque mali*, Tac. *Ann.* 3.2.5 (Germanicus' funeral): *praecedebant incompta signa, uersi fasces.* For reversal of norms as a key element in Roman funeral rites see Scheid (1984).

8. Alludes to Tib. 2.6.15–16: *acer Amor, fractas utinam, tua tela, sagittas, | si licet, extinctas aspiciamque faces.* The broken bow and arrows also reflect Roman practice. See e.g. *Epic. Drusi* 177: *consul init fractis maerentem fascibus urbem.* Both Tibullus and Ovid Romanize elements from Bion's *Adonis* (80–2): 'Weeping

254   *Commentary*

around him, the Loves groan aloud, cutting their hair for Adonis; one threw on arrows, one a bow, one a feather, another a quiver'.

9–12. aspice, demissis ut eat miserabilis alis
   pectoraque infesta tundat aperta manu.
excipiunt lacrimas sparsi per colla capilli
   oraque singultu concutiente sonant.
Continuing with the focus on Amor, the speaker draws attention to the god's appearance and behaviour: his wings and hair, his breast-beating and his sobs.

9. This is the last line for which we have the evidence of manuscript S (Cod. Sang. 864).

aspice: Singles out a particularly important figure. Cf. the beginning of Anchises' lament for Marcellus (*A.* 6.855–6): *aspice, ut insignis spoliis Marcellus opimis | ingreditur.*

demissis...alis: Perhaps recalls the association between grief and letting down one's hair e.g. *Her.* 10.137: *aspice demissos lugentis more capillos*, Prop. 2.24.52, Sen. *Tro.* 100.

miserabilis: Recalls the elegiac lover's conventional pose as *miser* (e.g. Tib. 1.2.91, Prop. 1.1.1, Ov. *Am.* 1.1.25: *me miserum! certas habuit puer ille sagittas*); and perhaps (though not without irony) Horace's description of Tibullus' poems as *miserabilis...elegos* (*Carm.* 1.33.2–3).

10. For this verbal pattern (AbVaB) in *Amores* see above on 3.6.56.

pectoraque...aperta: For the association between bare chests and mourning see e.g. 3.6.58, *Her.* 12.153, and *Met.* 2.339, 13.688–9: *apertae pectora matres | significant luctum.*

tundat: Suggests a more vigorous beating of the breast than the usual *plango*. See *A.* 1.481, 11.37–8, *Ars* 1.535 (Ariadne): *iamque iterum tundens mollissima pectora palmis*, *Met.* 8.536 (Meleager's sisters): *immemores decoris liuentia pectora tundunt.*

infesta...manu: Sometimes denoting outright hostility (e.g. Sen. *Thy.* 739 [Atreus killing Thyestes' third son]), the phrase here suggests Cupid's anger and the ferocity with which he pounds his breast.

11. excipiunt lacrimas: For *excipio* used of the absorption of liquid (as opposed to, say, collection in a *patera*) see e.g. *Met.* 9.131 (of Nessus' blood). Examples are collected at *TLL* 1253.51–70.

sparsi per colla capilli: For flowing hair as a sign of distress or mourning see e.g. *Her.* 15.73: *iacent collo sparsi sine lege capilli*, Sen. *Tro.* 85: *per colla fluant maesta capilli.*

12. singultu concutiente: Often used of powerful physical forces, *concutio* here suggests the intensity of Cupid's sorrow. For its use in connection with death see *Fast.* 2.846 (of dying Lucretia): *uisaque concussa dicta probare coma*, Stat. *Silu.* 5.1.179–80 (to a bereaved husband): *parce precor lacrimis, saeuo ne concute planctu | pectora.*

13–14. fratris in Aeneae sic illum funere dicunt
   egressum tectis, pulcher Iule, tuis.
The speaker now turns to simile, likening Amor's reaction to Tibullus' death to his response to that of Aeneas.

13. One implication of Aeneas' descent from Venus is that Rome's ultimate founder is Cupid's half-brother. Some Augustan poets seem to take the idea seriously (e.g. Tib. 2.5.39, Virg. *A.* 1.667). Ovid's Dido employs it sarcastically (*Her.* 7.31–2): *durumque amplectere fratrem, | frater Amor, castris militet ille tuis*, while the Exile's tone, when addressing Amor, is hard to gauge (*Pont.* 3.3.62): *ab Aenea est qui tibi fratre tuus.*

The simile surprises because while poets refer to Aeneas' apotheosis, they do not usually speak of his death e.g. Tib. 2.5.43–4: *illic sanctus eris, cum te ueneranda Numici | unda deum caelo miserit indigetem*, *A.* 1.259–60: *sublimemque feres ad sidera caeli | magnanimum Aenean*, *Met.* 14.600–8. Livy (1.2.6), by contrast, is doubtful about the hero's status and speaks of both burial and divinity.

dicunt: As Boyd (1997: 182) notes, this suggests an 'Alexandrian footnote'. If it is, the reference is obscure.

14. pulcher: This is Virgil's standard epithet for Iulus: *A.* 5.570, 7.107, 477–8, 9.293, 310. (When called Ascanius he is most commonly *puer.*)

15–16. nec minus est confusa Venus moriente Tibullo
   quam iuueni rupit cum ferus inguen aper.
For his second simile the speaker turns from Cupid to Venus, this time referring to Adonis' death without actually naming the youth.

15. Reference to the Adonis myth underlines Ovid's exploitation of Hellenistic predecessors, especially Bion's *Adonis*. See introduction, on line 8 above, and on lines 19–20.

It is striking, as McLennan (1972) points out, that this line which names Tibullus employs a third-foot weak caesura (- u // u), a marked feature of Tibullus' verse. Ceccarelli (71; see table 11) calculates that Tibullus employs the third-foot trochaic break in 19.81 per cent of his hexameters; the comparable figure for Ovid's erotic works is 8.68 per cent. See also on line 35 below.

16. For the boar's killing of Adonis see Bion, *Adonis* 7–12 and *Met.* 10.708–39.

17–18. at sacri uates et diuum cura uocamur;
   sunt etiam qui nos numen habere putent.

From the sorrow caused by Tibullus' death, the speaker now turns to the injustice of his fate.

17. Plainly alludes to Tib. 2.5.113–14, a couplet in which (a) he asserts divine concern for poets and (b) the phrase *sacer uates* is used for the first time:

> at tu, nam diuum seruat tutela poetas,
> praemoneo, uati parce, puella, sacro.

The wholly spondaic line (SSSS) perhaps undercuts the speaker's confidence in making this assertion.

sacri: For the sacred status of the *uates* see above on 3.1.19. For the phrase see also Tib. 2.5.114 (quoted above), Hor. *Carm.* 4.9.28: *carent quia uate sacro*, line 41 below, *Ars* 3.539: *insidiae sacris a uatibus absunt*, Calp. *Ecl.* 4.65, VF 6.114. Cf. *Ars* 3.403: *sacris…poetis, Rem.* 813: *reddetis sacro pia uota poetae.*

diuum cura: Rewrites Tibullus' *diuum…tutela*; see also *Ars* 3.405: *cura deum fuerant olim regumque poetae*, [Tib.] 3.4.43–4 (with Fulkerson [2017: ad loc.]): *salue, cura deum: casto nam rite poetae | Phoebusque et Bacchus Pieridesque fauent.*

uocamur: The first person plural implicitly links Ovid with Tibullus as a fellow elegist and poet. See also *nos* in the next line and the poem's conclusion. Note too that the speaker says 'we are called' not 'we are'.

18. The generic subjunctive (*sunt…qui…putent*; Woodcock [§§155–7]) both alludes to authority (i.e. Tibullus) and suggests this speaker's doubt. In *Ars* the Teacher uses the idea to persuade girls to sleep with poets (3.547–8): *uatibus Aoniis faciles estote, puellae: | numen inest illis, Pieridesque fauent.* See also *Fast.* 6.5: *est deus in nobis.*

19–20. scilicet omne sacrum mors importuna profanat,
   omnibus obscuras inicit illa manus.
But if poets are sacred, death violates everything sacred. Reed (1997b: 262) notes that this couplet 'corrects' Tibullus prayer at 1.3.4–5: *abstineas auidas, Mors, modo, nigra, manus. | abstineas, Mors atra, precor.* Bion's *Adonis* is closer to the mark (54–5): 'Persephone, take my husband; for you are much greater than me and everything beautiful rushes down to you'.

19. scilicet: Underlines the logical connection between this couplet and the previous one: if poets are sacred, the death of Tibullus proves that death violates all that we hold sacred.

importuna: Seems an even more powerful denunciatory term than those commonly used of death, terms like *atra, nigra* (Tib. 1.3.4, 5; Sen. *Oed.* 164, Stat. *Theb.* 4.528), *dura* (G. 3.68, A. 10.791, Luc. 6.772), *grauis* (38 below, *Met.* 3.471, Sen. *Thy.* 401), *immatura* (Catul. 96.5, Lucr. 5.221, A. 11.166, Luc. 5.117), and *saeua* (*Tr.* 1.4.27, Sen. *Tro.* 621, Luc. 2.100).

profanat: Underlines the sacrilegious nature of death's action in taking Tibullus. Cf. Dido's attack on Aeneas (*Her.* 7.129): *pone deos et quae tangendo sacra profanas*.

The verb is first used in this sense at Liv. 3.19.7.5 (*profanatis omnibus in cella Iouis optimi maximi*) and here. In earlier texts it means (*OLD* 1): 'to offer (in front of a temple, shrine)'.

20. obscuras...manus: Alludes to Tib. 1.3.4: *abstineas auidas mors modo nigra manus*, with *obscuras* picking up *nigra*. Even closer to Tibullus is *Am.* 2.6.39: *optima prima fere manibus rapiuntur auaris*.

inicit...manus: The phrase has legal overtones (e.g. *Dig.* 2.4.10.1.3). Ovid sometimes uses it of laying claim to a sexual partner (1.4.6, 40, 2.5.30, *Her.* 8.16, 12.158, *Ars* 1.116). Closer to our passage are *A.* 10.419 (of doomed Halaesus; with Servius: *et sermone usus est iuris*): *iniecere manum Parcae*, *Tr.* 3.7.35: *inicietque manum formae damnosa senectus*.

21–2. quid pater Ismario, quid mater profuit Orpheo?
carmine quid uictas obstipuisse feras?
To prove the claim that poets are not immune, the speaker now invokes the archetypal poet: even Orpheus died. It is perhaps not surprising that in a poem concerned with poetic genealogy (esp. 61–6) Ovid highlights the ancestry of each of his three examples, referring to Apollo as father of both Orpheus and Linus, and using a patronymic to designate Homer (25). For the dead poet as Orpheus see also [Moschus] *Lament for Bion* 17–18, 123–4 (Reed [1997b: 266]).

21. Repetition, separation of adjective and noun, and ellipse of the main verb (*profuit* needs to be understood with both *pater* and *mater*) result in a superbly crafted line which is balanced at the main caesura.

quid...profuit: For this question in funereal contexts see Tib. 1.3.23–4, 2.4.51, Prop. 3.18.11 (death of Marcellus), 4.11.11–12 (death of Cornelia). See also 33–4 below.

pater...mater: For Apollo as Orpheus' father see e.g. Pind. *Pyth.* 4.176, Apollod. 1.14.2; for Calliope as Orpheus' mother e.g. *Ecl.* 4.57, [Sen.] *Her. O.* 1034, Apollod. 1.14.2.

Ismario: For the association between Ismarus (a mountain in Thrace) and Orpheus see *Ecl.* 6.30: *nec tantum Rhodope miratur et Ismarus Orphea*, Prop. 2.13.6 (in a couplet which alludes to Orpheus; and in a poem which imagines the poet's funeral): *aut possim Ismaria ducere ualle feras*.

22. For Orpheus' power over nature see Simonides fr. 567 (Campbell [1991]): 'Countless birds used to fly above his head, fish leaped up straight out of the blue water at his lovely song', Aesch. *Ag.* 1629–30: 'You have a tongue opposite to

Orpheus; for he used to lead everything with delight from his voice', G. 4.510: *mulcentem tigris*, Prop. 3.2.3: *Orphea detinuisse feras et concita dicunt*, Ars 3.321: *saxa ferasque lyra mouit Rhodopeius Orpheus*, Met. 11.1–2: *carmine dum tali siluas animosque ferarum* | *Threicius uates et saxa sequentia ducit*.

**23–4. et Linon in siluis idem pater 'aelinon' altis
dicitur inuita concinuisse lyra.**
To the example of Orpheus can be added the case of Linus, a poet of lesser fame but similar ancestry.

23. et Linon…'aelinon': Linus occurs in the description of Achilles' shield at *Il.* 18.570: ἱμερόεν κιθάριζε, Λίνον δ' ὑπὸ καλὸν ἄειδε ('He played the lyre delightfully and accompanied his lovely singing 'Linus'). Coray (2018: 253) notes: 'Linos is a designation for a song…and in post-Homeric sources a mythical figure associated with music'.

Linus' name was thought to derive from the cry of mourning: *aelinon* (Edwards [1991: 225, on *Il.* 18.570]). Pindar makes the connection (fr. 128c.6 Race): ἁ μὲν εὐχαίταν Λίνον αἴλινον ὕμνει ('One sang *aelinos* for lovely-haired Linus'). The cry appears in all three fifth-century tragedians e.g. Aesch. *Ag.* 121 (with Fraenkel [1950: ad loc.]), 139, 159; Soph. *Aj.* 627, *Phil.* 218; Eur. *HF* 348, *Or.* 1395. More importantly for our purposes, it is the first word of [Moschus'] *Lament*: αἴλινά μοι στοναχεῖτε νάπαι ('Cry *aelina*, you groves'). It occurs in Latin only here.

The case for allusion to Prop. 2.13 is strengthened by the fact that Propertius also refers to Orpheus (quoted above on line 21) and Linus in successive couplets (2.13.7–8): *sed magis ut nostro stupefiat Cynthia uersu:* | *tunc ego sim Inachio notior arte Lino*. For discussion see Morgan (1977: 95–7). Virgil also links Orpheus and Linus (*Ecl.* 4.55–7), but not in the context of death. See also Stat. *Silu.* 5.54–5 (with Gibson [2006: ad loc.]).

Like most recent editors I print the reading of Y: *et Linon in siluis idem pater elinon altis*. P also begins with *et Linon*. The penultimate word, however, is hard to decipher. Kenney comments: eunon P (*ut uid.*). Ramirez de Verger (2) prefers Heinsius' emendation: *Aelinon…Aelinon*. Heinsius found the repetition 'charming' (*venusta…repetitione* 286). But etymological play makes the manuscript reading even more attractive.

idem pater: For Apollo as Linus' father see e.g. Theoc. 24.105–6, Paus. 2.19.8.1, Apollod. 1.14.2, *Ecl.* 4.56–7.

24. inuita…lyra: May suggest paternal distress or refer to the tradition that Apollo was responsible for Linus' death (Paus. 9.29.6, Diog. Laert. 1.4.6). For the phrase see Prop. 4.1b.74.

**25–6. adice Maeoniden, a quo ceu fonte perenni
uatum Pieriis ora rigantur aquis.**

Focus now shifts from mythical poets to the founder of the Greco-Roman literary tradition.

25. Maeoniden: The word's patronymic form suggests that Ovid alludes to the tradition that Homer's father was called Maeon. See 1.15.9 (with McKeown [1989: ad loc.]), *Fast.* 2.120, *Tr.* 1.1.47, 2.377, 4.10.22. Maeonides is a common synonym for Homer in the *Greek Anthology* (*PA* 5.30.2; 7.2.2, 15.2, 138.3, 213.8, 674.2; 9.28.6, 97.5, 192.2, 575.5).

Elsewhere Ovid uses *Maeonius* of either Homer or epic verse (*Ars* 2.4, *Rem.* 373, *Tr.* 1.6.21, *Pont.* 3.3.31, 4.12.27; see also Hor. *Carm.* 1.6.2 with Nisbet and Hubbard [1970: ad loc.]). The epithet suggests a connection with Maeonia, an alternative name for Lydia, Smyrna being one of the places that claimed Homer as a native son (e.g. Luc. 9.984 [quoted below on 29], Lucian *Ver. Hist.* 2.20.5).

While Ovid sometimes exploits Homer for humour (e.g. 1.8.61, 3.8.28), he also acknowledges his greatness (1.15.9–10: *uiuet Maeonides, Tenedos dum stabit et Ide, | dum rapidas Simois in mare uoluet aquas, Ars* 3.414, *Rem.* 365, *Tr.* 2.379, *Pont.* 2.10.13).

fonte perenni: The expression is commonly used of literal sources of water (Col. 1.5.1, Curt. 6.6.23, Liv. 1.21.3, Tac. *Hist.* 5.12.3). Metaphorical use is rare: Cic. *Mil.* 34 (of glory), *Her.* 8.64 (of tears). For *perennis* used of works of literature see Catul. 1.10, Hor. *Carm.* 3.30.1, Stat. *Silu.* 5.1.12.

26. The pentameter extends the metaphor by invoking the Pierian springs, a site sacred to the Muses e.g. Stat. *Silu.* 1.2.3–6: *procul ecce canoro | demigrant Helicone deae quatiuntque… | et de Pieriis uocalem fontibus undam,* [Tib.] 3.1.15–16.

uatum: For the connotations of *uates* see above on 3.1.19.

27–8. hunc quoque summa dies nigro submersit Auerno.
 defugiunt auidos carmina sola rogos.
But even if Homer's works constitute an 'unfailing spring', he himself was subject to death.

27. For the reminder that even Homer died see Lucr. 3.1037–8: *quorum unus Homerus | sceptra potitus eadem aliis sopitus quietest.*

summa dies: Used of supreme moments of crisis (e.g. *A.* 2.324–5: *uenit summa dies et ineluctabile tempus | Dardaniae,* Luc. 7.195: *uenit summa dies, geritur res maxima*), the phrase here marks the day of Homer's death.

nigro…Auerno: Avernus is described as *niger* only here and at Stat. *Theb.* 3.146. Darkness, however, is commonly ascribed to the underworld and its god.

28. For this verbal pattern (VaBbA) see on 3.1.7. Ovid reworks this line at *Tr.* 4.10.86: *et gracilis structos effugit umbra rogos.*

260   *Commentary*

The idea that a great poet's works survive has a long history. See e.g. Pind. *Nem.* 4.6: ῥῆμα δ' ἐργμάτων χρονιώτερον βιοτεύει ('The word lives for a longer time than deeds'), Plat. *Symp.* 209d. For Ovid's distinctive take on poetic immortality (viz. that his works will survive his body's annihilation) see 1.15.41–2: *ergo etiam cum me supremus adederit ignis,* | *uiuam, parsque mei multa superstes erit,* Met. 15.873–6, *Tr.* 3.7.50–2. The exiled Ovid alludes to our passage when hoping for complete personal extinction (*Tr.* 3.3.60): *effugiatque auidos pars mihi nulla rogos.* Propertius, at least for the sake of a brilliant poem, disagrees (4.7.2): *luridaque exstructos effugit umbra rogos.*

29–32. durat opus uatum: Troiani fama laboris
   tardaque nocturno tela retexta dolo;
sic Nemesis longum, sic Delia nomen habebunt,
   altera cura recens, altera primus amor.
As proof of the claim that 'poems escape the greedy funeral-pyre', the speaker offers two poets and their two works: Homer's *Iliad* and *Odyssey*, and Tibullus' *Elegies* Book 1 (Delia) and *Elegies* Book 2 (Nemesis).

29. durat opus uatum: Lucan reworks this line when claiming quasi-Homeric status for himself (9.984): *Zmyrnaei durabunt uatis honores.*

Goold's emendation *durant uatis opus* (1965: 54–5; printed in Showerman and Goold) is unnecessary. *uatum* looks back to the previous line's generalization and forward to the particular poets, Homer and Tibullus. P offers: *durus op̌at uatum* (with correction *dur*^{at}); Y: *durat opus uatum*. P's reading is, in Goold's words (55), 'an insignificant spoonerism'.

Troiani fama laboris: Captures the *Iliad*'s title if not its content.

30. Points to the *Odyssey* by referring to one of its most famous stories, Penelope's weaving and unravelling of Laertes' shroud (*Od.* 2.93–110, 19.137–56, 24.129–46). The line reworks Propertius' account of Penelope's trick (2.9.6): *nocturno soluens texta diurna dolo.*

dolo: Recalls the description of Penelope's trick as *dolos* e.g. *Od.* 2.93: ἡ δὲ δόλον τόνδ' ἄλλον ἐνὶ φρεσὶ μερμήριξε ('She devised this other deception [*dolon*] in her mind'). Although Ovid's Penelope does not explicitly refer to the shroud, she does have a particular interest in *dolus* (*Her.* 1.18): *flebam successu posse carere dolos.* See also 40, 42.

For this verbal pattern (abAVB), the third most frequent in *Amores*, see above on 3.2.40.

31. This is a beautifully crafted line. It employs balance at the main caesura, with each clause beginning with *sic* followed by a proper name; and uses the *apo koinou* construction (see above on line 1), with *nomen* supplied from the second clause in the first, and *longum* from the first in the second, and with Nemesis and Delia sharing the verb *habebunt*.

Commentary, 9.29-35   261

Nemesis...Delia: Delia is Tibullus' female beloved in his first book elegies, Nemesis in his second.

32. Like the previous line, this one is balanced at the main caesura. Here that balance is underlined by repetition of *altera* and by use of chiasmus (noun adjective... adjective noun).

cura: For the noun's erotic associations see above on 3.4.26.

33-4. quid uos sacra iuuant? quid nunc Aegyptia prosunt
   sistra? quid in uacuo secubuisse toro?
With these three questions the argument takes a different direction: first, it now engages with Tibullus' reflections on death (especially in 1.3) and, second, it underlines the pointlessness of Tibullus' concern with religious observance.

33. quid uos sacra iuuant? The question's form recalls *G.* 3.525 (of dying cattle): *quid labor aut benefacta iuuant?* Its content reminds the reader of Tibullus' emphasis on religious ritual e.g. 1.1.11-24, 1.3.23-34, 2.1, 2.5.

quid...prosunt | sistra? Recalls Tib. 1.3.23-4: *quid tua nunc Isis mihi, Delia, quid mihi prosunt | illa tua totiens aera repulsa manu?*

34. sistra: Ovid replaces Tibullan periphrasis ('hand-struck bronze') with the object's precise designation, *sistrum* (*OLD*: 'A metal rattle used in the worship of Isis'). See also 2.13.11 (to Isis): *per tua sistra precor,* Ars 3.635: *cum sedeat Phariae sistris operata iuuencae.*

quid in uacuo secubuisse toro? Summarizes the next couplet in the same poem (Tib. 1.3.25-6): *quidue, pie dum sacra colis, pureque lauari | te (memini) et puro secubuisse toro?* See also Tib. 1.2.77-8, Prop. 2.33a.17.

Periods of sexual abstinence were a familiar aspect of Isis' cult and a source of concern to elegiac lovers e.g. Prop. 2.33a, *Am.* 1.8.73-4. For abstinence from sex as part of Ceres' worship see on 3.10.

35-6. cum rapiunt mala fata bonos (ignoscite fasso)
   sollicitor nullos esse putare deos.
The fact that religious observance failed to protect Tibullus raises the possibility that gods do not exist. For apparent injustice leading to doubt about the gods' existence see above on 3.3.1.

35. McLennan (1972: 32) points out that this hexameter and the following two are notable for their use of a familiar Tibullan feature, the weak third-foot caesura (- u // u). See above on 15. The line is also notable for its simple language: death (or fate) is evil; Tibullus counts as a good and pious man.

(ignoscite fasso): Adapts the Tibullan lover's plea that Delia's husband (*coniunx* 1.6.15) forgive him when he acknowledges his adulteries (1.6.29): *ignosce fatenti.*

262   *Commentary*

The parenthesis undercuts the speaker's scepticism by acknowledging the gods' existence.

36. sollicitor: Here too the speaker stops short of scepticism: he is tempted but does not yield.

nullos esse deos: For the phrase used seriously see e.g. Cic. *N.D.* 1.123.5: *Posidonius disseruit... nullos esse deos Epicuro uideri*, Sen. *Med.* 1027 (Jason to Medea; with Boyle [2014: ad loc.]): *testare nullos esse, qua ueheris, deos.* Non-philosophers are more frivolous atheists e.g. Prop. 1.6.8 (Cynthia sees the lover's absence as proof that gods do not exist): *queritur nullos esse relicta deos*; Mart. 4.21.1–2 (Segius' wealth proves divine non-existence): *nullos esse deos, inane caelum | affirmat Segius.*

37–8. uiue pius: moriere pius; cole sacra: colentem
  mors grauis a templis in caua busta trahet.
From doubt about the gods' existence, the speaker moves to asserting the pointlessness of religious practice.

37. Punctuation of this line is disputed and important: some recent editors (Munari, Showerman and Goold, McKeown, and Ramirez de Verger [1]) punctuate strongly after *moriere*, while others (Kenney and Ramirez de Verger [2]) place a semicolon after the second *pius*; the issue matters because it affects the meaning of the line. If we turn to the major manuscripts we find that P offers no help (*Uiue pius mori^{e}re pius cole sacra colentem*). Y, however, punctuates after the second *pius*: *Viue pius. moriere pius. cole sacra. colentem.* (Though clearly visible in Y, this punctuation is not recorded by Munari [1965: 54].) I punctuate after *moriere pius*, not only because it has the support of a major manuscript, as well as Heinsius, Burman, Kenney, and Ramirez de Verger, but also because it produces a more powerful effect: *moriere pius* is stronger than *pius cole sacra.* When taken with *cole sacra, pius* is banal: we expect worshippers to be pious (cf. Tib. 1.3.25: *pie dum sacra colis*). *uiue pius: moriere pius*, by contrast, makes a powerful statement: piety makes no difference as to whether you live or die. In support of this view see Thomas (1965b); for the contrary view see Goold (1965: 55).

Marius compares Hor. *Carm.* 2.14.2–4: *nec pietas moram | rugis et instanti senectae | afferet.* See also Tib. 1.8.70: *nec prodest sanctis tura dedisse focis.*

38. Striking claim is followed by vivid image: death drags the worshipper to the grave. Here too phrasing is straightforward, with adjectives placed next to the nouns they qualify.

mors grauis: For *grauis* used of death and causes of death see *TLL* 2295.23–2296.8. Cf. *Met.* 3.471, *Tr.* 3.3.54, Sen. *Thy.* 401, Stat. *Silu.* 4.6.72–3.

39–40. carminibus confide bonis: iacet ecce Tibullus:
  uix manet e toto, parua quod urna capit.
As with piety, so with poetry: being a great poet is no protection from death.

Commentary, 9.36-43

39. Like lines 15, 35, and 37, this hexameter employs a weak caesura: *cārmĭnĭ̆|būs cōn|fĭdĕ // bŏ|nīs*. And like line 15 it names the poet who tended to favour this metrical form. The line is also notable for alliteration of *c* and *n* in words leading up to the climactic *Tibullus*.

iacet ecce Tibullus: Alludes to Tibullus' proposed epitaph (1.3.55-6): *hic iacet immiti consumptus morte Tibullus, | Messallam terra dum sequiturque mari. iacere* is regularly used to mean 'lie dead' (*OLD* 6, *TLL* 16.79-18.3).

40. toto: This is the reading of P and Y. It is preferable to *tanto*, found in some lesser manuscripts and printed by Kenney and McKeown. The previous line contrasts Tibullus' poetic achievement with the finality of death. The pentameter now draws out the implication of the hexameter's last three words: all that remains of Tibullus' whole body can be contained in a tiny urn (*parua... urna*). *tanto* weakens the point by invoking the notion of Tibullus' greatness. (For defence of *tanto* see Goold [1965: 56]. Note, however, that in Showerman and Goold he prints *toto*.)

parua...urna: For bodily remains reduced to the size of a tiny urn see *Met.* 12.615-16: *et de tam magno* (both 'great' and 'big') *restat Achille | nescio quid paruum, quod non bene compleat urnam*, Tr. 3.3.65: *ossa tamen facito parua referantur in urna*. Cf. Prop. 4.11.14: *en sum, quod digitis quinque legatur, onus*.

**41-2. tene, sacer uates, flammae rapuere rogales
pectoribus pasci nec timuere tuis?**
The speaker expresses shock (underlined by alliteration especially of *r* and *p*) that funeral flames could commit so appalling a sacrilege as consuming Tibullus' body.

41. tene: For initial use of *tu* in a similar context, with *ne* emphasizing the key word, see A. 11.42-3: *tene, inquit, miserande puer, cum laeta ueniret, | inuidit Fortuna mihi*.

sacer uates: For the phrase see above on 17.

rogales: Seems to be an Ovidian coinage picked up by Statius (*Theb.* 1.112): *igne rogali*.

42. pectoribus pasci: Alliteration of *p, c*, and *s* makes this a remarkable phrase. It suggests bestial feeding e.g. Mart. *Sp.* 7.1-2: *Prometheus | adsiduam nimio pectore pauit auem*. There is particular poignancy in the fire's feeding on the seat of the emotions (*OLD* 3a), especially love e.g. 1.1.26, 1.2.8; 3.2.40, 3.10.18, 3.11.2, 33.

**43-4. aurea sanctorum potuissent templa deorum
urere, quae tantum sustinuere nefas.**
Denunciation of the flames continues with the suggestion that burning Tibullus' body was tantamount to destroying temples of the gods.

43. The line impresses because of its internal rhyme and verbal patterning (abVAB; for the 'golden line' see above on 3.3.21). Ovid sometimes uses repetition of *orum* and *arum* to suggest horror e.g. *Her.* 11.111: *nate, dolor matris, rapidarum*

264   *Commentary*

praeda ferarum, Met. 7.8: *lexque datur Minyis magnorum horrenda laborum,* 12.219: *nam tibi, saeuorum saeuissime Centaurorum,* 13.763 (of the Cyclops): *uritur oblitus pecorum antrorumque suorum.* That seems appropriate here.

aurea...templa: For the phrase see Propertius, whose moralizing speaker seems to disapprove of current ways (4.1a.5): *fictilibus creuere deis haec aurea templa* and *Fast.* 1.223-4, where the speaker, Janus, is happy with both past and present practice: *nos quoque templa iuuant, quamuis antiqua probemus,* | *aurea.*

45-6. auertit uultus, Erycis quae possidet arces;
       sunt quoque qui lacrimas continuisse negant.
The speaker closes this phase of the argument with the claim that Venus could not bear to watch Tibullus' funeral.

45. auertit uultus: Averting one's gaze can be a sign of sorrow (e.g. Sen. *Phaed.* 886: *quidnam ora maesta auertis*) or embarrassment (e.g. *Tr.* 4.3.50: *auertis uultus et subit ora rubor*) or horror at a crime (e.g. [Quint.] *Decl.* 19.6.5: *ad quaedam facinora sufficit claudere oculos, uultus auertere, tacere*). All seem appropriate here.

Erycis...arces: For the introduction to Rome of the cult of Venus as goddess of Mt Eryx in Sicily, see Liv. 22.9.10. For Venus as *Erycina* see e.g. Catul. 64.72, Hor. *Carm.* 1.2.33, *Am.* 2.10.11, *Her.* 15.57, *Met.* 5.363. Ovid mentions her temple near the Colline gate (*Rem.* 549-50): *est prope Collinam templum uenerabile portam,* | *imposuit templo nomina celsus Eryx.*

46. sunt...qui...negant: The use of the indicative where we might expect a generic subjunctive suggests that the speaker has greater confidence when asserting Venus' sorrow than when claiming that poets have divine powers (see on 18 above). Cf. *Her.* 13.8: *et sunt quae uolui dicere multa tibi,* i.e. there are many things which I really wanted to say to you; *Met.* 5.42-3: *sunt qui Cephea dicunt* | *cum genero debere mori,* i.e. there are those who actually say that Cepheus should die.

lacrimas...continuisse: For the idea that gods cannot cry see e.g. Eur. *Hipp.* 1396 (Artemis to dying Hippolytus): ὁρῶ· κατ' ὄσσων δ' οὐ θέμις βαλεῖν δάκρυ ('I see you, but I am not allowed to cast a tear from my eyes'), *Met.* 2.621-2: *neque enim caelestia tingi* | *ora licet lacrimis, Fast.* 4.521: *neque enim lacrimare deorum est.* At Hom. *Il.* 16.459, by contrast, Zeus cries 'bloody tears' (αἱματοέσσας δὲ ψιάδας) for Sarpedon. In this case, Venus' reaction to Tibullus' death was closer to that of Homer's Zeus than Euripides' Artemis.

For the expression see e.g. Plaut. *Mos.* 822, *Am.* 1.14.51, *Her.* 15.174, *Ars* 2.70, 2.582, Sen. *Ep.* 99.20.3.

47-8. sed tamen hoc melius, quam si Phaeacia tellus
       ignotum uili supposuisset humo.
After denouncing Tibullus' funeral the speaker finds comfort: it could have been worse.

47. Phaeacia tellus: Alludes to Tib. 1.3.3: *me tenet...Phaeacia terris*. Pliny (*Nat.* 4.52.6) identifies Homeric Phaeacia (the island where Odysseus tells his tales), with Corcyra (modern Corfu).

48. ignotum: Transfers the site of Tibullus' sickness to the poet himself (1.3.3): *me tenet ignotis aegrum...terris.*

uili...humo: The juxtaposition is striking because *humus*, though used of burials (e.g. *A.* 9.214, Prop. 3.7.25), does not mean 'tomb'.

supposuisset: In funerary contexts the verb commonly denotes cremation (e.g. *A.* 11.119: *miseris supponite ciuibus ignem*, Prop. 2.13.31, Sil. 10.542-3). Ovid, however, uses it of burial in earth (cf. *Tr.* 3.3.68 [of Antigone]: *supposuit tumulo rege uetante soror*).

49-50. hic certe madidos fugientis pressit ocellos
 mater et in cineres ultima dona tulit.
At least Tibullus' mother was there to close his eyes.

49. hic: Means 'here', i.e. in Rome as opposed to Phaeacia. Allusion to Tib. 1.3.5 confirms this reading: *non hic mihi mater.*

Recent editors (apart from Showerman and Goold) print *hic* rather than *hinc*, found in P and Y. (In Y, however, a corrector has inserted *hic* above *hinc* in lines 59 and 61.) Although *hinc* has better manuscript support, *hic* gives better sense. Neither of the possible meanings of *hinc* works here: *OLD* 1: 'from here'; *OLD* 8a: 'from this fact or circumstance, hence'. Bornecque (1930) prints *hinc*, but offers *ici* ('here') as a translation presumably because 'from here' would be meaningless. Showerman and Goold opt for 'hence' and translate 'to this 'tis due'. *hinc* (*OLD* 8a), however, is a logical term and its use entails that the second claim results from the first. But the opposite is the case here: the judgement (it is better) flows from the fact (his mother was present).

madidos...ocellos: For the phrase see 3.6.57, where it is used of raped Ilia's distress.

fugientis: Use of simple *fugio* to mean 'die' seems exceptional. Other authors add words signifying 'life' or 'death' to clarify e.g. Sen. *Dial.* 6.25.1.4 (*ad Marciam*): *integer ille nihilque in terris relinquens sui fugit et totus excessit, Ep.* 24.25.1, Luc. 9.105; Stat. *Silu.* 3.3.186.

50. mater: One of Tibullus' complaints when apparently dying in Phaeacia was precisely his mother's absence (1.3.5-6): *non hic mihi mater | quae legat in maestos ossa perusta sinus*. Her presence makes death in Rome better.

ultima dona: Cf. *Her.* 7.192 (Dido to Anna): *iam dabis in cineres ultima dona meos*. What are these 'final gifts'? They might be the funeral ritual itself (e.g. Catul. 101.3-4: *ut te postremo donarem munere mortis | et mutam nequiquam alloquerer cinerem*) or some other kind of offering, perhaps flowers or hair or tears or perfumes or

266 Commentary

sacrificial victims (e.g. *A*. 6.883-4: *manibus date lilia plenis | purpureos spargam flores*; Prop. 1.17.21: *illa meo caros donasset funere crines*, *Met*. 13.427-8: *Hectoris in tumulo canum de uertice crinem, | inferias inopes, crinem lacrimasque reliquit*; *Pont*. 1.7.29: *cui nos et lacrimas, supremum in funere munus*; Prop. 2.13.30: *cum dabitur Syrio munere plenus onyx*, Tib. 1.3.7 [quoted below on 51]; *A*. 10.518-19: *quattuor hic iuuenes...|...inferias quos immolet umbris*).

51-2. hic soror in partem misera cum matre doloris
   uenit inornatas dilaniata comas.
And his sister was there too.

51. **hic:** See above on 49.

soror: Alludes to Tibullus' concern that dying in Phaeacia would prevent his sister's presence (1.3.7-8): *non soror, Assyrios cineri quae dedat odores | et fleat effusis ante sepulcra comis*.

52. **inornatas...comas:** May suggest the dishevelment associated with distress (e.g. *Met*. 5.472 [Ceres]: *inornatos laniauit diua capillos*) or simple lack of adornment (e.g. *Met*. 1.497-8 [Apollo and Daphne]: *spectat inornatos collo pendere capillos | et 'quid, si comantur?' ait*). In this context the former is more likely.

dilaniata: Perfect participle passive with a retained accusative. Cf. *Her*. 12.157-8 (Medea catching sight of Jason's wedding procession): *uix me continui, quin dilaniata capillos | clamarem*.

53-4. cumque tuis sua iunxerunt Nemesisque priorque
   oscula nec solos destituere rogos.
Members of Tibullus' family were not the only ones present: so were both his girlfriends. When picturing his death, Tibullus had imagined Delia giving him kisses mixed with tears (*lacrimis oscula mixta* 1.1.62). Here, however, he receives the combined kisses of mother, sister, and two mistresses. The presence of the latter makes Tibullus' death congruent with his life. Cf. the hope of one Ovidian lover (2.10.37-8): *atque aliquis nostro lacrimans in funere dicat: | 'conueniens uitae mors fuit ista tuae'*.

53. The absence of a third-foot caesura makes this a remarkable line, throwing *iunxerunt* into particular prominence and emphasizing perhaps the multitude of mourners. For the absence of a third-foot caesura see above on 3.1.25.

Nemesis: Tibullus' lover in Book 2, poems 3-6.

priorque: This apparently dismissive term identifies Tibullus' first mistress, Delia, with the book in which she appears, the first book of elegies.

54. Reworks line 28 above. Poetry may abandon the poet's funeral pyre, but his girlfriends don't.

oscula: For a girlfriend's final kisses see Tib. 1.1.62 (quoted above) and Prop. 2.13.29: *osculaque in gelidis pones suprema labellis*.

55-8. Delia discedens 'felicius' inquit 'amata
   sum tibi; uixisti, dum tuus ignis eram'.
cui Nemesis 'quid' ait 'tibi sunt mea damna dolori?
   me tenuit moriens deficiente manu'.
The presence of two girlfriends, however, leads to an unseemly squabble as Delia and Nemesis argue over the nature of their relationship with the dead poet.

55. Delia: The name recalls Delia's presence at the poet's imagined funeral in Tibullus' first poem (1.1.61): *flebis et arsuro positum me, Delia, lecto*.

56. tibi: For dative of the agent after a perfect passive see Pinkster (1.245).

uixisti: Often used to signify life's completion (e.g. *A*. 4.653: *uixi et quem dederat cursum Fortuna peregi*, Sil. 13.270: *hactenus est uixisse satis*), the perfect tense of *uiuo* here underlines the fact that Tibullus did not die on Delia's watch.

57-8. Nemesis responds to Delia's spite with an equally spiteful remark. (For the wholly dactylic couplet see above on 3.2.1–2.)

58. Reworks Tib. 1.1.60: *te teneam moriens deficiente manu*. As Cornacchia (1989: 102) notes, Nemesis responds to her rival by 'stealing a verse written for her'.

59-60. si tamen e nobis aliquid nisi nomen et umbra
   restat, in Elysia ualle Tibullus erit.
In this final phase of the argument the speaker changes course, imagining that Tibullus continues to have some bodily reality.

59. In *Tr*. 4.10 Ovid combines reworked versions of this line and 28 above (85–6): *si tamen extinctis aliquid nisi nomina restat | et gracilis structos effugit umbra rogos*.

aliquid…restat: For this phrase used of post-mortem survival see e.g. Prop. 2.34.53 *nec si post Stygias aliquid restabimus undas*, *Tr*. 4.10.85 (just quoted).

nomen et umbra: The speaker contrasts the insubstantiality connoted by *nomen* and *umbra* (*nomen* [OLD 16], *umbra* [OLD 9]), with Tibullus' substantial existence in the underworld. Unlike the inhabitants of Virgil's underworld (e.g. *A*. 6.264, 401), Tibullus (here at least) is not an *umbra*. (For the shift in *umbra*'s meaning see below on 65.) For these nouns combined to similar effect see Luc. 2.302–3: *tuumque | nomen, Libertas, et inanem persequar umbram*.

60. Elysia ualle: Recalls Tibullus' own prediction of his post-mortem destiny (1.3.57–8): *sed me, quod facilis tenero sum semper amori, | ipsa Venus campos ducet in Elysios*.

For Tibullus in the Elysian fields (along with Virgil, who also died in 19 BCE) see Domitius Marsus, an epigrammatist of the Augustan period (fr. 180 Hollis). For discussion of Marsus' double epitaph see Morgan (2010: 366–7).

61–4. obuius huic uenias hedera iuuenalia cinctus
   tempora cum Caluo, docte Catulle, tuo;
tu quoque, si falsum est temerati crimen amici,
   sanguinis atque animae prodige Galle tuae.

If Tibullus is in the underworld, Catullus, his fellow love-poet Calvus, and Gallus should come to meet their successor.

Reed (1997b: 265–6) compares this list of poets with that of [Moschus]. The Greek poet's catalogue, however, is a long list of mourners (70–97) including non-pastoral poets like Homer and Hesiod. Ovid, by contrast, imagines only three, Tibullus' fellow love poets, greeting their colleague in the underworld. Closer is Ovid's own catalogue of birds (2.6.49–58) welcoming Corinna's parrot to Elysium.

61. uenias: This is the reading of P and Y. Some editors prefer *uenies*, found in lesser manuscripts (Kenney's ω). There is no compelling reason for choosing a future indicative over a jussive or optative subjunctive.

hedera...cinctus: For the association between ivy and poetry see e.g. *Ecl.* 7.25: *hedera crescentem ornate poetam*, *Met.* 5.338 (Calliope), *Fast.* 5.79–80 (also Calliope).

iuuenalia: Born somewhere between 55 and 48 BCE, Tibullus was relatively young when he died. Marsus' description of his death as *non... aequa* underlines the age difference between the elegist and the epic poet: Virgil was 51 when he died, Tibullus around 30.

62. Caluo: C. Licinius Calvus (born 82 BCE [Plin. *Nat.* 7.165.5]) was a poet and friend of Catullus. Propertius speaks of him as a love poet (2.34.89–90): *haec etiam docti confessa est pagina Calui, | cum caneret miserae funera Quintiliae*, while Ovid draws attention to his adulteries (*Tr.* 2.431–2): *par fuit exigui similisque licentia Calui, | detexit uariis qui sua furta modis*. For the remains of his poetry see Hollis frr. 19–42.

docte: The epithet is often applied to the Muses (e.g. *Ars* 2.425: *docta... Erato*, 3.411–12: *doctis |... Musis*), poets (e.g. Tib. 1.4.61, Prop. 2.34.89 [quoted above], *Ars* 3.551) and girlfriends (e.g. Catul. 35.17, Prop. 2.11.6, 2.13.11, *Am.* 2.4.17).

Catulle: Addressing Catullus underlines his importance: Calvus is his sidekick. Elsewhere Ovid treats Catullus as Verona's pride (3.15.7) and as a predecessor in erotic poetry (*Tr.* 2.427–10). Catullus is called *doctus* by the author of [Tib.] 3.6.41 and Martial (7.99.7, 8.73.8, 14.100.1, 14.152.1).

63–4. If Catullus and Calvus share a couplet, Gallus has one to himself. His importance for Ovid is underlined by frequency of references (Catullus is named

Commentary, 9.61-7

three times in Ovid's work, Gallus nine, including three in 1.15.29-30); and by the fact that Ovid positions Gallus as the first and himself as fourth in the line of love elegists: (*Tr.* 4.10.53-4). See also *Rem.* 763-6 where Ovid, having listed four Greek love poets, names an equivalent Roman quartet: Tibullus, Propertius, Gallus, and himself.

63. si falsum est temerati crimen amici: Propertius had also placed Gallus in the underworld (2.34.91-2): *et modo formosa quam multa Lycoride Gallus | mortuus inferna uulnera lauit aqua*. Ovid, however, presents Gallus' existence in Elysium as conditional on his innocence because he had fallen foul of Augustus. *temerati...amici* may reflect the language of formal 'renunciation of friendship'. (For discussion see Rogers [1959] and Wardle [2014: on Suet. *Aug.* 66.2]). The exiled Ovid presents Gallus' punishment as resulting from excessive freedom of speech (*Tr.* 2.445-6): *non fuit opprobrio celebrasse Lycorida Gallo, | sed linguam nimio non tenuisse mero*.

64. The language reflects the fact that Gallus felt obliged to commit suicide (Suet. *Aug.* 66.2.4, Dio 53.23-24).

65-6. his comes umbra tua est, siqua est modo corporis umbra;
   auxisti numeros, culte Tibulle, pios.
If Gallus' place in Elysium is questionable, Tibullus' right to remain among the pious dead is not.

65. umbra...umbra: Here the speaker both applies and withholds the conventional term for the underworld's inhabitants. If Tibullus was said in line 59 to be more substantial than a shadow, here he is an *umbra*, but only if such things exist.

66. numeros...pios: For Tibullus' piety see above on 33-4.

culte Tibulle: For Tibullus as *cultus* see 1.15.27-8: *donec erunt ignes arcusque Cupidinis arma, | discentur numeri, culte Tibulle, tui*. There, as here, it suggests the elegance (cf. Quint. 10.1.93.2: *tersus atque elegans maxime uidetur auctor Tibullus*) of the poet's works and perhaps of the poet himself.

For *cultus* as a critical term applicable to all of Ovid's early works see *Ars* 3.341-6. Martial applies it to elegy as a whole: 5.30.4: *cultis aut elegia comis*.

67-8. ossa quieta, precor, tuta requiescite in urna,
   et sit humus cineri non onerosa tuo.
The poem closes quietly with a variation on traditional prayers for the dead and allusion to Tibullus (2.4.49-50): *et 'bene' discedens dicet 'placideque quiescas, | terraque securae sit super ossa leuis'* and Propertius (1.17.23-4): *illa meum extremo clamasset puluere nomen, | ut mihi non ullo pondere terra foret.*

67. ossa quieta: Reference to bones is not surprising in a funerary poem. An apostrophe to bones, however, is unique.

270 Commentary

tutā requiescite in urnā: The epithet is transferred. The speaker is presumably concerned about the bones' safety rather than the urn's. For the connection between enallage and pathos see above on 3.

The similarity to this passage of Met. 4.166 (the burial of Pyramus and Thisbe): <u>una</u> requiescit in <u>urna</u> underlines an important difference. Here the tone is solemn; there verbal play undercuts apparent seriousness.

68. For the wish that the earth lie lightly upon the dead person's remains see e.g. Eur. Alc. 462–3: κοῦφα σοι | χθὼν ἐπάνωθε πέσοι, γύναι ('May the earth fall lightly upon you, lady'), Tib. 2.4.50 (quoted above), Prop. 1.17.24 (quoted above), Ars 3.740: *hoc faciet positae te mihi, terra, leuem*, Mart. 9.29.11 (using the standard inscriptional formula): *sit tibi terra leuis*; and with a twist: Sen. Phaed. 1280 (Theseus cursing Phaedra): *grauisque tellus impio capiti incubet*. For further examples in Greek literature and Latin inscriptions see Lattimore (1962: 65–74).

3.10: PRAYER TO CERES

Am. 3.10 brings together elements usually kept separate in love elegy: an erotic problem and a mythological tale. In this it resembles 3.6.[1] But where 3.6 draws upon a well-known part of Roman legend, the story of Ilia's rape, 3.10 reworks an obscure slice of Greek mythology, the tale of Ceres' sexual relationship with a hero called Iasion or Iasius.[2]

What then is the problem? It is one familiar from Tibullus, Propertius, and *Amores* 1.8: a mistress's commitment to a religious cult may require sexual abstinence. Both Tibullus and Propertius had complained that their girlfriend's worship of Isis forced them to sleep alone (Tib. 1.3.23–6; Prop. 2.33a); while in Propertius and Ovid brothel-keepers advise their protegees to use Isis as a pretext for withholding sex. Thus Acanthis gives this advice (Prop. 4.5.33–4): *denique ubi amplexu Venerem promiseris empto,* | *fac simules puros Isidos esse dies* ('Then when you have promised Venus and sold him an embrace, pretend that these are Isis' sex-free days'), while Dipsas counsels (*Am.* 1.8.73–4): *saepe nega noctes. capitis modo finge dolorem,* | *et modo, quae causas praebeat, Isis erit* ('Deny nights often. Now pretend you have a headache, now there will be Isis to offer an excuse'). In 3.10, however, it is not a foreign goddess who causes problems but local Ceres.

And the myth? The best-known part of Ceres' legend, familiar from the *Homeric Hymn to Demeter* and Ovid's own accounts in *Metamorphoses* and *Fasti*, concerns the goddess's search for Proserpina. This, however, is not the portion of

---

[1] Lenz (1933: 311) observes that there are no narrative poems outside Book 3. He includes 3.6, 3.10, and (with reservations) 3.13.
[2] Ovid calls him 'Iasius' here but 'Iasion' at Met. 9.423 and Tr. 2.300. In Greek sources the form 'Iasion' is more common.

the story that Ovid tells here. Rather he rewrites a story found in Homer and Hesiod: the tale of Demeter's affair with Iasion/Iasius. Here is Homer's version (*Od.* 5.125–8):

ὡς δ' ὁπότ' Ἰασίωνι ἐϋπλόκαμος Δημήτηρ,
ᾧ θυμῷ εἴξασα, μίγη φιλότητι καὶ εὐνῇ
νειῷ ἔνι τριπόλῳ· οὐδὲ δὴν ἦεν ἄπυστος
Ζεύς, ὅς μιν κατέπεφνε βαλὼν ἀργῆτι κεραυνῷ.

As when lovely-haired Demeter, yielding to her passion, mingled in love and in bed with Iasion in thrice-ploughed fallow land; nor was Zeus unaware for long: he killed him, striking with a bright thunderbolt.

Hesiod adds a location but omits the killing (*Theog.* 969–71):

Δημήτηρ μὲν Πλοῦτον ἐγείνατο δῖα θεάων,
Ἰασίῳ ἥρωι μιγεῖσ' ἐρατῇ φιλότητι
νειῷ ἔνι τριπόλῳ, Κρήτης ἐν πίονι δήμῳ.

Demeter, bright among goddesses, gave birth to Wealth, mingling in passionate love with the hero Iasius in thrice-ploughed fallow land in the rich country of Crete.

Ovid's innovation is to transform these brief stories into an extended narrative.[3]

How is this transformation achieved? Ovid takes his basic outline from Homer and Hesiod. Other elements derive from other sources. The (possibly false) Cretan claim to have nurtured the infant Jupiter (19–24) comes from Callimachus' *Hymn to Zeus* (4–9), while the crop failures resulting from the goddess's obsession with Iasius (29–34), reflect those caused by her unhappiness with the treatment of Persephone in the *Homeric Hymn to Demeter* (305–9, 351–4, 450–6). But Ovid's most striking innovation is to employ this newly-created myth to 'prove' that Ceres has no right to demand celibacy of her worshippers.

If 3.10's myth seems indebted to Homer, Hesiod, and other Greeks, the argument itself points to a Roman model: Propertius. In Prop. 2.33a the lover begins by stating his complaint (1–6): Cynthia's dedication to Isis means that the lovers will be separated for ten days; recounts the story of Io, who was commonly identified with the Egyptian goddess,[4] arguing (7–14) that Juno's cruelty, particularly transformation into a cow, is responsible for Isis' arrogance; and closes the poem (15–22) with a xenophobic attack on a foreign divinity.

The argument of 3.10 takes the same logical form, moving from complaint through myth to renewed criticism of the goddess. There are, however, important

---

[3] There are no extended accounts of Demeter's relationship with Iasius/Iasion in Greek literature. References to the affair are brief and depend on the reader's knowledge of Homer and/or Hesiod e.g. Theoc. *Id.* 3.50, Athen. *Deipn.* 13.20.37, Diod. Sic. 5.49, 77, Nonn. *Dion.* 5.518.
[4] E.g. Prop. 2.28a.17–18, *Am.* 2.2.45–6, *Her.* 14.85–6, *Met.* 1.747, *Tr.* 2.297–8, VF 4.416–18, Hyg. *Fab.* 145.

272   *Commentary*

differences. First, if Isis was Egyptian, Ceres was celebrated by the Roman state. Not surprisingly Ovid's poem is less hostile to his divine addressee. Second, 3.10 contains elements familiar from poetic and actual hymns, most notably a listing of the goddess's gifts and attributes. The Propertian lover, by contrast, questions why the goddess has come to the city, reminds her of the enmity between Tiber and Nile, and threatens her with expulsion from Rome. Third, whereas Propertius alludes enigmatically to details from a familiar myth, Ovid tells at length a story compounded of pre-existing elements, but essentially one of his own creation.

Secondary literature: Lenz (1933); Le Bonniec (1958: 404–12); Boyd (1997: 67–79).

1–2. Annua uenerunt Cerealis tempora sacri:
    secubat in uacuo sola puella toro.
A brisk opening establishes the lover's problem: because of Ceres' festival his girlfriend won't sleep with him.

1. What festival is this? For readers of *Fasti* the most obvious candidate is the Cerialia held on 11–19 April. This spring celebration, however, sems not to have been associated with celibacy. But another festival of Ceres, the *sacrum anniuersarium Cereris*, was held in summer to mark the recovery of Proserpina. This ritual was associated with women's abstinence from food and sex. (Le Bonniec [1958: 404–12] sets out the literary and non-literary evidence for this nine-day period of celibacy, the *castus/castum Cereris*. For the phrase see *Fest.* p. 154.58. See also Fantham [1998: 167–8].) Reference at the end of the poem (45–6) to the discovery of Ceres' daughter and her rule over the underworld confirms that this is the festival which prompts the lover's complaint.

Tibullus had linked Ceres with both chastity and purification of the fields (2.1, esp. 11–12): *uos quoque abesse procul iubeo, discedat ab aris, | cui tulit hesterna gaudia nocte Venus*. Still more important is the preface to Myrrha's story, combining a harvest festival, female celibacy, and allusion to this line (*Met.* 10.431–5):

> festa piae Cereris celebrabant annua matres
> illa, quibus niuea uelatae corpora ueste
> primitias frugum dant spicea serta suarum
> perque nouem noctes uenerem tactusque uiriles
> in uetitis numerant.

2. secubat in uacuo...toro: Recalls references in both Tibullus and Ovid to religious worship separating lovers (Tib. 1.3.26): *te memini et puro secubuisse toro; Am.* 3.9.34: *quid in uacuo secubuisse toro?* Propertius had made a similar complaint in different terms (2.33a.17): *quid tibi prodest uiduas dormire puellas?* For similar language in different contexts see *Am.* 2.19.42: *cur totiens uacuo secubet ipsa toro*, *Ars* 2.370 (of Helen): *et timet in uacuo sola cubare toro*.

For this variation on the golden line (VabBA) see above on 3.1.11.

Commentary, 10.1-7

3-4. flaua Ceres, tenues spicis redimita capillos,
   cur inhibes sacris commoda nostra tuis?
The lover turns now to addressing the goddess, singling out her particular attributes and posing a personal question.

3. flaua Ceres: The epithet reflects both literary tradition (e.g. ξανθὴ Δημήτηρ ['golden Demeter'] Hom. *Il*. 5.500, *Hymn. Hom. Dem*. 302; *flaua Ceres* Tib. 1.1.15, G. 1.96, Luc. 4.412) and the actual colour of ripe grain. Servius (on G. 1.96) explains: FLAVA CERES... *'flava' dicitur propter aristarum colorem in maturitate*.

spicis redimita: Alludes to Tibullus' description of the goddess (1.1.15-16): *flaua Ceres, tibi sit nostro de rure corona | spicea*. Both here and in Tibullus reference to ears of grain suggests a harvest celebration, i.e. a summer festival. Cf. Sen. *Oed*. 49-51 on the effects of plague: *denegat fructum Ceres | adulta, et altis flaua cum spicis tremat, | arente culmo sterilis emoritur seges*.

4. For this verbal pattern (VABba) see above on 3.1.30.

commoda: A polite euphemism replaces the more usual *gaudia* (e.g. 2.3.2, 3.7.63 [with note above], *Ars* 3.805).

nostra tuis: The juxtaposition of singular ('your' i.e. of Ceres) and plural ('our' i.e. of my girlfriend and me) underlines the claim that Ceres is robbing two people of sexual pleasure. For the idea of mutual satisfaction see e.g. 1.10.31: *et uendit quod utrumque iuuat quod uterque petebat*, *Ars* 2.682, 3.794.

5-6. te, dea, munificam gentes, ubi quaeque, loquuntur,
   nec minus humanis inuidet ulla bonis.
The lover continues his prayer to the goddess, contrasting her spite in this matter with her usual benevolence.

5. te, dea: Perhaps recalls (ironically?) Lucretius' prayer to Venus (1.6): *te, dea, te fugiunt uenti, te nubila caeli*.

ubi quaeque: Recent editors follow Munari in printing this, the reading of Y and possibly P. Kenney (1958: 65) pointed out the parallel with *A*. 7.400: *io matres, audite, ubi quaeque* ('everywhere'), *Latinae*. See also *Ars* 2.627 (noted by Kenney in his apparatus): *scilicet excuties omnes, ubi quaeque, puellas*, Stat. *Theb*. 11.183: *conueniant ubi quaeque nurus matresque Pelasgae*. Some twentieth-century editors printed *ubiquaque*, a word which occurs nowhere in classical Latin.

6. nec minus: Understatement highlights Ceres' generosity to humankind.

7-10. ante nec hirsuti torrebant farra coloni,
   nec notum terris area nomen erat,
sed glandem quercus, oracula prima, ferebant;
   haec erat et teneri caespitis herba cibus.

This picture of the pre-agricultural world, though given a distinctly Ovidian twist, is consistent with both naturalistic and theistic accounts of early human life. Lucretius, for example, imagines that before the invention of the plough humans ate what earth produced of its own accord (5.937–8) and cared for themselves among *glandiferas...quercus* (5.939). Virgil, Tibullus, and Ovid attribute the shift from acorns to grains to Ceres or other rustic gods e.g. *G*. 1.7–8, Tib. 2.1.37–8, *Fast*. 4.401–2.

7. hirsuti...coloni: The epithet suggests disdain. Cf. *Ars* 1.107–8 (of early Romans), *Met*. 13.766 (of Polyphemus), *Tr*. 2.259 (of Ennius' poetry): *sumpserit Annales (nihil est hirsutius illis)*.

torrebant farra: Reference to emmer wheat underlines the lover's contempt for the past: we are talking about a time before even that antiquated grain.

That first-century Romans thought of *far* as old-fashioned is clear. They noted, as Spurr (1986: 11) points out, that emmer was used in ancient rituals (e.g. in a form of marriage known as *confarreatio*) and that it is the only grain mentioned in the Twelve Tables. Garnsey (1999: 120) observes: 'For the Romans, the most ancient wheat was *far*, emmer wheat (*Triticum dicoccum*)'.

For the roasting of emmer, with particular stress on the variety's outdatedness, see *Fast*. 2.519–21, 6.313. See also Var. *R*. 1.63.1.8, 1.69.1.1, Manil. 5.282–3, Plin. *Nat*. 18.7.6.

9. glandem: For acorns as early human food see e.g. Tib. 2.3.69, *Met*. 1.106, *Fast*. 4.399.

oracula prima: Recalls Dodona, a shrine of Zeus in Epirus, famous for its oracular oak trees (e.g. Hom. *Od*. 14.327–8, 19.296–7). Virgil also links Dodona's oracle with acorns and the invention of agriculture (*G*. 1.8, 148–9).

10. For grass (and leaves) as primitive food see *Fast*. 4.397–8: *et modo carpebant uiuax e caespite gramen, | nunc epulae tenera fronde cacumen erant*.

11–14. prima Ceres docuit turgescere semen in agris
    falce coloratas subsecuitque comas.
prima iugis tauros supponere colla coegit
    et ueterem curuo dente reuellit humum.

From describing the pre-agricultural world, the lover turns to Ceres' achievements in the cultivation of grain and the invention of ploughing. These lines, as Du Quesnay (1973: 25) notes, 'adapt' or rather correct Tibullus' praise of Osiris (1.7.29–31).

11. prima Ceres: In the *Homeric Hymn* Demeter both blights (305–9) and revives agriculture (471). In Roman tradition, however, Ceres is humanity's teacher e.g. Lucr. 5.14–15: *namque Ceres fertur fruges...mortalibus instituisse*, *G*. 1.147–8, *Met*. 5.341–2, *Fast*. 4.401–2.

12. falce coloratas...comas: Adapts Tibullus' description of pruning vines (1.7.34): *hic uiridem dura caedere falce comam*. For *comae* as ears of grain see Tib. 2.1.47–8 (with Maltby [2002: ad loc.]): *rura ferunt messes, calidi cum sideris aestu | deponit flauas annua terra comas*; Prop. 4.2.14: *et coma lactenti spicea fruge tumet*. *coloratas* is equivalent to Tibullus' *flauas*.

subsecuitque: Regularly used of harvesting various kinds of leaves and grasses (e.g. Varr. *R.* 1.49.1.4, *Med.* 36, *Ars* 1.300, *Fast.* 4.438).

13–14. Virgil and Ovid attribute the invention of the plough to Ceres (*G.* 1.163: *Eleusinae matris*; *Fast.* 4.403: *illa iugo tauros collum praebere coegit*), while Tibullus gives credit to rustic gods more generally (2.1.41–2: *illi etiam tauros primi docuisse feruntur | seruitium*). For a similar description of ploughing see *Rem.* 171–2: *colla iube domitos oneri supponere tauros, | sauciet ut duram uomer aduncus humum*.

13. iugis tauros...coegit: Cf. Hypsipyle's description of Medea's control of Jason (*Her.* 6.97): *scilicet ut tauros, ita te iuga ferre coegit*.

14. For this verbal pattern (abBVA) see above on 3.2.66.

curuo...dente: For the *dens* as the tip of the ploughshare (*uomer*) see *G.* 1.261–2: *durum procudit arator | uomeris obtunsi dentem*, Col. 10.1.1.69: *curui uomere dentis*.

15–16. hanc quisquam lacrimis laetari credit amantum
    et bene tormentis secubituque coli?
While listing a divinity's gifts is a conventional part of prayer, the lover's inference is not: given all the evidence for Ceres' benevolence, no one could suppose that she expects lovers to sleep apart.

15. lacrimis laetari: Ceres could not be so cruel as to rejoice in another's sorrow. Cf. Deianira's view of Iole's reaction to her pain (*Met.* 9.144): *paelex lacrimis laetabitur istis*.

16. tormentis secubituque: The phrase is best treated as a hendiadys (see above on 3.7.4), i.e. 'torture and sleeping apart' = 'the torture of sleeping apart'. The claim is histrionic: in a world where actual torture is commonplace, sleeping alone hardly counts. Cf. Prop. 3.5.39, *Met.* 3.694–5, *Ib.* 189: *in te transcribet ueterum tormenta reorum*.

bene...coli: Cf. Dido's attack on Aeneas' *pietas* (*Her.* 7.130): *non bene caelestis impia dextra colit*.

17–18. nec tamen est, quamuis agros amet illa feraces,
    rustica nec uiduum pectus amoris habet.
By way of transition to the story of Ceres' passion, the lover argues that a fertility goddess must be susceptible to love.

17. agros amet illa feraces: Perhaps recalls the lover's description of his homeland (2.16.7): *terra ferax Cereris multoque feracior uuis*.

18. rustica: For the resonance of this adjective see above on 3.1.43. Its use here is paradoxical: the quintessential country goddess is declared to be unrustic. For a similar paradoxical use see Phaedra's comment (*Her.* 4.102): *si Venerem tollas, rustica silua tua est*.

uiduum: For *uiduus* as 'loveless' with a dependent noun see 2.10.17 (*uiduo...cubili*) and 3.5.42 (*uiduo...toro*), *Her.* 1.81 (*uiduo...lecto*). For *uiduus* followed by a genitive (only here in Ovid) see *OLD* 4.

19–20. Cretes erunt testes; nec fingunt omnia Cretes.
    Crete nutrito terra superba Ioue.
The shift to narrative is made in a remarkable couplet, with a framed hexameter (*Cretes...Cretes*), with anadiplosis (*Cretes* | *Crete*) and anaphora (*Cretes...*| *Crete*). All this is done to underline the infant Jupiter's association with Crete.

19. nec fingunt omnia Cretes: The lover's confidence in the Cretans (well, they don't always lie) reverses Callimachus' acceptance of Epimenides' dictum (*Hymn* 1.8): Κρῆτες ἀεὶ ψεῦσται ('Cretans are always liars').

20. Faced with choosing between Arcadia and Crete as the birthplace of Zeus, Callimachus (*Hymn* 1.5–7) had picked Arcadia. Ovid's lover makes the opposite choice.

21–2. illic sideream mundi qui temperat arcem
    exiguus tenero lac bibit ore puer.
In terms at first grand and then lowly the lover develops the claim that Crete is the place where Jupiter was raised.

21. sideream...arcem: The language is exalted. *sidereus* is found primarily in epic and tragedy e.g. *A.* 10.2–3: *conciliumque uocat diuum pater atque hominum rex* | *sideream in sedem*, 12.166–7; *Met.* 4.169, Sen. *Phaed.* 677–8; while *arx* used of the heavens is very much high style e.g. *A.* 1.250, *Met.* 1.27–8, 15.858–9: *Iuppiter arces* | *temperat aetherias*.

temperat: Suggests majestic rule e.g. *A.* 1.146 (of Neptune): *uastas aperit Syrtis et temperat aequor*, *Met.* 1.770, 15.869.

22. The contrast with the hexameter could hardly be greater, with both *exiguus* and *tenero...ore* suggesting the infant Jupiter's vulnerability.

23–4. magna fides testi: testis laudatur alumno.
    fassuram Cererem crimina nostra puto.
In solemn language the lover declares that he has a witness far superior to the Cretans to support his accusations against Ceres.

23. For repetition and polyptoton used as an elegant frame for the main caesura see above on 3.2.32.

magna fides: Encapsulates a highly-prized Roman value e.g. Nep. *Iph.* 3.2.3: *bonus uero ciuis fideque magna*, A. 11.55: *haec mea magna fides?*

fides testi: The phrase has a strongly legal flavour e.g. Cic. *Q. Rosc.* 45.8, *Flac.* 60.4, *Caec.* 3.12, *Phil.* 11.5.5.

24. fassuram…crimina: The reason for highly-charged moral and legal language becomes clear: the lover is prosecuting Ceres.

nostra: This is the reading of the main manuscripts P and Y. Kenney and McKeown prefer *nota* found in ω (i.e. many minor manuscripts). One objection to *nota* is that the story, though hinted at in Homer and Hesiod, is not 'well-known'.

25–6. uiderat Iasium Cretaea diua sub Ida
   figentem certa terga ferina manu.
The narrative proper now begins with Ceres catching sight of the Iasius. Perhaps not surprisingly, in the lines that follow the lover alludes to *Heroides* 4, the letter in which Phaedra attempts to seduce Hippolytus, a youth who is both a hunter and her stepson.

25. Iasium: Ovid adopts the Hesiodic spelling (and scansion: *Ĭăsĭŭm*) of the hero's name. At *Met.* 9.422–3 (*queritur canescere mitis | Iasiona Ceres*) and *Tr.* 2.300 (*in Cerere Iasion*) he prefers the Homeric form.

Cretaea…sub Ida: Hesiod (*Theog.* 971) places the affair on Crete. Ida is labelled 'Cretan' (*OLD* 2) to distinguish it from Ida near Troy (*OLD* 1).

26. For this verbal pattern (VaBbA) see above on 3.1.7. Neither Homer nor Hesiod suggests that Ceres' beloved is a hunter.

27–8. uidit, et ut tenerae flammam rapuere medullae,
   hinc pudor, ex illa parte trahebat amor.
Catching sight of Iasius leads to instant love.

27. uidit: Repetition of a form of *uideo* from the previous hexameter underlines the importance of the gaze in generating sexual passion. While usually male (see above on 3.2.67), the gaze is sometimes female. See e.g. Phaedra's focus on Hippolytus' physical appearance at *Her.* 4.67–84. (For Phaedra's gaze see Davis [1995: 45–7].)

flammam…medullae: For love as a flame which works upon the marrow see e.g. Catul. 100.7, A. 4.66, *Her.* 4.15: *ut nostras auido fouet igne medullas.*

28. pudor…amor: For the opposition between shame/modesty and love see e.g. A. 4.54–5, 1.2.32, *Her.* 4.9: *pudor est miscendus amori.*

29–30. uictus amore pudor: sulcos arere uideres
   et sata cum minima parte redire sui.
Ceres' surrender to sexual passion and consequent neglect of her duties lead to agricultural disaster of the kind that followed Demeter's search for Persephone (*Hymn. Hom. Dem.* 305–7): 'She made it a year most terrible, most horrible for humans over the nourishing earth. Nor did the land send up what was sown. For lovely-garlanded Demeter hid it'.

29. uictus amore: For the metaphor of conquest by love see e.g. *Her.* 4.152–3: *certi siquid haberet amor | uicta precor, Fast.* 2.585.

30. cum minima parte sui: This of course defeats the farmers' expectations: seeds are sown in the hope of profit not loss e.g. Tib. 2.6.21–2, *Rem.* 173–4, *Pont.* 1.5.26: *et sata cum multo faenore reddit ager.*

31–4. cum bene iactati pulsarant arua ligones,
   ruperat et duram uomer aduncus humum,
seminaque in latos ierant aequaliter agros
   irrita decepti uota colentis erant.
The lover now recalls the description of crop failure found in the *Homeric Hymn* (308–9): 'The oxen were trying to drag many curved ploughs over the ploughlands uselessly, and much white barley fell to the earth fruitlessly'.

31. iactati…ligones: For *iacto* used of wielding agricultural implements (*OLD* 6b) see *G.* 2.355: *duros iactare bidentis,* Calp. *Ecl.* 4.117–18.

32. For this verbal pattern (VaBbA) see above on 3.1.7.

aduncus: This is Ovid's preferred epithet for a ploughshare (*Ars* 1.474, 725; *Rem.* 172, *Fast.* 2.295, 4.297, *Pont.* 4.10.6. Cf. *Hymn. Hom. Dem.* 308: καμπύλ' ἄροτρα ('curved ploughs')), Lucr. 1.313–14: *uncus…uomer, G.* 2.223: *uomeris unci.*

34. For this verbal pattern (abABV) see above on 3.6.4.

35–6. diua potens frugum siluis cessabat in altis;
   deciderant longae spicea serta comae.
And why did crops fail? Because agriculture's goddess spent her time idling in the forest.

35. diua potens frugum: Poets combine *potens* with an area of control (in the genitive) as a way of referring to a divinity e.g. *A.* 3.528: *tempestatumque potentes,* Hor. *Carm.* 1.3.1, 3.25.14, *Saec.* 1, *Met.* 9.315, Sen. *Her. F.* 300.

36. For this variation on the golden line (VabBA) see above on 3.1.11.
For Ceres' characteristic garland of grain see e.g. Tib. 1.1.15–16, Hor. *Saec.* 29–30, *Met.* 10.433, *Fast.* 4.615–16: *uultumque Ceres animumque recepit, | imposuitque suae spicea serta comae.* The fallen garland marks Ceres' failure to perform her duty.

37–8. sola fuit Crete fecundo fertilis anno:
  omnia, qua tulerat se dea, messis erat.
But if crops failed throughout the world that year, Ceres' presence ensured success on Crete.

37. fuit…fecundo fertilis: Alliteration of *f* and the juxtaposition of synonyms meaning 'fruitful' underlines the abundance of the Cretan harvest.

fecundo: Is rarely used of periods of time (*TLL* 419.16–20). But see *Fast.* 3.243 (of spring): *tempora…fecunda*, 4.671: *fecundior annus*.

38. tulerat se: As befits a goddess, the language is epic e.g. Enn. *Ann.* sedinc. 537 Goldberg and Manuwald (1): *fert sese campi per caerula laetaque prata, A.* 1.314, 3.598–9, 5.289–90, 6.879, 11.762, Sil. 1.497, 5.492, 14.317.

39–40. ipse locus nemorum canebat frugibus Ide
  et ferus in silua farra metebat aper.
Even Mt Ida, a place famous for forests not ploughlands, was white with grain.

39. ipse: Most editors print *ipse*. Némethy, Showerman and Goold, and Ramirez de Verger (2) prefer *ipsa*. While *ipsa* is possible, *ipse* yields good sense: 'Ida, the very home of forests', i.e. Ida, a place particularly associated with woodlands (and not agriculture). For Cretan Ida's sylvan fame see e.g. *Ars* 1.289–90 (of Pasiphae's bull): *forte sub umbrosis nemorosae uallibus Idae | candidus, armenti gloria, taurus erat, Fast.* 5.115–16.

canebat: For *caneo* used of ripe grain see *Met.* 1.110: *nec renouatus ager grauidis canebat aristis*.

40. farra: Reminds us that Ceres' affair with Iasius happened in the remote past. For *far* as an ancient grain see above on 7.

metebat: Given that boars do not actually harvest crops, the choice of verb is clearly ironic. For a similar use of *meto* see *Met.* 8.290–2 (the Calydonian boar).

41–2. optauit Minos similes sibi legifer annos;
  optasset Cereris longus ut esset amor.
The lover completes the narrative by drawing attention to another consequence of the bumper harvest: the Cretan king's pleasure.

41. Minos…legifer: The adjective, which occurs only twice in Latin poetry (and in Apuleius), is transferred from Ceres (*A.* 4.58: *legiferae Cereri*) to Minos. Ceres' negligence means that she no longer deserves her Virgilian epithet.

42. optasset: This is the reading of P and Y. Older editors printed *optauit*. Kenney (1958: 66) observed: 'The general avoidance of *optasset* is odd; in my opinion it gives the only pointed sense: "Minos prayed for other such years; what he should

280   Commentary

have prayed for..." How can Minos be supposed to have known what was going on?' Subsequent editors have rightly followed his advice.

longus...amor: Minos' hope for an enduring love affair would be entirely self-interested. For the phrase see (1.6.5), *Ars* (1.49): *materiam longo qui quaeris amori*. Cf. Catul. 76.13, Prop. 1.19.26.

43–4. qui tibi secubitus tristes, dea flaua, fuissent,
   hos cogor sacris nunc ego ferre tuis.
The lover now recalls his opening argument and draws the story's moral: the sex that the goddess once enjoyed she now denies to others.

   qui...| hos is the reading of P and Y and was printed in all editions before Heinsius. Heinsius preferred *quod...| hoc*, which he claimed to have found in his Palatinus. Munari reports in his apparatus that he was unable to find this reading anywhere. With one exception, subsequent editors have printed *qui...| hos*. Showerman and Goold retain *quod...| hoc*, perhaps a relic of Showerman (1914). *qui...| hos* makes good sense; *quod...| hoc* is no improvement.

43. qui: The relative pronoun precedes its 'antecedent'. The placing of the two pronouns one above the other is particularly effective.

secubitus: Recalls *secubat* (2) and *secubuitque* (16).

dea flaua: Recalls *flaua Ceres* (3).

44. sacris...tuis: The echoic effect produced by placing *sacris* at the caesura and *tuis* at the end of the line throws otherwise inoffensive *tuis* into prominence and so underlines the lover's accusation: it's your fault.

45–6. cur ego sim tristis, cum sit tibi nata reperta
   regnaque quam Iuno sorte minora regat?
Further, now that Proserpina has been recovered there is no reason for the lover to feel distressed.

45. Reference to the recovery of Proserpina reminds readers (a) that Ovid has extended Homer's and Hesiod's story of Iasion/Iasius by tacking on the best-known portion of Ceres' myth and (b) that the occasion for this enforced celibacy is the *sacrum anniuersarium Cereris* (see above on 1).

46. regnaque quam Iuno sorte minora regat: The expression is condensed: *Iuno* = *regna Iunonis*. See 1.8.25 (with McKeown [1989]): *nulli tua forma secunda est*, i.e. second to no one else's beauty; 2.6.62 (with McKeown [1998]): *ora fuere mihi plus aue docta loqui*, i.e. more skilled than any other bird's.

sorte: Refers to the allocation of realms between Jupiter, Pluto, and Neptune (*Il.* 15.187–93; *OLD* 4b).

minora: Manuscripts are divided between *minore* (P) and *minora* (apparently a correction of *minore* in Y). The parallels with 1.8.25 (*secunda*) and 2.6.62 (*plus docta*) support *minora*. *minora* also yields better sense: the point is to flatter Ceres (your daughter's kingdom is inferior only to Juno's) not to remind her that Pluto came off third best.

47–8. festa dies ueneremque uocat cantusque merumque;
  haec decet ad dominos munera ferre deos.
The lover closes with a witty combination of solemnity and self-interest, arguing that this is not a genuine holiday at all: real festivals involve song, wine, and sex.

47. festa dies: The lover wishes that Ceres' festival were more like those of Anna Perenna or Flora, festivals which involved wine, song, and dance (*Fast.* 3.525–6, 531–2, 535–8, 5.335–44); and, in the case of Flora, sexual high jinks on stage (5.347–50).

ueneremque: For the goddess's name used of a sexual partner or sex itself see e.g. 1.4.66, 1.10.33, 2.4.40, 3.14.24, *Her.* 3.116, 16.160, *Ars* 1.275, 386, 2.414, 3.609, *Rem.* 405.

ueneremque...cantusque merumque: Repeated *que*, a feature typical of the high style (see above on 3.1.32), adds gravity to the line, a gravity undercut by its content.

48. dominos...deos: For the idea see Cic. *Leg.* 2.15.8–10: *sit igitur hoc iam a principio persuasum ciuibus, dominos esse omnium rerum ac moderatores deos*. Ovid seems to be the only poet to use the phrase: *Her.* 4.12, *Pont.* 1.9.36, 2.2.12. (On Hor. *Carm.* 1.1.6 see Nisbet and Hubbard [1970] and Mayer [2012].)

3.11: REFLECTIONS ON CATULLUS

3.11: One poem or two?

Before Müller's edition of Ovid's *Carmina Amatoria* (1861) all editors printed 3.11 as a single poem. In his dissertation Müller (1856: 91) had argued (a) that lines 27–32 would make an appropriate ending to a poem because they restate the argument set out in lines 1–6 and (b) that lines 33–4 contradict that conclusion and launch a new analysis. He proposed therefore that 3.11 was originally a set of paired poems in the manner of 1.11 and 1.12 (Nape and the writing tablets) and 2.13 and 2.14 (Corinna's abortion).[1] Since 1861 there has been disagreement, with some editors accepting Müller's position (Ehwald, Némethy, Brandt,

---

[1] For these paired poems see Introduction §3. A divided 3.11 would actually be very different from those poems because lines 33–52 do not constitute, to use J. T. Davis's term (1977: 19), a 'dramatic sequel'.

Bornecque, Munari, Kenney, Showerman and Goold, and Ramirez de Verger [1]) and others rejecting it (Merkel [1862], Riese [1871], Edwards [1898], McKeown, and Ramirez de Verger [2]).

Although the Gallus papyrus provides evidence that the Romans used division signs and increased spacing to mark the end of one poem and the beginning of the next,[2] those conventions were lost in the shift from papyrus roll to codex. The medieval scribes who wrote P and Y (and indeed R and S) capitalized the first word of each line and used a larger capital to mark the beginning of a new poem. While the left-hand margin of the relevant section of P (lines 23–33) is severely damaged, there appears to be insufficient space for an initial capital at line 33, the point at which Müller proposed to divide the poem. Y's scribe clearly treats 3.11 as a single poem, using larger capitals only at 3.11.1 (*Multa diuque tuli*) and 3.12.1 (*Quis fuit ille dies*).

That, however, is not the end of the matter. Errors occur. Munari (1965: 17) noted, for example, that non-existent divisions are marked in Y: 'In six verses of the *Amores* the first letter is larger than usual, as if the copyist wished to indicate the beginning of a new elegy.'[3] Munari also notes (1965: 60) that in P a larger capital wrongly suggests that a new poem begins at 3.7.19: *A pudet annorum*. And the opposite also happens. Scribes sometimes fail to mark the end of one poem and the beginning of the next. In R and S, for example, there are no divisions between 1.Epigram, 1.1, 1.2, and 1.3; while in P there is nothing to mark the beginning of 2.19.[4] The evidence of medieval manuscripts is not enough to resolve the issue.

What then of 3.11? What is the evidence for treating lines 1–52 as a single unit? First there is the manuscript tradition: all known manuscripts treat this as a single poem. Second, taken together, these lines are perhaps more self-analytical than any other group of lines in Book 3. Third, and this is related to the second point, these lines engage explicitly with Catullus' struggle to understand and control his passion for Lesbia, alluding to two of Catullus' most famous poems, poem 8 (especially line 11: *perfer, obdura* ['endure, be strong']); cf. 3.11.7: *perfer et obdura* ['endure and be strong']); and poem 85 (1: *odi et amo* ['I hate and I love']; cf. 3.11.34: *amor...odium* ['love...hate'], 35: *odero...amabo*, 36: *amat...odit*, 43: *odium...amorem*).

It is notable, however, that the lover alludes consistently to Catullus 8 in lines 1–32 and to Catullus 85 in lines 33–52. Related to this is the fact that he adopts contradictory positions, with lines 1–32 proclaiming that he is now free of love, and lines 33–52 acknowledging that he is caught up in a struggle between love and hate. Note too that lines 33–52, responding as they do to Catullus 8, work

---

[2] See Anderson, Parsons, and Nisbet (1979: 129–30).
[3] Munari's examples are: 1.2.51, 1.4.13, 1.6.9, 17, 27, 2.3.15.
[4] Damon (1990: 273) lists additional examples of 'run-on-poems' and 'false poem divisions'. I have included in the text only examples which I have been able to verify myself.

very differently from 1–32, with the exploration of paradox being its primary mode. What makes this question so difficult is the sudden change in stance: there is no bridge passage like that which unites the two halves of 3.12 (13–18).

Also important is the naval metaphor at 29–30: *iam mea uotiua puppis redimita corona | lenta tumescentes aequoris audit aquas* ('and now my ship, crowned with votive garlands, hears unmoved the sea's swelling waters'). These lines suggest closure because they refer to the practice of garlanding a ship at the conclusion of a safe voyage.[5] They allude, moreover, to Propertius' declaration that his affair with Cynthia is over (3.24.15–16): *ecce coronatae portum tetigere carinae, | traiectae Syrtes, ancora iacta mihi est* ('My ship has touched harbour, garlanded, the Syrtes have been passed and my anchor dropped'). But what do these lines close? A section or a whole poem? If we turn to line 51 we find that the speaker invokes and reverses the closural effect of the naval image: *lintea dem potius uentisque ferentibus utar* ('may I rather spread my sails and experience favourable winds').

On balance, it seems likely that 3.11 should be read as a single poem held together by its focus on Catullan themes. Just as 3.9 engages with Tibullus and 3.12 with Propertius, so 3.11 reflects upon different aspects of the Catullan experience.

3.11

In this poem's first section the lover addresses himself.[6] His meditation begins (1–8) and ends (27–32) by asserting that he is free from love. In 9–26 he recalls the experience of sexual obsession, speaking only of the suffering he has endured: of resting on hard ground, of his mistress's lies and deceptions, of the pain and embarrassment caused by rivals.

If we turn to comparison with Catullus 8, as the quotation at line 7 suggests we should, we find a similar structure but a different story. Both poems frame an account of the experience of love with a focus on the present. Catullus, however, begins and ends not with propositions but self-exhortation (1–2): *miser Catulle, desinas ineptire, | et quod uides perisse perditum ducas* ('Wretched Catullus, you should stop being stupid, and count as lost what you see has perished'); (19): *at tu, Catulle, destinatus obdura* ('but you, Catullus, be resolved, be strong'). Catullus, moreover, becomes so sentimental that he can summarize the affair in the following words (8): *fulsere uere candidi tibi soles* ('truly then the sun shone

---

[5] See e.g. *G*. 1.303–4 (quoted below on 29). At *A*. 4.418 garlanding marks both an end and a beginning: *puppibus et laeti nautae imposuere coronas*; so too at *Her*. 15.211–12: *siue redis, puppique tuae uotiua parantur | munera*. In his later works Ovid continues to mark endings with reference to sea voyages (e.g. *Ars* 1.772, 3.748, *Rem*. 811–12, *Fast*. 2.863–4).

[6] The poem is not addressed to 'the beloved' or 'Ovid's mistress', as Cairns (1972: 80; 1979: 125) and McKeown (1998: 169) assert. As in Catul. 8, the speaker uses the second person when addressing both himself and his absent girlfriend. Neither Catul. 8 nor 3.11 fits Cairns's (1972: 80) definition of the 'genre renuntiatio amoris'.

284   *Commentary*

for you'). Consequently it is not surprising that the increasingly passionate questions (16–18) which he imagines putting to his girlfriend suggest loss of self-control and that his final command lacks conviction.

Lines 9–26 diverge widely from the Catullan model, recalling not the republican poet's works but the Ovidian lover's earlier experiences. He recalls, for example, being a locked-out lover (9–12; cf. 1.6, 2.19.21–4), his girlfriend's perjuries (21–2; cf. 3.3), her use of secret messages (23–4; cf. 1.4.17–20, 2.5.15–18, 2.19.41–2), feigned illness (cf. 1.8.73, 2.19.11–12), and exploitation of rivals (26; cf. 1.8.95).

The conclusion (27–32), however, reverts to Catullan themes and language: *duraui* (27; cf. *obdura* [11], *obdurat* [12]), *obdura* [19]); *ferendis* (27; cf. *perfer* [11]); *desine* (31; cf. *desinas* [1]); *perdere* (cf. 32 *perditum* [2]). But these similarities underline differences. First, Ovid's lover uses indicatives and imperatives not subjunctives: *duraui* ('I have grown strong' 27), *quaere* ('look for' 28), *desine…perdere* ('stop…wasting' 31–2) to emphasize his achievement in escaping love's toils. Second, this section's final line underlines success by responding to Catullus' opening exhortation *desinas ineptire* ('stop being stupid' 1) with a statement of fact: *non ego nunc stultus, ut ante fui* ('I am no longer as foolish as I was' 32).

The second section (33–52) reworks another poem of Catullus, this time exploring his most famous couplet (85):

> odi et amo. quare id faciam fortasse requiris.
> nescio, sed fieri sentio et excrucior.

I hate and I love. How I do this, perhaps you ask. I do not know, but I feel it happening and I am tortured.

Catullus presents a paradox. His first three words set out a contradiction: the poet experiences both love and hate. He then imagines a reader's reaction: how is this possible? The pentameter fails to answer the question: there is no explanation, only pain.

In 85 Catullus juxtaposes love and hate. Elsewhere he attempts to make sense of the paradox, by distinguishing between different kinds of emotion (72.5–8):[7]

> nunc te cognoui: quare etsi impensius uror,
> multo mi tamen es uilior et leuior.
> 'qui potis est?' inquis. quod amantem iniuria talis
> cogit amare magis, sed bene uelle minus.

Now I know you: so even though I burn more intensely, to me you are much cheaper and more trifling. 'How is this possible?', you say. Because such a wrong compels a lover to love more, but like less.

---

[7] For the contrast between love (*amare*) and liking (*bene uelle*) see also Catul. 75.3–4.

Commentary, 11.1-3   285

In different words, the lover poses the question of poem 85: 'How is this possible?' Now, however, he has an answer: he distinguishes passion from respect, love from affection.

Obsessive repetition of the words 'love' and 'hate' links lines 33-52 to Catullus 85. But the attempt to comprehend the Catullan paradox at length connects this section with poem 72. Here, however, Catullus' eight lines of analysis have grown into a twenty-line meditation.

Secondary Literature: Müller (1856); Lee (1962: 160-4); Williams (1968: 506-10); Cairns (1972: 138-40); Frécaut (1972: 188-90); Morgan (1977: 83-5; 97-98); Cairns (1979); Courtney (1987); Damon (1990); Heyworth (1995); Perkins (2002); Milnor (2014: 89-90; 206-8); Knox (2018); Graverini (2019).

1-2. Multa diuque tuli; uitiis patientia uicta est:
cede fatigato pectore, turpis amor.
The lover begins with a bold declaration: I can take no more; this relationship is over.

1. A wholly dactylic line (DDDD) perhaps underlines the lover's confidence.

Multa diuque tuli: Quotes an earlier complaint against a husband too tolerant of his wife's adulteries (2.19.49). Here the lover's protest is less cynical: he can no longer endure his girlfriend's faults.

uitiis: Given this line's clear allusions to 2.19, *uitium* here may recall that lover's perverse use of the word to denote his own masochism (9) and a husband's acquiescence (58). Here it is used in the expected way, as at e.g. 2.4.1-2: *non ego mendosos ausim defendere mores | falsaque pro uitiis arma mouere meis*.

patientia: Recalls the cynical conclusion of the previous book (2.19.59): *quin alium, quem tanta iuuat patientia, quaeris?* (These are the only occurrences of *patientia* in *Amores*.) There the lover's patience amounted to tolerating a husband's indifference to his wife's adulteries; here it is used, in the normal way, of tolerating a girlfriend's faults.

2. **turpis amor:** This love is 'shameful' because the beloved is unworthy. See e.g. Hor. S. 1.4.111, Prop. 2.16.36, 3.21.33, *Rem.* 64, *Ib.* 295.

amor: Whether to treat 'love' as a common or proper noun is an editorial decision. Here 'love' hovers between abstraction and personification. But see below on 5.

3-4. scilicet asserui iam me fugique catenas
et quae non puduit ferre, tulisse pudet.
Consequently the lover has now escaped love's slavery and shame.

3. **scilicet:** Sometimes used sarcastically, the particle seems unironic here.

asserui…me: Originally a legal term for liberation of the enslaved (*TLL* 1A: *technice in re publica et re iudicaria*), *assero* here recalls the *seruitium amoris*. Although infrequent in *Amores* (1.2.18, 1.3.5, 2.17.1–2), it is important in *Her.* 20 and 21 (Ziogas [2021: Chapter 4]). For references see above on 3.8.14.

catenas: For love's chains see 1.2.30: *et noua captiua uincula mente feram*. Elsewhere in *Amores*, Ovid associates *catenae* with actual slavery (e.g. 1.6.1, 2.2.41).

4. Interweaving of verbs and tenses brilliantly encapsulates the lover's feelings about past and present.

5–6. uicimus et domitum pedibus calcamus Amorem.
   uenerunt capiti cornua sera meo.
Not only has he escaped slavery but the lover has a victory over Love and regained his sense of masculine pride.

5. The lover's language suggests military conquest. See e.g. *Pont.* 4.7.47–8 (addressed to a successful general): *ense tuo factos <u>calcabas uictor</u> aceruos | impositoque Getes <u>sub pede</u> multus erat*. It also recalls and reverses Love's dominion over the Propertian lover (1.1.4): *et caput impositis pressit Amor pedibus*, (2.30a.7–8). Cf. *Rem.* 530: *et tua saeuus Amor sub pede colla premit?*

uicimus: Recalls *uicta est* in 1. Patience conquered leads to conquest.

Amorem: As in Prop. 1.1.4 and 2.30a.7–8, reference to trampling or crushing underfoot suggests personification.

6. For this verbal pattern (VABba) see above on 3.1.30.

cornua: For horns as a sign of defiance or pride (*TLL* 973.21–39, *OLD* 1d) see e.g. Plaut. *Pseud.* 1021, Hor. *Carm.* 3.21.18 (with Nisbet and Rudd [2004]), *Ars* 1.239, *Tr.* 4.9.27: *iam feror in pugnas et nondum cornua sumpsi*.

7–8. perfer et obdura. dolor hic tibi proderit olim:
   saepe tulit lassis sucus amarus opem.
This phase of the argument closes confidently: if the lover shows strength his health will be restored.

7. **perfer et obdura:** Adapts Catul. 8.11: *sed obstinata mente perfer, obdura*. (Adaptation is necessary because Catullus employs an iambic metre: *pĕrfĕr, ŏbdūrā*.) Quotation underlines reversal: the Catullan lover has been discarded (8.9): *nunc iam illa non uult*; this lover rejects his mistress.

Ovid recycles Catullus' words in surprising contexts: when encouraging the student-lover to be persistent (*Ars* 2.178): *perfer et obdura: postmodo mitis erit*; and when writing to his wife (*Tr.* 5.11.7): *perfer et obdura. multo grauiora tulisti*.

dolor hic tibi proderit olim: Perhaps recalls *A.* 1.203: *forsan et haec olim meminisse iuuabit*, particularly if *iuuabit* is taken to mean 'help' rather than 'give pleasure'.

8. lassis: For *lassus* as 'sick' (*OLD* 3) see 2.13.2: *in dubio uitae lassa Corinna iacet*. At 13 it has a different meaning.

sucus amarus: For the phrase's medical connotations see e.g. *Her.* 20.183–4, *Ars* 2.335–6, *Rem.* 227–8: *saepe bibi sucos, quamuis inuitus, amaros | aeger*. The medical writer Celsus recommends the 'juice of bitter nuts' (4.31.7.5, 6.7.8c.3).

Medical language invokes the idea that sexual passion is a form of disease. Pervasive in Euripides' *Hippolytus*, a play in which νόσος ('disease') and cognates occur 23 times, the trope is common in love elegy (e.g. Catul. 76.25 [cf. 83.4 where *sana* means 'free of love'], Prop. 1.1.26–7, 2.1.57–8; Tib. 2.3.13–14) and central to *Remedia Amoris*.

9–12. ergo ego sustinui, foribus tam saepe repulsus,
   ingenuum dura ponere corpus humo?
ergo ego nescio cui, quem tu complexa tenebas,
   excubui clausam seruus ut ante domum?
Moralizing now gives way to urgent questions. Repetition of *ergo ego* at the beginning of each hexameter underlines the lover's indignation (cf. *Pont.* 4.14.17, 19), while the combination of two of elegy's best-known tropes, the *exclusus amator* and the *seruitium amoris*, emphasizes his degradation.

9. ergo ego: The phrase is used by Cicero (e.g. *Phil.* 2.30.5: *ergo ego sceleratus appellor?*), Livy (2.40.8), Propertius (3.21.17), Ovid (e.g. 1.4.3, 1.7.11, *Her.* 10.119, *Met.* 7.51, 7.172, 9.182, 9.513), and others to express resentment.

sustinui: Underlines the speaker's inability to believe what has happened. Cf. *Her.* 5.31–2: *Xanthe, retro propera, uersaeque recurrite lymphae! | sustinet Oenonen deseruisse Paris*, *Met.* 6.563.

McKeown (1989: on 1.7.49–50) notes that Livy and Ovid are the earliest authors to use an infinitive after *sustineo*. For examples see *OLD sustineo* 6.

foribus...repulsus: Exclusion from the mistress's house is a commonplace of Latin love poetry e.g. Hor. *Carm.* 3.10 (with Nisbet and Rudd [2004]), Tib. 1.2.7–14, Prop. 1.16 (with Fedeli [1980]), *Am.* 1.6 (with McKeown [1987]). For the phrase see Hor. *S.* 2.7.90.

10. For the verbal pattern (the golden line: abVAB) see above on 3.3.21.

ingenuum...corpus: The adjective is ambiguous between 'freeborn' (*OLD* 2) and 'delicate' (*OLD* 3c). The first sense arises from context (note especially 3–4) and is reinforced by the contrast with *seruus* in 12. *ingenuus* invokes the lover's legal status and suggests that lying on the ground outside a woman's house is slave-like. (For the *seruitium amoris* see above on 3.) Cf. *Ars* 2.215–16 where the Teacher

288   *Commentary*

sees holding a woman's mirror as unworthy of a free man: *nec tibi turpe puta (quamuis sit turpe, placebit), | ingenua speculum sustinuisse manu.* Juxtaposition with *dura* activates the sense of 'delicate' and highlights the discomfort of lying on the ground. Cf. *Tr.* 1.5.71–2 (contrasting Ulysses with the exiled poet): *illi corpus erat durum patiensque laborum: | inualidae uires ingenuaeque mihi.* For *ingenuus* as 'delicate' see also 1.7.50, 1.14.52 (of his girlfriend's face): *ingenuas...genas*.

For the concept of the *ingenuum corpus* see Oenone's rejection of a rapist's 'reward' (*Her.* 5.143–4): *nec pretium stupri gemmas aurumque poposci: | turpiter ingenuum munera corpus emunt.* Here *ingenuum* underlines Oenone's sense of honour and self-worth. (For discussion of this passage see Introduction §11.)

ponere corpus humo: Ovid's Teacher actually encourages excluded lovers to lie on the ground (*Ars* 2.523–4): *clausa tibi fuerit promissa ianua nocte: | perfer et immunda ponere corpus humo.* At *Tr.* 1.2.54 the same phrase is used of dying: *in solita moriens ponere corpus humo.*

11. complexa tenebas: For the phrase used in a similarly dismissive context see 1.13.39: *at si quem manibus Cephalum complexa teneres,* where *quem...Cephalum* ('some Cephalus or other') is almost equivalent to *nescio cui quem.*

12. As in the previous couplet, the lover combines two major elegiac tropes, the *exclusus amator* and *seruitium amoris.*

ut seruus: Reinforces *ingenuus* in the sense of 'free-born' in the previous couplet. For the excluded lover as slave-like see Tib. 1.1.55–6: *me retinent uinctum formosae uincla puellae, | et sedeo duras ianitor ante fores.*

clausam...domum: For the phrase see Tib. 2.4.22: *ne iaceam clausam flebilis ante domum.*

13–16. uidi, cum foribus lassus prodiret amator,
    inualidum referens emeritumque latus.
hoc tamen est leuius, quam quod sum uisus ab illo:
    eueniat nostris hostibus ille pudor.
Urgent questions are followed by an appeal to autopsy: he has actually seen and been seen by worn-out lovers leaving his girlfriend's house.

13. lassus...amator: For *lassus* as 'sexually exhausted' see 1.5.25, 3.7.80.

14. Describes in polite terms what Catullus (6.13) had called *latera ecfututa.* For *latus* as a sexual term see above on 3.7.36.

emeritumque: Maltby (2002: 334) notes that Tibullus is the first to use *emereo* in the sexual sense of 'service' (1.9.59–60): *nec lasciua soror dicatur plura bibisse | pocula uel plures emeruisse uiros.* See also *Am.* 2.8.24: *unum est e dominis emeruisse satis.*

16. eueniat…hostibus: Ovid particularly favours this form of curse: 2.10.16, 17, Her. 16.219, Ars 3.247, Fast. 3.494, Pont. 4.6.35. Cf. Aesch. PV 864: τοιάδ' ἐπ' ἐχθροὺς ἐμοὺς ἔλθοι Κύπρις ('May a Cypris like this come upon my enemies'), Prop. 3.8.20: *hostibus eueniat lenta puella meis.*

17-18. quando ego non fixus lateri patienter adhaesi,
  ipse tuus custos, ipse uir, ipse comes?
Prompted perhaps by self-pity, the lover now protests against the injustice of his treatment.

17. The lover claims loyalty to his mistress in terms that recall the devoted service of an impoverished Tibullan lover (1.5.61-2): *pauper erit praesto semper, te pauper adibit | primus et in tenero fixus erit latere.* (For the servility of this Tibullan lover see Putnam [1973: 106], Murgatroyd [1991: 182], Maltby [2002: 257].)

fixus lateri…adhaesi: The language here (unlike that of Tibullus, if Putnam and Maltby are right) suggests devotion rather than sexual passion. Cf. Virgil's description of Aeneas and Pallas (*A*. 10.160-1): *Pallasque sinistro | adfixus lateri iam quaerit sidera.*

patienter: The adverb perhaps implies enslavement. See e.g. 1.14.25 (of hair submitting to torture): *quam se praebuerunt ferro patienter et igni,* Her. 20.88-90 (Acontius promising to be Cydippe's slave): *'quam patienter amat!' | ipsa tibi dices, ubi uideris omnia ferri: | 'tam bene qui seruit, seruiat iste mihi!'*

18. Outlines the three roles that the lover played in his girlfriend's life. Two of these are typically performed by a wealthy man's inferiors.

custos: In *Amores* guards are usually enslaved. See above on 3.4.36.

uir: While the term can be ambiguous between 'husband' (*OLD* 2a) and 'lover' (*OLD* 2b), there is no uncertainty here: this man is a former lover.

comes: As Maltby (2002: 331) notes, the term often implies lower rank (*OLD* 2, 3, 4b). Here it continues the reference to Tib. 1.5, with the 'companion' clearing the street of crowds for his mistress (63-4): *pauper in angusto fidus comes agmine turbae | subicietque manus efficietque uiam.* See also Tib. 1.9.42 where the 'companion' complains that he has held a (literal) torch for his girlfriend: *ipse comes multa lumina nocte tuli.* Cf. *Met.* 3.574-5: *comitem famulumque sacrorum | cepimus,* 6.649.

19-20. scilicet et populo per me comitata placebas:
  causa fuit multis noster amoris amor.
Not only has he protected her, but the lover has made his mistress universally well-known.

19. populo…placebas: The phrase is sometimes used of literary or theatrical popularity (e.g. Ter. *An.* 3, *Pont.* 2.4.15). When addressed to a woman, however, it implies prostitution. See Sen. *Con.* 1.2.7.9: 'You stood with prostitutes (*meretricibus*), you stood adorned in such a way that you could be attractive to the people (*populo placere*), in the clothes which a pimp had given you'. For *placeo* in the sense of 'be sexually attractive to' see on 3.2.35.

per me comitata: This resembles (but is not identical to) the claim made in 3.12 that it is the lover's poetry which has made his mistress famous. Here it is their relationship which has established his mistress's reputation.

20. Internal rhyme (*multis…amoris*) and polyptoton (*amoris amor*) make this a particularly effective line.

21–2. turpia quid referam uanae mendacia linguae
    et periuratos in mea damna deos?
From talking up the benefits he has conferred upon his mistress, the lover now begins to list his complaints. Here he denounces her dishonesty, as he did in 3.3.

21. For the verbal pattern (aVbAB) see above on 3.6.16.

mendacia: That mistresses lie is an elegiac commonplace e.g. Prop. 2.17.1, 2.26a.3, *Am.* 2.19.11, 3.3.10, 44.

22. periuratos…deos: For a girlfriend's perjuries see Tib. 1.9.29–40, Prop. 1.8a.17, 1.15.25, 35–8, *Am.* 1.8.85, 3.3.3, 21, 36.

23–32: Manuscript damage means that the beginnings of these lines are missing from P.

23–4. quid iuuenum tacitos inter conuiuia nutus
    uerbaque compositis dissimulata notis?
This complaint about furtive messages reworks the instructions of Tibullus' Venus (1.2.21–2): *illa uiro coram nutus conferre loquaces | blandaque compositis abdere uerba notis* and summarizes the Ovidian lover's advice to his girlfriend (1.4.15–28). For detailed discussion of secret signs in elegy see McKeown (1989: 85–6) on 1.4.17–28.

23. For nods as communication between lovers see Tib. 1.2.21, 1.6.19, 1.8.1, *Am.* 1.4.17, 2.5.16, *Her.* 16.258, *Ars* 1.138. Repetition of *quid* (from 21) supplies *referam* as the main verb.

24. compositis…notis: Cf. Tib. 1.2.22, *Pont.* 3.3.58: *credor adulterii composuisse notas*.

uerbaque…dissimulata: Cf. *A.* 1.710 (of Cupid as Iulus): *simulataque uerba*, *Pont.* 3.9.40: *uerbaque profectu dissimulata carent*.

Commentary, 11.19-30   291

25-6. dicta erat aegra mihi: praeceps amensque cucurri.
ueni, et riuali non erat aegra meo.
While the complaint that mistresses feign sickness (often headaches) is conventional, the couplet's structure is not: repetition combined with polyptoton underlines the girlfriend's deceitfulness: *erat aegra mihi...non erat aegra meo*. Striking too is the drama, because here the lover reports not his girlfriend's trick but the means by which it was uncovered.

25. For the fake illness see Plaut. *Truc.* 632 (Phronesium the *meretrix*): *nam mihi de uento miserae condoluit caput*, Tib. 1.6.36, 2.6.49-50, *Am.* 1.8.73: *capitis modo finge dolorem*, 2.19.11-12.

26. For the value of rivals in keeping lovers on their toes see *Ars* 3.593-4: *postmodo riualem partitaque foedera lecti | sentiat*.

27-8. his et quae taceo duraui saepe ferendis:
quaere alium pro me, qui queat ista pati.
The lover concludes his argument with a series of closural gestures. In this couplet he employs ring composition, repeating words from his opening argument: *duraui* (cf. *obdura* 7), *ferendis* (cf. *tuli* 1, *tulisse* 4, *perfer* 7), *pati* (cf. *patientia* 1).

27. duraui: Suggests that the lover has obeyed his own command (7): *perfer et obdura*.

28. pati: Given that the lover's *patientia* (1) is no more, his girlfriend will need another to *pati* her faults.

29-30. iam mea uotiua puppis redimita corona
lenta tumescentes aequoris audit aquas.
Reference to the practice of garlanding a ship's stern at the end of a voyage constitutes a second closural move.

29. meă uotiuā...redimită coronā: For Ovid's fondness for interweaving four words ending in *a* see Introduction §10 and on 3.4.16.
   For the practice of garlanding ships at the end of a sea voyage see *G.* 1.303-4, *Rem.* 811-12: *hoc opus exegi: fessae date serta carinae; | contigimus portus, quo mihi cursus erat*. Like Propertius (3.24.15-16, quoted in the introduction above), Ovid extends the image to mark the end of a love affair, an extension made easier by poets' treatment of the sea as an emblem of love e.g. Hor. *Carm.* 1.5.13-16, *PA* 12.156.5-6: τυφλὰ δ', ὅπως ναυηγὸς ἐν οἴδματι, κύματα μετρῶν | δινεῦμαι, μεγάλῳ χείματι πλαζόμενος ('Like a shipwrecked man in the swelling surge, counting the blind waves, I whirl about baffled by a great storm').

30. lenta: For *lentus* as 'unmoved' see 1.6.15, 41; 2.19.51; 3.6.60. Cf. Seneca's use of *lentus* of an unresponsive harbour rather than a ship (*Med.* 622-3): *Aulis amissi memor inde regis | portibus lentis retinet carinas*.

**31–2. desine blanditias et uerba potentia quondam
perdere: non ego nunc stultus, ut ante fui.**
As an additional closural gesture the lover tells himself to stop and contrasts his past with his present state.

31. desine: For this verb used to mark closure see Catul. 21.12, 23.27, 69.10, 103.3, *Ecl.* 9.66, Hor. *Carm.* 1.23.11, 3.3.70, Prop. 1.5.31, *Am.* 1.10.64.

32. non ego nunc stultus, ut ante fui: Responds to Catullus' self-exhortation *desinas ineptire* (8.1) with a firm claim to success.

**33–4. luctantur pectusque leue in contraria tendunt
hac amor hac odium. sed, puto, uincit amor.**
The lover launches a new phase in his self-analysis with a less than pithy statement of the Catullan paradox, a paradox that he resolves before the couplet is complete.

33. luctantur…tendunt: Framing the hexameter with two main verbs and postponing the subject until the beginning of the pentameter makes for a striking opening to this new phase of the argument.

pectusque leue: The language is typical of Ovid, not Catullus. For Catullus it is Lesbia who is *leuis* (72.6; quoted in the introduction above); for Ovid it is elegy itself that is 'lightweight' (1.1.19, 2.1.21, 3.1.41).

34. hac amor, hac odium: While the opposition between love and hate is found in Hellenistic poetry (e.g. *PA* 5.107, 12.172), Catullus seems exceptional in presenting the lover as experiencing these emotions simultaneously.

The phrase perhaps recalls Propertius' drunken return to Cynthia (1.3.14): *hac Amor hac Liber, durus uterque deus*. For similar internal conflict see Ovid's Dido (*Her.* 7.29–30):

> non tamen Aenean, quamuis male cogitat, <u>odi</u>,
> sed queror infidum questaque peius <u>amo</u>.

puto: For the scansion *putŏ* see above on 3.1.8.

uincit amor: While Catullus seems to treat love and hate as equally powerful, Ovid's lover, if hesitantly, sees love as the more potent force.

**35–6. odero, si potero; si non, inuitus amabo.
nec iuga taurus amat; quae tamen odit, habet.**
But if love currently holds the upper hand, the lover will attempt to reverse that situation: he will hate or at least love against his will.

35. This is a remarkable line. Like 33, it is framed by two main verbs . Here we also have balanced clauses flanking the main caesura in the Ovidian manner (see above on 3.2.11).

Commentary, 11.31–5 293

But this line presents a problem. Heinsius bracketed the couplet in his text and commented (290): *Distichon hoc Ovidianum non videtur esse*. Kenney (1962: 13) agreed: '3.11.35–36, <was> rightly condemned by Heinsius'. Neither editor gives reasons. Courtney (1987: 7), however, does:

First, their jerky character is quite unlike the Ovidian flow. Second, the announcement of future intent is premature and disruptive at this point. Third, the scansion *oderŏ* is not Ovidian.

None of these criticisms is persuasive. First, Ovid's writing is sometimes 'jerky'. See e.g. *Her.* 14.106: *tu tibi dux comiti, tu comes ipsa duci*, a pentameter which, despite its lack of 'Ovidian flow' (it consists of eight words), displays typical Ovidian skill in its use of balance, repetition, and variation. Second, this is not a not narrative poem: it presents a series of arguments not a plot. Third, *odero* occurs nowhere else in Latin poetry. Leaving aside this occurrence, we have no evidence for its scansion, Ovidian or otherwise. Note too that Courtney's conclusion (1987: 8) that 'Ovid...confines himself to two clearly-defined classes... proper names...and compounds of iambic words' is based on a question-begging argument.

But we do know that Ovid sometimes treats final *o* as short e.g. *putŏ*, just three words away in the previous line. Platnauer (1951: 52) notes that Ovid treats final *o* as short in trisyllabic words (*Her.* 18.203: *desinŏ*; *Pont.* 1.1.25: *conferŏ*) and in futures/future perfects (*Tr.* 4.10.130: *erŏ*; *Her.* 17.260: *dabŏ*; and *Am.* 3.11.35: *oderŏ*).

On the other hand, this line is supported by older evidence than almost any other verse in Ovid. Our oldest manuscript, P, is no older than the ninth century. This line, however, combined with a garbled version of Prop. 1.1.5 (*donec me docuit castas odisse puellas*), occurs in a graffito from Pompeii which must have been written no later than 79 CE (*CIL* 4.1520):

> candida me docuit nigras
> odisse puellas <u>odero si potero sed non inuitus</u>
> <u>amabo</u>
> scripsit Venus fisica Pompeiana

It seems extraordinary to reject such a well-attested line.

For Ovid in Pompeii see Graverini (2013–14; 2019), Milnor (2014: Chapters 3 and 4). Graverini (2019: 32) notes that *Amores, Heroides*, and *Tristia* were particularly popular.

odero si potero: Metrical mirroring (*ōdĕrŏ...pŏtĕrō*) and rhyme underline a paradox: the lover claims that he can choose which emotions he will have.

inuitus amabo: Acknowledges the Catullan claim that we can love against our will (cf. 72.8: *cogit amare*).

36. The conventional image of bull and yoke/plough (e.g. *PA* 12.149.3, Prop. 2.3.47–8, *Am.* 1.2.13–14, *Ars* 1.471, *Her.* 4.21, *Rem.* 235) restates the lover's position in less paradoxical language: the bull dislikes the plough, but endures what he hates.

37–8. nequitiam fugio, fugientem forma reducit;
auersor morum crimina, corpus amo.

This couplet offers different formulations, the second more blunt than the first, in a second attempt at unravelling the initial paradox: the lover is attracted by his girlfriend's body but loathes her behaviour.

37. This is another brilliant line, with repetition framing the main caesura (*fugio // fugientem*) and alliteration of *f* used to underline both the lover's attempt to escape and the reason for his failure. For this type of framing see above on 3.2.32.

nequitiam: For the poet-lover's characteristic *nequitia* see 2.1.2: *ille ego nequitiae Naso poeta meae* and 3.1.17 (with discussion above): *nequitiam uinosa tuam conuiuia narrant*. Here, however, the context suggests that depravity is primarily the girlfriend's.

forma: Perhaps recalls Catullus' defining epithet for Lesbia *formosa* (86.1, 3, 5). See below on 41.

38. Framed by powerfully emotive words which recall Catullus' own, the line attempts another resolution: the lover lusts after his girlfriend's body but is repulsed by her character and habits.

auersor: Equivalent to *odi*, this verb is used of Daphne's attitude to suitors (*Met.* 1.478: *illa auersata petentes*) and the nurse's reaction to Myrrha's incestuous desires (*Met.* 10.394: *auersata gemit*). It conveys a powerful sense of revulsion.

39–40. sic ego nec sine te nec tecum uiuere possum,
et uideor uoti nescius esse mei.

What are the consequences of living a paradox? Confusion.

39. As Barchiesi (2001b: 155–6) pointed out, the sentiment recalls a speech given in 131 BCE by the censor Q. Caecilius Macedonicus, a speech invoked by the *princeps* in support of the *lex Iulia de maritandis ordinibus* (Gel. 1.6.2.3): 'Since nature has handed down that it is not possible to live with them very agreeably, nor at all without them...'. (For Augustus' use of the speech see Liv. *Per.* 59.15, Suet. *Aug.* 89.2.)

The idea was old long before Macedonicus. The leader of the men's chorus in Aristophanes' *Lysistrata* refers to 'that proverb' (ἐκεῖνο τοὔπος) (1039): οὔτε σὺν πανωλέθροισιν οὔτ' ἄνευ πανωλέθρων ('neither with the ruinous creatures nor without the ruinous creatures'). Martial virtually quotes Ovid (12.46): *difficilis facilis, iucundus acerbus es idem | nec tecum possum uiuere, nec sine te.*

40. uoti nescius: Elsewhere Ovid uses the phrase of his student's confusion (*Ars* 1.64): *cogeris uoti nescius esse tui* and Myrrha's quandary (*Met.* 10.481): *tum nescia uoti*.

41–2. aut formosa fores minus aut minus improba uellem:
 non facit ad mores tam bona forma malos.
If only she did not combine beauty with wickedness.

41. The line is carefully crafted with carefully placed alliteration of *f* and *m*, with key terms occupying the second and second-last positions, and with *minus aut minus* as the centrepiece.

formosa: Recalls not only *forma* (37) but Catullus' definition of Lesbia's beauty (86.5–6): *Lesbia formosa est, quae cum pulcherrima tota est, | tum omnibus una omnes surripuit Veneres.*

improba: Although Catullus does not use this term of Lesbia (he reserves it for *cinaedi* [57.1, 10] and an incestuous mother [64.403]), he acknowledges her infidelity in even his most besotted moments (68b.135–6): *quae tamen etsi uno non est contenta Catullo, | rara uerecundae furta feremus erae.* Elsewhere no pejorative epithet is needed (e.g. 11.17–20, 58).

42–50. Manuscript damage means that the beginnings of these lines are missing from P.

42. facit ad: For the idiom (first found in Ovid) see 1.2.16, *Her.* 6.128, 14.56, 15.8, 16.192, *Ars* 3.540 (Gibson [2003]: 'colloquial'), *Tr.* 1.10.44. (*TLL* 122.42–123.15 gives further examples.)

43–4. facta merent odium, facies exorat amorem:
 me miserum! uitiis plus ualet illa suis.
This couplet offers a final attempt at coming to grips with the Catullan paradox: while her beauty demands love, her deeds warrant hate.

43. This is another superbly constructed line with each half beginning *fac-*, with echoic syntax (subject verb object), and with the key terms of the Catullan paradox placed at the end of each clause.

44. me miserum: Recalls a moment of Catullan self-pity (76.19): *me miserum aspicite.*

uitiis…ualet: The lover closes this phase of the argument with one last paradox. A *uitium* is a weakness, 'a flaw' (*OLD* 2). In this case, however, weakness is a source of strength.

45–8. parce, per o lecti socialia iura, per omnes
 qui dant fallendos se tibi saepe deos,
perque tuam faciem magni mihi numinis instar,
 perque tuos oculos qui rapuere meos.
From reflection on the nature of his predicament the lover turns to a direct and sustained appeal to his girlfriend, begging her to show some pity. While the request itself takes only a single word (*parce*), the plea is highly rhetorical, elaborated over two couplets, and articulated by repetition of *per.*

Commentary

45–6. Interruption of the first appeal with a reminder of the mistress's many perjuries postpones the noun to follow *per omnes* and produces vertical agreement: *per omnes | ... deos*.

45. parce: The placing of *parce* as the appeal's first word, recalls a number of urgent requests in Tibullus: 1.3.51 (to Jupiter): *parce, pater*, 1.4.83: *parce, puer*, 1.5.7 (to Delia): *parce tamen*.

per o: While separation of *per* from its noun in appeals is commonplace (Pease [1935: on *A*. 4.314]), there is only one other example of *per* followed by the interjection *o* (*Met*. 14.372 [Circe to Picus]): *per o tua lumina*. In both cases *o* underlines the intensity of the speaker's feelings.

lecti socialia iura: Recalls Catullus' treatment of his relationship with Lesbia as a *foedus* (76.3, 87.3, 109.6: *aeternum hoc sanctae foedus amicitiae*) and Propertius' insistence on a formal agreement with Cynthia (3.20.15–24). Closest, however, is Tib. 1.5.7: *parce tamen, per te furtiui foedera lecti*. But where Tibullus' description of the bed as *furtiuus* implies adultery, Ovid's suggests a marriage-like relationship (*socialia*). See e.g. *Her*. 4.17 [of Phaedra's marriage to Theseus]: *non ego nequitia socialia foedera rumpam*, 12.139 [of the wedding hymn for Jason and Creusa]: *tibiaque effundit socialia carmina uobis*).

46. dant: Heinsius' emendation *dent*, adopted by Ramirez de Verger, is unnecessary. Both P and Y read *dant*.

fallendos...deos: Behind Tibullus' declaration and this one, as McKeown (1987: 41–2) observes, lies Homeric Hera's oath to Zeus (*Il*. 15.36–9): 'Let Earth know this and wide Heaven above, and the down-trickling water of Styx, which is the greatest oath and most dreadful for the blessed gods, and your sacred head and our shared bed of marriage, by which I would never swear in vain'. Reference to Hera's misleading oath is an appropriate way of reminding the lover's girlfriend of her frequent perjuries. It may also recall Catullus' declaration of his own honesty (76.3–4): *nec foedere in ullo | diuum ad fallendos numine abusum homines*.

47. Perhaps alludes to Tib. 1.5.8: *per Venerem quaeso compositumque caput*.

magni numinis mihi instar: The phrase is recycled at Mart. 7.12.11 and Sil. 13.623.

48. Reworks 2.19.19: *tu quoque, quae nostros rapuisti nuper ocellos*. For the importance of the eyes in creating erotic attraction see e.g. Prop. 1.1.1, *Her*. 12.36, *Met*. 14.372–3: *per o, tua lumina, dixit, | quae mea ceperunt*.

49–50. quidquid eris, mea semper eris; tu selige tantum,
  me quoque uelle uelis, anne coactus amem.
Having pleaded for mercy, the lover now surrenders: his mistress will decide whether he is to be a willing or unwilling lover.

49. In the simplest possible language the lover submits to his beloved.

50. Reworks the language of Catul. 72.8: *cogit amare magis, sed bene uelle minus*, with both lovers acknowledging their lack of freedom. Omission of *utrum* (commonly used to introduce alternative indirect questions, but never in Ovid) and juxtaposition of forms of *uolo* create initial puzzlement, but underline the lover's lack of will.

uelle uelis: For the same words in an equally paradoxical context see *Her.* 21.58 (accepting, with Kenney [1996], the manuscript reading): *me, precor, ut serues, perdere, uelle uelis*, i.e. 'I beg you, please be willing to destroy me in order to save my life'.

51–12.26: These lines are almost entirely unreadable in P.

51–2. lintea dem potius uentisque ferentibus utar
et, quam, si nolim, cogar amare, uelim.
The poem closes with hope that the relationship might work and with yet another paradox involving the willingness and/or unwillingness to love.

51. The hope for plain sailing recalls both the nautical metaphor in 29–30 and Tibullus' choice of image for his own failure (1.5.75–6): *nescio quid furtiuus amor parat. utere quaeso, | dum licet: in liquida nat tibi linter aqua.*

lintea dem: Apparently a Virgilian coinage (*A.* 3.686), *lintea dare* varies the more common *uela dare* (*OLD uelum* 2a). See also *Her.* 3.58, 21.80, *Rem.* 266, *Met.* 3.640, 7.40.

uentisque ferentibus: This is perhaps another Virgilian coinage (*A.* 3.473, 4.430 [with Servius ad loc.: *bene flantes*]) picked up by Ovid (*Her.* 16.127, *Tr.* 1.2.73).

52. The poem closes with a dazzling (if puzzling) line which combines the ideas of compulsion with willingness and unwillingness. As at line 50, the reader's bewilderment reflects the lover's entanglement in contradiction.
For similarly paradoxical play with Catullus' *odi et amo* see 2.4.5: *odi nec possum cupiens non esse quod odi*.
I print Kenney's version of this line. Its paradoxical character has caused difficulties for scribes and editors alike. Y offers *Vt qui si nolim cogar amare uelim*. A second hand, however, has written *quamquam* above *qui si nolim* and almost completely obliterated *uelim* (the *l* is still visible) replacing it with *tamen* (Munari [1965: 55]). (Unfortunately, P is unreadable at this point.) Other manuscripts offer other readings. In the first printed edition Johannes Andreas (1471) offered *ut quam si nolim: cogar amare tamen*. Subsequent editors from Calfurnio (1474) to Weise (1845) printed *ut quamuis nolim, cogar amare tamen*. *tamen*, however, as Tarrant (2007: 102) points out, is 'flat'. (Of the 826 examples in Ovid, only eleven occur at the end of a line [*Her.* 20.44, *Ars* 1.228, 478, 664, 700, *Rem.* 440, *Fast.* 2.688, *Tr.* 1.5.82, 5.13.16, *Pont.* 1.8.30, 4.8.2], none at the end of a book or poem.) Müller (1861) restored *uelim*. Most recent editors (including Munari, Showerman

and Goold, and McKeown) print Madvig's (1873: 69) conjecture: *ut, quam, si nolim, cogar amare, uelim.* Madvig explained: *Hoc est: ut uelim eam amare, quam, si nolim, cogar tamen* ('This means: So that I might be willing to love her, whom, if I were unwilling, I would nevertheless be forced to love'). This has the advantage of yielding in equally striking form a sense close to that of line 50. Kenney's *et* instead of *ut* transforms *uelim* into an optative subjunctive and creates an attractive couplet that offers two wishes, the first employing metaphor, the second paradox.

Ramirez de Verger (2) accepts the reading of P6 (= Kenney's Ph) and prints: *quam, quamuis nolim, cogar amare tamen.* The combination *quam quamuis* is unattractive and is found nowhere in Latin literature. For *tamen* see above.

3.12: REFLECTIONS ON PROPERTIUS

Why write erotic elegy? If we can believe Propertius, it is falling in love that prompts a poet to write love poetry.[1] He claims that his talent, his *ingenium*, is inspired by a girl, that his talent is powerless without her (2.1.4: *ingenium nobis ipsa puella facit*; 2.30b.40: *nam sine te nostrum non ualet ingenium*). And he advises others to do the same: when they fall in love serious poets should switch to writing poems that girls would like to hear (1.9.14); they should take love poets like Philetas and Callimachus as their models (2.34.31-2). In other words, they should follow the example set by so many Roman predecessors (Varro, Calvus, Catullus, Gallus, Propertius himself [2.24.81-94]) and write love poetry.

But what good is erotic elegy? If we look again to Propertius, we discover that it will make a poet famous (1.7.9-10, 2.7.17-18, 2.13a.8, 3.2.25-6). But if the poet wins fame, how does his girlfriend benefit? She too can win renown (2.5.6), especially for beauty (2.25.3): *ista meis fiet notissima forma libellis* ('that beauty of yours will be made famous by my books'); (3.2.18): *carmina erunt formae tot monumenta tuae* ('my poems will be so many reminders of your beauty').

But a girl's fame can generate fear (2.19.31-2) because fame can turn into notoriety:

> quin ego in assidua metuam tua nomina lingua:[2]
> absenti nemo non nocuisse uelit.

[Nothing can stop me] from fearing your name on a busy tongue: there is no one who would not willingly harm the absent.

---

[1] That 3.12 engages with Propertius has long been recognized. For detailed discussion see e.g. Luck (1961: 173-93). His repeated characterization of 3.12 as Propertian 'parody', however, is not persuasive.

[2] The text of this line is insecure. For discussion see Fedeli (2005: ad loc.) and Heyworth (2007a: ad loc.). I favour Lee's (1994) interpretation: 'Stop me...from fearing that your fame will be on every tongue'.

And a girl's desire or need for gifts can result in accusations of greed (2.16.11–12):

> Cynthia non sequitur fasces nec curat honores:
> semper amatorum ponderat una sinus.

Cynthia does not follow the fasces or care for office: she in particular always weighs her lovers' purses.

And claims of avarice can lead to hints of prostitution. Thus the Propertian lover contrasts women from the remote past with their modern descendants (2.16.21–2):

> numquam uenales essent ad munus amicae,
> atque una fieret cana puella domo.

Never then would girlfriends be on sale for gifts, and a girl would grow grey in just one house.

A girlfriend's fame has its perils.

When we turn to Ovid we find similar anxieties. Like his Propertian equivalent, the Ovidian lover expects fame, fame that he will share with his girlfriend (1.3.25–6):[3]

> nos quoque per totum pariter cantabimur orbem,
> iunctaque semper erunt nomina nostra tuis.[4]

In the same way I too will be sung throughout the whole world,[5] and my name will always be linked with yours.

But he is also troubled by his girlfriend's greed (1.10.11): *cur sim mutatus, quaeris? quia munera poscis* ('You ask why I've changed? Because you demand presents'). And if Propertius hints at prostitution, Ovid is explicit (1.10.21–2):

> stat meretrix certo cuiuis mercabilis aere,
> et miseras iusso corpore quaerit opes.

The prostitute stands for purchase by anyone at a fixed price and acquires wretched money with her body on demand.

It is noteworthy that Propertius uses *meretrix* ('prostitute') once; and then only as an insult: Cleopatra is the 'prostitute queen of incestuous Canopus' (*incesti meretrix regina Canopi* 3.11.39). Tibullus does not use the term at all.[6]

---

[3] For the speaker of 1.3 as Ovidian lover see lines 7–8.
[4] See also 1.15.7–8: *mihi fama perennis | quaeritur, in toto semper ut orbe canar* ('I seek enduring fame, so that I be sung always in the whole world').
[5] I take *nos...cantabimur* as plural for singular and not as a true plural because otherwise *nostra* in the next line (an unambiguous example of plural for singular) is awkward.
[6] Tibullus, however, does share the other elegists' anxieties, treating a boy's wanting gifts (*munera uelle* 1.4.58) as tantamount to selling love (*Venerem...uendere* 1.4.59, *uendit amorem* 1.4.67).

But 3.12 does not merely focus on difficulties implicit in Propertius' account of his relationship with Cynthia. Rather the poem highlights a deeper problem in the apparently autobiographical approach to love elegy which Propertius represents.[7] Taking as its springboard an alleged event in the poet-lover's life (Corinna's resort to prostitution), the poem underlines the fictional character of *Amores* (and of elegiac poetry more generally). As Bretzigheimer (2001: 165) observes, 3.12 offers 'reflection on the relationship between poetry and truth' and warns readers against confusing poetry with life.

Secondary literature: Luck (1969: 173–93); Stroh (1971: 157–73); Morgan (1977: 48–50, 99–102); McKeown (1979); J. T. Davis (1980); Greene (1994); Fear (2000); Bretzigheimer (2001: 165–77); Heyworth (2009); Lowe (2018); Oliensis (2019: 48–51).

1–2. Quis fuit ille dies, quo tristia semper amanti
   omina non albae concinuistis aues?
The lover launches the poem with a puzzling question (really an exclamation) addressed to birds of ill omen.

1. Quis fuit ille dies: Later poets follow Ovid in using the phrase to suggest disaster e.g. Luc. 2.99 (of Marius seizing Rome), Stat. *Theb.* 1.166 (of Eteocles taking sole power), 12.698 (of Creon renewing war).

semper amanti: Alludes to Prop. 1.16.47–8: *sic ego nunc dominae uitiis et semper amantis | fletibus*. Fedeli (1980: ad loc.) notes that allusion is secured by word placement and enjambment; and that *semper* is effectively adjectival (= *sempiternus*) both here and in Propertius. See also *Am.* 1.9.28: *miseri semper amantis*, where *semper* is to be construed with both *miseri* and *amantis*.

2. Reworks Prop. 2.28.38: *nigraque funestum concinit omen auis*, with *non albae* replacing *nigra*; see also 2.20.5–6. Close allusion to Propertius signals engagement with Propertian issues.

3–4. quodue putem sidus nostris occurrere fatis,
   quosue deos in me bella mouere querar?
From unfavourable omens the lover turns histrionically to the malevolent forces that they might signify: the stars and the gods.

3. Perhaps recalls Prop. 1.20.3: *saepe imprudenti fortuna occurrit amanti*.

4. bella mouere: The phrase suggests matters of great moment affecting nations not individuals e.g. *G.* 1.509: *hinc mouet Euphrates, illinc Germania bellum*, *Am.* 2.12.21–2: *femina Troianos iterum noua bella mouere | impulit in regno, iuste Latine, tuo*. For less serious uses see Hor. *Carm.* 4.1.1–2 (of Venus), *Am.* 2.6.25 (of a dead parrot).

---

[7] For Propertius' 'fictitious realism' see Wallis (2018: 202).

Commentary, 12.1–8

5–6. quae modo dicta mea est, quam coepi solus amare,
cum multis uereor ne sit habenda mihi.
The lover turns now from inflated language to plain statement of the cause of his anxiety: he may have to share his girlfriend with other men. Martial uses similar language of a husband who shares his wife (3.26.5–6): *omnia solus habes—hoc me puta uelle negare— | uxorem sed habes, Candide, cum populo.*

5. quae modo dicta mea est: Quotes Prop. 2.8.6: *nec mea dicetur, quae modo dicta mea est*. It is reasonable to infer that the lover refers to Corinna because (a) he names her at line 16 and because (b) he alludes to *Am.* 1.5 at line 12, the first Corinna poem in the collection.

modo: The adverb implies that the lover's relationship with Corinna is a new one. If *Amores* purported to be an autobiographical text, this poem would come early in the collection.

6. If 2.8's Propertian lover is concerned with losing his mistress to another man, Ovid's is troubled by his girlfriend's having sex with many.

cum multis: Deianira speaks of herself in similar terms (*Her.* 9.137): *me quoque cum multis, sed me sine crimine amasti.*

7–8. fallimur, an nostris innotuit illa libellis?
sic erit: ingenio prostitit illa meo.
And how is it that she has become so well known? The poet's books have made his mistress famous and enabled her to practise prostitution.

7. nostris…libellis: For a girlfriend's fame won through books see Prop. 2.24a.1–2: *tu loqueris, cum sis iam noto fabula libro | et tua sit toto Cynthia lecta foro* (where *Cynthia* is also the book's name), 2.25.3 (quoted above in the introduction), 3.2.17: *fortunata, meo si qua es celebrata libello*. See also *Am.* 1.10.59–60: *est quoque carminibus meritas celebrare puellas | dos mea; quam uolui, nota fit arte mea.*

innotuit: *innotesco* is rare in verse, occurring only here and in Phaedrus (1.10.1, 16.32). While sometimes positive or neutral in sense, it is frequently pejorative e.g. Liv. 22.61.4.2, Phaed. 1.10.1, Val. Max. 8.14(ext).3.19.

8. sic erit: Found in comedy (Pl. *Ps.* 677, Ter. *Ad.* 182, *Eu.* 1058, *Hau.* 1014, *Ph.* 801) the idiom ('that's right') is perhaps colloquial. Ovid uses it only here and at 1.2.7.

ingenio…meo: For *ingenium* see above on 3.1.25.

prostitit: Like Catullus (110.7–8 [denouncing Aufillena's desire for gifts]): *plus quam meretricis auarae <est>, | quae sese toto corpore prostituit*), but unlike Tibullus and Propertius, Ovid is explicit in his references to prostitution (1.10.17, 42; 3.14.11).

9–10. et merito: quid enim formae praeconia feci?
   uendibilis culpa facta puella mea est.
In fact the poet's work has transformed his girlfriend into a commodity for sale.

9. et merito: Here the adverb acknowledges fault. See also Prop. 1.17.1 (the lover caught in a storm): *et merito, quoniam potui fugisse puellam*; *Met.* 9.585–6 (Byblis having tried to seduce her brother): '*et merito, quid enim temeraria uulneris huius | indicium feci?*' Sometimes it does the opposite and asserts entitlement e.g. *Met.* 6.687 (Boreas claims a right to rape): '*et merito!' dixit, 'quid enim mea tela reliqui?*'

formae praeconia: A *praeco* is both an announcer (*OLD* 1) and an auctioneer (*OLD* 2). (On the role of the *praeco* see Fear [2000] and Lowe [2018].) The term can be used positively e.g. Cic. *Arch.* 24.4, *Ars* 1.623, 3.535, *Pont.* 4.8.45: *carmina uestrarum peragunt praeconia laudum*. Here, however, it clearly has the negative sense of 'auctioneer', as at Catul. 106: *cum puero bello praeconem qui uidet esse | quid credat nisi se uendere discupere?* As Stroh (1971: 162 n. 74) points out, the *Amores*-lover aspires to the role of poetic herald (*Dichterherold*), but turns out to be an auctioneer.

10. For the interweaving of four words ending in *a* see above on 3.4.16.

uendibilis: Rare in poetry (Horace uses it of an unsaleable farm at *Ep.* 1.17.47: *et fundus nec uendibilis*), the word astonishes with its bluntness. *mercabilis* at 1.10.21 (quoted above in the introduction) has a similar effect.

11–12. me lenone placet, duce me perductus amator,
   ianua per nostras est adaperta manus.
The blunt language continues with the lover seeing himself as a pimp, as a version of Dipsas, the procuress of 1.8, or the indulgent husband of 2.19.

11. me lenone: While the *lena* is a familiar figure in elegy, including *Amores* (Tib. 1.5.47–58, 2.6.41–54, Prop. 4.5, *Am.* 1.8, 3.5.39–40), her male equivalent occurs only in Ovid (1.10.23, 2.19.57). If it is extraordinary for the poet to call a husband a 'pimp' (*cum lenone marito* 2.19.57), it is still more extraordinary to find him applying that label to himself.

perductus: For *perduco* used of drawing young men into sex see e.g. Ter. *An.* 80–1, Sen. *Con.* 2.1.35.12, Apul. *Met.* 9.20.1: *solum perducit…amatorem strenuum infert adusque dominae cubiculum*.

12. adaperta: Allusion to 1.5 (*pars adaperta fuit* 3), the lover's first account of sex with Corinna, implies that she used that poem as a form of advertising. Even there she is likened to a well-known courtesan (1.5.12): *et multis Lais amata uiris*. (The first two appearances of *adaperio* in verse are at 1.5.3 and here. See also *Met.* 5.193, 14.740.)

13–14. an prosint dubium, nocuerunt carmina semper;
   inuidiae nostris illa fuere bonis.

Now follows a six-line transition linking the poem's two major sections, the first (1–12) concerned with the corrupting effects of love elegy, the second (19–40) with the fictional character of poetry.

13. an prosint dubium: Invokes and immediately dismisses the debate as to whether the aim of poetry is utility or pleasure (e.g. Hor. *Ars* 333: *aut prodesse uolunt aut delectare poetae*). Poetry is not helpful.

That poetry can harm its author is a major focus of the exile poetry e.g. *Tr.* 3.7.27, 3.14.5–6, *Pont.* 1.2.133–4, 4.13.41: *carmina nil prosunt, nocuerunt carmina quondam*, 4.14.17, *Ib.* 5. Tibullus takes a similar view (2.4.13–15).

14. inuidiae: For the predicative dative of this noun see above on 3.3.17. Recalls the poet-lover's concern with *liuor* (1.15.1, 39; *Rem.* 365, 369, 389).

15–16. cum Thebae, cum Troia foret, cum Caesaris acta,
   ingenium mouit sola Corinna meum.
The poet-lover now rewrites the manifesto that opens Propertius' second book. The earlier elegist had rejected subjects like Thebes and Troy and Caesar's achievements in favour of the girl who inspired him. This elegist, however, regrets writing about a girl when there was a wealth of epic material to choose from.

15. Thebae: Munari prints *Thebe*, found in Y and other manuscripts. Elsewhere Ovid uses the spelling *Thebe* for the individual (3.6.33, 34) and *Thebae* for the city. See Kenney (1958: 66).

Recalls three of the epic subjects that Propertius rejects (2.1.21): *nec ueteres Thebas, nec Pergama*; (2.1.25): *bellaque resque tui... Caesaris*. For a similar refusal to write about Thebes and Troy see Prop. 3.9.37–42.

16. Alludes to the source of Propertius' inspiration (2.1.4): *ingenium nobis ipsa puella facit*. Ovid's lover makes a similar claim in a poem addressed to Corinna (2.17.34): *ingenio causas tu dabis una meo*. See also *Tr.* 4.10.59–60.

Corinna: Although the lover insists upon the importance of Corinna as inspiration, he refers to her only infrequently. So far in Book 3 she has been named by Elegy (3.1.49) and referred to as a former girlfriend (3.7.25). Her name will not occur again. (For Corinna's role in *Amores* see Introduction §7.)

17–18. auersis utinam tetigissem carmina Musis,
   Phoebus et inceptum destituisset opus!
Not only does the poet-lover regret writing elegy, he regrets writing poetry at all, explicitly rejecting the divinities who had helped Propertius (1.8b.41–2): *sunt igitur Musae, neque amanti tardus Apollo, | quis ego fretus amo*; and whose priest he claimed to be (*Am.* 3.8.23): *ille ego Musarum purus Phoebique sacerdos*.

17. auersis...Musis: For *auersus* used of hostile divinities see e.g. *A.* 1.482 (Minerva): *diua...auersa*, Prop. 4.1b.73: *auersus...Apollo*, *Fast.* 1.60: *auerso...Marte*.

304   Commentary

19-20. nec tamen ut testes mos est audire poetas:
      malueram uerbis pondus abesse meis.
With these lines the poet-lover shifts the argument from authorial regret at writing poetry to the folly of readers who take poets at their word, believing everything they write. As evidence of readerly stupidity he introduces a list of stories invented by poets which no one could possibly believe. While the mythological catalogue is characteristic of Propertius (1.2.15-20, 1.3.1-6, 1.15.9-22, 2.14.1-18, 3.19.11-28), none is as extensive as this one, which takes up fully half the poem. On the other hand, as Luck (1961: 189) pointed out, 'most of these exempla are actually found in Propertius'.

The catalogue is carefully organized. It focuses primarily on a set of hybrid or monstrous creatures (21-8) and a series of transformations (31-8); but it also includes an introductory couplet (19-20), a two-line transition with stories from the *Odyssey* (29-30), and a final couplet recording remarkable events (39-40).

19. nec tamen: Manuscripts' *nec* is preferable to Hall's (1999: 98) *at*. The point is that while readers do not usually treat poets as reliable witnesses, they have done so in this case.

testes...poetas: For the distinction between the evidential value of poetry and legal testimony see Cic. *Leg.* 1.4.11: 'But, my dear Titus, some of those people show their ignorance who in a proof of this kind insist on accuracy as if they were dealing with a witness in court (*a teste*) and not a poet (*a poeta*)'.

20. malueram: The pluperfect indicative is regularly used in hypothetical expressions in both verse and prose (Pinkster [1.460]). Here it has a metrical advantage: the pluperfect subjunctive will not scan in dactylic verse (*māluīssem*). Cf. *Her.* 7.43: *quod tibi malueram, sine me debere procellis.*

Hall (1999: 99) suggests *maluerim* 'reported by Munari from the Hamilton manuscript' and 'infinitely preferable' because 'the optative, not the affirmative, mood is what we need here'. The reading of Y is *malueram*. Another hand has written *i* above the second *a*. Normal Latin idiom supports *malueram*.

uerbis pondus: Perhaps recalls Propertius' treatment of this idea: the words of poet-lovers usually lack weight: 2.22b.44: *quid iuuat, heu, nullo pondere uerba loqui?*; 3.7.44: *uerbaque duxisset pondus habere mea.* See also *Am.* 3.3.19 (with note above), *Her.* 3.98, 6.110, *Tr.* 1.6.17-18, *Pont.* 3.9.49-50. The concept of verbal weight is important in Cicero's rhetorical works e.g. *de Orat.* 2.73.2, *Part.* 19.13, *Orat.* 26.6, 197.6, *Brut.* 141.4, 265.10.

21-2. per nos Scylla patri caros furata capillos
      pube premit rabidos inguinibusque canes;
As if to underline myth's unbelievability, the speaker immediately combines the tales of two well-known women: of Scylla, daughter of Nisus, the princess of Megara who stole her father's hair and whose story is first found in Aeschylus

Commentary, 12.19-23

(*Cho.* 613-22; with Garvie [1986: ad loc.]); and of Scylla, daughter of Phorcys, the monster familiar from Homer's *Odyssey* (12.85-126, 223-59).
Poets sometimes keep the two Scyllas separate: (Nisus' daughter): *G.* 1.404-9, Prop. 3.19.21-6, *Met.* 8.1-151; (Phorcys' daughter): *Met.* 13.898-14.74. And sometimes they combine them: *Ecl.* 6.74-7, Prop. 4.4.39-40, *Ars* 1.331-2, *Rem.* 737, *Fast.* 4.500. For the two Scyllas see e.g. Hinds (1993: 11-21), Fantham (1998: 187), Kenney (2011: 222), and Cowan (2017).
Ovid adapts this couplet at *Ars* 1.331-2: *filia purpureos Niso furata capillos | pube premit rabidos inguinibusque canes.*

21. per nos: Tibullus had asserted the importance of poetry and poets in keeping myths alive: 1.4.63-4: *carmine purpurea est Nisi coma: carmina ni sint, | ex umero Pelopis non nituisset ebur.* Throughout the catalogue that follows the poet-lover is even more insistent than Tibullus: *nos...nos* (23), *idem...porreximus* (25), *fecimus* (27), *inclusimus* (29), *fecimus* (31), until the point no longer needs explicit repetition (33-40).

caros...capillos: Nisus' hair is 'precious' because his life depends on it. Scylla takes a different view at *Met.* 8.79: *ille* [i.e. Nisus' hair] *mihi est auro pretiosior.*

22. premit: For this sense of *premo* ('keep shut in or confined') see *OLD* 28. For a similar description of Scylla see *Met.* 14.66-7, where *coercet* replaces *premit: statque canum rabie subiectaque terga ferarum | inguinibus truncis uteroque exstante coercet.*

rabidos: Y reads *rapidos.* While this is possible, the quotation of this line at *Ars* 1.332, where *rabidos* is well attested, makes *rabidos* attractive. Showerman and Goold claim that P reads *rapidos.* P is unreadable at this point. See above on 3.11.51-2.

inguinibusque canes: Alludes to Prop. 4.4.40: *candidaque in saeuos inguina uersa canes.*

**23-4. nos pedibus pinnas dedimus, nos crinibus angues:
uictor Abantiades alite fertur equo.**
Now follows an oblique account of Perseus' killing of Medusa, oblique because Medusa is not named and because Perseus is referred to as Abantiades, a patronymic (great grandson of Abas) which has no precedent in Greek or Roman literature.

23. pedibus pinnas: For Perseus' winged feet see *Ars* 2.644: *mobilis in gemino cui pede pinna fuit, Fast.* 3.454.

dedimus: Particularly striking here and in the following couplets (25-31) is the agency which the speaker claims for poets: we are the ones who put wings on Perseus' feet, snakes on Medusa's head, and so on.

crinibus angues: For Medusa's snaky hair see *Met.* 4.791-2 (a question put to Perseus): *cur sola sororum | gesserit alternis immixtos crinibus angues.*

24. uictor...alite fertur equo: If, as seems likely, the winged horse is Pegasus, this must refer to a time after Medusa's decapitation, because Pegasus was born from Medusa's blood (*Met.* 4.785–6). The emphatic placing of *uictor* confirms this: the 'conqueror' of Medusa rode the winged horse.

Bellerophon, not Perseus, is Pegasus' usual rider. It is important to note, however, that both Catullus and Propertius name Perseus and Pegasus in successive lines in such a way that a reader might conclude that Perseus rides Pegasus: Catul. 58b.2–3 (Mynors [1958]): *non Ladas ego pinnipesue Perseus, | non si Pegaseo ferar uolatu*; Prop. 2.30a.3–4: *non si Pegaseo uecteris in aere dorso, | nec tibi si Persei mouerit ala pedes.* Ovid's speaker makes the reader's conclusion explicit.

Abantiades: The patronymic (Perseus' male ancestors were Jupiter, Acrisius, and Abas) is an Ovidian coinage used only of Perseus (*Met.* 4.607, 673; 5.138, 236: *uictor Abantiades*, and *Ib.* 463). Marius (78) argued that *Abantiades* refers to Bellerophon. Micyllus (pp. 367–8) tried to circumvent the problem of Perseus riding Pegasus by arguing that *fertur* means 'is famous for'. Burman (525) rightly rejected both arguments.

25–6. idem per spatium Tityon porreximus ingens,
   et tria uipereo fecimus ora cani;
For his third fiction, the speaker turns to the underworld, naming one of its criminal inhabitants and describing its fantastical guardian. Here he alludes to a passage in Propertius which questions the truth of underworld tales, including those of Tityos and Cerberus: (3.5.43–5):

> num tribus infernum custodit faucibus antrum
>   Cerberus, et Tityo iugera pauca nouem,
> an ficta in miseras descendit fabula gentes.

25. Recalls Tibullus' description of the punishment of the giant who attempted to rape Latona (1.3.75): *porrectusque nouem Tityos per iugera.* See also *A.* 6.595–7: *nec non et Tityon,... | cernere erat, per tota nouem cui iugera corpus | porrigitur.*

idem...porreximus: See above on 21 and 23. Where Virgil and Tibullus use the passive voice, our speaker prefers the active: we poets did this.

26. For the golden line (abVAB) see above on 3.3.21. Here the verbal pattern underlines the connection with Prop. 3.5.43–5 (quoted above), a passage which employs golden lines in both hexameters.

tria...ora: For Cerberus' three mouths see e.g. *G.* 4.483, *Met.* 4.450–1: *tria Cerberus extulit ora | et tres latratus semel edidit.*

uipereo: The epithet was coined by Virgil (*A.* 6.281, 7.351, 7.753). Ovid uses it of mythological monsters e.g. the Colchian serpent's teeth (*Her.* 6.33, *Met.* 7.122), the Theban serpent's teeth (*Met.* 3.103, 4.573), an Erinys (*Met.* 4.491), Medusa (*Met.* 4.615), and the Furies (*Met.* 6.662).

fecimus: For *facio* (also at 27 and 31 below) used of artistic creation, see the account of Arachne's weaving (*Met.* 6.108: *fecit et Asterien*, 109: *fecit... Ledam*).

27-3.14.2: These lines are missing from P.

27-8. fecimus Enceladon iaculantem mille lacertis,
   ambiguae captos uirginis ore uiros.
Next are hybrid creatures invented by epic poets.

27. Enceladon: For Enceladus as one of the Giants see e.g. Eur. *HF* 908, *A.* 4.178-9, Hor. *Carm.* 3.4.56-8. For the Giants' hybrid character see *Met.* 1.184: *anguipedum*, *Tr.* 4.7.17: *serpentipedesque Gigantas*. For Gigantomachy as a typically epic subject see Prop. 2.1.39-40: *sed neque Phlegraeos Iouis Enceladique tumultus | intonet angusto pectore Callimachus*, *Am.* 2.1.11-16.

iaculantem...lacertis: Cf. Hor. *Carm.* 3.4.56, *Met.* 14.184 *uasta Giganteo iaculantem saxa lacerto*.

28. ambiguae...uirginis: The hybridity of the Sirens is post-Homeric. In the *Odyssey* they are women who lure sailors to their deaths with song (*Od.* 12.39-54, 165-200). In AR (4.898-9) and Ovid (*Met.* 5.552-3; cf. *Ars* 3.311: *monstra*), by contrast, they have the appearance of both birds and virgins. For Propertius they are simply one of the perils faced by Ulysses (3.12.34): *Sirenum surdo remige adisse lacus*. (For discussion of the Sirens in earlier literature and the visual arts see Heubeck and Hoekstra [1989: 118-20]).

29-30. Aeolios Ithacis inclusimus utribus Euros;
   proditor in medio Tantalus amne sitit.
From the Sirens the speaker turns to two more Odyssean episodes, Aeolus' bag of winds (*Od.* 10.19-75) and Tantalus' thirst (*Od.* 11.582-92).

29. For this variation of the golden line in which paired adjectives and nouns enclose a centrally placed verb (abVBA) see 2.1.6, 2.4.27, 30; 2.9.12, 22; *Her.* 9.77, 16.46, 110; 18.131.

Aeolios...Euros: Homer's Aeolus gives Odysseus a bag containing Zephyrus (*Od.* 10.25), i.e. the west wind. Ovid perhaps corrects the Homeric account for, as Heubeck and Hoekstra note (1989: 44), Aeolus gives Odysseus the wrong wind: 'The bag is not in any case required for the homeward journey, since Aeolus sends the west wind'.

30. proditor: While there is consensus on the nature of Tantalus' punishment (to be tempted eternally by drink and food), there is no agreement on its cause. Homer does not explain. This description (for *proditor* as 'betrayer of secrets' see *TLL* 1617.38-61) is consistent with Ovid's treatment of Tantalus as guilty of speaking too much: 2.2.44, 3.7.51 (with note above), *Ars* 2.606.

   Luck (1961: 190) notes that Propertius mentions this myth at 2.17.5-6, 3.5.42, and 4.11.24. It would be difficult, however, to argue that Ovid alludes to these passages.

31–2. de Niobe silicem, de uirgine fecimus ursam.
   concinit Odrysium Cecropis ales Ityn;
From well-known Homeric stories, the poet-lover turns to tales of transformation.

31. de Niobe silicem: Niobe's story, told by Achilles in *Iliad* (24.602–21), makes an effective transition: from Tantalus to a daughter of Tantalus; from Homer to myths of metamorphosis (*Il.* 24.617: λίθος περ ἐοῦσα 'although she was a stone'). For Ovid's version see *Met.* 6.148–312. See also Prop. 2.20.7–8, 3.10.8: *et Niobae lacrimas supprimat ipse lapis.*

de uirgine...ursam: Perhaps alludes to Prop. 2.28.23: *Callisto Arcadios errauerat ursa per agros.* Ovid tells Callisto's story at length at *Met.* 2.401–530 (where, as here, she remains unnamed) and *Fast.* 2.153–192.

fecimus: For unbelievability of metamorphic stories see *Tr.* 2.64: *in non credendos corpora uersa modos.*

32. For the verbal pattern (VabBA) see above on 3.1.11.
   Lament for Itys (Itylus) symbolizes mourning in Homer and Virgil (*Od.* 19.518–23, *G.* 4.511–15), with the lamentation of Penelope and Orpheus being likened to the nightingale's song (*Od.* 19.518: ἀηδών, *G.* 4.511: *philomela*).
   This line reworks (or is reworked by) *Her.* 15.154: *concinit Ismarium Daulias ales Ityn.* (For discussion of the connection see Thorsen [2014: 52–3].) Ovid tells the story of Tereus' rape of Philomela and of Procne's revenge in gruesome detail at *Met.* 6.424–674. For Propertius' treatment of the myth see 3.10.10: *increpet absumptum nec sua mater Ityn.*

concinit: Catullus had used the same verb of mourning for Itys (65.13–14): *qualia sub densis ramorum concinit umbris | Daulias, absumpti fata gemens Ityli.*

Odrysium: The epithet is used by poets to mean 'Thracian', the Odrysii being a people of that region (*Pont.* 1.8.15). Ovid uses it at *Ars* 2.130 (of Rhesus), *Rem.* 459 (of Tereus), *Met.* 6.490 (of Tereus), and *Met.* 13.554 (of Polymestor). Here it is applied to Tereus' son, killed by his mother and aunt, and eaten by his father.

Cecropis ales: Refers to Procne, daughter of Athenian king Pandion (*Cecropis* = 'Athenian'), who mourns for her dead son.

33–4. Iuppiter aut in aues aut se transformat in aurum
   aut secat imposita uirgine taurus aquas.
Taking up the theme suggested by the transformation of Callisto in the previous couplet, the lover now names various kinds of disguise that Jupiter had adopted in order to rape. For the god's propensity to adopt the form of a bird or bull see 1.10.7–8: *aquilamque in te taurumque timebam, | et quidquid magno de Ioue fecit amor.*

33. Iuppiter aut in aues: There are several examples of Jupiter transforming himself into a bird for sexual purposes: Asterie (*Met.* 6.108), Ganymede (Hor. *Carm.* 4.4.1–4, *Met.* 10.155–8), and Leda (1.10.7–8, *Her.* 17.55–6, *Met.* 6.109).

in aurum: For Jupiter's transformation into a shower of gold when raping Danae see Hor. *Carm.* 3.16.1–8, *Met.* 4.611: *quem pluuio Danae conceperat auro*, *Met.* 6.113: *aureus ut Danaen*. For Ovid's treatment of Danae in *Amores* see above on 3.4.21–2 and 3.8.29–34. Propertius (2.20.9–12, 2.32.59–60) refers to Danae, but omits the shower of gold.

34. For Jupiter's abduction of Europa in the form of a bull see *Ars* 1.323–4, 3.252: *uecta boue*, *Met.* 2.833–3.2, 6.103–7. Propertius (2.28.52) merely names Europa as one of many beautiful women in the underworld.

35–6. Protea quid referam Thebanaque semina, dentes,
   qui uomerent flammas ore, fuisse boues,
Now follow three couplets which constitute a single sentence: a list of transformations (35–8) and remarkable events (39–40).

35. Protea: The shape-shifting god is primarily familiar from Homer (*Od.* 4.351–570), Virgil (*G.* 4.387–452), and Ovid (*Met.* 8.725–37). He is not mentioned by Propertius.

quid referam…?: This question is frequently used to introduce a new element in a poetic catalogue e.g. Tib. 1.7.17 (of possible subjects for poetry), *Am.* 3.6.33, *Her.* 12.129 (of Medea's services to Jason), *Ars* 1.283 (of lustful women). At *Am.* 1.5.23, by contrast, it terminates a list: *singula quid referam?*

Thebanaque semina, dentes: Refers to the teeth sown by Cadmus at Thebes and Jason at Colchis; and the self-slaying earthborn men at both Thebes and Colchis. For Aeetes' possession of the Theban dragon's teeth see AR 3.1177–9, VF 7.282–3 (with Davis [2020: ad loc.]).

36. Since Cadmus does not employ fire-breathing oxen (*Met.* 3.101–5), this refers to Jason's ploughing at Colchis. See e.g. AR 3.410, Prop. 3.11.9–10: *Colchis flagrantis adamantina sub iuga tauros | egit et armigera proelia seuit humo*, *Met.* 7.104–5.

37–8. flere genis electra tuas, auriga, sorores,
   quaeque rates fuerint, nunc maris esse deas,
Now follow two enigmatic transformations: the tears of Phaethon's sisters into amber and Aeneas' ships into goddesses. Neither story is found in Propertius.

37. flere…electra…sorores: For the association between Phaethon's sisters (the Heliades) and amber tears see e.g. Eur. *Hipp.* 738–41: 'Where into the dark swell the unhappy girls, in sorrow for Phaethon, let drop the amber-bright gleam of their tears'; AR 4.603–6: 'Round about the maiden Heliades, confined in tall

310   Commentary

poplars, in sorrow shed a plaintive wail, and pour forth from their eyes shining drops of amber to the ground'; *Met.* 2.364–6.

auriga: The classic version of Phaethon's attempt to guide the sun's chariot is *Met.* 1.747–2.400. The story had been told in two now-fragmentary tragedies, Aeschylus' *Heliades* and Euripides' *Phaethon*.

38. For the metamorphosis of Aeneas' ships see *A.* 9.77–122, *Met.* 14.527–65.

39–40. auersumque diem mensis furialibus Atrei,
    duraque percussam saxa secuta lyram?
The catalogue closes not with transformations, but with remarkable events: the Sun-god's revulsion at Atreus' monstrous banquet and Amphion's founding of Thebes.

39. The story of the sun's revulsion at Atreus' murder of his nephews and Thyestes' cannibalism is as old as Sophocles (*PA* 9.98). For this myth on the republican stage see Boyle (2017: lxxii – lxxviii). For us the classic version of this story is Seneca's *Thyestes*.

auersumque diem: For this language see *Tr.* 2.391–2: *si non Aeropen frater sceleratus amasset, | auersos Solis non legeremus equos* and Sen. *Thy.* 1035–6: *hoc est deos quod puduit, hoc egit diem | auersum in ortus.*

40. For Amphion's creation of the walls of Thebes with music see Prop. 1.9.9–10: *quid tibi nunc misero prodest graue dicere carmen | aut Amphioniae moenia flere lyrae?*; 3.2.5–6: *saxa Cithaeronis Thebanam agitata per artem | sponte sua in muri membra coisse ferunt.*

For this verbal pattern (abAVB), the third most frequent in *Amores*, see above on 3.2.40.

41–2. exit in immensum fecunda licentia uatum,
    obligat historica nec sua uerba fide.
The poet-lover begins his conclusion by asserting the well-recognized freedom of poets to create fictions.

The idea that poets deal in falsehoods is at least as old as the Hesiodic Muses: 'We know how to speak many falsehoods that resemble reality' (*Theog.* 27). For Ovid's career-long insistence on the fictional character of poetry and myth see on 3.6.17–18.

41. exit: For the idea of exceeding boundaries see *OLD exeo* 13, *TLL* 1365.5–22.

in immensum: The phrase is effectively adverbial (as Bömer [1969] notes on *Met.* 2.220). See also *Met.* 4.661, Sen. *Ep.* 39.5.5, Luc. 2.663.

licentia uatum: For the idea of 'poetic licence' in diction: see e.g. Cic. *de Orat.* 1.70.2, 3.153.3: *poetarum licentiae, Orat.* 68.3; in accuracy: see e.g. Col. 9.2.2.7:

poeticae magis licentiae quam nostrae fidei concesserim; in choice of subject matter: see e.g. Hor. *Ars* 9–11 (where *uenia* equals *licentia*): '*pictoribus atque poetis | quidlibet audendi semper fuit aequa potestas*'. | *scimus, et hanc ueniam petimusque damusque uicissim*.

42. For the verbal pattern (VabBA) see above on 3.1.11.

historica...fide: The language perhaps invokes prose discussions of the differences between kinds of writing (e.g. Cic. *Orat.* 68.13, *Top.* 78.10), because, as Oliensis (2019: 49, n. 117) notes, *historicus* is a prosaic word, which occurs here for the first time in verse. The poet-lover makes the distinction that Aristotle had made at *Poetics* 1451b4: 'But they differ in this way: in so far as one tells what did happen, the other the kinds of things that could happen'.

43–4. et mea debuerat falso laudata uideri
    femina; credulitas nunc mihi uestra nocet.
The poem ends with the application of literary theory to this particular case: I write fiction and the gullibility of readers is doing me harm.

But 3.12's final couplet does more than this because it alludes to 'an ambitiously closural poem' of Propertius (Wallis [2018: 201]). In Book 3's penultimate poem the Propertian lover had rebuked Cynthia for arrogance, for taking pride in the beauty which the poet had bestowed upon her. He points out, however, that the Cynthia in his poems is not a real individual (3.24.1–6):

> falsa est ista tuae, mulier, fiducia formae,
>   olim oculis nimium facta superba meis.
> noster amor talis tribuit tibi, Cynthia, laudes:
>   uersibus insignem te pudet esse meis.
> mixtam te uaria laudaui saepe figura,
>   ut, quod non esses, esse putaret amor.

In 3.24 the Propertian lover not only renounces love; he reveals that his apparently (auto)biographical text is actually fiction. *Am.* 3.12 extends the Propertian lover's argument by claiming that readerly misunderstanding actually harms the poet.

43. falso: Recalls the first word of Prop. 3.24. The argument is one that the poet pressed with greater urgency from exile e.g. *Tr.* 2.339–40, *Tr.* 4.10.60.

laudata: Evokes the praises heaped on Cynthia: *laudes* (3.24.3), *laudaui* (3.24.5).

44. credulitas...uestra: In the last line the poem takes a surprising turn, switching from the third to second person. Who is gullible here? Unlike Prop. 3.24, this poem is not addressed to a girlfriend and so the credulity cannot be hers. The problem lies with readers who fail to read correctly. Cf. *Tr.* 2.275–6: *sic igitur carmen, recta si mente legatur, | constabit nulli posse nocere meum*.

Ovid is the first to use *credulitas* in poetry. He regularly treats it as a major fault e.g. 3.3.24, *Her*. 12.120 (with Davis [2012: 41]), 17.39, *Met*. 15.498, *Pont*. 2.4.32.

3.13: JUNO'S FALISCAN FESTIVAL

Am. 3.13 stands out as the only non-erotic work in three books of love poems. Its position between 3.12, an argument triggered by the claim that the poet's mistress behaves like a prostitute, and 3.14, a rebuke to his girlfriend for failing to conceal her infidelities, only underlines its exceptional character. The focus of this poem is participation in a religious festival in a country town.

And yet the poem is not without parallel in love elegy. Munari (103) notes that 3.13.5 seems to allude to Prop. 4.8.4 (see below). Miller (1991: 52) points out other connections, including reference to a local cult of Juno, the steepness of the ground to be traversed, and the role of virgins in performance of the rites. We might also compare *Am*. 3.2 with 3.13 because both poems are set in a real place, the Circus Maximus and the town of Falerii (modern Civita Castellana, about 62 kms north of the centre of Rome); and both depict a religious procession (*pompa*: 3.2.43, 44, 61; 3.13.12, 29, 31). Another possibility is 3.10 because it is prompted by a festival of Ceres. It must be said, however, that these three poems are very different from 3.13 because none is seriously concerned with religious ritual. In Prop. 4.8 Cynthia's alleged participation in a pilgrimage[1] provides the lover with an opportunity for sexual shenanigans on the Esquiline; in *Am*. 3.2 the real focus is on the speaker's attempts to pick up the girl sitting next to him; while in 3.10 the lover rails against Ceres because her cult involves abstinence from sex.

It is Tibullus who provides the most obvious models for *Am*. 3.13, especially 2.1 and 2.5. The first poem of Book 2 dramatizes a religious ceremony, beginning with words that recall the customary request for silence (2.1.1): *quisquis adest, faueat* ('Whoever is present, be propitious'). And it soon becomes clear that the speaker is engaged in a ritual purification of the countryside (2.1.17): *di patrii, purgamus agros, purgamus agrestes* ('gods of our fathers, we cleanse the fields, we cleanse the people of the fields'). Then follows a celebration of country gods and of the countryside itself. Although 2.5 lacks the rural elements of 2.1, it begins in a similar way, this time with an emphasis on priestly dignity (2.5.1): *Phoebe faue: nouus ingreditur tua templa sacerdos* ('Phoebus, be propitious: a new priest enters your temple'). Like *Am*. 3.13, and unlike Prop. 4.8, *Am*. 3.2, and 3.10, these poems of Tibullus are seriously concerned with the description and enactment of religious ceremonies.

---

[1] The Propertian lover is sceptical of the motive for Cynthia's travel (4.8.16): *causa fuit Iuno, sed mage causa Venus* ('The reason given was Juno, but Venus was the real reason').

But if 3.13 has clear affinities with the work of other elegists, it is unique in one particular: the poet refers to his wife. The presence of a wife in the antepenultimate poem of the final book of Augustan love elegy can only upset the reader's expectations. Central to the genre as practised by Gallus, Tibullus, Propertius, and Ovid himself, is the idea that the poet-lover is erotically obsessed with a woman whom he cannot marry. And now, close to the end of the final book, a married man takes centre stage.

How are we to respond to this? Some turn to biography. Lenz (1958: 257-8; 1972: 229-30) saw the poem as an expression of gratitude to his wife for introducing the future poet of the *Fasti* to Italian history and religion. Green (1982: 334) speculated on the identity of this wife: 'Ovid's Faliscan wife cannot be his third, who was Roman-born, and this leaves us hesitating between the two earlier marriages, neither of which lasted long', while Schmitzer (2013: 61) claimed that the presence of Ovid's wife represents an 'incursion of reality into the fictionalized world of elegy that transcends generic boundaries'. But for anyone reading these poems in order (and the papyrus scroll encourages serial reading) this seems an extraordinary claim to make, because only four lines earlier the poet had warned against (auto)biographical readings of his work (3.12.41-2). Why should we suppose that when Ovid speaks as a lover, he is indulging in fiction, but that when he represents himself as a dutiful husband he is telling the truth? In my view, 3.13 exposes the fictionality of the elegiac genre not by allowing an 'incursion of reality', but by setting up an alternative fiction.[2] I do not deny that Ovid sometimes includes genuine autobiographical elements in *Amores* (as in 1.3, 2.1, 2.16, 2.18, and 3.15), but I do claim that the world of this collection is overwhelmingly fictional. Even if Ovid had a 'Faliscan wife', we cannot be confident that this journey ever took place.

Secondary literature: Lenz (1958/1972); Cahoon (1983); Miller (1991: 50-7, 69-74, 80-1); Boyd (1997: 51-3); Farrell (2014); Oliensis (2019: 39-40, 46-52).

On Falerii and Juno Curitis: Strabo (5.2.9); Dionysius of Halicarnassus (*Ant. Rom.* 1.21); Pliny (*Nat.* 3.51.7); Frederiksen and Ward Perkins (1957: 128-46, 190); Ferri (2011).

1-2. Cum mihi pomiferis coniunx foret orta Faliscis,
    moenia contigimus uicta, Camille, tibi.
3.13's opening couplet shocks, not because its content is so outrageous but because it is so innocent: the poet is travelling with his wife to Falerii.

1. pomiferis...Faliscis: Suggesting primarily orchard fruit (3.6.46, Calp. *Ecl.* 2.64-5), the adjective is perhaps used loosely. In antiquity Falerii was famous for

---

[2] Oliensis (2019: 51) seems to adopt a similar view when she speaks of 3.13 as 'making a strategic move that benefits Naso'.

314 Commentary

its cattle (see below on 13–14), while in modern times the area is best known for grain and wine, not fruit. Perhaps because the town's name, Fălĕrĭi, cannot be accommodated in dactylic verse, poets name only the people, the Falisci, not the place.

coniunx: Placed in the centre of the line just after the caesura, this is the line's most striking word. Elsewhere in *Amores* it is used of angry husbands (1.10.2) or unfaithful wives (*adultera coniunx* 3.4.37). Here it denotes a pious wife accompanied by a dutiful husband.

foret orta Faliscis: Suggests that the speaker's wife was born in Falerii.

Farrell (2014: 232) notes that *orior* is 'very commonly used in phrases that refer not to the immediate circumstances of a person's birth, but to their more distant ancestry'. It is true that *orior* is sometimes used in this way: e.g. *A.* 1.626 (Greek Teucer claims Trojan ancestry): *seque ortum antiqua Teucrorum a stirpe uolebat; Fast.* 3.425 (of Augustus): *ortus ab Aenea*. But such cases are obvious and rare: at *A.* 1.626 *antiqua* makes it clear that Teucer is not claiming Trojan parents, while at *Fast.* 3.425 no reader will suppose that Augustus is actually Aeneas' son. As evidence Farrell cites *TLL orior* IIc (998.73–999.18). Most of the examples given, however, do not support his case. To cite only Ovidian instances see *Ars* 3.409: *Ennius emeruit, Calabris in montibus ortus* (Ennius actually came from Calabria), *Met.* 15.60: *uir fuit hic ortu Samius* (Pythagoras really was from Samos), *Fast.* 3.631: *orta Tyro est* (Anna is from Tyre).

2. Camille: Reference to Camillus adds glamour but misleads. Livy (5.27) and Plutarch (*Cam.* 9–11) record a moralizing (and probably fictitious) tale whereby the Faliscans willingly surrendered their town to Camillus in 394 BCE. That town, however, no longer existed. It was destroyed by the Romans in 241 BCE and replaced by a new settlement, Falerii Novi, some five kms to the west (Frederiksen and Ward Perkins [1957: 128, 131]). Ovid mentions the crushing of Falerii when discussing the cult of Minerva Capta (*Fast.* 3.843–4): *an quia perdomitis ad nos captiua Faliscis | uenit?*

3–4. casta sacerdotes Iunoni festa parabant
 et celebres ludos indigenamque bouem.
And the reason for the trip? A festival of Juno involving shows and the sacrifice of a cow.

3. casta: Means both 'holy' (*OLD* 3) and 'chaste' (*OLD* 4). Not surprisingly, it is common in religious contexts: e.g. of *ludi* (Cic. *Har.* 24.10 [the Megalesia]: *qui sunt more institutisque maxime casti, sollemnes, religiosi*), of ceremonial torches (*A.* 7.71: *castis adolet dum altaria taedis*), and rituals (Stat. *Ach.* 1.370: *castisque accedere sacris*). It is particularly appropriate for this festival which is (a) held in honour of Juno, goddess of marriage, and (b) performed by virginal girls (25–6).

Commentary, 13.2–7

For the importance of chastity in the performance of Juno's rituals see e.g. Liv. 27.37.10.2 and Sil. 7.77–8.

Iunoni: For the association between Falerii and Juno see *Fast.* 6.49: *Iunonicolasque Faliscos*. Dionysius of Halicarnassus underlines the importance of Juno's Faliscan temple (*Ant. Rom.* 1.21.2.1): πάντων δὲ περιφανέστατον μνημεῖον…ὁ τῆς Ἥρας νεὼς ἐν Φαλερίῳ ('The most conspicuous reminder…is the temple of Hera at Falerii').

4. ludos: For *ludi* as part of religious ritual see above on 3.2.43.

indigenamque bouem: The sacrifice of a cow to Juno is conventional (e.g. G. 3.532, Liv. 27.37.11.3). See also the inscriptional record of the Secular Games of 17 BCE (Schnegg [2020: 119, p. 30]):

⟨A(nte) D(iem)⟩ IV NONAS IVN(ias) IN CAPITOL[io i]NMOLAVIT IVNONI REGINAE BOVEM FEMIN[am propriam Achiuo ritu].

For the local cattle see 13–14 below. Columella observes that homegrown oxen were more highly prized than outsiders (6.2.12.5): *longeque omnis bos indigena melior est quam peregrinus*.

5–6. grande morae pretium ritus cognoscere, quamuis
 difficilis cliuis huc uia praebet iter.
Although the journey is difficult (with the run of three words ending in *-is* perhaps underlining its unpleasantness; cf. 1.12.20 [of birds of ill omen]: *uulturis in ramis et strigis oua tulit*, 2.1.32: *Haemoniis flebilis Hector equis*, Her. 7.135 (of Dido's unborn child): *accedet fatis matris miserabilis infans*), getting to know the rites is worthwhile.

5. morae pretium: For the phrase (a mainly poetic variation on the common *pretium operae*) see *OLD pretium* 2: '(with gen.)…*pretium morae*, a return for time spent'. Ovid also uses the expression (perhaps a Virgilian invention [A. 9.232]), at 2.14.26: *est pretium paruae non leue uita morae*, Her. 7.74: *grande morae pretium tuta futura uia est*.

6. difficilis cliuis: Frederiksen and Ward Perkins (1957: 129) note that 'Falerii Veteres, like its medieval and modern successor, stands at the centre of a radiating series of deep vertical gullies and elevated tufa promontories'.

7–8. stat uetus et densa praenubilus arbore lucus;
 aspice, concedes numinis esse locum.
Having suggested the journey's difficulty, the husband now turns to the destination and describes the setting for the sacred ceremonies. His language explicitly recalls the description of the fictional grove of Book 3's opening poem.

316   Commentary

7. stat uetus...lucus: Quotes 3.1.1: *stat uetus...silua*.

Frederiksen and Ward Perkins (1957: 129-30) place the shrine of Juno Curitis on the left bank of the Rio Maggiore, a little to the north of Falerii Veteres.

praenubilus: The word occurs only here (*hapax legomenon*). OLD: 'with adjectives *prae-* indicates eminence in the quality concerned'.

8. concedes numinis esse locum: Almost quotes 3.1.2: *credibile est illi numen inesse loco*. The difference, however, is important. Where the poet of 3.1 is mildly sceptical, the husband of 3.12 is unreservedly pious.

Y reads: *concedes nume̢ᶦnis esse locum*. Showerman and Goold follow Heinsius in printing: *concedas numen inesse loco*. Heinsius cites *Fast.* 3.295-6 as parallel: *lucus Auentino suberat niger ilicis umbra,* | *quo posses uiso dicere 'numen inest'*. The resemblance is hardly a reason for change. In this context the subjunctive *concedas* would introduce an inappropriately hesitant note.

9-10. accipit ara preces uotiuaque tura piorum,
    ara per antiquas facta sine arte manus.
From general description of the place, the husband now turns to the altar as a site of prayer and as an embodiment of ancient piety.

9. For the burning of incense as part of religious practice see above on 3.3.33. For the combination of prayer with incense-burning see e.g. *Met.* 6.164, 9.159.

10. ara per antiquas facta...manus: The antiquity of the altar is evidence of its sanctity. See e.g. *Met.* 7.74, 15.686 (Aesculapius): *flectit et antiquas abiturus respicit aras*.

sine arte: While lack of art is sometimes treated as a fault in Ovid's erotic poetry (e.g. 1.15.19, *Ars* 1.106, 113, 3.42), here it is evidence of honest devotion.

11-12. huc, ubi praesonuit sollemni tibia cantu,
    it per uelatas annua pompa uias.
The husband now begins his account of the first phase of the ceremony: the procession of animals for sacrifice at Juno's temple.

11. huc: At this point our sole major manuscript Y offers H^(hic)*anc*. *Hanc* makes no sense. Before Heinsius editors printed *hic*. But this is no improvement because the procession must move either to (*huc*) or from (*hinc*) the altar. Heinsius printed *hinc* in his text, but recommended reading *huc* (292): 'Lege *Huc*'. Recent editors (apart from Showerman and Goold: *hinc*) favour *huc*. Given that the first stage of sacrifice involves animals being led *to* an altar (Beard, North, and Price [1998b: 148]), and given that the following lines are devoted to describing a parade of sacrificial animals, *huc* is clearly right.

praesonuit: An Ovidian coinage, this verb occurs only here and at Calp. *Ecl.* 4.66.

tibia: A flutelike musical instrument, which seems to be primarily (but not exclusively) associated with joyful occasions e.g. Lucr. 4.584–5: *dulcisque querellas, | tibia quas fundit, Her.* 12.139–40, *Met.* 4.761–2, *Fast.* 6.659–60.

For the phrase *tibia cantu* see Catul. 64.264, Tib. 1.7.47, *A.* 9.618.

12. annua pompa: Frederiksen and Ward Perkins argue that the procession took place on the road leading from Falerii Novi to Juno's temple (1957: 46): 'The preparations were presumably made in Falerii Novi, where inscriptions record the *pontifex sacrarius Iunonis Quiritis*; moreover we may be sure that in Ovid's day nothing remained on the old site. Hence the Via Sacra, as indeed its name would suggest, was probably the road along which the procession moved to the temple'.

For this verbal pattern (VabBA) see above on 3.1.11.

13–14. ducuntur niueae populo plaudente iuuencae,
   quas aluit campis herba Falisca suis,
The first sacrificial victims are the white heifers for which Falerii was famous.

13. niueae…iuuencae: White cattle were prized. In myth they are associated with Pasiphae (*Ecl.* 6.46), Aristaeus (*G.* 1.15), Apollo ([Tib.] 3.4.67), and Io (*Met.* 1.652). Ovid implies their suitability for sacrifice (*Met.* 10.272; a festival of Venus): *conciderant ictae niuea ceruice iuuencae.* Pliny suggests that it was the water that made Faliscan cattle white (*Nat.* 2.230.1): *in Falisco omnis aqua pota candidos boues facit.*

14. Ovid recycles this line when describing the sacrifices on the Capitol for inauguration of the consuls (*Fast.* 1.83–4): *colla rudes operum praebent ferienda iuuenci, | quos aluit campis herba Falisca suis, Pont.* 4.4.31–2, 4.8.41–2.

15–16. et uituli nondum metuenda fronte minaces
   et minor ex humili uictima porcus hara
Next come calves and a pig.

15. Emphasis on the calf's youth may be intended to arouse pathos or (perhaps more likely) to be purely descriptive. For the sacrifice of a calf see Lucr. 2.352–4, a passage to which Ovid alludes at *Rem.* 184, *Met.* 2.623–5, 15.464–5, *Fast.* 4.459–60.

16. Perhaps alludes to Tib. 1.10.26: *hostiaque e plena rustica porcus hara.* For the possible etymological connection between *hara* and *hostia/uictima* see Maltby (2002: ad loc.).

17–18. duxque gregis cornu per tempora dura recuruo.
   inuisa est dominae sola capella deae:
The speaker concludes his description of the parade by noting the presence of a ram and the absence of a she-goat.

318 Commentary

17. duxque gregis: This phrase is used of either a ram (e.g. Tib. 1.10.10: *securus sparsas dux gregis inter oues*, *Met.* 7.311, Sen. *Tro.* 1035, *Thy.* 226) or a bull (*Ars* 1.326 [Pasiphae's bull], Sen. *Phaed.* 116 [also Pasiphae's bull]). Here the context requires a ram, because (a) cattle have already been mentioned and (b) a ram is needed to complete the *suouetaurilia*, the killing of a pig, a ram, and a bull, a common form of public and private sacrifice (Beard, North, and Price [1998b: 151–3]).

18. Juno's hatred of the she-goat is found only here.

**19–20. illius indicio siluis inuenta sub altis
dicitur inceptam destituisse fugam.**
As explanation for Juno's hostility, the speaker offers an aetiological story involving a goat that that betrays the goddess's hiding-place. This myth of a tattletale goat resembles stories told in *Metamorphoses* and *Fasti* of humans and animals punished by the gods for revealing the truth: the talkative crow and raven (*Met.* 2.531–611), Ocyroe (2.633–75), and Battus (2.687–707); the noisy ass (*Fast.* 1.393–440, 6.319–348), prophetic birds (1.441–56), and Lara (2.599–616). For discussion of the *Metamorphoses* stories see Keith (1992) and Davis (2016: 189–97).

19. indicio: *index* and *indicium* are key terms in the some of the relevant stories in *Metamorphoses* and *Fasti* (*Met.* 2.546, 706, *Fast.* 1.450, 6.346).

20. Burman (528: n. 19) observes that there are two stories of Juno's flight, first, when Jupiter attempted to seduce her by disguising himself as a cuckoo (Paus. 2.17.4), and, second, when the gods fled to Egypt (*Met.* 5.321–4). Neither myth seems pertinent.

**21–2. nunc quoque per pueros iaculis incessitur index
et pretium auctori uulneris ipsa datur.**
The story of the she-goat's betrayal of the goddess's whereabouts explains why, as part of Juno's ritual, boys throw missiles at a goat. For a similar account of the origins of a ceremony involving cruelty to animals see *Fast.* 4.681–712, explaining why Romans set fire to foxes.

**23–4. qua uentura dea est, iuuenes timidaeque puellae
praeuerrunt latas ueste iacente uias.**
From the parade of sacrificial animals, the speaker now turns to describing the procession which leads the goddess from her temple along the sacred way towards Falerii.

23. qua uentura dea est: For the sacred way see above on 12.

iuuenes timidaeque puellae: For the participation of young men and women in religious rituals see e.g. Hor. *Carm.* 1.21.1–2, 3.1.4, 3.14.10, *Saec.* 6: *uirgines lectas puerosque castos* (with Schnegg [2020: 20, p. 16]: PVEROS VIRGINESQVE

PATRIMOS MATRIM[osque]). While Ovid uses the phrase *timidae puellae* in different ways (e.g. 1.7.45 [of his girlfriend's fear after being struck], 2.6.43 [of Corinna's fear for her parrot], *Rem.* 33 [of girls afraid of being caught]), here it suggests *pudor*. For the association of timidity with modesty see e.g. 1.5.8: *qua timidus latebras speret habere pudor, Ars* 3.699 [of Procris]: *coniugis ad timidas aliquis male sedulus aures*.

24. praeuerrunt: The verb occurs only here. This is the poem's second *hapax legomenon* involving the prefix *prae-*. (See above on 7.) Here it indicates that the young men and women lead the goddess along the sacred way.

praeuerrunt...ueste: For 'sweeping' the ground with trailing garments see e.g. *Met.* 11.166 and Stat. *Ach.* 1.262–3.

25–6. uirginei crines auro gemmaque premuntur,
  et tegit auratos palla superba pedes;
Now the speaker employs high-flown language to describe the rich and elaborate clothing worn by female participants in the ceremony. For similarly sumptuous adornment see Cydippe's preparations for worshipping Apollo and Diana (*Her.* 21.89–90): *ipsa dedit gemmas digitis et crinibus aurum, | et uestes umeris induit ipsa meis*.

25. uirginei crines: *uirgineus* is an almost exclusively poetic word (the exception is Col. 9.4.4.2). For 'virginal hair' see *Fast.* 2.560: *uirgineas...comas*, Sen. *Ag*. 312–13, Stat. *Theb.* 2.255.

auro gemmaque: The combination of course implies great wealth (e.g. *A*. 1.655, 728). For their use in a procession see 1.2.41–2 (Cupid's triumph).

premuntur: Use of this verb for hair decoration (*TLL* 1169.46–63) is purely poetic e.g. *A*. 4.148: *fronde premit crinem*, 5.556, *Fast*. 4.517–18, Stat. *Silu*. 1.2.228.

26. For this verbal pattern (VaBbA) see above on 3.1.7.

auratos...pedes: The adjective is primarily poetic (*TLL auro* 1521.66–7). Virgil (*A*. 5.250: *chlamydem auratam*) and Ovid (*Her*. 13.32: *aurata...ueste*, *Met*. 8.448, 14.263) use *auratus* of clothing. The whole expression, however, is an elaborate way of referring to golden foot-bindings, as *TLL* 1521.40–1 suggests, or golden shoes.

palla superba: When used of clothing *superbus* perhaps suggests huge expense: see e.g. *A*. 1.639: *arte laboratae uestes ostroque superbo*.

27–8. more patrum Graio uelatae uestibus albis
  tradita supposito uertice sacra ferunt.
The husband now emphasizes the Greek character of the ceremony. The contemporary antiquarian, Dionysius of Halicarnassus, makes a similar point (*Ant. Rom.* 1.21.2.3): 'The temple of Hera in Falerii was constructed as at Argos. Here the

manner of sacrificing was also the same: holy women serving the precinct, and a girl free of marriage called the 'basket-carrier' (*kanēphoros*) beginning the sacrifices, and choruses of virgins singing to the goddess in ancestral hymns'.

27. more…Graio: Refers to Roman ceremonies which included Greek elements, such as the starting of sacrifices in the morning and concluding them in the evening, the involvement of a bareheaded priest (*aperto capite*), the wearing of a laurel wreath, and the occasional use of Greek words. For sacrifice to Juno 'in the Greek manner' see the inscriptional record of the Secular Games of 204 CE (Schnegg 2020 [183, p. 310]): IMMOL[avit I]VNONI REGINAE VACCAM ALB(am) GRAECO ACHIVO RIT [u. On the significance of sacrifice *Graeco ritu* see Scheid (1995).

28. The white-robed maidens presumably include Dionysius' 'basket-carrier'. For this verbal pattern (abBAV) see above on 3.2.42.

29–30. ore fauent populi tum cum uenit aurea pompa,
  ipsa sacerdotes subsequiturque suas.
The body of the procession now follows with the goddess's statue coming last of all.

29. ore fauent: For the use of *faueo* in religious contexts see above on 3.2.43.

  ore is the reading of Y and most other manuscripts. Goold argues for *ora*, with *populi* becoming genitive singular because 'the mention of *populi* ("nations") is ridiculous'. However, (a) the ablative is normal after this verb (e.g. Enn. *Ann.* 16.426: *ore fauentes*, A. 5.71: *ore fauete omnes*, Ib. 98: *quisquis ades sacris, ore fauete, meis*) and (b) the use of plural for singular is not unusual in Ovid, even with *populus* (e.g. *Met.* 6.92: *populisque*, i.e. the Pygmean people; 7.523: *populis*, i.e. the Aeginetan people; 8.298: *populi*, i.e. the Calydonian people); *Fast.* 1.38: *cum rudibus populis*, i.e. the Roman people).

aurea pompa: For the phrase see 3.2.44.

30. ipsa: Underlines the importance of the goddess as the procession's climactic figure.

31–2. Argiua est pompae facies; Agamemnone caeso
  et scelus et patrias fugit Halaesus opes
The Greek form of the ritual requires explanation. The procession is not only Greek in form but Argive, a 'fact' that can be explained by an appeal to a familiar myth.

31. Argiua…facies: Dionysius of Halicarnassus (*Ant. Rom.* 1.21.2; quoted above on 27–8) had emphasized Falerii's Argive connection, while Pliny reports Cato as noting the town's Argive origins (*Nat.* 3.51.7): *intus coloniae Falisca, Argis orta, ut auctor est Cato.*

32. Halaesus: For Virgil Halaesus is Agamemnon's son (A. 7.723-4): *hinc Agamemnonius, Troiani nominis hostis, | curru iungit Halaesus.* Ovid not only makes him a son of Agamemnon but links his name with that of Falerii (*Fast.* 4.73-4): *uenerat Atridae fatis agitatus Halaesus, | a quo se dictam terra Falisca putat.*

33-4. iamque pererratis profugus terraque fretoque
moenia felici condidit alta manu.
But if Virgil knows that Halaesus was a son of Agamemnon, Ovid's dutiful husband can tell us more: he was the founder of Falerii.

33. pererratis profugus terraque fretoque: Alludes to the *Aeneid*'s opening lines, particularly 1.2-3: *profugus Lauiniaque uenit | litora, multum ille et terris iactatus et alto.* As Boyd (1997: 52) notes, allusion to the Virgil sets up a contrast between Juno as 'implacable enemy' of Aeneas and Rome, and as protector of Halaesus and Falerii.

34. moenia condidit...alta: Continues allusion to *Aeneid*'s proem, this time to lines 5 and 7: *dum conderet urbem... altae moenia Romae.*
   Perhaps influenced by the proximity of *manus* Y reads *apta*, not *alta*. (For *apta manus* see e.g. *Her.* 3.70, *Ars* 1.693, *Fast.* 4.774.) While it is not clear what *apta* might mean in this context, *alta*, which has some manuscript support, underlines the Virgilian connection.

35-6. ille suos docuit Iunonia sacra Faliscos.
sint mihi, sint populo semper amica suo.
The poem closes with the claim that Halaesus taught these rites and a prayer that they might continue to benefit both speaker and townspeople.

36. sint...sint: This reading is offered by most manuscripts (including Y) and printed by most editors. In his fourth edition Munari printed *sit*, a suggestion of Francius (Burman: ad loc.) that was endorsed by Lee (1952: 176). For defence of *sint* see Kenney (1958: 66). For *amicus* as 'dear' see (*TLL* 1904.6-38, *OLD* 5; e.g. Hor. *Carm.* 4.6.41-3: *ego dis amicum,... reddidi carmen,* Prop. 2.16.26: *formosis leuitas semper amica fuit.*

3.14: CONCEAL YOUR INFIDELITIES

As the last erotic poem in *Amores*, 3.14 surprises. When taking leave of love elegy, the Propertian lover said farewell to Cynthia (3.24, 3.25). This seems a suitable way of ending a set of love poems and we might expect a similar gesture here. But Ovid's lover has no such option, because in Book 3 Corinna already belongs to his past: she was his student (3.1.49: *didicit* ['she learned']), his sexual partner (3.7.26: *memini* ['I remember']), and his inspiration (3.12.16: *ingenium mouit* ['she stirred

322   Commentary

my talent']). While Corinna was a major figure in Book 2, she has had virtually no role to play in Book 3.

It is recapitulation of episodes in earlier parts of the collection that makes 3.14 an effective closural poem. Its opening line, for example, recalls the beginning of 3.7 (*At non formosa est* ['No, she wasn't lovely', i.e. 'Yes, she was lovely'] / *cum sis formosa* ['because you're lovely']),[1] while its reference to prostitution (9-12) recalls 1.10 (esp. 21-2) and 3.12 (esp. 7-8); and its description of sexual activity (21-6) supplies what was missing from 1.5 (25: *cetera quis nescit?* ['Who does not know the rest?']).[2] 3.14's use of legal language also connects it with 1.4 (I will lay claim to you),[3] 2.7 (Don't accuse me),[4] and 3.3 (My girlfriend perjured herself).[5]

But closest of all is 2.5. Both poems are explicit in their use of legal terminology and both are founded on the premise that the lover's mistress has been unfaithful. In 2.5, however, the lover makes the mistake of believing the evidence of his eyes, while in 3.14 he undertakes to accept any lie that his girlfriend tells. The connection is secured by the use of the phrase *non feci* ('not guilty') in both poems (2.5.10, 3.14.48). The legal significance of that phrase is made clear by Cicero when he sets out the two responses that a defendant can make to a criminal accusation (*Inu.* 1.10.7): *non feci aut iure feci* ('Not guilty' or 'I was right to do it'). Perhaps not surprisingly the phrase occurs nowhere else in poetry.

Also striking is the fact that in both poems the lover adopts a number of courtroom roles. In 2.5 he plays the part of prosecutor (7-8). Not only that, he is both witness (*uidi* ['I saw'] 13, 15, 23) and judge (*liquet* ['it is clear'] 24).[6] When we turn to 3.14 we find that the lover adds to these the task of censor (*nostra... censura* 3), an official, who, like the *princeps* himself,[7] was responsible for the supervision of public morality.

By constructing 3.14 as one side of a courtroom drama, Ovid reminds his readers that the law now governed (or attempted to govern) sexual morality. He also, as Stroh and others have argued,[8] points to a flaw in the *lex Iulia de adulteriis coercendis*, viz. that a husband who failed to detect his wife's adulteries could not be found guilty of *lenocinium* and was therefore innocent before the law.[9]

---

[1] For allusion to 3.7 see below on 21-6.
[2] I this point to Bretzigheimer (2001: 40).
[3] For the law in 1.4 see e.g. J. T. Davis (1993), Miller (2003: 177-80), Ziogas (2021: 93-104).
[4] For the law in 2.7 see e.g. Watson (1983), Gebhardt (2009: 169-71), Ziogas (2021: 117-23).
[5] For more details see below.
[6] For *liquet* as a judicial term see Gebhardt (2009: 173).
[7] *RG* 6.1 (Cooley [2009]): *cu[rator legum et morum...]* / ἐπιμελετὴς τῶν τε νόμων καὶ τῶν τρόπων ('supervisor of laws and morals'). (I quote the Greek because most of the Latin is an editorial supplement.) Cf. *Tr.* 2.233-4: *urbs quoque te et legum lassat tutela tuarum | et morum* ('The city wearies you as well as guardianship of your laws and morals').
[8] Stroh (1979: 341-3), McGinn (1998: 235), Gebhardt (2009: 175-6).
[9] For the charge of *lenocinium* see above on 3.4.45-6.

Commentary, 14.1-3   323

As Gebhardt puts it (2009: 176), 'a husband could invoke his *credulitas* to escape prosecution'.

Secondary literature: Luck (1969: 173-80); Frécaut (1972: 190-2); Morgan (1977: 102-104); Bretzigheimer (2001: 38-41, 142-6), Gebhardt (2009: 175-7); Lui in Morwood et al. (2011: 27-32); Ingleheart and Radice (2012); Oliensis (2019: 81-7); Ziogas (2021: 75-92).

1-2. Non ego, ne pecces, cum sis formosa, recuso,
  sed ne sit misero scire necesse mihi;
While the hexameter offers a careful if convoluted attempt at stating what the lover does not object to (note the line's lack of fluency, the placing of *ne pecces* before *recuso*, the way in which the causal clause interrupts the main construction), the pentameter sets out bluntly what he wants: ignorance.

1. non ego: Makes a striking opening to a poem because it immediately prompts questions: If *you* don't, then who does?, Then what *do* you do? It is used by the lover at 2.4.1 when refusing to defend his morals: *non ego mendosos ausim defendere mores*; and by the pickup artist as a prelude to stating his real intentions at 3.2.1: *non ego nobilium sedeo studiosus equorum*.

pecces: For *peccare* used of adultery see above on 3.4.9.

cum sis formosa: Recalls both the gods' unwillingness to punish to lovely girls (3.3.31): *formosas superi metuunt offendere laesi* and the lover's failure (3.7.1): *at non formosa est*.

recuso: As Ziogas (2021: 81) observes 'the legalistic *recuso* evokes right from the beginning the setting of a trial'. Here, however, we have a prosecutor who refuses to object to wrongdoing. For the legal resonance of *recuso* see *OLD* 1: 'leg. To put in an objection, demur', *TLL β: spectat ad leges* 463.71-464.50.

2. ne sit...scire necesse: For the desirability of ignorance see [Tib.] 3.20.1-2: *rumor ait crebro nostram peccare puellam: | nunc ego me surdis auribus esse uelim*.

misero...mihi: Recalls the conventional lover's pose as *miser*. See above on 3.9.9.

3-4. nec te nostra iubet fieri censura pudicam
  sed tamen ut temptes dissimulare rogat.
Not content with presenting himself as a prosecutor unwilling to do his job, the lover takes on the role of reluctant censor, one who insists on the appearance, but not the substance of sexual morality.

3. Although lines 3-8 are very difficult to read, the evidence of P resumes at this point.

nostra...censura: Equates the lover with one of the two officials appointed under the Republic to register and regulate Rome's citizenry and implicitly with the *princeps* himself. (For Augustus as at least quasi-censor see *RG* 6.1 [quoted in note 7 above], *Fast.* 6.647: *sic agitur censura*, Suet. *Aug.* 27.5.3: *recepit et morum legumque regimen aeque perpetuum*, Cass. Dio 54.10.5: 'Having been invited, he was elected supervisor of morals for five years and accepted the power of the censors for the same period'.) At *Ars* 2.387 the Teacher adopts a similarly flippant attitude to the censorship: *nec mea uos uni damnat censura puellae*. He takes it more seriously when it is applied to his own work (*Rem.* 362): *quorum censura Musa proterua mea est*.

Here the censor's failure to enforce *pudicitia* establishes the truth of the adulterer's (entirely cynical) argument in the first ten lines of 3.4, viz. that when it comes to morality an individual's inner commitments are more important that external controls.

pudicam: The adjective is used of women in *Amores* only here and at 13 below. In both cases it is a virtue to be faked not practised. Dipsas, the brothel-keeper of 1.8, (esp. 43: *casta est, quam nemo rogauit*) and the aspiring adulterer of 3.4 (esp. 41: *quo tibi formosam, si non nisi casta placebat?*) express similar contempt for conventional morality.

4. dissimulare: For the benefits of simulating *pudor* see 1.8.35-6 (Dipsas again): *decet alba quidem pudor ora, sed iste, | si simules, prodest; uerus obesse solet*.

5-6. non peccat, quaecumque potest peccasse negare,
   solaque famosam culpa professa facit.
Repetition and alliteration (especially of *p* and *f*) are used here to underline the importance of a policy of stout denial.

5. peccat...peccasse: For similar use of repetition to give a paradoxical case an air of logical necessity see 3.4.9-10: *cui peccare licet, peccat minus; ipsa potestas | semina nequitiae languidiora facit*.

6. In 3.12 the poet-lover argued a slightly different case: it was his poetry that made his girlfriend famous (7): *fallimur, an nostris innotuit illa libellis?* Here it is a woman's admission of guilt that brings infamy.

famosam: As at 3.6.78, where raped Ilia uses it of her own sense of shame, the word is pejorative.

professa: Often used of commitment to a profession (*OLD* 5, *TLL* 1721.25-46), *profiteor* may suggest prostitution in this context. See e.g. *Fast.* 4.865-6: *numina, uulgares, Veneris celebrate, puellae: | multa professarum quaestibus apta Venus*, Suet. *Tib.* 35.2.1: 'Notorious women (*feminae famosae*) had begun to profess that they were prostitutes (*lenocinium profiteri*) in order to avoid the punishment of the law and to be released from the rights and status of being a *matrona*'. If so, it foreshadows the explicit references to prostitution in 9-12.

7-8. quis furor est, quae nocte latent, in luce fateri,
   et quae clam facias facta referre palam?
Using antithesis (*nocte/luce, clam/palam*), the lover underlines the perversity of his girlfriend's behaviour: instead of denying her misdeeds she actually makes them public.

7. quis furor est: The question is appropriate to more serious contexts (e.g. *A.* 5.670 [Ascanius sees the Trojan fleet ablaze]: *quis furor iste nouus?*, Tib. 1.10.33: *quis furor est atram bellis accersere mortem?*, Luc. 1.8: *quis furor, o ciues*). Here its use seems histrionic. Cf. *Ars* 3.172 (criticism of expensive clothes): *quis furor est census corpore ferre suos!*

quae nocte latent: Night offers both concealment of wrongdoing (e.g. Hom. *Il.* 3.11, Enn. *Phoen.* [Goldberg and Manuwald 2] fr. 109.4: *res obnoxiosae nocte in obscura latent*, Catul. 62.34, *A.* 8.658) and opportunities for sex (e.g. *A.* 11.736, Prop. 2.15.1, *Her.* 13.105: *nox grata puellis*). Here night conceals sexual wrongdoing.

8. facias facta: For polyptoton used to frame the main caesura see on 3.2.32.

9-10. ignoto meretrix corpus iunctura Quiriti
   opposita populum summouet ante sera;
The lover follows the previous couplet's tactfully phrased question with an insulting comparison: even a prostitute has sex behind closed doors.

9. The line is carefully structured with the central word *corpus* framed by a chiastic arrangement of noun and adjectives (aBbA).

ignoto...Quiriti: The singular *Quiriti* emphasizes the prostitute's concern for privacy: she has sex with one citizen and excludes the *populus*. As Porphyrio notes on Hor. *Carm.* 2.7.3, the singular is rare: *attende singulari numero dictum, quod non facile apud ueteres inuenias*. See also 1.7.29, *Met.* 14.823, *Tr.* 2.569. For the plural *Quirites* see above on 3.2.73.

meretrix: Recalls the lover's denunciation of gift-giving (1.10.21): *stat meretrix certo cuiuis mercabilis aere* and the suggestion that the lover's girlfriend has become a prostitute (see introduction to 3.12).

corpus iunctura: For *iungo* in sexual contexts see Adams (1982: 179-80). The phrase seems polite e.g. Lucr. 5.962, *Her.* 9.134, *Met.* 9.470.

10. opposita...sera: For the phrase see *Ars* 2.244: *atque erit opposita ianua fulta sera*, *Fast.* 1.266: *dempserat oppositas inuidiosa seras*.

11-12. tu tua prostitues famae peccata sinistrae,
   commissi perages indiciumque tui?
From insulting comparison the lover shifts to asking an equally offensive question.

326 Commentary

11. tu tua: Ovid is fond of combining a pronoun with its corresponding possessive adjective. For *tu/te tua* see *Her.* 7.87, 18.97, 19.184, *Met.* 2.177, 683, *Fast.* 1.481. For the more frequent *me mea* see above on 3.2.48 and 3.6.100. Here alliteration and assonance underline they key verb: *tu tua prostitues*.

prostitues: While here the verb has the sense 'to expose to public shame' (*OLD* 2; citing this passage), the context reminds readers that the verb's primary meaning is 'to prostitute' (*OLD* 1).

peccata: For *peccare* and illicit sex see above on 3.4.9.

12. commissi: May reflect the language of Augustus' moral legislation. *Dig.* 48.2.3.pr.2–4 lays out the form of an indictment for adultery: 'In the presence of that praetor or consul, Lucius Titius announced that he was accusing Maevia of committing adultery (*adulterium commisisse*) with Gaius Seius under the Julian Law on Adultery'. See also *Ars* 2.365 (with Janka [1997: ad loc.], who notes the legal terminology): *nil Helene peccat, nihil hic committit adulter.*

indiciumque: For *indicium* as legal evidence or testimony see *TLL* 1145.82–1147.7.

13–14. sit tibi mens melior, saltemue imitare pudicas,
 teque probam, quamuis non eris, esse putem.
The lover now offers advice: either mend your morals or pretend to.

13. mens melior: For moralizing writers *mens bona* is a virtue to be prized (e.g. Cic. *Tusc.* 5.67.3: *quid est autem in homine sagaci ac bona mente melius?*). For others it is a quality overthrown by sexual passion (e.g. *Am.* 1.2.31: *Mens Bona ducetur manibus post terga retortis*) or regained when passion wanes (Prop. 3.24.19–20): *Mens Bona, si qua dea es, tua me in sacraria dono.* | *exciderunt surdo tot mea uota Ioui.* Here, however, *mens melior* is no more than avoiding infidelity.

14. imitare pudicas: If she cannot be faithful, she should join a category of girls the lover fancies (2.4.15–16): *aspera si uisa est rigidasque imitata Sabinas,* | *uelle, sed ex alto dissimulare puto.*

pudicas |…probam: Alludes to Catullus (42.24: *pudica et proba*) and Horace (*Epod.* 17.40: *tu pudica, tu proba*), both addressing women who are neither chaste nor virtuous.

quamuis non eris: Use of the indicative after *quamuis* perhaps underlines the actual situation (she will not be chaste) and the lover's choice to be deceived. (In *Amores* Ovid shows a slight preference for the indicative after *quamuis*, rather than the subjunctive.)

15–16. quae facis, haec facito: tantum fecisse negato
 nec pudeat coram uerba modesta loqui.
From wish and polite suggestion the lover now turns to blunt commands: do what you like, but deny that you're doing it.

15. The line is remarkable for its use of three different forms of *facio* and its placing of legal imperatives at the main caesura and the end of the line.

facis...facito...fecisse: For similar play with multiple forms of the same verb see *Ars* 1.454: *ne dederit gratis quae dedit, usque dabit*, *Met.* 10.302–3: *nec credite factum, | uel, si credetis, facti quoque credite poenam.*

facito...negato: The speaker states his demands in legal language. For the future imperative as characteristic of legislative texts see Woodcock (§127) and Pinkster (1.517–20). For the legal connotations of the future imperative in *Am.* 1.4 see J. T. Davis (1993) and Ziogas (2021: 94). Particularly pertinent here is the stated intent of the 'The Julian law on the suppression of adultery' (*Dig.* 48.5.13.pr.1): *haec uerba legis 'ne quis posthac stuprum adulterium facito sciens dolo malo'* ('These are the words of the law: "After this no one shall commit *stuprum* or adultery knowingly and with malicious intent"').

16. nec pudeat: Change of construction marks a change in tone, with *ne* and the present subjunctive being used 'for a milder form of advice' (Pinkster [1.499]).

coram: Means both 'in public' (*OLD* 2b: e.g. *Met.* 9.560: *et damus amplexus, et iungimus oscula coram* [i.e. sister and brother may embrace and kiss openly]); and 'in my presence' (*OLD* 1: e.g. *Her.* 16.283–4 [Paris to Helen]: *sed coram ut plura loquamur, | excipe me lecto nocte silente tuo*). Both meanings seem appropriate. The lover wants his girlfriend to behave modestly in public (cf. *palam* 8) and to lie to him in person.

uerba modesta: Implies an apparent commitment to conventional moral values, especially *pudor* (see above on 3.6.67). The idea that decorous speech might be source of shame is paradoxical.

17–18. est qui nequitiam locus exigat; omnibus illum
    deliciis imple, stet procul inde pudor.
Having insisted that his girlfriend seem self-controlled in public, the lover argues that she should throw off all restraint in private.

17. est qui...locus exigat: For the expression see *Her.* 7.58: *perfidiae poenas exigit ille locus* (i.e. the sea will punish Aeneas' treachery), *Fast.* 4.417: *exigit ipse locus raptus ut uirginis edam* (i.e. this point in my text requires this story). Here the *locus* is the bedroom, a place characterized by *nequitia* (hence the generic subjunctive [see on 3.9.18] *exigat*).

nequitia: For *nequitia* as a defining quality of both elegiac lover and beloved see on 3.1.17 and 3.11.37.

18. deliciis: For *deliciae* as sexual pleasure see Catul. 45.24, 74.2, Prop. 2.15.2: *lectule deliciis facte beate meis*, *Her.* 15.138, *Ars* 3.649. Adams (1982: 196–7) notes that it was a popular term in the late Republic for extra-marital affairs. For *deliciae* as 'erotic verse' or 'love affairs' see below on 3.15.4.

stet procul inde pudor: While the language recalls Tibullan Priapus' praise of a boy (1.4.14: *uirgineus teneras stat pudor ante genas*), the rejection of conventional morality is closer to the *Amores*-poet's ban on the narrow-minded (2.1.3): *procul hinc, procul este, seueri!* Here, however, the lover pleads that a liberated woman (she is by no means narrow-minded) abandon all pretence of shame.

pudor: As in 2.5, another poem in which legal terminology is important, *pudor* is a key concept here. *pudor* and cognates occur six times in 3.14. Although the word occurs only once in 2.5 (at line 34), its significance there is highlighted by five similes imaging its effect upon the defendant's face (35–40).

19–20. hinc simul exieris, lasciuia protinus omnis
    absit, et in lecto crimina pone tuo.
In this and the next three couplets the lover prescribes rules of behaviour for different places. Once she goes outside (*hinc*), the girlfriend should behave with modesty. In bed (*illic* 21, 23, 25), however, her conduct should be very different.

19. lasciuia: Sometimes used of the lover's own behaviour (1.4.21, 2.10.27), *lasciuia* here implies an indulgent attitude towards the girl's actions. For the wider importance of this term see on 3.1.43.

20. crimina pone: Continues the legal language, a *crimen* being 'an indictment, charge, accusation' (*OLD* 1) or 'a misdeed, crime' (*OLD* 4). For *crimen* in a similar quasi-legal context see also 2.7.1: *ergo sufficiam reus in noua crimina semper?*, 28: *me non admissi criminis esse reum*.

Here the lover advises his girlfriend to lay aside (*OLD pono* 10) her crimes, i.e. pretend they didn't happen. But what are they? Polite society may object to her exercise of sexual freedom, the lover to her lack of loyalty to him.

21–2. illic nec tunicam tibi sit posuisse pudori
    nec femori impositum sustinuisse femur;
The sexual explicitness of the advice given in this and the next two couplets recalls the description of the disappointed girlfriend's attempts to arouse the impotent lover in 3.7 (esp. 9–12).

21. tunicam...posuisse: When outside the girl should leave her 'crimes' behind; in bed it's her tunic that she should leave behind.

pudori: The idea that taking off her clothes should not be a cause of shame seems paradoxical.

22. Recalls the lover's advice to his girlfriend at 1.4.43: *nec femori committe femur* (1.4 being another poem which exploits legal terminology; see above on 15); his attitude to a female critic at 2.4.22: *culpantis cupiam sustinuisse femur*; and the disappointed girl's attempts to excite her lover at 3.7.10: *lasciuum femori supposuitque femur*.

sustinuisse: For this verb in sexual contexts see 2.4.22 (quoted above), 3.2.30 (with note): *optauit manibus sustinuisse suis*, 3.7.26: *me memini numeros sustinuisse nouem*.

**23-4. illic purpureis condatur lingua labellis,
   inque modos uenerem mille figuret amor;**
Allusion to 3.7 continues with reference to deep kissing and the variety of sexual positions.

23. Reworks one of the dissatisfied girl's attempts to arouse her partner (3.7.9): *osculaque inseruit cupida luctantia lingua*. For deep kissing see 2.5.24, 57-8, *Her.* 15.129-30, and Tib. 1.8.37-8.

purpureis...labellis: The adjective is frequently applied to clothes (*TLL* 2708.12-34) and flowers (*TLL* 2711.19-59). When used of the mouth, as at Catul. 45.12: *illo purpureo ore suauiata*, (with Fordyce [1961: ad loc.]), it seems to suggest both redness and beauty. (Hor. *Carm.* 3.3.12: *purpureo bibet ore nectar*, of Augustus, is not helpful here.) Perhaps it also suggests the bruising that may result from vigorous kissing e.g. 1.7.41: *aptius impressis fuerat liuere labellis*. Cf. Catul. 8.18: *cui labella mordebis?*

24. modos: Recalls the lover's threat to Cypassis at 2.8.28: *narrabo dominae, quotque quibusque modis* and the sex he had hoped for at 3.7.64 (with note): *quos ego non finxi disposuique modos*.

modos...mille: For the multiplicity of sexual positions see *Ars* 2.679-80: *utque uelis, uenerem iungunt per mille figuras: | inuenit plures nulla tabella modos*.

ueneremque: For the goddess's name used of a sexual partner or sex itself see on 3.10.47.

**25-6. illic nec uoces nec uerba iuuantia cessent,
   spondaque lasciua mobilitate tremat.**
In the hexameter the lover recalls an activity present in 3.7, while in the pentameter he refers to one that was unfortunately absent. The whole couplet reworks (or is reworked by) *Her.* 15.47-8: *tunc te plus solito lasciuia nostra iuuabat, | crebraque mobilitas aptaque uerba ioco*.

25. uerba iuuantia: Recalls another of the girl's attempts to excite her partner (3.7.12): *et quae praeterea publica uerba iuuant*.

26. spondaque: Denoting the supporting framework (e.g. *Met.* 8.656: *lecto sponda pedibusque salignis*), the noun is used here of the whole couch.

lasciua: Perhaps recalls 3.7.10: *lasciuum...femur*.

mobilitate: For the lover's preference for vigorous female movement during sex see 2.4.13-14: *siue procax aliqua est, capior, quia rustica non est, | spemque dat in* *molli mobilis esse toro*. Lucretius claims that although men like women to move during intercourse (4.1276), movement is typical of *scorta* (4.1274), and not appropriate for wives (4.1268, 1277). Cf. Catul. 6, where a shaky bed (10 *tremulique… lecti*) is evidence that Flavius is having an affair with a *scortum* (4–5 *nescioquid febriculosi | scorti diligis*).

27–8. indue cum tunicis metuentem crimina uultum,
  et pudor obscenum diffiteatur opus.
But when it's all over and she goes outside the girl should adopt an air of modesty which denies the reality of sex work.

27. indue…uultum: For the expression see *A.* 1.684 (to Cupid): *notos pueri puer indue uultus, Met.* 8.853–4 (Erysichthon's daughter Mestra): *uultumque uirilem | induit,* Sen. *Med.* 751: *pessimos induta uultus, Ag.* 707: *induit uultus feros.*

cum tunicis: She should put on a modest look when she dons the tunic discarded at 21.

metuentem crimina: Suggests both fear of doing wrong and fear of being accused of doing wrong.

28. pudor: See above on 18.

obscenum…opus: For *opus* used of sexual activity (*OLD* 1d) see 1.4.48: *dulce… opus,* 2.10.36: *cum moriar, medium soluar et inter opus.* Here it may suggest that sex is the girl's occupation (*OLD* 2).

diffiteatur: The verb is rare, being used at Cic. *Fam.* 10.8.4.5, Col. 4.1.7.7, Quint. *Inst.* 2.17.5.2 and three times in Apuleius.

29–30. da populo, da uerba mihi: sine nescius errem,
  et liceat stulta credulitate frui.
The lover closes this stage of the argument with a request that his girlfriend deceive not only the outside world but himself.

29. da populo, da uerba mihi: Having asked that his girlfriend mislead Rome in general, the lover extends that request to himself: he too should be deceived. For the idiom *uerbum/uerba dare* meaning 'to deceive' see *OLD uerbum* 6. Cf. the advice the Teacher gives his male students at *Ars* 2.557–8: *quo magis, o iuuenes, deprendere parcite uestras: | peccent, peccantes uerba dedisse putent.*

  Lee (1968) punctuates: *da populo. da uerba mihi.* Assigning different meanings to *dare* is witty and attractive (for *dare* used in a sexual sense see on 3.8.34; Lee translates: 'Take whoever you please—provided you take me in'). The argument, however, requires a shift from the general (implied in 27–8, explicit in *populo*) to the particular (*mihi*), not a clever endorsement of promiscuity.

29. sine nescius errem: The Teacher takes the same view at *Ars* 2.555: *sed melius nescisse fuit.*

Commentary, 14.27–36   331

30. stulta credulitate: Recalls 3.3.24: *et stulta populos credulitate mouet*. Allusion underlines a change in attitude. In 3.3 the lover protested against his girlfriend's lies; in 3.14 he prefers her falsehoods.

31–2. cur totiens uideo mitti recipique tabellas?
   cur pressus prior est interiorque torus?
Having asked his girlfriend to lie, the lover now puts a series of questions asking why he has to *see* so much evidence of infidelity. First comes the circumstantial evidence: exchanges of letters and a messy bed.

31. For *tabellae* as evidence of infidelity see 2.5.5 (it's not just letters): *non mihi deceptae nudant tua facta tabellae*, 2.19.41: *quas ferat et referat sollers ancilla tabellas*. For the use of letters more generally see 1.11 and 1.12, *Ars* 1.437–40, 3.619–30.

32. This girlfriend clearly follows Dipsas' advice (1.8.97): *ille uiri uideat toto uestigia lecto*. Propertius' Cynthia, by contrast, seems innocent (2.29b.35–6): *apparent non ulla toro uestigia presso, | signa uolutantis nec iacuisse duos*.

prior est interiorque torus: Suggests of course that the bed has had two occupants. Cf. 1.5.2, where *medio…toro* implies that the lover expects to sleep alone. See also 2.10.17–18, *Her.* 19.158: *ponuntur medio cur mea membra toro?*
   Epic. Drusi (*Consolation to Livia*) 328 implies that the man occupies the outer part of the bed: *quaeris et in uacui parte priore tori?* The medical writer Marcellus confirms this (1.57 [Helmreich 1889: p. 34]): *si spondam lecti priorem, qua uir cubat, perunxeris*.

33–4. cur plus quam somno turbatos esse capillos
   collaque conspicio dentis habere notam?
Next comes personal evidence: disordered hair and love bites.

33. Spondees (SSSS) perhaps give this question a mock solemnity.

34. Recalls and even quotes 1.7.41–2: *aptius impressis fuerat liuere labellis | et collum blandi dentis habere notam*. Here too the girlfriend follows Dipsas' advice, ensuring that her lover see (1.8.98): *factaque lasciui̱s̱ liuida colla notis*. See also Tib. 1.6.13–14, 1.8.38, Prop. 4.3.25–6.

35–6. tantum non oculos crimen deducis ad ipsos;
   si dubitas famae parcere, parce mihi.
The lover has seen so much evidence of his girlfriend's infidelity. So what should she do? Make it less obvious.

35. tantum non: See *OLD tantum* 11: 'Only just not, all but, almost'. *OLD* cites only prose examples.

36. si dubitas famae parcere: So far, however, she has shown no concern for her reputation (6, 11).

parcere, parce: Recalls the lover's request to a lying girlfriend (3.3.48): *aut oculis certe parce, puella, meis.*

parce mihi: Spare the lover what? Presumably the visual evidence of her infidelity.

**37-8. mens abit et morior, quotiens peccasse fateris,
   perque meos artus frigida gutta fluit.**
And why does he request that she conceal her promiscuity? Because the effect is devastating on both mind and body. In this and the next couplet the lover uses allusion to Sappho and Catullus to articulate his predicament.

37. mens abit et morior: Ovid's Lucretia (*Fast.* 2.753) describes her thoughts in identical terms. While this man and Lucretia are very different (see Robinson [2011: ad loc.]), they have in common despair at the prospect of losing their beloved.

38. frigida gutta fluit: As in Catul. 51, the lover describes the physical symptoms caused by evidence of his beloved's infidelity (51.9–12). The details here, however, are closer to Sappho fr. 31, the poem that Catullus adapts, than to Catul. 51.

Unfortunately Sappho's text is disputed. Page (1955), for example, printed (31.13): κὰδ δέ μ' ἴδρως ψῦχρος ἔχει ('A cold sweat possesses me'), while Campbell (1990) offered: κὰδε δέ μ' ἴδρως κακχέεται ('A sweat pours down from me'). *frigida gutta* points to Page's version, while *gutta fluit* looks to Campbell's.

For similar description of physical distress see Arethusa's words (*Met.* 5.632–3): *occupat obsessos sudor mihi frigidus artus, | caeruleaeque cadunt toto de corpore guttae* and Lucretia's self-description at *Fast.* 2.754: *gelidum pectora frigus habet.*

**39-40. tunc amo, tunc odi frustra, quod amare necesse est
   tunc ego, sed tecum, mortuus esse uelim.**
To be more precise, the effect is that described concisely by Catullus in poem 85 and analysed in detail by Ovid in 3.11.

39. tunc amo, tunc odi…| tunc: Threefold repetition of *tunc* underlines the fact, as in Catul. 85 (*odi et amo* 1) and 3.11 (*hac amor hac odium* 34), the lover experiences contradictory emotions simultaneously.

amo: For the scansion (*amŏ*) see above on 3.1.8.

odi frustra: Recalls 3.11.34: *sed, puto, uincit amor.*

quod amare necesse est: Alludes to 3.11.52: *et, quam, si nolim, cogar amare, uelim.*

40. mortuus esse uelim: Recalls Sappho fr. 31.15–16 (Campbell: 1990): τεθνάκην δ' ὀλίγω 'πιδεύης | φαίνομ' ἔμ' αὔτ[ᾳ ('To myself I seem little short of dying') and possibly Catul. 51.11–12 (Mynors: 1958): *gemina teguntur | lumina nocte.* (I understand this as a reference to death. Cf. the Homeric formula [*Il.* 4.461 and 11

Commentary, 14.37-44 333

more times]: τὸν δὲ σκότος ὄσσε κάλυψεν ['Darkness covered both his eyes']. Catullus' text, however, is doubtful at this point.)

**41-2. nil equidem inquiram, nec quae celare parabis
insequar, et falli muneris instar erit.**
If knowledge causes distress, then it's better not to ask and even to be deceived.

41. nil equidem inquiram: Whereas 2.19's adulterer urged an acquiescent husband to ask questions (39-40): *incipe...* | *quaerere*, this lover has decided to ask none.

nec celare parabis | insequar: The decision not to probe becomes advice in *Ars* (2.555): *sed melius nescisse fuit: sine furta tegantur*. The Tibullan lover, by contrast, takes the view that concealment is impossible 1.9.23: *nec tibi celandi spes sit peccare paranti*.

42. falli muneris instar erit: In his willingness to be deceived this lover resembles the lover of 2.9 who hoped to be misled (43): *me modo decipiant uoces fallacis amicae* and the adulterer of 2.19 who advised his mistress to cheat (33): *siqua uolet regnare diu, deludat amantem*.

muneris instar: The phrase only occurs in Ovid. In *Ars* the Teacher advises that rape (1.676) and books of poetry (2.285-6) can be viewed as gifts.

**43-6. si tamen in media deprensa tenebere culpa,
et fuerint oculis probra uidenda meis,
quae bene uisa mihi fuerint, bene uisa negato:
concedent uerbis lumina nostra tuis.**
But suppose that the policy of not asking does not suffice; suppose that the lover actually sees his girlfriend being unfaithful. In that case he will believe her denials and not the evidence of his eyes. Like Bagoas' owner, he will choose self-deception over knowledge: (2.2.57-8): *uiderit ipse licet, credet tamen ille neganti* | *damnabitque oculos et sibi uerba dabit*.

43. in media...culpa: The expression is doubly striking, first because *medius* is normally used of space or time (though see *OLD* 7) and, second, because while *culpa* is regularly used of sexual misconduct (*OLD* 3b), its use as a euphemism for sexual intercourse is exceptional. For similar euphemistic expressions see 2.10.36, *Ars* 3.796, *Rem.* 357.

deprensa: The verb is commonly used, especially in Ovid, in contexts of sexual wrongdoing e.g. Catul. 56.5-6: *deprendi modo pupulum puellae* | *trusantem*; *Am.* 1.9.39: *Mars quoque deprensus fabrilia uincula sensit*; *Ars* 2.313, 377, 557, 593; 3.717.

44. For this verbal pattern (VABba), also used at line 46, see on 3.1.30.

probra: This powerful word of condemnation is mainly used of sexual crimes in Ovid e.g. *Her.* 17.208 (Helen of herself), *Ars* 3.49 (of Helen), 3.716 (Procris imagining Aura's misdeeds): *atque oculis probra uidenda tuis*, Ib. 565-6 (of Adonis, as child of incest).

45. Repetition of forms of *uideo* combined with the future imperative *negato* suggest allusion to Prop. (2.18a.3): *si quid uidisti, semper uidisse negato*. Unfortunately the state of Propertius' text renders the point of such a reference obscure.

The line's dactylic character (DDDD) perhaps underlines the offhand nature of the speaker's suspension of disbelief.

bene uisa: For *uidere bene* as 'see clearly, correctly' see *TLL bonus (bene)* 2116.27-40. Repetition reinforces the lover's advice to his girlfriend: simply deny the reality of what I have actually seen.

negato: For the future imperative see above on 15.

46: If the dactyls in 45 make the lover's request seem offhand, the spondees here imply utter seriousness.

47-8. prona tibi uinci cupientem uincere palma est,
  sit modo 'non feci' dicere lingua memor.
With an initially puzzling hexameter and a straightforward pentameter, the lover offers his girlfriend an easy win: all she has to say is 'not guilty'.

47. The line is artfully constructed with *cupientem* flanked by forms of *uinco*, and forms of *uinco* surrounded by an adjective and noun in agreement, both beginning with *p*.

uinci...uincere: Perhaps alludes to 1.5.15-16: *tamquam quae uincere nollet, | uicta est non aegre proditione sua*, where verbal play involving *uinco* is combined with an easy victory.

uincere: For *uincere* in legal contexts (*OLD* 5) see 2.5.7-8: *o utinam arguerem sic, ut non uincere possem | me miserum! quare tam bona causa mea est?*, 2.7.1-2: *ergo sufficiam reus in noua crimina semper? | ut uincam*.

palma: For the association with victory see on 1.2.82.

48. non feci: For the legal significance of this phrase and its connection with 2.5.10 see introduction above.

49-50. cum tibi contingat uerbis superare duobus,
  etsi non causa, iudice uince tuo.
If she says 'not guilty' she will win, not because her case is sound, but because the judge is on her side.

49. contingat: For this verb used intransitively with the dative see on 3.2.8.

50. Like the husband in 2.2, this lover is a biased judge: (2.2.55-6): *culpa nec ex facili quamuis manifesta probatur; | iudicis illa sui tuta fauore uenit*, (61-2): *quid dispar certamen inis? tibi uerbera uicto | adsunt, in gremio iudicis illa sedet*.

3.15: GOODBYE, LOVE ELEGY

The final poem in an Augustan poetry book often takes the form of a poetic signature. The closing lines of Virgil's *Georgics* (4.565-6), for example, define their author as the poet of the *Eclogues* and *Georgics*. More elaborate is the last poem in Horace's three-book collection of *Odes*. There the lyric poet signals closure in the poem's first word (*Exegi*, 'I have finished'), lays claim to poetic permanence (3.30.1-9), refers to his homeland Apulia (10-12), and sets out the nature of his achievement (12-16). When we turn to Propertius the situation is more complex. At the end of Book 1 the poet refers to the civil wars (especially the destruction of Perusia) and defines himself as a native of Umbria (1.22.9-10), while in the last poem of Book 2 the elegist asserts his place in the tradition of erotic poetry as embodied in the works of Varro, Catullus, Calvus, and Gallus (2.34.85-94).[1] *Am.* 3.15 clearly belongs in this category of *sphragis-* or signature-poems.

But so too do poems at the end of Books 1 and 2. In 1.15 we find a poet even more assertive than Propertius or Horace. Like Propertius, he claims affinity with predecessors, but he names not only love poets like Callimachus, Tibullus, and Gallus, but also epic poets like Homer, Ennius, Varro, and Virgil; and dramatists like Sophocles, Menander, and Accius. And like Horace he claims that his works will endure. But while Horace claimed that he would not wholly die (*non omnis moriar* 6), Ovid aspires to worldwide fame (*in toto semper ut orbe canar* 1.15.8) and immortality (*uiuam* 42). If we turn to 2.18 (the book's penultimate poem, but a signature-poem nevertheless), we find a work primarily concerned with defending the poet's achievement. But where Horace made his claim in relatively abstract terms (he was the first to bring lyric measures to Italy [3.30.13-14]), Ovid reviews his works thus far, mentioning his tragedy (15-16), *Ars Amatoria* (2.18.19: *artes... Amoris*),[2] and listing nine of his *Heroides*.[3]

Am. 3.15 clearly has elements in common with the signature-poems of Horace and Propertius. Like Horace in *Carm.* 3.30 and Propertius in 1.22, Ovid asserts an ethnic identity: he is from Sulmo in the territory of the Paeligni. But Propertius did more than remind readers that he was from Umbria: he devoted most of 1.22 (6 lines in a ten-line poem) to the destruction of Perusia during the civil war. Ovid follows suit and recalls the role of the Paeligni during Rome's war with the Italian allies (3.15.9-10). And while Propertius compared himself to his predecessors in the field of erotic poetry (2.34.85-94), Ovid claims equality with Catullus and Virgil (7-8). If 3.15 seems closer in subject matter to Propertius 1.22 and 3.15, it is closer in tone to *Carm.* 3.30. Propertius modestly raises the possibility

---

[1] While the conclusion to Propertius' third book is the most elaborate of all (with 3.23 reporting the loss of the poet's writing tablets, 3.24 declaring that the lover's relationship with Cynthia is over, and 3.25 looking forward to Cynthia's old age), it cannot be said to constitute a poetic signature.
[2] For discussion of this reference to *Ars Amatoria* see Introduction §2.
[3] In 2.18 he mentions the following: Penelope (21), Phyllis (22), Oenone (23), Canace (23), Hypsipyle and Medea (23), Phaedra (24), Dido (25), and Sappho (26).

that Fame might add him to the list of love poets (2.34.94: *si...Fama...uolet* ['If Fame is willing']). Horace and Ovid, by contrast, are confident of their work's immortality (*Carm*. 3.30.6–7): *non omnis moriar multaque pars mei | uitabit Libitinam* ('I will not wholly die and a great part of me will escape Death'); (*Am*. 3.15.20): *post mea mansurum fata superstes opus* ('work destined to live on after my death').

But if the last poem in *Amores* shares features with final poems in Horace and Propertius, its connections with the poems which introduce all three books of *Amores* are equally important. Thus 3.15 begins by addressing Venus as mother of the Cupid who intervened in 1.1 and actually addresses the god (and his mother) at line 15: *culte puer*. It also recalls the opening of 2.1 (*hoc quoque composui Paelignis natus aquosis*) when it reminds the reader of the poet's ethnic affiliations (3, 8, 11), and of 3.1 when it signals a shift to more serious forms of poetry (3.1.23: *thyrso...grauiore*, 3.15.17: *thyrso grauiore*). 3.15 engages not only with the signature poems of Horace and Propertius but with earlier reflections in earlier books on the nature of Ovid's poetry.

Secondary literature: Schmitzer (1994); Boyd (1997: 200–202); Oliensis (2019: 78–82, 85–7)

1–2. Quaere nouum uatem, tenerorum mater Amorum:
   raditur hic elegis ultima meta meis;
In firm if polite language, the elegist tells Venus that she needs to find a new poet. This one is finished with love elegy.

1. uatem: Alludes to Cupid's original command (1.1.24): *quodque canas, uates, accipe dixit opus*. That task is now complete. (For *uates* more generally see on 3.1.19.)

tenerorum...Amorum: The phrase makes an appropriate closural gesture through allusion to 3.1.69–70: *teneri properentur Amores, | dum uacat: a tergo grandius urget opus*, lines which both end a poem and foreshadow the conclusion of the poet's commitment to love elegy. See also 2.18.4 (a quasi-closural poem): *et tener ausuros grandia frangit Amor*, 2.18.19: *artes teneri profitemur Amoris*.

These words define not Venus but the poet himself in his proposed epitaph (*Tr*. 3.3.73) and in the opening words of his autobiography (*Tr*. 4.10.1). (For *tener* used of *amor/Amor* see above on 3.1.69.)

mater Amorum: Rewrites Horace's less than flattering references to Venus: *Carm*. 1.19.1: *mater saeua Cupidinum*, 4.1.4–5: *dulcium | mater saeua Cupidinum*. Ovid varies the phrase at *Her*. 7.59: *mater Amorum*, 16.203: *uolucrum...mater Amorum*, *Fast*. 4.1: *geminorum mater Amorum*.

Nisbet and Hubbard (1970: 239) and Thomas (2011: 89–90) note Greek antecedents for the phrase e.g. Pind. *Enc.* fr. 122.4–6 Race: ματέρ' ἐρώτων...πρὸς Ἀφροδίταν ('to Aphrodite mother of the Erotes'), *PA* (Philodemus) 10.21.2: Κύπρι Πόθων μῆτερ ἀελλοπόδων ('Cypris, mother of storm-footed Desires').

Commentary, 15.1–5 337

2. Pindar speaks of the 'chariot of the Muses/Pierians' (*Ol.* 9.81, *Pyth.* 10.65). For the poem itself as chariot see Callim. *Aet.* fr. 1.25–8 Harder; and *Ars* 1.39–40, 264, 2.426, 3.467–8, 809–10, *Rem.* 394, *Fasti* 1.25, 2.360, 4.10, 6.585–6.

raditur: This is Heinsius' emendation of *traditur* found in manuscripts. (Y clearly reads *Traditur*. P seems to offer *traditur* but a stain makes the text difficult to read). For discussion see West (1973: 142).

raditur...meta: For the tight turn see 3.2.12 (with note above): *nunc stringam metas interiore rota*. For *meta* as a poetic goal see Prop. 4.1a.69–70: *sacra deosque canam et cognomina prisca locorum:* | *has meus ad metas sudet oportet equus*.

3–4. quos ego composui, Paeligni ruris alumnus,
   (nec me deliciae dedecuere meae)
Having announced that *Amores* are about to end, the poet turns to self-definition: he identifies as a Paelignian and a love poet.

3. Reasserts the poet's connection with the Paeligni by quoting 2.1.1, changing only *hoc* to *quos*. See also 2.16.1, 5, 37. The association becomes even more important in the exile poetry: *Fast.* 3.95, 4.685, *Pont.* 1.8.42, 4.14.49: *gens mea Paeligni regioque domestica Sulmo*. For similar emphasis on a poet's regional origins see Hor. *S.* 1.5.77–8, *Carm.* 3.4.9, 3.30.10–12, Prop. 1.22; 4.1.63–4, 121–6.

Paeligni: The territory of the Paeligni (whose main towns, according to Pliny [*Nat.* 3.106.6] were Corfinium, Superaequum, and Sulmo) lies in the Abruzzi to the east of Rome (90 Roman miles according to *Tr.* 4.10.4, 160 kms according to Google maps).

composui: The Exile employs similar language when referring to *Amores* (*Tr.* 2.361): *denique composui teneros non solus amores/Amores*. For *compono* used of writing verse see *TLL* 2125.55–2126.21.

4. Alliteration and assonance are marked in this line, with alliteration of *m* (*me...meae*) framing alliteration of *d* and *c* (*deliciae dedecuere*).

deliciae: For *deliciae* as 'erotic verse' see *Tr.* 2.78, 349: *sic ego delicias et mollia carmina feci*, 5.1.15–16. But the meaning 'love affairs' is also present. For this see e.g. *Tr.* 2.367–8: *nec tibi, Battiade, nocuit, quod saepe legenti* | *delicias uersu fassus es ipse tuas*.

5–6. si quid id est, usque a proauis uetus ordinis heres,
   non modo militiae turbine factus eques.
From region and occupation as markers of identity, the speaker turns to social class: he comes from a long-standing equestrian family.

5. Recalls the lover's claim that he had inherited membership of the equestrian order (1.3.8): *nostri sanguinis auctor eques*. See also *Tr.* 2.89–90, 541–2, *Fast.* 2.127–8.

6. Emphasis on inherited as opposed to parvenu status distinguishes the speaker from 3.8's ex-soldier (9–10): *ecce, recens diues parto per uulnera censu | praefertur nobis sanguine pastus eques*. The exiled Ovid repeats these lines with slight variation at *Tr*. 4.10.7–8: *si quid id est, usque a proauis uetus ordinis heres, | non modo fortunae munere factus eques*, deleting only the reference to the now distant civil war (*militiae turbine*). Schmitzer (1994: 108) argues for anti-Horatian polemic behind this claim, Horace having gained equestrian status through military service (Armstrong [1986]).

7–8. Mantua Vergilio gaudet Verona Catullo;
   Paelignae dicar gloria gentis ego,
From socio-legal status, the speaker turns to two of his greatest predecessors, both of whom had identified closely with cities in northern Italy. For similar juxtaposition of Catullus and Virgil see Mart. 1.61.1–2, 14.195.

7. This line is artfully phrased with *gaudet* placed centrally, with alliteration and assonance linking the nouns which frame the verb (*Vergilio… Verona*), and with a city's name preceding each poet's name.

Mantua Vergilio: For Virgil's association with Mantua see *Ecl*. 9.27–8, *G*. 2.198, 3.12, *A*. 10.200 (with Malamud [1998]).

Verona Catullo: For Catullus and Verona see Catul. 35.3, 67.34, 68a.27.

8. This is the last line for which we have the evidence of P.

dicar: Schmitzer (1994: 109) notes an allusion to Horace's claim to Apulian origins (*Carm*. 3.30.10): *dicar qua uiolens obstrepit Aufidus*.

gloria gentis: The phrase has an epic ring e.g. *A*. 6.767: *Procas, Troianae gloria gentis*, *Met*. 12.530: *Lapithaeae gloria gentis*. Cf. Hom. *Il*. 9.673 (and five more times): μέγα κῦδος Ἀχαιῶν ('great glory of the Achaeans').

9–10. quam sua libertas ad honesta coegerat arma,
   cum timuit socias anxia Roma manus.
And what can be said of the Paelignian people? They fought against the Romans in the Social War of 91–89 BCE. They were among the leaders of the rebellion, with the allied capital being Corfinium, the principal city in Paelignian territory (Vell. 2.16.4.6). Closest to this passage are Virgil's references to the sufferings of Mantua (*Ecl*. 9.27–8, *G*. 2.198) and the closing poems of Propertius' *Monobiblos*, 1.21 being spoken by a dead victim and 1.22 emphasizing the destruction caused by civil war.

9. sua libertas: In Ovid *libertas* commonly denotes sexual freedom (*Her*. 17.154, *Ars* 2.590, 3.604, *Rem*. 385, 662), or personal freedom of speech (*Her*. 15.68, *Met*. 1.757, 9.559), or an individual's legal status (2.2.15, 40, 2.7.21, *Ars* 2.289). Here it has its full political force (*OLD* 2): 'the political status of a sovereign people'. For the physical embodiment of this ideal see *Fast.* 4.623–4: *hac quoque, ni fallor, populo dignissima nostro | atria Libertas coepit habere sua*.

ad honesta...arma: Unlike Virgil and Propertius, Ovid's speaker talks not of suffering but the justice of his people's cause. For *honestus* used of a just reason for war see Liv. 37.54.15.1: *alia enim aliis et honesta et probabilis est causa armorum*.

10. For this verbal pattern (VabBA) see on 3.1.11.

timuit...anxia Roma: For this war between Rome and the Italian allies, a two-year war which involved several Roman defeats and the deaths of two consuls see Vell. 2.16.4.

socias...manus: The phrase underlines the horror of civil war. For similar usage see VF 3.30–1 (with Manuwald [2015: ad loc.]): *ut socias in nocte manus utque impia bella | conserat et saeuis erroribus implicet urbem*.

manus: May mean either 'hand' (*OLD* 8: 'the hand as the instrument of violence') or 'troops' (*OLD* 22: 'an armed force').

11–12. atque aliquis spectans hospes Sulmonis aquosi
   moenia, quae campi iugera pauca tenent,
The poet now imagines what a stranger might think of his hometown, Sulmo. (On Sulmo as a literary landscape in 2.16 see Boyd [1997: 53–61].)

11. Sulmonis aquosi: For Sulmo as a well-watered place see 2.1.1: *Paelignis natus aquosis*, 2.16.2, 5, *Tr.* 4.10.3. See also Plin. *Nat.* 17.250.

12. iugera pauca: For Sulmo's territory as small see 2.16.2: *parua*, *Fast.* 4.685–6: *hac ego Paelignos, natalia rura, petebam, | parua*.

13–14. 'quae tantum' dicet 'potuistis ferre poetam,
   quantulacumque estis, uos ego magna uoco'.
The couplet is remarkable for its use of similar-sounding words with opposed meanings at the beginning of the hexameter and pentameter. Quasi-anaphora underlines the contrast between the poet's greatness and the town's smallness.

For the idea that talent confers greatness on a poet's homeland see Prop. 4.1a.65–6: *scandentis quisquis cernit de uallibus arces, | ingenio muros aestimet ille meo*, 4.1b.125–6: *scandentisque Asis consurgit uertice murus, | murus ab ingenio notior ille tuo*.

13. quae: This is Marius' correction of *quem* found in most manuscripts (including Y).

dicet: This, the reading of Y, is printed by most editors. Showerman and Goold, however, follow Riese (1871), Edwards (1898), Ehwald (1903), and Brandt in preferring F's *dicat*. The future makes for a strong assertion. The advantage of the subjunctive is not clear.

14. quantulacumque: The word occurs here for the first time in verse. The effect may be humorous: for a word denoting smallness it seems very big. See also *Ars* 3.264 (with Gibson's [2003: ad loc.] comment: 'The imposing five-syllable length of the adjective contrasts comically with the addressee's lack of stature'): *inque tuo iaceas quantulacumque toro, Fast.* 3.572, 4.516, *Pont.* 4.15.14. After Ovid it is used only by Martial and (possibly) Juvenal.

15–16. culte puer puerique parens Amathusia culti,
   aurea de campo uellite signa meo.
Having told Venus directly in line 1 that she would need to find a new poet, our speaker now employs elaborate language and metaphor to resign his post.
15. This is a remarkable line, with repetition of forms of *cultus* used to frame the line, with repetition of forms of *puer* (combined with *parens*) used to create alliteration of *p* and *r* in the centre, and with a weak main caesura combined with a high-flown Greek adjective giving the line a distinctly Hellenic feel.

For the weak caesura see on 3.9.15, 35, and 39. Platnauer (1951: 9–10) notes that Ovid uses a weak main caesura in 7.5 per cent of hexameters in *Amores*. The corresponding figure for Callimachus' *Bath of Pallas* is 57 per cent.

puer puerique: Wills (1996: 255–6) compares *Met.* 15.861–5 and argues that Ovid uses this form of repetition ('genitival subordination') in *sphragis*-poems.

Amathusia: Derived from the town of Amathus on Crete, a place particularly associated with Aphrodite/Venus (e.g. Paus. 9.41.2.5, Catul. 36.14, *A.* 10.51: *est Amathus, est celsa mihi Paphus atque Cythera*), the adjective is an appropriate epithet of Venus. While the adjective Ἀμαθούσιος (Amathousios) occurs, it is not used in Greek literature as a title of Aphrodite. Its first occurrence is in Catul. 68b.51.

16. For this verbal pattern (aBVAb) see on 3.6.6.

aurea…signa: Venus' standards are golden because she herself is golden (e.g. Hom. *Il.* 3.64 (and five more times), *A.* 10.16, *Her.* 16.35, *Met.* 10.277). For Venus' standards see *Fast.* 4.7 (poet addresses the goddess): *saucius an sanus numquid tua signa reliqui?*

uellite signa: Use of standard military terminology (e.g. Liv. 3.50.11.3, *A.* 11.19) invokes the idea that the lover is a kind of soldier (see on 3.7.68).

17–18. corniger increpuit thyrso grauiore Lyaeus:
   pulsanda est magnis area maior equis.
Having said farewell to Venus and Cupid, the poet now promises to honour the commitment made in 3.1 that he would abandon elegy for tragedy.

17. corniger…Lyaeus: For Bacchus, god of tragedy, as horned see e.g. Soph. 959.2–3 Lloyd-Jones (1996): ὁ βούκερως | Ἴακχος ('ox-horned Iacchus'), Eur.

Bacch. 100 (with Dodds [1960: ad loc.]), Hor. *Carm.* 2.19.29–30 (with Nisbet and Hubbard [1978: ad loc.]), Sen. *Phaed.* 756, VF 1.726, 2.271, 5.79, *LIMC* III.1.154–9: 3. Dionysos tauromorphos.

increpuit: Alludes as a closural gesture to the last poem of Horace's final book of *Odes* (*Carm.* 4.15.1–2): *Phoebus uolentem proelia me loqui | uictas et urbis increpuit lyra*. Ovid alludes to both *Carm.* 4.1 and this line in *Fasti*'s closing couplet (6.811–12): *sic cecinit Clio, doctae adsensere sorores; | adnuit Alcides increpuitque lyram*. See also 2.11.32, *Her.* 3.118.

thyrso grauiore: Alludes to Tragedy's impatient criticism (3.1.23): *tempus erat thyrso pulsum grauiore moueri*.

18. area: Recalls Tragedy's view of the poet's likely response to her criticisms (3.1.26): '*haec animo' dices 'area facta meo est*'. Now, however, the poet is ready for 'a larger area'. The Teacher employs similar language when contrasting *Fasti* with the youthful *Amores* (*Fast.* 4.9–10): *quae decuit primis sine crimine lusimus annis; | nunc teritur nostris area maior equis*.

19–20. imbelles elegi, genialis Musa, ualete,
    post mea mansurum fata superstes opus.
Finally the poet bids farewell to elegiac verse and predicts that his work will endure.

19. imbelles elegi: For the conventional opposition between love elegy and war see e.g. Tib. 1.1, Prop. 3.5, and *Am.* 1.15 (esp. 3–4). Ovid, however, presents the elegiac metre as 'light' (2.1.21: *elegosque leues*, *Pont.* 4.5.1: *leues elegi*), i.e. as intrinsically 'unwarlike' (e.g. 1.1). In later works he expresses anxiety about elegy's ability to handle grander themes (*Fast.* 2.3–4, 125–6, *Pont.* 3.4.85).

genialis Musa: For *genialis* as 'cheerful' see *Ars* 3.327 (of a musical instrument), *Met.* 4.14: *genialis consitor uuae* (cf. Tib. 2.3.63: *iucundae consitor uuae*), 13.929: *genialia serta*, *Fast.* 3.523: *Annae festum geniale Perennae*. The poet is about to exchange love elegy's cheerful Muse for Tragedy.

20. Another closural gesture, this line recalls not only Hor. *Carm* 3.30 (esp. 6–7) but also the last line of Book 1's final poem (42): *uiuam, parsque mei multa superstes erit*. For an even grander invocation of Horace's closing claim to immortality see *Met.* 15.871–9.

Bibliography

1. Latin Texts: Editions, Commentaries, Translations

Andreas, J. (1471), *Publii Ovidii Nasonis Opera*. Rome.
Bailey, C. (1947), *Titi Lucreti Cari De Rerum Natura Libri Sex*. Edited with Prolegomena, Critical Apparatus, Translation, and Commentary, 3 vols. Oxford.
Barber, E. A. (1960), *Sexti Properti Carmina* 2 edn. Oxford.
Barchiesi, A. (1992), *P. Ouidii Nasonis Epistulae Heroidum 1–3*. Florence.
Barchiesi, A. (2005), *Ovidio, Metamorfosi*, Vol. 1 (Libri I–II). Milan.
Barchiesi, A. and Rosati, G. (2007), *Ovidio, Metamorfosi*, Vol. 2 (Libri III–IV). Milan.
Bertini, F. (2017), *Publio Ovidio Nasone: Amori* 6 edn. Milan.
Bömer, F. (1958), *P. Ouidius Naso: Die Fasten. Band II: Kommentar*. Heidelberg.
Bömer, F. (1969), *P. Ouidius Naso, Metamorphosen: Kommentar Buch I–III*. Heidelberg.
Bömer, F. (1976), *P. Ouidius Naso, Metamorphosen: Kommentar Buch IV–V*. Heidelberg.
Bömer, F. (1977), *P. Ouidius Naso, Metamorphosen: Kommentar Buch VIII–IX*. Heidelberg.
Booth, J. (1991), *Ovid Amores II*. Warminster.
Bornecque, H. (1930), *Ovide: Les Amours*. Paris.
Boyle, A. J. (2014), *Seneca: Medea*. Oxford.
Boyle, A. J. (2017), *Seneca: Thyestes*. Oxford.
Brandt, P. (1911), *P. Ouidi Nasonis Amorum Libri Tres*. Leipzig.
Burman, P. (1727), *Publii Ouidii Nasonis Opera Omnia IV. Voluminibus Comprehensa; cum integris Jacobi Micylli, Herculis Ciofani, et Danielis Heinsii notis, et Nicolai Heinsii curis secundis… cura et studio Petri Burmanni*, 4 vols. Amsterdam.
Calfurnio, G. (1474), *Publii Ouidii Nasonis Opera*. Venice.
Camps, W. A. (1967), *Propertius: Elegies* Book 2. Cambridge.
Casali, S. (1995), *P. Ouidii Nasonis: Heroidum Epistula IX. Deianira Herculi*. Florence.
Celsanus, B. (1484), *Publii Ovidii Nasonis Opera*. Venice.
Clausen, W. V. (1994), *A Commentary on Virgil, Eclogues*. Oxford.
Cooley, A. E. (2009), *Res Gestae Diui Augusti: Text, Translation, and Commentary*. Cambridge.
Dangel, J. (1995), *Accius. Oeuvres: Fragments*. Paris.
Davis, P. J. (2020), *Valerius Flaccus: Argonautica Book 7*. Edited with Introduction, Translation, and Commentary. Oxford.
Duemmler, E. (1881), *Poetae Latini Aevi Carolini*. Berlin.
Edwards, G. M. (1898), 'Amorum Libri III', in Postgate, J. P. (Ed.), *P. Ovidi Nasonis Opera ex Corpore Poetarum Latinorum a Iohanne Percival Postgate Edito, 1*. London, 93–152.
Edwards, M. W. (1991), *The Iliad: A Commentary. Volume V: Books 17–20*. Cambridge.
Ehwald, R. (1903), *P. Ouidius Naso ex Rudolphi Merkelii Recognitione edidit R. Ehwald. Tom. I*. Leipzig.
Fantham, E. (1998), *Ovid: Fasti Book 4*. Cambridge.
Fedeli, P. (1980), *Sesto Properzio. Il primo libro delle Elegie: Introduzione, testo critico e commento a cura di Paolo Fedeli*. Florence.
Fedeli, P. (1994), *Sexti Properti Elegiarum Libri IV*. Stuttgart.

Fedeli, P. (2005), *Properzio: Elegie Libro II. Introduzione, Testo e Commento.* Cambridge.
Fordyce, C. J. (1961), *Catullus: A Commentary.* Oxford.
Fulkerson, L. (2017), *A Literary Commentary on the Elegies of the Appendix Tibulliana.* Oxford.
Gibson, B. J. (2006), *Statius, Siluae 5* Edited with an Introduction, Translation, and Commentary by Bruce Gibson. Oxford.
Gibson, R. K. (2003), *Ovid: Ars Amatoria Book 3.* Cambridge.
Goldberg, S. M. and Manuwald, G. (2018a), *Fragmentary Republican Latin. Ennius. Testimonia. Epic Fragments.* Cambridge, Mass.
Goldberg, S. M. and Manuwald, G. (2018b), *Fragmentary Republican Latin. Ennius. Dramatic Fragments, Minor Works.* Cambridge Mass.
Goold, G. P. (1990), *Propertius: Elegies.* Cambridge, Mass.
Gowers, E. (2012), *Horace: Satires Book I.* Cambridge.
Green, P. (1982), *Ovid: The Erotic Poems.* Harmondsworth.
Green, S. J. (2004), *Ovid, Fasti I: A Commentary.* Leiden.
Harder, R. and Marg, W. (1956), *Publius Ouidius Naso: Liebesgedichte.* Munich.
Hardie, P. R. (1994), *Virgil: Aeneid Book IX.* Cambridge.
Harrison, S. (2017), *Horace: Odes Book II.* Cambridge.
Heinsius, D. (1629), *Pub. Ouidii Nasonis Opera Daniel Heinsius Textum Recensuit.* Leyden.
Heinsius, N. (1658), *Publii Ouidii Nasonis Operum Tomus I. Scripta Amatoria Complexus.* Amsterdam.
Helmreich, G. (1889), *Marcelli de Medicamentis Liber.* Leipzig.
Helzle, M. (2003), *Ovids Epistulae ex Ponto: Buch I-II Kommentar.* Heidelberg.
Hexter, R., Pfuntner, L., and Haynes, J. (2020), *Appendix Ovidiana: Latin Poems Ascribed to Ovid in the Middle Ages.* Cambridge, Mass.
Heyworth, S. J. (2007a), *Cynthia: A Companion to the Text of Propertius.* Oxford.
Heyworth, S. J. (2007b), *Sexti Properti Elegos.* Oxford.
Heyworth, S. J. (2019), *Ovid Fasti Book III.* Cambridge.
Heyworth, S. J. and Morwood, J. H. W. (2011), *A Commentary on Propertius Book 3.* Oxford.
Hill, D. E. (1985), *Ovid: Metamorphoses I-IV.* Warminster.
Hollis, A. S. (1977), *Ovid: Ars Amatoria Book I.* Oxford.
Hollis, A. S. (2007), *Fragments of Roman Poetry c. 60 BC-AD 20.* Oxford.
Holzberg, N. (2014), *Publius Ouidius Naso: Liebesgedichte. Amores* 2 edn. Berlin.
Horsfall, N. (2000), *Virgil, Aeneid 7: A Commentary.* Leiden.
Horsfall, N. (2013), *Virgil, Aeneid 6: A Commentary.* Berlin.
Hutchinson, G. (2006), *Propertius: Elegies Book IV.* Cambridge.
Ingleheart, J. (2010), *A Commentary on Ovid, Tristia, Book 2.* Oxford.
Ingleheart, J. and Radice, K. (2012), *Ovid Amores III. A Selection: 2, 4, 5, 14.* London.
Janka, M. (1997), *Ovid, Ars Amatoria: Buch 2: Kommentar.* Heidelberg.
Johnson, M. (2016), *Ovid on Cosmetics: Medicamina Faciei Femineae and Related Texts.* London.
Kenney, E. J. (1961), *P. Ouidi Nasonis: Amores; Medicamina Faciei Femineae; Ars Amatoria; Remedia Amoris.* 1 edn. Oxford.
Kenney, E. J. (1994), *P. Ouidi Nasonis: Amores; Medicamina Faciei Femineae; Ars Amatoria; Remedia Amoris.* 2 edn. Oxford.
Kenney, E. J. (1996), *Ovid Heroides XVI-XXI.* Cambridge.
Kenney, E. J. (2011), *Ovidio, Metamorfosi, Vol. 4 (Libri VII-IX).* Milan.
Knox, P. E. (1995), *Ovid, Heroides: Select Epistles.* Cambridge.
Lee, G. (1968), *Ovid's Amores.* London.
Lee, G. (1994), *Propertius: The Poems.* Oxford.

Lenz, F. W. (1966), *Ovid: Die Liebeselegien*. Berlin.
Littlewood, R. J. (2006), *A Commentary on Ovid: Fasti Book 6*. Oxford.
Luck, G. (1977), *P. Ouidius Naso Tristia. Band II. Kommentar*. Heidelberg.
Maltby, R. (2002), *Tibullus: Elegies. Text, Introduction and Commentary*. Cambridge.
Manuwald, G. (2015), *Valerius Flaccus: Argonautica 3*. Cambridge.
Marius Niger (1518), *P. Ouidii Nasonis Amorum Libri Tres, de Medicamine Faciei Libellus: et Nux*. Venice.
Marlowe, C. (1603), *Ouid's Elegies: 3 Bookes*. Middlebourgh.
Marx, F. (1904), *C. Lucilii Carminum Reliquiae*. Leipzig.
Mayer, R. (1994), *Horace Epistles Book I*. Cambridge.
Mayer, R. (2012), *Horace Odes Book I*. Cambridge.
McGill, S. (2020), *Virgil: Aeneid Book XI*. Cambridge.
McKeown, J. C. (1987), *Ovid: Amores. Text, Prolegomena, and Commentary. I. Text and Prolegomena*. Liverpool.
McKeown, J. C. (1989), *Ovid: Amores. Text, Prolegomena, and Commentary. II. A Commentary on Book One*. Leeds.
McKeown, J. C. (1998), *Ovid: Amores. Text, Prolegomena, and Commentary. III. A Commentary on Book Two*. Leeds.
Melville, A. D. (1989), *Ovid: The Love Poems*.
Merkel, R. (1862), *P. Ovidius Naso. Tom. I. Amores, Epistulae. De Medic. Fac. Ars Amat. Remedia Amoris*. Leipzig.
Micyllus, I. (1549), *P. Ouidii Nasonis Poetae Sulmonensis Opera Quae Vocantur Amatoria*. Basel.
Müller, L. (1861), *P. Ouidii Nasonis Carmina Amatoria*. Berlin.
Munari, F. (1970), *P. Ouidii Nasonis Amores: Testo, Introduzione, Traduzione e Note di Franco Munari* 5 edn. Florence.
Murgatroyd, P. (1991), *Tibullus I: A Commentary on the First Book of the Elegies of Albius Tibullus*. Bedminster.
Mynors, R. A. B. (1958), *C. Valerii Catulli Carmina*. Oxford.
Mynors, R. A. B. (1990), *Virgil: Georgics*. Edited with a Commentary by R. A. B. Mynors. Oxford.
Naugerius, A. (1515), *P. Ouidii Nasonis...Heroidum Epistolae, Amorum Libri III, De Arte Amandi Libri III, De Remedio Amoris Libri II, De Medicamine Faciei*. Venice.
Némethy, G. (1907), *P. Ouidii Nasonis Amores*. Budapest.
Nisbet, R. G. M. and Hubbard, M. A. (1970), *Commentary on Horace: Odes Book I*. Oxford.
Nisbet, R. G. M. and Hubbard, M. A. (1978), *Commentary on Horace: Odes Book II*. Oxford.
Nisbet, R. G. M. and Rudd, N. (2004), *Commentary on Horace: Odes Book III*. Oxford.
Parkes, R. (2012), *Statius, Thebaid 4*. Edited with an Introduction, Translation, and Commentary. Oxford.
Pease, A. S. (1935), *Publi Vergili Maronis Aeneidos Liber Quartus*. Cambridge, Mass.
Pestelli, A. (2007), *P. Ovidii Nasonis Heroidum Epistula VIII: Hermione Oresti*. Florence.
Putnam, M. C. J. (1973), *Tibullus: A Commentary*. Norman, Oklahoma.
Ramirez de Verger, A. (2006), *Publius Ouidius Naso. Carmina Amatoria*. 2 edn. Munich.
Ramirez de Verger, A. and Socas, F. (1991), *Ovidio. Obra Amatoria I: Amores*. Madrid.
Reed, J. D. (2013), *Ovidio, Metamorfosi, Vol. 5 (Libri X–XII)*. Milan.
Ribbeck, O. (1897), *Scaenicae Romanorum Poesis Fragmenta Tertiis Curis Recognouit Otto Ribbeck. Volumen I. Tragicorum Fragmenta*. Leipzig.
Riese, A. (1871), *P. Ouidii Nasonis Carmina. Vol. I: Heroides. Amores. Med. Formae. Ars Amatoria. Remedia Amoris. Poetae Ouidiani*. Leipzig.
Robinson, M. (2011), *A Commentary on Ovid's Fasti, Book 2*. Oxford.

Rosati, G. (1989), *Publio Ovidio Nasone, Lettere di eroine; Introduzione, traduzione e note di Gianpiero Rosati*. Milan.
Schnegg, B. (2020), *Die Inschriften zu den Ludi Saeculares*. Acta Ludorum Saecularium. Berlin.
Showerman, G. (1914), *Ovid: Heroides and Amores*. 1 edn. London.
Showerman, G. and Goold, G. P. (1977), *Ovid: Heroides and Amores*. 2 edn. Cambridge, Mass.
Skutsch, O. (1985), *The Annals of Quintus Ennius*. Oxford.
Tarrant, R. J. (2012), *Virgil: Aeneid Book XII*. Cambridge.
Thomas, R. F. (2011), *Horace: Odes Book IV and Carmen Saeculare*. Cambridge.
Tissol, G. (2014), *Ovid Epistulae ex Ponto I*. Cambridge.
Wardle, D. (2014), *Suetonius: Life of Augustus*. Oxford.
Warmington, E. H. (1936), *Remains of Old Latin 2: Livius Andronicus, Naevius, Pacuvius and Accius*. Cambridge, Mass.
Watson, L. C. (2003), *A Commentary on Horace's Epodes*. Oxford.
Weise, C. H. (1845), *P. Ouidii Nasonis Opera Omnia. Tomus I: Heroides, Amores, Ars Amatoria. Remedia Amoris*. Leipzig.
Zangemeister, C. (1871), *Corpus Inscriptionum Latinarum Consilio et Auctoritate Academiae Litterarum Regiae Borussicae Editum. Volumen Quartum. Inscriptiones Parietariae Pompeianae Herculanenses Stabianae*. Berlin.

2. Other Works

Acosta-Hughes, B. (2002), *Polyeideia: The Iambi of Callimachus and the Archaic Iambic Tradition*. Berkeley.
Adams, J. N. (1982), *The Latin Sexual Vocabulary*. London.
Anderson, R. D., Parsons, P. J., and Nisbet, R. G. M. (1979), 'Elegiacs by Gallus from Qasr Ibrîm', *Journal of Roman Studies* 69: 125–55.
Anderson, W. S. (1968), 'Brooks Otis, Ovid as an Epic Poet', *American Journal of Philology* 89: 93–104.
Armstrong, D. (1986), 'Horatius Eques et Scriba: Satires 1.6 and 2.7', *TAPA* 116: 255–88.
Armstrong, R. (2019), *Vergil's Green Thoughts. Plants, Humans, and the Divine*. Oxford.
Asquith, H. (2005), 'From Genealogy to Catalogue: The Hellenistic Adaptation of Hesiodic Catalogue Form', in Hunter, R. (ed.), *The Hesiodic Catalogue of Women. Constructions and Reconstructions*. Cambridge, 266–86.
Baeza Angulo, E. F. (1989), 'Ovidio, *Amores* III.7', *Faventia* 11: 25–58.
Barchiesi, A. (1989), 'Voci e istanze narrative nelle *Metamorfosi* di Ovidio', *Materiali e Discussioni per l'analisi dei testi classici* 23: 55–97.
Barchiesi, A. (1995), 'Review of *Die Briefpaare in Ovids Heroides: Tradition und Innovation* by Cornelia Hintermeier', *Journal of Roman Studies* 85: 325–7.
Barchiesi, A. (1997), *The Poet and the Prince: Ovid and Augustan Discourse*. Berkeley and Los Angeles.
Barchiesi, A. (1999), 'Vers une histoire à rebours de l'élégie latine: les *Héroïdes* "doubles" (16–21)', in Fabre-Serris, J. and Deremetz, A. (eds.), *Élégie et épopée dans la poésie ovidienne (Héroïdes et Amours): En hommage à Simone Viarre*. Paris, 53–67.
Barchiesi, A. (2001a), 'Voices and Narrative "Instances" in the *Metamorphoses*', in Fox, M. and Marchesi, S. (eds.), *Speaking Volumes: Narrative and Intertext in Ovid and Other Latin Poets*. London, 49–78.

Barchiesi, A. (2001b), 'Allusion and Society: Ovid the Censor', in Fox, M. and Marchesi, S. (eds.), *Speaking Volumes: Narrative and Intertext in Ovid and Other Latin Poets*. London, 155-61.
Barchiesi, A. (2002), 'Martial Arts. Mars Ultor in the Forum Augustum: A Verbal Monument', in Herbert-Brown, G. (ed.), *Ovid's Fasti: Historical Readings at Its Bimillennium*. Oxford, 1-22.
Barchiesi, A. (2011), 'Roman Callimachus', in Acosta-Hughes, B., Lehnus, L., and Stephens, S. (eds.), *Brill's Companion to Callimachus*. Leiden, 511-33.
Barchiesi, A. and Hardie, P. (2010), 'The Ovidian Career Model: Ovid, Gallus, Apuleius, Boccaccio', in Hardie, P. and Moore, H. (eds.), *Classical Literary Careers and their Reception*. Cambridge, 59-88.
Barsby, J. (1996), 'Ovid's *Amores* and Roman Comedy', *Papers of the Leeds International Latin Seminar* 9: 135-57.
Beard, M., North, J., and Price, S. (1998a), *Religions of Rome. Volume 1. A History*. Cambridge.
Beard, M., North, J., and Price, S. (1998b), *Religions of Rome. Volume 2. A Sourcebook*. Cambridge.
Berger, A. (1953), *Encyclopedic Dictionary of Roman Law*. Philadelphia.
Bertini, F. (1976), 'La Ringkomposition negli *Amores* ovidiani e l'autenticità dell'elegia III.5', *Rivista di Cultura Classica e Medioevale* 17: 151-60.
Bowie, E. L. (1993), 'Lies, Fiction and Slander in Early Greek Poetry', in Gill, C. and Wiseman, T. P. (eds.), *Lies and Fiction in the Ancient World*. Liverpool, 1-37.
Boyd, B. W. (1997), *Ovid's Literary Loves: Influence and Innovation in the Amores*. Ann Arbor.
Boyd, B. W. (2002), 'The *Amores*: The Invention of Ovid', in Boyd, B. W. (ed.), *Brill's Companion to Ovid*. Leiden, 91-116.
Boyle, A. J. (1997a), 'Postscripts from the Edge: Exilic *Fasti* and Imperialised Rome', *Ramus* 26: 7-28.
Boyle, A. J. (1997b), *Tragic Seneca: An Essay in the Theatrical Tradition*. London.
Boyle, A. J. (2003), *Ovid and the Monuments: A Poet's Rome*. Bendigo.
Boyle, A. J. (2006), *An Introduction to Roman Tragedy*. London.
Brecke, I. (2021), 'Rape and Violence in Terence's *Eunuchus* and Ovid's Love Elegies', in Thorsen, T. S., Brecke, I., and Harrison, S. (eds.), *Greek and Latin Love: The Poetic Connection*. Berlin, 83-104.
Bretzigheimer, G. (2001), *Ovids Amores: Poetik in der Erotik*. Tübingen.
Buchan, M. (1995), 'Ovidius Imperamator: Beginnings and Endings of Love Poems and Empire in the *Amores*', *Arethusa* 28: 53-83.
Cahoon, L. (1983), 'Juno's Chaste Festival and Ovid's Wanton Loves: *Amores* 3.13', *Classical Antiquity* 2: 1-8.
Cahoon, L. (1984), 'The Parrot and the Poet. The Function of Ovid's Funeral Elegies', *Classical Journal* 80: 27-35.
Cahoon, L. (1985), 'A Program for Betrayal. Ovidian *nequitia* in *Amores* 1.1, 2.1, and 3.1', *Helios* 12: 29-39.
Cahoon, L. (1988), 'The Bed as Battlefield: Erotic Conquest and Military Metaphor in Ovid's *Amores*', *TAPA* 118: 293-307.
Cairns, F. (1972), *Generic Composition in Greek and Roman Poetry*. Edinburgh.
Cairns, F. (1979), 'Self-Imitation within a Generic Framework. Ovid, *Amores* 2.9 and 3.11 and the *Renuntiatio Amoris*', in Woodman, T. and West, D. (eds.), *Creative Imitation and Latin Literature*. Cambridge, 121-41.

Cairns, F. (2012), 'The Genre "Oaristys", in *Roman Lyric. Collected Papers on Catullus and Horace*. Berlin, 47-76.
Cameron, A. (1968), 'The First Edition of Ovid's *Amores*', *Classical Quarterly* 18: 320-33.
Cameron, A. (1995), *Callimachus and His Critics*. Princeton.
Campbell, D. A. (1990), *Greek Lyric I: Sappho and Alcaeus*. Cambridge, Mass.
Campbell, D. A. (1991), *Greek Lyric III: Stesichorus, Ibycus, Simonides, and Others*. Cambridge, Mass.
Ceccarelli, L. (2018), *Contributions to the History of the Latin Elegiac Distich*. Turnhout.
Chandezon, C. (2015), 'Animals, Meat, and Alimentary By-Products: Patterns of Production and Consumption', in Wilkins, J. and Nadeau, R. (eds.), *A Companion to Food in the Ancient World*. Chichester, 135-46.
Claridge, A. (1998), *Rome: An Oxford Archaeological Guide*. Oxford.Coarelli, F. (2007), *Rome and Environs: An Archaeological Guide*. trans. Clauss, J. J. and Mackay, P. A. Berkeley.
Collard, C. and Cropp, M. (2008), *Euripides Fragments. Oedipus – Chrysippus. Other Fragments*. Cambridge, Mass.
Connor, P. (1974), 'His Dupes and Accomplices: A Study of Ovid the Illusionist in the *Amores*', *Ramus* 3: 18-40.
Connors, C. (1994), 'Ennius, Ovid and Representations of Ilia', *Materiali e discussioni per l'analisi dei testi classici* 32: 99-112.
Conrad, C. (1965), 'Traditional Patterns of Word-Order in Latin Epic from Ennius to Vergil', *Harvard Studies in Classical Philology* 69: 195-258.
Conte, G. B. (2007), *The Poetry of Pathos: Studies in Virgilian Epic*. Oxford.
Coray, M. (2018), *Homer's Iliad: The Basel Commentary. Book XVIII*. Trans. Millis, B. W., Strack, S., and Olson, S. D. Berlin.
Cornacchia, G. A. (1989), 'Ovidio, *Am*. 3,9,58: Nota di lettura', in *Mnemosynum: Studi in Onore di Alfredo Ghiselli*. Bologna.
Courtney, E. (1987), 'Quotation, Interpolation, Transposition', *Hermathena* 143: 7-18.
Courtney, E. (1988), 'Some Literary Jokes in Ovid's *Amores*', in Horsfall, N. (ed.), *Vir bonus discendi peritus: Studies in Celebration of Otto Skutsch's Eightieth Birthday*, Bulletin supplement (University of London. Institute of Classical Studies) 51. London, 10-23.
Cowan, R. (2017), 'Ovid, Virgil and the Echoing Rocks of the Two Scyllas', *Cambridge Classical Journal* 63: 1-18.
D'anna, G. (1999), '*Recusatio* e poesia di corteggiamento negli *Amores* di Ovidio', in Schubert, W. (ed.), *Ovid. Werk und Wirkung. Festgabe für Michael Von Albrecht zum 65. Geburtstag*, Studien Zur Klassischen Philologie, 1. Frankfurt, 67-78.
Damon, C. (1990), 'Poem Divisions, Paired Poems and *Amores* 2.9 and 3.11', *TAPA* 120: 269-90.
Davenport, C. (2019), *A History of the Roman Equestrian Order*. Cambridge.
Davies, M. (2013), '*Stat Vetus...Silva*: Burlesque and Parody in Ovid *Amores* 3.1 and Persius Satire 5.132-53', *Prometheus: Rivista quadrimestrale di studi classici* 2: 165-76.
Davis, J. T. (1977), *Dramatic Pairings in the Elegies of Propertius and Ovid*. Bern.
Davis, J. T. (1979), 'Dramatic and Comic Devices in *Amores* 3.2', *Hermes* 107: 51-69.
Davis, J. T. (1980), 'Exempla and Anti-Exempla in the *Amores* of Ovid', *Latomus* 39: 412-17.
Davis, J. T. (1981), '*Risit Amor*: Aspects of Literary Burlesque in Ovid's *Amores*', in Haase, W. (ed.), *Aufstieg und Niedergang der römischen Welt*, II.31.4. Berlin, 2460-506.
Davis, J. T. (1993), 'Thou Shalt Not Cuddle: *Amores* 1.4 and the Law', *Syllecta Classica* 4: 65-9.
Davis, P. J. (1983), '*Vindicat omnes natura sibi*: A Reading of Seneca's *Phaedra*', *Ramus* 12: 114-27.
Davis, P. J. (1995), 'Rewriting Euripides: Ovid, *Heroides* 4', *Scholia* 4: 41-55.

Davis, P. J. (2003), *Seneca: Thyestes*. London.
Davis, P. J. (2006), *Ovid and Augustus: A Political Reading of Ovid's Erotic Poetry*. London.
Davis, P. J. (2010), 'Jason at Colchis: Technology and Human Progress in Valerius Flaccus', *Ramus* 39: 1–13.
Davis, P. J. (2012), '"A Simple Girl"? Medea in Ovid *Heroides* 12', *Ramus* 41: 33–48.
Davis, P. J. (2016), 'Freedom of Speech in Virgil and Ovid', in Mitsis, P. and Ziogas, I. (eds.), *Wordplay and Powerplay in Latin Poetry*. Berlin, 183–98.
De Boer, K. R. (2010), 'Verbera, Catenae, Concubitus: Slaves, Violence and Vulnerability in Ovid's *Amores*', (University of North Carolina at Chapel Hill).
De Boer, K. R. (2021), 'Violence and Vulnerability in Ovid's *Amores* 1.5–8', *American Journal of Philology* 142: 259–86.
De Vasconcellos, P. S. (2017), 'Images of Dead Poets in Roman Elegiac and Lyric Underworld', *Revista Classica* 30: 47–74.
Della Corte, F. (1972), 'L'elegia del sogno (Ovid. *Am*. III 5)', *Studi classici in onore di Quintino Cataudella*, 3. Catania, 319–30.
Delvigo, M. L. (2019), 'Virgilio, Ovidio e l'esegesi Virgiliana Antica', in Bessone, F. and Stroppa, S. (eds.), *Lettori Latini e Italiani di Ovidio: Atti del convegno, Università di Torino, 9–10 Novembre 2017*. Pisa, 51–8.
Delz, J. (1983), 'Die Hörner des Achelous (Ov. *Epist*. 9.139 und *Met*. 9.98)', *Museum Helveticum*: 123–4.
Deremetz, A. (1999), 'Visages des genres dans l'élégie Ovidienne: *Amores* 1,1 et 3,1', in Fabre-Serris, J. and Deremetz, A. (eds.), *Élégie et épopée dans la poésie Ovidienne (Héroïdes et Amours): En hommage à Simone Viarre*. Paris, 71–84.
DiLuzio, M. J. (2016), *A Place at the Altar: Priestesses in Republican Rome*. Princeton.
Dodds, E. R. (1960), *Euripides' Bacchae*. 2nd edn. Oxford.
Dodge, H. (1999), 'Amusing the Masses: Buildings for Entertainment, and Leisure in the Roman World', in Potter, D. S. and Mattingly, D. J. (eds.), *Life, Death, and Entertainment in the Roman Empire*. Ann Arbor, 205–55.
Drinkwater, M. O. (2013), '*Militia Amoris*: Fighting in Love's Army', in Thorsen, T. S. (ed.), *The Cambridge Companion to Latin Love Elegy*. Cambridge, 194–206.
Dryden, J. (1685), *Sylvæ: Or, the Second Part of Poetical Miscellanies*. London.
Du Quesnay, I. M. L. (1973), 'The *Amores*', in Binns, J. W. (ed.), *Ovid*. London, 1–48.
Due, O. S. (1980), '*Amores* und Abtreibung: Ov. "Am." II 13 & 14', *Classica et mediaevalia* 32: 133–50.
Elsner, J. and Sharrock, A. (1991), 'Re-Viewing Pygmalion', *Ramus* 20: 149–82.
Farrell, J. (2014), 'The Poet in an Artificial Landscape: Ovid at Falerii (*Amores*, 3.13)', in Nelis, D. P. and Royo, M. (eds.), *Lire la ville: Fragments d'une archéologie littéraire de Rome antique*. Paris, 215–36.
Fear, T. (2000), 'The Poet as Pimp: Elegiac Seduction in the Time of Augustus', *Arethusa* 33: 217–40.
Feeney, D. (1991), *The Gods in Epic: Poets and Critics of the Classical Tradition*. Oxford.
Feeney, D. (1998), *Literature and Religion at Rome: Cultures, Contexts and Beliefs*. Cambridge.
Feeney, D. (2011), '*Hic finis fandi*: On the Absence of Punctuation for the Endings (and Beginnings) of Speeches in Latin Poetic Texts', *Materiali e discussioni per l'analisi dei testi classici* 66: 45–91.
Ferri, G. (2011), 'Due divinità di Falerii Veteres: Giunone Curite e Minerva Capta', *Mélanges de l'École française de Rome* 123: 145–56.
Fitzgerald, W. (1988), 'Power and Impotence in Horace's *Epodes*', *Ramus* 17: 176–91.
Fitzgerald, W. (2000), *Slavery and the Roman Literary Imagination*. Cambridge.

Flemming, R. (1999), 'Quae corpore quaestum facit: The Sexual Economy of Female Prostitution in the Roman Empire', Journal of Roman Studies 89.
Fraenkel, E. (1950), Aeschylus Agamemnon. Edited with a Commentary by Eduard Fraenkel, 3 vols. Oxford.
Frampton, S. A. (2019), Empire of Letters: Writing in Roman Literature and Thought from Lucretius to Ovid. New York.
Fränkel, H. F. (1945), Ovid: A Poet between Two Worlds. Berkeley and Los Angeles.
Frécaut, J. M. (1968), 'Vérité et fiction dans deux poèmes des Amours d'Ovide, 1.5 et 3.5', Latomus 27: 350–61.
Frécaut, J. M. (1972), L'esprit et l'humour chez Ovide. Grenoble.
Frederiksen, M. W. and Ward Perkins, J. B. (1957), 'The Ancient Road Systems of the Central and Northern Ager Faliscus (Notes on Southern Etruria, 2)', Papers of the British School at Rome 25: 67–203.
Fulkerson, L. (2013), 'Seruitium Amoris: The Interplay of Dominance, Gender and Poetry', in Thorsen, T. S. (ed.), The Cambridge Companion to Latin Love Elegy. Cambridge, 180–93.
Fulkerson, L. (2022), 'Elegy, Tragedy, and the Choice of Ovid (Amores 3.1)', in Volk, K. and Williams, G. D. (eds.), Philosophy in Ovid, Ovid as Philosopher. Oxford, 49–62.
Gale, M. R. (1997), 'Propertius 2.7: Militia Amoris and the Ironies of Elegy', Journal of Roman Studies 87: 77–91.
Gale, M. R. (2021), 'Catullus and Augustan Poetry', in Du Quesnay, I. and Woodman, T. (eds.), The Cambridge Companion to Catullus. Cambridge, 219–41.
Gamel, M.-K. (1989), 'Non sine caede: Abortion Politics and Poetics in Ovid's Amores', Helios 16: 183–206.
Gardner, H. H. (2013), Gendering Time in Augustan Love Elegy. Oxford.
Garnsey, P. (1999), Food and Society in Classical Antiquity. Cambridge.
Gärtner, T. (2011), 'Das Erlebnis der Impotenz: Zur Genese, Struktur und Rezeption von Ov., Am. III.7', Latomus 70: 103–23.
Garvie, A. F. (1986), Aeschlyus Choephori. Edited with Introduction and Commentary by A. F. Garvie. Oxford.
Gebhardt, U. C. J. (2009), Sermo Iuris: Rechtssprache und Recht in der Augusteischen Dichtung. Leiden.
Ghisalberti, F. (1946), 'Mediaeval Biographies of Ovid', Journal of the Warburg and Courtauld Institutes 9: 10–59.
Goold, G. P. (1965), 'Amatoria Critica', Harvard Studies in Classical Philology 69: 1–107.
Gow, A. S. F. and Page, D. L. (1968), The Greek Anthology: The Garland of Philip and Some Contemporary Epigrams, 2 vols. Cambridge.
Grant, L. (2019), Latin Erotic Elegy and the Shaping of Sixteenth-Century English Love Poetry. Cambridge.
Graverini, L. (2012–13), 'Ovidian Graffiti: Love, Genre and Gender on a Wall in Pompeii. A New Study of CIL IV 5296 – CLE 950', Incontri di Filologia Classica 12: 1–28.
Graverini, L. (2019), 'Ovidio a Pompei', in Bessone, F. and Stroppa, S. (eds.), Lettori latini e italiani di Ovidio: Atti del Convegno, Università di Torino, 9–10 Novembre 2017. Pisa, 27–39.
Greene, E. (1994), 'Sexual Politics in Ovid's Amores: 3.4, 3.8, and 3.12', Classical Philology 89: 344–50.
Greene, E. (1999), 'Travesties of Love: Violence and Voyeurism in Ovid, Amores 1.7', Classical World 92: 409–18.
Hall, J. B. (1999), 'Critical Observations on the Text of Ovid's Amatory Works', in Braund, S. M. and Mayer, R. (eds.), Amor: Roma. Love and Latin Literature. Cambridge, 94–103.

BIBLIOGRAPHY   351

Hampel, E. (1908), *De apostrophae apud Romanorum poetas usu*. Jena.
Harder, A. (2012), *Callimachus: Aetia*, 2 vols. Oxford.
Hardie, P. R. (2002), 'Ovid and Early Imperial Literature', in Hardie, P. (ed.), *Cambridge Companion to Ovid*. Cambridge, 34–45.
Harrison, S. (2002), 'Ovid and Genre: Evolutions of an Elegist', in Hardie, P. (ed.), *Cambridge Companion to Ovid*. Cambridge, 79–94.
Harvey, A. E. (1955), 'The Classification of Greek Lyric Poetry', *Classical Quarterly* 5: 157–75.
Haynes, J. (2015), 'Citations of Ovid in Virgil's Ancient Commentators', in Kraus, C. S. and Stray, C. (eds.), *Classical Commentaries: Explorations in a Scholarly Genre*. Oxford, 216–32.
Hedicke, E. (1905), *Edmundi Hedickii Studia Bentleiana: V. Ouidius Bentleianus*. Freienwald.
Henderson, J. (1991, 1992), 'Wrapping up the Case. Reading Ovid, *Amores* 2.7 (+8)', *Materiali e discussioni per l'analisi dei testi classici* 27, 28: 37–88, 27–84.
Henderson, J. (2002), 'A Doo-Dah-Doo-Dah-Dey at the Races: Ovid *Amores* 3.2 and the Personal Politics of the Circus Maximus', *Classical Antiquity* 21: 41–66.
Heubeck, A. and Hoekstra, A. (1989), *A Commentary on Homer's Odyssey. Volume II: Books IX–XVI*. Oxford.
Heyworth, S. J. (1995), 'Dividing Poems', in Pecere, O. and Reeve, M. D. (eds.), *Formative Stages of Classical Traditions: Latin Texts from Antiquity to the Renaissance*. Spoleto, 117–48.
Heyworth, S. J. (2009), 'Propertius and Ovid', in Knox, P. E. (ed.), *A Companion to Ovid*. Malden, Mass., 265–78.
Heyworth, S. J. (2011), in Morwood, J., et al., 'Explorations of Ovid, *Amores* 3.2, 3.4, 3.5, and 3.14', *Greece and Rome* 58: 21–6.
Heyworth, S. J. (2016), 'Authenticity and Other Textual Problems in *Heroides* 16', in Hunter, R. and Oakley, S. P. (eds.), *Latin Literature and Its Transmission: Papers in Honour of Michael Reeve*. Cambridge, 142–70.
Hinds, S. (1987), 'Generalising About Ovid', *Ramus*: 4–31 = (2006), 'Generalising About Ovid', in Knox, P. E. (ed.), *Oxford Readings in Ovid*. Oxford, 15–50.
Hinds, S. (1993), 'Medea in Ovid. Scenes from the Life of an Intertextual Heroine', *Materiali e discussioni per l'analisi dei testi classici* 30: 9–47.
Hinds, S. (1998), *Allusion and Intertext: Dynamics of Appropriation in Roman Poetry*. Cambridge.
Hofstaedter, J. R. (1973), 'The Structure of Ovid's *Amores*, Book I' (Ohio State University).
Holmes, N. (1995), '*Gaudia Nostra*: A Hexameter-Ending in Elegy', *Classical Quarterly* 45: 500–3.
Holzberg, N. (2002), *Ovid: The Poet and His Work*. trans. Goshgarian, G. M. Ithaca.
Holzberg, N. (2009), 'Ovid, *Amores* 3.7: A Poem between Two Genres', *Latomus* 68: 933–40.
Housman, A. E. (1889), 'Horatiana (Continued)', *Journal of Philology* 18: 1–35.
Housman, A. E. (1909), '*Vester = Tuus*', *Classical Quarterly* 3: 244–48.
Housman, A. E. (1927), 'Prosody and Method', *Classical Quarterly* 21: 1–12.
Humphrey, J. H. (1986), *Roman Circuses: Arenas for Chariot Racing*. London.
Hunt, A. (2016), *Reviving Roman Religion: Sacred Trees in the Roman World*. Cambridge.
Hunter, R. L. (1989), *Apollonius of Rhodes: Argonautica Book III*. Cambridge.
Hunter, R. L. (2005), 'The Hesiodic Catalogue and Hellenistic Poetry', in Hunter, R. (ed.), *The Hesiodic Catalogue of Women. Constructions and Reconstructions*. Cambridge, 239–65.
Huskey, S. J. (2005), 'In Memory of Tibullus: Ovid's Remembrance of Tibullus 1.3 in *Amores* 3.9 and *Tristia* 3.3', *Arethusa* 38: 367–86.

Hutchinson, G. O. (2008), 'Ovid, *Amores* 3: The Book', in *Talking Books: Readings in Hellenistic and Roman Books of Poetry*. Oxford, 177-99.
Ingleheart, J. (2021), '*Amores* Plural: Ovidian Homoerotics in the Elegies', in Thorsen, T. S., Brecke, I., and Harrison, S. (eds.), *Greek and Latin Love: The Poetic Connection*. Berlin, 185-212.
James, S. L. (1997), 'Slave-Rape and Female Silence in Ovid's Love Poetry', *Helios* 24: 60-76.
James, S. L. (2003), *Learned Girls and Male Persuasion: Gender and Reading in Roman Love Elegy*. Berkeley and Los Angeles.
Karakasis, E. (2010), 'Generic Consciousness and Diction in Ovid: A Reading of *Amores* 3.1', *Rivista di filologia e di istruzione classica* 138: 128-42.
Kaster, R. A. (1997), 'The Shame of the Romans', *TAPA* 1997: 1-19.
Keith, A. M. (1992), *The Play of Fictions: Studies in Ovid's Metamorphoses Book 2*. Ann Arbor.
Keith, A. M. (1994), '*Corpus Eroticum*: Elegiac Poets and Elegiac *Puellae* in Ovid's *Amores*', *Classical World* 88: 27-40.
Kennedy, D. F. (1993), *The Arts of Love: Five Studies in the Discourse of Roman Elegy*. Cambridge.
Kenney, E. J. (1958), 'Notes on Ovid', *Classical Quarterly* 8: 54-66.
Kenney, E. J. (1959), 'Notes on Ovid: II', *Classical Quarterly* 9: 240-60.
Kenney, E. J. (1962), 'The Manuscript Tradition of Ovid's *Amores, Ars Amatoria*, and *Remedia Amoris*', *Classical Quarterly* 12: 1-31.
Kenney, E. J. (1966), 'First Thoughts on the Hamiltonensis', *Classical Review* 16: 267-70.
Kenney, E. J. (1969a), 'Ovid and the Law', *Yale Classical Studies* 21: 241-63.
Kenney, E. J. (1969b), 'On the *Somnium* Attributed to Ovid', *Agon* 3: 1-14.
Kenney, E. J. (1976), 'Ovidius Prooemians', *Proceedings of the Cambridge Philological Society* 202: 46-53.
Kenney, E. J. (2002), 'Ovid's Language and Style', in Boyd, B. W. (ed.), *Brill's Companion to Ovid*. Leiden, 27-89.
Kershaw, A. (1986), '*Amores* 3.1.53 ff.', *Mnemosyne* 39: 407-8.
Knox, P. E. (1986), *Ovid's Metamorphoses and the Traditions of Augustan Poetry*. Cambridge.
Knox, P. E. (2009a), 'A Poet's Life', in Knox, P. E. (ed.), *A Companion to Ovid*. Malden Mass., 3-7.
Knox, P. E. (2009b), 'Lost and Spurious Works', in Knox, P. E. (ed.), *A Companion to Ovid*. Malden Mass., 207-16.
Knox, P. E. (2018), 'A Known Unknown in Pompeian Graffiti?', in Knox, P. E., Pelliccia, H., and Sens, A. (eds.), *They Keep It All Hid: Augustan Poetry, Its Antecedents and Reception*. Berlin, 29-40.
Krevans, N. (2011), 'Callimachus' Philology', in Acosta-Hughes, B., Lehnus, L., and Stephens, S. (eds.), *Brill's Companion to Callimachus*. Leiden, 118-33.
Lateiner, D. (1978), 'Ovid's Homage to Callimachus and Alexandrian Poetic Theory (*Am*. 2, 19)', *Hermes* 106: 188-96.
Lateiner, D. (1990), 'Mimetic Syntax: Metaphor from Word Order, Especially in Ovid', *American Journal of Philology* 111: 205-37.
Latham, J. A. (2016), *Performance, Memory, and Processions in Ancient Rome: The Pompa Circensis from the Republic to Late Antiquity*. New York.
Lattimore, R. (1962), *Themes in Greek and Latin Epitaphs*. Urbana.
Lavery, H. (2016), *The Impotency Poem from Ancient Latin to Restoration English Literature*. Farnham.
Lawrence, C. P. (1973), 'The Structure of Ovid's *Amores*, Book II', (Ohio State University).

Le Bonniec, H. (1958), *Le Culte de Cérès à Rome*. Paris.
Lee, A. G. (1952), 'The *Amores* of Ovid' (Review of P. *Ovidi Nasonis Amores*: A cura di Franco Munari), *Classical Review* 2: 175-7.
Lee, A. G. (1962), 'Tenerorum Lusor Amorum', in Sullivan, J. P. (ed.), *Critical Essays on Roman Literature: Elegy and Lyric*. London, 149-80.
Lennon, J. J. (2014), *Pollution and Religion in Ancient Rome*. Cambridge.
Lenz, F. W. (1933), 'Ceresfest: Eine Studie zu Ovid Amores, 3.10', *Studi Italiani di Filologia Classica* 10: 299-313.
Lenz, F. W. (1958), 'Junofest (Ovid *Amores* III 13). Eine Studie zu Ovids elegischer Erzählungskunst', *Fabula* 1: 255-62 (= Lenz [1972: 227-34]).
Lenz, F. W. (ed.), (1972), *Opuscula Selecta*. Amsterdam.
Lindner, M. M. (2015), *Portraits of the Vestal Virgins, Priestesses of Ancient Rome*. Ann Arbor.
Lloyd-Jones, H. (1996), *Sophocles: Fragments*. Cambridge, Mass.
Lörcher, G. (1975), *Der Aufbau der drei Bücher von Ovids Amores*. Amsterdam.
Lowe, D. M. (2018), 'Loud and Proud: The Voice of the *praeco* in Roman Love Elegy', in Matzner, S. and Harrison, S. (eds.), *Complex Inferiorities: The Poetics of the Weaker Voice in Latin Literature*. Oxford, 149-68.
Luce, T. J. (1990), 'Livy, Augustus, and the Forum Augustum', in Raaflaub, K. A. and Toher, M. (eds.), *Between Republic and Empire: Interpretations of Augustus and His Principate*. Berkeley, 123-38.
Luck, G. (1961), *Die römische Liebeselegie*. Heidelberg.
Luck, G. (1969), *The Latin Love Elegy*. London.
Lyne, R. O. A. M. (1979), '*Seruitium Amoris*', *Classical Quarterly* 29: 117-30.
Lyne, R. O. A. M. (1980), *The Latin Love Poets from Catullus to Horace*. Oxford.
Madvig, I. N. (1873), *Adversaria Critica ad Scriptores Graecos et Latinos. Vol. II. Emendationes Latinae*. Copenhagen.
Malamud, M. (1998), 'Gnawing at the End of the Rope: Poets on the Field in Two Vergilian Catalogues', *Ramus* 27: 95-126.
Maltby, R. (1991), *A Lexicon of Ancient Latin Etymologies*. Leeds.
Maltby, R. (2009), 'Tibullus and Ovid', in Knox, P. E. (ed.), *A Companion to Ovid*. Malden Mass., 279-93.
Martelli, F. (2013), *Ovid's Revisions: The Editor as Author*. Cambridge.
Martín Puente, C. (2012), 'La Elegía *Amores* III 5: Posible indicio del perfeccionismo de Ovidio', *Antigüedad y Cristianismo: Monografías históricas sobre la antigüedad tardía* 29: 337-45.
Mauger-Plichon, B. (1999), 'Ovide et l'expression du fiasco', *Via Latina* 154: 23-37.
Mazzoli, G. (1999), 'Tragedia vs. Elegia: Genesi e rifrazioni d'una 'scena' metapoetica Ovidiana (*Am*. 3, 1)', in Schubert, W. (ed.), *Ovid. Werk und Wirkung: Festgabe für Michael Von Albrecht zum 65. Geburtstag*, Studien zur klassischen Philologie, 1. Frankfurt, 137-52.
McCaffrey, D. V. (1974), 'The Thematic Arrangement of Ovid's *Amores*', (University of Michigan).
McCarthy, K. (1998), '*Servitium Amoris: Amor Servitii*', in Murnaghan, S. and Joshel, S. R. (eds.), *Women and Slaves in Greco-Roman Culture*. London, 174-92.
McGinn, T. A. J. (1998), *Prostitution, Sexuality, and the Law in Ancient Rome*. New York.
McKeown, J. C. (1979), 'Ovid, *Amores* 3.12', *Papers of the Liverpool Latin Seminar* 2: 163-77.
McKeown, J. C. (2002), 'The Authenticity of *Amores* 3.5', in Miller, J. F., Damon, C., and Myers, K. S. (eds.), *Vertis in Usum: Studies in Honor of Edward Courtney*. Munich, 114-28.
McLennan, G. (1972), 'Arte Allusiva and Ovidian Metrics', *Hermes* 100: 495-6.

354 BIBLIOGRAPHY

Miller, J. F. (1989), 'Ovidius Imitator Sui: Fasti 4.179ff and Amores 3.2.43ff', Rheinisches Museum für Philologie 132: 403-5.
Miller, J. F. (1991), Ovid's Elegiac Festivals. Frankfurt.
Miller, J. F. (1993), 'Ovidian Allusion and the Vocabulary of Memory', Materiali e discussioni per l'analisi dei testi classici 30: 153-64 = (2006), 'Ovidian Allusion and the Vocabulary of Memory', in Knox, P. (ed.), Oxford Readings in Ovid. Oxford, 86-99.
Miller, P. A. (2003), Subjecting Verses: Latin Erotic Elegy and the Emergence of the Real. Princeton.
Milnor, K. (2014), Graffiti and the Literary Landscape in Roman Pompeii. Oxford.
Morgan, K. (1977), Ovid's Art of Imitation: Propertius in the Amores. Leiden.
Morgan, L. (2010), Musa Pedestris: Metre and Meaning in Roman Verse. Oxford.
Morwood, J., et al. (2011), 'Explorations of Ovid, Amores 3.2, 3.4, 3.5, and 3.14', Greece and Rome 58: 14-32.
Most, G. W. (2018), Hesiod: The Shield, Catalogue of Women, and Other Fragments. Cambridge, Mass.
Müller, L. (1856), 'De Ovidi Amorum libris', Philologus 11: 60-91.
Müller, L. (1863), 'Zur Kritik des ersten Theils der ovidischen Dichtungen', Rheinisches Museum für Philologie 18: 71-90.
Munari, F. (1948), 'Sugli Amores di Ovidio', Studi italiani di filologia classica 23, 113-52.
Munari, F. (1965), Il Codice Hamilton 471 di Ovidio. Rome.
Murgatroyd, P. (1975), 'Militia Amoris and the Roman Elegists', Latomus 34: 59-79.
Murgatroyd, P. (1981), 'Seruitium Amoris and the Roman Elegists', Latomus 40: 589-606.
Nagy, B. (2023), 'Some Stylometric Remarks on Ovid's Heroides and the Epistula Sapphus', Digital Scholarship in the Humanities 38: 1-17 https://doi.org/10.1093/llc/fqac098.
Navarro Antolín, F. (1996), 'Ingenium dominae lena mouebit anus. La auara puella en los Amores de Ovidio: Am. I.8, I.10, III.5, III.8', in Arcaz, J. L., Laguna Mariscal, G., and Ramírez de Verger, A. (eds.), La Obra Amatoria De Ovidio Madrid, 65-94.
Newlands, C. E. (1995), Playing with Time: Ovid and the Fasti. Ithaca.
O'Hara, J. J. (1990), Death and the Optimistic Prophecy in Vergil's Aeneid. Princeton.
O'Hara, J. J. (2007), Inconsistency in Roman Epic: Studies in Catullus, Lucretius, Vergil, Ovid and Lucan. Cambridge.
Obermayer, H. P. (1998), Martial und der Diskurs über männliche "Homosexualität" in der Literatur der frühen Kaiserzeit. Tübingen.
Ogden, D. (2002), Magic, Witchcraft, and Ghosts in the Greek and Roman Worlds: A Source Book. New York.
Oliensis, E. (2019), Loving Writing/Ovid's Amores. Cambridge.
Oliver, R. P. (1945), 'The First Edition of the Amores', TAPA 76: 191-215.
Otto, A. (1890), Die Sprichwörter und sprichwörtlichen Redensarten der Römer. Leipzig.
Page, D. (1955), Sappho and Alcaeus: An Introduction to the Study of Ancient Lesbian Poetry. Oxford.
Parker, D. (1969), 'The Ovidian Coda', Arion 8: 80-97.
Perkins, C. A. (1993), 'Love's Arrows Lost: Tibullan Parody in Amores 3.9', Classical World 86: 459-66.
Perkins, C. A. (2000), 'Ovid's Erotic Vates', Helios 27: 53-61.
Perkins, C. A. (2002), 'Protest and Paradox in Ovid, Amores 3.11', Classical World 95: 117-25.
Perkins, C. A. (2011), 'The Figure of Elegy in Amores 3.1: Elegy as puella, Elegy as poeta, puella as poeta', Classical World 104: 313-31.
Perkins, C. A. (2015), 'Ovid Breaks the Law: Amores 3.2 and the Edictum de adtemptata pudicitia', Paideia: Rivista letteraria di informazione bibliografica 70: 137-53.
Pfeiffer, R. (1949-53), Callimachus, 2 vols. Oxford.

BIBLIOGRAPHY 355

Pichon, R. (1902), *De sermone amatorio apud latinos elegiarum scriptores*. Paris.
Pietropaolo, M. (2020), *The Grotesque in Roman Love Elegy*. Cambridge.
Pinkster, H. (2015), *Oxford Latin Syntax: 1. The Simple Clause*. Oxford.
Pinkster, H. (2021), *Oxford Latin Syntax: 2. The Complex Sentence and Discourse*. Oxford.
Platnauer, M. (1951), *Latin Elegiac Verse: A Study of the Metrical Usages of Tibullus, Propertius and Ovid*. Cambridge.
Port, W. (1926), 'Die Anordnung in Gedichtbüchern augusteischer Zeit', *Philologus* 81: 280-308, 427-68.
Powell, J. U. (1925), *Collectanea Alexandrina: reliquiae minores poetarum Graecorum aetatis Ptolemaicae 323-146 A.C., epicorum, elegiacorum, lyricorum, ethicorum*. Oxford.
Race, W. H. (1997), *Pindar, Nemean Odes. Isthmian Odes. Fragments*. Cambridge, Mass.
Rambaux, C. (1985), *Trois analyses de l'amour: Catulle, Poésies: Ovide, Les Amours: Apulée, Le conte de Psyché*. Paris.
Ramirez de Verger, A. (1999), 'Figurae Veneris (Ov. Ars 3.769-88)', in Schubert, W. (ed.), *Ovid: Werk und Wirkung. Festgabe für Michael von Albrecht zum 65. Geburtstag*, Studien zur klassischen Philologie, 1. Frankfurt, 237-43.
Ramsby, T. (2005), 'Striving for Permanence: Ovid's Funerary Inscriptions', *Classical Journal* 100: 365-91.
Rawson, E. (1987), 'Discrimina Ordinum: The *Lex Iulia Theatralis*', *Papers of the British School at Rome* 55: 83-114.
Reed, J. D. (1997a), *Bion of Smyrna: The Fragments and the Adonis*. Cambridge.
Reed, J. D. (1997b), 'Ovid's Elegy on Tibullus and Its Models', *Classical Philology* 92: 260-9.
Richardson, L. (1992), *A New Topographical Dictionary of Ancient Rome*. Baltimore.
Richlin, A. (1992), *The Garden of Priapus: Sexuality and Aggression in Roman Humor*. 2 edn. New York.
Richlin, A. (2014), 'Reading Ovid's Rapes', in *Arguments with Silence. Writing the History of Roman Women*. Ann Arbor, 130-65.
Richmond, J. A. (1981), 'Doubtful Works Ascribed to Ovid', in *Aufstieg und Niedergang der römischen Welt* 2.31.4. Berlin, 2744-83.
Rogers, R. S. (1959), 'The Emperor's Displeasure: *amicitiam renuntiare*', *TAPA* 90: 224-37.
Rogerson, A. (2017), *Virgil's Ascanius: Imagining the Future in the Aeneid*. Cambridge.
Rosati, G. (1983), *Narciso e Pigmalione: Illusione e spettacolo nelle Metamorfosi di Ovidio*. Florence.
Ross, D. O. (1969), *Style and Tradition in Catullus*. Cambridge, Mass.
Ross, D. O. (1975), *Backgrounds to Augustan Poetry: Gallus, Elegy, and Rome*. Cambridge.
Scheid, J. (1984), 'Contraria facere: Renversements et déplacements dans les rites funéraires', *Annali di Archeologia e Storia Antica / Dipartimento di Studi del Mondo Classico e del Mediterraneo Antico* 6: 117-39.
Scheid, J. (1995), 'Graeco Ritu: A Typically Roman Way of Honoring the Gods', *Harvard Studies in Classical Philology* 97: 15-31.
Schmitzer, U. (1994), 'Non modo militiae turbine factus eques: Ovids Selbstbewusstsein und die Polemik gegen Horaz in der Elegie Am. 3, 15', *Philologus* 138: 101-17.
Schmitzer, U. (2013), 'Strategien der Selbstkanonisierung bei Ovid', in Schmitzer, U. (ed.), *Enzyklopädie der Philologie: Themen und Methoden der klassischen Philologie heute*. Göttingen, 51-83.
Schrijvers, P. H. (1976), 'O Tragoedia tu labor aeternus. Étude sur l'élégie III,I des *Amores* d'Ovide', in Bremer, J. M., Radt, S. L., and Ruijgh, C. J. (eds.), *Miscellanea Tragica in Honorem J. C. Kamerbeek*. Amsterdam, 405-24.
Schwarz, H. (1952), 'Stil und Komposition in Ovids *Amores*' (University of Göttingen).
Scioli, E. (2015), *Dream, Fantasy, and Visual Art in Roman Elegy*. Madison.

Semmlinger, L. (1988), 'Zur Echtheit der Elegie *De Somnio*' = Ovid, *Amores* 3, 5', in Kindermann, U., Maaz, W., and Wagner, F. (eds.), *Festschrift für Paul Klopsch*. Göppingen, 455-75.
Sharrock, A. R. (1995), 'The Drooping Rose: Elegiac Failure in *Amores* 3.7', *Ramus* 24: 152-80.
Sharrock, A. R. (2013), 'The *Poeta-Amator*, *Nequitia* and *Recusatio*', in Thorsen, T. S. (ed.), *The Cambridge Companion to Love Elegy*. Cambridge, 151-65.
Shea, K. J. (2011), '(Re)Visions of Love: Augustan Visual Culture in Ovid's *Amores*', (Rutgers, State University of New Jersey).
Spurr, M. S. (1986), *Arable Cultivation in Italy c. 200 B.C. - A.D. 100*. London.
Starnone, V. (2019), 'The *faber* and the *saga*: Pygmalion between the *eburnea uirgo* and the *truncus iners*', *Classical Quarterly* 69: 309-18.
Stevenson, J. (2005), *Women Latin Poets: Language, Gender, and Authority from Antiquity to the Eighteenth Century*. Oxford.
Stroh, W. (1971), *Die römische Liebeselegie als werbende Dichtung*. Amsterdam.
Stroh, W. (1979), 'Ovids Liebeskunst und die Ehegesetze des Augustus', *Gymnasium* 86: 323-52.
Strong, A. K. (2016), *Prostitutes and Matrons in the Roman World*. Cambridge.
Suter, A. (1989), 'Ovid, from Image to Narrative: *Amores* 1.8 and 3.6', *Classical World* 83: 15-20.
Syme, R. (1978), *History in Ovid*. Oxford.
Talbert, R. J. A. (1984), *The Senate of Imperial Rome*. Princeton.
Taplin, O. (1986), 'Fifth-Century Tragedy and Comedy: A Synkrisis', *Journal of Hellenic Studies* 106: 163-74.
Tarrant, R. (2007), 'Ovid's Amatory Works', *Classical Review* 57: 102-4.
Tarrant, R. J. (1995), 'Ovid and the Failure of Rhetoric', in Innes, D., Hine, H., and Pelling, C. (eds.), *Ethics and Rhetoric. Classical Essays for Donald Russell on His Seventy-Fifth Birthday*. Oxford, 63-74.
Taylor, J. H. (1970), '*Amores* 3.9: A Farewell to Elegy', *Latomus* 29: 474-7.
Thomas, E. (1965a), 'A Comparative Analysis of Ovid, *Amores*, II.6 and III.9', *Latomus* 24: 599-609.
Thomas, E. (1965b), 'Ovid, *Amores* III.9.35-40', *Classical Review* 15: 149-51.
Thomas, E. (1969), 'Ovid at the Races, *Amores* 3.2 and *Ars Amatoria* 1.135-164', in Bibauw, J. (ed.), *Hommages a Marcel Renard*. Brussels, 710-24.
Thorsen, T. S. (2006), '*Scribentis Imagines* in Ovidian Authorship and Scholarship: A Study of the *Epistula Sapphus* (*Heroides* 15)' (University of Bergen).
Thorsen, T. S. (2013), 'Ovid the Love Elegist', in Thorsen, T. S. (ed.), *The Cambridge Companion to Love Elegy*. Cambridge, 114-29.
Thorsen, T. S. (2014), *Ovid's Early Poetry. From His Single Heroides to His Remedia Amoris*. Cambridge.
Thorsen, T. S. (2018), 'Intrepid Intratextuality: The Epistolary Pair of Leander and Hero (*Heroides* 18-19) and the End of Ovid's Poetic Career', in Harrison, S. J., Frangoulidis, S., and Papanghelis, T. (eds.), *Intratextuality and Latin Literature*. Berlin, 257-72.
Tissol, G. (1997), *The Face of Nature: Wit, Narrative, and Cosmic Origins in Ovid's Metamorphoses*. Princeton.
Treggiari, S. (1991), *Roman Marriage: Iusti Coniuges from the Time of Cicero to the Time of Ulpian*. Oxford.
Tueller, M. A. and Paton, W. R. (2014-), *The Greek Anthology*, 5 vols. Cambridge, Mass.
Volk, K. (2005), '*Ille Ego*: (Mis)Reading Ovid's Elegiac Persona', *Antike und Abendland* 51: 83-96.

Wallis, J. (2018), *Introspection and Engagement in Propertius: A Study of Book 3*. Cambridge.
Watson, L. (2019), *Magic in Ancient Greece and Rome*. London.
Watson, P. A. (1983), 'Ovid *Amores* 2.7 and 8: The Disingenuous Defence', *Wiener Studien* NF 17: 91–103.
Watts, W. J. (1973), 'Ovid, the Law and Roman Society on Abortion', *Acta Classica* 16: 89–102.
Weinlich, B. (1999), *Ovids Amores: Gedichtfolge und Handlungsablauf*. Stuttgart.
Welch, T. S. (2012), 'Elegy and the Monuments', in Gold, B. K. (ed.), *A Companion to Roman Love Elegy*. Malden, Mass., 103–18.
West, M. L. (1973), *Textual Criticism and Editorial Technique*. Stuttgart.
West, M. L. (2003a), '*Iliad* and *Aethiopis*', *Classical Quarterly* 53: 1–14.
West, M. L. (2003b), *Greek Epic Fragments*. Cambridge, Mass.
Westerhold, J. A. (2016), 'Ovid's Epic Forest: A Note on *Amores* 3.1.1–6', *Classical Quarterly* 63: 899–903.
Wilkinson, L. P. (1955), *Ovid Recalled*. Cambridge.
Wilkinson, L. P. (1963), *Golden Latin Artistry*. Cambridge.
Williams, F. (2003), 'The Hands of Death: Ovid *Amores* 3.9.20', *American Journal of Philology* 124: 225–34.
Williams, G. (1968), *Tradition and Originality in Roman Poetry*. Oxford.
Wills, J. (1996), *Repetition in Latin Poetry: Figures of Allusion*. Oxford.
Wimmel, W. (1960), *Kallimachos in Rom: die Nachfolge seines apologetischen Dichtens in der Augusteerzeit*. Wiesbaden.
Wise, J. (2019), 'Subaltern Women, Sexual Violence, and Trauma in Ovid's *Amores*', in Karanika, A. and Panoussi, V. (eds.), *Emotional Trauma in Greece and Rome: Representations and Reactions*. London.
Woodcock, E. C. (1959), *A New Latin Syntax*. London.
Wray, D. L. (2007), 'Wood: Statius's *Siluae* and the Poetics of Genius', *Arethusa* 40: 127–43.
Wright, J. W. (1674), *Thyestes: A Tragedy, Translated out of Seneca: To Which Is Added Mock-Thyestes, in Burlesque*. London: T. R. and N. T. for Allen Banks.
Wyke, M. (2002), *The Roman Mistress: Ancient and Modern Representations*. Oxford.
Wyke, M. (2006), 'Reading Female Flesh: *Amores* 3.1', in Knox, P. (ed.), *Oxford Readings in Ovid*. Oxford, 169–204.
Zanker, P. (1988), *The Power of Images in the Age of Augustus*. trans. Shapiro, A. Michigan.
Zetzel, J. E. G. (1996), 'Poetic Baldness and Its Cure', *Materiali e discussioni per l'analisi dei testi classici* 36: 73–100.
Zgoll, C. (2010), 'Crossroads Narrative or Beauty Contest? Role-Play in Ovid, *Amores* 3.1', *Digressus* 10: 97–111 = (2010), 'Ovids heimliches Bündnis mit Venus im Eröffnungsgedicht des dritten Amoresbuches', *Antike und Abendland* 56: 159–73.
Zimmermann Damer, E. (2019), *In the Flesh: Embodied Identities in Roman Elegy*. Madison.
Ziogas, I. (2016), 'Love Elegy and Legal Language in Ovid', in Mitsis, P. and Ziogas, I. (eds.), *Wordplay and Powerplay in Latin Poetry*. Berlin, 213–39.
Ziogas, I. (2021), *Law and Love in Ovid: Courting Justice in the Age of Augustus*. Oxford.
Zwierlein, O. (1999), *Die Ovid- und Vergil-Revision in tiberischer Zeit. Vol. 1: Prolegomena*. Berlin.

1. Latin Words

adulter/adultera 11, 83, 84, 90, 139, 142, 149, 150, 152, 153, 194, 314
aelinon 250, 258
albeo 164
area 85–6, 341
artes ingenuae 230

blanditiae 91, 116, 207, 220
blandus/blanda 116, 219

caesaries 87, 88
candidus/candida 127, 161, 162, 201, 206, 210
carcer 98, 101–2, 118–19, 121
castus/casta 141–2, 154, 203, 218, 272, 314, 318, 324
Cinyreius 174
coniunx 11, 139, 153, 158, 162, 167, 313, 314
contraho 95
corpus 142, 143, 150, 152, 212, 236, 253, 287–8, 325
cothurnus 80, 82, 87–8, 95
credulitas 8, 132, 311–12, 323, 331
cultus 90, 186, 188, 203, 269
custos 11, 92, 93, 140, 141, 143, 152, 248, 249

Danaeius 174
deliciae 327, 337
deuota 202, 211, 212
doctus 268
domina 9, 17, 104, 105, 116, 122, 162, 167, 171, 172, 232
dominus 207, 224, 281
dos 230
durus/dura 93, 98, 140, 237, 288

ecquis 82
egelidus 12
elegeia 79, 249, 252
eques 1, 228, 232, 233, 234, 246, 337–8

falsum iurare 129, 137
far 274
fidem fallere 125, 126
flaua 210, 273, 275, 280
fons 77, 198, 199, 213, 259

garrulus 163, 218
grauis 75, 85, 88–9, 220, 246, 262, 336, 341

heu 235

infelix 101, 120
ingenium 85–6, 141, 167, 231, 232, 243, 298, 301, 303, 321–2
ingenuus/ingenua 139, 151, 152, 230, 287–8
instita 138
inuidia 130, 176, 303
iuuenis 148, 177, 209, 318
iuuo 31, 177, 207, 221, 261, 287, 329

languidus/languida 144, 204, 223, 226
lasciuia 88, 91, 328, 329
lasciuus/lasciua 91, 206, 328, 329
latus 106, 214, 234, 288
legifer 279
legitimus 197–8
lena 91, 158, 163, 167, 302
leno, lenocinium 91, 138, 139, 155, 302, 322, 324
leuis 89, 90, 220, 270, 284, 292, 341
libertas 151, 152, 338–9
licentia 97, 268, 310–11
linea 105
liuor 164, 168, 303
lutulentus 199

Maeonides 259
maritus 139, 149, 150, 154, 158, 162, 248
materia 85–6, 90
Mauors 132, 133, 181
membra 207, 223, 226
mendacium 175
meretrix 10, 236, 290, 291, 299, 301, 325
merito 302
mollities 235

natura 243
nequitia 83, 144, 236, 294, 327
neruus 214
nil agis 140, 141
nobilis 99
nomen 96, 128, 131–2, 198, 252, 267
non feci 322, 334

opus 78, 85, 136, 224, 253, 260, 330

palla 81, 188, 319
pallidus 178
pallium 106-7
pariter 204
pauper 228, 246, 247, 289
pecco 143-4, 323, 324, 326
perfida 128
pes 80, 128, 173-4, 187, 286, 306, 318
pompa 112-13, 117, 312, 317, 320
pondus 130, 208, 304
praeconia 302
propago 191
prostituo 326
pudica 324, 326
pudicitia 324
pudor 84, 191-2, 194, 209, 215, 225, 277, 319, 324, 327, 328, 330
puella 86, 104-5, 105-6, 137, 139, 141, 149, 151, 162, 167, 202, 205, 219, 293, 298, 318

Quirites 120, 325

ruricola 115
rusticus/rustica 90-1, 115, 152-3, 197, 276

sceptrum 3, 75, 80, 81, 82, 95
semiuir 12
septena 183, 233
serua 152
seruitium 9, 234, 275, 286, 287, 288
seruus 151, 152, 287, 288
silu 75-6
sollicitare fidem 92
spolia opima 171
stola 106-7, 138, 141
succingo 109

tabella 111, 331
tener/tenera 86-7, 96, 115, 132, 141, 190, 218, 230, 276
thyrsus 75, 85, 336, 341
turpis, turpiter 150, 194, 216, 232, 240, 285, 288

uates 76, 78, 84, 96, 250, 252, 256, 259, 263, 336
uir 9, 12, 139, 140, 141, 154, 167, 209, 216, 221, 229, 289
uita 234
uitium 80, 144, 285, 295
uitta 18, 138, 141, 188-9, 194
uoluptas 145, 150-1, 207, 229
uxor 139-40, 153, 162, 301

2. Passages Quoted from Latin and Greek Texts

Accius (Warmington)
fr. 162   104
fr. 244   89

Acta ludorum saecularium (Schnegg)
20, p. 16   318–19
119, p. 30   315
183, p. 310   320

Aeschylus
Ag. 1629–30   257–8
PV 864   289

Apollodorus
2.1.3–5   177

Apollonius of Rhodes
2.2–4   177
3.532   172
4.603–6   309–10
fr. 5.1 (Powell)   183

Apuleius
Metamorphoses (Golden Ass)
2.10   88
2.29.13   212
9.20.1   302

Aristophanes
Frogs 124–5   207
Lysistrata 1039   294

Aristotle
Poetics 1451b4   311

Arrian
Epict. 2.20.34.5   144

Artemidorus
1.2.11   158 n. 14
2.20.50   163

Bion
Adonis
1   250 n. 8
54–5   256
80–2   253–4

Caesar
Gal. 2.21.5.4   234

Callimachus
Aetia (Harder)
fr. 1.24   80
fr. 7.11–14   79
fr. 7a.14–15   183
fr. 384.31–2 (Pfeiffer)   183
Epigram AP 5.6   123
Epigram AP 28.1–4   169
Hymn 1 (to Zeus) 8   276
Hymn 2 (to Apollo) 105–12   169
Hymn 2 (to Apollo) 110–11   237
Hymn 4 (to Delos) 112   180
Iambics 3 (fr. 193.col. 6.34–5 Pfeiffer)   230

Cassius Dio
54.10.5   324

Catullus
1.1   232
3.1   116
3.17–18   88
6.4–5   330
6.10   330
6.13   214, 288
8.1–2   283, 284, 292
8.8   283
8.9   286
8.11   286
8.15   200
8.18   329
8.19   283
11.7   183
17.18–19   208
22.4–5   191
25.3   223
32.8   211
32.11   225
42.24   326
45.1–2   247
45.12   329
45.13   233

362 PASSAGES QUOTED FROM LATIN AND GREEK TEXTS

46.1	12	*Planc.* 59.13	88
50.14–15	223	*Sen.* 29.10	205
51.11–12	332	*Top.* 73.4	130
56.5–6	333	*Tusc.* 1.37.5	77
58b.2–3	306	*Tusc.* 5.55.16	144
62.5	96	*Tusc.* 5.67.3	326
64.7	242	*Ver.* 2.1.11	131
64.63	210		
64.295	235	CIL	
64.370	208	4.1520	293
65.13–14	308	4.5296.3	126
66.8	88		
68b.135–6	295	Columella	
69.2	206	6.2.12.5	315
72.5–8	284	7.6.4.5	162
72.8	293, 297	8.2.11.5	162
76.3–4	296	9.2.2.7	310
76.19	295	10.1.1.69	276
85	332	10.1.1.138	186
86.1–2, 294	128	12.1.1	162
86.5–6	295	Curtius Rufus	
101.3–4	265	4.1.21	213
101.6	235		
106	302	Diodorus Siculus	
109.1	233	4.73.4–5	103
109.6	296		
110.7–8	301	Dionysius of Halicarnassus	
		Ant. Rom.	
Celsus		1.21.2.1	315
3.6.1	146	3.68.3.6	101
		7.72.13	112
Censorinus		8.89.5.3	188
14.2	177		
		Ennius (Goldberg and Manuwald)	
Cicero		*Ann.*	
de Orat. 3.153.3	310	1.35	190
de Orat. 3.177.7	222	1.39–40	187, 188
Fam. 14.2.3.7	233	1.44–5	191, 196
Fam. 14.4.1.9	233	1.49	190
Flac. 98.14	233	1.50	188
Har. 24.10	314	1.79–81	118
Inu. 1.10.7	322	6.175	76
Leg. 1.4.11	304	6.190	216
Leg. 2.15.8–10	281	14.377	242
Leg. 2.24.12	218	16.426	320
N.D. 1.79	80	sedinc. 535–6	145
N.D. 1.123.5	262	sedinc. 537	279
N.D. 2.67.11	194	*Euh.* 10	236
N.D. 2.112.14	199	*Phoen.* fr.109.4	325
Off. 1.39	126		
Off. 1.60	217	*Epicedion Drusi* (*Consolation to Livia*)	
Off. 1.105.11	131	40	252
Off. 3.104	125	141–2	253
Off. 3.108.2	129	177	253
Parad. 3.20.13	144	253	164
Phil. 2.30.5	287	328	331

PASSAGES QUOTED FROM LATIN AND GREEK TEXTS 363

Euripides		14.293–4	103
Alc. 462–3	270	15.36–9	296
Bacch. 526–7	136	16.459	264
Bacch. 596–9	135	18.104	204
Hipp. 738–41	310–11	18.570	258
Hipp. 1396	264	20.73–4	178
Med. 28–9	220	23.338–40	102
fr. 1061 (Collard and Cropp)	140	24.85–6	251
fr. 1063 (Collard and Cropp)	140	24.617	308

Fronto		*Odyssey*	
Aurel. 2.1.2.4	246	2.93	260
		5.125–8	271
Gallus (Hollis)		10.341	226
145.1	83	11.235–54	184
Gellius		11.243–4	185
1.6.2.3	294	11.300	115
12.1.17.4–6	152	15.52	174
12.2.5.3	238	15.121	174
		18.248–9	128
Greek Anthology (PA)		19.518	308
5.6	123	20.73–4	178
5.30.3–4	248	22.330–1	221
5.50.1	228 n. 8		
5.129.8	223	Horace	
10.21.2	336	*Ars Poetica*	
11.29.3–4	223	9–11	311
11.30.1–2	210	38–9	86
11.30.2	211	75	249
11.30.3–4	223	278–9	82
12.156.5–6	291	279–80	88
12.173.5–6	148	333	303
12.216	223	351–2	134
12.232.1–4	223		
		Carmen Saeculare	
Hesiod		6	318
Catalogue of Women fr. 73 Most	124		
Theogony 27	175, 310	*Carmina (Odes)*	
Theogony 969–71	271	1.1.4–5	102
Works 111	240	1.1.35	84
Works 117–18	241	1.2.2–4	135
Works 232–3	241	1.3.25–6	146
		1.3.34–8	244
Homer		1.7.5	227
Homeric Hymn to Demeter		1.7.13–14	185–6
305–7	278	1.15.22	215
308	278	1.17.7	162
308–9	278	1.19.1	336
		1.23.5–6	166
Iliad		1.23.11–12	223
1.102	174	1.33.2–3	254
2.599	222	1.33.9	150
3.237	115	2.1.40	90
4.461	332	2.8	124
7.322	174	2.8.1–2	131
9.673	338	2.8.6	128
11.492–5	172–3	2.8.10–11	136
13.112	175		

364 PASSAGES QUOTED FROM LATIN AND GREEK TEXTS

2.8.11–12	129	50.16.42	150
2.14.2–4	262	50.16.239.1	151
3.1.2–4	236		
3.1.11	247	Juvenal	
3.3.1	82	6.196–7	219
3.3.12	329	9.34	214
3.7.1	189	11.201–2	106
3.7.21	220	13.27	183
3.16.8	239		
3.16.9–11	239	Livy	
3.16.11–13	241	1.4.2.2	187
3.19.27	223	3.19.7.5	257
3.26.10	206	6.12.8.4	235
3.29.6	186	37.54.15.1	339
3.30.1	147	39.52.1.5	179
3.30.6	335	40.56.9	208
3.30.6–7	336		
3.30.10	338	Lucan	
4.1.4–5	336	1.8	325
4.3.22–3	2 n. 15, 84	1.180	247
4.6.41–3	321	2.302–3	267
4.9.28	256	3.109–11	245
4.15.1–2	341	4.96	241
		4.223–4	246
Epistles		4.248	234
1.2.7	231	6.39–40	243
1.5.12–14	217	6.589	191
1.17.47	302	6.822	212
2.1.225	94, 238	7.195	259
		8.494–5	154
Epodes		9.984	260
2.26	77	Lucilius (Marx)	
11.8	84	1305	101
11.11–12	231		
17.40	326	Lucretius	
17.54	220	1.6	273
		1.42	191
Satires		1.230–1	152
1.8.1	208	1.313–14	278
1.8.30	212	1.922–3	85
1.8.30–1	226	3.135	247
2.4.70	185	3.1037–8	259
		4.421	187
Hyginus		4.584–5	317
Astr. 2.12.1.6	234	5.14–15	274
Fab. 63.1	240	5.1112	223
		5.1241–2	241
Justinian's *Digest*			
4.4.37.7–11	153	Manilius	
8.3.38	172	4.863	199
13.5.1	126		
34.2.23.2	107	Marcellus (Helmreich)	
38.1.38	236	*de Medicamentis* 1.57 (p. 34)	331
48.2.3.pr.2–4	326		
48.5.2.2	155	Martial	
48.5.13.pr.1	327	1.53.10	134
48.5.30.3	155	3.2.1	171

PASSAGES QUOTED FROM LATIN AND GREEK TEXTS 365

3.26.5–6	301	1.4.43	328
4.21.1–2	262	1.4.43–4	206
5.30.4	269	1.4.48	330
6.23.3	219	1.4.53	83
6.42.19–20	201	1.4.61	151
6.86.5	247	1.5.2	331
9.29.11	270	1.5.3	302
10.68.10	219	1.5.8	319
11.9.1	253	1.5.9	93, 128, 233
11.81.3	208	1.5.9–10	14
11.104.7	107	1.5.12	302
12.46	294	1.5.15–16	334
13.99	120	1.5.19	215
Sp. 7.1–2	263	1.5.23	309
		1.5.25	111, 215
[Moschus]		1.6.1	152
Lament for Bion		1.6.7–8	93
1	250, 258	1.6.49	88
7	250	1.6.62	93, 141
8	250	1.7.1	244
11	250	1.7.11–13	18
51	250	1.7.13–14	108
68–9	250	1.7.17	189
		1.7.18	226
Nepos		1.7.19	94
Iph. 3.2.3	277	1.7.21	136
		1.7.27	244
Nonnus		1.7.35	126
Dion. 7.212	181	1.7.41	329
		1.7.41–2	331
Ovid		1.7.49–50	186
Amores		1.7.67–8	18
1.Epigr.1–2	3	1.8.1–2	167
1.Epigr.1	232	1.8.3	107
1.1.1–2	85	1.8.6	213
1.1.19	90	1.8.25	280
1.1.24	78, 96, 336	1.8.25–6	203
1.1.25	119, 254	1.8.31	129
1.2.1	125	1.8.31–2	107
1.2.8	84	1.8.35–6	324
1.2.19	107, 129	1.8.42	153
1.2.30	286	1.8.43	142, 203
1.2.31	326	1.8.43–4	154
1.2.35	91, 117, 221	1.8.47	148, 163
1.2.39–40	114	1.8.57–8	233
1.2.42	205	1.8.61	238
1.2.50	219	1.8.62	144, 232
1.3.3–4	117	1.8.73	291
1.3.7–9	228	1.8.73–4	271
1.3.8	234	1.8.86	125
1.3.18	101	1.8.97	331
1.3.21	146	1.8.98	331
1.3.25–6	299	1.8.113–14	201
1.4.27	205	1.9.1–2	108
1.4.32	205	1.9.22	178
1.4.41	110		

1.9.28	300	2.1.22	237
1.9.29	225	2.1.26	213
1.9.39	333	2.1.27–8	91
1.9.40	9	2.1.32	315
1.10.4	240	2.1.33–4	237
1.10.7–8	308	2.2.3–4	78
1.10.11	299	2.2.4	162
1.10.17–18	241	2.2.15–16	151
1.10.21	325	2.2.17	152
1.10.21–2	10, 236, 299	2.2.43–4	218
1.10.25	159	2.2.45–6	146
1.10.31	274	2.2.55–6	334
1.10.35–6	229	2.2.57–8	333
1.10.41–2	241	2.2.61–2	334
1.10.46	135	2.3.2	197
1.10.59–60	230, 301	2.3.3	207
1.11.9	190	2.3.7	208
1.11.11	76, 196	2.3.17	103
1.12.9	219	2.4.1	323
1.12.20	315	2.4.1–2	83, 285
1.13.20	130	2.4.3	236
1.13.25	218	2.4.5	297
1.13.37	216	2.4.13–14	329
1.13.39	288	2.4.15	248
1.13.47	103, 123	2.4.15–16	326
1.14.15–16	9	2.4.16	219
1.14.25	9, 289	2.4.21–2	109
1.14.33	89	2.4.22	328
1.14.33–4	109	2.4.33–4	128
1.14.39	214	2.4.35	128
1.14.46	2	2.4.39	149
1.14.51	119	2.4.45	220
1.14.52	288	2.5.5	331
1.15.2	237	2.5.7–8	334
1.15.3–4	229	2.5.8	119
1.15.7–8	96, 299 n. 4	2.5.25	210
1.15.8	335	2.5.25–8	217
1.15.9–10	259	2.5.38	214
1.15.13–14	86	2.5.43	100
1.15.15	82	2.5.58	205
1.15.19	86	2.6.4	1.8.6
1.15.23–4	89	2.6.39	257
1.15.27–8	269	2.6.40	209
1.15.35	210	2.6.50	160
1.15.41–2	260	2.6.62	280, 281
1.15.42	96	2.7.1	328
2.1.1	83, 336, 339	2.7.1–2	334
2.1.1–2	83	2.7.9	168
2.1.2	236, 294	2.7.17	233
2.1.3	239, 328	2.7.28	329
2.1.3–4	6	2.8.6	209
2.1.5	168	2.8.24	288
2.1.12	95	2.8.27–8	221
2.1.21	91, 116, 341	2.8.28	329

PASSAGES QUOTED FROM LATIN AND GREEK TEXTS 367

2.9.43	333	2.19.19	296
2.9.49	90	2.19.27–8	148
2.10.4	147	2.19.29–30	146
2.10.5	203	2.19.33	333
2.10.14	110	2.19.39–40	333
2.10.15–16	154	2.19.41	331
2.10.17	276	2.19.44	85
2.10.17–18	168	2.19.51–2	150
2.10.25	163	2.19.53	152
2.10.26	202	2.19.55–6	151
2.10.27–8	209	2.19.57	197
2.10.31–2	236	2.19.59	285
2.10.35	101		
2.10.36	331	*Ars Amatoria*	
2.10.37–8	266	1.17–18	84
2.11.36	221	1.40	173
2.12.2	121, 240	1.43	163
2.12.2–4	11	1.49	280
2.12.9	179	1.64	294
2.12.21–2	300	1.99	100
2.12.25–6	158	1.129	189
2.13.1–2	16	1.135	99
2.13.2	287	1.136	106
2.13.11	261	1.139–42	105
2.13.15–16	17	1.144	207
2.13.21	96	1.146	99
2.13.23	134	1.147–8	112
2.14.7–8	152	1.148	114, 116
2.14.17–18	11	1.149–50	112
2.14.23–5	214	1.151–2	112
2.14.26	315	1.153–4	106
2.15.1	176	1.155–6	107
2.15.25	225	1.157–8	106
2.16.2	339	1.161	111
2.16.5–6	160	1.191–2	160
2.16.7	161, 205, 277	1.206	95
2.16.9–10	160	1.274–5	142
2.17.21	89	1.289–90	279
2.17.22	96	1.331–2	305
2.17.27–8	94	1.349–50	165
2.17.34	303	1.358	117
2.18.3	78	1.362	116
2.18.4	336	1.454	327
2.18.13–14	75	1.459	237
2.18.13–16	80	1.461	246
2.18.14	78	1.511	203
2.18.15	87	1.518	121
2.18.15–18	3–4	1.529	93
2.18.19	335, 336	1.531–2	193
2.18.19–20	4	1.532	192
2.19.4	149	1.535	254
2.19.5	204	1.573	236
2.19.7–8	217	1.621–2	128
2.19.17–18	207	1.631–2	117

1.633	123	3.298	237
1.635	129	3.298–9	81
1.637–8	134	3.303–4	81
1.643	227	3.311	307
1.669	110	3.321	258
1.672	90	3.341–2	203
1.691	119	3.343–4	3
1.698	209	3.346	78
1.729	178	3.396	102
1.749	150	3.403	256
2.43	167	3.405	257
2.53	143	3.407–8	84
2.110	196	3.409	314
2.131–5	165	3.411–12	268
2.159–60	207	3.431–2	252
2.178	286	3.480	207
2.215–16	287–8	3.524	207
2.231	200	3.538	92
2.244	325	3.539	256
2.277–8	231, 246	3.542	78
2.279–80	238	3.547–8	76
2.365	144, 326	3.552	119
2.369	153	3.578	178
2.370	272	3.593–4	291
2.387	324	3.612	185
2.400	141	3.615–16	151
2.425	268	3.699	319
2.426	102	3.716	333–4
2.433–4	102	3.735–6	120
2.523–4	288	3.740	270
2.552	231	3.775–6	108
2.555	330, 333	3.794	205
2.557–8	330	3.799	214
2.599–600	87		
2.627	273	*Epistulae ex Ponto*	
2.635	93	1.4.4	177
2.644	305	1.5.26	278
2.663–4	154	1.5.37–8	126
2.672–4	244	1.7.5–6	127
2.679–80	329	1.7.29	266
2.682	197	1.9.39	198
2.685	142, 240	2.5.37–8	161
2.713–14	234–5	2.5.38	206
3.15–16	147, 179	2.8.29	196
3.27	91	2.10.49	178
3.53–4	165	3.1.7	117
3.58	86	3.1.9	117
3.96	227	3.1.9–10	224
3.127–8	90	3.3.3–4	208
3.172	325	3.3.29	73
3.185–7	191	3.3.29–30	2
3.186	199	3.3.58	290
3.211	134	3.3.62	255
3.264	340	3.4.105	243

PASSAGES QUOTED FROM LATIN AND GREEK TEXTS 369

3.6.59–60	127	3.171–2	165
3.9.40	290	3.243	279
4.4.25	246	3.295–6	160, 316
4.5.1	341	3.306	244
4.5.3	80	3.420	128
4.7.47–8	286	3.425	314
4.8.45	302	3.495	80
4.13.41	303	3.523	341
4.14.49	337	3.545	135
4.16.29	88	3.631	314
		3.645	92–3
Fasti		3.697	185
1.38	320	3.839–40	243
1.60	303	3.843–4	314
1.71	113	4.1	116
1.83–4	317	4.7	340
1.142	84	4.9	87
1.199	153	4.9–10	341
1.217–18	246	4.71	186
1.223–4	231, 264	4.73–4	321
1.266	325	4.111	98
1.553	221	4.215	95
1.557	93	4.217	95
2.3–6	90	4.313	141
2.6	87	4.365–6	107
2.89	163	4.383	233
2.121	237	4.391	113
2.139	141	4.397–8	274
2.145	189	4.401–2	241
2.170	194	4.403	275
2.309–10	79	4.417	327
2.333	83	4.426	187
2.349–50	110	4.427	160
2.386	119	4.521	264
2.435–6	76	4.555	178
2.475–6	245	4.615–16	278
2.560	319	4.623–4	339
2.717	178	4.649–50	76
2.754	332	4.671	279
2.778–9	127	4.685–6	339
2.784	234	4.691	165
2.803–4	195	4.865–6	324
2.805	178	4.940	199
2.805–6	127	4.948	97
2.807	141	5.351–2	137
2.819–20	194	5.597	120
2.826	227	5.638	187
2.841	118	5.699	115
2.846	123, 255	6.5	256
2.859	253	6.6	94
3.13	188	6.49	315
3.21–2	153, 187	6.123–5	141
3.29–30	188	6.187	216
3.62	153	6.253–4	175
3.157	191		

370 PASSAGES QUOTED FROM LATIN AND GREEK TEXTS

6.405	113	7.58	327
6.440	209	7.59	336
6.647	324	7.74	315
6.811–12	341	7.123–4	201
		7.129	257
Halieutica		7.130	275
119	163	7.132	217
		7.135	135
Heroides		7.147–8	161
1.18	260	7.192	265
1.49	148	9.2	136
1.77–8	90	9.127	81
1.81	276	9.137	301
2.26	251	9.139	182
2.59–60	193	10.73	117–18
3.3	93	10.137	254
3.5–6	160	10.138	192
3.24	190	11.35	159
3.26	126	11.91–2	186
3.35–6	152	11.95	165
3.38	147	11.111	263–4
3.47	204	11.120	103
3.82	200	12.82	118
3.105–10	129	12.139	296
3.114	176	12.140	252
4.9	277	12.157–8	266
4.15	277	12.198	204
4.17	296	13.8	264
4.34	150	13.29	204
4.63	111	13.32	319
4.73–4	154	13.34	232
4.87	109	13.105	325
4.102	276	13.133	150
4.131–2	91	14.106	293
4.149	225	15.5–6	90
4.152–3	278	15.7	79, 249
5.31–2	287	15.21	87
5.54	242	15.47–8	329
5.71–2	186	15.55	175
5.115	119	15.64	225
5.117–18	108	15.73	254
5.133	142	15.95	121
5.133–4	126	15.96	117
5.140–4	18–19	15.107–8	118
6.17	136	15.116	253
6.19	212	15.152	77
6.47–8	197	15.154	308
6.87	172	15.158	77
6.91	213	15.211–12	283 n. 5
6.91–2	212	16.23–4	132
6.97	275	16.85–6	161
6.152	253	16.93	205
7.29–30	292	16.149–53	17
7.31–2	255	16.203	116
7.43	304		

16.267	336	1.136	242
16.283–4	327	1.139	241
16.368	147	1.139–40	241
17.3–4	92	1.152	245
17.51	200	1.178–80	87
17.180	100	1.184	307
17.222	191	1.422	183
18.30	142	1.427–8	209
18.73	161	1.478	294
18.105	110	1.497–8	266
18.166	119	1.498–9	128
19.158	331	1.566–7	123
19.177	188	1.721	147
19.205	106	2.200	103
20.19–20	117	2.313	110
20.31–2	127	2.418	75–6
20.55–6	103, 128	2.464	126
20.57	205	2.547–8	163
20.61–2	110	2.621–2	264
20.88–90	289	2.627	179
20.119–20	126	2.770–1	204
20.129–30	232	2.852–3	161
20.140–1	240	2.863	110
21.58	297	3.5	178
21.89–90	319	3.28	76
21.103	100	3.32	181
21.156	223	3.57	145–6
21.217	128	3.98	100
21.228	223	3.132–3	216
21.242	192	3.148–9	109
		3.198	174
Ibis		3.308–9	135
14	200	3.420	128
98	320	3.423	127
188	243	3.482	127
189	275	3.531–2	181
		3.574–5	289
Medicamina		4.14	341
1	237	4.51–2	106
18–19	79	4.137	247
39	213	4.142	100
40	213	4.156	179
83	134	4.166	270
		4.205	226
Medea		4.358	207
2	233	4.359	195
		4.450–1	306
Metamorphoses		4.611	309
1.4	238	4.776–7	195
1.79	253	4.791–2	305
1.96	242	4.803	168
1.97	243	5.1	174
1.101–2	241	5.42–3	264
1.110	279	5.122	226
1.112	241		
1.123–4	174		

372 PASSAGES QUOTED FROM LATIN AND GREEK TEXTS

5.236	306	9.560	328
5.336	78	9.585–6	302
5.472	266	9.614	190
5.576	200	9.711	178
5.600	187	10.152	90
5.632–3	332	10.171	225
6.59–60	109	10.258	164
6.78	133	10.272	317
6.92	320	10.275	205
6.108	307, 309	10.302–3	327
6.109	307	10.394	294
6.113	309	10.431–5	272
6.116–17	185	10.481	294
6.131	196	10.515–17	109
6.228	103	10.516	116
6.251	132	10.556–7	165
6.358–9	165	10.573	129
6.492	110	10.594–5	127
6.547	220	10.628	176
6.551	132	10.689	223
6.635	179	11.1–2	258
6.687	302	11.52–3	252
7.8	264	11.219–20	216
7.202	111	11.252	145
7.204	14 n. 50, 146	11.314	127
7.394	212	11.488	110
7.523	320	11.552–3	187
7.593–5	162	11.676	165
7.704–5	117	11.767–8	90
7.720–1	92	12.80–1	236
7.724–5	142	12.187–8	215
7.788	244	12.219	264
8.13	113	12.492	132
8.38–9	107	12.530	338
8.79	305	12.606	146
8.170	233	12.615–16	263
8.237–8	116	13.48	220
8.298	320	13.150	166
8.329	76	13.241	147
8.477	178	13.427–8	266
8.536	254	13.453	225
8.612–13	175	13.488	253
8.614–15	175	13.491	189
8.656	329	13.517	194
8.785–6	154	13.550	189
8.814	154	13.558–9	129
8.853–4	330	13.569–70	252
9.144	275	13.688–9	254
9.203–4	125	13.762	177
9.322–3	137	13.763	264
9.408	179	13.776	81
9.422–3	277	13.843–4	201
9.456	210	13.929	341
9.461–2	203	14.66–7	305

PASSAGES QUOTED FROM LATIN AND GREEK TEXTS 373

14.81	131	1.5.71–2	288
14.184	307	1.8.48	209
14.372	297	2.12	136
14.372–3	297	2.63	85
14.396	132	2.63–4	175
14.430	237	2.64	308
14.522	136	2.212	140
15.38	187	2.259	274
15.60	314	2.275–6	311
15.181	110	2.279–80	83
15.186–7	127	2.283–4	97
15.218	115	2.300	277
15.343–4	127	2.327	80
15.466–7	236	2.339–40	2
15.529	147	2.342	243
15.677	113	2.349	338
15.686	316	2.349–50	84
15.813	147	2.359	87
15.829–30	231	2.361	96, 337
15.858–9	276	2.367–8	337
15.879	166	2.381	88
		2.391–2	310
Remedia Amoris		2.424	86
71–2	107	2.431–2	268
77	204	2.445–6	269
133	144	2.449	92
171–2	275	2.455	164
214	126	2.553–4	80
227–8	287	3.3.51	193
232	150	3.3.60	260
303	126	3.3.65	263
330	91	3.3.68	265
362	324	3.3.73	96, 230
379	79, 116	3.7.35	257
385–6	107	3.8.1–2	175
403–4	207	3.8.5–6	175
431	219	3.8.11–12	160
504	226	3.8.12	175
530	286	3.8.41	178
549–50	264	3.9.2	231
555–6	166	3.10.78	136
757	230	3.11.51	136
758	230	4.1.43	85
811–12	291	4.1.73–4	234
813	256	4.3.50	194
		4.6.43	142
Tristia		4.7.17	307
1.1.1	171	4.9.27	287
1.1.1–2	232	4.10.1	87
1.1.15–16	80	4.10.7–8	338
1.1.57	126	4.10.51–4	15
1.1.105–6	103	4.10.53–4	228 n. 2
1.2.54	288	4.10.57–8	3
1.3.18	253	4.10.59–60	167
1.5.55–6	90		

374 PASSAGES QUOTED FROM LATIN AND GREEK TEXTS

4.10.61–2	3	Hor. *Carm.* 1.33.2	252
4.10.67–8	84	Hor. *Carm.* 2.7.3	325
4.10.85–6	267	Hor. *Carm.* 2.8.1	124
4.10.86	259	Hor. *S.* 1.10.36–7	171
4.10.129	166	Hor. *S.* 2.3.25–6	83
5.1.5–6	249		
5.3.29–30	135	*Priapea*	
5.7.11–12	127	20.1–2	133
5.7.55	236		
5.11.7	286	Propertius	
		1.1.1	8, 88, 92
Paul the Deacon		1.1.4	286
14.4	159	1.1.5	293
		1.2.1–3	79
Petronius		1.2.1	15, 233
88.2.1	230	1.2.19–20	104
132.9.3	224	1.3.14	292
		1.3.16	224, 225
Phaedrus		1.3.37–8	226
1.3.7	165	1.4.14	110
		1.5.21	178
Pindar		1.5.26	84
Enc. fr. 122.4–6	336	1.6.8	125
Nem. 4.6	260	1.6.25–6	83
Ol. 9.81	337	1.6.29–30	10, 229
Pyth. 9.15–17	180	1.6.29	114
Pyth. 10.65	337	1.7.8	78
fr. 128c.6 (Race)	258	1.8b.41–2	303
		1.8b.45	179
Plato		1.9.9–10	310
Crat. 395c–d3	78	1.9.11	238
		1.9.30–2	220
Plautus		1.11.10	146
Amphitryo 882–3	227	1.13.21–2	185
Casina 135	233	1.15.22	253
Menaechmi 369–70	197	1.15.33–4	229
Mercator 501	189	1.16.21	82
Stichus 333	197	1.16.47–8	300
Truculentus 632	291	1.17.1	302
		1.17.1–2	125
Pliny (elder)		1.17.21	108
Natural History		1.17.23	108
2.230.1	317	1.17.23–4	269
3.51.7	321	1.20.3	300
7.6.6	175	2.1.4	298, 303
14.5.2	246	2.1.21	303
24.24.8	207	2.1.25	213, 303
28.19.1	213	2.1.39–40	307
34.147.2–5	190	2.1.41	140
		2.1.41–2	10
Pliny (younger)		2.1.42	11
Ep. 4.15.2.3	145	2.2.5–6	128
Pan. 4.4.2	222	2.3.11–12	127
Pan. 49.8.3	173	2.3.14	128
		2.5.1–2	83
Plutarch		2.6.21	227
Moralia fr. 141.10	144		
Porphyrio			
Hor. *Carm.* 1.1.22	77		

2.6.32	146	2.32.59–60	147
2.6.39–40	140	2.33a.12	163
2.7.15	229	2.33a.17	261, 272
2.8.6	301	2.33b.38	238
2.8.11–12	129	2.34.44	140
2.8.29	253	2.34.53	267
2.9.6	260	2.34.57	223
2.9.7–8	148	2.34.59	223
2.10.12	95	2.34.89–90	268
2.10.19	238	2.34.91–2	269
2.12.2	91	2.34.94	336
2.12.22	90	3.1.1–4	77
2.13.6	257	3.1.3	236
2.13.7–8	258	3.1.5	77
2.13.29	267	3.1.38	73
2.13.30	266	3.2.3	258
2.13.46	215	3.2.5–6	310
2.15.2	327	3.2.17	301
2.15.12	103	3.2.18	298
2.15.39	238	3.3.1	73, 78
2.16.11–12	299	3.3.13–14	77
2.16.16	239	3.3.15–16	78
2.16.21–2	299	3.3.27–8	77
2.16.23–4	233	3.3.28	73
2.16.26	154, 321	3.5.1	114
2.16.47–8	124	3.5.9–10	142
2.18.3	78	3.5.43–5	306
2.18.7	216	3.7.44	305
2.18.27–8	15	3.7.72	237
2.19.3–4	153	3.8.6	186
2.19.31–2	298	3.8.20	289
2.19.41	331	3.10.8	308
2.19.42	272	3.10.10	308
2.20.11	248	3.11.9–10	309
2.20.21–2	83	3.11.39	299
2.20.23–4	89	3.12.34	307
2.22a.23–4	135, 201	3.19.13–14	185
2.22b.44	304	3.20.3	140–1
2.23.9	93	3.22.23	187
2.23.19	151	3.24.1–6	311
2.24a.1–2	301	3.24.3	311
2.24c.37–8	228	3.24.5	311
2.25.3	298	3.24.13–14	111
2.25.3–4	232	3.24.15–16	283
2.26b.25	248	3.24.19–20	326
2.26b.28	248	4.1a.5	264
2.28.5–6	16	4.1a.65–6	339
2.28.23	308	4.1a.69–70	337
2.28.38	300	4.1b.73	303
2.29b.35–6	331	4.1b.125–6	339
2.29b.37–8	168	4.1b.135	14
2.30a.3–4	306	4.1b.145–6	140
2.30b.13	141	4.2.14	275
2.30b.40	298	4.2.62	115
2.32.47	140	4.4.37	247

4.4.40	305	Med. 696–7	221
4.5.27–8	175	Med. 751	330
4.5.33–4	270	Med. 1020	195
4.7.2	260	Med. 1027	125
4.7.81	185	Nat. 4a.2.12	183
4.7.93	247	Oed. 49–51	273
4.8.75	78	Phaed. 384	89
4.10.20	146	Phaed. 459–60	141
4.11.14	263	Phaed. 508	77
		Phaed. 547–8	234
Quintilian		Phaed. 654	115
Inst.		Phaed. 668	227
1.8.5	89	Phaed. 683–4	110
1.8.6	89	Phaed. 886	264
10.1.66.3	88	Phaed. 886–7	195
10.1.89	86	Phaed. 1112	198
10.1.93.2	269	Phaed. 1174	128
10.1.93.3	91	Phaed. 1280	270
		Phoen. 588–9	126
[Quintilian]		Thy. 467–8	173
Decl. 19.6.5	264	Thy. 863–4	199
		Thy. 1035–6	310
Sallust		Thy. 1101–2	198
Iug. 46.8.3	247	Tro. 64	189
Sappho		Tro. 85	254
fr. 31.13	332	Tro. 212	215
fr. 31.15–16	332	[Sen.] Her. O.	
		523–4	213
Scholia to Callimachus			
Ia. 3 (fr. 193.6.34–5)	231	Servius	
		Virg. A. 1.273	186–7
Scholia to Homer's Iliad		Virg. A. 2.374	207
13.685	180	Virg. A. 2.392	186
		Virg. A. 4.430	297
Seneca (elder)		Virg. A. 5.71	113
Con. 1.2.7.9	290	Virg. A. 6.552	220
Con. 2.1.17.12	246	Virg. A. 6.596	213
Con. ex. 2.2.1.36	80	Virg. A. 8.610	12
Con. 2.2.12.12	12	Virg. A. 10.419	257
Con. 2.5.14.8	208	Virg. A. 11.93	253
Suas. 6.27.1	238	Virg. A. 12.139	132
		Virg. Ecl. 1.52	78
Seneca (younger)		Virg. Ecl. 6.54	156
Ag. 707	330	Virg. G. 1.96	273
Dial. 6.23.3	217		
Dial. 6.25.1.4	265	SHA Alexander Severus	
Ep. 5.3.2	246	29.2.1	218
Ep. 41.3	76		
Ep. 58.15.5	222	Silius Italicus	
Ep. 76.31	82	4.214	233
Ep. 88.2.1	230	5.158–9	164
Ep. 117.16	217	7.339–40	173
Med. 99–100	127	12.236–8	234
Med. 285–8	118	13.270	267
Med. 331–2	243	15.23–4	79
Med. 622–3	291	15.30	74 n. 3

PASSAGES QUOTED FROM LATIN AND GREEK TEXTS 377

15.71–2	94	1.1.15–16	80
16.175	246	1.1.25	228
16.360–1	120	1.1.55–6	288
Simonides (Campbell)		1.1.56	237
fr. 567	257	1.1.57–8	229
		1.1.58	237
Sophocles		1.1.60	267
fr. 959.2–3 (Lloyd-Jones)	340	1.1.61	267
Phil. 422	215	1.1.62	267
Statius		1.1.73	90
Achilleid		1.1.75–6	10
1.327	159	1.2.5	93
1.370	314	1.2.21–2	290
		1.3.3	265
Siluae		1.3.4	257
1.2.3–6	259	1.3.4–5	256
4.7.1–4	95	1.3.5	265
5.1.179–80	255	1.3.5–6	265
Thebaid		1.3.7–8	266
1.112	263	1.3.23–4	261
1.428–9	132	1.3.25–6	261
1.572–3	148	1.3.26	272
1.680	181	1.3.41	241
2.466	81	1.3.43–4	242
4.345	181	1.3.45	241
4.761–2	159	1.3.51	296
6.446	119	1.3.55–6	263
11.100–1	244	1.3.57–8	267
11.183	273	1.3.75	306
Suetonius		1.4.14	328
Aug. 27.5.3	324	1.4.23–4	123
Cal. 55.2	121	1.4.40	144
Tib. 35.2.1	324	1.4.42	199
Vit. 7.1	121	1.4.57–8	230
		1.4.63–4	305
Tacitus		1.4.83	296
Ann. 1.66.1	145	1.5.7	296
Ann. 3.2.5	253	1.5.8	296
Ann. 4.38.17–19	245	1.5.39–44	202
Ann. 13.2.7	151	1.5.41	212
Ann. 13.3.15	166	1.5.44	210
Dial. 30.4	230	1.5.57	76
Tertullian		1.5.61–2	289
de Spectaculis		1.5.63–4	289
9	121	1.5.75–6	297
		1.6.9–10	92
Theocritus		1.6.12	92
3.15	177	1.6.29	261
Theodulf of Orleans		1.6.67–8	141
3.6	159	1.6.75	141
		1.7.34	275
Tibullus		1.8.18	212
1.1.5	228	1.8.37–8	206
1.1.7–8	91	1.8.53–4	93

378 PASSAGES QUOTED FROM LATIN AND GREEK TEXTS

1.8.70	134	Virgil	
1.8.75–6	93	*Aeneid*	
1.9.3–4	131	1.2–3	321
1.9.5–6	129	1.5	321
1.9.23	333	1.7	321
1.9.42	289	1.8	127
1.9.59–60	288	1.48–9	134
1.9.63–4	222	1.146	276
1.9.74	203	1.147	172
1.10.10	318	1.203	287
1.10.26	146	1.259–60	255
1.10.33	325	1.292	245
1.10.40	146	1.337	82
1.10.49–50	141	1.345	227
1.10.51	130	1.403–4	79
1.10.61	80	1.482	303
2.1.1	312	1.626	314
2.1.11–12	218	1.639	319
2.1.17	313	1.684	330
2.1.41–2	275	1.710	290
2.1.47–8	275	2.108–9	192
2.2.3	134	2.198	179
2.3.4	91	2.296–7	194
2.3.33–4	229	2.324–5	259
2.3.37	244	2.476–7	101
2.3.53–4	79	2.557	208
2.3.63	115	2.792–3	192
2.4.13	14	3.56–7	243
2.4.22	288	3.208	242
2.4.49–50	269	3.386	226
2.5.1	312	3.528	278
2.5.43–4	255	3.658	189
2.5.113–14	253	4.1	148
2.6.1	238	4.8	130
2.6.15–16	253	4.23	235
[Tibullus]		4.58	279
3.4.43–4	256	4.148	319
3.4.55–6	166	4.314–19	117
3.4.73	177	4.324	132
3.6.44	137	4.325–6	194
3.7.36	82	4.381	126
3.20.1–2	323	4.489	172
		4.590	210
Valerius Flaccus		4.653	267
2.555–6	196	4.690–1	192
3.30–1	339	5.71	113, 320
5.513	132	5.163	121
6.443	213	5.250	319
7.602	242	5.609–10	253
Varro		5.670	325
L. 5.153.4	118	5.673–4	234
L. 6.9.2	201	6.179	76
R. 1.29.2.1	242	6.226–8	193

6.314	173	12.68–9	127
6.471	190	12.225–6	198
6.595–7	306	12.723	174
6.673	198	12.827	191
6.707–8	161	12.870	192
6.767	338	12.898	242
6.791	84		
6.855–6	254	*Eclogues*	
6.870–1	191	1.4–5	78
6.882	235	1.65	199
6.883–4	266	4.30	241
7.41	84	4.32–3	243
7.45	85	4.41	241
7.71	314	5.44	200
7.180	241	6.4–5	238
7.273	166	6.5	73
7.400	273	6.8	80
7.444	247	6.27–8	237
7.640	132	6.30	257
7.723–4	321	6.54	156, 163
8.18	174	6.71	237
8.39	198	6.74–6	181
8.196–7	93	7.7	162
8.230–1	182	7.12–13	172
8.351–2	76	7.25	268
8.453	241	7.61–2	88
8.458	82	8.43	177
8.621	132	8.80–1	212
8.707–8	111	9.28	200
9.51	82	9.40–1	161
9.279	247	10.22–3	148
9.435–6	223	10.28	82
9.607	231	10.66	206
9.625	116		
9.631	132	*Georgics*	
9.634	126	1.40	116
10.2–3	276	1.92	201
10.51	340	1.126–7	242
10.151	81	1.163	275
10.160–1	289	1.261–2	275
10.261–2	234	1.509	300
10.419	257	2.35	237
10.518–19	266	2.223	278
10.537–8	189	2.355	278
11.42–3	263	2.459	244
11.55	277	3.6–8	103
11.93	253	3.47	198
11.119	265	3.106–7	102
11.371	216	3.125	162
11.582–4	148	3.267	117
11.716	196	3.294	95
11.849	132	3.501–2	215
12.65	127	3.525	261
		4.300–1	145

4.361	185	Xenophon	
4.374	77	*Memorabilia*	
4.412	145	2.1.21.4–22.9	74
4.510	258		
4.511	308		

3. General Index

Accius 87, 88, 89, 104, 157, 335
Achilles 119, 126, 146, 152, 159, 165, 204, 209, 251, 258, 308
Acrisius 147, 239, 240, 306
Andromeda 108, 130
Anio 11, 19, 83, 185–92, 195–6
Apollodorus 130, 177, 178, 183, 184, 257, 258
Apollonius of Rhodes 104, 172, 177, 183, 309–10
Argo 242
Artemidorus 158 n. 14, 163
Ascanius/Iulus 126, 255, 290, 325
Atalanta 18, 108, 127, 129, 205
Augustus
  deification 244–5
  marriage legislation 11, 138–40, 294, 324, 326
  myth of Rome's foundation 11–12, 141, 171, 245, 314
Aulus Gellius 152, 172, 238

Bion 249–50, 253, 255, 256
Briseis 108, 126, 129, 152, 234
Burman, Pieter 101, 152, 176, 183, 206, 214, 232, 240, 262, 306, 318, 321

Cadmus 182, 216, 309
Caecilius Macedonicus, Q. 294
Caesar, Julius 191, 238, 245
Callimachus 74, 79, 80, 86, 98, 123, 169–71, 180, 183, 228 n. 8, 231, 237, 238, 271, 276, 298, 307, 335, 340
Calvus 250, 268, 298, 335
Campus Martius 247
Catullus 6, 8, 10 n. 40, 12, 15, 76, 86, 88, 91, 96, 100, 105, 111, 115, 122, 128, 130, 142, 154, 161, 176, 183, 189, 191, 195, 196, 200, 201, 203, 211, 213, 214, 217, 220, 223, 225, 231, 232, 233, 235, 240, 242, 247, 250, 252, 256, 259, 264, 265, 268, 277, 280, 281–98, 308, 317, 325, 326, 327, 329, 330, 332, 333, 335, 338, 340
celibacy 271, 272, 280
Celsus 146, 287
Ceres 154, 182, 213, 218, 241, 261, 266, 270–81, 312
Circe 212, 226, 296
Circus Maximus 5 n. 26, 97–123, 312
Crete 271, 276, 277, 279, 340

Danae 139, 147, 174, 239, 240, 241, 309
Demeter 271, 273, 274, 278
Dido 120, 126, 131, 132, 135, 159, 190, 192, 194, 195, 201, 210, 216, 227, 235, 255, 257, 265, 275, 292, 315, 335 n. 3
Diodorus Siculus 103, 104, 181, 183
Dionysius of Halicarnassus 97 n. 2, 99, 101, 112, 113, 114, 313, 315, 319, 320
dreams 5, 73, 155–69, 187, 191
Dryden, John 14, 131

elegiac poetry/poets
  love as disease 287
  metre 12–14, 73, 80, 83, 85, 86, 89, 94, 96, 99, 101, 102, 104, 109, 116, 122, 136, 153, 173, 193, 196, 207, 208, 209, 249, 251, 252, 256, 267, 285, 304, 314, 331, 334, 341
  peace and war 10, 114, 229, 233–4, 246, 335, 338, 339, 341
  poverty and wealth 9–10, 217, 227–9, 231, 233, 235, 246–9
  social status 1, 138, 227–9, 232–3, 234, 246, 337–8
emmer 274
Ennius 75 n. 4, 76, 80, 86, 125, 170, 187, 188, 190, 191, 196, 249 n. 1, 274, 314, 335
Euripides 16, 135, 136, 140, 180, 182, 264, 287, 310
Europa 309

Falerii 312–21

Gallus 15, 82, 83, 89, 105, 228, 237, 250, 251, 268–9, 282, 298, 313, 335

Heinsius, Nicolaus 87, 93, 95, 101, 104, 156, 160, 173, 178, 180, 183, 204, 206, 214, 219, 222, 232, 247, 258, 262, 280, 293, 296, 316, 337
Hesiod 73, 123, 124, 163, 170, 171, 175, 210, 240, 241, 252, 268, 271, 277, 280, 310
Homer 102, 115, 117, 127, 128, 147, 170, 172–3, 174, 178, 180, 181, 184–5, 204, 215, 222, 221, 224, 226, 238, 257, 258, 259, 260, 264, 265, 268, 271, 273, 274, 277, 280, 296, 305, 307, 308, 309, 325, 332, 335, 338, 340
Horace 2, 77, 78, 80, 81, 82, 83, 84, 85, 86, 88, 90, 95, 100, 102, 113, 114, 115, 119, 124–5, 127,

382 GENERAL INDEX

128, 129, 130, 131, 134, 135, 136, 141, 142, 144, 146, 147, 150, 151, 154, 158-9, 162, 165, 166, 167, 171, 172, 176, 185, 186, 189, 193, 195, 199, 201, 202, 204, 206, 208, 211, 212, 213, 214, 215, 217, 218, 220, 223, 227, 231, 232, 236, 237, 238, 239, 240, 241, 242, 244, 247, 249, 252, 254, 256, 259, 262, 264, 278, 281, 285, 286, 287, 291, 292, 300, 302, 303, 307, 309, 311, 318, 326, 335-6, 338, 341
Hypsipyle 212, 216, 275, 335 n. 3

Iasion/Iasius 270-1, 277, 280
Ilia/Rea Silvia 11-12, 19, 83, 84, 103, 107, 153, 171, 185-96, 210, 265, 270, 325
impotence 9, 201-27, 328
Isis 17, 219, 261, 270, 271, 272
Itys 308

Jason 103, 118, 127, 180, 184, 195, 216, 225, 242, 252, 262, 266, 275, 296, 309
Julian law on the suppression of adultery 10-11, 138, 153, 154, 155, 322, 326, 327
Julian law on upper-class marriage 138, 294
Juno 6, 134, 136, 192, 271, 281, 312-21
Justinian's *Digest* 91, 107, 126, 150, 151, 153, 154, 155, 236, 249, 257, 326, 327

Linus 257, 258
Lucan 76, 88, 102, 115, 125, 133, 134, 144, 154, 166, 169 n. 1, 172, 183, 184, 189, 191, 193, 211, 212, 213, 220, 234, 241, 243, 245, 246, 247, 256, 259, 260, 265, 267, 273, 300, 310, 325
Lucretia 123, 141, 192, 194, 195, 224, 227, 255, 332
Lucretius 85, 95, 100, 142, 152, 184, 187, 190, 191, 197, 199, 200, 218, 222, 223, 231, 232, 241, 247, 256, 259, 273, 274, 278, 317, 325, 330
Lygdamus 158, 166, 177

magic 212-14, 226
Marius (Domenico Mario Negri) 88, 148, 150, 155 n. 1, 173, 178, 183, 206, 214, 217, 232, 240, 262, 306, 339
Marlowe, Christopher 88, 143, 219, 240
Mars 11, 19, 103, 114, 132, 133, 153, 166, 181, 186, 187, 188, 211, 333
Medea 111, 118, 172, 195, 212, 216, 225, 252, 262, 266, 275, 309, 336
Medusa 174, 305-6
Memnon 251
Micyllus (Jacob Moltzer) 82, 101, 183, 206, 214, 232, 306
Milanion 108-9
[Moschus] 249-50, 251, 257, 258, 268

Naugerius, Andreas (Andrea Navagero) 101, 183, 206, 214, 232
Nicaenetus 170
Nile 183, 184, 198, 201, 272
Niobe 103, 178, 308

Odysseus/Ulysses 90, 108, 147, 157, 179, 184, 221, 226, 265, 288, 307
Oenomaus 103-4
Oenone 18-19, 119, 126, 142, 287, 288, 335 n. 3
Orpheus 90, 220, 252, 257-8, 308
Ovid
  Amores:
  abortion 9, 11, 16, 17, 152, 156, 202, 281
  Alexandrian footnote 178, 180, 183, 211, 255
  alliteration 77, 78, 103, 105, 106, 109, 110, 114, 116, 117, 118, 121, 122, 126, 129, 130, 131, 136, 137, 138, 142, 154, 164, 173, 182, 189, 194, 197, 198, 199, 200, 204, 207, 215, 221, 223, 224, 235, 263, 279, 294, 295, 324, 326, 337, 338
  aposiopesis 108
  apostrophe 103, 108, 112, 120, 176, 182, 243, 251, 269
  assonance 105, 106, 122, 129, 130, 173, 174, 197, 237, 326, 337, 338
  balance at main caesura 13, 103, 110, 116, 117, 128, 136, 146, 153, 173, 185, 203, 204, 205, 214-15, 251, 257, 260, 261, 292
  chiasmus 115, 122, 251, 261
  Corinna 7, 8, 9, 10, 11, 14, 16-17, 18, 86, 92-3, 97, 108, 139, 145, 167, 189, 190, 202, 203, 209, 211, 215, 227, 232, 233, 240, 268, 281, 287, 300, 301, 302, 303, 319, 321, 322
  date 2-4, 83-4, 85, 138-9
  design of collection 4-6
  elision 186, 189-90, 195, 200, 201
  etymology 131, 151, 177, 209, 221, 235, 252, 258, 317
  hendiadys 204, 275
  hyperbaton 14, 157, 161
  interweaving of words ending in *a* 14, 145, 206, 207, 227, 291, 302
  paradox 7, 80, 105, 108, 130, 132, 136, 141, 144, 145, 169, 178, 184, 211, 276, 283, 284-5, 292, 293, 294, 297, 298, 324, 327, 328
  patronymics 185, 221, 257, 259, 306
  persuasion 98-9, 119, 169
  politics 1, 9, 10-12, 171, 244-5, 246, 247, 338
  polyptoton framing the main caesura 109, 163, 232, 277, 294, 325, 340
  Pompeii 126, 293
  prostitution 10, 19, 91, 97, 106, 138, 236, 290, 299-300, 301, 312, 322, 324, 325, 326
  punctuation 104, 122-3, 214-15, 262, 330

rape and sexual violence 9, 11, 17–19, 141, 153, 171, 174, 177, 179, 182, 184, 185, 186, 187, 188, 189, 191, 192, 194, 195, 196, 216, 227, 239, 265, 270, 302, 306, 308, 324, 333
rhyme 13, 101, 102, 104, 117, 147, 263, 290, 293
similes 18, 109, 127, 161, 162, 164, 210, 255, 328
stage directions 88, 123, 165
symmetry 5, 109, 117, 131, 146, 198
verbal patterning 12–14, 79, 81, 83, 84, 87, 109, 111, 112, 118, 121, 131, 145, 155, 159, 160, 161, 162, 166, 172, 174, 175, 188, 189, 197, 242, 252, 253, 254, 259, 260, 263, 273, 275, 277, 278, 286, 287, 290, 306, 308, 310, 311, 317, 319, 320, 333, 339, 340
Ovid's life 1, 8, 300, 313

pandering 91, 138, 139, 155, 302, 322, 324
Paul the Deacon 159
Penelope 90, 108, 128, 147–8, 157, 260, 308, 335 n. 3
Perseus 174, 196, 226, 240, 305–6
Phaeacia 265, 266
Phanocles 170
Philodemus 148, 202, 210, 211, 336
Philomela 92, 103, 194, 220, 224
Procne 308
Propertius 1 n. 1, 6, 7, 8, 10, 11, 14, 15, 16, 17, 73, 74, 77, 78, 79, 80, 82, 83, 84, 86, 88, 89, 90, 91, 92, 93, 94, 95, 100, 102, 103, 105, 108, 110, 111, 114, 115, 116, 119, 120, 122, 124, 125, 127, 128, 130, 135, 136, 138, 140, 141, 142, 144, 145, 146, 147, 148, 149, 153, 154, 157, 161, 163, 168, 171, 172, 175, 178, 179, 180, 185, 187, 189, 190, 193, 195, 201, 202, 204, 206, 207, 208, 210, 211, 213, 215, 216, 217, 218, 219, 220, 221, 223, 224, 225, 226, 227, 228, 229, 230, 232, 233, 234, 236, 237, 238, 239, 247, 248, 250, 253, 254, 257, 258, 260, 261, 262, 263, 264, 265, 266, 267, 268, 269, 270, 271, 272, 275, 280, 283, 285, 286, 287, 289, 290, 291, 292, 293, 294, 296, 298–312, 313, 321, 325, 326, 327, 331, 334, 335, 336, 337, 338, 339, 341
Proserpina 187, 270, 272, 280

Quintilian 75 n. 4, 86, 88, 89, 91, 133, 264, 269, 330
Quirinus 153, 244–5

Romulus and Remus 11, 141, 153, 171, 186, 187, 245

Sappho 77, 85, 89, 91, 113, 117, 225, 249, 332, 335 n. 3

Scylla (daughter of Nisus) 141, 177, 181, 304, 305
Scylla (daughter of Phorcys) 177, 181, 305
Secular Games 315, 320
Semele 135–6
Seneca (elder) 11, 80, 81, 87, 208, 239
Seneca (younger) 16 n. 56, 76, 77, 81, 85, 89, 103, 110, 115, 118, 125, 126, 127, 128, 129, 131, 134, 141, 144, 145, 151, 153, 159, 163, 164, 172, 173, 182, 183, 184, 189, 192, 195, 198, 199, 213, 214, 216, 217, 218, 221, 222, 223, 227, 230, 234, 238, 243, 246, 252, 254, 256, 257, 291, 310
Servius 12, 77, 113, 132, 156, 163, 177, 186–7, 189, 191, 192, 199, 207, 213, 220, 253, 257, 278, 273, 297
Silius Italicus 74 n. 3, 79, 81, 94, 115, 120, 142, 153, 173
Sirens 307
slavery 8, 9, 76, 107, 138, 139, 151–2, 169, 176, 196, 202, 227, 230, 232, 243, 248, 285, 286, 287, 288, 289
Statius 76, 77, 81, 96, 100, 102, 115, 116, 119, 127, 131, 133, 144, 145, 148, 154, 159, 173, 174, 181, 184, 190, 216, 241, 244, 255, 256, 258, 259, 262, 263, 265, 273, 300, 314, 319

Tacitus 99, 145, 150, 166, 230, 245, 253, 259
Tantalus 104, 218, 307, 308
Tereus 92, 103, 110, 194, 222, 308
Theocritus 98, 171, 177, 226, 250 n. 8, 258, 271 n. 3
Theodulf of Orleans 159
Tibullus 2, 6, 7, 8, 9, 10, 14, 15, 16, 17, 76, 78, 79, 80, 82, 84, 86, 88, 89, 90, 91, 92, 93, 94, 96, 98, 105, 107, 111, 113, 114, 115, 116, 119, 125, 127, 130, 131, 134, 135, 138, 140, 141, 143, 144, 146, 149, 159, 176, 183, 186, 187, 189, 190, 193, 194, 199, 202, 203, 204, 206, 207, 208, 210, 211, 212, 213, 218, 219, 220, 222, 224, 228, 229, 230, 232, 234, 235, 237, 238, 240, 241, 242, 243, 244, 249–70, 272, 273, 274, 275, 278, 283, 287, 288, 289, 290, 291, 296, 297, 299, 301, 302, 303, 305, 306, 309, 312, 313, 317, 318, 325, 329, 331, 335, 341

Vestal Virgins 19, 83, 188–9, 190, 193, 194, 196, 209, 210
Virgil 11, 12, 16, 73, 76, 77, 78, 79, 80, 81, 82, 83, 84, 85, 86, 87, 88, 93, 94, 95, 100, 101, 102, 103, 109, 111, 113, 116, 117, 118, 119, 120, 126, 127, 130, 132, 133, 134, 141, 142, 144, 145, 147, 148, 153, 154, 156, 159, 161, 162, 163, 164, 165, 166, 168, 170, 172, 173, 174,

176, 177, 179, 180, 181, 182, 183, 184, 185,
186, 189, 190, 191, 192, 193, 194, 195, 196,
198, 199, 200, 201, 206, 207, 208, 210, 211,
212, 213, 215, 216, 220, 221, 223, 225, 226,
227, 231, 235, 237, 238, 240, 241, 242, 243,
245, 247, 251, 252, 253, 254, 255, 256, 257,
258, 259, 261, 263, 265, 266, 267, 268, 273,
274, 275, 277, 278, 279, 280, 283 n. 5, 287,
289, 290, 291, 292, 296, 297, 300, 303, 305,
306, 307, 308, 309, 310, 314, 315, 317, 319,
320, 321, 325, 330, 335, 338, 339, 340

witchcraft 172, 211–14, 226

Xenophon 74, 80